D0893681

ABOUT THE AUTHOR

 Jim Willis, a minister with the United Church of Christ (UCC) for thirty years, served as adjunct professor of comparative religion and cross-cultural studies at Mt. Wachusett Community College until his retirement in 2003. He also finds the time to be a part-time carpenter and writer. He recorded and produced two albums of gospel music while serving as writer, producer, and host of the "Through the Bible" series, a daily drive-time radio program.

His hobby—some would say obsession—is long-distance bicycle riding. He has biked across the country from west to east and south to north, has traveled the length of the Connecticut River and the length and breadth of Massachusetts, and has ridden extensively in New England, the Midwest, the West, and the Southeast. He describes his travels in *Journey Home: The Inner Life of a Long-Distance Bicycle Rider,* published in 2000.

After graduating from the Eastman School of Music in Rochester, New York, during the 1960s, Willis was a high school band and orchestra teacher during the week, a symphony trombonist on weekends, a jazz musician at night, and a choral conductor on Sunday mornings. He became an ordained minister in 1972 and earned his master's degree in theology from Andover Newton Theological School in 1991.

He and his wife, Barbara, now live in Arizona, where Willis serves as senior pastor to the United Churches Fellowship, UCC, in the border town of Nogales.

Other Visible Ink Press titles distributed by Omnigraphics

The Astrology Book (0-7808-0719-7)

Black Firsts, 2nd Ed. (1-57859-153-8)

Black Heroes (0-7808-0728-6)

The Fortune-Telling Book (0-7808-0720-0)

The Handy Dinosaur Answer Book (0-7808-0724-3)

The Handy Ocean Answer Book (0-7808-0725-1)

The Handy Physics Answer Book (0-7808-0723-5)

The Handy Politics Answer Book (0-7808-0726-X)

The Handy Science Answer Book (0-7808-0727-8)

Real Ghosts, Restless Spirits, and Haunted Places (0-7808-0721-9)

The Religion Book (0-7808-0722-7)

Unexplained! 2nd Ed. (0-7808-0715-4)

The Vampire Book (0-7808-0716-2)

The Werewolf Book (0-7808-0717-0)

The Witch Book (0-7808-0718-9)

www.omnigraphics.com

The Religion Book

Places, Prophets, Saints, and Seers

To Barb and Jan
From different sides of the generation gap they listen for the music of God—
And dance to her tune

The Religion Book

Places, Prophets, Saints, and Seers

JIM WILLIS

DETROIT

The Religion Book
Places, Prophets, Saints, and Seers

Copyright 2004 by Visible Ink Press®

This publication is a creative work fully protected by all applicable copyright laws, as well as by misappropriation, trade secret, unfair competition, and other applicable laws.

No part of this book may be reproduced in any form without permission in writing from the publisher, except by a reviewer who wishes to quote brief passages in connection with a review written for inclusion in a magazine or newspaper.

All rights to this publication will be vigorously defended.

Visible Ink Press®
43311 Joy Rd. #414
Canton, MI 48187-2075

Visible Ink Press is a registered trademark of Visible Ink Press LLC.

Art Director: Mary Claire Krzewinski
Typesetting: The Graphix Group

ISBN 0-7808-0722-7

Front cover art, *Tower of Babel*, by Pieter Brueghel, the Elder, reprinted by permission of the Bridgeman Art Library International.

Cataloging-in-Publication Data is on file with the Library of Congress.

Printed in the United States of America

All rights reserved

10 9 8 7 6 5 4 3 2 1

Casebound editions published exclusively for Omnigraphics

info@omnigraphics.com
1-800-875-1340
Editorial Office: 615 Griswold St.
Detroit, MI 48226
www.omnigraphics.com

CONTENTS

INTRODUCTION

The subjects covered in this volume are as old as the human race and as new as today's newspaper headlines. They are presented not to be judged as much as to inform, explain, and enlighten.

The Religion Book: Places, Prophets, Saints, and Seers offers a broad overview of religion through the millennia, providing nearly 300 entries and 100 photos. Covered in-depth are the five well-established and documented world religions—Hinduism, Buddhism, Judaism, Christianity, and Islam—that have supported and informed lives for thousands of years. You will also read about spiritual practices of the ancients that have been rediscovered through archaeological evidence and oral history. Druidism and goddess worship, the Red Paint culture, Native North American spirituality, and the ancient Celts still speak to people, especially as new information is uncovered and published. Some of their ancient wisdom is being melded into what is often referred to as New Age religion. The modern resurgence of Wicca is only one example.

Readers will encounter holy places such as Jerusalem, Mecca, and Amesbury, England, near Stonehenge; prophets from the pages of the Bible and Zoroastrian scriptures; founders such as Jesus, Moses, Siddhartha, and Joseph Smith; saints like the apostle Paul and Francis of Assisi; seers, including Wiccan priestess Laurie Cabot; and charismatic leaders like David Koresh. A few figures from popular legend and folklore appear as well, including King Arthur, Merlin, and even the Abominable Snowman. Angels and demons have their place, along with in-depth discussions about how creeds, doctrines, and dogmas came to be established.

The Religion Book discusses religious movements, such as the Great Awakening of the eighteenth century and the Death of God movement of the 1960s, as well as more secular movements inspired by religion, including the environmental and civil rights movements. It examines various approaches to religion and religious study, such as the historical/critical method of biblical scholarship and the "conservative versus liberal" debates that span the Protestant Reformation of the sixteenth century, the Scopes "Monkey Trial" of the 1920s, the modern-day appointment of openly gay clergy, and beyond.

If what you are looking for is not listed alphabetically as an individual entry, it is likely included under a related subject. Cross-references throughout the book, as well as the comprehensive index, explain where to find what you seek. Within an entry, more cross-references lead to related topics. "Abraham," for instance, leads to "Judaism, Development of," which links to "Ark of the Covenant," and so on. Or "Abraham" might lead to "Islam, Development of," which will direct you to "Muhammad." The list of resources at the end of the book provides valuable direction on acquiring more information about the topics covered.

Origins of Religion

Archaeology has unearthed ritual burial sites going back to the time of the Neanderthal, some twenty-five thousand years ago. Our first ancestors likely would not have gone to the trouble of burying their loved ones with prized hand axes and implements unless they were convinced those items would be needed in the next life. But this kind of planning for "the next life" is evidence of a spiritual concept of life extending beyond the physical, mortal one. In other words, early humans were likely practicing a basic form of religion. A good case can even be made that the advent of religion was a primary building block for the development of humanity.

Two common theories explain the existence of religion. One is that religion is entirely a human invention. This was the view of Karl Marx, who said, "Man makes religion; religion does not make man.... Religion is the sigh of the oppressed creature … the opium of the people." Others believe a spiritual reality exists that various cultures tap into and express in their own unique ways. There are planes of existence, according to this view. A spiritual plane exists that is separated from the material world we normally experience. It is "outside" or "other." But it is not separated from us by an impermeable barrier. The wall is full of doors and windows. Religion is a major access point, allowing us to catch glimpses of what's happening on the other side.

To use a computer metaphor, the spiritual plane is the hardware that contains the "works." Religions are the software that access that hardware. This metaphor is valuable because it sheds light on the age-old hindrance to peaceful religious coexistence. Any software will work fine as long as its rules are followed. But you can't mix software very well. They don't use the same language, so they don't speak to each other. Hence, what works for one individual or culture might not be of any use to a different individual or culture. Each software producer, of course, rightly claims that its own product works best, because for them, at least, it does. But it takes a while to really get to know the ins and outs of a piece of software. You can read about its claims, but to really get to know how to use it takes time, effort, and application.

Pondering this issue, I wondered if I ought to offer my own thoughts on the matter—the culmination of thirty years of religious study—and "interpret" the material I would be presenting. But as soon as I framed the question, the answer became obvious. It simply is not my job, within the confines of this book, to judge or interpret

THE RELIGION BOOK: PLACES, PROPHETS, SAINTS, AND SEERS

anyone else's religion. *The Religion Book,* therefore, presents not one person's interpretation but the histories and the stories themselves.

Where it might be enlightening, the book examines the often conflicting theories and interpretations of spiritual and historical matters. For instance: Was there really a man named Noah who built an ark? Judeo-Christian-Islamic tradition, along with that of many indigenous peoples, tells the story of such a man, so the story is presented here, along with various schools of interpretation as to what the story means. But the final judgment will have to be made in the mind of each reader.

ACKNOWLEDGMENTS

A book of this size and scope can never be considered to be the work of only one person. Hundreds of people have left their mark.

Way back in 1969, when I was a public school music teacher, nightclub musician, and trombonist with the Syracuse symphony, I was also a part-time choir director at the Baptist Church in Macedon, New York. The folks there thought it might be a good idea if, on Laity Sunday, I gave a sermon entitled, "Why Music in the Church?" John Blyth, organist, good friend, and musical colleague, put them up to it. It was my first experience in a church pulpit. They told me they thought I might have a future as a preacher. We all laughed. I'm sure all of them have forgotten the incident by now. But I never have.

Since then I have delivered thousands of sermons, requiring even more thousands of hours of preparation, questions, struggles, and long nights. Always before me was the thought that people deserved answers and serious commitment each and every Sunday morning.

For three years I had the privilege of serving, for one month every summer, a small Baptist Church on North Haven Island off the coast of Maine. One Saturday evening the news flashed around the island that former President Jimmy Carter was a guest at the home of one of his former ambassadors. And I was preaching at the Baptist Church! His only other option was the Episcopal Church down island. I figured I had it made. The world's most famous Baptist was about to hear me preach. I had never worked so hard on a sermon in my life! Every reference was checked thoroughly, every point supported with a spiffy, down-home but elegant illustration.

On Sunday morning Mr. and Mrs. Carter, accompanied by Secretary of State Cyrus Vance, waved as they drove by the parsonage. It turned out his host was an Episcopalian, and the Carters, then as now, were unfailingly polite and gracious to their hosts. But as I stood in the pulpit that Sunday morning I had an epiphany. If I had worked this hard to prepare a sermon for a president, the common, workaday people, who had problems just as real and important as a former world leader, deserved no less. I shared my thoughts with the congregation. A deacon came up to me after the service with tears in his eyes. "Jimmy Carter must be a hell of a Sunday school teacher," he said. "That was the best lesson I ever heard and he wasn't even here!" (By the way, the contest turned out to be a tie. The Carters attended the Episcopal Church that day, but we had more people out. The Baptists figured they had at least won a moral victory.)

Congregations such as those at North Haven Island helped me prepare to write this book. And the folks who came to worship services and Bible studies in Royalston, Townsend, and New Salem, Massachusetts, who were part of my life for thirty years, asked the probing questions and demanded nothing less than my best. Those people, along with my wonderful students at Mount Wachusett Community College, really shaped my journey and made me who I am today.

Individual people helped, as well. Professor Gabriel Fackre at Andover Newton Theological School is an insightful mentor who has the brilliant mind of a systematic theologian and the compassionate heart of a pastor. He quite literally changed my life. Thanks, Gabe!

An author is nothing without an editor. Christa Gainor is part writer, part psychologist, part cheerleader, part coach, and all heart. Besides that, I got to officiate at her wedding. Not even torrential rains can dampen her spirits. And now she's a mother! I envy her son, Joey. He's got a great set of parents! Bob—thanks for putting up with my many e-mails and calls.

Also at Visible Ink Press, thank you to publishers Martin Connors and Roger Jänecke, cover and interior designer Mary Claire Krzewinski, copyeditor Judy Galens, proofreaders Dana Barnes and Roger Matuz, indexer Larry Baker, permissions manager Christopher Scanlon, photo digitizer Robert Huffman, and typesetter Marco Di Vita of the Graphix Group.

To me a computer is just a big typewriter. When I needed help setting up all the programs that would free me to write, my daughter showed up, spent all the time she needed to spend, and showed me how to make technology work for me instead of against me. Jan—you're the greatest!

Finally, I have to mention the behind-the-scenes coauthor of this book. Writing is a solitary sport. But when you ascend from a bout with the muse, excited and invigorated, someone has to listen to your enthusiasm, support you with a pat on the head, and then have the courage to bring you down to earth by saying, "What did you mean by this?" My wife is more than a helper, more than a critic, more than editor, and more than a support group. She is an inspiration, a joy, and a soul mate. Thank you, Barbara. I never could have done it without you!

Adam and Marianna, thanks for sharing your mother. Jim and Jan, thanks for making me feel that what your father said was important when you took notes while visiting his college courses. Dad, thanks for everything. And Dot, neither one of us will ever forget the trip to Israel!

And to all of you—have a great journey!

AARON

(See also Ark of the Covenant; Burning Bush; Moses)

Aaron, the brother of Moses, was the first High Priest of Israel and patriarch of the family called Kohen. (This name is sometimes spelled Cohen; it comes from the Hebrew word for priest and, in biblical times, referred to those who conducted worship at the ancient Temple.)

When Moses, confronted by God at the burning bush, complained that his public speaking ability was not adequate for the task of calling on Pharaoh to release the Hebrew people from bondage in Egypt, his older brother Aaron was called upon to become his spokesman (Exodus, chapters 6 and 7). Thus it was that Aaron, standing before Pharaoh, performed the miracles of turning his staff into a serpent and calling forth the first three of ten plagues that persuaded Pharaoh to release the Hebrews.

In the wilderness journey following Passover, when the people of Israel complained about God's leadership, Aaron was named High Priest. As such, he conducted the first worship services held in the Tent of Meeting, sometimes called the Tabernacle in the Wilderness. The vestments he wore were made according to the instructions of God, and the ritual he instituted lasted for more than five hundred years, until the destruction of the Second Temple at Jerusalem in 70 CE.

Sources:
Bridger, David, ed. *The New Jewish Encyclopedia*. New York: Behrman House, 1962.

ABEL *see* Cain and Abel

ABOMINABLE SNOWMAN

In 1832, B. H. Hodson, a British representative writing from Nepal, described a creature that allegedly attacked a group of his servants. Members of the local population

Aaron, the priestly brother of Moses. *Fortean Picture Library.*

told him he had described a Raksha, from the Sanskrit for "demon." This appears to be the first Western report of an unsubstantiated, many say mythical, beast who stands some seven to nine feet tall, is very hairy, and leaves behind mysterious footprints along with what is often described as a very disagreeable odor.

Since then similar reports have come from China, Vietnam, Siberia, Canada, and northwestern sections of the United States. The creature is called Yeti, Bigfoot, Sasquatch, Abominable Snowman, and even, in a Hollywood movie, "Hairy," a creature who moves in with the Henderson family.

Usually it is reported that indigenous people, including Buddhist monks living in a monastery in Nepal, take for granted the existence of these creatures. But the first reported name, "demon," suggests the existence of a religious mythology.

Three main categories of theories seem to have formed concerning religious or psychological ways of understanding the Abominable Snowman/Big Foot phenomenon:

1. Because no hard evidence has yet been fully accepted by the scientific community, the creature does not exist except as a mythological personification of normal human fears—a way of explaining the unknown, as perhaps Greek and Roman mythologies do.

2. Such creatures possibly exist, and their discovery may point to earlier evolutionary human ancestors or cousins.

3. Such creatures exist and various cults have formed around them, each with its own explanation of where the creatures came from and why they are here. One theory says that when three of the Ten Lost Tribes of Israel migrated to the Americas sometime after the eighth century BCE (see Babylonian Captivity; Book of Mormon; and Eliot, John), descendants of Goliath of Gath, whose ancestors are thought to be the "giants" described in the Bible in Numbers 13, came with them. When Goliath, the nine-foot-tall Philistine warrior, was slain by David, the shepherd boy, he apparently left behind relatives who, by all accounts, were much more peace-loving than he was. This view is substantiated by 1 Chronicles 20, which speaks of "brothers" of "Goliath, slain by David." Other accounts seem to associate Yetis with the UFO culture, identifying them either as aliens or creatures contacted by aliens in the distant past, and with whom the aliens are possibly still in touch. Still others see in the Abominable Snowman a godlike or demonlike creature existing outside normal human understanding.

This mythology is perhaps most evident in the religious traditions of Indian communities found throughout North America, but best illustrated by stories told in the northern Plains cultures. Peter Matthiessen, while doing research for his book *In the Spirit of Crazy Horse*, discovered that many Indian elders knew of and had seen

> a messenger who appears in evil times as a warning from the Creator that man's disrespect for His sacred instructions has upset the harmony and balance of existence … He has strong spirit powers and sometimes takes the form of a huge, hairy man. In recent years this primordial being has appeared near Indian communities from the northern Plains states to far northern Alberta and throughout the Pacific northwest.

So great is the mystery surrounding this creature that he is sometimes alluded to only as "That-One-You-Are-Speaking-About." Others simply call him the "Big Man."

Perhaps illustrating a marriage of traditional indigenous beliefs with Christianity, some Indian elders believe the creature to be *Unk-cegi,* which means "Brown Earth,"

The Abominable Snowman, by Ivan Sanderson. *Fortean Picture Library.*

or, less delicately, "Brown Dung," the filth of creation. The story goes that Unk-cegi lived long ago during the time of the big animals but was drowned with them during the Great Flood. He was safely buried for a long time, but now that the white man had been burrowing deep and exploding bombs under the earth in a relentless search for minerals, the spirit of Unk-cegi has been released through the resultant fissures to roam the earth in warning. As the time of the end grows nearer, according to the belief, there will be more and more sightings.

Sources:

Coleman, Loren. *The Field Guide to Bigfoot, Yeti, and Other Mystery Primates.* Worldwide, 1999.

Douglas, J. D., Emory Stevens Bucke et al, eds. *American Folklore and Legend.* Pleasantville, NY: Reader's Digest Association, 1978.

Matthiessen, Peter, *In the Spirit of Crazy Horse.* Viking Press, New York, 1983.

ABORTION

Heartfelt feelings about abortion have both galvanized and polarized the religious community. Fundamentalist Protestants and traditional Roman Catholics, people who normally would have little in common theologically, find themselves marching together in picket lines across the street from pro-choice rallies. Conservative Jews join hands with evangelical Christians to sponsor local chapters of Operation Rescue in an attempt to shut down neighborhood abortion clinics. In many communities, women who have had abortions are either ostracized by their religious family or live lives consumed by guilt and feelings of hypocrisy when they attempt to keep their secret hidden.

At issue is the religious definition of when life begins. People who believe that life begins at conception, and that this life is morally and legally independent from the mother, generally label themselves pro-life. Others believe that life begins at a later point—for many, that point is reached when the fetus becomes viable, meaning that it could survive outside the mother's body. Many people try to take into account concerns such as the health, survival, and quality of life for both mother and fetus. Those who believe that abortion is an issue best decided by the pregnant woman label themselves pro-choice.

Religious people on both sides of the issue consider life sacred and a gift from God. As always, there are those who use religious arguments to buttress emotional positions. From the political/religious right comes the argument that the miracle of life is in God's hands and God's hands alone. From the political/religious left comes the argument that with the gift of life comes the God-given responsibility to care for that life, a responsibility that can only belong to the woman who carries the life within her own body.

Both the *Washington Times* and *Christianity Today* magazine credit the Republican stand on "abortion and family values" with the party's political victories in the 2002 elections. But FoxNews exit polls revealed that only 16 percent of voters polled were active in the "Conservative Christian political movement."

Some have attempted compromises, suggesting that abortion is wrong except in certain cases, such as when the woman has become pregnant as a result of rape or incest, or when carrying a child to term will endanger the health of the mother. Many opponents of abortion urge women with unwanted pregnancies to consider adoption rather than abortion.

One of the major problems confronting people who want to know what various religions say about the issue is that in almost every case, the "rank and file" disagree among themselves. The "official" Roman Catholic position concerning birth control, for instance, is that artificial birth control is forbidden by the church. But unofficial polls repeatedly show that the overwhelming opinion of American Catholics is at odds with church doctrine. Even many priests, asked for their opinion "off the record," testify that they are in disagreement with the Vatican. In other words, it can be said that the Catholic Church says artificial birth control is a sin, but Catholics do not. Likewise, the official positions held by various religions concerning abortion may not reflect the views of a number of their adherents.

Below are some of the positions held by various religions.

In Strict Opposition

"Abortion is wrong under any circumstance." This position is held by Buddhist and Hindu sects that have chosen to commit themselves on the question. Their feeling is that all life is sacred. Many Buddhists and Hindus will not destroy any life, even going to the trouble of sweeping the streets before them to prevent stepping on insects. Destroying life builds bad Karma for the next life (see Buddhism; Hinduism; Jainism). According to these beliefs, abortion at any stage of development is wrong.

This position is also held by the Roman Catholic Church and the Jehovah's Witnesses, along with some Baptist denominations (see entries under each). They don't use the same justification as the Buddhists and Hindus, because they don't believe in reincarnation. But their official statements indicate the belief that all life is sacred and that the taking of any human life, at any stage of development, is a sin.

Some Exceptions

"Abortion is wrong unless the mother's life is threatened." This position has been, since 1989, the official stance of the Anglican Church. It is also the stand taken by most Presbyterian churches, the United Church of Christ, and most Lutheran churches. Some add that the rape of the mother justifies abortion.

A Middle Ground

"Abortion is allowed up to a certain point of fetal development." This position is held by Sikhs and some Muslims, as well as by the Supreme Court of the United States. The problem becomes trying to determine when that point is reached. Some Muslims, for instance, place it at 40 days, others at 120 days. This is when the fetus is said to be "ensouled." After the soul is melded with the body, abortion is considered to be murder. Sikhs don't go so far as to set a date. They just allow abortion at any time up to a "medically safe" point.

A Pro-choice Position

"Abortion is a decision best left up to the mother." This position is held by the Unitarian Universalist Society and the Reform branch of Judaism. It is probably safe to say that, at least in America, it is also the quiet position held by the majority of women in the religions discussed so far. The feeling in these groups is that abortion is simply too important and personal a choice for anyone to make for anyone else.

Some religious groups have simply refused to go on record with an opinion. Conservative Jews, for instance, are divided on the subject. Orthodox Jews advise women to consult with their rabbi before coming to a decision.

The traditional American Indian and Eskimo belief is that abortion is wrong, but the infant can and should be adopted by members of the tribe if, for any reason, the mother cannot or will not raise the child.

A variety of websites are listed below for more in-depth study concerning religious positions on this very personal and controversial subject.

Sources:
Childbirth by Choice Trust. http://www.cbctrust.com. September 14, 2003.
Religious Coalition for Reproductive Choice. http://www.rcrc.org/. September 14, 2003.
Religious Tolerance.org. http://www.religioustolerance.org. September 14, 2003.

ABRAHAM

No colossus stands astride the monotheistic religious history of the world quite like Abraham. Three world religions—Judaism, Christianity, and Islam—trace their ancestry back to him. He is considered to be the father of both Judaism and Islam, through his sons Isaac and Ishmael, respectively, and the spiritual father of Christianity, according to Paul's letter to the Romans, chapter 4, verse 1. Indeed, except for the name of Jesus, Abraham's name appears more times in the Christian New Testament than does any other.

Although scholars will probably always wonder whether he was an actual man or a composite of characters, his story, set in about 2000 BCE, is told in a straightforward, historical manner beginning in the book of Genesis, chapter 12.

He is first introduced as Abram (the name means "exalted father"), living in Ur of the Chaldees, in what is now Iraq. The ancient city of Ur, a Sumerian capital, has been excavated. As a result of archaeological work done there, many believe it has been demonstrated that a people called Hapiru, or Hebrew, lived in Ur until about the

Abraham offering his son Isaac as a sacrifice to God. *Fortean Picture Library.*

time of the biblical narrative. They apparently migrated to Haran, in northern Mesopotamia, and then, it is assumed, to Canaan, later called Palestine, now Israel. Critical scholarship, however, like all sciences, is continually in flux, and it must be noted that further research sheds doubt on the connection.

Abraham is presented as a man of great faith although, like most biblical heroes, his feet of clay make him disarmingly appealing. The religious "call" that begins his story occurs in Genesis 12:

> Now the Lord said to Abram, "Go from your father's house to the land I will show you. And I will make of you a great nation, and I will bless you and make your name great, so that you will be a blessing. I will bless those who bless you, and him who curses you I will curse; and by you all the families of the earth shall bless themselves."

"So Abram departed," according to the Bible, without a single word of protest or explanation. This act of unquestioning faith became the foundation for three religions.

After demonstrating this faith, however, Abram does an unexpected thing. He goes to Canaan as instructed, but at the first sign of famine, he continues on to Egypt. While there he is so worried about the Egyptian response to the beauty of his wife, Sarai, that he passes her off as his half-sister so no one will kill him in the hopes of marrying his widow. His plot almost backfires, and Sarai barely escapes becoming a member of Pharaoh's harem.

When Abram does return to Canaan, his name is changed to Abraham, which means "father of a multitude." It is by this name, and his wife's new name of Sarah, that they are known by three world religions. Abraham promises to remain faithful to his covenant with God, and circumcision will be the physical sign of that covenant, so as to set apart his descendants forever (see Circumcision).

Abraham is told that he and his wife will have a son whose ancestors will grow to become a great nation. When the miracle of birth fails to materialize (the couple is, after all, more than ninety years old), Sarah decides Abraham should father a baby by her Egyptian servant, Hagar. This practice was apparently fairly common in those days. A woman incapable of bearing children would often adopt as her own the child of her husband and a household servant.

The baby boy born of this union was named Ishmael. It is from Ishmael, the firstborn, that Muslims believe the religion of Islam begins. Significantly, the Hebrew Bible inserts an editorial at this point. Ishmael is called "a wild ass of a man" whose "hand will be against every man and every man's hand against him; and he shall dwell against all his kinsmen" (Genesis 16:12).

All was not happy in the tents of Abraham, however. Right after Ishmael was born, Sarah gave birth to her own son, naming him Isaac. This being a patriarchal social system, she believed Hagar, her servant, now felt superior to her, having given birth to Abraham's firstborn son. Casting Hagar and her son Ishmael out into the desert, Sarah began to raise Isaac, who was to become father to the Hebrew people.

Thus in these two sons is prophesied two great peoples who, it is said, will forevermore be in competition.

Abraham's complete story is recounted in the rest of the book of Genesis, but a few highlights are especially important.

In Genesis 14:17–24, the mysterious Melchizedek appears. Chedorlaoma, king of Elam, had captured Abraham's kinsman, Lot. Abraham and his family army attacked by night, effecting a rescue. Upon Abraham's return from the battle, Melchizedek, "king of Salem" and "priest of the most high God," appears on the scene, offering a blessing and a gift of bread and wine. Abraham promptly gives him a tithe, or one-tenth, of the spoils captured in battle. This action is never explained. Indeed, Melchizedek is never mentioned again in the Hebrew Bible, except for an enigmatic reference in Psalm 110. "The Lord says to my Lord ... You are a priest forever after the order of Melchizedek." The Christian author of the book of Hebrews, however, uses this passage to form the basis for a central New Testament theology of "The Melchizedek Priesthood" of Christ. Jesus Christ, the "Prince of Peace," is described as both priest and king, gives his followers bread and wine, and is deserving of their tithes and offerings (Hebrews 7:1–4).

Also central to Abraham's story is the aborted sacrifice of Isaac, his son. In Genesis 22, God tells Abraham to offer a sacrifice in the hills of Moriah. Today many Jews believe this to be the place in Jerusalem where the important Muslim mosque called the Dome of the Rock now stands. Its familiar golden roof dominates pictures of the Jerusalem skyline.

Because child sacrifice was practiced in the Canaanite religion of those days, this story is not quite so outlandish as may appear to modern sensibilities. What may seem strange, however, was that Isaac was "the promised seed" who was to become the "father of a multitude." How was he to fulfill his destiny if he were killed? The question was answered when God provided a ram, caught in nearby bushes, that became Isaac's substitute.

The story is interpreted three different ways by three different religions. Besides being a test of faith, Jews see this as a foreshadowing of the sacrificial system later inaugurated by Moses and brought to its highest expression in the Temple of Solomon, built a thousand years later on this same spot of ground. Animal sacrifice as substitutionary atonement for sin here replaces human sacrifice, a step up on the religious evolutionary scale.

Christian theologians take the story further, saying that Jesus, the Son of God, himself became "the Lamb of God" that would replace the animal sacrifice. Because the crucifixion took place in the same geographical area, a progression is seen on this spot of ground that leads from human to animal to God becoming the substitute for the guilty sinner in need of atonement. In other words, Abraham's son could be spared; God's son could not.

Muslims have another version of the story. The events are the same but the place and people change. The name of Abraham's son and the place of the sacrifice are not mentioned in the Qur'an; it is usually understood that it was Ishmael, the first-born, who was offered. And the place of sacrifice was not the scene of present-day Jerusalem, but rather south, in Mecca. According to Muslim belief, Abraham and Ishmael practiced true faith in God by "submitting." The word "Muslim" means "a submitter." Tradition states that Abraham brought Ishmael to Mecca when Sarah forced them to leave. Later, Ishmael and Abraham together rebuilt in Mecca the Kaaba (shrine) that had been destroyed by Noah's flood. There they prayed that Allah would raise up from their descendants a messenger who would declare God's revelations and teach wisdom. This messenger, Muslims believe, was Muhammad.

Abraham, then, is the most revered patriarch of the major monotheistic religions. Although views about him differ widely depending on which religion's scriptures are consulted, his story, as interpreted by Jews, Christians, and Muslims, has undeniably affected the course of human history.

Sources:

Bridger, David, ed. *The New Jewish Encyclopedia*. New York: Behrman House, 1962.

Bucke, Emory Stevens et al, eds. *The Interpreter's Dictionary of the Bible*. 4 vols. New York: Abingdon Press, 1962.

The Holy Qur'an, trans. with a commentary by Abdullah Yusuf Ali. Beirut, Lebanon: Dar Al Arabia, 1968.

May, Herbert G., and Bruce M. Metzger, eds. *The New Oxford Annotated Bible with the Apocrypha*. Rev. ed. New York: Oxford University Press, 1973.

Szulc, Tad. "Journey of Faith." *National Geographic*, December 2001.

ADAM AND EVE

(See also Lilith)

According to Genesis, the first book of the Jewish and Christian Bible, the first man and woman were created on the sixth day of Creation, "in the image of God." Two accounts are given. In Genesis 1, "male and female" were created together (see Lilith). In Genesis 2, the first man was created, and when "God saw that it was not good that the man should be alone," a "helper fit for him" was created from one of the man's ribs.

Because the man was created "from the dust of the ground" (Adamah, in Hebrew), he was called "Adam." The name "Eve" comes from the Hebrew Havvah, meaning "life-bearer."

Their home is said to be in the garden called Eden, in the region where the Tigris and Euphrates flowed, along with two other now-unidentifiable rivers.

Their life was said to be innocence itself, existing in total harmony with each other and their environment, with no need for clothes or covering, and with God, who "walked in the garden in the cool of the evening."

All this changed in Genesis 3. It was then that temptation, in the form of the "forbidden fruit," led to sin and the fall of the human race. A serpent, identified much later by Christians as "that old serpent, the Devil and Satan" (Revelation 20), appeared to Eve and tempted her to eat the fruit of the one forbidden tree, the tree of the knowledge of good and evil. Succumbing to three temptations—of the eye ("it was a delight to the eye"), the flesh (it was "good for food"), and pride (it was "to be desired to make one wise")—she ate of the fruit and gave some to Adam, who joined her in breaking God's command.

When their act was discovered, punishment followed. Eve was to bring forth children in pain and her "desire [was] to be for her husband, [who would] rule over [her]." Adam, because he "listened to the voice of [his] wife," was destined to work in the fields and henceforth earn his daily bread "by the sweat of [his] brow."

"The Fall of Man," by Hans Sebald Behan, represents Adam and Eve's expulsion from the Garden of Eden. *Fortean Picture Library.*

Children were born to them. After Cain, the firstborn, killed his brother Abel and departed to build a city, their third son, Seth, was born. Seth carried on the lineage of the rest of the human race through his descendant, Noah. Although

Adam was said in Genesis 5:4 to have fathered "other sons and daughters," they are not named.

There are at least three ways to view the story of Adam and Eve.

1. As a historical account of what actually happened. Since the events occurred at the beginning of Creation, it is impossible either to prove or disprove this view.

2. As an early origin myth attempting to explain, among others things, how the human race came to exist and why a "good" God could have created a "good" creation that seems to possess "bad" qualities.

3. As a metaphor expressing the oral memory of historical evolution. In other words, our ancestors did once walk the forest, eating what the trees offered, until they learned to grow crops "by the sweat of their brow." The "good old days" of gathering in the forest are pictured as a "Garden of Eden," better than the drudgery of the tasks of plowing and weeding.

However the story is read, it has become a source of rich spiritual and philosophical exploration. Many different religious discussions have centered on treasures to be mined from this vein.

Mary Baker Eddy, the founder of Christian Science, sees in the name Adam a metaphor for "a dam," or an obstruction. In this case the dam does not restrict the course of water, but of thought. In other words, our original male parent was the first to lose, or block, the purity of a perfect, "good" way of viewing the world. Since then, we are all doomed to see the illusion of death and sickness rather than the reality of life and wholeness.

Daniel Quinn, in novels exploring present-day life and how it came to be this way, sees in the story of Adam and Eve—and later, Cain and Abel—a retelling of what actually occurred during the agricultural revolution. Cain, the agriculturalist, killed Abel, the nomadic shepherd, and went out to build a city. Historically, this progression took place when humans developed a stable food supply. "Civilization," including the building of cities and the invention of writing, marked the beginning of what we now call history. In other words, the story of Adam and Eve is a myth describing the hinge between prehistory and history. Because the Bible places the story six to eight thousand years ago, the same date historians use to mark the first agricultural revolution, Quinn makes a compelling case (see Agricultural Revolution).

Joseph Campbell saw in the story another example of the universal myth he called "the one forbidden thing," retold in almost every culture to deal with the "problem" of evil, or why bad things happen to good people (see Evil).

Christian theologians ever since the apostle Paul have used Genesis 3 to explain the need for the sacrifice of the Son of God. When Adam and Eve were cast out of the garden, "an angel with a flaming sword" guarded the entrance. This was the angel of death, blocking the way back to Eden. Union with God is impossible without death because, in the words of Saint Paul, "the wages of sin is death" (Romans 6:23). Being descendants of Adam and Eve, all humans have inherited their "original sin." An old New England spelling primer, dating back to 1691, put it simply: "In Adam's fall, we sinned all." Christians thus see Jesus as "the second Adam," who came to undo or atone for the sin of the first Adam. In 1 Corinthians Paul writes, "In Adam we all die … but in Christ, the second Adam, we shall all be made alive."

In the Qur'an, Muslims read that after Adam was created the angels were told to bow down to him. Iblis, the Satan figure, "refused and was haughty: he was one of those who rejected Faith" (2:33–37). Thus Iblis was cast into hell not because he hated God, but rather because he loved God too much to worship another created being.

Sources:
Bridger, David, ed. *The New Jewish Encyclopedia*. New York: Behrman House, 1962.
Campbell, Joseph. *The Power of Myth*. New York: Doubleday, 1988.
Dawood, N. J., trans. *The Koran*, 5th rev. ed. New York: Penguin Classics, 1990.
Eddy, Mary Baker. *Science and Health with a Key to the Scriptures*. Christian Science Publications, 1875.
The Holy Bible, New International Version. Grand Rapids, MI: Zondervan Bible Publishers, 1978.
Quinn, Daniel. *Ishmael*. New York: Bantam/Turner Books, 1995.

ADVENT *see* **Christianity, Calendar of**

AFTERLIFE

The earliest evidence we have of early humans, the Neanderthal, consists of grave burials. As early as 25,000 years ago, people began to bury their dead with what appears to be religious intent. Skeletons have been found in graves containing hand axes and weapons, perhaps implying a belief that the dead would need them in a life following this one. An argument could thus be advanced that belief in an afterlife was among the first human religious convictions.

Afterlife is a fundamental belief of most religious traditions, and its interpretation falls into one of three basic categories:

A Place

Probably the first belief in afterlife was that a person goes somewhere when departing this life. Often religions describe this place as an ideal environment projected from surroundings with which the culture is already familiar: the rich hunting ground of Plains Indian culture, the recycled earth of the Hebrew prophets, the "Holy City" of the Christian New Testament, and the heavenly oasis of Islam. Egyptian embalmers went to great extremes to prepare their nobility for this place, not only building great pyramids for entrance halls but also providing wealth to cover traveling expenses and to ensure a continuation of lifestyle in the life to come.

Often this place of eternal joy and contentment is contrasted with a place of torment for those who fail to attain the ethical righteousness a religion calls for. Either a fiery hell or a nebulous place of darkness awaits the unworthy, sometimes preceded

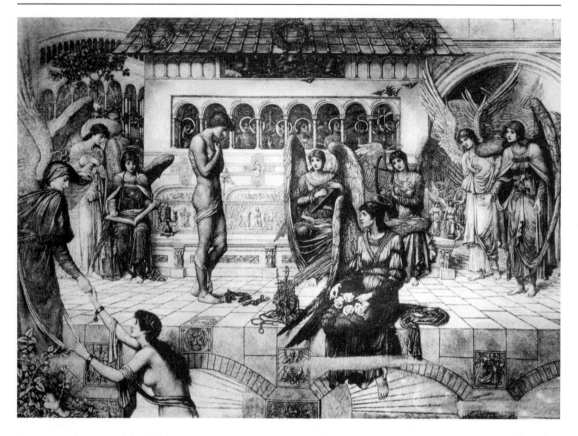

Engraving depicting the afterlife by J. M. Strudwick, 1891, entitled "The Ramparts of God's House." *Fortean Picture Library.*

by a "waiting room" or purgatory, where debts must be paid or choices made concerning eternity.

In some traditions, the spirit of the deceased stays where he or she lived during life. In Shinto it is not uncommon for ancestors, accustomed to receiving offerings and prayers from their descendants, to speak through the lips of shamans. "Haunted" houses are said to be home to ghosts or shades of previous owners. The famous magician Harry Houdini promised to communicate from the place of the dead if at all possible; after years of seances, usually held at Halloween—traditionally said to be the time when the veil between this world and the next is stretched the thinnest—his wife finally gave up in despair. Sir Arthur Conan Doyle, author of the Sherlock Holmes mysteries, spent the last years of his life exploring ways to pierce the barrier between life and death.

Many "after-death" experiences have been recorded by people considered clinically dead and then revived. They commonly report having seen a tunnel of light leading to a beautiful place of fields and flowers, a Being of Light radiating warmth and love, and reunion with loved ones. These experiences have been reported by both religious and nonreligious people, and they are the subject of considerable debate. Some see these descriptions as proof of afterlife, others as a chemical reaction in the brain rendering near-death visions of culturally familiar concepts of heaven.

A Consciousness

Sometimes afterlife is described in terms of a drop of water returning to the ocean. This is the view of the Buddhist Nirvana and New Age thought; it is also found in ancient Hinduism. In this interpretation, universal consciousness has taken on human form. Then, after spending a few years or lifetimes on Earth gathering experience, it returns to the consciousness of the cosmos, uniting again in the wholeness encompassing both time and space.

A Process

As expressed in the Tibetan Book of the Dead, this view of afterlife sees a procession of incarnations. Life is described as the perpetually turning wheel of samsara, in which people live out a series of reincarnations, driven by Karma accumulated in past lives (see Karma). Exploration of past lives helps in the understanding of why things happen in the present life. The process is, for all practical purposes, endless, though the goal is moksha, eventual release of the now fully formed individual into the eternal consciousness. In Hinduism, atman, the individual soul, merges with brahman, the universal consciousness. The Buddha was said to have achieved Nirvana upon his death and is even now drawing unto himself the Buddha consciousness inherent in every human.

Sources:
Hagen, Steve. *Buddhism Plain and Simple*. Boston: Charles E. Tuttle Co., 1997.
The Holy Qur'an, trans. with a commentary by Abdullah Yusuf Ali. Beirut, Lebanon: Dar Al Arabia, 1968.
Lewis, James R. *The Death and Afterlife Book*. Detroit, MI: Visible Ink Press, 2001.
May, Herbert G., and Bruce M. Metzger, eds. *The New Oxford Annotated Bible with the Apocrypha*. Rev. ed. New York: Oxford University Press, 1973.
Szulc, Tad. "Journey of Faith." *National Geographic*, December 2001.
Tibetan Book of the Dead. New York: Oxford University Press, 1960.

AGNI

Agni is the Hindu god of fire, from whose name are derived the English words "igneous" and "ignite."

The harnessing of fire was one of the first crucial steps humans had to take in order to advance. The fire sacrifice is one of the earliest of religious rituals, brought down through the famous Khyber Pass around 1500 BCE by Indo-European Aryans and imposed upon the existing culture of India. This migration began what we now call intellectual Hinduism. The world's first scripture, the Hindu Rig Veda, appeared at about this time. It told of Agni, the magician of fire, existing on Earth not only to consume but also to give warmth and to help in cooking food. In the atmosphere, he is the lightning. In the sky, the sun. Inhabiting all three levels of the cosmos—Earth, sky, and atmosphere—he is able to bear prayers and sacrifices to the gods.

Gradually Agni became internalized. Fire is a mystery and burns within Earth and the sun. But the fire of life also burns within each human. Sometimes it even breaks out in fever during times of emotional turmoil or illness. Agni, then, dwells within as well as without.

Although the Sanskrit doctrine of *tat tvam asi*, "thou art that" (see Brahman/Atman), had not yet been fully developed, it was a small but formative step to picture Agni as the fire of life itself. Within humans burned the fire that is at the very heart of the universe.

Sri Aurobindo (1872–1950), the Indian spiritual master, has written:

The Vedic deity Agni is the first of the powers that have issued from the vast and secret Godhead. Agni is the form, the fire, the forceful heat and flaming will of this Divinity. [The word Agni] means a burning brightness, whence its use for fire. When man, awakened from his night, wills to offer his inner and outer activities to the gods of a truer and higher existence and so to arise out of mortality into the far-off immortality, it is this flame of upward aspiring Force and Will that he must kindle; into this fire he must cast the sacrifice.

Thus Agni, oldest of the Hindu gods, evolved into a metaphor for creativity and spiritual yearning.

Sources:
Fisher, Mary Pat. *Living Religions*. 3rd ed. Upper Saddle River, NJ: Prentice Hall, 1991.
Sri Aurobindo. *The Immortal Fire*. Auroville, India: Auropublications, 1974.

AGNOSTICISM/THEISM/ATHEISM

Agnosticism is a middle position concerning belief in the divine. Theists believe in the existence of God, or the reality of, in the words of Joseph Campbell, an "invisible plane" supporting the visible context of everyday life. Atheists do not. They believe all reality can be explained by scientifically reasoned principles and that there is no reason to postulate spiritual forces beyond perceived phenomena. In short, the material realm of the cosmos contains all that exists (see Anthropomorphism).

The word "agnostic" derives from "gnosis," which means knowledge, or the condition of knowing. An agnostic is one who professes not to know. The word is used in two different religious conceptions:

1. A person may claim that knowledge of God is unknowable to anyone; that God is above human categories of thought and thus impossible to know or understand with human sensibilities. In other words, God may or may not exist, and it is impossible for humans to know.

2. A person may claim that he or she has not experienced the divine and therefore cannot demonstrate personal knowledge of a deity.

Joseph Campbell, author of such books as *The Masks of God* and *The Hero with a Thousand Faces,* has associated the words theist and atheist with the tendency to connect religious myth to historical fact. In an interview with Bill Moyers televised by PBS, he somewhat facetiously divided the world into two camps. Those in one camp, he explained, believe their religious myths are historically accurate explanations of how things occurred. These, he said, are called theists. Those in the other group—knowing, for example, that God didn't create the world in six literal days—refuse to acknowledge the historical accuracy of their culture's mythology and are labeled atheists. In Campbell's view, the two words are arbitrary designations based not on belief but rather on mythological interpretation.

Sources:
Campbell, Joseph. *The Power of Myth*. New York: Doubleday, 1988.
Webster's Third New International Dictionary and Seven Language Dictionary. 3 vols. Chicago: William Benton, 1966.

AGRICULTURAL REVOLUTION

Ten to twelve thousand years ago, what has been called the agricultural revolution began to alter completely almost every aspect of human life and religious history. By six thousand years ago its results were seen in some of the oldest cities in the world. In Jericho, perhaps the oldest continually inhabited city in existence, and Ur, purported to be the home of Abraham and the Hapiru (see Abraham), complex lifestyles developed when people discovered both the blessings and curses resulting from a fixed, stable home.

The agricultural revolution marks the beginning of what we now call civilization or recorded history. When people discovered the benefits of cultivation and a predictable food source, the results were dramatic. In Mesopotamia and Egypt, populations exploded as large crops farmed by few people could support larger families and communities. Cities evolved as more people settled in one place. This shift led to specialization of occupations and the beginning of formal political and economic systems. As one city traded with another, the invention of writing made it possible both to communicate and keep track of wealth.

But there was a dark side to this revolution. Stored wealth invited the temptation to manipulate the food supply. The "haves" grew to dominate the "have-nots." Social class stratas inevitably followed. Competition over the best fields and the pressure of overcrowding led to warfare between cities. The drudgery of the field replaced the sport of the hunt. The drawbacks were accepted, however, because of the utility and obvious advantage of a reliable food supply.

The agricultural revolution led to significant changes in world religions. Wars and armies tended to encourage the concept of male, warlike, tribal gods, capable of defending cities and cultures, rather than the female mother-earth goddesses of pastoral peoples. Gods such as Baal of the Canaanites and Jehovah of the Israelites tended to require more and bloodier sacrifices to prove their superiority over the gods of other indigenous people. Specialization of occupations led to professional clergy, along with the temples and traditional styles of worship inherent in formal religions. The invention of writing led to organized, systematic scriptures. Once beliefs were written down, they tended to become codified, in contrast to the fluid, evolving patterns of oral mythology. Written scriptures also tended to follow analytical patterns of thought, departing from the imaginative, intuitive patterns of oral culture. Over time, religions tended to become increasingly hierarchical and dominated by men.

These changes did not happen right away. But by 4000 BCE, in the Tigris/Euphrates and Nile River valleys, the agricultural revolution was undeniably underway.

Biblical historian Daniel Quinn has made the case that a description of the process can be found in the third and fourth chapters of Genesis and is a part of Judaism, Christianity, and Islam. Here, Adam and Eve, having left the delights of the traditional gathering lifestyle they knew in the Garden of Eden, are now forced to earn their food by the drudgery of work in the field. Their son Cain, the new agriculturist, presents an offering from his garden to the traditional God of his parents. It is rejected in favor of the traditional sacrifice of his brother Abel, the pastoral herdsman. A revolution breaks out between the old tradition of pastoral migration and the new style of agricultural independence. Agriculture wins. Cain kills his brother. But he is driven from the presence of the old God, the old way of doing things. The implication is that he must find a new God, one who accepts the modern lifestyle.

The first thing Cain does is build a city, and his descendants proceed to develop not only agriculture, but also the industry of Tubal-Cain, the bronze-age forger, and the music of Jubal, "the father of all who play the harp and flute." Also at this time Lamech marries two women and vows vengeance on anyone who injures him. As humankind experiences a population explosion, corruption and violence grow so severe that God finally decides to destroy everything with a great flood. Thus, way back in the early chapters of Genesis, we read about urban development, agriculture, the growth of industry, the music business, bigamy and adultery, revenge, population explosion, corruption, violence, and natural disaster. Seen in this way, it reads like a modern-day morning newspaper.

In the biblical account, this is all placed about six thousand years ago in Mesopotamia, precisely when and where the agricultural revolution was changing the world. So when conservative scholars of Jewish, Christian, and Islamic belief say that the world began six to ten thousand years ago, perhaps they might more accurately say that the world of modern civilization, or written history, began at that time.

Whether Genesis contains the remembered oral record of human history is, of course, a matter of interpretation and religious belief. But the agricultural revolution has undoubtedly led to the way of life we now take for granted. Male-dominated hierarchical religious systems did tend to overcome goddess-based religious traditions as civilization spread. Leaders of wars even today use the tribal terminology of "our God against your God," a practice as old as that used by conflicting cities six thousand years ago as they fought for natural resources. Overcrowded cities and population centers are still recognized as hotbeds of crime and violence.

Sources:
Ellwood, Robert S., and Barbara A. McGraw. *Many Peoples, Many Faiths*. 6th ed. Upper Saddle River, NJ: Prentice Hall, 1999.

May, Herbert G., and Bruce M. Metzger, eds. *The New Oxford Annotated Bible with the Apocrypha.* Rev. ed. New York: Oxford University Press, 1973.

Quinn, Daniel. *Ishmael.* New York: Bantam/Turner Books, 1995.

AHRIMAN *see* **Ahura Mazda/Ahriman**

AHURA MAZDA/AHRIMAN

(See also Apocalypse; Babylonian Captivity; Zoroastrianism)

Ahura Mazda is the Zoroastrian high god of light. According to tradition, he is using humankind to defeat Ahriman, or Angra Mainyu, the devil figure of darkness, who has come to Earth to tempt humans away from the light. A battle of light and darkness, good and evil, is being waged that will end at the last judgment, when light will triumph and a new, purified Earth will enter into its prophesied eternal age of destiny.

Sources:

Campbell, Joseph. *The Inner Reaches of Outer Space: Metaphor As Myth and As Religion.* New York: Harper & Row, 1986.

Ellwood, Robert S., and Barbara A. McGraw. *Many Peoples, Many Faiths.* 6th ed. Upper Saddle River, NJ: Prentice Hall, 1999.

ALCOHOL

(See also Eucharist)

Religions seem to have a difficult time analyzing their relationship with alcohol, especially wine. Significantly, another name for alcohol is "spirits." Conversations with the psychologist Carl Jung led Bill W., cofounder of Alcoholics Anonymous (AA), to believe the only way to deal with "demon drink" was to enlist the aid of a "higher power." Breaking free from the "possession" of alcohol involved a battle of the gods. In a letter to Bill W., Jung wrote that the "craving for alcohol [is] the equivalent, on a low level, of the spiritual thirst of our whole being for wholeness, expressed in medieval language: the union with God ... 'alcohol' in Latin is *spiritus*, and you use the same word for the highest religious experience as well as the most depraving poison." Jean Shinoda Bolen, in her book *Gods in Everyman,* draws on this insight to affirm the basic tenet of AA: "When the use of alcohol or any other substance is motivated by Dionysus, a man or woman is seeking communion through these means; when this is the case, it's no wonder that a relationship with God helps bring about sobriety."

According to mythology, it was the Roman god Dionysus—earlier called Bacchus by the Greeks—who brought wine to the human race. A son of Zeus by Semele, a mortal woman, Dionysus was the god of wine and ecstasy. He was also the most human of the gods, and in his presence people are driven not only to great heights of spiritual awareness but also to depths of depression.

An ambivalent relationship exists between many religions and alcohol. Muslims and some conservative Christians forbid it. Christian women's temperance groups helped to bring about Prohibition in the United States. So runs the advice of good King Solomon in Proverbs 23:29–32:

Who has woe? Who has sorrow? Who has needless bruises? Who has bloodshot eyes? Those who linger over wine. Drink not the wine when it is red … in the end it bites like a snake and poisons like a viper.

Yet Noah—father of us all, according to Judeo-Christian scripture—didn't heed the word. The first thing he did after coming ashore after the flood was plant a vineyard, make some wine, and get inebriated (Genesis 20:21–23).

And the apostle Paul, in his first letter to young Timothy, pastor of the church at Ephesus, advised him to "Stop drinking only water, and use a little wine for the sake of your stomach" (1 Timothy 5:23).

Such is the nature of the modern-day cult of Dionysus. On the one hand we rage against his worship, calling it "Bacchanal." On the other, we elevate his gift of wine to the realm of the sacred, surround it with mystery, lift it high at the altar, watch it mystically transform into the blood of God, and then drink it.

Sources:

Bolen, Jean Shinola, M.D. *Gods in Everyman*. San Francisco: Harper & Row Publishers, 1989.

The Holy Bible, New International Version. Grand Rapids, MI: Zondervan Bible Publishers, 1978.

ALEXANDRIA

Alexander the Great's (356–323 BCE) conquests created the largest empire in the world to that time. He planned to build a great city in Egypt and call it Alexandria. When he died suddenly and mysteriously in 323 BCE, his plans were continued by Ptolemy, one of his four major generals and king of Egypt. Alexandria soon became the most important city of the African continent and the intellectual capital of the world.

Its library became the acknowledged center of learning, with an estimated 400,000 to 500,000 works along with priceless treasures of art and antiquity. As scholars flocked there to study, a blend of Greek, Hebrew, Egyptian, Chaldean, and Persian mysticism developed that, centuries later, was to blossom into a school of learning and a cult of Alexandrian alchemists who taught their secrets of chemical philosophies only to the initiated. Alchemy was not simply an attempt to turn base metals into gold. It was a metaphysical attempt to discover the very composition of how the world was made—the very structure of the cosmos.

In 80 BCE Roman emperor Julius Caesar invaded Egypt. A fire, attributed to warships burning in the Alexandrian harbor, spread to land and destroyed a major part of the collection of the library, but Alexandria still exerted a great intellectual influence over the Western world.

By the third century CE, the condition of the Roman Empire had deteriorated. Although Alexandria was second only to Rome in prestige, its time was limited. When Constantine, emperor of Rome, made Christianity the state religion in the early fourth century, it became the recognized duty of the state to eliminate all forms of what was considered idolatry and paganism, including representations of such in literature. In 389 CE, Theodosius called for the final destruction of paganism. Although the university in

Alexandria struggled on, by 415 the frenzied, zealous religious mobs ruled, and the wonderful library, along with its priceless scrolls and artifacts, was burned to the ground.

What was not generally known was that many of the Greek and Egyptian texts had been translated to Arabian and Syrian languages and carried to other places of learning. When Muslim influence swept as far east as Spain and Morocco in the seventh and eighth centuries, much learning attributed to Islamic scholars was, in fact, knowledge that had been preserved from the time of the Alexandria academic community. The alchemists' cult of chemistry had been somewhat preserved, but we will never fully know what has been lost.

Alexandria was also an important Jewish center of learning and culture. It was here that scholars labored to translate the Hebrew Bible into Greek for the benefit of Jews living abroad. This translation was called the Septuagint, so named because it was thought to be the work of seventy scholars.

Meanwhile, Alexandria was becoming important in Christian history. Egyptian Christianity is attributed to the missionary efforts of the apostle Mark, the man generally credited with the authorship of the second Gospel of the New Testament. It was the home and final battleground of Gnosticism (see Gnosticism), an early group of Christians, later declared heretical, who believed Jesus imparted a secret knowledge, or *gnosis*, to a select group of apostles. Some of their writings, including the Gospel of Thomas, thought to have been lost forever along with other Coptic writings, have been discovered within the last fifty years.

Origen, writing from Alexandria in the third century, was one of the first Christian scholars to treat biblical passages metaphorically rather than literally. In his *On First Principles*, he writes:

> Now what man of intelligence will believe that the first and the second and the third day, and the evening and the morning existed without the sun and the moon and the stars? And that the first day, if we may so call it, was even without a heaven (Gen.1:5–13)? And who is so silly as to believe that God, after the manner of a farmer, "planted a paradise eastward in Eden," and set in it a visible and palpable "tree of life," of such a sort that anyone who tasted its fruit with his bodily teeth would gain life; and again that one could partake of "good and evil" by masticating the fruit taken from the tree of that name (Gen. 2:8, 9)? And when God is said to "walk in the paradise in the cool of the day" and Adam to hide himself behind a tree, I do not think anyone will doubt that these are figurative expressions which indicate certain mysteries through a semblance of history and not through actual events (Gen. 3:8).

Augustine (354–430 CE), Bishop of Hippo in North Africa and intimate with Alexandrian tradition, believed the Greek neo-Platonists were right when they described a universal, cosmic hierarchy, descending from an eternal, intelligible God. His *City of God*, inspired by the fall of Rome in 410, criticized "pagan" religious, natural philosophy. Rumors were circulating that Rome fell because it had deserted its ancient religion. Augustine disputed these rumors in his book that describes two cities built on love. The earthly city is built on love of self. The city of God is built on love of God. Although they intermingle, they are at war. Earthly cities are destined to fall, but according to Augustine, the city of God will remain forever.

Sources:

Abdel-Reheem, Hamed, ed. "Technical Arts Related to Alchemy in Old Egypt." *The Alchemy Website*. http://www.levity.com/alchemy/islam07.html. April 22, 2002.

Bridger, David, ed. *The New Jewish Encyclopedia*. New York: Behrman House, 1962.

Douglas, J. D., ed. *The New International Dictionary of the Christian Church*. Grand Rapids, MI: Zondervan Publishing, 1974.

Fisher, Mary Pat, and Lee W. Bailey. *An Anthology of Living Religions*. Upper Saddle River, NJ: Prentice Hall, 2000.

Origen. "On First Principles," in Hugh T. Kerr, ed., *Readings in Christian Thought*. Nashville, TN: Abingdon Press, 1966.

ALLAH

Although the Qur'an of Islam lists ninety-nine names for God, it says most emphatically that *la ilah illa' Allah*—"there is no God but Allah." Allah is not so much a name as a title. The word means "the God," and it is the name revealed to the prophet Muhammad of the god worshiped by other "people of the book"—that is, Christians and Jews—although they use other names.

Because the Qur'an cannot be translated—that is, any translation is considered merely a study aid, not the true Qur'an—these words are an approximation, but they carry the weight and the essential meaning of Allah.

> There is no god but he; That is the witness of Allah, His angels, and those endued with knowledge, standing firm on justice. There is no god but he, the Exalted in Power, the Wise. (Qur'an 3:18)

> He it is Who created the heavens and the earth in Six Days, and is moreover firmly established on the Throne [of Authority]. He knows what enters within the earth and what comes forth out of it, what comes down from heaven and what mounts up to it. And he is with you wheresoever ye may be. And Allah sees well all that you do. (57:4)

> To Allah belongeth all that is in the heavens and on the earth. Whether ye show what is in your minds or conceal it, Allah calleth you to account for it. He forgiveth whom he pleaseth, and punisheth whom He pleaseth, for Allah hath power over all things. (2:284)

> He is the First and the Last, and the Outward and the Inward; and he is the Knower of all things. (57:3)

Sources:

Fisher, Mary Pat, and Lee W. Bailey. *An Anthology of Living Religions*. Upper Saddle River, NJ: Prentice Hall, 2000.

The Holy Qur'an, trans. with a commentary by Abdullah Yusuf Ali. Beirut, Lebanon: Dar Al Arabia, 1968.

ALMSGIVING (ZAKAT) *see* **Islam**

ALTAR

The original meaning of the word signified a raised structure, usually of stone, later of bronze, where sacrifices were offered or incense burned. Altars served as the focus of communal worship. Although the structures have been called by different names, all religions that share the element of sacrifice have used altars. Usually a severe ritual was enacted, with priests or shamans leading the rite while a congregation looked on. The offering consisted of everything from the plant material used in goddess worship to the animal sacrifices of Judaism and the elaborate human sacrifices of Canaanite and Olmec worship. Later, especially in Christianity, a table was substituted, often called a Communion Table, because here were placed the elements of the communion meal, which celebrated the sacrifice of Jesus.

Sources:

Bridger, David, ed. *The New Jewish Encyclopedia*. New York: Behrman House, 1962.

Bucke, Emory Stevens et al, eds. *The Interpreter's Dictionary of the Bible*. 4 vols. New York: Abingdon Press, 1962.

Webster's Third New International Dictionary and Seven Language Dictionary. 3 vols. Chicago: William Benton, 1966.

AMBROSE *see* Augustine

The altar in Breedon-on-the-Hill church, Leicestershire, England. *Fortean Picture Library.*

AMESBURY

(See also Ley Lines)

The town of Amesbury, located about eighty miles west of London, England, lies in an area of ancient and continued holiness. Nearby, on the Salisbury Plain in Wiltshire, is Stonehenge, one of the most ancient megalithic structures. A little to the north is the Avebury stone circle, scene of a religious tradition going back some four thousand years.

Welsh historians believe that during the Middle Ages, a monastery was located in Amesbury, but a consensus seems to have developed that in the time of Ambrosias Aurelianus, uncle to the fabled King Arthur, it was a garrison for troops, and the place was named Ambrosiani after Ambrosias.

In the Arthurian legends, it was in Amesbury that Guinevere, after her affair with Lancelot and banishment following Arthur's death, became a nun and lived out

Amesbury, an important site of Arthurian legends, is near the pre-Christian site of Stonehenge. *Fortean Picture Library.*

her days. Although modern writers more than earlier scribes seem to emphasize the importance of Amesbury in the Arthurian legends, John Masefield, in his poem, "Gwenivere Tells," has Guinevere remembering:

> Anon I made profession, and took vows
> As nun encloistered: I became Christ's spouse,
> At Amesbury, as Abbess to the house.
> I changed my ermines for a goathair stole,
> I broke my beauty there, with dule and dole,
> But love remained a flame within my soul.

Thus at Amesbury we find a curious but fairly common occurrence. One religious tradition, in this case the stone-building culture of prehistorical Stonehenge, is superseded by a completely different religious tradition. In this case, it is the legend of King Arthur's court and the search for the grail from Christ's last supper—the legend marking the transition from paganism to Christianity.

Sources:
James, Simon. *The World of the Celts.* New York: Thames and Hudson, 1993.

Jones, Prudence, and Nigel Pennick. *A History of Pagan Europe*. New York: Routledge, 1995.

Keyes, Bradley. "Stonehenge." *The Active Mind*. http://www.activemind.com/Mysterious/Topics/Stonehenge/index.html. April 25, 2002.

Llywelyn, Morga. *Druids*. New York: Ivy Books, 1991.

Masefield, John. "Amesbury." *Arthurian Sites in England*. http://www.uidaho.edu/student_orgs/arthurian_legend/england/sites/amesbury.httm. April 25, 2002.

AMISH

(See also Anabaptists; Mennonites)

When the Mennonites, lineal descendants of the Anabaptist movement in Europe, migrated to the United States from Switzerland, a splinter group broke away. This group believed wholeheartedly in the biblical command to "come out from them and be ye separate." Taking their name from Jakob Ammann, these were the Amish, and they have ever since retained their traditional lifestyle. They embrace pacifism and avoid many modern conveniences, such as electricity and automobiles, used by the "English" (as they call non-Amish) out in "the world." Instead they have continued to practice what they call their "plain" lifestyle, believing God intended people to live in redemptive community. Their beautifully kept farms have become tourist attractions, most notably in the Pennsylvania Dutch country, where it is common to see bearded farmers and women wearing traditional head coverings called *kapps* driving along country roads in horse-drawn black buggies. Popular restaurants in Amish communities offer some of the finest examples of American home cooking, featuring the traditional seven sweets and seven sours. But all this is surface appeal covering a deeply rooted, biblically based spiritual conviction that has been the driving force of their sect's strength for generations.

Sources:

Hostetler, John A. *The Amish*. Scottdale, PA: Herald Press, 1995.

AMITABHA BUDDHA

(See also Buddhism, Development of)

The founder of what is now called Pure Land Buddhism, Amitabha was the "Buddha of Boundless Light" who was said to have promised the creation of a special place of bliss (the Pure Land) open to all who called upon his name. For many Buddhists in China and Japan, Amitabha has become "the Buddha," expressing universal Buddha nature.

Sources:

Ellwood, Robert S., and Barbara A. McGraw. *Many Peoples, Many Faiths*. 6th ed. Upper Saddle River, NJ: Prentice Hall, 1999.

AMULET *see* Healing Effigy/Amulet/Talisman/Fetish

ANABAPTISTS

In the years following Christianity's sixteenth-century Protestant Reformation, freedom from the rigid structures of the Roman Catholic Church resulted in movements far removed from Martin Luther's original ideas of reforming the church of his day. Once the process began, various groups quickly formed what later would be called denominations. Points of theology became catalysts for fervent debate. With the invention of the printing press in the fifteenth century, debates spread quickly. Followers of charismatic leaders like John Calvin and Ulrich Zwingli could distribute convincing sermons and rebuttals to masses of people hungry for spiritual direction.

By 1523, especially in Zurich, Moravia, and the Netherlands, baptism was the topic of conversation that caught the attention of leaders such as Conrad Grebel, Balthasar Hubmaier, and Feliz Manz. At this time, the long-revered custom was that children should be baptized. This sacrament, in the words of the *Book of Worship of the United Church of Christ*, "was the mark of their acceptance into the care of Christ's church, the sign and seal of their participation in God's forgiveness, and [the] beginning of their growth into full Christian faith and life." Because the children were not old enough to be able to make the commitment themselves, their parents and godparents stood in for them. When the children matured to an age of understanding, they then confirmed for themselves their baptism vows.

But for some reformers, biblical precedent seemed to imply that only people who had attained the age of responsibility could be capable of promising their lives to Jesus and the church. Because these theologians could find no scriptural pattern for the two-part process of baptism/confirmation, they began to insist on adult baptism, often called believer's baptism. This meant that people who had already been baptized as infants were baptized again, this time by full immersion into water, following the pattern set by John the Baptist in the Jordan River.

These people were called Anabaptists, "ana" meaning "again." They would lead the way for groups such as the Mennonites and various Baptist denominations.

They were, of course, persecuted. Established religions, both Catholic and Protestant, took exception to the fact that their infant baptism was deemed less than adequate, let alone heretical.

But baptism was only the beginning. Anabaptists soon became known as a radical wing of the Protestant Reformation. Along with a strict policy of baptized, believers-only membership in the church, they insisted on strict conservative biblical interpretation with a literal reading of the Bible as history and dogma.

Sources:
Douglas, J. D., ed. *The New International Dictionary of the Christian Church*. Grand Rapids, MI: Zondervan Publishing, 1974.

ANALECTS *see* Confucian Texts

ANASAZI *see* Kiva

ANGEL

(See also Devil/Demons)

Monotheistic religions arising in the Middle East tended to see a separation between the material world and the spiritual. A wall stands between the experience of everyday life and life that is "other," above or beyond our physical environment. One realm exists for humankind and another for God. On this material side exist space and time.

On the transcendent side, infinity and eternity. The wall of separation is not solid but contains windows that enable at least partial communication or mystic vision to take place. The apostle Paul described this concept in 1 Corinthians 13: "Now we see through a glass, darkly, but then we shall see face to face."

One method of communication is for God to use messengers to bridge the gap, to move through the wall and carry God's messages to humans and human prayers to God.

The word "angel," from the Greek *angelos*, means "messenger." Although the concept of angels becomes more fully developed in later monotheistic religions, it is found in early Canaanite mythological poems and Persian Zoroastrianism. Ancient Hittite texts going back to a time when God was perceived as feminine describe groups of "fairy messengers" attending the mother-goddess.

Although popular misconceptions involve people becoming angels when they die, Judaism, Christianity, and Islam all teach that angels are a separate species created before humans. Probably because these are historically male-dominated religions, angels are usually depicted as being masculine, even though they are said to be either sexless or above sex. In one early exception to this

Image of an angel appearing to shepherds, from Thomas Heywood's *Hierarchie*, 1635. *Fortean Picture Library.*

notion of sexlessness, a passage in Genesis 6 explains that the judgment of Noah's flood was brought about in part because "the sons of God" (a phrase often interpreted to mean angels) "saw that the daughters of men" (that is, human women) "were beautiful, and they married any of them they chose." The offspring of these unions were the Nephilim, a mysterious term often translated as "giants" but defined in the Bible as "the heroes of old."

Although angelic myths differ, all describe a war in heaven that caused one-third of the angels to sin. They became the demons of Judeo/Christian teaching and a category within the "jinns" of Islam, creatures of smokeless fire. The fallen angels were led by the being Jews and Christians call "the Satan" (the accuser). Muslims call him Iblis.

In Christian scripture, angels generally appear in human form. An angel ordered Abraham to refrain from sacrificing his son Isaac (Gen. 22:11). Angels appeared to Ishmael, Jacob, Moses, Joshua, and Muhammad. Either two or three (the account in Genesis 18 and 19 is unclear) had dinner with Abraham on their way to destroy Sodom and Gomorrah.

THE RELIGION BOOK: PLACES, PROPHETS, SAINTS, AND SEERS

By the time of the sixth century BCE, angels were beginning to be defined more clearly. While earlier texts spoke simply of "the sons of God" or "holy ones," their hierarchy began to be revealed. By the thirteenth century CE, Saint Thomas Aquinas listed nine "choirs" or ranks of angels, beginning with the seraphim and continuing through cherubim, thrones, dominions, virtues, powers, principalities, archangels, and angels. We also learn of the angelic choir who sing eternally in heaven and have been known to give concerts on Earth, specifically to a group of shepherds on the first Christmas.

In Genesis 3 we learn of "cherubim [with] a flaming sword flashing back and forth to guard the tree of life." This image is quite different from the cute, chubby variety often portrayed in popular culture. Isaiah describes his vision of six-winged seraphim standing in the presence of God. They "were calling to one another" (Isaiah 6:3):

Holy, holy, holy is the Lord Almighty;
the whole earth is full of his glory.

And in the book of Hebrews, chapter 13, verse 2, readers are reminded: "Do not forget to entertain strangers, for by doing so some people have entertained angels without knowing it."

The apostle Paul understood the church to be the fulfillment of God's eternal plan. It was a mystery revealed to him that "Gentiles are heirs together with Israel." But the purpose of this plan was to demonstrate the "manifold wisdom of God" to "principalities and powers [rulers and authorities; ranks of angels] in the heavens" (Ephesians 3).

Even the individual names of angels are revealed in some cases. From Apocryphal books of the Bible we learn of the names Raphael and Uriel. From the book of Daniel we read about Michael, said to be "captain of the Lord's hosts."

One ecumenical angel who seems to be very busy is Gabriel. He first appears bearing a message to the Jewish patriot, Daniel. Later he comes to Mary to tell her she is about to become the mother of Jesus, the founder of Christianity. Still later he appears to Muhammad, escorting him on his famous "night journey" to the seventh heaven, a journey that marked the beginnings of Islam.

Walter Wink has written an important series of three books about the language of power in the New Testament. His thesis is that early writers intuitively grasped spiritual realities present in the human condition, labeling them "angels." In the New Testament book of Revelation, chapters 2 and 3, letters are addressed to the "angels of the seven churches." Could it be, he asks, that human institutions develop spiritual realities? In other words, when churches, schools, corporations, and even governments exist long enough, a spirit of tradition, perhaps even a metaphysical reality, forms that becomes bigger than the institution itself. What is "the spirit of America"? Why are soldiers ready to die for it? Why can we fire an entire corporate board of directors, hire new people, and still see no substantial change in the organization? Why does it not seem to matter much to average Americans when Republicans replace Democrats? Do power and tradition combine to form a spiritual but tangible reality? By asking the question, Wink does not imply that an organization attracts or becomes possessed by a passing spirit. Instead, he suggests that such an entity actually develops a "spirit" or tangible tradition of its own. This, he says, is what was intuitively recognized by the early authors, who labeled such a tradition an "angel."

In the case of the seven angels of the book of Revelation, Wink implied that for substantial change to occur, the very "angel" or spirit of the church had to be changed, a far-reaching implication as well for governments and corporations today.

Sources:

Bridger, David, ed. *The New Jewish Encyclopedia*. New York: Behrman House, 1962.
Bucke, Emory Stevens et al, eds. *The Interpreter's Dictionary of the Bible*. 4 vols. New York: Abingdon Press, 1962.
Douglas, J. D., ed. *The New International Dictionary of the Christian Church*. Grand Rapids, MI: Zondervan Publishing, 1974.
The Holy Qur'an, trans. with a commentary by Abdullah Yusuf Ali. Beirut, Lebanon: Dar Al Arabia, 1968.
May, Herbert G., and Bruce M. Metzger, eds. *The New Oxford Annotated Bible with the Apocrypha*. Rev. ed. New York: Oxford University Press, 1973.
Wink, Walter. *Naming the Powers*. Philadelphia: Fortress Press, c. 1984.

ANGLICAN CHURCH

(See also Episcopal Church)

The word "Anglican" means "of England"; the Anglican Church is also known as the Church of England, but it now exists worldwide.

Although Angelicans claim apostolic succession, an unbroken line of apostles going back to Peter, Anglicans officially broke away from Rome in 1536. They were one of the many—and sometimes violent—reform movements following Martin Luther's posting of his Ninety-five Theses, the event that marked the beginning of the Protestant Reformation.

As with most historical stories, there is a simple view, popularly accepted, and a more complex one that, perhaps, tells the real story.

The popular perception, especially in the United States, is that King Henry VIII wanted a divorce and the Pope wouldn't grant it. So he simply declared the Church of England separate from Rome and dissolved the monasteries and abbeys. Anglicans still considered themselves to be the true church, but, following the tradition of the Eastern Orthodox Church division of 1054, they now existed with a distinct identity.

As with most history, there is a more complex story. A careful reading of the historical record shows a series of disputes between Henry VIII and Rome throughout his reign. The divorce issue was simply one of many disagreements, some religious and some political, that split Rome and England.

What holds the Anglican Church together is not necessarily its English identity, although members do celebrate their tradition. The church finds its identity in the Bible, in their Articles of Religion, and especially in the Book of Common Prayer, first produced in 1549. Here the Latin liturgy of Rome was altered, simplified, and translated into English. The revision of 1662 has become the basis for most modern Anglican liturgy, so that the words and "feel" of worship are familiar to Anglicans no matter where they worship around the world.

In July 2002 the British government announced the appointment of the Most Reverend Rowan Williams, Bishop of Monmouth and Archbishop of Wales, to the position of 104th Archbishop of Canterbury, leader of the Anglican Church. The Reverend Williams is an outspoken liberal, questioning traditional church views on all kinds of hot-button issues such as gay rights, women's rights, and the church's history concerning rights in general. He also happens to be the first archbishop to wear a beard. On the evening of July 24th he was both lauded by the BBC and ridiculed, along with the whole Anglican Church and most participants of English religious society, by Pat Robertson on the *700 Club* television show.

It's not easy being archbishop. Reverend Williams responded simply by asking people to pray.

Sources:
"Church History." *The Anglican Domain.* http://www.anglican.org/church/ChurchHistory.html. May 2, 2002.
Douglas, J. D., ed. *The New International Dictionary of the Christian Church.* Grand Rapids, MI: Zondervan Publishing, 1974.

ANGRA MAINYU *see* **Ahura Mazda/Ahriman**

ANIMISM

Animism is the belief that spirits dwell within people and objects, in effect "animating" them. Sir Edward Tylor, a late-nineteenth-century anthropologist, developed the theory for which he coined the term "animism." He believed religious thought originated in primitive people through their experience of death and dreams. They experienced the loss of a member of their tribe or family and then experienced that person again through a dream or remembrance. So the idea arose that the spirit (*anima*) or soul of the person had left the mortal body and now existed in another form. As people began to worship the more powerful of these spirits, religion was born. Tylor didn't fix any rigid structure to this evolution but offered the postulate that a belief in animism may have led to more generalized deities and finally the worship of a single god. (Many twentieth-century anthropologists have largely rejected this evolutionary form of religion.)

Sir James Frazier, who believed the first human attempts to systematize these spirits led to the formation of religious rituals, developed the theory further. He saw the development of the concept of personal gods as the direct result of shamans who "adopted" a special spirit as their own object of veneration. Sigmund Freud later constructed a psychological model, including the view that belief in a personal god is a projection of a father figure growing out of a human need to feel protected and secure.

Animism is found in many indigenous religions worldwide, and it is an almost universal component of regional folklore. After the famous lost colony of Roanoke disappeared in 1590, many Christian colonists believed the spirit of Virginia Dare, the first baby born in the New World, could be seen on moonlit nights in the body of a white deer, ghosting through the forest.

Science, rather than putting to rest the ancient religion, has given proponents new ways of conceptualizing their beliefs. If energy cannot be destroyed, they claim, but only changed to a different form, why is it not possible to conceive of the notion that life energy, upon the death of the body, takes on a new shape?

Thus, animism, interpreted anew, might demonstrate how religion evolves and adapts to changing times and new paradigms.

Sources:
American Folklore and Legend. Pleasantville, NY: Reader's Digest Association, 1978.
Frazer, James George. *The Golden Bough.* 3rd ed. 1935, Touchstone Books, 1996.
Ludwig, Theodore M. *The Sacred Paths: Understanding the Religions of the World.* 2nd ed. Upper Saddle River, NJ: Prentice Hall, 1996.
Tylor, E. B. *Primitive Culture.* 1871, reprinted in *The Collected Works of E. B. Tylor.* New York: Routledge, 1994.

ANTHROPOCENTRISM

Webster's dictionary gives three meanings for the word *anthropocentrism*. Taken together, they lead to a specific mode of religious thought that has affected the course of human history.

1. Considering man to be the central or most significant fact of the universe.
2. Assuming man to be the measure of all things.
3. Interpreting or regarding the world in terms of human values and experiences.

Pantheism, on the other hand, is the belief that one absolute reality exists everywhere and in everything. Indigenous pantheistic religions that view humans as part of a whole, neither more nor less important than the animals and plants existing in the environment, tend to view Earth as a living, breathing entity. In this view, Earth is the very body of the divine, so the sacred becomes feminine, the goddess, from whose womb all life springs.

This view is by no means limited to primitive people. Recently one name for the goddess, Gaia, has been resurrected by science to describe the contemporary unifying principle of the earth itself as a living organism, with all systems of life and energy combining to produce the "balance of nature" as we experience it (see Gaia Principle). The Gaia principle is what some religions have called Mother Earth or the Divine Mother Goddess.

But once humans become the center and culminating fact of creation (anthropocentrism), the psychology of religious thought immediately changes. Rather than becoming a living framework for the very existence of the balance of nature, Earth becomes a smorgasbord of natural resources put here for human consumption and exploitation. Humans then live "on" Earth rather than "in" it.

This view is expressed in the first chapter of the Jewish/Christian Bible:

God blessed them and said to them, "Be fruitful and multiply, fill the earth and subdue it. Rule over the fish of the sea and the birds of the air and over every living creature that moves on the ground. I give you every seed-bearing plant on the face of the whole earth and every tree that has fruit with seed in it. They will be yours for food." (Gen. 1:28, 29)

It is probably not a coincidence that once this view became scriptural dogma, and wherever it was introduced into indigenous cultures, conditions quickly changed. Masculine-dominated religious systems quickly replaced the feminine. Nature became something to subdue "by the sweat of your brow," in the words of Genesis 3. Pantheism, respect for Mother Earth, and worship of the goddess became worship of the God. Humans were now separate from nature, and religions developed hierarchical structures.

An example of these conflicting religious views can be seen in the European invasion of New England beginning in the seventeenth century. Puritan preachers such as Cotton Mather thundered warnings from their Boston pulpits about the "howling wilderness" where "wild creatures" (meaning American Indians, presumably without souls) worshiping the "fiery worm who flies by night" practiced all sorts of "abominations." The wilderness was to be tamed. Wolves, trees, bears, panthers, and Indians were to be removed because they hindered the spread of humans who were put on Earth "to subdue it." It became the "Puritan ethic" to work hard to subdue a wild land for the glory of God. The concept of manifest destiny spread this doctrine from sea to shining sea in less than two centuries.

Deep Ecology environmentalists today place what they consider to be exploitation of natural resources into the realm of religious holy war (see Deep Ecology). They believe that both so-called tree-huggers and oil-drilling companies are products of certain religious ideologies.

English historian and philosopher Arnold Toynbee said it this way:

If I am right in my diagnosis of mankind's present-day distress, the remedy lies in reverting from the world view of monotheism to the world view of pantheism, which is older and was once universal.

Sources:
Campbell, Joseph. *The Power of Myth*. New York: Doubleday, 1988.
Gaskell, G. A. *Dictionary of All Scriptures and Myths*. New York: Gramercy Books, 1960.
Mitchell, John Hanson. *Ceremonial Time*. New York: Warner Books, 1984.
The New Oxford Annotated Bible with the Apocrypha. Rev. ed. New York: Oxford University Press, 1973.
Toynbee, Arnold J. *A Study of History*. London, 1934.
Webster's Third New International Dictionary and Seven Language Dictionary. 3 vols. Chicago: William Benton, 1966.

ANTHROPOMORPHISM

Religions are typically expressed in anthropomorphic ways. The term comes from the Greek *anthropos* ("man") and *morphe* ("form") and refers to the human tendency to visualize nonhuman concepts in human form. We say the waters of a placid lake "lie still." A fire "rages" within a forest. Gods, spirits, and abominable snowmen take on human attributes.

This concept is summarized by Kurtis Schaeffer of the University of Alabama in a review of Stewart Guthrie's book *Faces in the Clouds: A New Theory of Religion:*

> Our tendency to find human characteristics in the non-human world stems from a deep-seated perceptual strategy: in the face of pervasive (if mostly unconscious) uncertainty about what we see, we bet on the most meaningful interpretation we can. If we are in the woods and see a dark shape that might be a bear or a boulder, for example, it is good policy to think it is a bear. If we are mistaken, we lose little, and if we are right, we gain much. So in scanning the world we always look for what most concerns us—living things, and especially human ones. Even animals watch for human attributes, as when birds avoid scarecrows. In short, we follow the principle, better safe than sorry.

Genesis teaches that humans were created in the image of God (although the television character Archie Bunker of *All in the Family* fame would later remark, "I won't say you can't tell us apart"). Some posit that, in art and literature, humans have recreated God in our image, both "Father God" and "Mother Earth."

Although all religions, even pantheistic ones, tend to see God or gods in human form, anthropomorphic expression of the divine found full expression in the Greek pantheon. Gods were, quite literally, made in the image of men. This tendency, however, was predated by biblical descriptions of God as a being with human form (Exodus 15:3)—with feet (Genesis 3:8), hands (Exodus 24:11), a mouth (Numbers 12:8), and heart (Hosea 11:8)—while at the same time displaying human emotions (Exodus 20:5). To be sure, when God is described as "a consuming fire," natural forces as well have been called upon to conceptualize the divine.

Much later, the Qur'an attributes noble human emotions to Allah, calling him "most merciful" and reminding us that "Allah heareth and knoweth all things."

Biblical writers must have been aware of this tendency, because they grappled with the problem of reducing spirit to human language. In the Greek Septuagint version of the Hebrew Bible, Alexandrian Jewish scholars felt the need to freely translate a few texts. Because the Israelites "saw no form" at Mount Sinai on the occasion of the delivery of the Ten Commandments, resulting in the instructions to make no images or idols of the divine, the translators felt free to add a descriptive word or two from time to time. Where Numbers 12:8 says, "I will speak with Him mouth to mouth," the Greek version reads, "I will speak to Him mouth to mouth apparently."

Perhaps it was the problem of anthropomorphism that caused early Hindu writers to insist that Brahman, the ultimate, universal creative principle, could not be "soiled by the tongue." The Upanishads describe Brahman as "Him the eye does not see, nor the tongue express, nor the mind grasp." Although there are said to be thirty-three million gods in India, ultimately all are faces of the inexpressible Brahman.

Sources:

Ellwood, Robert S., and Barbara A. McGraw. *Many Peoples, Many Faiths.* 6th ed. Upper Saddle River, NJ: Prentice Hall, 1999.

Guthrie, Stewart Elliot. *Faces in the Clouds: A New Theory of Religion.* New York: Oxford University Press, 1995.

The Holy Qur'an. Trans. with a commentary by Abdullah Yusuf Ali. Beirut, Lebanon: Dar Al Arabia, 1968.

Prabhupada, A. C. Bhaktivedanata Swami. *Bhagavad-Gita As It Is.* Los Angeles: Bhaktivedanta Book Trust, 1986.

The Septuagint Version of the Bible. Grand Rapids, MI: Zondervan Publishing, 1970.

Schaeffer, Kurtis. Review of *Faces in the Clouds: A New Theory of Religion,* by Stewart Elliot Guthrie. http://www.as.ua.edu/rel/faces.html. October 7, 2003.

ANTICHRIST

(See also Apocalypse; Armageddon)

For all the coverage in movies, television shows, books, and sermons, the Antichrist gets surprisingly little space in the Christian New Testament. Popular conservative theology paints a detailed picture of the mysterious being who will appear at the end of time to mimic and challenge Jesus Christ before his Second Coming. Antichrist is "the man of sin" who, along with his sidekick, "the false prophet," will rule over a ten-kingdom federation of nations that will introduce worldwide governmental control, forcing all who wish to "buy and sell" to receive "the mark of the beast" on their hand or forehead. His mystical number is 666. Although he will eventually be destroyed at the battle of Armageddon and the return of Christ, many conservative students of prophecy believe he will first deceive the nations of the earth. This deception will occur during the seven-year period of Tribulation following the Rapture, or "snatching away," of the faithful who are still living "at the sound of the trumpet" of God. Following their disappearance, the Antichrist will deceive the nations, causing three and a half years of peace, followed by three and a half years of deception and warfare called the Great Tribulation. Then Christ will return at the Second Coming and destroy him, along with the false prophet. Satan, the power behind Antichrist, will be imprisoned for a thousand years. This is the Millennium, during which the earth will be recycled for use during a time of peace, when "the lamb will lay down with the lion and a little child will lead them." Although his destruction is predetermined, Satan will be given a brief period of time to live following his release. But, along with the Antichrist and his false prophet, the devil is doomed to failure.

This view of coming attractions begins with only four verses in the Bible, all found in 1 and 2 John, in which the Antichrist is depicted as a "spirit [that] shall come." This spirit will "deny the Father … and is a deceiver." John even says, "there are many antichrists."

These verses are the only ones in which the word "antichrist" appears in Christian scripture. The rest of the story comes from interpretations based on differing opinions coaxed out of the book of Revelation, perhaps the most disputed book in the New Testament.

Although he wasn't the first, Hal Lindsey was perhaps the most popular modern exponent of Antichrist lore. His book *The Late Great Planet Earth*, first published in the 1970s, sold millions of copies and led the way for the best-selling "Left Behind" series of novels by Tim LaHaye and Jerry B. Jenkins that occupied the top of the fiction charts beginning in the mid-1990s.

Antichrist lore is a modern phenomenon. There is no tradition of antichrist legend, except for the occasional labeling of perceived enemies as "antichrist" when disagreements arose. Martin Luther, for instance, called the Pope "antichrist."

This fact does not deter modern writers. They point to Daniel 12:9, which says, "these things will be sealed up until the time of the end." Because the "elect" now understand the truth of the Antichrist, that is only proof that we are living in "the time of the end" when "all these things must come to pass."

People have long tried to decipher the mysterious sign of the Antichrist, the numbers 666. Some, using a form of numerology, have assigned numerical values to letters to derive the number 666 by adding up the values of the letters in certain words, names, or phrases. One

Engraving entitled "The Reign of Antichrist" by Michael Volgemuth from *Liber Chronicarum,* 1493. **Fortean Picture Library.**

result of this formula was the Greek word *Latéinos* for "Latin Kingdom," referring to the Roman Catholic Church. During the "shuttle diplomacy" of the 1970s it was discovered that the last name of Henry Kissinger, through a formula in which A=1x6, B=2x6, etc., added up to 666. This conclusion was presented by some as "proof" that Dr. Kissinger was about to design a Middle East peace treaty ushering in the time of deception that would prepare the way for the Antichrist and his one-world government. Later, some observers considered the birthmark on the forehead of Mikhail Gorbachev, general secretary and president of the U.S.S.R., the "mark of the beast," which pointed to him as a potential Antichrist candidate.

Since then new candidates have appeared from time to time. Following the field of eschatology (end-time theology) requires a breadth of biblical knowledge. Events are strung together from Genesis to Revelation. Single verses from separate books of the Bible are placed out of their local context into a bigger scheme. Because many people don't have this kind of background, it is easy to be convinced of the truth of the story without realizing that the only references referring to the Antichrist by name are found in 1 John 2:18, 2:22, and 4:3, and in 2 John 2:18.

Sources:

Bucke, Emory Stevens et al, eds. *The Interpreter's Dictionary of the Bible*. 4 vols. New York: Abingdon Press, 1962.

Douglas, J. D., ed. *The New International Dictionary of the Christian Church*. Grand Rapids, MI: Zondervan Publishing, 1974.

May, Herbert G., and Bruce M. Metzger, eds. *The New Oxford Annotated Bible with the Apocrypha*. Rev. ed. New York: Oxford University Press, 1973.

Strong, James. *The Exhaustive Concordance of the Bible*. New York: Abingdon Press, 1890.

APOCALYPSE

(See also Antichrist; Armageddon)

The term "apocalypse" refers to the end of time. One of the biggest differences between the Eastern thought of, for example, Hinduism and Buddhism and the Western thought of Judaism, Christianity, and Islam is the concept of time. Followers of Western, monotheistic religions tend to view time as linear, with a beginning and end, and often have a difficult time even imagining another way of thinking. It just seems obvious, under such a frame of reference, that everything started at some time in the past and will end at some time in the future. In religions arising out of Eastern thought, however, time is circular, repeating itself endlessly. For most of humankind's existence, linear thinking was not even an option.

When thinking in terms of a beginning and an end, however, the mind immediately jumps to how the end will come and what happens next. The study of the end of time is called eschatology. When visions of the end were experienced and written down, usually in intricate symbolism that only the initiated would understand, the writing was called apocalyptic writing. One notable book in this tradition is the book of Revelation in the Christian New Testament, often called the Apocalypse of Saint John. But there were many, many more books like this that didn't pass muster for the final biblical cut.

An early instance of apocalyptic writing appears in Persian Zoroastrianism. Zoroaster, called Zarathustra by the Greeks, lived in 550 BCE, though some sources place him as early as 1000 BCE. A good case can be made that the religion he founded was the first monotheistic religion. Although most people assume Judaism takes this honor, until the Babylonian captivity, when Jews first experienced Persian religion, their writing was filled with sentences such as, "Jehovah is a mighty God, and a great God above all gods" (Psalm 95:3). The phrase "all gods" suggests that Judaism was not yet monotheistic.

The principal concept of Zoroastrian apocalyptic writing is dualism. A battle between good and evil is being carried out on planet Earth. The good god, Ahura Mazda, is using humankind to bait Ahriman, the evil god, into the world. Ahriman will tempt humans, who, by resisting, will wear him down so that he can eventually be destroyed. History will end at the last judgment, and a new, purified Earth will be formed. Humans will be rewarded with Paradise, an ideal heavenly realm with a divine court abiding over the blessed, or hell, which is not eternal but will purify the wicked along with Earth. Just before this happens, Zoroaster will return as a prophet

Engraving of the four horsemen of the Apocalypse, one of the visions from the book of Revelation. The horsemen are predicted to ride during an apocalyptic period with wars, weather changes, earthquakes, and plagues, heralding the end of the world. *Fortean Picture Library.*

conceived by a virgin with his own seed, which has been stored in a mountain lake. A prophet will then appear in this way every thousand years until the final restoration of the world, three thousand years later.

When the Jews returned from the Babylonian/Persian captivity, their writings showed evidence of the kind of apocalyptic literature they encountered there. The later prophets of Judaism, beginning with Daniel, wrote with "good against evil" and "light against dark" imagery. The Dead Sea Scrolls left by the Essene community make it clear that apocalyptic theology was a potent force in their struggle against Roman oppression.

It may well have been a sense of apocalyptic curiosity that prompted some Zoroastrian priests, called "Magi" or "Wise Men," to make the long journey to Bethlehem. They had seen an astrological event in the heavens that signaled the birth of the "King of the Jews."

The Qur'an of Islam continues the tradition of monotheistic apocalyptic writing:

Then, on the Day of Judgment, he will cover them with shame, and say, "Where are my partners concerning whom ye used to dispute with the godly?" ... To those who do good, there is good in this world, and the Home of the righteous, gardens of Eternity which they will enter: beneath them flow pleasant rivers: they will have all that they wish: thus doth Allah reward the righteous, (namely) those whose lives the angels take in a state of purity, saying (to them), "peace be on you; enter ye the Garden, because of (the good) which ye did (in the world)." (16:27–32)

Apocalyptic literature of all monotheistic religions shares a sense of linear time, a fiery judgment delivered from the mouth of God or his messenger, rewards for the blessed, and punishment for the wicked. Believers look forward to the next life and a cessation of the bitterness of this one, with the hope of hearing something like: "Blessed are those who wash their robes, that they may have the right to the tree of life and may go through the gates into the city.... Whoever is thirsty, let him come" (Revelation 22:14, 17).

Sources:

Bucke, Emory Stevens et al, eds. *The Interpreter's Dictionary of the Bible*. 4 vols. New York: Abingdon Press, 1962.

Ellwood, Robert S., and Barbara A. McGraw. *Many Peoples, Many Faiths*. 6th ed. Upper Saddle River, NJ: Prentice Hall, 1999.

Fisher, Mary Pat, and Lee W. Bailey. *An Anthology of Living Religions*. Upper Saddle River, NJ: Prentice Hall, 2000.

The Holy Qur'an, trans. with a commentary by Abdullah Yusuf Ali. Beirut, Lebanon: Dar Al Arabia, 1968.

LaSor, William Sanford. *The Dead Sea Scrolls and the Christian Faith*. Chicago: Moody Press, 1956.

May, Herbert G., and Bruce M. Metzger, eds. *The New Oxford Annotated Bible with the Apocrypha*. Rev. ed. New York: Oxford University Press, 1973.

APOCRYPHA

Between 90 and 98 CE, Jewish scholars met at Jamania and established the criteria for the books of the Hebrew Bible that would later be adopted as part of Christianity's official biblical canon—the "canonical books." Criteria of antiquity, language, and moral integrity were established. Books that failed to meet the criteria came to be called "apocryphal."

The word is a Greek plural neuter adjective meaning "hidden." As a literary term it was first applied to books containing esoteric wisdom deemed too sensitive for the uninitiated. Hence, it was a term of honor among scholars. But after the destruction of the Temple at Jerusalem in 70 CE, its meaning gradually evolved to mean "spurious" or even "heretical."

When it came time for the New Testament canon to be "fixed" at the Council of Hippo in 393 CE, the criteria were established that each book had to have been written by an apostle or someone close to an apostle, and each had to have been traditionally used in public worship.

The term apocryphal is now applied to books not included in the official canon of the Bible but often included, especially in Protestant Bibles, as a section between the Old and New Testaments. Such writings include additions to the book of Esther, the Prayer of Azariah and the Song of the Three Young Men, Psalm 151, and the books of Baruch, Bel and the Dragon, Ecclesiasticus, 1 and 2 Esdras, Letter of Jeremiah, Judith, 1–4 Maccabees, Prayer of Manasseh, Susanna, Tobit, and Wisdom of Solomon. Orthodox, Roman, and Protestant churches differ regarding the importance and content of these sections.

Jerome, writing in the early fifth century, was probably the first to use the term "Apocrypha" to describe noncanonical books. He believed apocryphal books should be read for edification but not "for confirming the authority of church dogmas." Because of their acceptance in church tradition, he felt compelled to include them in his famous Latin Bible, *The Vulgate*, which became the official translation of the Roman Catholic Church.

In the Greek Orthodox Church all but four books of the Apocrypha were accepted as canonical. After the Reformation of the sixteenth century, most Protestants generally ignored the Apocrypha. Martin Luther added the Apocrypha to the end of his German translation while commenting, "These books are not held equal to the sacred Scriptures but are useful and good for reading." That statement probably marked the beginning of the end for the study of the Apocrypha in most Protestant circles. Because they were placed together in a group, they were easy to remove, and most Protestant Bibles do not contain even a mention of such books.

Sources:

Douglas, J. D., ed. *The New International Dictionary of the Christian Church*. Grand Rapids, MI: Zondervan Publishing, 1974.

The Lost Books of the Bible and the Forgotten Books of Eden. Cleveland, OH: World Syndicate Publishing, 1926.

May, Herbert G., and Bruce M. Metzger, eds. *The New Oxford Annotated Bible with the Apocrypha*. Rev. ed. New York: Oxford University Press, 1973.

APOLOGISTS

An apologist is one who speaks or writes in defense of a faith or cause. The term has come to be used to describe a group of second-century Church fathers who wrote letters defending the new faith of Christianity.

The earliest of them is unknown, although his apology, *To Diognetus*, still survives. Perhaps the most well known of the early apologists is Justin (c. 100–c. 165), whose death for the faith earned him the name Justin Martyr. Tertullian (c. 155 or 160–c. 225) is still remembered for his work, *Apology*.

The importance of these works is that historians, by studying them, can learn about the early objections to Christianity as well as the manner in which educated members of the church responded to them. This leads to an understanding of how Christian theology evolved through the very act of responding to early criticism.

Sources:

Gonzalez, Justo L. *The Story of Christianity*. 2 vols. New York: Harper & Row, 1985.

Webster's Third New International Dictionary and Seven Language Dictionary. 3 vols. Chicago: William Benton, 1966.

APOSTASY *see* Excommunication/Apostasy

APOSTLE *see* Disciple/Apostle

APOSTLES' CREED *see* Gnosticism

AQUARIUS, AGE OF

(See also Astrology)

Aquarius is the eleventh sign of the Zodiac. The song "Age of Aquarius" from the rock musical *Hair* speaks of Earth entering into a new stage of religious development. Jeff Jawer, astrologer and founder of StarIQ.com, writes:

> The great ages are a result of the wobble of the Earth's pole on its axis. The cycle of approximately 26,000 years gives rise to twelve ages of about 2,160 years each. The beginning of an age occurs when the vernal equinox (sun at zero degrees of Aries) enters a new constellation. This precession of the equinoxes moves backward in the Zodiac, thus the shift from the twelfth sign Pisces (the fish) into the eleventh sign Aquarius. Due to conflicting interpretations on the boundaries of the constellations, there is a wide range of dates given as the beginning of the Age of Aquarius, from as early as the 1600's to as late as the 2400's. As with any slow cycle, it's likely that the transition process can cover a good deal of time, perhaps centuries.

According to astrologers, the Piscean Age was one of systemic religious hierarchies. They do not wonder that early Christians adopted the sign of Pisces, the fish, as their secret sign and signal. Aquarius, however, signals freedom, awareness of spiritual possibilities, and individual paths to God.

But change brings confusion. Astrologers warn that the accepted but outgrown elements of the past often seem to conflict with the unknown future. In times of stress it is easy to harden opinions and seek to continue on familiar paths, even if those paths have not led out of the forest. Such conditions, they say, may have contributed to "us against them" thinking, sixties activism, post-9/11 tension, racial bigotry, and religious warfare.

Philosophical writer I. M. Oderberg points out that the themes of Aquarius have been anticipated with mystic religious movements within major institutional traditions. Buddhism and Hinduism have always allowed personal, individual expression. But within Judaism, the Kabbalah has a mystic history going back to the Middle Ages. Sufi has offered an alternative tradition within Islam that is at once personal, flamboyant, individualistic, and meditative. The discovery of Gnostic gospels such as the Gospel of Thomas has caused a great stir in Christian circles. People who never considered anything but what they regard as traditional Christianity seem fascinated that there were once other ways to approach Christianity. The mystical, highly individualistic trend of the charismatic movement has swept the denominations.

Astrologers can't yet say what they believe will emerge in this Age of Aquarius. Some see an advanced stage of religious development in their observation that people are giving themselves permission to pick and choose from differing traditions, building their own belief systems from the wealth of what has come before and separating themselves from institutionalized power structures.

Sources:
Focht, Doug. "The Age of Aquarius?" *Bible Search.* http://www.biblesearch.com/articles/articl14.htm. May 9, 2002.
Jawer, Jeff. "From Pisces to Aquarius: The Epochal Shift That Is Shaking Our World." *StarIQ.com.* http://www.stariq.com/Main/Articles/P0003036.htm. May 9, 2002.
Lewis, James R. *The Astrology Book: The Encyclopedia of Heavenly Influences.* 2nd ed. Detroit: Visible Ink Press, 2003.
Oderberg, I. M. "Religion in the Age of Aquarius." *Theosophy Northwest.* http://www.theosophy-nw.org/theosnw/world/general/rel-imo.htm. May 9, 2002.

AQUINAS, THOMAS

Thomas Aquinas (1224–1274), a Dominican scholar, is recognized as one of the greatest systematic theologians. His system has become known as Thomism, and his crowning work, *Summa Theologica,* is often compared with a vast Gothic cathedral. In the words of theologian Justo Gonzalaz, it is "an imposing monument in which each element of creation and the history of salvation has a place and stands in perfect balance and symmetry." Aquinas was one of the school of theologians whose body of work is called scholasticism because its methodology was forged in academic institutions that would later grow into what we know as universities. One of their main contributions to the field of theology was the reintroduction of the thought and wisdom of the Greek philosopher Aristotle. This movement introduced the process of logic and science into what had been, until scholasticism, mainly a field dominated by faith and acceptance of doctrine. For instance, in his famous "five ways," or arguments for the existence of God, Aquinas was able to produce a logical, philosophical "proof" that God was real, based not on scriptural passages to be accepted without question but on a step-by-step system of logic. Religion thus became something to be thought about and pondered with the analytical left side of the brain, rather than a feeling intuited by the right. He helped to elevate the study of religion to an academic science, integrated with the humanities.

People have argued ever since that there is a dark side to this achievement. Twentieth-century *Star Trek*–influenced Christians have even been known to call Thomas "the Vulcan's theologian." Treating Christianity as an intellectual endeavor can produce a dry, logical religion void of warmth, love, grace, and magic, much like actor Leonard Nimoy's portrayal of the television show's methodical Mr. Spock from the Vulcan planet. But Saint Thomas himself argued that he never intended his logical theological system to replace grace and mystery. Rather, he intended it as a healthy proof that truth incorporates both.

Sources:
Gonzalez, Justo L. *The Story of Christianity.* 2 vols. New York: Harper & Row, 1985.

THE RELIGION BOOK: PLACES, PROPHETS, SAINTS, AND SEERS

ARABS

The term Arab originally meant a member of the Semitic race of people of the Arabian Peninsula east of Palestine. They were the nomadic Bedouins of the desert. Today, Arabs live throughout the world, including parts or all of Algeria, Bahrain, Djibouti, Egypt, Iraq, Jordan, Kuwait, Lebanon, Libya, Mauritania, Morocco, Oman, Qatar, Saudi Arabia, Somalia, Sudan, Syria, Tunisia, United Arab Emirates, and Yemen. Some Arabs hold Israeli citizenship. (Note that Iran is not an Arab country. Its roots go back to ancient Persia, with a totally different history and culture.) Although not all Arabs speak Arabic, the language is one of the great unifying and distinguishing characteristics of the people, even though dialects differ from place to place.

It is a common misconception that Islam is a unifying force in the Arab world. The truth is that only about 12 percent of Arabs worldwide are Muslims. Not all Arab traditions are Islamic, and Islam does not unite Arabs. Muhammad once commented, "The desert Arabians are most confirmed in unbelief and hypocrisy." There are more Muslims in Indonesia alone than in all Arab countries combined. Some thirty million Chinese are Muslim. In many countries, Muslim and Christian Arabs live side by side, although it is true that in most Arab countries, Islam is the predominate religion. In the Middle East it is not uncommon to meet Arab Muslims, Christians, Druze, and Jews all living within a few blocks of each other.

During the time of the Crusades in the Middle Ages, it became the custom of Christians to use the terms "Muslim," "Pagan," "Turk," "Infidel," and "Arab" almost interchangeably. Today, the Western "man on the street" usually thinks "Muslim" when he hears the word "Arab." This misapprehension is the result of mistaking religion for culture.

Sources:
Hooker, Richard. "Muhammad, Messenger of God." http://www.wsu.edu/~dee/ISLAM/MUHAM.HTM. June 6, 1999.
"One Hundred Questions and Answers about Arab Americans." *Detroit Free Press* http://www.freep.com/jobspage/arabs/. September 25, 2003.

ARCHAEOLOGY

Archaeology is considered by many to be the point where science and religion overlap. Religious myths or stories make up much of the background of religious studies. Archaeology is the science that literally digs into those stories, not to prove their historicity as much as to lend insight into the flesh-and-blood people who were at their core. It is an exact science, requiring academic training as well as fieldwork, with specializations having developed in extremely minute fields of study.

Religions existing in cultures without written languages, such as those of Central and South America and the prehistoric cultures of Europe, would be completely unknown without the science of archaeology.

Cutting-edge science and religion are often perceived to be at odds. But there is no question that, on purely philosophical grounds, both share a common goal. Through different disciplines, both search for truth.

Ancient Khirbet Qumran ruins, which lie on the northwestern shore of the Dead Sea in Jordan, are above the caves in which the Dead Sea Scrolls were discovered in 1947. Such sites are studied to lend insight into religious history and practices. *AP/Wide World Photos*.

ARIUS

Christian doctrine that is now considered traditional usually did not arrive on the scene fully developed. At one point, controversy surrounded much of what is accepted and cherished today. A study of controversies, debates, church councils, and resulting creeds reveals an evolving process of what has come to be known as systematic theology. Because the losers were usually declared heretical, many of their arguments have been lost to the general churchgoing public. But a few votes one way or another at critical times in the councils of church history might have completely changed the way Christian doctrine is understood today. Although by modern standards some of these debates may seem quite trivial and inconsequential, at the time people were willing to, and often did, put their lives on the line.

An example of this process is seen in an early but significant debate sparked by the teaching of Arius, one of the most prestigious and popular presbyters, or Christian leaders, of the city of Alexandria. Now called the Arian controversy, it led directly to the first great ecumenical, or universal, council of the church. Meeting in Nicea, a city in Asia Minor, a council of, according to some records, 318 bishops met in 325 CE. As a result of its debate, the council drafted the famous Nicene Creed, still used regularly as a statement of faith in many churches. Its specific declaration sounds stilted to modern ears, but it was a very exact and debated point:

> We believe in one Lord, Jesus Christ, the only Son of God, begotten of the Father from all time: God from God, Light from Light, very God from very God, begotten, not made, one in being with the Father. Through Him all things were made.... He was crucified for us.... He suffered, died and was buried ... He descended into hell ... He arose on the third day.... He entered into heaven and is seated on the right hand of the Father ... From thence He shall come to judge the quick and the dead.

The debate began with controversy over the logical consequences resulting from biblical interpretation. The text that best illustrates the controversy is found in the Gospel of John, chapter 1:

> In the beginning was the Word, and the Word was with God, and the Word was God. He was in the beginning with God. All things were made through Him and without Him was not anything made that was made. In Him was light, and the light was the life of men ... and the Word became flesh and dwelt among us.

When the first Christians began to preach their message, Roman intelligentsia often considered them ignorant atheists because they had no visible gods. Christians countered these claims with arguments of the Greek philosophers. The apostle Paul once argued that the Greek "unknown god," the god believed to be above the Cosmos, was in fact the Christian God (Acts 17). This no doubt appealed to the Athenians. But it was a dangerous argument because it removed from theology the argument of revelation preached by the prophets and other biblical writers. It moved the discussion about the nature of God to the field of analytical argument. Since Greek philosophy postulated perfection as immutable, impassable, and fixed, these attributes came to be accepted as the God of scripture.

So where does "the Word" of John's Gospel fit in? Arius's view, phrased in his words, said, "there was when He was not." In other words, first and always came the immutable God, then, proceeding from God, came "the Word." Since "the Word became flesh and dwelt among us," it logically follows that "the Word," the voice of God, was Jesus. So there must have been a time when Jesus "was not."

Alexander, Bishop of Egypt, decreed this heretical. He taught that Jesus existed eternally with the Father. It is important to understand that both sides believed "the Word" existed before the incarnation. Arius, however, believed that "the Word" was the first creation of God, made before anything else.

Put simply, if asked to build a fence between God and Creation, Arius would put "the Word" on the Creation side of the fence, while his opposition would place "the Word" on the side of the eternal Father.

Both sides, of course, had proof texts and logical arguments. But Arius lost, and the result was what now is understood as the doctrine of the Trinity. Arius believed such a result violated the concept of one God—monotheism. Those who came to be known as Trinitarians believed they had answered the question by pointing out that God is one, expressed in three "persons"—Father, Son, and Holy Spirit—separate, equal, and one.

This is the concept the bishops tried to express in the Creed of Nicea, composing in detail the awkward but specific description of Jesus Christ as "begotten of the Father" but "from all eternity." He was "very God from very God" and "one in being with the Father," but "through Him all things were made." In other words, Jesus, the second entity of the Trinity, existed before Creation, and is, indeed, God.

Sources:
Gonzalez, Justo L. *The Story of Christianity.* 2 vols. New York: Harper & Row, 1985.
May, Herbert G., and Bruce M. Metzger, eds. *The New Oxford Annotated Bible with the Apocrypha.* Rev. ed. New York: Oxford University Press, 1973.

ARK OF THE COVENANT

(See also Tabernacle in the Wilderness)

When Moses received from God the Law delivered to the Israelites after their escape from Egypt, he was told to build an ark upon which the glory of God would rest.

"Ark" comes from the Greek word for chest. "Covenant" means contract or agreement. The ark became a constant reminder of God's contract with his chosen people.

It was a box about two and a half feet high and wide, and four and a half feet long. It was made of wood and covered with gold leaf. It was transported by means of two long poles and placed within the Holy of Holies, the inner sanctuary, in the Tabernacle or Tent of Meeting during the forty years the Israelites wandered in the wilderness. After the conquest of Canaan it was housed in the sanctuary at Shiloh,

Made of acacia wood and clad in gold, the Ark of the Covenant was built to house and transport the tablets of the Law. It is renowned for its mysterious powers against the enemies of Israel. *Fortean Picture Library.*

and it was later brought by King David to the site of the future Temple at Jerusalem. This was the occasion that so inspired David that he "danced before the Lord," much to the disgust of his wife (see David, King).

When the Babylonians destroyed Solomon's Temple in 586 BCE, the ark disappeared. Although many have tried to locate it (including Indiana Jones in the movie *Raiders of the Lost Ark*), its location has remained a mystery ever since. Some think it is hidden away in a temple in Ethiopia, brought there by the son of Solomon and the Queen of Sheba. Others believe it is hidden in the caves of Qumran or buried under the Temple Mount. Still others believe it destroyed.

Three symbolic objects were placed within the ark. Each recalled stories that, when taken together, represented the very essence of Judaism. (The stories are found in the biblical books Exodus and Numbers.)

The first object was the stone tablet containing the Ten Commandments. These represented God's law. But the people had broken God's law. While Moses was on Sinai receiving instructions that forbade the worship of idols, the people were down below dancing around a golden calf. The tablets would forever symbolize the people's rejection of God's law.

The second was a pot of manna. "Manna" literally means, "What is it?" When the people needed food in the desert, God told Moses to have them go outside and gather a daily supply of a light bread that would form with the dew each morning. Only one day's supply could be gathered because it would spoil if hoarded. The bread gathered on Friday would keep for an extra day so the people would not have to break the Sabbath commandment forbidding work on the seventh day. When the people went outside on the first morning to discover the miracle of God's provision, they saw the manna and said, "What is it?" The idea was to teach the people to trust in God's daily provision. But after the novelty wore off, the people complained, longing for "the leeks and onions of Egypt." So manna came to represent their rejection of God's provision.

The third item was "Aaron's rod that budded." Aaron, Moses' brother, had been selected by God to be High Priest. But the people wanted to elect their own leaders. They complained to Moses, who passed the word on to God. So Moses was told to have each tribe select a candidate for High Priest. Each would place his "rod," or walking staff, in the ground to be inspected during the next morning's convocation. The rod that "budded," or took root, would indicate God's choice. The implication was that God's leaders bear fruit.

Of course Aaron's rod produced a bud, and he went on to become the first High Priest of Israel. But the people would always be reminded that they had rejected God's leadership.

On the cover of the ark stood the Mercy Seat. Two carved angels, one on each side with their arched wings meeting in the middle, looked down at the ark's contents. There they saw rejection—rejection of God's law, God's provision, and God's leadership. That doesn't leave a lot more of God left to reject.

But on one day a year, the Day of Atonement, Yom Kippur, the High Priest sprinkled the blood of a sacrificial lamb on the Mercy Seat. On that day the angels would see not rejection but the blood of the innocent substitute, and the sins of the people would be atoned for.

Much speculation has arisen over the true meaning of the ark. Because the Bible makes a special point of saying Moses' face glowed when he came out from the visible presence of God, some have speculated it contained a source of light. It was said that at the ark Moses would hear the voice of God. This has sparked wild tales of it being a transmitter through which Moses was in contact with aliens from outer space, using details supplied from their blueprints to build the ark to their specifications. Because of the ark's supposed ability to inspire armies in war, and because at least one man is said to have died after he touched it without proper consecration, speculation arose as to its mystical or military powers.

The Ark of the Covenant is surrounded by mystery. Perhaps it still awaits discovery, resting in its 3,500-year-old hiding place. But its meaning to the Israelites was clear: the ark reminded them of their contract with the God who chose them to be a special people.

Sources:

Bridger, David, ed. *The New Jewish Encyclopedia*. New York: Behrman House, 1962.

May, Herbert G., and Bruce M. Metzger, eds. *The New Oxford Annotated Bible with the Apocrypha*. Rev. ed. New York: Oxford University Press, 1973.

The Septuagint Version of the Old Testament. Grand Rapids, MI: Zondervan Publishing, 1974.

ARMAGEDDON

(See also Antichrist; Apocalypse)

The sixth angel poured out his bowl on the great river Euphrates, and its waters were dried up to prepare the way for the kings of the east. Then I saw three evil spirits … the spirits of demons … and they went out to the kings of the whole world, to gather them for battle on the great day of God Almighty … they gathered the kings together in the place that in Hebrew is called Armageddon. (Revelation 16:12–16)

Thus the book of Revelation describes events leading up to the last battle of the world, which ends with the coming of the "rider on a white horse." The rider's name is "Faithful and True," and he defeats the armies of the Antichrist in the climactic battle of history that takes place in the valley of Mount Megiddo, an immense plain in Israel.

Unfortunately, although the writer says Armageddon is a Hebrew word, it appears nowhere in Hebrew literature and there is some doubt as to its proper spelling in Greek. So aside from the highly symbolic language of this one sentence in the Bible, there is no other frame of reference or explanation available.

Although conservative Christian scholarship holds to its meaning as a culminating, definitive battle between God and Satan, the word is usually now employed metaphorically to indicate either a definitive personal battle or the ultimate result of a nuclear war. In the latter sense, the spirit of the book of Revelation is called upon, if not its literal or historical context.

Sources:

May, Herbert G., and Bruce M. Metzger, eds. *The New Oxford Annotated Bible with the Apocrypha*. Rev. ed. New York: Oxford University Press, 1973.

ARMINIUS, JACOB *see* **Calvin, John, and Jacobus Arminius**

ARTHUR

The stories of King Arthur and the Knights of the Round Table can be read on many levels. They are, at the very least, entertaining adventure tales. On a deeper level, they are a rich mythological source, examining the depths of human nature from ancient Celtic myth to medieval Christian values. Certainly there are those who read them to discover more about what was going in the historical period in which they were written. But fascinating insights can also be derived by reading them from a religious perspective.

Arthur is portrayed as a hinge between two worlds. Assisted by the wizard Merlin, who is perhaps a Druid, Arthur stands as the last of the pagan kings, but with

Engraving depicting the death of King Arthur, based on an 1869 painting by Joseph Noel Patton. *Fortean Picture Library.*

a foot in the Christian world as well. Seen in this light, the Arthurian legend is the story of all the gods becoming one God, of pagan Europe being transformed to Christianity. When young Arthur draws Excalibur from the stone, he is freeing the source of magic from the dark, hard places of the earth and exposing them to work in the air and light of day. He never really becomes a Christian, however, so at his death the sword, having done its work, is returned to the Lady of the Lake, the goddess. The sword is represented now by the many pagan customs "baptized" or adapted and wielded by Christianity. Easter celebrations, bunnies and eggs, Christmas trees and lights—all are examples of Excalibur, still flashing in the light of triumphant Christianity. But rest assured, the legend reminds us, that when the male God of Christianity has done his work, the sword will be returned to its rightful owner, the goddess, who has been the real source of power all along.

In the fifth century, Rome was pressured to draw its legions back from England to protect itself from the Barbarian hordes nipping away at its borders. The Pax Romana, or Peace of Rome, was removed. It had been a peace enforced by the sword, but a peace nevertheless. The crust of Roman civilization in Britain began to crumble under invasion from without and rebellion from within. Christianity had been the official religion of Rome, but it had never managed to eliminate the pagan religion that had been at the heart of the people of Britain, who now looked for protection so they could plow their fields and support their families. They needed leadership. But they were also searching for spiritual nourishment. Many had adopted the new religion but would not forsake the old. The shrines of roadside gods still held peasant offerings. Christian bishops battled pagan priests for the soul of Britain, and both needed political protection from Saxon ships pillaging their shores.

This is the drama into which Arthur, if he ever lived at all, was born. His birth and ascension were magical. Merlin, the mysterious, shadowy background figure, seems to be at home in both mystical Avalon and the castle of Camelot, a Druid who has elements of Mithras, the soldier's god, and Christ. He is, of course, suspected by all and accepted by none but Arthur, but his magic and insight guide the young king to establish, for a short time, an empire open to all.

By the time of the Middle Ages the stories take on a distinctly Christian aura with the Grail legends. The Holy Grail was the cup from which Jesus drank at the Last Supper. Brought to England, some say by angels, others by Joseph of Arimathea, it was hidden away, to be found only by the pure of heart.

At this point it is important to remember that the Grail legend predates Christianity by centuries. Celtic lore refers to several magic cauldrons that heroes undergo quests to find. It was another pagan myth that, like the Christmas tree, the Easter bunny, and the Yule Log, was "baptized" by the church to incorporate pagan customs the people refused to abandon.

But to study the Grail legends is to delve into the very heart of religion and human psychology. Galahad, who achieved the quest, becomes a study of purity and noble purpose. Thirteenth-century German poet Wolfram von Eschenbach's Parzival discovers the Fisher King (keeper of the Holy Grail), drinks from the Grail, and becomes the Grail King himself. When he is baptized by its water, an inscription appears on the cup: "If any member of this community should, by the grace of God, become the ruler of an alien people, let him see to it that they are given their rights."

Joseph Campbell believes this to be the first time in history that such a thought was expressed. The idea that a king must rule in the name of his people, rather than in his own name, didn't come to fruition until the signing of the Magna Carta in 1215.

When Parzival meets a hermit he is told, "You, through your tenacity of purpose, have changed God's law." The idea of a human being wrestling with God and winning is new to Christianity, although the Hebrew Bible tells the story going back all the way to Jacob in the book of Genesis.

We see here the concept of evolving religion. Paganism is enveloped by Christianity. Christianity adapts to the importance of the individual over the divine right of feudal lords.

This idea is captured beautifully by Mary Stewart in her recent series of books based on the legend of Merlin. In the final scene of *The Hollow Hills*, Arthur has drawn the sword from the stone and Merlin is left alone where magic fire has scoured the pagan altar. Merlin speaks:

> I carried the nine lamps out of the chapel. Come daylight, I would take them where they now belonged, up to the caves of the hollow hills, where their gods had gone … my sight blurred and darkened as if still blind with vision, or with tears…. The tears showed me the altar now, bare of the nine-fold light that had pleasured the old, small gods; bare of the soldier's sword and the name of the soldier's god. All it held now was the hilt of the sword standing in the stone like a cross, and the letters still deep and distinct above it: TO HIM UNCONQUERED.

Sources:
Campbell, Joseph. *Transformations of Myth Through Time*. New York: Harper & Row, 1990.
Stewart, Mary. *The Hollow Hills*. New York: Fawcett Books Group, 1973.

ARTS

The very first human art we know about may have been inspired by religion. The cave paintings of ancient humans, such as those at Lascaux, France, discovered in 1940 and dating to approximately 30,000 BCE, inspire awe and wonder. What source of pigment and light did they use? Why travel a mile down into the bowels of the earth through dark, dank, dangerous passageways to produce these masterpieces?

Cave art was possibly used in religious rites associated with hunting cultures. If they were offered to the gods of the hunt, as some archaeologists believe, the cave paintings would have been religiously inspired works of art, as opposed to the art of personal adornment. Since then, religion has continued to inspire art of all kinds.

Bach, Handel, Beethoven, and Mozart are four composers among hundreds whose work is performed weekly in places of worship and regularly in secular concert halls as well. Michelangelo's paintings, not least the ceiling of the Sistine Chapel, attract thousands to Rome each year. Literary works like *Ben-Hur*, about a Palestinian Jew battling the Roman empire at the time of Jesus, still inspire Hollywood to make epic films. John Milton's *Paradise Lost* is required reading at colleges and universities. The Japanese form of Haiku poetry is a distinct part of Zen Buddhism, allowing bright but fragile images to pierce through a very strict literary form. Hindu goddess statues, even a very ancient figure in the lotus position, are still being uncovered by the archaeologist's brush.

Because religious-inspired art was an early form of human expression and appears in all cultures, a good argument can be made that art is what makes us human, separates us from the rest of the animal kingdom, and provides a window through which we see that which is "other," spiritual, or eternal. In short, it can be said that art is a medium of expression by which we experience divinity.

Sources:
Campbell, Joseph. *The Power of Myth*. New York: Doubleday, 1988.

ARYANS

The group of people who migrated from their original Indo-European homeland stretching from Eastern Europe to Central Asia called themselves Aryans ("noble ones").

Beginning around 1500 BCE, some migrated down through the Khyber Pass into India, superimposing their pastoral lifestyle over the agricultural customs of the indigenous people, and forming the background for Hinduism.

Others moved eastward into present-day Iran, building the foundation of what would become Persian Zoroastrianism. Their language, Sanskrit, is closely related to other Indo-European languages, as is their culture and religion. Yet another group migrated westward into Europe, eventually becoming Greeks, Romans, and Germanic peoples, Slavs and Balts.

Eventually, of course, the migration jumped the Atlantic and asserted itself among the indigenous peoples in what is now North America.

Aryans have historically been identified as a warring culture. They were originally tribal, with each tribe headed by a war chief. Because they had domesticated the horse and invented the chariot, they were a fierce opponent in battle, and their early skills in metallurgy produced superior weaponry.

Aryans produced the very first scriptures. Although they did not possess a written language, they composed hymns and ritual verses known as Vedas, transmitted orally in priestly families and castes. Vedas were thought to be timeless, eternal truths heard by the rishis, the seer-prophets of old. After the invention of writing, Vedas became the foundation of Hinduism. The Rig Veda is the oldest, containing more than one thousand hymns.

The word for God in Sanskrit is *deva*, meaning "shining" or "auspicious." By this, Aryans referred to the powers experienced in the various aspects of nature—wind, fire, water, speech, and consciousness.

Aryans must be separated from Aryanism. "Aryan" simply denotes ancestry. Aryanism, according to Webster's dictionary, was the doctrine put forth by Nazi leader Adolf Hitler that Aryan people "possess superior capacities for government, social organization and civilization." This is the "superior race" doctrine that led to the formulation of what was to be the "Thousand-Year Reich," an ultra-nationalistic German regime headed by Hitler. Under his leadership, the Nazis conducted a systematic slaughter of several million people they had labeled non-Aryans, including Jews, Poles, and Roma (Gypsies). Germany's defeat in World War II ended the Thousand-Year Reich, but various hate groups, who often use religion to justify their bigotry, still carry on the philosophy.

Sources:
Ludwig, Theodore M. *The Sacred Paths: Understanding the Religions of the World.* 2nd ed. Upper Saddle River, NJ: Prentice Hall, 1996.
Webster's Third New International Dictionary and Seven Language Dictionary. 3 vols. Chicago: William Benton, 1966.

ASCETIC

Ascetics practice extremely focused religion, employing various techniques to bring about spiritual discipline. From Hindus to Buddhists, from Jews to Christians to Muslims, virtually every world religion and most indigenous ones have ascetics.

Native American vision quests included denying oneself food and water. Christian monks sat on poles and scourged themselves with whips. The Buddha himself followed the path of asceticism, reaching the point of eating just one grain of rice a day, though it was only in his abandonment of asceticism that he found enlightenment. Some Jains go to extreme degrees to break down the fleshly "crust" formed by Karma.

The idea is that by denying oneself and punishing the "flesh," the spirit will be free to dominate and come into its own. This view always sees the spirit as somehow being "trapped" in the body. The body, with its appetites and desires, is generally seen as evil. Asceticism is the attempt to break free, and it is a direct opposite to so-called wholeness religious movements.

Sources:
Ellwood, Robert S., and Barbara A. McGraw. *Many Peoples, Many Faiths*. 6th ed. Upper Saddle River, NJ: Prentice Hall, 1999.
Renard, John. *The Handy Religion Answer Book*. Detroit: Visible Ink Press, 2002.

ASSEMBLIES OF GOD

(See also Pentecostalism)

The Methodist Church has come to know many divisions over the years. William Booth, founder of the Salvation Army, was originally a Methodist. Many of the so-called holiness denominations, chief among them being the Church of the Nazarene, were formed because it was thought Methodism had moved too far away from the message preached by its founder, Charles Wesley.

In 1906, at the Azusa Street Mission in Los Angeles, California, a Methodist-sponsored revival of "Pentecostal Power" broke out. People claimed to have been "baptized by the Holy Spirit" in the manner evidenced on the birthday of the Church during the celebration of Pentecost in the time of the Apostles (Acts 2). People speaking in tongues and miracles of healing roused people to a spiritual frenzy. The people who attended those meetings spread their enthusiasm throughout the United States, and the Pentecostal movement began.

In 1914 the director of a Pentecostal publication called for a great meeting of "believers in the baptism of the Holy Spirit." Out of that meeting, the Assemblies of God was born.

Assemblies of God is now a worldwide Protestant denomination following Methodist Church polity but emphasizing the need to be both "born again" and "baptized by the Holy Spirit as evidenced by the gift of speaking in tongues." This experience is called "the second blessing" and usually happens after a person has been "saved" by accepting the Lord Jesus Christ as his or her personal savior. The second blessing is evidence of a "spiritual in-filling," and biblical evidence for the experience comes mostly from the book of Acts and from Paul's letters.

Woodcut of an astrologer, by Albtecht Durer, 1498. *Fortean Picture Library.*

Sources:
Hudson, Winthrop S. *Religion in America.* New York: Charles Scribner, 1965.

ASTROLOGY

(See also Aquarius)

As people began to consider the seemingly infinite universe, they wondered whether the stars could foretell future events and exercise control over human lives. A psalmist of the Bible wrote, "the heavens declare the glory of God" (Psalm 19:1). Zoroastrian astrologers called Magi traveled to Bethlehem at the birth of Jesus because they saw a "star" or sign in the heavens foretelling the birth of a Jewish king. Long before this, astrologers as far apart as Egypt, China, Peru, and England were building stone structures to aid in foretelling times and seasons based on the stars.

Good evidence has been presented that the pyramids of Giza mirror the stars of the constellation Orion. There appears to be astrological significance attached to many of the enigmatic stone circles of Western Europe, including Stonehenge. Indians of the American Southwest seem to have been very aware of the significance of astral events, recording them on pictographs scattered throughout Arizona and New Mexico. Chinese mythology makes mention of comets and stars that are now followed by astronomers.

When the comet Hale-Bopp stood high in the sky during the spring evenings of 1997, groups such as the Heaven's Gate cult were sure it was a prophecy portending either doom or salvation for the human race (see Cults).

Such age-old wonder at the heavens perhaps naturally gave rise to astrology, the study of the stars. Astrology, a form of which is found in nearly all cultures, is a vast field of study that focuses on the correlations between celestial events and humanly meaningful events. While not a religion in itself, astrology has been put to use in many religious contexts. As astrologer James R. Lewis notes in *The Astrology Book:* "Most people are familiar with only a tiny portion of the science of the stars, namely the 12 signs of the Zodiac as they relate to the personality of individuals and the use of astrology for divinatory purposes"—that is, the horoscope as it appears in daily newspapers. Such horoscopes are based on a person's sun sign—which one of twelve constellations the sun appeared in, from the perspective of his or her birthplace, at the time of the person's birth. The positions of other heavenly bodies also make up one's so-called natal chart, which most astrologers are careful to note does not so much predict a person's future as describe possible influences, likely tendencies, or the overall nature of one's personality—information one can use to set the course of one's own life. The same process can be applied to analyze the circumstances of any other event, past or potential, such as a wedding.

Sources:
Hitching, Francis. *Earth Magic*. New York: William Morrow & Company, 1977.
Lewis, James R. *The Astrology Book: The Encyclopedia of Heavenly Influences*. 2nd ed. Detroit: Visible Ink Press, 2003.

ATHEISM *see* Agnosticism/Theism/Atheism

ATLANTIS *see* New Age Religions

ATMAN *see* Brahman/Atman

ATTILA THE HUN

Christians in the fifth century called Attila, war leader of the Huns, "the Scourge of God." He has become an almost mythical figure. Richard Wagner was so taken with the warrior's exploits that his famous opera cycle, *The Ring of the Nibelung*, was based on the story of Attila's battle with the Burgundian king, Gundahar, along with other historical figures like Queen Brynhild.

Attila invaded Italy in 452 CE. When the city of Aquileia fell to his army, the road was open all the way to Rome. The empire was by this time divided into West (governed by Rome) and East (governed by Constantinople). The Roman West was weak, both in character and in military strength. The Eastern empire left no doubt that they did not want to intervene. So Leo "the Great," who has been called the first pope in the modern sense, went to talk to Attila personally.

One of history's mysteries occurred at that meeting. No one knows what was said between the two leaders. Legends later reported that Attila had a vision of Saints Peter and Paul marching with the pope. Whatever he saw, Attila decided not to attack Rome. He turned north instead and died shortly thereafter.

Leo was still Bishop of Rome when Vandals attacked in 455. He was unable to prevent the sacking of the city. But he was able to arrange a treaty with them, so at least the city was not burned to the ground.

Such negotiations helped Leo's reputation and gave him great political and spiritual clout. Lost to history is the substance of the sermon that made Attila, "the Scourge of God," see the light.

Sources:
Gonzalez, Justo L. *The Story of Christianity*. 2 vols. New York: Harper & Row, 1985.
Jones, Prudence, and Nigel Pennick. *A History of Pagan Europe*. New York: Routledge, 1995.

AUGUSTINE

(See also Alexandria; Calvin, John, and Jacobus Arminius)

Augustine of Hippo (354–430 CE) was a professor of rhetoric, born in the little town of Tagaste, North Africa. The purpose of rhetoric, as practiced in those days, was not to

Augustine of Hippo, one of the Latin fathers of the Church, lived and taught in Roman North Africa. *Fortean Picture Library.*

deliver truth. That was left to the philosophers. Students of rhetoric learned to present clear and forceful arguments for whatever they were called to defend.

Augustine had a problem, however. He was forced to study and teach the works of Cicero, the famous orator of classical Rome. And Cicero was a philosopher who very much cared about truth. It was while studying his works that Augustine came to a conviction that style was worthless without substance.

This decision led him to the study of Manicheism. Mani, its third-century founder, was convinced that the Zoroastrian concept of "light" battling "darkness" was true, but he interpreted the struggle as a battle between spirit and matter. Manichean mythology explained that light and darkness had somehow mingled within each individual. Salvation consisted of separating the two so as to prepare the human spirit for its return to pure light. Mani believed this principle had been revealed to Buddha, Zoroaster, and Jesus.

Augustine responded favorably to Manicheism for two reasons.

First, any teacher of rhetoric must consider the language of the Bible to be inelegant, at best. To a professor like Augustine, some of it must have appeared positively barbaric.

Second, Augustine had a real problem with the Christian concept of evil (see Evil). How did a "good" God allow evil into the universe, especially after pronouncing Creation "very good"? If evil came from God, God couldn't be good. And if it didn't, God couldn't be all-powerful. It was as simple, and as complex, as that.

But Augustine was simply too intelligent for his Manichean teachers to handle. Their explanations didn't help him in his quest. So he turned to Neoplatonism.

This philosophy was very popular at the time, and it appealed to Augustine because it had religious overtones. It was a philosophical discipline that sought to reach the "One," the source of all being. Neoplatonists taught that all reality derived from one principle that was totally good. The more one understood the good, the further one moved from evil. Moral evil consists of looking away from the One and living in the world of contradictions and inferior ideas. So Augustine became convinced that evil was not a thing, but rather a direction—away from the One and the Good.

This notion seemed to satisfy him until he agreed to listen to a series of sermons preached by Ambrose, at that time the most famous preacher in Milan.

Although he attended at first just to listen to Ambrose's rhetoric, he was soon captivated by his message.

The key, according to Ambrose, was that the Bible was to be interpreted allegorically, not literally. This was Augustine's answer; it allowed him to reconcile what he had previously seen as the inherent contradictions of Christianity. He didn't need to check his great intellect at the door of the church. He decided to become a Christian.

At first he was confused about the fact that he rather liked the good life that seemed to be anathema to the Christian community. His famous prayer reveals that struggle. "God, give me chastity and continence; but not too soon!"

Through years of intellectual and emotional struggle, however, Augustine persevered to emerge as one of the leading intellectual Christian philosophers and theologians. His closely reasoned arguments against what are now called heresies; his spiritual autobiography, *Confessions*; and his monumental *City of God* are still required readings at most seminaries.

He eventually became the favorite theologian of the sixteenth-century Protestant Reformers, and he is today considered the most influential Western theologian of both the Protestant and Catholic traditions.

Sources:

Gonzalez, Justo L. *The Story of Christianity*. 2 vols. New York: Harper & Row, 1985.

AUM SHINRI KYO *see* Cult

Avatar

(See also Bhagavad-Gita; Hinduism)

Vishnu is the Hindu god of goodness. He has come to Earth when needed in the past in a series of so-called descents or avatars. These are incarnations. Tradition says there will be ten of them, nine of which have already passed:

A dwarf who saved the world from a demon.
Prince Rama, defender of the good.
Krishna, the poet and warrior who reestablished the principles of religion.
A fish that rescued the first man, Manu, from a worldwide flood.
A tortoise.
A boar.
A man-lion.
A warrior hero.
Prince Gautama, the Buddha.
Yet to come: A messiah with a sword of flame who will come at the end of the fourth period of the world to save the righteous and destroy the wicked. He will be riding a white horse.

Sources:

Ellwood, Robert S., and Barbara A. McGraw. *Many Peoples, Many Faiths*. 6th ed. Upper Saddle River, NJ: Prentice Hall, 1999.

BABYLONIAN CAPTIVITY

(See also Solomon)

The Babylonian captivity refers to Babylon's capture of the Hebrew people of Judah in the sixth century BCE.

The Northern and Southern Kingdoms

Israel reached the height of its political power about 1000 BCE. Under the rule of King Solomon, Jerusalem was enlarged, a palace and the first great temple were constructed, and a wall was built surrounding the city. Part of the wall still stands (see Wailing Wall).

When Solomon died, his son Rehoboam lacked the strength of character and charisma necessary to hold the kingdom together (see Judaism, Development of). Civil war broke out, and Israel was divided into two countries. The Northern Kingdom, consisting of a population descended from ten of the original twelve tribes of Israel, retained the name Israel. The Southern Kingdom, consisting of descendants of the tribes of Benjamin and Judah, was known as the House of David, or simply Judah.

Although Judah was vastly outnumbered, two important political and religious considerations gave it the advantage. First of all, Judah's kings continued the bloodline of the respected King David. Second, and most important, mighty Jerusalem was its capital city and the home of the Great Temple, the only place sacrifice could be offered. Israel may have made up most of the "body" of the Hebrew people, but Judah housed its soul.

This situation prevailed for some three hundred years. The biblical books of Kings and Chronicles tell a story of intrigue, war, and conflict that prompted warnings and admonitions from the Hebrew prophets. In the early years of the eighth century

BCE, Israel fell to Assyria. Although Jerusalem was besieged as well, it resisted success-fully, aided by a plague that broke out in the camp of the enemy, forcing the Assyrians to withdraw. Biblical history records that the Northern Kingdom, or Israel, was taken off into captivity and oblivion, forever after known as the Ten Lost Tribes of Israel.

The Lost Tribes of Israel

There are many theories purporting to locate the tribes. Herbert W. Arm-strong, founder of the Worldwide Church of God, declared their final resting place to be Europe. In his view, known as the "British-Israel" theory, the tribe of Ephraim set-tled in Britain, and Armstrong insisted that "the Queen of England sits on the throne of David." Mannaseh, following the prophecy of Genesis 48:14, became the "fruitful vine" who "climbed over the wall" to America. Even now, according to Armstrong, the Western nations, ignorant of their heritage, await the coming of the Promised One, for "the scepter will not depart from Judah, nor the ruler's staff from between his feet, until he comes to whom it belongs, and the obedience of the nations is his."

Joseph Smith, founder of the Church of Jesus Christ of Latter-day Saints, the Mormons, claimed to have been shown golden plates hidden on Hill Cumorah in Palmyra, New York. These plates, when translated, became the Book of Mormon. It tells the story of how three of the Ten Lost Tribes migrated to the Americas, mingling with the local populations to produce the great Central American civilizations exist-ing in the sixteenth century at the time of European contact.

Others have followed historical clues leading south to Ethiopia where, in 1930, Emperor Haile Selassie came to power, calling himself "the Lion of the Tribe of Judah." Before his rise to power, Haile Selassie's name was Ras Tafari Makonnen. Descendants of African slaves living in Jamaica believed his ascension to the throne was a fulfillment of prophecy. Believing themselves to be descendants of one of the lost tribes, and Haile Selassie to be a descendant of King David, they established the religion of Rastafarianism. Ethiopia is one of the supposed hiding places of the lost Ark of the Covenant. The Queen of Sheba, mentioned in the book of Kings, is thought by some to be Ethiopian. She visited King Solomon in Jerusalem, and tradi-tion has it she returned home with a son, whose descendants spirited away the Ark of the Covenant before the Babylonians could capture it (see Ark of the Covenant).

Another theory says simply that Jews from the north returned to live with their brothers and sisters following the release of the Southern Kingdom from their Babylonian captivity.

What really happened to Israel will probably never be known for sure. What we do know is that Assyria sent her own colonists to live in the land they now called Samaria. This colonization was the root of the conflict between Jews and Samaritans that would be so prevalent seven hundred years later, prompting Jesus' familiar parable of the Good Samaritan, found in Luke 10.

The Captivity

Judah, the Southern Kingdom of Israel, lived on as an independent nation until 586 BCE. Through the work of good kings like Hezekiah and Josiah, the people underwent periods of revival and renewal. But major prophets such as Ezekiel and Jeremiah foretold their end. It happened, according to 2 Kings 25, at the hands of Nebuchadnezzar, king of Babylon. After a fierce, prolonged siege, the walls of Jerusalem were breached and the city, along with its beautiful Temple, destroyed. The Ark of the Covenant disappeared. The Temple furnishings were carted back to Babylon. The cream of Israel's youth, including a young man named Daniel who would gain fame and recognition in a lion's den, were carried away from their home and spiritual center. In the stark words of 2 Kings 25:21, "So Judah went into captivity, away from her land."

While Judah was in captivity, something very important happened to direct the course of Judaism and its offshoots, Christianity and Islam. The religion of Judaism became solidly monotheistic. Judaism is often thought of as a monotheistic religion going all the way back to Abraham, or at least as far back as Moses. But even the Ten Commandments delivered at Sinai leave room for polytheism: "I am the Lord your God … You shall have no other gods before me" (Exodus 20:2, 3). Strict monotheism would not recognize "other gods." The Psalms continue this theme. The Hebrew God YHVH, translated into English as Yahveh or Jehovah, is said to be superior to the "gods of the nations." Worship of the Canaanite God, Baal, was a constant problem addressed by the Hebrew prophets. Idol worship in the tradition of Jeroboam, son of Nebat (1 Kings 16:31), plagued the religious leaders for generations, causing Israel to sin again and again, according to the religious historians who compiled Kings and Chronicles. Indeed, the prophets said this was the very sin that, along with the neglect of the command to follow a Sabbath rest for their fields, caused God to allow the Babylonian captivity in the first place (2 Chronicles 36:15–21).

The captivity lasted for some generations. While some Jews eventually returned to Judah, others remained in Babylon, which later became Persia. The captivity can be said to have ended with the rebuilding of Jerusalem and the Temple, described in the books of Ezra and Nehemiah.

After the Captivity

After Judah's return from captivity, idol worship is never mentioned again. What happened to the Hebrews in the generations of their exile that caused this change?

Some say the people had learned their lesson. They repented of their sin and scourged the last vestige of idol worship out of their religion, as God had planned.

Others suspect Persian influences. A few years after the captivity, Babylon was surrounded by Persian armies. The city was considered to be impregnable, and the Babylonians thought they could attain victory simply by sitting behind their very secure walls and admiring their famous hanging gardens until the Persians got tired and left.

According to Daniel 5, the Babylonian king Belshazzar decided to celebrate early the departure of the Persians and threw a victory party. In the midst of the drunken revelry someone got the idea that it might be a good time to bring out the golden dishes and cups stolen from the Temple at Jerusalem. In judgment against this blasphemy, the God of the Hebrews brought the party to an abrupt halt. The fingers of a man's hand appeared in the air and began to inscribe a message. The "writing on the wall" came directly to the point: "You have been weighed in the balance and found wanting" (Daniel 5:27). The reign of Babylon was over. That very night the river supplying water to the city was dammed. Persian soldiers, entering under the walls by means of the dry riverbed, conquered the city. Babylon was no more.

The religion practiced by the Persians was Zoroastrianism, a strict—and perhaps the first—monotheistic religion (see Apocalypse). Traces of Persian religion are found throughout Judaism after the return. Monotheism is there, certainly, but also Zoroastrian apocalyptic ideas about duality, prophecy, and the nature of good and evil. Although the Bible never mentions Zoroastrianism, it certainly seems more than coincidental that so much of its influence, especially monotheism, appears in Judaism right after the Jews' first encounter with it.

It was during the Persian rule that the events of the book of Esther take place. Esther is the only book of the Bible that never once, except possibly in code, uses the word "God." It is a fascinating story about a Hebrew peasant who becomes Queen of Persia, saving the Hebrew people.

Some followers of the Baha'i faith see in this story a contact with Persian culture and faith that would later explain how the God of the Hebrews and Allah of Islam are in fact one and the same. Just as Persian religion and political influence aided the Hebrew people, Judaism quite literally "wed" itself to Persian culture when the Jewish woman described in the book of Esther married the Persian king, saving Judaism. This mix of cultures flowered centuries later in Persian Islam, ultimately influencing Baha'u'llah, the founder of Baha'i (see Baha'i).

The books of Ezra and Nehemiah tell how, by command of Artaxerxes, king of Persia, Jerusalem and the Temple were rebuilt. Daniel, writing from captivity, foretells the coming of the Greeks and Romans and introduces true apocalyptic literature into the Hebrew Bible, with dates and times coded so as not to be understood "until the time of the end" (Daniel 12:4). Some Christians even refer to the book of Daniel as the Little Book of Revelation (see Apocalypse). (It is important to note that many Christian scholars believe the book of Daniel was written by at least two different authors, one of whom lived after the time of Rome but dated his book back to the time of the captivity so as to make it appear he was writing prophecy rather than history.)

Even though the Hebrews returned to Jerusalem to rebuild, they were not free from outside rule. First the Persians, then the Greeks, and finally the Romans claimed power. Until 70 CE, the city of Jerusalem and the Temple remained standing as the center of Jewish life. But after their destruction by Titus and the Roman legions, the Jews were expelled into the great Diaspora. Dating from the time prior to the Babylonian captivity, Israel would not know true independence again until the United Nations vote of 1947 granted them a shared state with the Palestinians, a vote that eventually led to the creation of the State of Israel.

Sources:

The Book of Mormon. Trans. Joseph Smith. Salt Lake City: The Church of Jesus Christ of Latter-day Saints, 1980.

Bridger, David, ed. *The New Jewish Encyclopedia*. New York: Behrman House, 1962.

THE RELIGION BOOK: PLACES, PROPHETS, SAINTS, AND SEERS

May, Herbert G., and Bruce M. Metzger, eds. *The New Oxford Annotated Bible with the Apocrypha*. Rev. ed. New York: Oxford University Press, 1973.

BACH, JOHANN SEBASTIAN

Anyone who has attended Protestant worship services for any length of time has experienced in some way the music of Johann Sebastian Bach (1685–1750). Raised in the Lutheran tradition, Bach is history's most prolific composer of church music and one of the true musical giants. During his lifetime Bach was recognized as a brilliant organist, but the people of his day—possibly because they lived at a time of fluctuating musical tastes—didn't really appreciate his genius as a composer. He died in 1750, but it wasn't until Felix Mendelssohn revived the *Saint Matthew Passion* in 1829 that Bach finally took the place he holds today as one of the most respected composers of all time. His organ music, choral cantatas, and instrumental works have become standard repertoire for church musicians, and beloved hymns like "Sleepers Awake," "A Mighty Fortress Is Our God," and "Break Forth, O Beauteous Heavenly Light" are in every hymn book.

Johann Sebastian Bach, the great German composer, spent much of his career serving as organist and music director for a Lutheran church in Leipzing. *The Art Archive/ Society of the Friends of Music Vienna/Dagli Orti.*

Sources:

Douglas, J. D., ed. *The New International Dictionary of the Christian Church*. Grand Rapids, MI: Zondervan Publishing, 1974.

BAHA'I

In 1844 a Muslim named Ali Muhhamad Shirazi declared himself the spokesman for the twelfth Imam, or prayer leader, anticipated by some Shi'ite Muslims ever since the ninth century. Calling himself Bab-ud-Din, the "Gate of Faith," he introduced sweeping reforms into Islam, such as raising the status of women. A group of followers gathered around him, calling themselves Babis, "followers of the Bab." Although Bab-ud-Din was executed in 1850, he believed he had prepared the way for another who would found a worldwide religion.

A follower who escaped after the execution believed himself to be the predicted one. Mirza Husayn Ali took the name Baha'u'llah, "Glory of Allah," in 1863, and those who followed him became known as Baha'is.

Imprisoned in Acre, Turkey, Baha'u'llah was still able to receive guests and write. After his death in 1892, his son Abdul Baha took over the movement, traveling and lecturing extensively, eventually even receiving knighthood in England for his work promoting world peace.

Now, having moved far away from Islam, Baha'i is recognized as a separate religion.

Baha'u'llah's emphasis was on unity. He believed his religion to be the culmination of all the religions of the world, though he didn't seek to overthrow any of them. He taught that the Qur'an should be interpreted allegorically and was equal to the scriptures of all other religions. He did not believe in the existence of angels or spirits, and he felt that heaven and hell are symbolic conditions of the soul, not literal places.

He taught his followers that all religions come from the same source, and that divine revelation is continuous and progressive. Messengers of God, according to the teachings of Baha'u'llah, include Moses, Zoroaster, Jesus, Muhammad, and the Buddha. Baha'u'llah was the most recent, the Manifestation of God for the New Era. His was one of the first world religions to preach the unity of the whole human race and to teach that all religions are the work of one God.

Communal worship takes place in members' homes, consisting of prayer and readings from various scriptures and Baha'u'llah's writings. The Baha'i vision is positive and world-embracing, seeking the elimination of war and armaments and the formation of a world tribunal for settling disputes.

Some five million followers carry the vision throughout the world.

Sources:
Ludwig, Theodore M. *The Sacred Paths: Understanding the Religions of the World*. 2nd ed. Upper Saddle River, NJ: Prentice Hall, 1996.

BANTU

The rich culture of the Bantu people of Africa, south of the Congo River, includes several hundred languages and many different religious traditions. At the height of the slave trade, Islam had spread into the remote interior of the Bantus' homeland, while Catholicism vied for control of the coast. Countless thousands of Bantus were captured by Muslim slavers. Then they were marched to the coasts, where Catholic priests, who wanted to ensure their salvation, baptized them. Finally, they were loaded into the holds of Protestant-owned ships from America. They were then taken to different points of destination to work as slaves for the remainder of their lives.

But whether they were taken to the cane fields of Cuba or the cotton plantations of Georgia, they placed their own unique brand of spirituality upon their culture. The Voodoo of Haiti and New Orleans, the Rastafarianism of Jamaica, the unique song form of the black American spiritual, the philosophies of the Black Muslims, the southern gospel tradition of Protestant worship—all owe their very existence to people who absorbed the religion of their persecutors but refused to surrender their unique spirituality.

In South Africa today, the term Bantu is used to refer to the indigenous African population that was subject to the policies of Apartheid, the strict segregation of the black and white populations.

BAPTISM

(See also Anabaptists; Baptist; Sacrament)

Baptism is a sacrament ("sacred secret") common to all Christian traditions. Practiced by religious traditions worldwide, it became associated with the early Christian movement following the baptism of Jesus of Nazareth by John, called the Baptist or the Baptizer. Jesus would later issue a Great Commission to his church:

> Go ye into all the world and preach the Gospel, baptizing them in the name of the Father, the Son and the Holy Spirit. (Matthew 28:19)

Two forms of baptism are in use today. Some Christians practice "believer's baptism." Adults are baptized, usually immersed fully in water, upon their confession of faith that Jesus Christ is Lord and Savior. This affirmation declares they have become "born again."

Others practice infant baptism. Babies are baptized by sprinkling drops of water on their foreheads. Parents or godparents make baptism vows, awaiting the child's coming of age when the child personally confirms those vows and makes his or her "confirmation." After a period of study, usually in a series of classes, a public service is held where the child is received into church membership and, if not allowed already according to the dictates of the denomination, receives or "makes" his or her first communion.

A few traditions view baptism as the mark of salvation. They believe that with few exceptions, only those baptized will receive entrance into heaven. But most Christian traditions believe baptism to be an outward sign of an inward reality. Those baptized have been "cleansed of sin" by God, "washed clean" by the sacrifice of Jesus Christ.

Sources:
Douglas, J. D., ed. *The New International Dictionary of the Christian Church*. Grand Rapids, MI: Zondervan Publishing, 1974.

BAPTIST

"Baptist," to many people, means Southern Baptist and brings to mind two of its most famous adherents, the Reverend Billy Graham and, until he left the denomination in 2000, former U.S. president Jimmy Carter. But although the Southern Baptist Convention is the largest Protestant denomination in the United States, there are many more Baptist denominations, ranging from the mainline American Baptist Church to the smaller Conservative Baptists and Baptist General Conference. Then there are less well known Baptist denominations such as the Six Principle Baptists, Independent Baptists, and Charismatic Baptists.

Baptists came to America with the Puritan Roger Williams, who settled Providence, Rhode Island, in 1636. They have always been reluctant to force creeds and formulas, but, although their denominations are legion, they share certain doctrines and theological positions.

First, they practice adult baptism, almost always by full immersion in water. To be accepted into church membership, individuals must publicly confess conversion to

Pope John Paul II baptizes a child held by his mother in the Sistine Chapel at the Vatican during a special Mass, a traditional papal commemoration of Jesus' baptism in the River Jordan. *AP/Wide World Photos*.

Jesus Christ as Lord and Savior. This means they have become, in the words of John 3:3, "born again," or spiritually awakened to God. Having thus "accepted Jesus into their hearts" and received God's forgiveness for their sins, believers are baptized, usually in a public ceremony, "in the name of the Father, the Son, and the Holy Spirit."

Second, Baptists tend to be conservative in theology, ranging from fundamentalists to evangelicals (see Evangelical; Fundamentalism). Christ is generally acknowledged as sole and absolute spiritual authority, speaking to each believer individually. The Bible is God's voice in all matters relating to faith and practice.

Third, Baptists practice congregational autonomy. Each congregation, although belonging to the denomination, is free to own its own buildings, call its own pastors, elect its own deacons, and manage its own affairs free from denominational hierarchy.

Fourth, worship is generally nonliturgical, featuring music, preaching, and teaching.

A recent and ongoing theological power struggle within the Southern Baptist Convention illustrates the tension between Baptist church polity and individual expression. Sensing erosion of fundamental theology, a group of conservatives, employing organizational techniques similar to those used in political parties, were able to fill key positions on both elected and appointed boards and committees within the convention during its 2000 annual spring meeting. After obtaining control, they proceeded to set forth a doctrinal agenda they believed was within the framework of traditional Baptist tradition. "The Baptist Faith and Message" is the denomination's chief doctrinal statement. All missionaries and teaching professors must affirm it to receive denominational support. Arguments erupted when it was amended to say that women must "submit graciously to their husbands" and could no longer hold pastoral teaching positions in the church. Because individual churches call their own pastors, the rule could not be enforced at the local level. But seminaries supported by the convention were urged to examine the classroom lectures of teaching professors, some of whom were respected women academics. A few of these professors were released, not explicitly because they were women, but because they taught theological positions contrary to those supported by the convention. Many churches stopped paying denominational dues and dropped their traditional monetary support of convention-based mission works. A church split loomed and is still a very real possibility. In 1985 more than 45,000 people attended the convention. In 2002 fewer than 9,500 registered.

The situation illustrates a fundamental question inherent in religious organizations that stress individual freedom. It is a question that has been asked again and again ever since Martin Luther sparked the Protestant Reformation, and it is at the core of why Christianity is so divided as a whole and even within individual denominations. If religion is fundamentally a personal choice, how do people band together for the common good? Put in other words, who determines, in a democratically based institution, what the fundamental belief structure is going to be? Every time a vote is taken, are the losers forced to change their religious beliefs? If they don't change their beliefs, must they drop out to form yet another Christian denomination? How far out can theological lines be drawn and still maintain traditional identity, especially when facing a changing secular culture? How long does tradition continue before it becomes dogma, especially in a church that originally formed by breaking traditional dogmas?

Sources:
Breed, Allen G. "Baptist Leader Sees a 'New Day.'" *Boston Globe*, June 13, 2002.

Douglas, J. D., ed. *The New International Dictionary of the Christian Church*. Grand Rapids, MI: Zondervan Publishing, 1974.

Bar/Bat Mitzva

In Hebrew tradition, public prayer can take place when ten male adults, a group known collectively as the Minyan, gather in congregation. When a boy reaches the age of thirteen, he is considered old enough to participate in the Minyan and assume the duties of an adult Jew: to read Torah, and, among traditional Jews, to wear phylacteries (in Hebrew, *tefillin*; small boxes, bound to the left arm and the forehead, containing scriptural passages) during morning weekday prayers.

The occasion that marks this passage, usually taking place on the first Sabbath following a young man's thirteenth birthday, is called Bar Mitzva. Many Jewish congregations have also instituted a similar ceremony for girls, called Bat Mitzva.

At the ceremony, the new adult is generally honored with an Aliyah, a ritual in which he or she is invited to ascend the Bimah, the platform in the synagogue, and recite a blessing over the Torah, usually reading the Haftarah, the selection from the prophets read immediately after the Torah reading.

A Bar or Bat Mitzva is a joyful time of "coming out" that marks an important transition. The congregation is saying, in effect, "You are no longer a child. Now you are an adult. Take up your responsibilities."

Sources:
Bridger, David, ed. *The New Jewish Encyclopedia*. New York: Behrman House, 1962.
Ellwood, Robert S., and Barbara A. McGraw. *Many Peoples, Many Faiths*. 6th ed. Upper Saddle River, NJ: Prentice Hall, 1999.

BELTAIN *see* **Paganism, Calendar of**

Benedictines

(See also Catholicism)

Benedict of Nursia was a devout Roman Catholic who lived from 480 to 550 CE. Although he was not an ordained priest, those who follow his Benedictine Rule today generally study for the priesthood.

Benedictines are a contemplative order of monks and nuns, usually living communally and reaching for a deeper relationship with God through prayer, meditation, and community service as part of the Roman Catholic Church.

Sources:
Renard, John. *The Handy Religion Answer Book*. Detroit: Visible Ink Press, 2002.

BERG, DAVID *see* **Cult**

Bethlehem

Bethlehem means "House of Bread." The earliest mention of this famous town is in the Amarna letters of the fourteenth century BCE. They mention an early Hebrew settlement—"Bit-Lahmi" (Bethlehem) that "has gone over to the Apiru" (Hebrews).

Bethlehem's Old City as it appears today in Israel. *AP/Wide World Photos.*

Less than three hundred years later it was the birthplace of King David, who won fame by slaying Goliath and began his rise to power.

A thousand years after that, Bethlehem became immortalized as the birthplace of Jesus of Nazareth. With shepherds and kings leading the charge, tourists have filled its streets ever since. Dozens of Christmas carols have waxed eloquent over its "dark streets" shining with "the everlasting light," which makes recent tragedies it has witnessed seem ironic, to say the least.

Because Bethlehem is a Palestinian city, it is frequently the scene of Palestinian celebrations—and just as frequently a scene of Israeli and Palestinian violence.

In April and May 2002, the cathedral built to honor the traditional place of Jesus' birth became a fortress, surrounded by an Israeli army, defended by Muslim soldiers, whose wounded were tended by Christian priests and nuns—truly the dark side of ecumenical relations.

Sources:
Bucke, Emory Stevens et al, eds. *The Interpreter's Dictionary of the Bible*. 4 vols. New York: Abingdon Press, 1962.

BHAGAVAD-GITA

(See also Agni; Aryans; Brahman/Atman; Hinduism)

The Bhagavad-Gita is part of the Hindu Mahabharata, an epic Sanskrit scripture about the history of the ancient world, the story of a great war between cousins over the succession to the throne of an Aryan state. The Bhagavad-Gita, however, is widely published and read by itself, separate from the Mahabharata.

Hindu scriptures are some of the oldest in the world. The Vedas, developed by ancient Aryans and brought to India around 1500 BCE, are myths of ancient gods (devas, or "shining ones"). The Upanishads of about 500 BCE deal with levels of consciousness and the practice of meditation. In effect, the Upanishads moved the outward myth inward.

But after Buddhism split away from Hinduism a concern arose among Hindus to govern and organize society. This concern was stressed, at about 100 BCE, first in the Laws of Manu (the "Way of Society") that detail the four ends of man: pleasure (*kama*), gain (*artha*), righteousness (*dharma*), and liberation (*moksha*). These translate loosely into the four stages of life: student, householder, hermit, and renuncient.

The Laws of Manu were followed, four hundred years later, by the Yoga Sutras (the "Way of the Yogi"), an attempt to delve further into techniques of yoga meditation. The practitioner needs to follow eight limbs, or steps: nonviolence (truthfulness, celibacy, refraining from stealing, and avoiding greed), purity (contentment, mortification, study, and devotion), posture, breath control, withdrawal of attention from the senses, concentration, meditation, and contemplation. When the practice is mastered, the result is a heightened awareness not even suspected by most people. The Yoga Sutras tell how to read minds and discern thoughts, walk on water, fly through the air, levitate, become as small as an atom, and be impervious to hunger and thirst.

Both of these responses to Buddhism, the Laws of Manu and the Yoga Sutras, come together in the Bhagavad-Gita ("Song of the Lord").

Robert S. Ellwood and Barbara A. McGraw, in their book *Many Peoples, Many Faiths*, eloquently sum up the story told in the Bhagavad-Gita:

> Prince Arjuna, whose charioteer is the heroic god Krishna in human form, is setting out to lead his army into bloody battle against the foe. Appalled at what he is about to do, Arjuna pauses in deep moral distress. The book is a series of answers that Krishna gives the prince in answer to his irresolution. It discourses on why Arjuna can and must fight, but its implications go much further than this. The pacifist Gandhi greatly treasured this book, taking it as an allegory of nonviolent struggle against injustice and for spiritual purity.

Sources:

Ellwood, Robert S., and Barbara A. McGraw. *Many Peoples, Many Faiths*. 6th ed. Upper Saddle River, NJ: Prentice Hall, 1999.

Prabhupada, A. C. Bhaktivedanata Swami. *Bhagavad-Gita As It Is*. Los Angeles: Bhaktivedanta Book Trust, 1986.

BHAKTI

(See also Brahman/Atman)

To follow a Hindu spiritual path is to follow Bhakti, or dedication to a personal deity of love, mercy, and grace who calls for devotion and surrender. This concept is similar in practice, if not in theology, to the Christian concept of salvation. Hindus prefer the word devotion, a personal response to the feeling that one is separated from the ground of one's being. Although the Hindu concept of "God" is far different from the traditional Western understanding, in Bhakti a chosen deity manifests itself to the individual and calls for personal devotion. The deity is only one expression of the divine, which is unknowable and impossible to define.

Sources:
Ellwood, Robert S., and Barbara A. McGraw. *Many Peoples, Many Faiths*. 6th ed. Upper Saddle River, NJ: Prentice Hall, 1999.
Renard, John. *The Handy Religion Answer Book*. Detroit: Visible Ink Press, 2002.

BIBLE

(See also Apocrypha; Literary Criticism/Historical Critical Method; Tanakh)

The Bible is a library of books containing the scriptures of two religions. The Hebrew scriptures have been adopted by Christians and labeled the Old Testament. These thirty-nine books were written before the birth of Jesus. The twenty-seven books of the New Testament are the product of the Christian movement following the birthday of the church on the day of Pentecost, sometime around 30–33 CE.

The names "Old" and "New" Testaments come from the New Testament book of Hebrews, chapter 8, which in turn quotes the Old Testament book of Jeremiah, chapter 31:

> The time is coming, declares the Lord, when I will make a new covenant [testament] with the house of Israel and with the house of Judah. It will not be like the covenant I made with their fathers when I took them by the hand to lead them out of Egypt, because they did not remain faithful to my covenant, and I turned away from them, declares the Lord. This is the covenant I will make with the house of Israel after that time, declares the Lord. I will put my laws in their minds and write them on their hearts. I will be their God, and they will be my people. No longer will a man teach his neighbor, or a man his brother, saying, "Know the Lord," because they will all know me, from the least of them to the greatest. For I will forgive their wickedness and will remember their sins no more.

Then follows an editorial comment by the Christian author of Hebrews: "By calling this covenant 'new,' he has made the first one obsolete."

Christianity was, at first, considered a reform movement of Judaism. All of its first converts were Jewish. But when the apostle Paul freed Gentile converts from the Jewish requirements of circumcision and kosher food restrictions, they began to think of themselves as the "new" Israel, related to Abraham not by blood but by spirit. The only scripture familiar to the new Church was the Hebrew Bible, and it was quoted freely in their writings, which, when brought together some three hundred years later, would be called the New Testament. (The process is explained under the entry on Apocrypha).

The Story of the Bible

The Bible, written by many authors over the course of more than one thousand years, tells a single story. The individual books are divided into chapters and verses for easy identification. Genesis 3:15–18, for instance, means that the passage quoted is from Genesis (the first book of the Bible), chapter three, verses fifteen through eighteen. With so many different translations and editions, identification by page number is simply not feasible. This refinement, however, was not found in the original manuscripts. It is the result of an editorial decision made in the Middle Ages.

The first eleven chapters of Genesis contain a prologue to the main story:

Chapters 1 and 2: Creation.
Chapter 3: The Fall. Adam and Eve are expelled from Eden.
Chapter 4: Cain murders Abel and goes forth to populate the earth.
Chapters 5 through 9: As evil spreads throughout the earth, God destroys humankind with a great flood.
Chapter 10: The Table of Nations. An explanation of how each human race descended from one of the three sons of Noah.
Chapter 11: The Tower of Babel. An explanation of why different races speak different languages.

In chapter 12 the main story of the Bible begins. Abraham answers the call of God, who tells him to "leave your country, your people and your father's household to go to the land I will show you." By following this command to migrate to the land now called Israel, Abraham sets in motion the long story of his descendants that occupies the rest of the Bible. Genesis tells the story of how Isaac, his son, becomes the father of Jacob and Esau. Jacob's name is changed to Israel when he wrestles with an unknown antagonist all night. His sparring partner is finally revealed to be none other than God. Israel means "he struggles with God." Jacob, now called Israel, fathers twelve sons. Their descendants, known as the Twelve Tribes of Israel, are forever after called *bene Yisrael*, "children of Israel."

Their occupation of the land promised them by God, the Promised Land, is interrupted by a four-hundred-year captivity in Egypt (described in the book of Exodus). But under Moses they finally break free and begin their journey to the place they will forever call home (see Passover). If the Hebrew race began with Abraham, it can be said that the Jewish religion began with Moses. In the forty-year period of desert wandering following their escape from Egypt, the Hebrews were given the Law at Sinai and developed Tabernacle worship. The children of Israel became a unified people with a clear goal (detailed in Exodus through Deuteronomy). Their conquest of the Promised Land (Joshua through Ruth) began a long journey leading to great heights of glory under David and Solomon and great depths of despair in captivity in foreign lands (Samuel through Nehemiah; see Babylonian Captivity). Wisdom was acquired at a great price and expressed beautifully by many different writers (Job through Solomon's Song). The Hebrew prophets (Isaiah through Malachi) would time and again call upon the people to return to the path of God begun by their ancestors so many generations earlier.

The New Testament finds the Jews living in Israel, now called Palestine, under Roman rule. Jesus Christ is born in Bethlehem. His story is told in four Gospels, called Matthew, Mark, Luke, and John (see Gospel). His followers come to believe he is the Messiah anticipated by the Hebrew prophets, and they are soon called Christians. They proceed to spread his message throughout the Roman empire (described in the book of Acts). The first great Christian missionary, the apostle Paul, writes epistles, or letters, to the many churches he establishes (Romans through Philemon). Other letters written by different apostles (Hebrews through Revelation) follow these.

Taken together, Christians understand the Old and New Testaments of the Bible to tell the story of the human race. In the beginning, the first human parents are cast out of the Garden of Eden to keep them from the Tree of Life. Eating its fruit in their sinful state would have opened the doors to an eternity of evil. But that evil is addressed by God and paid for at Calvary (see Christ/Jesus of Nazareth). The way to the Tree of Life is opened once again. The final chapter of the Bible pictures the tree now standing in the New Jerusalem, "come down from heaven as a bride prepared for her bridegroom ... and the leaves of the tree are for the healing of the nations. No longer will there be any curse" (Revelation 22:2, 3).

Biblical Interpretation

What divides Bible scholars today is interpretation. How should the Bible be read? Who really wrote it? Is it a history textbook? Is it a book of ethics? What does it mean when Paul claims that "all Scripture is inspired by God" (2 Timothy 3:16)? Are Christians bound by the cultural patterns of the authors? If so, slavery and subjugation of women seem to be ordained by God, since both seem to have Paul's approval (Ephesians 6:5 and 1 Corinthians 14:34). And what about the stories of rape, murder, and incest committed by people who seem to have God's blessing? Are they in the same category as the texts that outline moral behavior?

Answers to these questions form the basis of a great divide in the Church today. How scholars approach the subject of biblical interpretation immediately labels them. Dr. Gabriel Fackre of Andover Newton Theological School has prepared the following chart to help explain basic Christian theological positions in regard to biblical interpretation:

Biblical View	Definition	Popular Label
Oracular	"The Bible was dictated by God to human authors."	Extreme fundamentalism
Inerrancy	"The autographs of the Bible are without error in all matters about which it chooses to speak."	Fundamentalism/ evangelicalism/charismatic

Biblical View	Definition	Popular Label
Infallibility	"The Bible is the authority in all matters pertaining to faith and life."	Moderate evangelicalism
Conceptual	"We are not to be concerned with the *words* of the Bible but rather with the *ideas* they convey."	Liberal evangelicalism/mainstream
Historical	"The Bible reveals what God *did* and *does*, not what God *said*."	Mainstream/liberal
Christological	"The Bible is a medium for knowing Jesus Christ."	Liberal

The matter of scriptural interpretation continues to divide not only the Christian community, but Muslims and Jews as well. Whenever a holy book is read, assumptions have to be made. What was in the mind of the original author? Is the author even who he claims to be? Does the intention of the author determine our interpretation, or is the author being used by a Higher Power? Are secrets or even codes planted within scripture that are intended to remain hidden until the time arrives to which they apply? Are doctrines based on eternal truth or culturally conditioned behavior?

Sources:

Fackre, Gabriel. *The Christian Story*, Vol. 2. Grand Rapids, MI: Erdmans, 1986.

Helms, Randel McCraw. *Who Wrote the Gospels?* Altadena, CA: Millennium Press, 1997.

Kirsch, Jonathan. *The Harlot by the Side of the Road.* New York: Balantine Books, 1997.

May, Herbert G., and Bruce M. Metzger, eds. *The New Oxford Annotated Bible with the Apocrypha*. Rev. ed. New York: Oxford University Press, 1973.

BLACK ELK

Black Elk was an Oglala Sioux *wichasha wakon* (holy man or priest). A second cousin to Crazy Horse, he knew the old war chief well.

In August 1930 a Nebraska writer named John G. Neihardt met Black Elk while doing research on American Indian history. Black Elk, who did not speak English, was said to have remarked to his interpreter, "As I sit here, I can feel in this man beside me a strong desire to know the things of the Other World. He has been sent to learn what I know, and I will teach him."

The world is richer because he did. Neihardt's book, *Black Elk Speaks,* is one of the great religious books written on the American continent. Not only has it introduced Lakota religious concepts to non-Indians, it has reintroduced countless Indian young people to their roots, whether or not they are from the Plains Indian culture.

Black Elk shared the spiritual framework of the pipe ceremonies and his vision of the "hoop" of his people, delving into what it meant to be a Sioux religious leader and what it means to be an Indian. He shared stories from his youth, remembering bison hunts and Custer's Last Stand. He described the first great vision that set him apart, and he recalled the final days of Wounded Knee.

In his senior years he returned to Harney Peak, where he had experienced his first great vision, filled with images of flying horses and mystical appearances. Here he had heard the sun singing as it rose:

> With a visible face I am appearing,
> In a sacred manner I appear.
> For the greening earth a pleasantness I make.
> The center of the nation's hoop I have made pleasant.
> With visible face, behold me!
> The four-leggeds and two-leggeds, I have made them to walk;
> The wings of the air, I have made them to fly.
> With visible face I appear.
> My day, I have made it holy.

Now, on his final trip to the place of his vision, Black Elk offered a prayer for all his people who had been so cruelly displaced and abused:

> With tears running, O Great Spirit, my Grandfather—with running tears I must say now that the tree has never bloomed. A pitiful old man, you see me here, and I have fallen away and have done nothing. Here at the center of the world, when you took me when I was young and taught me; here, old, I stand, and the tree is withered, Grandfather, my Grandfather. Again, and maybe the last time on this earth, I recall the great vision you sent me. It may be that some little root of the sacred tree still lives. Nourish it then, that it may leaf and bloom and fill with singing birds. Hear me, not for myself, but for my people.

Neihardt says that on the trip up the mountain the sun had been shining. As Black Elk prayed the sky clouded over and it began to rain. With tears running down his face, the old man repeated: "Hear me in my sorrow, for I may never call again. O make my people live."

"And in a little while," Neihardt tells us, "the sky was clear again."

Sources:
Neihardt, John G. *Black Elk Speaks*. Lincoln, NE: University of Nebraska Press, 1961.

BLACK MUSLIMS

Elijah Muhammad (1897–1975) was one of the most influential Muslim leaders among Americans of African descent. During the tumultuous 1960s, the black community throughout the United States became a scene of missionary activity and was mobilized as never before. Although the Nation of Islam, developed by Elijah Muhammad, was often accused of preaching unorthodox doctrine compared to Islamic tradition, its teachings concerning the separation of black and white America and the dignity of African descent touched a chord that resonated throughout the black community. Since then the movement has moved closer to traditional Islam, and its best-known adherent, Malcolm X (1925–1965), supported this trend, especially toward the end of his life. Today the mainstream of African-American Islam strives to be associated with Islam, rather than to be known as a protest to white America. But

Bronze statue of Bodhisattva Maitreya. Bodhisattva is a Sanskrit term that translates as: enlightenment (Bodhi) and being (sattva). *The Art Archive/ Musée Guimet Paris/Dagli Orti.*

splinter Black Muslim groups carry on. Perhaps the best-known spokesman of the Nation of Islam is the controversial minister Louis Farrakhan (b. 1933), whose Million Man March on Washington mobilized much of the black community around the issue of the father's role in the family. Minister Farrakhan is noted for his call for unity and the need for African Americans to separate themselves from what he sees as continued white oppression in the wake of so many centuries of slavery. He is also, however, widely criticized for what are seen as racist, sexist, bigoted, and anti-Semitic views.

Sources:

Ellwood, Robert S., and Barbara A. McGraw. *Many Peoples, Many Faiths.* 6th ed. Upper Saddle River, NJ: Prentice Hall, 1999.

BLACK STONE

(See also Islam)

Islamic tradition says the black stone built into the foundation of the Kaaba in Mecca was given to Abraham and his son Ishmael by the angel Gabriel as a sign of God's pleasure. Many archaeologists believe it had been a meteor, and some stories say it fell to Earth when Adam and Eve were evicted from Eden.

However it happened, a journey to the black stone of Mecca is part of the pilgrimage required of all Muslims and is holy to all who finally visit the place toward which they have faced each time they prayed.

Sources:

Ludwig, Theodore M. *The Sacred Paths: Understanding the Religions of the World.* 2nd ed. Upper Saddle River, NJ: Prentice Hall, 1996.

BODHISATTVA

In Mahayana Buddhism, a Bodhisattva is one who has attained enlightenment, whose Buddha nature has found peace, but who has renounced Nirvana for the sake of helping others in their journey to liberation from suffering.

Sources:

Ellwood, Robert S., and Barbara A. McGraw. *Many Peoples, Many Faiths.* 6th ed. Upper Saddle River, NJ: Prentice Hall, 1999.

BOOK OF MORMON

(See also Babylonian Captivity; Mormons/Church of Jesus Christ of Latter-day Saints)

The Book of Mormon is Joseph Smith's translation of golden plates said to be shown him by the angel Moroni beginning on September 21, 1823, in Palmyra, New York. Covering the time from roughly 600 BCE to 421 CE, they tell the story of how God preserved a people in the Americas who would reveal God's plan during the latter days of earthly life.

Mormons read the Book of Mormon along with the Bible, calling it another testament of Jesus Christ.

Sources:

The Book of Mormon. Trans. Joseph Smith. Salt Lake City, UT: The Church of Jesus Christ of Latter-day Saints, 1980.

BRAHMAN/ATMAN

(See also Hinduism)

A succinct definition of Hinduism might read, "The Universe is profoundly One." This unity can best be understood by exploring the Hindu concepts of Brahman and Atman.

The Upanishads, which form part of the Hindu scripture, speak of Brahman as "Him the eye does not see, nor the tongue express, nor the mind grasp." Brahman is not a God, but rather the ultimate, unexplainable principle encompassing all of creation. Because creation preceded language, words cannot grasp the totality of Brahman. Any and every definition falls short. Brahman then becomes a word used to speak of what can be called a "macro" metaphysical principle.

But there is also a "micro" metaphysical principle. The subtle presence intuited within, identified as "soul" or "self" by other traditions, is called Atman. Atman, thus, perceives Brahman. But this perception leads to a central meditation discovered by the Hindu rishis, or sages, described in the Chandogya Upanishad:

> In the beginning there was Existence alone—One only, without a second. He, the One [Brahman], thought to himself: "Let me be many, let me grow forth." Thus out of himself he projected the universe, and having projected out of himself the universe, he entered into every being. All that is has its self in him alone. Of all things he is the subtle essence. He is the truth. He is the Self. And that ... THAT ART THOU!

When one discovers that Atman, the inner self, and Brahman, the essence of the universe, are indeed one, the experienced result is said to be one of immense peace and harmony, of coming home. The human perception of life is often that of a small, fragile being gazing out into an infinite, unknowable space. Hinduism teaches that the intuitive leap of realizing "that art thou" tells us we belong. We have a place. We are one with the stars and the consciousness that brought them into being.

Sources:

Fisher, Mary Pat, and Lee W. Bailey. *An Anthology of Living Religions*. Upper Saddle River, NJ: Prentice Hall, 2000.

Vedanta Society of Southern California. *The Upanishads*. Swami Prabhavananda and Frederick Manchester, trans. New York: Mentor Books, 1957.

BRANCH DAVIDIANS *see* **Cult**

BUDDHA

(See also Hinduism)

The legend of Prince Siddhartha Gautama, who became known to the world as the Buddha, has many versions. But certain facts of the story are known:

Siddhartha was born around 563 BCE to the Sakya clan in Lumbini, located near the Nepal/India border. A Brahmin priest visited the family compound and prophesied that the young prince would grow up to be either an emperor or a Buddha, an Enlightened One.

The child's father wanted the boy to grow up to be an emperor, so he sequestered young Siddhartha within the walls of the palace, hoping to discourage any untoward spiritual development by supplying everything the young man desired in the way of material delights.

But young men are curious, so one day Siddhartha had his chariot driver take him out into the real world. There he saw four sights that changed the course of his life and of history.

The first thing he saw was an old man. From this he learned that every life will come to an end.

The second thing he saw was a man suffering from a hideous disease. From this he discovered that all life is suffering.

Next, he caught his first glimpse of a corpse. He learned that death is real.

At this point Siddhartha reflected:

I also am subject to death and decay and am not free from the power of old age, sickness and death. Is it right that I should feel horror, repulsion and disgust when I see another in such plight? And when I reflected thus … all the joy of life which there is in life died within me.

What the story illustrates so far is a phenomenon known as the "frog in the kettle" syndrome. The syndrome takes its title from the supposed fact that if a frog is thrown into boiling water, its reaction to the sudden change of temperature is so great that it will immediately hop out to avoid being scalded. But if the same frog is placed in water at a temperature to which its body is accustomed, and if the water is gradually heated, the change will seem so slight that the frog will not notice its predicament until it is too late.

Most people, as they grow up, gradually become accustomed to the realities of life—great joys as well as great suffering—and they accept, as a matter of course, that this is the nature of what it means to be human. But Siddhartha, unaccustomed to suffering while growing up, became the frog that was thrown into the boiling water. It affected him drastically and changed his life. He spent the remainder of his life learning how to hop out of the kettle of suffering he had so suddenly been exposed to.

Bronze sculpture of Buddha in Batsford Park, Gloucestershire, England. *Fortean Picture Library.*

While contemplating all he had seen, still not understanding, he saw the fourth sight that would alter him so dramatically: he gazed upon a holy man who seemed quite content.

Siddhartha decided he had to study the meaning of life by becoming a holy man.

Siddhartha's father, by trying to keep him from seeking a spiritual path of wisdom, had instead catapulted the young man toward exactly that destiny.

At this point the story becomes legend and the details vary. Some versions have Siddhartha simply leaving home to begin his journey. Others provide more detail. A popular rendition, consistent with Siddhartha's personality in view of later events, tells how the young man went home to confront his family. When his father refused to let the boy leave, Siddhartha simply waited, saying he would not move until he had his father's consent. Dinnertime came and went. Siddhartha remained patiently in place. Bedtime came, and his father was sure that by morning the boy would return to his senses. But morning's light found the boy standing still, ready to have his way or die.

Needless to say, the young prince eventually got his way. Saying goodbye to his family (some versions include a young wife), Siddhartha, with his faithful charioteer, left the family compound and began a search for the meaning of life.

For six years he wandered and studied. He talked with Brahmins, Hindu holy men. He learned yoga disciplines and meditation. He practiced extreme asceticism, eventually cutting down to one grain of rice a day and deciding that since he could exist on one grain, why not try slicing it in half to make it last twice as long?

It is said he became so thin and emaciated that a person could grasp Siddhartha's backbone from the front.

Even after all this, enlightenment eluded him. By this time he had joined a group of traveling holy men, none of whom was making any more progress along the spiritual path than he was. Terribly discouraged, he resorted to what had worked with his father. Seating himself beneath the famous Bo tree (Bodhi-tree—"Tree of Knowledge"; some legends make it a fig tree) he vowed he would meditate there, not moving until he reached enlightenment or died.

There he passed through the four Hindu stages of consciousness. When thus prepared, Mara, an old Hindu god and devil figure, lured him with three temptations.

First came the temptation of the flesh. Three beautiful women walked by, begging him to follow.

Next came the temptation of the spirit. Ferocious demons attempted to frighten him enough to make him flee from his place beneath the Bo tree. Smiling, Siddhartha simply touched the earth upon which he sat, saying, in effect, "I have a right to be here and here I will stay!"

When these temptations proved inadequate, the devil switched to the subtle temptation of pride. Whispering in Siddhartha's ear, Mara congratulated him on his spiritual growth, telling him that his insights and dedication were too profound for normal people to understand and that it would be profitless to attempt to teach them to others.

Again, Siddhartha resisted.

With this final spiritual victory, he passed through all stages of awareness. He saw in a flash all his previous incarnations and understood their connectedness, how they had brought him to this point in time and place. Now he understood Karma at work. He sensed the guiding force that propels life forward. And, more important, in a sudden intuitive leap, he grasped how to break out of samsara, the wheel of life, death, and rebirth. He had achieved the goal of his quest. He had become the Buddha, the Enlightened One.

He called his insight the dharma, the Middle Way that leads between the poles of all opposites to Nirvana, the place beyond, which embraces all extremes.

The Buddha saw life in terms of duality, pairs of opposites. For every up, there is a down; for every left, a right. There cannot exist cold without heat, joy without sorrow. So one-half of every pair of opposites is uncomfortable. The natural human tendency is to identify with what is good, comfortable, or otherwise desirable. Buddha saw this was impossible. Unless both poles of opposites are embraced, one cannot be content, because both poles are real and make up the fabric of life. To remain insulated from one pole or the other is to live in denial. Eventually, even if we live in a palace, we must journey outside the walls and experience the reality that is life in all its totality. Denying or even ignoring death and sickness doesn't make them less real. All it does is produce anxiety because the human psyche knows they are inevitable.

Siddhartha condensed his insight into what he called the Four Noble Truths (see Buddhism). He taught these principles to the men with whom he had previously traveled. At first, when they saw him eating whole meals, they thought he had departed from the spiritual path. But, upon hearing his first sermon, the Deer Park Discourse, they realized he had attained his quest and become the Buddha. They became his disciples, and from this group of monks grew the religion we know today as Buddhism. An organization developed. Buddhism became the first great missionary religion, eventually spreading throughout the entire world.

One of the Buddha's disciples, Devadatta, tried to betray and kill him but was thwarted in his attempt. The Buddha lived for another forty-five years, teaching and delivering discourses, now called Sutras.

It is said that at the end the Buddha ate some tainted meat that led to his death. After forgiving the man who had given him the meat, his spoke his final wisdom:

1. Be ye lamps unto yourselves.
2. All compounds [aggregates, even people] are transitory.
3. Work out your own salvation with diligence.

With that, he breathed his last, departed samsara, and entered Nirvana, beyond all pairs of opposites, even the opposites of life and death. From this place of cosmic consciousness, existing always beyond time and place, the spirit of the Buddha is engaged in drawing the Buddha nature, inherent in every person, to himself.

Buddha and Christ

While Buddhism stands alone, irrespective of comparisons with other traditions, any reader familiar with the story of Jesus Christ, founder of Christianity, will have noticed the parallels between the legend of the life of the Buddha and the legend of Jesus Christ.

Both left their homes seeking the truth that exists beyond average human existence. Both were led into the wilderness, where they were tested by the devil with three temptations. Both gathered a group of disciples, one of whom became a betrayer. Both returned from their wilderness experience to preach a sermon summing up their teaching: Buddha delivered the Deer Park Discourse, Jesus preached the Sermon on the Mount.

Both died at the hands of other men, forgiving them before the end. Even their final wisdom is similar:

The Buddha

Be ye lamps unto yourselves.

All compounds are transitory.

Work out your own salvation with diligence.

The Christ

Ye are the light of the world.

Ye are not of this world even as I am not.

(Through the apostle Paul) Work out your own salvation with fear and trembling.

Such comparisons do not suggest that one religion is an imitation or copy of the other. It is obvious that the two rose independently of each other and stand as separate entities. There are many points of contrast between the two, especially in their teachings concerning the nature of God (many Buddhists do not believe in a personal deity), time (linear versus circular), and afterlife (heaven versus Nirvana).

But similarities also exist, pointing to a common human experience. Perhaps these similarities were best summed up in *Questions of Faith II: Who Is Jesus?* by Roy Sano, who was born into a Buddhist family but became a Methodist bishop: "When I converted to Christianity I wondered how I could still be a Buddhist. As time goes by I now wonder how I can be a Christian and *not* be a Buddhist!"

Sources:

Hagen, Steve. *Buddhism Plain and Simple*. Boston: Charles E. Tuttle Co., 1997.

Hesse, Herman. *Siddhartha*. New York: Bantam Books, 1951.

Kung, Hans, and Julia Ching. *Christianity and Chinese Religions*. New York: Doubleday, 1989.

Questions of Faith II: Who Is Jesus? (video). Nashville, TN: EcuFilm and the United Church of Christ.

BUDDHISM

(See also Buddha)

Buddhism is a humanistic philosophy with deep psychological insights. Some practitioners worship gods, others do not. The Buddha himself is not worshiped as a god, but he is venerated as a completed, spiritual teacher.

Buddhism's principal concept is that human consciousness can be transformed from attachment to ego, suffering, and objects of desire to the unattached bliss of Nirvana. The path of this transformation was demonstrated by the Buddha, an enlightened man who showed the way out of the wheel of life, death, and rebirth—the material world seemingly ruled by attachment and ignorance. Buddhism's fundamental practice is meditation, and its fundamental social expression is the Samgha, the order of priests.

One of the keys to understanding Buddhism is the concept of *anatman*, "no self." To understand *anatman*, we must begin with Buddha's Four Noble Truths: All life is suffering; suffering is caused by desire; there can be an end to desire; and to end desire, follow the Eightfold Path.

In the process of seeking for the meaning of life, Buddha came to realize that:

All Life Is Suffering

By this Buddha did not mean that life is a miserable experience. Rather, he was pointing out that even the most joyous moment contains the thought that the moment cannot last. Every life will come to an end. Everything is in the process of dying. At the moment of birth the journey begins toward death. The reality of death should be acknowledged, not denied or feared to the point of debilitation.

The Buddha would never discourage jogging, joining an exercise club, or pursuing a healthy diet. But he would insist these activities should be performed to enhance life, rather than to create the illusion that death can be postponed. The healthiest person alive will someday die. Hence, all life is suffering.

But the knowledge of death is not necessarily tragic. Death is a part of life. So what causes suffering? Is it simply the knowledge that good times don't last forever? No.

Suffering Is Caused by Desire

We want what we cannot have. We desire something because we believe it will bring happiness or release from sorrow. We attempt to hold on to joyous moments, trying to make them last forever. We gather things around us to protect us from suffering, so life becomes a matter of accumulating and desiring more of those things—a bigger house, a more suitable mate, better clothes, a more comfortable car, a higher-paying job that will provide more money to buy more things.

Buddha believed people consist of five *skandhas*, or bundles. Rather than consisting of a "soul" stuck in a body, people are made up of various parts, blending together to produce a whole. The five *skandhas* are:

Form (outward appearance)
Feelings (inward emotions)
Perceptions (how we visualize what we feel)
Impulses (Karmic dispositions—the forces that propel life forward toward a goal)
Background consciousness (that from which we spring and to which we return)

To see how these things work together, consider, as an example, an inner conversation before buying a new car:

That's a nice car. (The form of the car pleases us.)

I want that car! (We experience an inward emotion of desire.)

I can just see myself driving down the street. Imagine the stares of approval I'd get. (We visualize how we would feel.)

I deserve that car. It was meant for me! (We believe Karma, or fate, brought us to this place and time.)

I've always wanted a car like that! (We come to believe our purchase is somehow eternally predestined.)

Note the progress from *skandha* to *skandha*. Form stimulates feelings, which form perceptions, provoke impulses, and inform consciousness.

The problem, according to Buddha, is that most people get stuck on the word "I." "I" want, "I" feel, "I" visualize. But who is this "I"? "I" is obviously the villain of the piece, because it is this "I" who is setting in progress the chain of desires that lead to suffering. By saying "I," we demonstrate that we feel as though we are somehow an individual separate from the rest of the world. If "I" am "me," and "you" are "you," then we are obviously separate from each other. And if "I" desire something, then the "I" that desires must be an entity separate from the desire itself.

Buddha would say we are misreading the data. The "I" who sees and perceives is simply a phenomenon. It is an illusion. It does not really exist. It is a word expressing the way we perceive what is, in fact, the bundle of parts that make up our whole.

We are now approaching the point where we can begin to understand *anatman*. We have seen that suffering is caused by desire. Buddha came to realize that "desire" was the weak point. This is where Buddhism becomes positive.

There Can Be an End to Desire

Suffering is like fire. It needs fuel. Remove the fuel and the fire goes out. Desire is the fuel that feeds suffering. If the perceived "I" can stop desiring, suffering can be stopped. It's as simple (and as difficult) as that.

Follow the Eightfold Path

But how do we stop desiring? How do we control such a basic human tendency? The path is difficult. Buddha's Fourth Noble Truth describes it as the Eightfold Path:

Right Understanding (seeing through illusions such as the idea that wealth will bring happiness)
Right Thought or Motives (doing for others rather than for oneself)
Right Speech (even to ourselves—positive words are better than negative ones)
Right Action (doing nothing that would have to be kept hidden)
Right Livelihood (work must be consistent with beliefs)
Right Effort (constant awareness of the Eightfold Path)
Right Mindfulness (doing everything purposefully)
Right Meditation (final attainment of the trance state of *anatman*, "no self"; we understand that we are one with everything and connected to it all, without being aware that we are aware—we simply "are")

When we come to the point wherein the "I," the ego, has retreated, taking its proper place as simply a phenomenon, we are freed from the desires upon which the "I" has insisted. Once we are freed from desire, suffering cannot exist, because suffering is caused by desire.

Acceptance replaces desire, and there is a vast difference between the two. Acceptance has to do with embracing the duality of life as it is in the moment, not desiring to modify it, change it, or judge it. This is the Middle Way between the pairs of opposites, joy and sorrow. Instead of clinging to the joy and attempting to hold onto it by any and all methods, we accept joy when it comes just as we accept sorrow when it comes. And by seeking acceptance, we discover the Middle Way between joy and sorrow to the place of peace that embraces both. This is enlightenment.

Sources:

Ellwood, Robert S., and Barbara A. McGraw. *Many Peoples, Many Faiths*. 6th ed. Upper Saddle River, NJ: Prentice Hall, 1999.

Hagen, Steve. *Buddhism Plain and Simple*. Boston: Charles E. Tuttle Co., 1997.

Peterson, Michael et al. *Reason and Religious Belief: An Introduction to the Philosophy of Religion*. 2nd ed. New York: Oxford University Press, 1998.

BUDDHISM, DEVELOPMENT OF

When the Buddha preached his Deer Park Discourse and began to teach what he had discovered about the Middle Way, a group of disciples formed around him. At first these followers were men. But later on Buddha permitted women to join what became known as the Samgha, the order of monks.

The vow taken by these disciples consisted of "taking refuge" in the Three Jewels, sometimes called the Three Refuges. Monks would declare, "I take refuge in the Buddha. I take refuge in the dharma [Buddha's teaching]. I take refuge in the Samgha."

The life of a monk was regulated by ten rules. The rules prohibit:

Taking life
Taking what is not given
Sexual misconduct
Lying
Taking intoxicants
Eating to excess and eating after the noon hour
Watching or participating in dancing, singing, or shows
Adorning oneself with decorations or perfumes
Sleeping in a soft bed
Receiving gold and silver

The first five were for lay associates of the order. Monks practiced all ten.

After the death of a founder, religions seem to develop traditions and hierarchies. Just as Christianity would later divide into Catholic and Protestant, Buddhism separated into two great traditions, one of which would further divide, just as Protestantism did as the years went by.

Theravada

Of the two present-day traditions of Buddhism, the largest is sometimes called Hinayana, a disparaging term meaning "lesser vessel," in contrast with the second major tradition called Mahayana, or "great vessel." The largest sect of Hinayana is Theravada.

Theravada means "path of the elders." It is the Buddhism of Sri Lanka, Myanmar, Thailand, Cambodia, and Laos. This is the Buddhism of monks with shaved heads wearing saffron-yellow robes. The Buddha is venerated with statues showing him in three positions, each pointing to a specific aspect of his presence.

When the Buddha is shown in the well-known lotus (seated) position, the image is reminding us of the Buddha in his enlightenment. This is the position of meditation, and it pictures Buddha under the Bo tree where he discovered his insight.

When Buddha is standing, he is being represented as a teacher. Rather than leave Earth, Buddha chose the path of the Bodhisattva. Although this is a Mahayana term, it is used to describe an enlightened one who chooses to remain and teach others his dharma, or doctrine.

When Buddha is shown reclining, it is an image of his entry into Nirvana. Other religious traditions sometimes picture their founder "going" somewhere accompanied by lights and celestial messengers. In Buddhism the understanding is somewhat different. Buddha did not so much venture outward as turn inward. Just as a star collapses in on itself, becoming a black hole that draws everything into the void, Buddha is now drawing all things into Nirvana, the place with no dimension and no mass, the place beyond all pairs of opposites, the eternal consciousness from which all things come and to which all things return. Buddha consciousness is present in everything and all people. People don't normally experience it without training, but Buddhism teaches that all are a manifestation of it and will eventually come to understand that the life people think they are living, though real, is ultimately an illusion. But after many lives of discovery, we, like the Buddha, will "recline" and be freed from samsara and the suffering of life.

Some forms of Theravada Buddhism practice archaic customs of initiation. Because initiation rites are part of prehistoric religions, these customs might point to ancient religious influences that have been absorbed into its culture. This type of rite is a common religious practice; both Christianity and Judaism show similar characteristics in their rites of baptism and circumcision.

Mahayana

The second great tradition of Buddhism is Mahayana, "Great Vessel." This is the Buddhism of China, Korea, Japan, Tibet, Nepal, and Vietnam. Just as the Reformation quickly divided Protestants into different denominations, so Mahayana divided into different sects. They share a few aspects in common.

Foremost, Mahayana Buddhism emphasizes Buddha in his enlightenment, the presence of Buddha nature, and seeing the universe as Buddha came to see it.

The story is told that one day, soon after the Buddha's enlightenment, a man saw the Buddha walking toward him. The man had not heard of the Buddha, but he could see that there was something different about the stranger, so he was moved to ask, "Are you a god?" The Buddha answered, "No." The man asked, "Are you some kind of celestial being? An angel, perhaps?" Again the Buddha said, "No." "You're a magician, then? A sorcerer? A wizard?" the man queried. Once again the Buddha said, "No." "Well, then," the man asked, "what are you?" The Buddha replied, "I am awake."

Buddhism is full of such stories, illustrating that things are not necessarily as they appear to be.

Mahayana Buddhism calls the universe the Void because there is nothing in it that can be grasped. But "void" is only a metaphor. It doesn't mean that nothing exists; rather, it says that there is no standard of reality by which the universe can be understood. Samsara, the wheel of life, and Nirvana, the place beyond, are one and the same. One does not "go" to Nirvana. It is here, now. Everything is the same, but after enlightenment it is seen differently.

In his book *Buddhism, Plain and Simple,* Steve Hagen writes:

> The Buddha never considered himself to be something other than a human being—only someone who was fully awake. He never claimed to be a god, or even to be inspired by God. He attributed his realization and understanding solely to human endeavor and human ability.
>
> We call Gautama "The Buddha," but many other Buddhas, many other awakened human beings, exist, and have existed.... Buddha is not someone you pray to, or try to get something from. Nor is a Buddha someone you bow down to. A Buddha is simply a person who is awake—nothing more or less.

The story is told of a man who returned home from a trip only to find his house on fire. His children, as yet unaware of their danger, were playing inside. Not wanting to panic them and perhaps cause them to do something foolish in their distress, he yelled out, "I have presents!" Of course they came running out to him, away from the danger that was about to engulf them.

This story expresses the essence of Mahayana Buddhism. The Buddha saw fire engulfing the world and yelled to those who were not aware of their danger, "I have presents." The hope is that those who hear will come running out.

Four broad traditions, outlined below, have developed within Mahayana.

Mind-Only Buddhism

Mind-Only is perhaps best illustrated by the Buddhism of Tibet. Hindus called Tibet the land of Shiva. The Chinese called it Shangri-la. Sometimes Tibetan Buddhism is called Tantric Buddhism, or "Wisdom" Buddhism. But most know it as Vajrayana, the "Thunderbolt Vessel."

Legend relates how an ancient ruler sent his two wives down from the mountains to bring back information about the religions of the outside world. One went west to India and came back with a form of Hinduism. The other went east to China and came back with Buddhism. Thus it is that in Tibetan Buddhism we find a mixture of Buddhist philosophy and Hindu mysticism.

Vajrayana is the Buddhism of prayer wheels (spinning drums containing bits of sacred text) and the mystical chanting of "om," the primeval sound through which the world came into existence. Its most famous scripture is the Bardo Thodol, the Tibetan Book of the Dead, an account of the experiences of one who had died and is awaiting the next incarnation in a womb. Its clergy are called lamas, and the leading lama, the reincarnation of the Buddha of Compassion, is called the Dalai Lama, one of the most respected religious leaders in the world. When the Chinese government invaded Tibet in 1951, forcing the fourteenth Dalai Lama into exile, his example of courage in the face of injustice and uncomplaining valor in the most pressing of circumstances proved to the entire world the value of his religious convictions. His acceptance of the world as it is rather than as he might want it to be spoke more powerfully than any sermon could have done.

Practitioners of Tantric Buddhism create reality out of their minds. There is only one reality, and that is Buddha nature. But we do not perceive it even though we are all buddhas. What we perceive is not the true nature of the universe. It is, therefore, an illusion.

When the Dalai Lama was asked how he could respond to Chinese brutality with such serene composure, he replied:

Oh, anger still comes. But only like lightning, only for an instant. Hatred, ill feeling, hardly ever. But there's an ill feeling against negative emotion because that is the root of all suffering. When you think of the suffering of Samsara, it's worse than the suffering of Tibet.... The enemy teaches you inner strength. Your mind by nature is very soft, but when you have troubles, your mind gets strong.

Tantric Buddhists often chant mantras over and over to focus concentration. Spun out thousands of times on prayer wheels or placed on prayer flags (strips of cloth containing sacred text or petitions), the mantra is continued in the blowing of the wind. A favorite is the phrase associated with Avalokitesvara, the Bodhisattva of mercy: "Om mani padame hum." It stimulates awareness of the "jewel in the lotus of the heart," the treasure lying hidden within each of us.

Zen Buddhism

Another Mahayana tradition was transmitted to China around 50 CE. Known there as Ch'an, it migrated to Japan, picking up elements of Taoism along the way. This tradition is now known to the world as Zen Buddhism.

Tradition has it that as Buddha sat teaching his disciples he picked up a flower and smiled. Only one disciple, Kashyapa, smiled back and understood. The flower and the smile conveyed what words could not.

The "secret of the smile" was passed down through monks and eventually found its way to Japan, embodying the essential practice of Zen Buddhism. Zen tries to bring students to a sudden, intuitive grasp of Mahayana Buddhism, that is, the truth of non-dualism. Making distinctions keeps people from understanding that they, and everything else, are Buddha nature. Zen strives to bring a student to *satori*, a sudden, intuitive awakening to the fact that the mind has a non-self-conscious union with ultimate reality.

Through thinking and worrying and trying to figure everything out, we get in our own way. And how does the student strive to correct this? By not striving.

Zen meditation is often described as "sitting quietly, doing nothing." The mind is seen as a quiet pool of water. When it is still, it will reflect the reality all around it. When troubled, everything is distorted.

Zen masters developed many teaching devices, some of them quite brutal in their directness. Koans, unsolvable riddles, are often used. Probably the most famous is the one that, quite possibly, no master has ever used: "What is the sound of one hand clapping?"

Modern Westerners unfamiliar with Zen might understand something about the purpose of Koans if they think about a computer analogy. Computers, like minds, can process information very quickly. But they don't understand any of it. They are not conscious. They are not purposeful. Human minds, however, are both conscious and purposeful. If the mind starts acting too much like a computer, perhaps the best way to deal with it is to jam it, to cause it to lock up. By contemplating a riddle with no solution, the conscious mind may, for an instant, lock up, allowing intuition and understanding to connect with ultimate reality. Words would not be able to describe the result. Trying to explain the unexplainable thing you have just experienced is impossible. If it could be explained, you wouldn't have to go through all the difficulty of Zen studies.

Someone once asked a Zen master, "What is the first principle of Zen?" The master replied, "If I told you, it would be the second principle."

Another teaching device is the Mondo. Mondos are dialogues or stories with a message, such as the following:

A senior monk and a novice were caught in a cloudburst as they walked along the way. After the storm had passed, the senior monk noticed a girl standing at the edge of a mud puddle that completely blocked the road. She was trying to find a way across. Without hesitating, he picked the girl up and carried her across, saving her from ruining her clothes. The two monks continued on together but the novice was shocked into complete silence. They were members of an order that forbade contact with women, and the novice didn't know what to think of the scene he had just witnessed. As the afternoon wore on, he finally could remain silent no more. "Master," he asked, "how could you have touched that girl when such an act is expressly forbidden by our order?" The Master replied, "Are you still carrying that girl around? I put her down hours ago!"

Zen practitioners have developed many ways of expressing purposefulness. One of the most beautiful is the form of poetry known as haiku. Haiku exhibits a rigid structure, usually consisting of three lines: the first line has five syllables, the second has seven, the third has five. But within this rigid structure lies a fragile beauty. A shimmering, transparent word picture is painted that can be grasped by the mind but never fully translated into words. The following comes from poet Joe Eldredge's "Island Haiku":

Tall rooms of damp fog
Step softly ashore to dry
In the July sun.

Zen in the Art of Archery, by Eugin Herrigal, has made famous the technique of "becoming one with the target." Olympic athletes now call it "visualizing."

The famous Japanese tea ceremony brings purposefulness into everyday life, creating an art form out of a daily ritual. The movie *The Karate Kid II* contains a beautiful "East meets West" scene in which the American hero is gently but firmly reminded, by a simple look accompanied by no words at all, that jokes have no part in an ancient ritual that has become a religious ceremony.

The point of these exercises is to *experience* what one is doing rather than just float on the surface of life. After satori, things appear the same to everyone else, but the enlightened one has broken through to see the reality. This notion is expressed by the seventeenth-century Zen master Shido Bunan, as quoted in *The World of the Buddha*:

The moon's the same old moon,
The flowers exactly as they were,
Yet I've become the thingness
Of all the things I see.

Pure Land Buddhism

Even though Zen produced profound results, because its inner awareness is so all-consuming, it was difficult for laity to give the time and effort (the Zen master would probably prefer the word "non-effort") needed for its practice. Other forms of Buddhism arose in India and the Far East that had greater popular appeal. Pure Land Buddhism was one such tradition.

Amida Buddha (Amitabha in Sanskrit) is known as the "Buddha of Boundless Light." He is said to have promised the creation of a special place of bliss (the "Pure Land," sometimes called the "Western Paradise"), open to all who called upon his name.

Some visualize this Pure Land to be somewhat similar to the Western concept of heaven. Others see it as a metaphor for the mystical experience of enlightenment in this life.

However interpreted, in Pure Land we find parallels to the Christian concept of "dying" to this life and being "reborn" into a new one. Pure Land's symbol is the lotus, a beautiful flower growing from the muck and mire of suffering and human ignorance.

For great numbers of people in China and Japan, Amitabha has become "the Buddha." To them, he is, in effect, universal Buddha nature.

Nichiren

In contrast to the intensely personal nature of the three expressions of Buddhism explored so far, a thirteenth-century Japanese fisherman's son stressed the importance of social reform. The movement bearing his name is called Nichiren.

Nichiren emphasizes the Buddhist scriptures called Lotus Sutra. These are a large collection of teachings, parables, verses, and descriptions of those who supported the teachings of the World-Honored One, the Buddha. Particular attention is paid to the Bodhisattva of Superb Action, a Buddhist missionary devoted to spreading the Perfect Truth, and the Bodhisattva Ever-Abused, who was persecuted because he believed Buddha nature is found in everyone.

The mantra chanted by Nichiren and his followers in meditation, even today repeated for hours on end, is "Namu myoho rengekyo." This mantra refers to faith in the entire Lotus Sutra. As the phrase is slowly repeated, it works inwardly, revealing its depths to the practitioner in ways beyond thought and understanding.

Nichiren social activists have built seventy Peace Pagodas scattered throughout Japan, England, Austria, and the United States. All have been built with donated materials by resident monks, nuns, and local volunteers, and all are dedicated to world peace. Marches, sometimes cross-country treks, are held to draw attention to the peace movement. Participants bow to the Buddha presence of everyone they meet and spread joy through chanting, often accompanied by the beating of small drums.

In 1995 Nichiren activists traveled from Auschwitz to Hiroshima and Nagasaki to celebrate the fiftieth anniversary of the end of World War II. In the summer of 2002, a march from Washington State to Washington, D.C., in the United States drew attention to the cause of world peace as a response to terrorism.

Whether these many expressions of Buddhism are considered religions or philosophies, one thing is certain: Buddhism has demonstrated itself to be a life-changing practice. The differing traditions emphasize the same underlying principle: human consciousness can be transformed from attachment to ego, suffering, and desire to the unattached bliss of Nirvana.

Sources:
Ellwood, Robert S., and Barbara A. McGraw. *Many Peoples, Many Faiths*. 6th ed. Upper Saddle River, NJ: Prentice Hall, 1999.
Fisher, Mary Pat. *Living Religions*. 3rd ed. Upper Saddle River, NJ: Prentice Hall, 1991.
Fisher, Mary Pat, and Lee W. Bailey. *An Anthology of Living Religions*. Upper Saddle River, NJ: Prentice Hall, 2000.
Hagen, Steve. *Buddhism Plain and Simple*. Boston: Charles E. Tuttle Co., 1997.
Hudson, Winthrop S. *Religion in America*. New York: Charles Scribner, 1965.
Ludwig, Theodore M. *The Sacred Paths: Understanding the Religions of the World*. 2nd ed. Upper Saddle River, NJ: Prentice Hall, 1996.
Stryk, Lucien, ed. *The World of the Buddha*. New York: Doubleday, Anchor Books, 1969.

BURIAL CUSTOMS

The very first religious ritual of which there is evidence seems to have been a funeral service. Archaeologists have discovered Neanderthal grave burials, dating back to 60,000 BCE, in which the dead are buried with animal antlers, tools, and floral arrangements. Although we will never know for sure, this certainly seems to indicate a religious ritual demonstrating a belief in an afterlife. Why else would precious tools, which took a lot of effort and time to make, be buried with the corpse?

Although some tribes exist whose people simply run away from their dead, the vast majority of cultures practice funeral rituals and practices that have three things in common:

1. Some type of funeral rite or ceremony is conducted indicating respect for the dead or death itself.

A burial ritual in Calcutta, India. *Fortean Picture Library.*

2. The dead are placed in an area that has either been previously recognized as sacred or becomes sacred after the ceremony.
3. The dead are memorialized or remembered.

Because we know of no cultures prior to the Neanderthal, and because these practices arose at the time of our own ancestors during the Cro-Magnon period, the burial ritual must be considered to be among the very first religious practices, if not *the* very first, of the human race.

Perhaps because of biological processes of decay, fear seems to be universally present in the face of death. The corpse is considered "unclean." The Polynesian word *tabu* (sometimes spelled *kapu* in English) and its English equivalents, defilement and pollution, express this thought. In the Bible, the book of Numbers 5:2 reads, "Whosoever is unclean by the dead shall be put outside the camp, that they defile not the camp in the midst of which the Lord dwells."

Fire (cremation) was often used to destroy evil spirits believed to be present in the body, but most cultures bury their dead to remove the corpse from human contact. "A shallow grave" is often considered a disparaging term, only to be dug as a last resort when circumstances do not permit anything else. Otherwise, "six feet under," the average height of a man, seems to be the rule.

Some of the Rocky Mountain Indians of the American West practiced a ritual that is the opposite of burial: the dead were not buried, but elevated. Elaborate rituals and taboos consecrated holy ground where corpses, along with many rich possessions, were placed on scaffolds built six feet or more above the earth. These above-ground cemeteries were sacred, as is so beautifully illustrated in the sensitive treatment given to the custom in the movie *Jeremiah Johnson*, starring Robert Redford.

Barrows of stone are built by many cultures, ranging from simple stone cemetery markers to caves of earth and rock. These are eclipsed by the great pyramids of Egypt, certainly the most elaborate "barrows" of them all.

If the Egyptians were not the first to practice embalming, they at least perfected the art. Belief in an afterlife was so strongly developed that a new king's first order of business was to begin building his tomb. The Egyptians and Chinese were famous for lavishly providing for their leader's future lifestyle in the hereafter.

According to the practices of some cultures, the greatest sign of respect for the passing of a loved one is self-mutilation or even death. When a Hawaiian *alii*, or member of the royalty, died, it was considered proper to mark the occasion by knocking out one's teeth and gouging out one's own eyes. In Japan the custom arose that at least twenty or thirty of a rich lord's slaves were ordered to commit hara-kiri, ritual suicide. And pity the poor Hindu wives who were expected to throw themselves onto their dearly departed husband's funeral pyre. Meanwhile, in Fiji it was considered correct for not only wives but also friends to be strangled after a loved one's death. The thought was that the dead deserved company in the hereafter.

Customs differ by gender in some cultures. Cochieans bury their women, while their men are suspended from trees. Sometimes women are buried, while men are cremated. There is an African custom practiced by some tribes in which men are meticulously buried facing north while women face south.

When we think of these traditions, it is quite natural to think we have outgrown primitive superstition and ritual. But many customs practiced today have their basis in such practices. When movies or television shows depict a doctor somberly drawing a sheet over the face of a person who just died, it is seen as a dramatic action conveying the finality of death. But this custom began long ago. Ancient tradition holds that the spirit of the deceased escapes through the mouth. Covering the face is an attempt to prolong life by preventing the spirit from leaving. Some cultures even held the mouth and nose of a sick person shut to prevent death.

Today's "wakes" began as a gathering to keep watch over the dead, hoping that the spirit would return. (Conversely, some say the wakes served to make sure the deceased really was dead, not just comatose.) But just in case the returning spirit was not in good humor, "mourning clothes" were worn as disguises in hopes that the malignant spirit, not recognizing those gathered, would become confused and leave

Moses and the burning bush, where the voice of God appeared to him in flames of fire to tell Moses to lead his people out of Egypt. *Fortean Picture Library.*

them alone. Candles would be lit because fire was known to discourage such spirits, and bells were rung to frighten them away.

In early Christianity, holy water was sprinkled on the body to protect it from demons. Floral offerings were intended to gain favor with the spirit of the deceased. Funeral music began with the chanting of priests to placate departed spirits.

At military funerals it is the custom to fire a rifle volley. This tradition is mirrored by the tribal practice of throwing spears or shooting arrows over the body in an attempt to dislodge the spirits gathered there.

This is not to say that modern funeral customs are simply superstition. They may have begun that way, but contemporary psychology recognizes the importance of ritual for human closure at the time of loss. Funeral ritual serves an important psychological purpose.

Sources:

"History of Funeral Customs." *Wyoming Funeral Directors Association.* http://www.wyfda. org/public/basics_2.html. May 27, 2002.

BURNING BUSH

(See also Moses; Red Paint People)

The third chapter of Exodus explains that Moses, soon to become the deliverer of the Hebrew people, fled from the wrath of the Egyptian Pharaoh. Forty years later, while tending the sheep of Jethro, his Midianite father-in-law, Moses heard the voice of God speaking to him from a bush that burned but was not consumed by the fire. Here Moses learned the name by which God would henceforth be called: "I Am Who I Am."

Although the monks at Saint Catherine's monastery at Mount Sinai have for generations cultivated a thorn bush of the species *rubus collinus*, thought to be the kind of bush Moses would have seen, no one knows for sure what kind of bush it was or even where the incident happened.

The significance of the burning bush lies in the fact that this dramatic event marked a transition in Moses' life. He became aware of the presence of the God of his ancestors, reluctantly left the safety of a comfortable, quiet life, and began a journey into history and legend.

Sources:

Bridger, David, ed. *The New Jewish Encyclopedia*. New York: Behrman House, 1962.

May, Herbert G., and Bruce M. Metzger, eds. *The New Oxford Annotated Bible with the Apocrypha*. Rev. ed. New York: Oxford University Press, 1973.

CABOT, LAURIE

(See also Wicca)

For two hundred years witches have tried to keep a low profile, especially in Salem, Massachusetts, scene of the famous Salem witch trials. But Laurie Cabot, known as the Official Witch of Salem, has chosen to deliberately defy tradition in an attempt to draw public awareness to the misunderstood religion of witchcraft known as Wicca.

She is an ordained high priestess of the craft and carries on the religious tradition practiced by her Celtic ancestors. Founder of the Cabot Tradition of the Science of Witchcraft and the Witches' League for Public Awareness, she has devoted her life to correcting public misconceptions about her religion through her books, public appearances, and teaching career.

Sources:
LaurieCabot.com http://www.lauriecabot.com. September 14, 2003.

CAESAR, JULIUS

Julius Caesar (100–44 BCE) is best known as the emperor who united Rome and built the foundation for its European domination. Popularized by his own writings and those of such notables as William Shakespeare, his story has become legend.

What is not so well documented is the cost of his endeavors to the storehouse of Western religious thought. While serving as captain of the armies of Rome, Caesar was well aware that his political future depended upon military victories to the north and west of Italy. To achieve those victories he was willing to do almost anything, including tearing the spiritual heart out of his enemies.

Julius Caesar. *Fortean Picture Library.*

Knowing the popular will to resist him depended upon the influence of the Druids, the indigenous religious leaders of Gaul, Caesar set out to destroy completely the Druidic priesthood and all semblance of the religion that had, for untold generations, united the people of present-day France. The sacred groves of the Druids were destroyed. Any practice of indigenous paganism was outlawed. One by one, local traditions were rooted out and eliminated. A powerful propaganda campaign was launched, with Caesar's own Gallic Wars leading the way. And, since history is written by the victors, a religion that served the people of Western Europe for hundreds, if not thousands, of years was almost lost to human memory. Only in the past few decades have we begun to understand the religious history of a culture that connected people to the earth and empowered them in their daily lives.

Caesar also made a second-hand contribution to Christian history. In 46 BCE he commissioned a calendar that was henceforth called the Julian Calendar. The month of July still bears his name. With modifications and corrections ordered by Pope Gregory XIII in 1582, it became the Gregorian calendar used today.

Sources:

Jones, Prudence, and Nigel Pennick. *A History of Pagan Europe.* New York: Routledge, 1995.
Llywelyn, Morgan. *Druids.* New York: Ivy Books, 1991.

CAIN AND ABEL

(See also Agricultural Revolution)

According to the Bible, Cain and Abel were the first two sons born to Adam and Eve after their expulsion from the Garden of Eden. (Genesis 5:4 adds the fact that many other children came later.) In a fit of jealous rage, Cain, the first agriculturist, murdered his brother Abel, the sheepherder, because God accepted Abel's sacrifice but rejected Cain's.

When God banished him, Cain feared he would be persecuted because of his crime. God placed upon him "the mark of Cain" to warn any who might harm him. Much speculation has centered upon this mysterious "mark." No indication is given in the Bible as to what constituted the mark of Cain. It is simply presented as history.

Cain migrated to "the land of Nod, east of Eden." "Nod" means "wandering," so this might be describing a condition rather than a place, but Cain's first act was to build a city.

The story of Cain and Abel raises questions for some readers of the Bible. First, if Cain and Abel were the only two young people in the world, and one murdered the other, why would the survivor require a mark to protect him from others? Second, when Cain established his city, who populated it? Such questions reveal the questioner's method of biblical interpretation. Those who ask such questions are demanding that the story be read as history. They either accept scripture as true or reject it as irrelevant based on their own personal bias. Those who think such questions are insignificant are reading scripture mythologically or allegorically.

Genesis 4 tells Cain's story, and it has been interpreted in many different ways. Some Christians understand it to mean God rejected Cain's "religion of works" in favor of Abel's "religion of blood sacrifice." Here they find the root of the doctrine that salvation comes through the blood sacrifice of Jesus rather than humans "being good enough" or "working hard enough" to earn it (see Covenant). Later, blood sacrifice of animals was developed by the Hebrew people during the time of Moses (see Judaism, Development of).

Sources:
Bridger, David, ed. *The New Jewish Encyclopedia*. New York: Behrman House, 1962.
May, Herbert G., and Bruce M. Metzger, eds. *The New Oxford Annotated Bible with the Apocrypha*. Rev. ed. New York: Oxford University Press, 1973.

CALDRON/CAULDRON

Double, double, toil and trouble—
Fire burn and caldron bubble.
(William Shakespeare, *MacBeth*, Act IV, Scene 1)

Even before the witches of Shakespeare's *MacBeth* cackled their way onto the stage of popular imagery, caldrons have been understood to be symbols of "the witches brew."

The plain and simple fact, however, is that some herbs need preparation not requiring "eye of newt" or "wing of bat." A caldron was the kitchen implement of choice used by women who prepared natural materials gathered from field and forest. When early Christian theology, separated as it was from nature and fueled by religious bigotry, declared many of these women to be witches, the scene of three old hags gathered around a caldron in the moonlight became yet another caricature used to frighten superstitious churchgoers, sometimes with tragic results for the innocent.

Sources:
Webster's Third New International Dictionary and Seven Language Dictionary. 3 vols. Chicago: William Benton, 1966.

CALIPHATE

When Muhammad died he left no clearly designated successor to lead the new Muslim movement. This led to an immediate division in Islam.

Traditionalists believed Abu-Bakr, one of the Prophet's friends (some say he was a father-in-law) and among the first of his converts, was meant to step into Muhammad's place. People of this tradition became known as Sunnis. Others chose to follow Ali, the prophet's cousin and son-in-law. These people came to be known as Shi'ites (from Shia Ali—"the party of Ali").

The leaders of each party were called caliphs, and their successors formed the caliphate.

Sources:
Ellwood, Robert S., and Barbara A. McGraw. *Many Peoples, Many Faiths.* 6th ed. Upper Saddle River, NJ: Prentice Hall, 1999.

CALVARY/GOLGOTHA

Luke 23:33 says Jesus was crucified in Jerusalem at the place called Calvary. The other Gospels use the term Golgotha, "the place of the skull."

This discrepancy has led to a difference of opinion about the location of the crucifixion. In the fifth century the emperor Constantine's mother, guided by a vision, located a split rock, supposedly cracked by the earthquake that occurred at Christ's death. A cathedral was built on the spot where today stands the Church of the Holy Sepulcher. But in the nineteenth century a rocky hill resembling a skull became another candidate, even though the Bible does not mention a hill. A very early tradition says "the place of the skull" referred to the fact that Adam's skull was supposed to be buried there, but this is unprovable and highly unlikely.

Sources:
Douglas, J. D., ed. *The New International Dictionary of the Christian Church.* Grand Rapids, MI: Zondervan Publishing, 1974.

CALVIN, JOHN, AND JACOBUS ARMINIUS

Following the Protestant Reformation biblical studies took a dramatic turn. By the seventeenth century the Reformed tradition determined what would thereafter be its orthodoxy. The reformer who most influenced this position was John Calvin.

One of the points of Calvin's theology concerned the doctrine of predestination. Calvin was convinced that human beings were totally depraved. There is no good in a person at all, not even enough to want to be saved from sin. That doesn't mean people always do bad things. There is, after all, God's Common Grace at work in the world, available to all.

But in terms of salvation and being "godlike," the human race is without hope. So how could a sinful human being choose to accept God's saving grace?

The answer was to be found in Romans 8:29: "For those God foreknew He also predestined to be conformed to the likeness of his Son … and those He predestined He also called."

Calvin believed the choice for salvation was not a human choice but rather a divine one. From before the time of Creation, God predestined some to be saved. Calvin never went so far as to say that some were then predestined for hell, but that was the obvious conclusion most people drew.

There were those who drew back from the idea that a good God would create people who had no hope for salvation. One of these was a distinguished Dutch pastor and professor named Jacobus Arminius. Although his training had been thoroughly Calvinistic and had even taken place under the direction of Calvin's successor, when called upon to refute a scholar who rejected this aspect of reformed theology, Arminius came to the reluctant conclusion that he couldn't do it.

He still believed in predestination, but he came to understand that God predestined those who, based on God's foreknowledge, would have chosen salvation if they could. Of course, their depravity made such a choice impossible, so God had to step in and intervene.

John Calvin wrote a popular systematic presentation of Christian doctrine and life, *The Institutes,* in 1536, final edition in 1559. *Fortean Picture Library.*

Here the plot thickens, because this belief opened doors long thought closed forever. Way back in the sixth century, some of the most important works written by Augustine, the favorite theologian of the reformers, were published to oppose the views of Pelagius, a British monk, who believed humans had free will either to accept or oppose God. Pelagius had completely rejected original sin and the corruption of human nature that forces us to sin. This battle between Augustinians and Pelagians lasted seven years and was known as the Pelagian Controversy. The Pelagians were decreed heretical, and once the Church settles something it is reluctant to open the issue again.

Now along came the Arminians who, while distancing themselves from Pelagianism by insisting that it was only by the foreknowledge of God that people could do good, seemed to be skirting near the same, heretical ground.

In true Church fashion, a council was called. The Synod of Dort met from November 1618 to May 1619, and the two parties fought it out. In the end, the Synod affirmed five doctrines that the Arminians simply could not accept, and these five points became the basis of Calvinist theology. Students of theology remember them by use of the acrostic, TULIP:

T = Total depravity. Although a vestige of natural light remains within fallen humanity, human nature is so corrupt that the light cannot be used.

U = Unconditional election. The election of the saved is based not on God's foreknowledge of human response but only on the inscrutable will of God.

L = Limited atonement. Christ did not die for all humanity, but only for the elect, meaning those who are saved.

I = Irresistible grace. God's grace cannot be refused, for it is greater than human sin.

P = Perseverance of the saints. The elect cannot fall from grace, or choose not to be saved.

Those who accepted these five points, later amplified and detailed at the same Westminster Assembly that affirmed the Westminster Confession and the teaching device known as the Westminster Catechism used by many churches to this day, became known as Calvinists. Their descendants formed denominations we now know as Presbyterians, Reformed, and Congregationalists.

Those who rejected these points formed denominations represented by groups such as the Methodists and Baptist denominations of today.

It is important to understand that these people were not simply playing mind games and performing academic exercises. History was changed by what they decided. Lives were lost and wars fought. For example, when the Puritans landed on the shores of New England, they were staunch Calvinists. They had come to believe that, although good works could not earn salvation, actions were proof that salvation had been granted. And so the so-called Puritan ethic was born. The whole community examined an individual's life, because how a person behaved was the sign of God's work of grace.

Someone once said, "Puritanism is the fear that somewhere in the world, someone might be happy." They may not have been far from the truth. Where John Calvin had found great joy and relief in the idea of resting secure in the arms of God's grace, his followers followed a strict, judgmental religion far removed from his original understanding. These were the people who persecuted unmercifully anyone who was Catholic or Quaker and publicly punished those found guilty of violating the Puritans' narrow structure of community standards.

But their strict Calvinism convinced them of two things:

First, if God had predestined some to be saved, there must be "heathen Indians" out there somewhere who were simply waiting for correct teaching. Their Christian duty was to find them.

Second, if unsaved Indians were predestined for hell, it was the duty of Christians to fulfill God's will by putting them there.

Viewed in this light, King Philip's War, fought in the seventeenth century, perhaps the biggest per capita bloodbath ever fought on American soil, was a holy war between Christians and Indians. Of course it was also a political land struggle and a clash of weapon superiority, but published sermons of the time leave no doubt that the

Calvinist religious component of doing God's will justified the conflict in the minds of the Europeans.

Contemplating the carnage of only this one example reveals that, far from being simply academic exercises, religious doctrines and conflicts have been at the root of events that have caused real and undeniable damage.

Sources:
Gonzalez, Justo L. *The Story of Christianity*. 2 vols. New York: Harper & Row, 1985.
Hauptman, Laurence M., and James D. Wherry, eds. *The Pequots in Southern New England*. Norman: University of Oklahoma Press, 1990.
May, Herbert G., and Bruce M. Metzger, eds. *The New Oxford Annotated Bible with the Apocrypha*. Rev. ed. New York: Oxford University Press, 1973.

CANAANITE GODS, GODDESSES

Before the 1920s the only thing known about Canaanite religion was what appeared in the Hebrew Bible, written from a Jewish perspective. But thanks to painstaking research, archaeologists are now able to paint a better picture.

The principal deity of Canaanite religion is El, a sky god who was worshiped from time immemorial. The Hebrews appropriated his name, using it to form the many names of God found in the Bible, Elohim being the first. It is found also in the name given to Jacob, Israel ("he wrestles with El," meaning "God"), and is preserved in the name Allah (El-Yah), used by Muslims and Arab Christians. We find it as well in names of prophets such as Joel, Elijah, and Elisha.

El is the father of all gods and the supreme leader of all the gods of the mountains. That is why so much biblical literature describes Moses, Jesus, and others going up into the mountains to talk to him. In Canaanite literature El is pictured as an ancient, revered old man who likes to drink a lot and often gets drunk at parties.

Baal, El's son, and Baal's wife (or perhaps sister, concubine, or all three), Anat, were important earth gods—that is, gods of vegetation and fertility. They may be roughly compared to the Mesopotamian gods Tammuz and Ishtar. Sacrifices were made every year, especially at the Canaanite New Year festival, to ensure a good crop in the coming season. Together with Baal's consort, Astarte (Asherah, Ashtoreth), they were the principal gods so vilified by the Hebrew prophets. Worship of these gods was conducted by employing vivid sexual symbolism. Male worshipers, representing Baal, publicly joined sacred prostitutes, representing Astarte. These acts were considered an important sacrament to ensure fertility of the soil and bountiful harvests in the coming year. Needless to say, this kind of worship grated on Hebrew sensibilities, steeped as they were in the strict sexual codes of the book of Leviticus. (Even a cursory reading of the Bible, however, reveals that the sensibilities of the Hebrew prophets were outraged far more than those of the common people, who seemed rather intrigued with sacred prostitutes.)

Although there were many other lesser gods in the Canaanite pantheon, Molech deserves special attention, if only for the fact that he is such a historical enigma. Aside from the Hebrew Bible we know absolutely nothing about him. He figures prominently in the books of Leviticus, Kings, and Jeremiah as the object of God's wrath because he demanded infant sacrifice. This practice was so common that Abraham didn't bat an eye when God asked him to sacrifice his son Isaac.

But aside from the biblical references, which must be viewed as having a cultural bias against the Canaanites, Molech is not mentioned in any Canaanite texts yet discovered.

Sources:

Bucke, Emory Stevens et al, eds. *The Interpreter's Dictionary of the Bible.* 4 vols. New York: Abingdon Press, 1962.

"Canaanite Culture and Religion." *International World History Project.* http://ragz-international. com/canaanite_culture_and_religion.htm. September 14, 2003.

Canaanite Gods http://www-relg-studies.scu.edu/netcours/rs011/sess04/canangod.htm. 2002.

CASTANEDA, CARLOS

In the 1960s Carlos Castaneda wrote a series of books beginning with the cult classic, *The Teachings of Don Juan.* Don Juan was a Yaqui Indian shaman, or medicine man, who lived in the Sonoran desert, practicing his art in several mountain retreats. Because the books were full of mystical, obscure spiritual teachings involving psychedelic mushrooms and religious "trips," they fit right into the spiritual and religious drug culture of the 1960s. The main teaching was that the mind had to be "altered" in order to see reality. Western-oriented culture had so conditioned people to perceive life within a narrow band of reality that the only way to break out was to change frequencies, so to speak. Some Indian cultures had accomplished this with ascetic vision quests. Others, according to Don Juan, used peyote.

There was historic truth in this argument. People in many parts of the world have injested plants that produce hallucinogenic effects for religious ceremonies. When Dr. Timothy Leary of Harvard University urged a generation of young Americans to "tune in, turn on, and drop out," many of them used Carlos Castaneda's Don Juan as their spiritual guide.

But from within the Indian community there was quite a different response. At this time the American Indian movement was fighting a political battle for freedom and rights. Many of them did not want their movement sullied by white, middle-class (some would have said "pampered") college students following a fad and becoming "armchair Indians" by reading a book.

Vine Deloria Jr., in his book *God Is Red*, said it this way:

> The Don Juan books were just what young whites needed to bolster their shattering personal identities, and the books were extremely popular.… [But] people appeared to be divided on whether or not Castaneda had actually met any Indians, let alone studied under Don Juan. The consensus is that the religious experiences were either made up or came out of a sugar cube somewhere on the West Coast.

Sources:

Deloria, Vine, Jr. *God Is Red*. Golden: Fulcrum Publishing, 1994.

CASTE SYSTEM

Although the influence of the caste system in India is now weakening, especially since it "officially" ended with Indian independence, the system did exert a powerful hold for countless generations and continues to have an impact on Indian society. It seems to have been a product of the Aryan migration of 1500 BCE; it was perhaps utilized to control the indigenous population. Society was divided into five groups, and it was a tenet of Hinduism that the only way to advance to a higher group was to live an exemplary life, following the rules of the caste into which you were born. Then, in your next incarnation, your good Karma would propel you toward birth into a higher caste.

At the top of the system were the Brahmins. These were the priests and scholars. (Western knowledge of the caste system was prevalent enough that in New England the term "Boston Brahmin" became synonymous with wealthy, upper-class society.)

Next down the social scale were the Kshatriyas, the rulers and warriors. They were followed by merchants and tradesmen, called Vaishyas. Lower on the ladder were the Shudras, the peasants.

The dregs of society, about 20 percent of the population, were the "out-castes," those without a caste, also known as the "untouchables."

The system functioned by popular consent. Built into the Hindu religion was the belief that you simply did not associate with people of a lower caste. Vaishyas stood aside on the road whenever a Brahmin walked by, not even letting their shadows get in the way of the person of higher caste.

Although modern Westerners shake their heads at such beliefs, it must be remembered that in pre–Civil War America, religion was used to enforce a similar pattern of social behavior between people of different races.

No one knows exactly when the caste system began. But it may be significant to point out that when Westerners first discovered its existence, during British colonial expansion, there seemed to be a direct correlation between skin color and caste ranking. The lighter the skin, the higher the caste. Even the word Varna, a collective term naming the four castes, means "color" or "appearance." If the caste system was, indeed, an Aryan import, by observing Aryan history in other parts of the world it is hard not to draw the inference that it represented a system of domination by people of white skin who used religion to enforce imposed racism.

Sources:
Ellwood, Robert S., and Barbara A. McGraw. *Many Peoples, Many Faiths.* 6th ed. Upper Saddle
    River, NJ: Prentice Hall, 1999.

CATHOLICISM

(See also Christianity, Development of)

If the Christian Church were to be pictured as a river flowing from Jesus Christ down to the present day, Roman Catholicism would see itself as the main channel from which Orthodox and Protestant streams diverged. Catholics believe they practice

Painting of Pope Pius X (1835–1914), c. 1903. The pope is the spiritual leader and highest-ranking member of the Roman Catholic Church. *The Art Archive/Dagli Orti.*

apostolic succession, an unbroken line of leaders, now called popes, going back to the first Vicar of Christ, the apostle Peter.

Matthew 16:13–21 tells how Jesus met with his disciples in the region of Caesarea Philippi and asked them a penetrating question: Who did people say he was? The disciples gave all the current opinions: some say John the Baptist, others say Elijah, and still others, Jeremiah or one of the prophets.

But Jesus pressed them for their own opinion. It was Peter who gave him the answer he was waiting for, saying Jesus was the Christ, the Son of the living God.

Although it may be overly simplistic to put it this way, with that declaration the papacy began. Roman Catholics believe Jesus' next words established Peter and all his appointed successors as Christ's Vicars, ruling bishops, leaders of the church forever.

> I tell you that you are Peter [Greek *petros*, or "stone"], and on this rock [Greek *petra*, or "boulder"] I will build my church, and the gates of hell will not prevail against it. I will give you the keys to the kingdom of heaven; whatever you bind on earth will be bound in heaven; whatever you loose on earth will be loosed in heaven.

These are the words Catholics believe give the church God's authority to rule, to "bind and loose," on Earth. They establish the church as Christ's body, led by Christ's appointed custodian of apostolic tradition, elected ever since the Middle Ages by a college of cardinals, to be the Holy Father, the pope.

The word "hierarchy" comes from Greek words meaning "sacred leadership." The Catholic Church's hierarchy consists of lay worshipers led by trained deacons who are supervised by ordained priests. The parish priests report to area bishops ("overseers"). The pope is the bishop of Rome and appoints, from the ranks of bishops and archbishops, a college of cardinals. The top of the hierarchy resides in and leads from the Vatican, the papal palace in Rome. Alongside this official chain of command are various religious orders of monks and nuns, organized around specific areas of worship or service, and countless lay organizations and charities.

Although known for its pageantry, Catholic worship varies from one extreme to the other. While a papal ceremony may involve columns of red-hatted cardinals in splendid vestments accompanied by choirs of men and boys chanting Latin plainsong, other services may consist of a few worshipers, led by a priest, meeting in a backward outpost. Some gatherings may feature organ music and orchestras; others, simple guitar music.

What binds the various forms of Catholic worship are the words of the Mass and the celebration of the Eucharist. When the priest says the words, "This is my body … this is my blood," and the sacred host is mysteriously transformed into Christ's body and blood (see Eucharist), believers who receive the sacrament know that wherever they may be in the world, their brothers and sisters are hearing the same words and participating in the same mystery.

Although much has changed in the Catholic Church (see Vatican Councils), much has remained the same. Contemporary Catholic doctrine stands at the end of a long tradition. A few key symbols and teachings strike the outsider right away.

The Crucifix

Ever since the sixth century, the image of Jesus nailed to the cross has been the central symbol of the Catholic Church. It has two primary historic meanings.

The first is the obvious reference to the sacrifice of Jesus as the "Lamb of God," the centerpiece of the doctrine of substitutionary atonement. The crucifix is a visual reminder of the broken body and shed blood of Jesus, received by the sinner during Mass.

The second refers to the eventual triumph of good over evil. When Adam and Eve were cast out of the Garden of Eden, they were cut off from the fruit of the tree of life. In the book of Revelation this tree is pictured again on Earth at the end of time. There it is declared, "the leaves of the tree are for the healing of the nations" (Revelation 22:2). But that is yet in the future. In the meantime, Jesus on the cross *is* the "tree of life," offering healing for the nations. In this reading of the symbol, the cross is not an implement of torture but a victorious sign of freedom.

Sacraments

"Sacrament" means "sacred secret" or "sacred mystery." The Catholic Church recognizes seven sacraments, or means of grace, through which God imparts blessing to the believer: baptism, confirmation, Eucharist, penance, holy orders, matrimony, and final anointing (commonly called last rites). Usually these are administered only through an ordained priest.

Saints

Although all believers are called "saints," there have been special people throughout history who have exemplified what it means to be a Christian. Elevated through a long process to the position of sainthood, these saints intercede from heaven on behalf of those who pray to them. By following a calendar of saints' days throughout the year, Catholic families are constantly reminded to remember those who have gone before.

Roman Catholic depiction of intercession, with Christ and the Virgin Mary kneeling before God, by Hans Balding Grun. *Fortean Picture Library.*

Male Hierarchy

Although the Catholic Church has been criticized, especially in the last few years, for refusing to even talk about ordaining women as priests, it is really not fair for them to bear the blame alone. Many Protestant traditions and denominations have done the same (see Baptist). They have just not been powerful enough to draw public scrutiny.

Recent scandals involving pedophilia and active sexuality among priests and seminarians who have taken vows of celibacy, however, have focused media attention on the longstanding tradition of allowing only men to be ordained and to administer the sacraments in public worship. Although for years voices have been raised calling for equal standing for women, no action toward reform in this area has yet been officially discussed.

Sources:

Douglas, J. D., ed. *The New International Dictionary of the Christian Church.* Grand Rapids, MI: Zondervan Publishing, 1974.

Groome, Thomas H. "The Free Flow of Fresh Air." *Boston Globe*, May 19, 2002.

McDermott, Alice. "Do Not Perpetuate Our Tragic Flaw." *Boston Globe*, May16, 2002.

Renard, John. *The Handy Religion Answer Book.* Detroit: Visible Ink Press, 2002.

CELIBACY

Monastic orders of many religious traditions have rules concerning celibacy. Marriage and sexual union are forbidden for practical or spiritual reasons.

Sometimes, as in some Hindu and Buddhist traditions, sexual expression is considered to be a detriment to meditation and growth, a "giving in" to the body and its desires. Celibacy is then considered to be a form of asceticism.

In early Christianity, celibacy was inspired by the words of the apostle Paul advising that those who chose not to marry had more time to serve the Lord. He implied that sex, as opposed to spiritual work, was a base human need when he said it "was better to marry than to burn." And since the early church believed Jesus was soon to return, it didn't make much sense to settle into a stable home life that would not last much longer. Besides this, Jesus had said that "in heaven they neither marry nor are given in marriage." All these together seemed to imply marriage was for the weak, at best.

This notion was taken to its logical conclusion by the Shaker community in the United States. Nobody was allowed to have sex. The community only grew by conversions.

In Roman Catholic tradition, celibacy is seen as a crucial vow taken by ordained clergy to allow them both time and uninterrupted energy to devote to the practical matter of being available for ministry. It is not that clergy are not married. They are married to the church and are expected to give the same devotion to Christ as they would to earthly spouses. Although a mystique surrounding "unavailable" male priests and "pure" female nuns undoubtedly places celibate clergy on a pedestal in the popular psyche, this was not the official intention of the church.

Muirdach's Cross at Monasterboice. Contemporary carved Celtic crosses almost invariably signify a burial place, while the early freestanding or high crosses, some of which are more than 1,200 years old, were positioned as meeting places, often within a Celtic monastic settlement. *Fortean Picture Library.*

Sources:
Smart, Ninian. *The Religious Experience.* 5th ed. Upper Saddle River, NJ: Prentice Hall, 1996.

CELTIC

(See also Caesar, Julius)

Long before Rome conquered all of Europe, the people known as Celts (known by the Greeks as Keltoi) lived and practiced complex polytheistic religious traditions, including Druidism, from Britain and Ireland to Spain, France, southern Germany, and all the way to central Turkey.

But they had no written language. Until modern archaeology began to reveal the depths of their culture, all that was known about them came from folklore, oral history, and Roman writers, particularly the quite prejudiced work of Julius Caesar (*The Gallic War*), Polybius, and Strabo.

Caesar first spoke about Druids—intellectuals, judges, diviners, and mediators with the gods. But Celtic religion was widespread, and it varied from land to land. Lugh (the "shining light"), Teutates ("god of the tribe"), Andastra, Belenus, Artio ("the bear"), Camulos, Cernunnos ("the horned one," lord of the animals), and Vasio all had their followings.

As is the case with many indigenous religions, gods had their own locations. A god of the grove sacred to one tribe might be recognized by another tribe but not worshiped, because he or she didn't live nearby. Instead, this other tribe would tend to worship the god of the lake near where they lived.

Celtic religious practice points out an important theological truth. When gods or spirits arise within the context of a particular place, the people connect with their environment and treat it accordingly. Indigenous people who worship in this manner, whether they are European Celts, Japanese Shinto, or American Indians, know that their environment is their cathedral. They live in their church, the home of their god. This kind of connection cements the bond between the land and the people. To cut down the sacred grove of the Druids, to kill the buffalo of the Dakota people, or to strip-mine a Cherokee mountaintop is religious blasphemy. Indigenous religion cannot be transported to another place. Missionaries cannot carry that religion with them to indoctrinate a new culture.

People of Jewish, Christian, or Islamic traditions often failed to understand this point of view. And when they did understand it, they usually exploited it. A people cut off from the "ground of their being," their god, are a defeated people. Julius Caesar understood. When he burned the Druid sacred groves and toppled the standing stones, he tore the soul out of the Celtic people, and with it their will to resist. Celtic religion went underground, practiced by old women who remembered herb lore and snatches of forgotten prayers and rituals. It was found in men's secret societies and existed in overgrown roadside shrines in the hollow hills of dim legend and folklore.

Only now, through the patient work of archaeologists, are we beginning to discover how much was lost. And who is to say whether the terrible record of environmental catastrophe in Western civilization is not a result of practicing religion in a way that separated humans from, rather than connected them to, the land they call home?

Sources:
James, Simon. *The World of the Celts*. New York: Thames and Hudson, 1993.
Jones, Prudence, and Nigel Pennick. *A History of Pagan Europe*. New York: Routledge, 1995.

CHAKRA

In the Tantric Hinduism of India, the ancient practice of yoga is a form of meditation designed to bring spiritual power through seven chakras (circles) located between the base of the spine and the top of the head. Although in the therapeutic sense chakras are viewed as the places where *ch'i*, or life force, is often bound up or blocked, in the religious sense they represent psychological centers or planes of consciousness through which spiritual power flows. From first to last, chakras represent spiritual growth.

The first chakra is located at the base of the spine at the rectum. Its symbol is the serpent, coiled three and a half times, and it represents the basic human need for killing and eating. The serpent, in the words of Joseph Campbell, is:

> Nothing but a traveling esophagus going along just eating, eating, eating.... This is the sacramental mystery of food and eating.... In early mythologies [people] would thank the animal they were about to consume for having given of itself as a willing sacrifice. There's a wonderful saying in one of the Upanishads: "Oh wonderful ... I am food.... I am an eater of food." We don't think that way today about ourselves. But holding on to yourself and not letting yourself become food is the primary life-denying negative act. You're stopping the flow! And a yielding to the flow is the great mystery experience that goes with thanking an animal that is about to be eaten for having given of itself. You, too, will be given in time.

In short, the first chakra reminds us of our place in the universe—as part of the food chain. We don't just live in nature. We are a part of nature.

The second chakra is located at the sex organs. This represents the urge to procreate, to reproduce our species and ourselves.

The third chakra is located at the navel and represents the will to conquer, to master and subdue. It is no accident that Sicilian dons in the Mafia, the godfathers, were referred to by a Sicilian phrase that translates to "men with a belly." From the sumo wrestler to the professional football lineman, a big belly symbolizes power and force.

These first three chakra centers represent the animal instincts of eating, procreation, and mastery. When we move up to the fourth chakra we enter a new realm, opening up to compassion and spirituality.

The fourth chakra is at the level of the heart. According to tradition, the Buddha was born from his mother's side, at the level of the heart. When you "open your heart" to someone you are elevated above the level of the animal.

The fifth chakra is located at the level of the throat and symbolizes creativity and communication.

The sixth chakra is located at the forehead—the "third eye" often pictured on the forehead of representations of Buddha. This is the eye that sees inward—the center of intuition and understanding.

The culminating chakra is the *sahasrara,* the thousand-petaled lotus at the top of the head. This is the chakra of spiritual maturity, exploding upward and outward into understanding and enlightenment.

When spiritual energy is brought up from the level of the animal to the level of spiritual awareness, it wakes up to the real world—the world of god-consciousness.

Sources:

Campbell, Joseph. *The Power of Myth.* New York: Doubleday, 1988.

Ellwood, Robert S., and Barbara A. McGraw. *Many Peoples, Many Faiths.* 6th ed. Upper Saddle River, NJ: Prentice Hall, 1999.

CHANNELING *see* New Age Religions

CHARISMATIC MOVEMENT

Charis is the English transliteration of the Greek word for "grace." *Mata* is the Greek word meaning "gifts." *Charismata,* then, means "grace gifts," and the charismatic movement is the term given to the Christian movement that has swept across denominational lines, reaching its peak—at least in America—during the 1970s. It was "uptown" Pentecostalism, with all the holiness fever first evidenced at the 1906 Azusa Street Mission (see Assemblies of God) but now present within mainstream churches of traditional, upper-middle-class membership. Catholics, Episcopalians, Presbyterians, Methodists, and Baptists: all denominations began to experience, within their individual churches, the same phenomenon. It would typically begin with a few people feeling the need for a deeper, more fulfilling spirituality within the context of the tradition in which they were raised. Meeting in living rooms—often without clergy, who were sometimes suspicious and antagonistic—people would pray together and suddenly find themselves speaking in tongues (glossolalia), gripped by a fever of emotional fulfillment and a sense of God's presence. It was as if the Holy Spirit had taken control of them. The feeling of being right with God, totally in the present and cleansed of all sin, was one hardly ever experienced in formal church services. It was pure, simple, heartfelt religion, *experienced* rather than intellectualized. It swept the nation. *The PTL Club* (which originally stood for "Praise the Lord" but was later amended by host Jim Bakker to "People That Love") started its two-hour daily television run. Satellites and theme parks followed. Pat Robertson began *The 700 Club* and even campaigned for the Republican nomination for president in 1988 (he lost). Jimmy Swaggart had a host of radio stations airing his show, and the Oral Roberts ministry aired once again.

Most of the theology behind the charismatic movement comes from the apostle Paul. In 1 Corinthians 12 he offers a list of the "gifts of the Spirit" given by God: wisdom, knowledge, faith, healing, miracles, prophecy, discernment, tongues, and interpretation of tongues. In Romans 12 he adds the gifts of serving, teaching, encouraging, contributing, leading, and showing mercy. An additional gift of self-control is referred to in 1 Corinthians 7:7.

If it had not been for the gift of speaking in other tongues, and, to a lesser extent, the gift of healing, mainstream church hierarchy probably would have encouraged the movement. After all, who among the clergy is going to object if a parishioner suddenly feels the urge to exercise his gift of giving generously to the church?

But to have people suddenly stand up during the pastoral prayer, raise their hands toward heaven, and begin praying in an unintelligible language can be a bit disconcerting to a mainstream Sunday-morning crowd. Many clergy began to feel they had somehow missed the boat by failing to meet the spiritual needs of congregations who had grown used to a formal, spit-and-polish religion of the mind, not the emotional outburst of tongues-speaking Pentecostal power. Many clergy felt left out. They had prayed for so long that the church would be revived. Now it was happening, either in spite of them or without them. Up to then the emotional outbursts had been limited to mostly southern, small, poor, Pentecostal holiness churches. Now it seemed to be breaking out in more metropolitan areas, in Detroit, Chicago, Los Angeles, and even staid, conservative Boston.

Meetings were held and books were written. Discussions followed symposiums. Was it a movement of God? Or was it a work of, at best, hysterical women, who seemed to be at the forefront of the movement, or, at worst, the devil? Was America indeed in the throes of another Great Awakening (see Great Awakening)? Some preachers went to the extreme of throwing out any church members who dared rock the boat. Others capitalized and began to hold healing meetings.

Religious movements come and go. The American segment of the charismatic movement peaked and began to level off. Worldwide, however, especially in Asia, Latin America, and Africa, Christianity with a charismatic cast is growing as rapidly as Islam, and in some cases more rapidly. Trends suggest that by the year 2050 there will be three Christians for every two Muslims worldwide, most of whom will be described as charismatic Christians.

And it's still very much on the scene in American churches such as the Assemblies of God. Robert Duvall's 1997 movie *The Apostle* shows an example of Pentecostalism. But it was the popularity of the charismatic movement that helped green-light a picture Duvall had pushed for more than fifteen years. He wasn't making fun of the preaching style he portrayed; he really respected the talent of charismatic preachers. Prayer meetings are still held in people's homes, and clergy who came of age during the movement's high point still preach about the more spectacular "gifts of the spirit."

Only time will tell how the charismatic movement will shape our future. Jim Bakker went to jail for embezzlement; paroled after serving five years of a forty-five-year sentence, he launched a new television ministry. His former wife, Tammy Faye Bakker, has remarried and still makes the occasional television appearance. Jimmy Swaggart apologized for soliciting prostitutes but remains on the fringes. Pat Robertson lost the election but still has political clout. The Trinity Broadcasting Network is now the world's largest religious television network. The Sky Angel Christian satellite television network, brainchild of Robert Johnson, purports to "free Christian broadcasting from secular news." Tim LaHaye and Jerry B. Jenkins's apocalyptic "Left Behind" books top the charts. Although many churches have returned to preaching social involvement and a more cerebral sort of Gospel message, one has the feeling it is only a matter of time before things get shaken up again.

Sources:

Douglas, J. D., ed. *The New International Dictionary of the Christian Church.* Grand Rapids, MI: Zondervan Publishing, 1974.
Jenkins, Philip. "Growing the Flock." *Boston Globe,* June 23, 2002.

Ch'i

Western monotheistic religions tend to visualize a God "out there" or "up there," with whom humans respond, communicate, and live to please. Chinese religious traditions may worship God or, more frequently, gods, but in terms of day-to-day life, more emphasis is given to "balance." Ch'i is life force, the essence of what it is to be human. To be content, yin and yang, feminine and masculine principles, must be balanced and in harmony. Sometimes, as in Daoism and Confucianism, this balance is brought about through meditation and spiritual exercises. At other times the flow of ch'i is aided by acupuncture or herbal combinations (see Chakras).

Sources:

Ellwood, Robert S., and Barbara A. McGraw. *Many Peoples, Many Faiths.* 6th ed. Upper Saddle River, NJ: Prentice Hall, 1999.

CHILDREN OF GOD—"THE FAMILY" *see* **Cult**

Christ/Jesus of Nazareth

Just as "Buddha" is not a name, but rather a title given to Siddhartha Gautama, "Christ" is a title given to Jesus of Nazareth. The name comes from the Greek word *christos,* meaning "Anointed One." So although people often make reference to "Jesus Christ," the correct term is actually "Jesus, the Christ."

The title is given to the man Jesus of Nazareth (Jesus, from the town of Nazareth), who would have been known to his contemporaries as Yeshua ben Yosef (Joshua, son of Joseph). If Jesus' name had been transliterated directly from Hebrew into English, he would have been known to the world today as Joshua. But because the documents written about Jesus, the biblical Gospels, were written originally in Greek, the Hebrew Yeshua became the Greek transliteration Iasous. Iasous, transliterated

Seventeenth-century engraving of Jesus walking on water while Peter sinks, by Matthaus Merian. *Fortean Picture Library.*

much later, became the Latin Jesu and the English Jesus. So it remains an ironic quirk of linguistic fate that although Christians are told "there is no other name under heaven given to men by which we must be saved," the name they are given would not even have been recognized by Jesus' mother, let alone anyone living in Nazareth at the time.

The events of Jesus' life have been told many times in stories, songs, and movies. Although the four biblical Gospels do not always agree with each other about events and times, a composite story emerges that at least provides a framework for reconstructing the basic details.

The story begins with Luke's account of Mary, a maiden, perhaps a young teenager, who is engaged to a carpenter named Joseph. She is told by the angel Gabriel she is going to become the mother of one "who will be great and will be called the Son of the Most High."

"How will this be," Mary asked the angel, "since I am a virgin?"

The angel answered, "The Holy Spirit will come upon you … so the holy one about to be born will be called the Son of God."

In those days, becoming pregnant after betrothal was considered a crime punishable by stoning death if the future husband, knowing the child was not his, was of a mind to press charges. But Joseph received a confirmation visit from an angel. Risking social ostracism, he took Mary to be his wife, "but he had no union with her until she gave birth to a son."

Nine months later, Caesar Augustus issued an empire-wide taxation, requiring everyone to journey to his hometown to register and pay the required fee. The couple returned to Joseph's birthplace, Bethlehem, where Jesus was born in a stable, "because there was no room for them in the inn" (Luke 2:7).

There the family was visited by shepherds and, twelve days later, according to tradition, wise men, or Magi, from the East.

The Magi were the visitors who caused all the trouble. They had followed a star that led them not to Bethlehem but to Jerusalem, five miles away. There they inquired about the newly born "King of the Jews."

This was news to Herod, who, as king of Judea, thought *he* was "King of the Jews." Herod tried to use the Magi as spies to lead him to the baby. When this failed, he issued a decree often labeled in folklore as "the slaughter of the innocents," a command that all male babies under the age of two were to be killed. (This decree is why some believe the Magi's visit could have been as long as two years after Jesus' birth. There is a lot of difference between a newborn baby and a child of two. Besides this, though Luke's account has Mary and Joseph in a stable, Matthew, who describes the Magi, has them living in a house.)

Joseph and Mary escaped the slaughter by fleeing to Egypt, where they stayed until Herod died. They returned to Nazareth, where the Bible says nothing about Jesus' life for the next thirty years except for one intriguing story. Each year his family traveled to Jerusalem to celebrate Passover. When he was twelve, just about the age for a modern Bar Mitzva, the Gospel of Luke tells how his parents returned home only to discover young Jesus was not with them. This by no means reflected on their parenting skills. It would have been common to travel in large family groups. Mary and Joseph probably thought their son was with a relative. When they discovered his absence, however, they immediately returned to Jerusalem. They found him holding court with the Temple scholars and religious leaders, amazing them with his knowledge. When questioned by his parents, Jesus gave only an enigmatic reply: "Didn't you know I had to be in my Father's house?" (Luke 2:49). It was a portent of things to come.

Eighteen years went by, often referred to as "the silent years," before Jesus was heard from in scripture again. Many fanciful stories were later written about this period of his life. Middle Age monks and the Qur'an of Islam told of him playing with friends, forming toy doves out of clay and then "breathing life into them" so they could fly away. Some accounts tell of Jesus traveling to India and consulting with Hindu holy men and Buddhist Bodhisattvas. Others have him traveling to England, accompanying his uncle, Joseph of Arimathea, as he plied the tin trade. (Although the Bible mentions Joseph of Arimathea, it fails to make any family connections. He is simply known as "an upright man" who, after voting against the council that decided to arrest Jesus, offered his tomb as Jesus' burial vault.)

The only documentation for the story thus far is found in the first two chapters of the Gospels according to Matthew and Luke. The remaining Gospels according to Mark and John pick up the narrative beginning with Jesus' baptism.

John the Baptist had been preaching and baptizing people in the waters of the Jordan River. He called his trademark a "baptism of repentance." People flocked to hear him even though his preaching style could be called, at best, abrasive.

"You brood of vipers!" he said to the religious leaders of Jerusalem. "Who warned you to flee from the coming wrath?" (Matthew 3:7).

When Jesus stepped forward for baptism, John recognized in him the blessing of God, the promised one for whom John was preparing the way. Something happened, although the Gospels are not clear as to exactly what it was. The spirit of God, "like" or "in the form of" a dove, descended upon Jesus. Whether everyone saw it, or just Jesus and John, this event marked the beginning of Jesus' public ministry, which lasted (the four Gospels seem to disagree) either one or three years.

But before Jesus could begin his work, he had to overcome a trial. For forty days he was alone in the desert, tempted by the devil. Three times Satan appeared to him, first telling Jesus to make bread from stone and then to show off his powers as the son of God by leaping from the pinnacle of the Temple. Finally Jesus was offered "all the kingdoms of the world" if he would only bow down and worship Satan. But three times Jesus resisted by quoting Hebrew scripture. In the end, he passed the test. He was worthy to begin.

Calling twelve disciples to be his followers, Jesus began to preach, heal the sick, and teach, most often in the form of parables, stories with a message. His Sermon on the Mount, containing the famous Beatitudes and the Lord's Prayer, is full of passages that have become the standard fare of popular idiom: "Blessed are the meek, for they shall inherit the earth.... You are the salt of the earth.... You are the light of the world.... Love your enemies.... Our Father, Who art in heaven.... Do not store up for yourselves treasures on earth.... No man can serve two masters.... Consider the lilies.... Knock and the door will be opened.... Narrow is the gate that leads to Heaven."

Marcus Borg is a member of the Jesus Seminar, a group committed to what has sometimes been called the "search for the historical Jesus." In his book, *Meeting Jesus Again for the First Time*, he summarizes the life of Jesus in this way:

> The historical Jesus was a spirit person, one of those figures in human history with an experiential awareness of the reality of God.... He was a teacher of wisdom who regularly used the classic forms of wisdom speech (parables and memorable short sayings known as aphorisms) to teach a subversive and alternative wisdom.... Jesus was a social prophet, similar to the classic prophets of Israel. As such, he criticized the elites of his time, was an advocate of an alternative social vision, and was often in conflict with authorities.... He was a movement founder who brought into being a Jewish renewal or revitalization movement that challenged and shattered the social boundaries of his day, a movement that eventually became the Christian Church.

If Jesus had continued in the path of itinerant preacher and miracle worker, he no doubt would have faded away into history or at best be remembered as just another Jewish visionary. There were, in those days, many who made great claims to religious insight and each had a following. But it was what happened at the end of his life that gave rise to what would become the Christian religion.

Crucifixion was a common Roman form of execution. It was, by design, a very prolonged and painful way to die. Public, conspicuous death on a cross was meant to serve as a deterrent to other would-be criminals.

Jesus had become a threat to established religious and secular power. His triumphal entry into Jerusalem a few days before Passover had excited the crowds, who were already in a patriotic, religious frenzy. When they cut palm branches to place before him and threw down their garments along his path, they were, in effect, offering the "red carpet" treatment accorded to visiting dignitaries. But when they began to sing the coronation song from Psalm 118, "Blessed is he who comes in the name of the Lord.... Hosanna in the highest," there was no question that they were prepared to recognize him as the promised Messiah who would lead them to freedom from Rome and restore Jewish nationalism.

By allowing this to happen, Jesus was deliberately throwing down a challenge to both political and religious authority. When warned by religious leaders to "rebuke your disciples," to shut them up and forestall a riot, Jesus made his challenge obvious. "I tell you," he said, "if they keep quiet, the stones will cry out" (Luke 19:40). From that moment, his death by crucifixion was almost certain.

It happened less than a week later. On Thursday, while Jesus celebrated the Passover Seder meal with his followers, one of them, Judas, quietly slipped out into the night. After collecting his betrayal fee of thirty pieces of silver he led a group of Roman Centurions to the quiet garden where Jesus was praying while the disciples slept. After an all-night trial in which Pontius Pilate, the Roman governor, ineffectively tried to pass Jesus over to Jewish authorities, on Friday morning at about 9 o'clock, Jesus was crucified according to Roman custom. He died at about 3 o'clock in the afternoon and was taken off the cross just before sunset.

Because Sabbath laws forbid work on Saturday, Jesus' body was never fully prepared for burial. At first light on Sunday a group of women who had cared for Jesus went to his tomb, intending to complete the burial ritual. But on that morning, which became known as Easter, they found the tomb empty. They ran back to tell the scattered disciples Jesus' body was gone. He had risen from the dead. Very soon after, and for the next month and a half, others made the same claim. Some five hundred people, according to the apostle Paul (1 Corinthians 15:6), saw the resurrected Christ.

Ever since then, people have argued about what happened. Some say it was a hoax perpetrated by hysterical fanatics, and that perhaps the women who claimed to have gone to the tomb to honor the body actually took it. Others wonder whether someone else might have taken the body to deceive the disciples. Apologists, however, argue that such deception would have had little point. Furthermore, some doubt the claims, even the existence, of the eyewitnesses mentioned later by Paul, while apologists see no reason for such doubt.

Whether the story is historical truth or legend, one fact stands out. The early believers were so convinced that the events following the death of Jesus of Nazareth actually happened that they galvanized into a movement that has lasted right up to the present. In terms of sheer numbers, significance, and influence on later world history, Christianity is one of the biggest religions the world has ever known.

Sources:
Borg, Marcus J. *Meeting Jesus Again for the First Time*. San Francisco: HarperCollins, 1994.
May, Herbert G., and Bruce M. Metzger, eds. *The New Oxford Annotated Bible with the Apocrypha*. Rev. ed. New York: Oxford University Press, 1973.

CHRISTIAN SCIENCE

In 1990 the Church of Christ, Scientist, was in serious trouble. Enrollments were down, giving was down, and a disastrous attempt to begin a television station, the Monitor Channel, had cost the church some $316 million. The station's shutdown was soon followed by that of the money-losing Monitor Radio network. From an estimated 268,915 U.S. followers in 1936, membership had dropped to 106,000. The 11,200 healers that practiced in 1941 had seen their numbers shrink to only 1,820. Worse yet, a landmark Massachusetts criminal court had, amid much publicity, convicted David and Ginger Twitchel of manslaughter in the tragic death of their two-year-old son resulting from a bowel obstruction, a death the court thought could have been prevented if the parents had gone to a doctor instead of relying on a Christian Science practitioner.

But by 2000 things had changed considerably. Seven hundred new bookstores in Latin America now carry the religion's textbook and Bible companion, *Science and Health with Key to the Scriptures*. The book is sold at agricultural fairs in Africa and book fairs in Japan. Some 2,500 people filled an airport hanger in Kinshasa in the Congo to attend a Christian Science lecture.

Clearly the church has discovered a new and enthusiastic audience. In September 2002, the new Mary Baker Eddy Library for the Betterment of Humanity opened in Boston, right next to the mother church on Massachusetts Avenue. Clay Bennett, editorial cartoonist for the *Christian Science Monitor*, the newspaper begun by Mary Baker Eddy, won a Pulitzer Prize earlier in the year.

The world seems to have rediscovered the teachings of Mary Baker Eddy, founder of the Church of Christ, Scientist, popularly known as Christian Science.

The church's theological centerpiece and reason for being is based in its belief that the root of illness lies in the mind, not just the organs of the body. In *Science and Health* Eddy wrote: "A patient under the influence of mortal mind is healed only by removing the influence on him of this mind." She had come to this conclusion through her own experience of self-healing and a study of Jesus' cures as recorded in the Gospels. Since then countless case studies, probably at least one from every member of the church, have confirmed Eddy's thesis to the satisfaction of thousands of believers over the years. They flock to Christian Science Reading Rooms, located in most cities nationwide, to read and listen to lectures. During church services, pas-

Christian Science complex in Boston, Massachusetts, the organization's headquarters. *Fortean Picture Library.*

sages from the Bible are followed with readings from *Science and Health*. The Massachusetts Metaphysical College in Boston trains healers to aid recovery from illness by working with the patient to correct intellectual and spiritual obstructions caused by false thinking.

Eddy, while believing firmly that no one person should ever control any institution, especially the church she founded, was one of the most influential women of the nineteenth century. Given the sexism of that time, her church probably received less support than it would have had it been founded by a man. Even so, Christian Science thrived and is no doubt here to stay. The church has made some concessions. Whether or not members will see doctors during illness, especially the illness of a child, is left up to the individual. Like all churches, there are splits and divisions. Some people think the very fact of going to a doctor is a confession of faithlessness that will prevent healing. Others think there are times when medicine can be used as a physical crutch, needed until a spiritual healing takes place.

A lot of New Age thought is simply the rediscovery of ancient Eastern religion. The fact that so much of that thought resonates with Eddy's teachings has no doubt aided the surge of renewed interest in Christian Science, regarded by some as perhaps the first hundred-year-old New Age religion. But a faith with such a large base of anecdotal evidence and personal, eyewitness accounts of healing cannot be ignored. New ways of describing those healings and explaining the basis of Christian Science may be utilized, much to the dismay of fundamentalists within the organization. But in the words of Virginia Harris, chair of the church's board of directors, "I like change because it is progressive. The world goes forward, so no matter how much you whine or talk about the past you can't get back there.... [But] as you go forward with change, always [remain] true to who you are."

Sources:
Blanton, Kimberly. "The Gospel According to Virginia Harris." *Boston Globe Magazine*, June 16, 2002.

CHRISTIANITY

One billion, seven hundred eighty-three million, six hundred sixty thousand people—about one out of every three in the world today—claim Christianity as their religion. This makes Christianity by far the world's largest religion. But those people have such vastly different opinions as to its theological content that a single definition of Christianity is just about impossible.

There are, however, some common beliefs, although even these are subject to differing interpretations:

1. Jesus of Nazareth, by his death on the cross, provided redemption for humans who were separated from God because of sin. Some Christians view this literally as a historic act, part of God's new covenant with humankind. Others see the cross as a permanent symbol of the victory of good over evil. But the architecture of all Christian churches features, usually on prominent display, a cross. In Roman Catholic tradition it is a crucifix, the body of Jesus nailed to the cross, signifying Jesus' death. In Protestant tradition the cross is empty, emphasizing his resurrection.

2. Jesus, either literally or figuratively, was resurrected from the dead.

3. Baptism is the initiation into the religion.

4. A Communion meal (Eucharist, Lord's Supper, Communion, or Last Supper) involving bread and wine is a central liturgical element of worship.
5. There is one life to live on Earth, followed by an everlasting afterlife (usually in heaven or hell).
6. The Bible, consisting of both Old and New Testaments, although interpreted in different ways, is the standard by which Christians live.
7. There is only one universal Church.

It is this final point that confuses people unfamiliar with Christian history. There is a vast difference between the stately liturgy of an Orthodox High Mass, with vested clergy chanting hymns in Latin or Greek, enveloped with the smell of incense wafting heavenward, and that of the shouting, singing, foot-stomping southern revival tent-meeting. One might be forgiven for seeing no similarity between a quiet Quaker meeting, where there is no worship leader and long periods of time pass when nothing seems to be happening, and a Pentecostal song service featuring many people raising their hands toward heaven and praying aloud in unintelligible tongues. A large, mainstream church in suburban Illinois might be attended by seven or eight hundred worshipers wearing dresses or suits, dutifully following an order of service designed and printed using the latest desktop computer technology. Meanwhile, an Appalachian one-room log sanctuary might house a dozen ardent believers whose church service reaches its high point when the faithful drape poisonous rattlesnakes around their necks.

These examples illustrate the breadth of Christianity. Participants in one tradition often deny the orthodoxy of other traditions, but they all share the above-listed common beliefs based on the same Bible.

Perhaps the easiest way to understand all this is to contrast the two extremes of Christianity, while remembering that in between these two positions are many gradations embracing shades of meanings and differences.

Ever since the famous Scopes Trial held in the spring of 1925, these two contrasting interpretations have been labeled fundamentalist (conservative, religious right) and modernist (liberal, religious left). John Scopes was a science teacher in Tennessee, accused of breaking a new state law forbidding the teaching of evolution. Clarence Darrow, who faced the flamboyant prosecutor William Jennings Bryan, defended him. Scopes lost and was fined one hundred dollars. But the trial polarized Americans, many of whom thought Bryan and his fundamentalist witnesses looked old-fashioned and foolish. As far as public education was concerned, the liberals lost the battle but eventually won the war. The fundamentalist/modernist controversy, however, is still with us.

At issue is biblical interpretation. Is the Bible to be read literally or metaphorically? This is a central issue that polarizes Christianity.

Fundamentalists have developed an entire tradition of preaching, teaching, and singing around a historical, literal interpretation. The "old-time religion" of conservative Christianity is the fastest-growing religion in the world today, with television stations featuring *The 700 Club* and *The PTL Club* and with numerous preachers showcased on TBN (Trinity Broadcasting Network). The popular Bill Gaither "Homecoming" Gospel music concert series, held in big-venue halls and stadiums, attracts thousands of people to each show. Conservatives have organized politically into groups such as the Christian Coalition, with enough clout to field presidential candidates such as Pat Robertson. Tim LaHaye and Jerry B. Jenkins's "Left Behind" novels top the fiction charts.

Conservative Christians belong to every denomination. They may be called evangelicals, charismatics, pentecostals, or fundamentalists. But there are traditional, or conservative, Lutherans, Presbyterians, Methodists, and Catholics as well as Baptists and Seventh-day Adventists. The hymns may be different, and worship traditions vary, but generally, within the framework of their tradition, conservatives read the Bible as they would a historical textbook.

The message at the heart of conservative Christianity is that human beings are born sinners. (One illustration sometimes offered, though questioned by skeptics, is that babies have to be taught how to share and be good, while selfishness and bad behavior come naturally.) The original sin of Adam, parent of the human race, has been passed on to his offspring and renders all humans unworthy of God's grace and an afterlife with him in heaven. In order for humans to enter heaven and spend eternity with God, the problem of atonement or reconciliation with God has to be addressed.

This reconciliation was achieved when Jesus of Nazareth accepted humankind's collective punishment—death and separation from God—in their place. Through this substitutionary atonement, as it is called, Jesus earned God's grace for humankind, who had been unable to earn it for themselves.

The following story is frequently told to illustrate the conservative Christian concept of substitutionary atonement:

A driver is arrested for speeding. He is brought before a judge who is wearing a black robe, the symbol of authority. The judge is sitting behind a great, elevated bench and looks down at the accused. All the trappings of the room point to the fact that this judge is in control and holds the power of life and death.

"How do you plead?" asks the judge.

The accused knows he is guilty. He was speeding and breaking the laws of the land. There is no sense denying the fact. And this isn't the first time. He's done it before.

"Guilty, your honor."

The judge pronounces his sentence. "I fine you one hundred dollars."

"I'm guilty," says the accused, "but I don't have enough money. I deserve the penalty, but I cannot pay."

"Then you must go to jail," says the judge.

The accused is made ready to be led off to jail, but before he can be escorted from the courtroom the judge halts proceedings.

"Wait!" he says. Removing his robe, the symbol of authority, he comes out from behind the imposing bench. Now he looks just like everyone else. Standing next to the accused the judge reaches into his pocket and produces a one-hundred-dollar bill. Paying the fine for the guilty party, he says, "Do you accept this payment?"

"Yes," says the relieved speeder. "I'm guilty, but I accept your payment of my fine. In the eyes of justice, the very judge who was forced to sentence me has paid my penalty. He put aside his robe of honor to do it, coming down here to stand right beside me like a brother, but my sin is now and forever atoned for."

And then the final mystery is explained to the courtroom. The judge was both father and brother to the accused—father when judgment was pronounced and brother when payment was made. And yet, somehow, father and brother are one and the same.

This story illustrates the essence of conservative Christian theology. The transaction it represents occurred at a real place and time in history, centering on Jesus of Nazareth and the cross at Calvary, where Jesus, who was Lord and judge, also became "brother" to humankind by paying their penalty.

Jesus explained the crucifixion to his disciples when he gave them bread and wine to drink. "This is my body, broken for you," he said. "This is my blood, shed for you. Do this in remembrance of me."

Liberal Christians read the same biblical texts, but as metaphors, not historical fact. The virgin birth does not mean that a human woman was impregnated by God from on high, but rather that to be fully human one must be open to spirit, as Jesus was. It means humans are at once physical and spiritual. Miracles mean that all is possible to those who see past the immediacy of our environment, who look for the possible even in the face of impossibility. Liberals differentiate between the historical man, Jesus of Nazareth, and, to use theologian Macus Borg's term, the "post-Easter" Jesus. By that he means that the spirit of Jesus was so powerful that his disciples realized he was still very much with them in that he was infused into their very personalities and being. Anyone who has ever heard the internal reproving or affirming voice of a parent long since deceased understands how people live on in us as long as we are alive.

In short, according to liberal interpretation, the events described in the Bible are universal and true, at once particular to each individual and all-encompassing to the entire human race. Indeed, to limit the Gospel to a story about a Christian God who somehow needs to be appeased by a bloody, painful sacrifice is to not only miss the point, it is downright blasphemous.

Some liberals view conservatives as totally misunderstanding what the biblical writers were talking about. By emphasizing individual need for salvation, they argue, conservatives wrap themselves into a religious cocoon that closes out social responsibility. This is why pro-slavery, born-again preachers could completely miss the New Testament verses that spoke of people being "neither slave nor free, but one in Christ" as they delivered their sermons. This is why the Ku Klux Klan could burn crosses "in the name of Jesus" as they hung black men just because they were not white. Liberals suggest that to cling to a literal view of the Genesis Creation story is to miss the truth of how God, the consciousness of the universe, created humans as a part of the whole—the very "dust of the earth" from which we sprang.

Indeed, conservative baggage associated with the word "God" is so prevalent that some liberal theologians have tried to find new words to use in its place— "Ground of Being," "Source," and "First Cause," to list just a few.

Liberal Catholic priests, mindful of how exclusionary the word "Father" was to feminists, especially those who might not have had positive parental experience, began to baptize "in the name of the Creator, the Redeemer, and the Sustainer," instead of "Father, Son, and Holy Ghost." Conservatives from their own Church ruled such baptisms invalid.

Some swear that the name Christian can only be applied to those who believe that the facts of the Bible, especially those surrounding the life and ministry of Jesus, are historically true and accurate. Others insist this dishonors God and distorts the deepest and most profound metaphors God has given to the human race concerning what it means to be a child of God. As well, there is a vast middle ground between the extremes of conservative and liberal, and many Christians find themselves leaning sometimes toward aspects of one viewpoint, other times toward aspects of the other.

Sources:

Borg, Marcus J. *The God We Never Knew.* San Francisco: HarperCollins, 1997.

Borg, Marcus J. *Meeting Jesus Again for the First Time.* San Francisco: HarperCollins, 1994.

Fackre, Dorothy, and Gabriel Fackre. *Christian Basics.* Grand Rapids, MI: William B. Eerdmans Publishing Co., 1991.

Smart, Ninian. *The Religious Experience.* 5th ed. Upper Saddle River, NJ: Prentice Hall, 1996.

CHRISTIANITY, CALENDAR OF

Because much of the world uses the Christian calendar, it is important to understand the significance of Christian holidays, some of which have become almost secular events.

The calendar begins with the birth of Jesus of Nazareth, although that is much too simple a statement. First of all, no one knows when Jesus of Nazareth was born. Due to archaeological, astronomical, and linguistic studies, the best guess now is that Jesus was born sometime in what would today be dated as 6 BCE. And even that date requires explanation.

Many people mark time with the terms BC, "before Christ," and AD, "anno domini," which translates to "the year of our Lord." In recent times, however, recognizing how insensitive this terminology is to non-Christians, many have adopted the terms BCE, "before the common era," and CE, "common era." Thus, Jesus was born in 6 BCE, or six years earlier than he was thought to have been born when the modern calendar was first drawn up.

Advent

The Christian calendar begins with Advent. Christmas, the traditional celebration of the birth of Jesus, has been celebrated on December 25th ever since the early part of the fourth century. This was the day of the winter solstice, the shortest day of the year according to the Roman calendar. The tradition of Advent, of preparing for the Christmas celebration, began early in the Eastern Church, beginning on November 14th, the feast of Saint Philip.

In the West, the season begins on the Sunday closest to the feast of Saint Andrew, the disciple who most often brought people to meet Jesus. So for most Christians, Advent now marks the beginning of the Christian calendar, four Sundays of preparation prior to the celebration of the birth of Jesus. Christians see this as the turning point of human existence, when "God became flesh," when the divine took on human form, when the "author" wrote himself into the play and entered into history. The liturgical color is traditionally purple, the sign of penitence. Often a purple candle is lit at the beginning of each Sunday worship service, until the final white candle of the Advent wreath is lit on Christmas Eve. But on the third Sunday, Gaudete ("Rejoice") Sunday, it is traditional to light a rose-colored candle, signifying the joy to come.

Advent is usually celebrated with scripture readings, many of them from the prophet Isaiah, that prophesy not only the birth of Jesus, or his first advent, but his second advent, or Second Coming, as well. The traditional Old Testament readings were incorporated by George Frederick Handel to make up the text of the Advent section of his famous Oratorio, *Messiah*.

Christmas

The season of Advent ends with the celebration of Christmas. Christmas, or the "Mass of Christ," is the English word for the Feast of the Nativity, celebrated on December 25th. Evidence suggests that this holiday, now common throughout the world, was not celebrated until at least the fourth century. Although there is no way of knowing the actual birth date of Christ, we do know that December 25th was the date of a Roman festival known as the "birthday of the unconquered sun," recognizing the fact that the sun, after the winter solstice, begins to strengthen. When the early church discovered it could not stamp out the celebration of what they considered a pagan holiday, sometime around 336 CE they "baptized" it with the Christian name, "Feast of the Nativity of the Son of Righteousness."

Most of the symbols surrounding Christmas are pagan in origin. Candles and Christmas tree lights reflect attempts to light up the longest night of the year. Parties and gift-giving were the custom when celebrating the Roman Saturnalia festival from December 17th to the 24th. Christmas dinner and family reunions come from Germanic-Celtic Yule celebrations.

The modern American celebration is a very new custom. When the Puritans came to New England they objected to the very idea of Christmas. It was considered a pagan holiday. But Christmas seems to have a habit of gradually accumulating customs. As Christmas grows more each year into a secular and commercial holiday, American churches are experiencing a dilemma. Traditionally, Advent was a time for penitence, for sober reflection and music in minor keys. When Christmas finally came, it was celebrated for twelve days, until the Feast of the Epiphany. But with the cultural phenomenon of joyous celebration and the countdown of "shopping days until Christmas," with Christmas music filling airwaves and shopping malls even before Thanksgiving, it is becoming harder and harder to leave the culture behind at the sanctuary door on Sunday morning. And just when the church begins to celebrate on Christmas morning, social voices tire of the long party and begin preparations for the New Year celebration.

Individual churches are forced to deal with the problem in their own way. Some have simply dropped the Advent tradition to follow society, singing Christmas hymns beginning in early December. Others attempt to carry on, fighting a counter-culture struggle.

At Christmas the liturgical colors in the Church are changed to white. Catholic churches usually say three masses that day, to signify Christ's birth eternally in the bosom of the Father, in Mary's womb, and in the souls of the faithful.

The Christmas season traditionally continues for twelve days. The shepherds were said to have visited Jesus on the day of his birth, but tradition has it that the wise men visited him twelve days later, on the Feast of the Epiphany.

Epiphany

No one knows how many wise men, or Magi, visited Bethlehem. Because they brought three gifts—frankincense, gold, and myrrh—it is assumed there were three. Tradition has even given them names: Melchior, Belthasar, and Gaspar or Caspar. In 1162, Frederick Barbarossa claimed to have discovered their relics and brought them back to Germany, where they are enshrined in Cologne Cathedral.

The Adoration of the Magi became a popular subject of music and art. Gian Carlo Menotti's opera, *Amahl and the Night Visitors*, is performed each year before appreciative audiences, and the Magi often take important roles in epic books and movies, such as *Ben Hur*.

An epiphany is "an appearance or manifestation of God." This is what the Magi experienced, so the Feast of the Epiphany is sometimes called the "Little Christmas" and celebrated as such in many churches with Christmas carols and gifts. This is the day when churches from the Eastern tradition celebrate Christmas.

Six weeks after Epiphany the Church begins the celebration of Lent.

Lent

Jesus' experience of forty days in the wilderness preparing for his ministry prompted the Church to institute a period of forty days, not counting Sundays, when preparations are made to celebrate Easter. Because Lent is traditionally a time of fasting and penitence, a real blowout used to occur in the days just preceding it. New Orleans (along with many other communities) continues the tradition with Mardi Gras, "Fat Tuesday," the day before fasting begins. Some Christians "give up something for Lent," a daily reminder of the season. In liturgical traditions, ashes, an ancient sign of mourning, are made from burning the previous Palm Sunday's palm branches. The ashes are administered to the forehead of the faithful on Ash Wednesday, the beginning of Lent, as a reminder of the Old Testament tradition of repenting "in sackcloth and ashes."

Sundays are considered a weekly vacation during Lent. Rules are relaxed. Feasts are prepared. Many churches institute Sunday afternoon jazz concerts, a reminder that life is not all mourning and sadness.

But as meditation, introspection, and repentance return each Monday morning, Lent begins to move toward the celebration of Holy Week.

Holy Week

Palm Sunday is the beginning of the countdown. It marks the celebration of the day Jesus rode into Jerusalem and was welcomed as Messiah. It was a very public, triumphal entry, and the people cut down palm branches to strew in his path. But when Jesus threw the money changers out of the Temple and taught what was considered by the authorities to be subversive doctrine, he was seen as a threat to established authority.

For three days he spoke openly in the city. Then, on Thursday night, Jesus met with his disciples in an upper room to celebrate Passover. Here he instituted the meal called the Last Supper, or Communion. Ever since, this day has been called Maundy Thursday. "Maundy" comes from the Latin *Mandatum*, or mandate. The day is so named because it was on this night Jesus gave his disciples a new mandate, or command, to "love one another" (John 13:34).

That night Jesus was betrayed and arrested. He was crucified the next day, now called Good Friday. It is called "good" because of the benefits God accomplished, not because of the horrible act of crucifixion.

On Easter Sunday morning, Jesus is said to have risen from the dead. Again, as with many Christian traditions, there is evidence of pagan influence. Although the Eastern Church celebrates Easter on the same date every year, the holiday in the West is always held on the first Sunday following the first full moon after the spring equinox. Without knowing any better, if you were to watch a group of religious folk climb up a mountain on the first Sunday following the first full moon of the spring equinox, gathering there to sing hymns as the sun rose, you would suspect you were viewing a pagan celebration, especially when you walked home to exchange fertility symbols of eggs and bunnies and to share a meal of new spring lamb. In fact, this is a typical Christian Easter sunrise service.

Even the name "Easter" is a bit suspicious. It apparently derives from the name of an ancient Celtic pagan spring festival. But evidence suggests it was celebrated early on in Church history and was the traditional day for baptism and reception of new Church members. Modern Christians simply ignore the significance of Easter bunnies and colored eggs. They may be pagan fertility symbols, but they are still a lot of fun.

The liturgical color for the next seven weeks is white, but eight weeks after Easter the color becomes red, the color of celebration, as the Church remembers the Pentecost.

Pentecost

This is the day marking the birthday of the Church. Pentecost is a Jewish holiday. When Jews from all over made their way to Jerusalem to keep the feast, the disciples, according to Acts 2, were celebrating as well. They had met together and were praying when,

Suddenly a sound like the blowing of a violent wind came from heaven
and filled the whole house where they were sitting. They saw what

seemed to be tongues of fire that separated and came to rest on each of them. All of them were filled with the Holy Spirit and began to speak in other tongues as the Spirit enabled them.

This example of "Pentecostal power" marked the coming of the Spirit, the day the Church began. Jesus had promised to send his spirit, and when he did, it certainly attracted a crowd. The apostle Peter preached the first Christian sermon and three thousand people joined the festivities. The church was off to a flying start—"And the Lord added to their number daily those who were being saved" (Acts 2:47).

Today Pentecost is often celebrated with balloons and streamers, fitting for a birthday party.

Following the festivities of Pentecost, the Church begins a period known as "normal time." The liturgical color is green, and that continues until summer is over and Advent begins again. Other days are celebrated throughout the year that have special meaning to the Church as a whole, or to individual churches, but this cyclical series of celebrations is designed to provide a framework, illustrating the Christian story anew each year.

Sources:
Douglas, J. D., ed. *The New International Dictionary of the Christian Church*. Grand Rapids, MI: Zondervan Publishing, 1974.
Renard, John. *The Handy Religion Answer Book*. Detroit: Visible Ink Press, 2002.

CHRISTIANITY, DEVELOPMENT OF

(See also Ecumenism)

Volumes have been written about the development of Christianity. The Christian Church has influenced Western society and world events to a degree that would be difficult, if not impossible, to estimate.

The Early Church

For its first three centuries the early Church can perhaps best be described as an underground Jesus movement. Persecuted much of the time, the Church nevertheless made huge strides in its Great Commission. In Matthew 28, the Bible says Jesus met with his disciples and gave them their marching orders:

All authority in heaven and earth has been given to me. Therefore go and make disciples of all nations, baptizing them in the name of the Father and of the Son and of the Holy Spirit, and teaching them to observe everything I have commanded you. And surely I will be with you always, to the very end of the age.

Whether or not Jesus really said these words doesn't matter a great deal. The early Church believed them with such conviction that within only a few years they were given the name Christians, "followers of the Christ" (Acts 11:26), by the people of Antioch, and they were accused of "turning the world upside down with their preaching" by the authorities of Thessalonica (Acts 17:6).

Fueled by martyrdom, beginning with Stephen's death, described in Acts 7; led by patriarchs such as Peter, the acknowledged leader; and spread by missionaries such as Paul, Barnabus, and Timothy, the Church was able to take advantage of a unique social situation.

Rome ruled the world, and a common culture and language held sway. Pax romana, the peace of Rome, was enforced by the sword but at least ensured governmental stability. The saying was true that "all roads led to Rome." Infrastructure that would not be duplicated for a thousand years allowed armies to move quickly to outposts of the Western world; such roadways also allowed for the freedom of secure movement for willing missionaries.

It was a time when "diversity" and "inclusion" were watchwords, as long as Rome and the Caesar were acknowledged and put in their proper place at the top of the pecking order.

All of this made it possible for the educated, urbane, extremely talented Saul of Tarsus (see Paul, Saul of Tarsus) to move freely (at least when he wasn't in jail) about the entire Western world, planting churches and writing one-third of the New Testament during his downtime (awaiting trial after being arrested for preaching a "divisive" doctrine).

It was certainly not easy to be a Christian in those days. Waves of persecution broke upon the shores of the early Church. But in spite of it all, men such as Irenaeus, Clement of Alexandria, Tertullian, and Origen were able to forge the basis of modern theological Christian thought by writing, debating, accusing, and finally arriving at a kind of consensus, usually derived by declaring that their opponents were heretics.

On April 30, 311 CE, everything changed. Galerius, ruler of Rome and persecutor of Christians, had a change of heart. Convinced a severe illness he was experiencing was a punishment for his sins, he issued a decree, as recounted by Justo L. Gonzalez in his *Story of Christianity:*

> With all the laws which we have decreed for the good of the state, we have sought to restore the ancient rules and traditional discipline of the Romans. We have particularly sought to have Christians, who had abandoned the faith of their ancestors, return to the truth ... and we were forced to punish [them].... But there are many who persist in their opinions.... Therefore, moved by our mercy to be benevolent towards all, it has seemed just to us to extend to them our pardon, and allow them to be Christians once again, and once again gather in their assemblies, as long as they do not interfere with the public order.... In return for our tolerance, Christians will be required to pray to their God for us.

The prisons were opened and Christians poured out, bearing the marks of their torture but thankful for what they perceived as answered prayer. But the best was yet to come. Constantine was waiting in the wings. Rome, marked by violence and civil war, was about to get a new emperor who would, as the result of a dream, transform Christianity from a persecuted to a very powerful religion.

Gathering his army in Gaul, Constantine crossed the Alps and marched on Rome. Emperor Maxentius had a stronghold there, following the sudden death of

Galerius. No one will ever know what might have happened if Maxentius had simply hunkered down behind the strong walls of Rome and waited for Constantine to go away. Instead, he ignored the advice of his military leaders and took his cue from his religious augurs. Marching forth to war, he met Constantine on the plains surrounding Milvian Bridge.

On the eve of battle, Constantine had either a dream or a vision. Arguments abound as to what it was he really saw. Eusebius later wrote he had a vision in the sky of a cross and the letters IHS, which Constantine took for the Latin *in hoc signo*, "By this sign [you shall conquer]." Other historians say Constantine saw a superimposition of the Greek letters chi and rho. Since they are the first two letters of the name "Christ," this might have been interpreted as a Christian symbol.

Whatever happened, Constantine won the battle and became emperor of Rome. His conversion was not immediate. It took years. But when Constantine signed the Edict of Milan in 313, officially ending Christian persecution, Christianity was on its way to eventually becoming the state religion of Rome.

Now there were great questions that needed to be answered. What would happen when a simple religion begun by a carpenter and practiced by fishermen found itself surrounded by pomp and ceremony and power? Christianity had "gained the whole world." Now would it be able to keep its soul?

The Imperial Church

The effects of Constantine's conversion, if he ever did really convert, cannot be underestimated. He began traditions still felt deeply throughout Christianity.

Most evident was his church-building program. From simple meeting places, sometimes outdoors, other times in people's homes, Christians now found themselves worshiping in the prototypes of the great European cathedrals with their naves, atriums, and sanctuaries. After Constantine's time it was considered almost obligatory for rulers to build memorials to themselves by constructing basilicas. From Rome to the newly renovated and expanded Eastern capital of Constantinople, and on to the Church of the Nativity in the Holy Land, a wave of church building began that continued for centuries.

More subtle, but perhaps more important, was the work of theologians during Constantine's reign. Eusebius of Caesarea (c. 263–c. 339) almost single-handedly popularized a way of thinking that persists to this very day, even though church scholars rarely acknowledge the fact. His *History of the Church* did more than recount what happened during the first few hundred years of the Church. He presented the idea that Christianity was the ultimate goal of all human history, and that the Church was God's plan and humankind had finally reached the final pinnacle of success. And he associated that goal with the work of the Roman state. He believed God had used Rome all along. Church and state were intimately linked together in God's eternal plan.

Lest we scoff at this, seeing what happened to Rome, it might be good to remember that the United States of America was seen by many of its founders in a similar role. The Pilgrims came to the shores of the New World proclaiming they had found the "New Jerusalem."

The idea that God worked through national politics of power was not a new one. Only one witness, that of Israel during the time of David, needs to testify to illustrate that. But this was the first time Christianity was seen in this light by people of power. With Christianity now the "going thing" in the religious/political world of the West, the next six hundred years saw great change. Monks began going into the desert to contemplate God, and the monastic movement began. Men such as Athanasius, Basil, Gregory, Ambrose, Chrysostom, Jerome, and Augustine hammered out a theological framework that would last for centuries. The Bishop of Rome became, by default, the Western Pope. A missionary named Patrick went to Ireland.

But while all this was happening, the Eastern Church was drifting away. Culture, language, and theology all conspired to divide East and West, Rome and Constantinople. When the split finally came on June 16, 1054, it was because of a long history of differences. But on that day Cardinal Humbert, representing the Roman Catholic Pope Leo IX (who had just died, but no one in the East knew it yet), walked into the Cathedral of Saint Sophia and placed upon the altar a sentence of excommunication declared upon the ruler of the Eastern Orthodox Church, the "heretic" Michael Cerularius, and anyone who followed him. The split was final and stands to this day. Now the universal Church consisted of two churches, known as Roman Catholic and Eastern Orthodox, both claiming to be the "One Body of Christ on Earth." And that was only the beginning.

The Protestant Reformation

The fall of Rome around 400 CE did not hinder the growth of Christianity. Perhaps Edward Gibbon, in his book, *Decline and Fall of the Roman Empire*, written in 1788, said it best:

> While that great empire [Rome] was invaded by open violence and undermined by slow decay, a pure and humble religion gently insinuated itself into the minds of men, grew up in silence and obscurity, derived new vigor from opposition, and finally erected the triumphant banner of the cross on the ruin of the capitol.

With Saxons, Vikings, Visigoths, and Franks nibbling away at the borders, and Attila the Hun, the "Scourge of God," eyeing Rome itself, the empire fell apart. But the Church, for all its faults and power struggles, served as the glue to hold together at least a semblance of order. The Church ran the schools. The Church provided a social framework of common thought to bring some sense to the collapse of what was considered to be God's handiwork. Faulty, fallible, and flawed though it was, the Church was still there when the early Middle Age, a period known as the Dark Ages, finally came to a close.

By the end of the fifteenth century, reform movements were abroad. Christopher Columbus had "sailed the ocean blue" and discovered new worlds. The feudal system was coming to an end. Johannes Gutenberg's printing press was spewing forth ideas brought to the West by Byzantine scholars fleeing the Muslim invasion of Constantinople. The wisdom of ancient Greece had been rediscovered. People were chafing at the bit, and the Church really needed reforming. Sometimes there were two popes, even three, claiming power. Intrigue ran amuck at the highest levels of Church hierarchy. Souls were up for sale to the highest bidder. Johann Tetzel would ride into town to raise money for a new cathedral singing, "As soon as a coin in the coffer rings, a soul from Purgatory springs!"

The religious, intellectual forest was dry and ready to burn. Only a spark was needed.

That spark fell into the dry tinder on October 31, 1517. An obscure German Monk named Martin Luther had been struggling with the idea of "justification by faith." How does justification take place? Luther had been taught the phrase meant God brings "justice" to the sinner by punishing him. But Luther came to the conclusion that the "righteousness" he sought so strongly was free, a gift given not to those who had faith enough to receive it, but to all those to whom God wishes to bestow it.

When Luther first understood this he was moved to write:

> I felt that I had been born anew and that the gates of heaven had been opened. The whole of scripture gained a new meaning. And from that point on the phrase "the justice of God" no longer filled me with hatred, but rather became unspeakably sweet by virtue of a great love.

Compiling a list of ninety-five theses—ideas about which he wanted to debate the established Church—he nailed them to the door of the castle church in Wittenberg, Germany. Little did he understand what commotion he would cause. The world has never recovered. Challenge followed challenge, debate followed debate. The level of both heat and light elevated as it caught the public's attention.

Things came to a head at a church meeting, in this case a Diet (meaning "assembly") of the Empire, held in the town of Worms in 1521. Luther wasn't the only item on the menu. There was plenty of political maneuvering going on. But at least the world would forever be treated to the wonderful thought that Protestantism began with a "Diet of Worms." There, when confronted and told he was challenging the entire established order of the universe and all conceivable suburbs, Luther stood alone and cried, "My conscience is a prisoner of God's Word. I cannot and will not recant, for to disobey one's conscience is neither just nor safe. Here I stand. God help me. Amen."

He left the assembly, never to return. His followers formed their own church. Others, in turn, left them to start their own. Disagreements caused still others to do the same. Anabaptists and Mennonites broke fellowship with Lutherans and Calvinists, and so on. They weren't called "Protesters" for nothing.

It is intriguing to study Luther's Ninety-five Theses because, considering the amount of reform the Catholic Church has undergone in the last few hundred years, it is conceivable that if Martin Luther were alive today, he would still be Catholic.

The Church Today

Christians still say, without crossing their fingers behind their backs, that there is "One, Holy and Apostolic Church." But most know that there are at least three major divisions—Roman Catholic, Eastern Orthodox, and Protestant—and many more subdivisions. Within each of those subdivisions there are further divisions of conservative and liberal. Nevertheless, at least the theological spirit is willing when Christians of all brand names, types, and descriptions stand together in ecumenical gatherings to sing the great hymn, "Onward Christian Soldiers":

> We are not divided,
> All one body, we,
> One in hope and doctrine,
> One in charity.

It is easy to criticize the Church, given its checkered history. It is a very flawed institution. It has sponsored pogroms and crusades, wars and inquisitions. It has persecuted Jews, enslaved blacks, exterminated Indians, burned "witches," and held back women.

However, it has also funded relief institutions, educated millions of people, built hospitals, and undergirded countries otherwise destined for extinction. The Church has inspired some of the world's greatest art and music while saving countless lives.

It has provoked frustration and inspired brilliance. It has disappointed and miserably failed while at the same time fulfilling and gloriously succeeding. It is bane to some and blessing to others. If the Church is the "instrument" of God, it has shown God to be sometimes totally tone deaf. But at other times it has made wonderful music.

One cannot expect people who have been severely hurt by the Church to view it with compassion. But right or wrong, there have been those who served it with pure convictions. Like all human institutions it is flawed, sometimes terribly so. But in every generation there are those prophets who try to bring it back to its Great Commission.

Sources:

Barzun, Jacques. *From Dawn to Decadence: 1500 Years to the Present.* New York: HarperCollins, 2000.

Ellwood, Robert S., and Barbara A. McGraw. *Many Peoples, Many Faiths.* 6th ed. Upper Saddle River, NJ: Prentice Hall, 1999.

Gonzalez, Justo L. *The Story of Christianity.* 2 vols. New York: Harper & Row, 1985.

CHRISTMAS *see* Christianity, Calendar of

CHURCH OF CHRIST, SCIENTIST *see* Christian Science

CHURCH OF JESUS CHRIST OF LATTER-DAY SAINTS *see* Mormons/Church of Jesus Christ of Latter-day Saints

CHURCH OF THE NAZARENE

The Church of the Nazarene was organized on October 8, 1908, in Pilot Point, Texas. A union of holiness churches that had gradually pulled away from Methodism, Nazarenes were convinced their former denomination had not remained faithful to its Wesleyan-Arminian theological foundation (see Calvin, John, and Jacob Arminius).

In the words of their theological statement of faith:

Nazarenes believe that God calls Christians to a life of holy living that is marked by an act of God, cleaning the heart from original sin and filling the individual with love for God and humankind. This experience is marked by entire consecration of the believer to do God's will and is followed by a life of seeking to serve God through service to others.

Churches following holiness traditions sometimes respond slowly to social change. They take time to weigh progress, to see if it is in line with God's will. Although most mainstream Nazarene worshipers now embrace cultural changes and conveniences, it took a while for men to decide whether or not they should "adorn" themselves with jewelry such as wedding rings. One preacher, in 1967, finally gave in to social pressure and advised his congregation they could still be good Christians and watch television. He drew sustained applause when he added, "But not in my house!"

There are now some 1.4 million people enrolled as Nazarenes, and some twelve thousand churches around the world.

Sources:

Gonzalez, Justo L. *The Story of Christianity*. 2 vols. New York: Harper & Row, 1985.
"Who Are the Nazarenes?" *Church of the Nazarene*. http://www.nazarene.org/welcome/index.html.
September 14, 2003.

CIRCUMCISION

Although it is an ancient medical procedure dating back to primitive times and is practiced by Muslims, some Christians, and many nonreligious people, circumcision, called Brit Milah by the Jews, is specifically the sign of the Abrahamic covenant. Indeed, Abraham received his name as a direct result of obeying this commandment.

> "This is my covenant with you and your descendants after you, the covenant you are to keep: Every male among you shall be circumcised. You are to undergo circumcision, and it will be a sign of the covenant between me and you...." On that very day, Abraham took his son Ishmael and all those born in his household or bought with his money, every male in his household, and circumcised them, as God had told him. Abraham was ninety-nine years old when he was circumcised. (Genesis 17:9–11, 23–24)

One shudders to contemplate the picture of a ninety-nine-year-old man circumcising himself, but "it's in the book." Ever since, circumcision's influence has been so strong that, even today, Jews, many of whom do not regularly practice their religion, still obey this commandment. On the eighth day, Jewish boys have the foreskin of their penis surgically removed by the *mohel* (circumcisor) in the presence of the child's father and *sandek* (godfather) and the required Minyan (religious quorum). The child is usually named during the blessings recited at the completion of the operation.

The Bible treats a delicate subject (one that is rarely heard preached from the pulpit) with a rather shocking nonchalance at times. In the book of 1 Samuel, for instance, the future King David asks King Saul for his daughter's hand in marriage. Saul, jealous of David, grants the wish on one condition. David must offer, as a goodwill offering, "one hundred Philistine foreskins." Saul had an ulterior motive. He "thought to make David fall by the hands of the Philistines."

But Saul didn't take into account David's flair for the dramatic. He was presented not with one hundred foreskins, a gift presumably acquired only after deadly persuasion, but with two hundred.

This isn't the only instance in the Bible where this kind of thing goes on. Genesis 34 tells a similarly gruesome story. What is arguably the most difficult passage to understand in the entire Bible, Exodus 4:24–26, is about circumcision. Moses, the great Jewish liberator, has met God at the burning bush and agreed to go back to Egypt, stand before Pharaoh and say, "Let my people go!" But right in the middle of all this, after Moses has promised to do all God requires of him, three very strange and enigmatic verses are inserted into the well-known story.

At a lodging place on the way, the Lord met Moses and was about to kill him. But Zipporah, Moses' wife, "took a flint knife, cut off her son's foreskin and touched his feet with it. 'Surely you are a bridegroom of blood to me,' she said. So the Lord let Moses alone. At that time she said, 'A bridegroom of blood in regard of the circumcision.'"

And Moses, without any comment, continues on to Egypt and into the pages of history. Commentators have written, debated, editorialized, and moralized, but when all is said and done one gets the feeling everyone would have been a lot happier if this passage had simply been left out of the Bible. Jonathan Kirsch, in his book *The Harlot by the Side of the Road*, presents an excellent, no-holds-barred summary of the many opinions that have been offered attempting to explain this passage, and he arrives at a compelling conclusion:

> Like some grotesque insect preserved in biblical amber, the spare three lines of text in Exodus that describe God's night attack on Moses—and the blood ritual that Zipporah uses to defend her husband and son—suggest that the faith of the ancient Israelites was far stranger and richer than the biblical authors are willing to let on.

Even modern translations of the New Testament try to edit out mention of the "c" word, presumably for Sunday-morning consumption. When you hear a preacher proclaiming that "Jew and Gentile are one," chances are the original text says "circumcised and uncircumcised."

Sources:
Bridger, David, ed. *The New Jewish Encyclopedia*. New York: Behrman House, 1962.
Kirsch, Jonathan. *The Harlot by the Side of the Road*. New York: Ballantine Books, 1997.

COLUMBUS, CHRISTOPHER

Many have speculated about the background and religion of the "discoverer" of the New World. His childhood is shrouded in mystery and his motives full of language about "the glory of God." At times he seemed to be a Christian mystic. Later generations would laud him as God's instrument through which the "new" world was "opened" for Christianity. Still later ones would vilify him as bloodthirsty, greedy, and a poor navigator who failed to recognize where he'd landed.

The New Jewish Encyclopedia has this to say about him:

Investigations cast doubt as to his presumed Italian birth, and much evidence was forwarded to strengthen the belief that his parents were Marranos (secret Jews) who fled from Spain to Italy. It is known that his expedition was helped by Jewish scientists, financiers, and statesmen. Some historians believe that Queen Isabella did not actually pawn her jewels to finance the expedition, and that most of the funds came from the confiscated wealth of Spanish Jews, especially that of Luis de Santangel. A professing Jew, Abraham Zacuto, provided Columbus with scientific maps for the expedition, and a number of Marranos were members of his crew. It is recorded that the secret Jew, Luis de Torres, Columbus's interpreter, was the first white man who set foot on the soil of San Salvador, the first island of the New World to be discovered.

Spain and Italy have long argued and fought over who gets to claim Columbus and his discoveries. Perhaps history will someday prove that Israel, for better or for worse, holds the honor.

Engraving of Christopher Columbus near the time of his famous "discovery" of the Americas voyage. *Fortean Picture Library.*

Whatever his biological ancestry, however, and whether or not his exploration was funded by Christians or Jews, there is no question that his discoveries soon denigrated into a battleground between competing Christian sects, secular authorities, and political parties. Christian friars marched beside Conquistadors to "Christianize" the Native Americans after their inevitable defeat. Protestants in New England sought to bring about the "New Jerusalem" by building a "city set on a hill" for all to see, while excluding the "Popish" folks whose church had established footholds to the south and west. It was, and still is, a confusing time for those whose political and national ties differ from their religious convictions. The United States Constitution eventually separated church and state by decree, but the laws of other countries did not. Sometimes political powers held sway only because the power of the church allowed them to. Other times saw different problems.

All this points to the fact that Columbus sailed under competing, conflicting motives that prefigured what was to come. Official documents claim spiritual aims. He wanted to convert the "heathen" and spread the gospel. But, as always, political gain was everything. Riches, not only for the state but also for the explorer, figured heavily into the mix.

Confessional inside the Cathedral of St. Pol-de-Leon, Brittany, France. *Fortean Picture Library.*

Sources:
Bridger, David, ed. *The New Jewish Encyclopedia.* New York: Behrman House, 1962.

COMMUNION *see* **Eucharist**

CONFESSION

A Christian "confession" carries with it the meaning of agreeing to a particular statement of faith. For example, the minister sometimes invites a congregation to read the Apostles' Creed (see Gnosticism) by saying, "Let us together make our confession of faith."

But perhaps the most familiar meaning of the word refers to the Catholic tradition of confessing *ad auriculam,* "into the ear of" a priest. The practice began in the medieval church. The Fourth Lateran Council of 1215 declared confession had to be at least an annual event if the confessor wanted to receive the host during Eucharist. In the sixteenth century, in order to provide privacy and a more substantial ritual, confessional stalls began to be used.

It has always been the law of the land that anything said to a priest was absolutely confidential. The priest took a holy vow that he was bound not to reveal anything told him in the confessional. But recently, as a result of child-abuse scandals in the Catholic church, state legislatures are beginning to question the practice of excusing priests and ministers from lists of people, such as doctors and social workers, who are required to report instances of child abuse. In May 2002 the Commonwealth of Massachusetts, for example, eliminated from the list of exceptions ministers of denominations who did not use confessionals by tradition.

Terrorist threats raised more questions. If a terrorist, seeking to save his soul after committing murder, confesses to a priest bound by the power of the confessional, is the priest obligated to remain silent?

It remains to be seen how long the Church will be able to hold out from social pressure requiring, for the public good, at least some confidentiality to be discarded.

Sources:
"Clergy Gather to Learn New Law." *United Church News,* Framingham, MA: Massachusetts Conference, United Church of Christ, June 2002.
Douglas, J. D., ed. *The New International Dictionary of the Christian Church.* Grand Rapids, MI: Zondervan Publishing, 1974.

CONFUCIAN TEXTS

(See also Confucianism/Daoism)

Confucius wrote or edited a series of five works that formed the foundation of Confucianism. In the third century BCE they became formally known as the Wu Jing, or Five Classics. They consist of the Book of History, the Book of Poems, the Book of Change (Yi Jing or I Ching), the Spring and Autumn Annals, and the Book of Rites. Besides these texts, which form the basis for Confucian scholarship, a collection of his sayings was gathered shortly after his death. Called the Analects, they form the basis for the familiar Confucian stereotype:

Confucius says …

Is it not a pleasure to learn and to repeat or practice from time to time what has been learned? Is it not delightful to have friends come from afar? Is one not a superior man if he does not feel hurt even though he is not recognized?

When a man's father is alive, look at the bent of his will. When his father is dead, look at the bent of his conduct. If for three years he does not change from the way of his father, he may be called filial.

A ruler who governs his state by virtue is like the north polar star, which remains in place while all the other stars revolve around it.

A superior man in dealing with the world is not for anything or against anything. He follows righteousness as the standard.

Three other works, written shortly after Confucius' time, demonstrate his influence. The Book of Great Learning, the Book of Mean (the "Middle Way"), and the Book of Mencius have been elevated by many scholars to the rank of Confucian scripture. Mencius is second only to Confucius in the Confucian tradition, and he was a major commentator on the master.

Mencius said:

For a man to give full realization to his heart is for him to understand his own nature, and a man who knows his own nature will know Heaven.

Confucianism went through a period of revival with the spread of Buddhism in China. The Yi Jing became widely read, but it was interpreted in a metaphysical fashion quite different from the method of classical Confucianism. Chou Tun-I (1017–1073 CE) is considered by many to be the great interpreter of this movement. His *Explanation of the Diagram of the Great Ultimate* marked the beginning of what is now called Neo-Confucianism. Together with his contemporary Chang Tsai's *The Western Inscription*, this reinterpretation transferred Confucian thought to a spiritual plane that protected and nourished people during the twentieth-century communist onslaught that destroyed the political, social, and economic base of traditional Confucianism.

Sources:

Fisher, Mary Pat and Lee W. Bailey. *An Anthology of Living Religions*. Upper Saddle River, NJ: Prentice Hall, 2000.

Kung, Hans and Julia Ching. *Christianity and Chinese Religions*. New York: Doubleday, 1989.

A woman consulting the Yi Jing while performing divination with the aid of Chinese fortune sticks. *Fortean Picture Library.*

CONFUCIANISM/DAOISM

(See also Confucian Texts; Lao Tzu; Tao Te Ching)

From 403 to 221 BCE China was torn apart by a period of war and political struggle for power. All of society was affected. Inevitably, the innocent suffered the most. Even then, Eastern philosophical spirituality revolved around the balance of yin and yang, the two contrasting but all-encompassing principles of the Dao. People began to wonder what had gone wrong, what they had done to destroy the harmony of daily existence.

The times might be compared to the destructive, intergenerational conflicts experienced during the 1960s in America. Race and politics, even gender, were examined anew, traditional values were questioned, and liberal and conservative traditions developed.

The conservative response centered on the teachings of K'ung Ch'iu, or Confucius. His philosophy was not to change existing society, but to do it better. Be a better son, a better farmer, a better politician. He taught that people must become what, in fact, they really were, even though their actions often failed to demonstrate it.

His writings revolved around the concept of *ren* (virtue) and *li* (the potential to rise above the animal). He taught that if you go through the motions enough, whether you feel like it or not, you will acquire the habit of doing what is right.

Confucius personified the yang side of Chinese reality. He was rational, thoughtful, left-brained, and part of the establishment. His object was to reform existing institutions.

Laozi, or Lao Tzu (the name simply means "the old man"), is considered to be the architect of Daoism (or Taoism). He was a contemporary of Confucius, and some traditions claim they met. Confucius was said to have remarked, "Of birds, I know they have wings to fly with, of fish, that they have fins to swim with, of wild beasts, that they have feet to run with. For feet, there are traps, for fins, nets, for wings, arrows. But who knows how dragons surmount wind and cloud into heaven? This day I have seen Laozi and he is a dragon."

Lao Tzu was yin to Confucius's yang, the liberal to his conservative, the hippie to his establishment. He was romantic, intuitive, feelings-oriented, and right-brained. His thinking was that reason and society were not answers to the problem but had become the problem itself.

Tradition even casts him as the first "drop out." We are told that at the ripe old age of eighty (some legends say he was 160), he became disgusted with the hypocrisy and striving of the world. Mounting his water buffalo, he rode west to Tibet, pausing at the border only long enough to write the Tao Te Ching before disappearing into history.

In truth, most Chinese were so steeped in balance that they prudently adopted both approaches to their social problems. Confucianism spoke to their social and family needs. Siddhartha's Buddhism answered questions about life and death, and Lao Tzu's Daoism spoke to their inner nature. It came to be said that Chinese officials were Buddhist by religion, Confucian at work, and Daoist in retirement. (Perhaps the equivalent can be seen in a man who goes to church, synagogue, or mosque on the weekend, wears a suit to a weekday business meeting, and rides off on a Harley during his vacation.)

But in essence, what for Confucius was the sum total of the ideal society—order and material gain, structure and formal learning—was, for Lao Tzu, the epitome of death and decay.

Sources:

Ellwood, Robert S., and Barbara A. McGraw. *Many Peoples, Many Faiths.* 6th ed. Upper Saddle River, NJ: Prentice Hall, 1999.

Lao Tzu. *Tao Te Ching.* Trans. D. C. Lau. London: Penguin, 1963.

Wing-tsit Chan, trans. and comp. *A Sourcebook in Chinese Philosophy.* Princeton, NJ: Princeton University Press, 1963.

CONFUCIUS

Confucius (551–479 BCE) was born, lived, and died in the Chinese province of Lu. He was raised by his mother after his father died when Confucius was a young child. A member of the *ru* class, he learned the "six arts" of ceremony, music (in which he is said to have excelled), archery, charioteering, calligraphy, and arithmetic.

Early nineteenth-century French aquatint of Confucius, Chinese philosopher, teacher, and political theorist, whose ideas became known as Confucianism. *The Art Archive/The Art Archive.*

By the time he was thirty-two he was a teacher. This was about the time he was said to have visited with Lao Tzu (see Confucianism/ Daoism).

At the age of fifty-one he became active in political life. But after only four years he was forced to leave his position of influence. For about twelve years he wandered, hoping to be called back into active politics where he could use his influence, believing he had the answer for China's volatile social climate.

Although he never again filled an important political post, his writings exerted a profound influence on Chinese history. On the last day of his life Confucius is reported to have said, "The great mountain must collapse, the mighty beam must break and the wise man wither like a plant.... No wise ruler arises, and no one in the Empire wishes to make me his teacher. The hour of my death has come."

He died at the age of seventy-three, never knowing he would one day be acknowledged as one of the greatest philosophers the world has ever known. Twenty-five hundred years later, people would apply his wisdom to everyday problems by saying, "Confucius said...."

But all this took time. It wasn't until 56 CE that Chinese children began to offer sacrifices to him, and in 1908 he was finally granted a form of divinity when he was declared "equal with heaven and earth."

Meanwhile, Confucian scholars would pride themselves on studying his writings, showing their dedication by growing two-inch-long fingernails. After all, anyone with two-inch fingernails can't be doing any manual labor, so he must be studying. In this society, at least, the pen really was thought to be mightier than the sword.

Sources:

Ellwood, Robert S., and Barbara A. McGraw. *Many Peoples, Many Faiths.* 6th ed. Upper Saddle River, NJ: Prentice Hall, 1999.

Olsommer, Ronald Henry. *Confucius' Life.* http://www.olsommer.com/tsoh/textonly/conlife-t.html. September 29, 2003.

CONGREGATIONALISM

Congregationalism is a form of church government as well as a denominational tradition. It refers to the fact that the power of the denomination lies in individual congregations rather than in a hierarchy of bishops or priests. Every congregation owns its own property, elects its own minister, and decides its own policies. It is democracy in its purest form, with each church member having one vote. Not even the minister can veto or act against the will of the majority of the congregation.

The concept was brought to the shores of New England by the first European settlers. In 1648, the Pilgrims of Plymouth Plantation and the Puritans of the Massachusetts Bay Colony agreed on certain principles of church governance in a statement called the Cambridge Platform. In those days, church membership was a prerequisite for voting in secular elections (see Half-way Covenant). Although Puritan Roger Williams (1600–1683), founder of the State of Rhode Island, felt the church had too much say over the politics of the community, it was a long time before the white meeting house on the town common no longer served as the place of town meeting, with its minister as town moderator.

The first Congregationalists were staunch Calvinists. They believed that God, through his predestined will, had brought them to this "New Jerusalem" to subdue the Indians, kill off the wolves, and cut down the forests so honest farmers could build stone walls and harvest their crops. Remembered for their "scarlet letters" and community stocks, they were a no-nonsense people who also built Harvard University and sent forth their worshipers on only a minute's notice to fight the British.

Over the years, as was the case for most Protestant churches, they split and formed offshoot denominations. But their democratic form of church government led to some uniquely difficult historical dilemmas.

The Trinitarian/Unitarian split following the Revolutionary War offers a good illustration. A spirit of independence permeated New England. A new liberal social consciousness was abroad. Part of this consciousness, popular with shopkeepers and schoolteachers alike, was what was called "natural religion" or "essential Christianity." "Progress" was the new watchword, and part of progress meant freedom from church dogma as well as freedom from taxation without representation.

Many of the founding fathers, Thomas Jefferson being only one example, were not Christians so much as they were Deists. They believed in God but didn't accept the Trinitarian definition of God as Father, Son, and Holy Spirit interceding in human lives. They perceived God in Unitarian terms, with one aspect, not three, and as something like the "Great Watchmaker" (see God) who had wound up the universe and now expected it to run on its own.

Picture, now, a typical church scenario: It's time to call a new minister. The church in question has an even one hundred members, all of whom have one vote. After much discussion and argument, the church finally decides, by a vote of forty-nine to fifty-one, to call a preacher who was educated at conservative, Trinitarian Yale rather than liberal, Unitarian-leaning Harvard.

The people have voted, but there are still forty-nine closet Unitarians who are members of the church. And being stubborn Yankees, they will not quietly accept the decision of the majority. They might decide to build another church across the street and call the minister they voted for. Or they might decide to stay and fight a guerrilla war from within the ranks.

In an age of denominational organization, it was only a matter of time before churches started banding together in a formal way. The voluntary denomination known as Congregationalists, mostly in New England, began to morph and jockey for position in various ways. Some churches voted to stay independent of any denominational ties. Others joined together according to theological similarities. Groups such as the Conservative Christian Congregational Churches and the Congregational Christian Churches were formed. In 1957 the Congregational Christian Churches, a large group of predominantly liberal congregations especially concerned with what they considered key issues of social justice, voted to make an ecumenical attempt to undo the divisive aspect of the Protestant Reformation. Merging with the Evangelical and Reformed Church, another like-minded Protestant tradition, they formed the United Church of Christ (see United Church of Christ).

But again church polity raised some barriers. Theological talks of pulpit unity with a Lutheran denomination almost broke down when the structured Lutheran representatives asked, "All your churches are independent of one another. Who do we talk to?"

It is inevitable, given today's social pressure on growth and "bottom line" efficiency, that big churches tend to get bigger while small churches tend to struggle on, merge with other congregations, or simply grow old and die. Traditional Congregationalism is difficult to maintain. Although each church is independent, those who formalize ties necessarily have a central office or headquarters for mutual aid. The custom of paying, to denominational headquarters, what amounts to a "head tax" on each individual member is difficult for small churches to continue when they are desperately trying to maintain historic, old buildings according to modern building codes. The plaintive cry is heard often from the historic New England common, "Do we fix the steeple, build an access ramp, or give to the denomination's mission fund?"

Sources:
Hudson, Winthrop S. *Religion in America*. New York: Charles Scribner, 1965.
United Church of Christ. http://www.ucc.org/. September 14, 2003.

CONSUBSTANTIATION *see* Eucharist

CONTEMPLATION *see* Prayer/Meditation/Contemplation

COPTIC CHURCH

(See also Alexandria)

"Copt" comes from the Greek word *Aigyptos*. This, in turn, comes from *Hikaptah*, one of the names for Memphis, the first capital of ancient Egypt.

The Coptic Church traces its roots to Saint Mark, who is said to have brought Christianity to Egypt twelve years after Jesus' ascension. The Copts believe they are the fulfillment of the prophecy of Isaiah 19:19: "In that day there will be an altar to the Lord in the midst of the land of Egypt, and a pillar to the Lord at its border."

When Alexandria became a major presence in early Christianity, the Coptic Church was recognized as a center for learning. Much of currently accepted theology was hammered out there in the writings of major, foundation-building church theologians such as Origen and Augustine, the favorite of the Protestant Reformers.

Copts pride themselves as the ones who hosted the Holy Family when they were forced to flee Palestine after the birth of Jesus (see Christ/Jesus of Nazareth). The Nicene Creed, a statement of faith used in many churches to this day, was created under its tutelage. The Catechetical School of Alexandria, probably the oldest such school in the world, was founded there in 190 CE. Monasticism was born in Egypt when the Desert Fathers retreated there to pray, meditate, and contemplate. Saint Anthony, the world's first Christian monk, was a Coptic priest from Upper Egypt.

The prophet Muhammad was said to have had such respect for the Coptic Church that he warned his warriors to tread lightly in Egypt, "for they are your protégés and kith and kin." Because of this, Muslim scholars saved much of what otherwise might have been lost when European Christianity quite literally fanned the flames that led to the burning of the Alexandrian library.

Ever since the Council of Chalcedon in 451 CE, the Copts have been independent of European Christianity. At that council, as at other ecumenical councils, Church bishops met to settle matters of doctrine and practice—in this case, to address the heretical notion that Christ had only one nature rather than two. Here there is great disagreement. Church historians tend to argue, as did the fifth-century council, that Copts are monophysites—that is, believing that Christ had only one (divine) nature rather than, as the council determined, two natures, divine and human.

The Coptic Church insists they were misunderstood at that council. Their position is that Christ had two perfect natures, but that those natures were joined in one called "the nature of the incarnate word." They believe their expulsion was due to European bigotry; they claim the Europeans wanted to isolate and finally abolish the Egyptians, who had their own Pope and who were insisting church and state should be separate.

Although centered in Egypt, the Coptic Church has congregations scattered around the world. Some nine million Copts live in Egypt, almost one-fifth of the population. Although they practice many of the same sacraments and feast days of Roman Catholicism, they no doubt hold the record for serious fasting. Out of 365 days in the year, Copts fast for 210 of them, allowing no food or drink to be consumed between sunrise and sunset.

Sources:

Encyclopedia Coptica: The Christian Coptic Orthodox Church of Egypt. http://www.coptic.net/. September 14, 2003.

Gonzalez, Justo L. *The Story of Christianity.* 2 vols. New York: Harper & Row, 1985.

COSMOGONY

A religion's cosmogony is its model of the creation of the universe. Jewish, Christian, and Islamic cosmogony begins with a six-day period of activity some six to ten thousand years ago. Some believe this to be a symbolic myth, others a historical fact.

Hindu and Buddhist cosmogony, along with many indigenous traditions, involve a cyclical understanding of the concept of time. There is no beginning or end. The wheel of samsara, the unending wheel of life (see Hinduism), turns forever.

Scientific theories now postulate a Big Bang, a beginning point when both time and space began.

A religion's cosmogony is expressed in Creation myths, stories that explain how things began. Jewish stories of God's six-day work week are contrasted with Hindu concepts of Vishnu sleeping on the cosmic ocean and dreaming a world into existence.

But it is a mistake to choose a religion based on its cosmogony. Within each tradition there are those believers who accept the latest scientific evidence while maintaining their traditional mythology. Mythological cosmogonies were not meant simply to explain how the universe was created. They almost always have a spiritual, moral, or ethical point to make as well.

Sources:
Ludwig, Theodore M. *The Sacred Paths: Understanding the Religions of the World.* 2nd ed. Upper Saddle River, NJ: Prentice Hall, 1996.

COUNCILS see Vatican Councils

COVENANT

"Covenant" means "contract" or "promise."

In Judeo-Christian tradition, a covenant usually takes the form of God agreeing to do something provided the people play by the rules. The Hebrew patriarchs of the Old Testament, just like the inhabitants of Canaan with whom they lived, had pragmatic theologies. To them, "God" was not an abstract philosophical idea. Their approach was simple: their religions had to work, or they shopped elsewhere.

By way of illustration, Yahweh of the Hebrews was the warrior God who led them out of captivity by conquering the Egyptians. As long as they needed his help defeating the Canaanites they agreed to put him first, to "have no other gods before [him]." But when they settled in the Promised Land and needed fertile ground and good crops, they had no qualms about worshiping Baal and Astarte, the agricultural specialists.

With the advent of Christianity, theologians needed to explain why the God of the New Testament was so different from the God of the Old Testament, even though he was supposedly the same God, "who changest not." Soon after the Protestant Reformation, "covenant theology" was employed to formulate a systematic way to describe history as a series of developing, evolving covenants between God and the human race. The sixteenth-century reformers recognized two great covenants. The Old Covenant (Testament) is called the Covenant of Works. The New Covenant (Testament) has been named the Covenant of Grace. Under the first covenant, the provisions called for obeying the law to earn favor with God. Sabbath was celebrated on the seventh day, a well-earned rest after the labors of the long week of labor, following the commands of the law. But under the new covenant, God's grace comes first, an undeserved gift. Hence, worship was done on the first day of the week, after which the rest of the week was spent laboring to say "thank you" to God for the gift of grace already given, unearned but gratefully accepted. In this view, God's eternal covenant with Jesus Christ is fulfilled before the creation of the world, while all of human history is simply playing out the drama to its predestined conclusion.

But since the Reformation, some theologians have further refined the system by identifying in scripture a progressive, cumulative series of promises. Each was given when the human race was ready for it. Numerous covenants can be found in the Bible; below are several of the most significant.

The Covenant with Adam, part 1 (Genesis 2:17): The terms were simple. God instructed Adam and Eve not to eat a certain fruit, or they would die. (Adam ate the fruit, and "in Adam's fall, we sinned all," as the saying goes.)

The Covenant with Adam, part 2 (Genesis 3:15): Children of Adam and Eve were going to be constantly "at enmity" with Satan. (In many religious traditions, such enmity is continually emphasized.)

The Covenant with Noah (Genesis 9:1–17): This promise came with the sign of the rainbow. God said it was a reminder that "I will never again destroy the earth with a flood. Be fruitful and multiply." (God didn't destroy Earth again, and humans were fruitful and multiplied.)

The Covenant with Abraham (Genesis 12:1–3): God said to Abraham, the father of three world religions, "Leave here and go to Canaan. I will bless your descendants and curse your enemies." (Abraham kept his part of the bargain. Some would argue that both descendants and enemies received both blessing and curses.)

The Covenant with Moses (Exodus 19:5): "Obey the Commandments and you will be a 'holy people.' (The Israelites fudged on this one from time to time but are still known as "God's chosen people.")

The Palestinian Covenant (Deuteronomy 30:3): The covenant is here quoted exactly because it is causing tremendous political, personal, and national problems in our day.

> When all these blessings and curses I have set before you come upon you and you take them to heart wherever the Lord your God disperses you among the nations, and when you return to the Lord your God and obey him with all your heart and with all your soul according to everything I command you this day, then the Lord your God will restore your fortunes and have compassion on you and gather you again from all the nations where he has scattered you.

(This one is rather uncanny. Because many Jews believe it has come to pass exactly as promised over the last two thousand years, it provides justification for them to claim Israel as the fulfillment of God's promise. It also gives American conservative Christians and Jews justification for a government policy endorsing Israel over the Palestinians and converts a political land battle into a holy war. Meanwhile, the Palestinians, who live there too, wonder why they should be bound by the promise of someone else's God.

The Covenant with David (2 Samuel 7:12–16): God tells David, "I will make your name great, like the names of the greatest men on earth. And I will provide a place for my people Israel and will plant them so that they can have a home of their own and no longer be disturbed." (Well, the first provision was certainly fulfilled, as David's songs are widely read. And, although it took a long time, Israel has certainly been "planted." But the part about not being disturbed? Well, the Palestinians claim some promises, too.)

The "New Covenant" (Jeremiah 31:31–37): God says, "I will make a new covenant with the house of Israel.... I will put my law in their minds and write it on their hearts," instead of on tablets of stone. (The Christian Church claims to be the recipient of this promise, calling itself "the new Israel.")

Sources:

Bucke, Emory Stevens et al, eds. *The Interpreter's Dictionary of the Bible.* 4 vols. New York: Abingdon Press, 1962.

Scofield Reference Bible. Grand Rapids, MI: Zondervan Publishing. 1971.

CREATIONISM

"Creationism" is a politically loaded word today. The famous Scopes Trial (sometimes known as the Scopes Monkey Trial; see Christianity) held in Dayton, Tennessee, in 1925 inspired the play *Inherit the Wind* and put the issue of science vs. religion square into the realm of politics. (An apocryphal story from this time tells of a fundamentalist who, when told about Darwin's "newfangled" theory, prayed fervently, "Lord, make it not true. And if it is true, don't let anybody find out about it!") But the verdict (the evolutionists lost) didn't settle the argument. In 1987, the U.S. Supreme Court was still trying to settle it. They ruled that creationism is religion, not science, thus declaring the phrase "scientific creationism" an oxymoron.

But laws don't always change people's opinions. When Charles Darwin published his famous theory of evolution he sent shock waves through the religious public, who interpreted his ideas to mean there was no longer any need for God. If Creation came about by way of natural processes, to the proverbial man on the street it meant that science had replaced God. Because public opinion usually deals with extremes, people were divided into "Bible-believing Christians" or "godless atheists." The science/religion duality debate is still very much alive.

Lost in the popular argument, however, are nagging details that concerned the Supreme Court.

1. Science vs. religion is not an "either/or" duality. It is a continuum. There are at least ten different gradations in Christian interpretation alone. Christians who write books holding to one opinion often spend as much time railing against other Christians as they do against so-called godless scientists. And in truth, many of those same scientists are openly Christian and find no problem being both scientific and religious.

2. Other religions have creation myths differing from Judeo-Christian concepts. If creationism is to be taught in public schools, whether or not it is called "creation science," which brand is going to dominate the textbooks?

3. Arguments about Creation almost always become arguments about evolution. But describing the beginning of the universe is the specialty of the physicist and mathematician, while evolution moves to the realm of the biologist. Only the fundamentalist theologian dares put both disciplines under one roof. So which group of scientists does the theologian talk to when he wants to debate?

4. Although Christians seem to be at the forefront of the battle, the scriptures they invoke are really taken from the Hebrew Bible. So when we talk about "Christian" positions, we are talking about Jewish Creation stories, accepted by most Muslims as well. But Jews and Muslims, at least up to this point, haven't chosen to be as politically involved and "out front" in the creationism debate as conservative Christians.

To try to sort all this out, we begin with an overview of Christian positions concerning Creation. At the root of the argument is the fundamental religious problem of scriptural interpretation. If the Bible is the literal word of God (unless context makes it clear it is switching to metaphorical or poetical language), it has to be read the same way all the time. "Thou shalt not kill" means thou shalt not kill, ever. "Earth was created in six days" means Earth was created in six literal days, not six metaphorical periods of time. (Although, as explained below, some Christian positions draw the line here.) In other words, conservative Christians believe that people cannot superimpose ideas over the biblical text. One verse cannot be read literally and the next metaphorically unless the Bible clearly says to do so. If we adopt a "pick and choose" interpretation based on our own prejudice, we are guilty of editing God. There has to be clear biblical justification for doing so.

That biblical justification is at the very heart of the argument.

To understand why a literal interpretation demands a six-day Creation that occurred thousands, rather than billions, of years ago, we have to read some scripture and do some math.

> In the beginning, God created the heavens and the earth. Now the earth was [or became] without form and void ... and God said, "Let there be light, and there was light."

Six times, once at the beginning of each of those first six days, God repeats the command, "Let there be...." Each day, God speaks something new into being:

Day 1: light
Day 2: separation of waters above and below the firmament
Day 3: vegetation
Day 4: sun and moon
Day 5: fish and birds
Day 6: people

This is where the idea of a six-day Creation comes from. A simple, literal reading of Genesis provides that. But where in the Bible does it say this all happened only a few thousand years ago? To answer that question we have to turn to the "begats" in Genesis 5. This chapter outlines Adam's genealogy. "When Adam had lived 130 years, he begat Seth.... When Seth had lived 105 years, he begat Enosh...." And so on. By adding Adam's age at Seth's birth to Seth's age at Enosh's birth, and continuing on down the line through the chapter, we discover that 1,656 years passed between Adam's life and Noah's flood.

We then turn to Genesis 11 and find another list, beginning with Noah's son Shem, father of the "Shem-itic" or Semitic races. Continuing the same mathematical process, we discover Abraham was born 1,948 years after Adam.

But now we are in the realm of historical time. We know Abraham lived roughly 2,000 years before Jesus, and we live some 2,000 years after Jesus. We can now construct a rough timeline, rounded off to the nearest thousand years for the sake of simplicity:

Adam	Abraham	Jesus	Present
4000 BCE	2000 BCE	BCE/CE	2000 CE

This places Adam and Creation about six thousand years ago. James Ussher (1581–1656), an Irish archbishop, worked this timeline out in 1650. His date for Creation was 4004 BCE. Since then, even the most conservative theologians add a few thousand years. Adam and Eve, after all, could very well have spent some time in Eden, the "land that time forgot," before they ate the apple and started to beget children.

This timeline invites speculation both ways. A "line" begins somewhere, but it also ends somewhere. As soon as people began to look at history this way, they discovered that "six days" of Creation correspond to about six thousand years of history. In 2 Peter 3:8 it says, "With the Lord a day is like a thousand years...." This statement, coupled with the fact that Jesus is supposed to come back and reign for another "thousand-year day," called the millennium, caused great speculation at the turn of the last century. Does history so far point to the six-day "work week" of God, while the reign of Christ, the time of the "peaceable kingdom," corresponds to God's "rest day," thus placing us right near the end of time? This concern sparked a number of end-of-the-world theories as the twentieth century came to a close.

Given this framework, Christian creationism can be summarized in the following manner (we list here both the concept and the principal source defending it):

Christian Creationism Theories

Young-Earth creationism is the literal view of scripture outlined above, usually with the added point being made that Earth was created with an appearance of age. In other words, the first tree probably already had growth rings. Adam and Eve were already adults (presumably with belly buttons). Geological formations were either laid down as they now appear or are the result of Noah's flood. The flood caused fossil deposits and the extinction of many species that couldn't fit on the ark. It also explains the evidence of universal catastrophes that science often attributes to plate tectonics or meteor strikes. Young-Earth creationists coined the term "creation science" and are generally at the forefront of lawsuits and political test cases. They often stage debates with traditional scientists and are highly skilled and convincing when they do so. They have become experts in finding every difficulty not yet explained completely by current scientific hypothesis. (More information about young-Earth creationism can be found in *The Genesis Flood*, by John C. Whitcomb and Henry Madison Morris, and at the Institute for Creation Research in El Cajon, California.)

The following paragraphs explore several different theories that fall into the broader category of old-Earth creationism. These people accept the idea of an ancient earth, but various subgroups explain it in different ways. (Articles on such topics can often be found in periodicals such as *Perspectives on Science and Christian Faith* and *Christianity Today*.)

The gap theory is one subgroup of old-Earth creationism. An alternate translation of Genesis 1:1 reads: "The earth 'became' without form and void." In other words, Earth was originally created millions or even billions of years ago and was subsequently "blasted," presumably at the time of Satan's rebellion, "becoming" without "form and void." A gap exists between Creation and the re-Creation described in Genesis 1. It has been six thousand years since the time of Adam, not since the beginning of everything. So what do you do with the age of rocks and the disappearance of dinosaurs? Dump them into the gap! They all occurred before Adam and Eve. The obvious problem with this theory is that it opens more theological problems than it solves. Romans 5:12 declares that "death entered the world through sin." If there was no death before Adam's sin, what killed off the dinosaurs? (More information about the gap theory can be found in the *Scofield Reference Bible* and in Donald Grey Barnhouse's *The Invisible War*.)

The day-age theory suggests Creation days were long periods of time, not literal days. The order of events described in Genesis is similar to the order of geological periods defined by geologists. (For more information about the day-age theory, consult the Jehovah's Witnesses Watchtower Bible and Tract Society.)

Probably the most popular old-Earth creationism, intelligent design creationism seeks to integrate science and religion. In evolutionary or theistic creationism, God is the "why," evolution is the "how." A conservative approach would be to say that God created the species and evolution works only within species. In other words, God created dogs; evolution created great danes and dachshunds. A more liberal interpretation would say that science pretty much has it right. It has discovered the process by which God is still creating.

Materialistic creationism is a variation of liberal creationism. This approach goes one step further, insisting that God does not interfere at all with the process now that it has begun. It says nothing about the spiritual aspects of creationism because that does not fall under the scrutiny of science.

An even more liberal interpretation, really outside the category of religion, is sometimes called philosophical materialistic evolution. It says that evolution is a completely natural process, and that belief or unbelief in God has nothing to do with it."

Besides all these, there are a few Christian concepts that do not represent the mainstream of any Christian group.

The Flat Earth Society still exists, and they can be reached at the International Flat Earth Society, Box 2533, Lancaster, CA. With tongue firmly in cheek but a guileless countenance, adherents affirm that Earth is flat and is covered by the "firmament" described in Genesis 1:6–8. The waters of this firmament caused Noah's flood, and the Bible refers to such things as the "four corners of the earth" and "the circle (not globe) of the earth."

Geocentrism suggests that Earth is indeed a sphere, but, Galileo and the Hubble space telescope to the contrary, the sun is not the center of the solar system and Earth does not move. One proponent of this theory, Tom Willis (at http://www.csama.org/), was the one most responsible for the 2000 revision of the Kansas public school curriculum, which removed all references to evolution, Earth history, and science methodology. Geocentrists are a very small group, but they are obviously politically active.

Non-Christian Religious Creationism

Hinduism. According to Hinduism, this Earth is one of many that have existed in the past and will exist in the future. Metaphorically, Vishnu sleeps on the cosmic ocean, resting on a great serpent made up of the remains of the last universe before this one. The lotus of the universe grows from his navel. On the lotus sits Brahma, the Creator. Brahma opens his eyes and a world comes into being. One day in the life of Brahma is four billion, three hundred twenty million years, or one world cycle. When Brahma opens his eyes the dream is over until he closes them and dreams another cycle into existence.

Hindus believe all the gods are many faces of the one indescribable Brahman principle. Their myths are not intended to be read literally. Viewed metaphorically, the Hindu creation myth is a pretty good description of the cyclical nature of the universe.

American Indian Creationism. There is not one view that can be called *the* American Indian view. Tribes had too many stories to list them all. But a very rough synopsis emerges from these many myths.

People and animals are really one. Megafauna and giant people once existed together, but they shrunk in size after their "golden age" passed. Earth was ravaged by fire, sometimes water, and many tribes have stories relating how their ancestors came into this world through a hole in the ground, escaping from the world that was before. Others tell about receiving help from various animals.

Eastern Creationism (Buddhism, Confucianism, Daoism). The universe is an expression of the Dao, with no real beginning or end. This principle involves a conception of time difficult for Westerners to grasp. The Shinto of Japan is a little different. In this view the beginning is unknowable, but historic progress is important.

Nonreligious Origin Theories

Besides the religious myths already listed, there are many creation myths that fall more readily under the heading of "cultural." Greek, Canaanite, Persian, Babylonian, Norse, Olmec, and many more creation myths were all a central part of the religion of their cultures. But some of those cultures, in spite of having different religions, share the same creation stories. Other times, as in the case of Roman myths, a previous culture's cosmogony—in this case, that of Greece—was given a new twist to apply to current conditions, but otherwise left pretty much intact.

There are, of course, nonreligious views of how it all began, current scientific theory being the most common. As far as creationism is concerned, the main question remains the same: If "creationism" or "creation science" is going to be taught in public schools, which religion's views are going to be represented? The U.S. Supreme Court does not comprise—as the justices are sometimes portrayed—a bunch of "godless atheists." The judges are simply struggling with the views of conflicting religions, each of whom want their stories to be included.

Sources:

Barbour, Ian G. *When Science Meets Religion: Enemies, Strangers or Partners?* New York: Harper-Collins, 2000.

Barnhouse, Donald Grey. *The Invisible War.* Grand Rapids, MI: Zondervan Publishing, 1980.

Campbell, Joseph. *The Inner Reaches of Outer Space: Metaphor As Myth and As Religion.* New York: Harper & Row, 1986.

Deloria, Vine, Jr. *God Is Red.* Golden, CO: Fulcrum Publishing, 1994.

Gaskell, G. A. *Dictionary of All Scriptures and Myths.* New York: Gramercy Books, 1960.

Gould, Stephen Jay. *Rocks of Ages: Science & Religion in the Fullness of Life.* New York: Ballantine Publishing, 1999.

Isaac, Mark. "What Is Creationism?" *The Talk.Origins Archive.* http://www.talkorigins.org/faqs/wic.html. May 30, 2000.

Miller, Kenneth R. *Finding Darwin's God.* New York: HarperCollins, 2000.

"The Origin of the Universe, Earth, and Life." *National Academies Press.* http://www.nap.edu/html/creationism/origin.html. September 14, 2003.

Scofield Reference Bible. Grand Rapids, MI: Zondervan Publishing, 1971.

Teilhard de Chardin, Pierre. *The Appearance of Man.* New York: Harper & Row, 1956.

Whitcomb, John C., and Henry Madison Morris. *The Genesis Flood: The Biblical Record and Its Scientific Implications.* Nashua, NH: P&R Press, 1989.

CREED (CHRISTIAN)

The word "creed" comes from the Latin *credo*, which means, "I believe." It is a concise statement of faith or beliefs held by a religious institution, outlining and clarifying that which sets the institution apart from others.

The Apostles' Creed, the Nicene Creed, and the Westminster Confession are just three examples of the many creeds developed to define the Christian Church or an individual tradition within it.

There are many Christian traditions, Baptists and Quakers being only two, that do not promote the use of creeds. But the majority of Christian denominations, being so influenced by Greek, systematic thought, use creedal formulas, which new members are expected to affirm when being baptized or confirmed.

Sources:

Douglas, J. D., ed. *The New International Dictionary of the Christian Church.* Grand Rapids, MI: Zondervan Publishing, 1974.

CREED (KALIMA) *see* **Islam**

CRUCIFIX *see* **Catholicism**

Engraving entitled "Procession of the Crusaders Around the Walls of Jerusalem," from the 1892 edition of the *Illustrated History of England. Fortean Picture Library.*

CRUSADES

In the early years of the eleventh century the Christian Church had already split into two distinct bodies. The Eastern Church was fighting against the enemy they called "infidel Muslim Turks," who had conquered Jerusalem in 638 and were now knocking on the door of Constantinople, home of Byzantine (Eastern) Christianity.

With this as a background, Pope Urban II gave a speech on November 27, 1095, in Clermont, France. He called for the nobility of Western Europe to form armies, head east, assist the Byzantine brothers, and liberate the Holy City.

The response exceeded his wildest expectations. Waves of people decided to "go crusading." It must have seemed like a great deal. Serfs, trying in vain to support their families with the income from their few small acres, were promised indulgences, free food and board, and a chance to see the world.

Waves of inspired people headed east in the centuries to come. Fighting men, yes, but also women (many of whom apparently had visions of a steady income through prostitution) and children got caught up in religious fervor. Some armies, financed and led by wealthy, educated lords, did very well. Against all expectations they even captured Jerusalem on July 15, 1099, establishing Crusader states that would last for a few hundred years. Others, however, were a disgrace. Hopping off the boat in Constantinople, they killed anybody that didn't look like a European Christian, including turbaned Byzantine Christians, Jews, and innocent Arab merchants.

Although we can mark the beginning of the crusades, the end is subject to debate. The Spanish defeated the Muslim kingdom of Granada in 1492, recovering the peninsula the Muslims had seized back in 711. One of the reasons "Columbus sailed the ocean blue" was to find a new route to Jerusalem. Another was to acquire wealth to help the Spanish kings carry on the fight.

As late as 1798, Napoleon was "crusading" on Malta. Perhaps even 1945 might be considered the end of the Crusades. That was the year the Crusade tax, imposed on local dioceses during the eleventh century to help fund the first Crusade, was officially abolished in the Roman Catholic diocese of Pueblo, Colorado.

It is easy to criticize the Crusades. It is perhaps more difficult to explain why they came about. The Islamic jihad expanded rapidly following the death of the prophet Muhammad. In 635 Islam had conquered Damascus. Persia followed in 636, Jerusalem in 638, all of Egypt by 640. Spain, North Africa, the Middle East, India, Pakistan, and even parts of China quickly followed. Some historians have speculated that, if Charles Martel had not stemmed the tide at the battle of Tours in 732, all of Western Europe might have fallen to the Islamic offensive. There were undoubtedly some Crusaders who sincerely believed their violence toward the Muslims was justified by God's will; many Crusaders, however, were expressing hatred and bigotry toward an unfamiliar religion and culture, using religious doctrine as an excuse to seize territory and riches.

Sources:

Crawford, Paul. "Crusades." *The ORB: On-line Reference Book for Medieval Studies.* http://www.the-orb.net/encyclop/religion/crusades/crusade.html. September 14, 2003.

Ellwood, Robert S., and Barbara A. McGraw. *Many Peoples, Many Faiths.* 6th ed. Upper Saddle River, NJ: Prentice Hall, 1999.

CULT

"Cult" is a very subjective term. The dictionary says it is "a system of religious worship; devotion, homage to a person or thing." The classical definition is not negative at all. It merely describes a religious expression unique to a particular locale. Christianity was once considered a Jewish cult. But popular usage conjures up scenes of brainwashing, manipulation of the minds and lives of cult members, and a leader who is usually involved with some kind of sex scandal.

Dr. J. W. West, professor of psychiatry at the University of California, describes a cultic evolutionary process beginning with a charismatic leader who surrounds him/herself with a group of avid followers. As their adulation grows, the leader gradually begins to believe he/she is worthy of all the attention, slowly withdraws, and, enveloped by a veil of secrecy, rules from afar, often pushing the limits of power by demanding all sorts of activities that test the group's devotion.

Religion is powerful. It offers answers to basic questions about individual worth and human destiny. Group dynamics provide family security for people who are searching for love within a caring community. Add to this a strong parental figure who brings both structure and loving concern, and you have a powerful potion for troubled young people from dysfunctional families or at-risk communities.

In the mind of such a person the questions begin: What in the world has gone wrong with my life? Where do I look for peace and love? Who offers love and acceptance? What does the future hold? How do I find meaning in a troubled world?

And the answer comes: Follow the leader. If the leader is strong enough, has a new slant on a religious tradition or a new interpretation of scripture that makes sense, and can articulate that interpretation with enough charisma, a cult is born. It becomes a house of blocks. Each block of teaching may be only a little off, but the cumulative effect of line upon line and precept upon precept eventually brings the whole thing crashing down. To extend the building metaphor, a bridge only needs to be wrong by an inch or so every few feet to completely miss the opposite shore it was aiming for.

Cults that started out with the best of loving intentions have seen their members reduced to suicide in the jungles of Guyana or dying horribly in the flames of Waco.

Cults come and go and are far too numerous to list completely. One estimate is that there are 183,000 in Japan alone. But some have captured the public eye. Taken together, they offer a fairly thorough cross-section of cult life.

Jim Jones and the Jonestown Tragedy

In 1963 Jim Jones was pastor of the People's Temple Full Gospel Church, a Pentecostal church in Indianapolis. It was a rare (for that time) interracial congregation accustomed to faith healing, visions, toe-tapping music, and people being "slain in the spirit." Strangely, considering the church's holiness background, they even received occasional advice from a passing extraterrestrial or two.

So strong was the spiritual clout of Pastor Jones that many elderly worshipers signed over their earthly possessions to the church with the understanding that they would be taken care of as long as they lived. So it was not surprising when Jones moved the whole operation to California, partly to find greener pastures and partly to escape negative publicity that was beginning to appear in local papers.

When the government began investigating Jones's tax records and financial dealings, however, it wasn't long before the church moved to Guyana.

Rumors persist to this day that the cult had shady government ties and involvement with the Central Intelligence Agency (CIA). A former Jones cult member, Phil Kerns, insists that Jones was a Marxist who had numerous contacts with officials of both the Cuban and Soviet governments.

Documents now open to the public reveal CIA operations in Guyana. The famous government-sponsored LSD experiments were supposedly going on at the time. They were supposed to have been discontinued in 1973, but conspiracy theorists are quick to ask if Guyana was far enough away to continue the program in secrecy.

Whatever was going on behind the scenes, Jim Jones had a captive audience in his new home. Stories abound of child molestation, forced sex, and what resembled slave labor. Preaching services continued far into the night, and pity the poor person who fell asleep after working in the fields all day. Jones began to refer to his congregation as his "children." This is common in many Christian congregations who refer to their leader as "Father," sometimes even referring to him as "shepherd," which makes the congregants "sheep." When a leader is so elevated and people so demeaned, it is a sure indication of cultic evolution having reached dangerous levels.

During the first weeks of November 1978, Congressman Leo Ryan, with a small party, came to Guyana to investigate the cult. His whole party was assassinated on Jones's orders.

Apparently realizing that you can't kill a United States congressman, even on foreign soil, without being found out and hunted down, Jim Jones ordered the death of his entire community. On November 18, 1978, nine hundred people drank a mixture of Kool-aid and cyanide. A few, including Jones himself, were shot, either by their own hand or by someone else.

Why did the religious camp just happen to have that much cyanide on hand? What was Congressman Ryan going to report when he got home? Why didn't cult members rise up in unison and say, "Enough!" The facts are unclear. In 1980 the House Permanent Select Committee on Intelligence finished their investigation of the incident. They found no evidence of CIA involvement in what had become known as the Jonestown Massacre.

David Berg and the Children of God—"The Family"

David Berg began as a Christian missionary, but his ideas soon moved outside accepted Christian theology. Some have called him mad, others have said quirky, but he never seemed to inspire apathy. Even in death he has confused people, because there are those who swear he's still alive.

Working with dissatisfied California "hippies," Berg established a following and soon followed the classic cult pattern of withdrawal, eventually communicating with his followers only through the famous "Mo" letters, which can be still be found on the Internet at http://www.thefamily.org.

What attracted the public at large to "the Family," as his followers called themselves, was, as is often the case, sex. Berg's controversial encouragement of what he called "flirty fishing" caught the attention of newspapers and provided him his brief fling with fame. Taken from Jesus' words to his disciples, "Come with me and I will make you fishers of men" (Matthew 4:19), "flirty fishing" was a simple marketing technique given holy approval:

> What better way to show them the Love of God than to do your best to supply their desperately hungry needs for love, fellowship, companionship, mental and spiritual communication, and physical needs such as food, clothing, shelter, warmth, affection, a tender loving kiss, a soft embrace, the healing touch of your loving hands, the comforting feeling of your body next to theirs—and yes, even sex if need be! (Letter 79)

To a young person looking for spiritual direction in the sixties, this was something that couldn't be found at a Billy Graham rally! Needless to say, for the small group of people who formed the Family, it was a popular doctrine that encouraged converts, especially during a period when America was loosening up from what many described as sexual repression.

Some who knew Berg called him a warm, self-effacing, loving, and good-humored individual, with the genteel mannerisms of a kinder era. He constantly advised his followers to "hate the sin but love the sinner." There is no doubt that he began with a sincere effort to win people to Christ, and he probably thought that was what he was doing right up until his death. But because of his rather unique way of going about it, he will be remembered, at least by traditional Christianity, as the leader of a cult.

Heaven's Gate and Hale-Bopp

On March 26, 1997, many people throughout the world thrilled to the sight of the comet Hale-Bopp hanging overhead, its long tail lighting up the night sky. For some it brought delight and awe. For others, death.

A group known as Heaven's Gate, a cult made up of web-page designers and founded and led by a man named Marshall Applewhite, had decided they were being instructed to shed their "earthly containers" in order to be "beamed up" aboard a spacecraft following in the comet's wake. The cult members apparently died in orderly shifts, some helping others to drink a mixture of phenobarbital and vodka. A few, it was later discovered, had undergone voluntary castration in the months before the suicide.

The gate that gave the group its name is the portal through which people of Earth may enter the next sphere, where inhabitants of "the next level" dwell. The name comes from the Bible, Genesis 28:17. Jacob, grandson of Abraham, had fallen asleep at the place he subsequently called Beth-El ("House of God"). He dreamed he saw a ladder reaching up to heaven. Angels, messengers of God, climbed up and down to carry out their ministry. Perhaps inspired by the Ziggurats of the Babylonians, he raised a standing stone, the pillow on which he had slept, and exclaimed, "This is the gate of heaven!"

The thirty-nine members of the Heaven's Gate cult believed sincerely in the existence of this newest return, or opening, of the gate of heaven. They believed Jacob's experience was probably a contact with members of the higher sphere. Their days consisted of getting up in the morning; praying; dressing in black with severe GI haircuts; doing their work; forgoing sex, drugs, and alcohol; and staring at the heavens through a telescope, trying to spot the space ship that was coming for them.

According to the Heaven's Gate website (a mirror of which can be found at http://www.wave.net/upg/gate/, as the official site is now closed): "The window to Heaven will not open again until another civilization is planted and has reached sufficient maturity (according to the judgment of the next level)."

David Koresh and the Branch Davidians

The Branch Davidians trace their roots back to the Seventh-day Adventist Church, though they were expelled from the denomination as far back as 1930.

At that time Victor Houteff claimed to be a new prophet for the church, similar to the respected Ellen G. White. His claims were discounted and he was expelled from the church, but a number of people followed him. He started a new organization called the "Davidian Seventh-day Adventists" or "The Shepherd's Rod," both names referring back to King David. Houteff had found many prophetic passages in the psalms attributed to the famous "sweet singer" of Israel (see David, King). When he died in 1955, his widow took over his position, but her place was disputed by Ben Roden, who believed God had called him to lead the movement. It seems Mrs. Houteff had incorrectly determined that the world was going to end in 1959. When it didn't, her authority was undermined.

Roden left, taking a group of dissatisfied people with him, and formed the Branch Davidian Seventh-day Adventists. Like any good fundamentalist preacher, Roden studied his Bible, looking for clues illuminating the plan of God. Finding a lot of typology and symbolism in the Old Testament, he instituted many Hebrew feast days into the church's calendar, especially significant prophetical celebrations like Passover, Pentecost, the Day of Atonement, and the Feast of Tabernacles. He was convinced these carried special meaning, foreshadowing God's plan for the last days of human history.

When he died in 1978, his wife Lois became president of the church, introducing the idea that the Holy Spirit was the feminine aspect of the Trinity. It was during her leadership, in 1981, that a young man named Vernon Howell joined the group. Two years later he experienced his first vision from God. Although it took a few years and some political infighting, Howell emerged as president of the Branch Davidians, and in 1990 he changed his name to David Koresh.

Branch Davidians believe we are living in the last days of history and that they are God's true church. God has revealed what the future holds by "sealing up" the prophecies that describe the events of these days. In Daniel 12:9–13, the angel Gabriel says to Daniel: "… the words are closed up and sealed until the time of the end … none of the wicked will understand, but those who are wise will understand." David Koresh was considered to be one of "the wise." He believed he had found the key to the sealed prophecies by uncovering the truth of the mysterious "seven seals" in the second and third chapters of the book of Revelation. God's plan called for two revelations to humanity, foreshadowed by the two daily sacrifices kept in the Old Testament. The first, the "morning sacrifice," was fulfilled in Jesus Christ. The one who unlocks the key to understanding end-time prophecy will fulfill the second, the "evening sacrifice."

Enter David Koresh. His behavior was not that of a typical prophet. Sex and violence were not the hallmark of the "Prince of Peace." But this illustrates the need to understand the mind of a cultist. In the thinking of the Branch Davidians, Jesus was perfect. He was the unblemished sacrifice of the morning, before the day's sins manifested themselves. The evening sacrifice prefigured the Day of Atonement, the "sin offering." In Koresh, God was working through a sinful vessel who, like the prophet Jonah of old, was not chosen for his purity. Koresh was "spiritually blinded" just as Samson was before he died destroying the enemies of God. Koresh's sin merely proves God's choice.

Now, for a moment, enter the mind of a Branch Davidian during the days preceeding February 28, 1993. For months David Koresh has preached a brand new revelation, opening up mysterious scripture passages that no one has yet really explained. It all seems to make such perfect sense. Night after night he brilliantly ties together passages from all over the Bible, showing how Genesis brings out meanings in the Psalms, prophesied by Daniel and intimated in the parables of Jesus. He makes the whole Bible seem alive, uniformly woven of one cloth. And the news of the day seems to mirror exactly the truth you are hearing. The Bible in one hand, the *New York Times* in the other—history is unfolding right before your eyes. The "mystery of inequity" is at work in the corrupt government that, even now, has your compound under surveillance. This is it—this is the time! Jesus will actually return during your lifetime. The weapons that will be used against the evil one are stockpiled in the basement. If you die, it will be in a holy war against oppression. The "desire of the nations" will soon enter into the atmosphere of planet Earth, and Jesus is coming for you!

And then it all seems to come to a head. Prophecies had stated that the world will end filled with flames, noise, and confusion. There will be "weeping and wailing and gnashing of teeth." And that's what was happening outside in February 1993.

It is an absolute tragedy that no one involved with the forces of the Bureau of Alcohol, Tobacco, and Firearms (ATF) the night of February 28, 1993, seems to have understood the mind of a cultist. To the members of the ATF forces, the cult represented a threat to both the surrounding community and national security. They believed Koresh had stockpiled weapons and explosives. Surrounding the compound and "playing by the book," they had tried to tire the inhabitants by setting up huge loudspeakers and disrupting the cult members' sleep with loud rock music. They had tried reasoning and various psychological ploys. They never understood that they were creating exactly the type of confused scenario that David Koresh had prophesied. The ATF had fulfilled, in miniature, exactly the type of conditions described in the Bible. No one knows why the ATF attacked when they did, or what set off the fires. Some say it was Koresh, others the ATF. But the tanks, the fires, the shooting, and the confusion seemed to duplicate exactly the events of Revelation, chapter 9. To the believers inside, the world was coming to an end. After a fifty-one-day standoff, eighty Branch Davidians died, including seventeen children.

The Branch Davidian movement did not end at Waco. Those who didn't perish in the flames or from gunfire believed there was a good chance that Daniel's prophecy of "2,300 days" (Daniel 8:14) may have kicked in with the death of David Koresh on April 19, 1993. If so, a "cleansing of the sanctuary" would have occurred sometime during the year 2000. That didn't happen. But many believers, who still meet at the Mount Carmel ranch where the siege occurred, feel that somewhere in the Bible, there is an explanation, and they will search for it until they find it.

The International Society for Krishna Consciousness/ The Hare Krishna Movement

When Beatles guitarist George Harrison, after writing "My Sweet Lord" as a hymn to Krishna, donated an estate covering approximately twenty acres to the Hare Krishna movement, the society was just about at its apex. Founded in 1966 by Srila Prabhupada, Hare Krishna had an instant appeal to young Americans who were fed up with the Vietnam War and suburban life. When they joined the society, they became part of a strict Hindu sect that had originated in India.

It was powerful and yet, to observers, strange. The long hair they had worn as a badge of rebellion was replaced by shaved heads. Their parents' compulsory skirts and ties gave way to saffron robes. The freedom they had sung about in all-night sing-alongs melded into the strict discipline of chanting mantras by the hour.

Prabhupada had translated the Bhagavad-Gita, opening new ways of thinking to traditional Western kids. He was the father figure many had never known in the days of "commuter dads." The family of Hare Krishna offered peer support and comfort. For many of the believers, life seemed to make sense for the first time. "Walking through a wall of water" is how the movement describes conversion.

During the 1970s the Hare Krishnas bought acreage in West Virginia and Pennsylvania. They were able to purchase a building in downtown Manhattan and almost a whole city block on Watseka Avenue in Los Angeles. Thanks to the success of the Bhagavad-Gita translation, they had even opened their own publishing business.

But when Prabhupada died in 1977, the movement faced a crisis. He had appointed eleven men to lead zones scattered across the country. But they were not able to inspire the same devotion he had inspired. And with the burst of growth the movement had experienced, donations by frequent flyers at airports just wouldn't pay the bills anymore. Worse yet, rumors began to surface about compulsory sex, child molestation, and abuse. Lawsuits followed. Children had been placed in round-the-clock childcare under Hare Krishna guidance with the understanding they would be given spiritual guidance and training while their parents were free to work for the movement. But when those children grew old enough to talk about their experiences, horror stories abounded. Bankruptcy followed, along with disillusionment and even a few suicides.

Many of those who remain are disheartened, feeling let down by those who lost their idealism. Hinduism is, after all, a rich and ancient spiritual tradition nourishing countless people. It is by no stretch of the imagination a cult. But as we have seen so far, traditional Westerners as different as fervent Pentecostals, buttoned-down web-page designers, and radical Seventh-day Adventists can gather around charismatic leaders. Converted Western Hindus are no different.

Aum Shinri Kyo

In Japan, Shoko Asahara, an admirer of Adolf Hitler, believes the world is coming to an end. That's nothing new. A lot of people believe that. The problem is that he wants to help it happen.

Partially blind from birth, he attended a school for the blind and became an acupuncturist, opening up a folk medicine shop in 1980.

A true ecumenist, he studied Buddhism and Hinduism in the Himalayas, and he used insights gleaned from the book of Revelation in the Christian Bible and the writings of the sixteenth-century mystic Nostradamus to attract some twenty thousand followers worldwide to his movement, Aum Shinri Kyo. The word "Aum" comes from the famous Hindu mantra, "om," chanted by priests in meditation. Shinri Kyo means "supreme truth."

Asahara claims to have talked directly with people from the year 2006. It seems they have survived World War III. The causes for that war were rooted in the materialism exemplified by the United States.

Supreme truth, *Shinri kyo*, emphasizes traditional Japanese values as opposed to what is seen as the corruption of Western influence. Like most cultic beliefs, a feeling of "us" against "them" pervades the group. They have stockpiled biological and chemical weapons in preparation for the battle of Armageddon. Unfortunately, as reported by the *New York Times*, they have not been afraid to use them. At least nine attacks have been staged in Japan, with targets including the legislature, the Imperial Palace, the U.S. military base at Yokosuka, and the infamous Tokyo subway attack on March

20, 1995. Twelve people were killed and thousands injured in that attack after being exposed to sarin nerve gas.

More than one hundred members of the group have been arrested, with trials scheduled to last for many years. Membership has dropped to under seven thousand. In 1997 the Japanese government ruled they could no longer justify breaking up the movement since they could only identify about one thousand members, not enough to constitute a national threat.

Falun Gong

In 1999 the Chinese government began a crackdown aimed at "subversive" spiritual and religious groups guilty of "superstition." Falun Gong, until that time a respected organization under the National Qi Gong Federation, found itself the victim of a media propaganda smear campaign.

Qi Gong, sometimes referred to as "Chinese Yoga," is one of a family of physical/spiritual techniques, including martial arts and t'ai-chi chuan. Its purpose is to promote the flow of ch'i (life force) and wellness, and it is a spiritual exercise older than Christianity. Falun Gong is one of many expressions of Qi Gong. Developed by its founder, Li Hongzi, in 1951, Falun Gong took hold to become the largest expression of Qi Gong after Li left the Qi Gong Federation in 1998.

When Falun Gong found itself the victim of a propaganda campaign, however, members reacted with a demonstration with some ten thousand participants, held near the residences of some of China's leadership in Beijing. Because this was the largest demonstration of its kind ever seen in China, the regime reacted by labeling the group a cult, dispersing the demonstration, and declaring further activity unlawful. Further complicating the situation was the fact that some military and low-level political leaders were members of Falun Gong, practicing what had just been declared illegal. Tracts were printed and television personalities raved against the movement. Local leaders were arrested, and China asked the United States to arrest and evict Li, who had immigrated there—a request that was denied because of Chinese human rights abuses.

This would be just another case of civil persecution if it were not for one fact that arguably places Falun Gong within the "cult" category: that it is led by one charismatic figure. Master Li is the only living person authorized to teach the specific exercises of Falun Gong, and he believes Falun Gong to be unique to the "cultivation of Xinxing." This is a spiritual path, based on Buddhism and Confucianism, that promotes the three values of zhen (truthfulness), shan (benevolence), and rhen (forbearance). Li teaches the concepts of reincarnation and Karma as well, with the need to undergo "tribulation" so as to pay off karmic debt. He also believes in good and bad deities, and he thinks some reports about aliens may have confused beings from outer space with demonic forces. Indeed, to practice Falun Gong without recognizing its spiritual component may even induce a demonic element.

The symbol of Falun Gong is a Buddhist swastika in a circle, or disk, surrounded by four yin/yang symbols, the symbols of the Dao. The idea is to awaken and nourish spiritual energy, and practitioners believe that following its five disciplines or sets of exercises may cure some illnesses.

By persecuting Falun Gong, Chinese government officials have become the object of world criticism, and they have probably done more to publicize the movement in the West than its adherents ever would have.

Sources:

Aum Shinri Kyo 1/2. http://www.gbs.sha.bw.schule.de/tsld026.htm. September 29, 2003.

Engeler, Amy. "Testimony." *My Generation Magazine,* July/August 2002.

Hannaford, Alex. "Return to Waco." *The Guardian,* October 28, 2003.

"History of the Branch Davidians." *The Fountain of Language.* http://www.fountain.btinternet. co.uk/koresh/history.html. September 14, 2003.

Introvigne, Massimo. "Falun Gong 101." *CESNUR: Center for Studies on New Religions.* http:// www.cesnur.org/testi/falung101.htm. September 14, 2003.

"One Year Later, Heaven's Gate Suicide Leaves Only a Faint Trail." *CNN.com.* http://www. cnn.com/US/9803/25/heavens.gate, March 25, 1998.

Robinson, B. A. "Aum Shinri Kyo (Supreme Truth). *Religious Tolerance.org.* http://www. religioustolerance.org/dc_aumsh.htm. July 2000.

"A Tribute to the Man, His Mission, and His Message." *The Family.* http://www. thefamily.org/ ourfounder/tribute/tribute.htm. September 14, 2003.

DANCE, SACRED

Almost every religious tradition encompasses some kind of expression involving movement or dance. Indeed, dance may be the single oldest religious expression known to the human race. Probably the drum, in the form of a hollow log, was the first musical instrument invented. Such early drums were almost certainly used to accompany religious or ritual dancing. It is even conceivable, though we will never know for sure, that extinct relatives of humans such as the Neanderthal enjoyed sacred dance.

In Islam, followers of the mystical expression known in the West as Sufi practice a form of prayer involving dancing in tight circles while experiencing union with the divine, a spiritual ecstasy. Spectators called participants "whirling dervishes."

The Hebrew psalms often speak of "praising God with the dance." King David "danced before the Lord" when the Ark of the Covenant was brought home to Jerusalem, much to the disgust of Michal, the daughter of King Saul. You can almost hear the sarcasm dripping from her lips: "How the king of Israel has distinguished himself today, disrobing in the sight of slave girls as any vulgar fellow would!" (2 Samuel 6:20). (Michal, in response to her low rating of David's moves, was given the ultimate Hebrew Bible/Old Testament punishment by the male author of Samuel. "And Michal, daughter of Saul, had no children to the day of her death.")

The Christian tradition has either totally accepted dance or totally rejected it, depending on the source of its inspiration. If divinely inspired, dance is considered an expression of spirituality. Otherwise it is, at best, a means by which the devil traps the impressionable (as in the movie *Footloose*), or, at worst, an activity reserved for "pagans" (as illustrated by the obligatory "war dance" that motion-picture Indians always seem to engage in before fighting the cavalry the next day).

Sacred dance performed by so-called whirling dervishes, their arms extended, right palm facing up and left palm facing down, to signify energy from above passing through the body and into the earth. The Sheikh represents the sun and the Dervishes represent the planets turning around him in the solar system of Mevlana. *Fortean Picture Library.*

Sacred dance, however, is typically a matter of opposing theological expressions. On one extreme, "dancing in the aisles" is a Pentecostal tradition. When "the spirit moves," people get up and dance. At the other extreme, the liturgical dance of the formal Church comes from the controlled, rehearsed tradition of the classical ballet.

This tension has caused puzzlement in middle-of-the-road churches that simply don't know how to handle dance as a spiritual expression. Quite often when the opera *Amahl and the Night Visitors*, the story of the wise men and their journey to Bethlehem, is performed in church sanctuaries, the pastor puts his foot down and eliminates the rustic peasant dancing scene.

There is, however, some recent evidence that conservative opinions concerning secular dance are beginning to change. In an article entitled "Footloose," which appeared in the *Boston Globe* on March 30, 2003, Naomi Schaefer reported that Wheaton College, known for asking every prospective student the question, "Have you accepted Jesus Christ as your personal Savior?" has recently made national news by allowing students to dance in public as long as they are not on campus. Previous school policy of the institution called by some the "Evangelical Harvard" not only forbade dancing, but faculty could be relieved of their duties if they were seen drinking a glass of wine in a restaurant. The school's director for orientation was quoted as saying, "If there is a group still offended by dancing, it's a small minority."

Probably the most well known and imitated sacred dance is found at the American Indian pow-wow. Dance is a central component of Indian spiritual life. Even though it has been commercialized, it remains an important part of religious ceremony. Manny Twofeathers, in his book *The Road to the Sundance*, eloquently describes his own spiritual journey and awakening to the mysticism of sacred dance associated with the Plains tribes. Especially accessible to non-Indians is the experience John Hanson Mitchell relates in his book *Ceremonial Time*. In the course of his study, Mitchell discovered that the people who lived on the land tended to have a completely different conception of time than he did. In trying to understand, he invited three Indian friends to accompany him to Forge Pond, near Route 2 in central Massachusetts. The three decided to find out for themselves which of their ancestors might still be around.

Mitchell is a typical modern man who writes and edits a magazine during a normal workday. His reaction to what happened that night is one that many could identify with. In his words:

> "Suddenly [Tonupasqua] rose to her feet and began to shift back and forth, her rounded body cutting off the glimmering lights of the civilized world across the lake. Nompenekit joined her, and after a minute or two, White Bird got up and began to shuffle his feet forward and backward. Then, abruptly, as if he had been seized by pain, White Bird threw up his right arm and crouched over, shouting in the high, unintelligible phrases known technically as vocables—meaningless words that traditional Indians use to accompany their dances. Crouching over, his right arm still raised, and his left arm crooked uncomfortably behind his back, he began to circle around the pipe, crossing his left leg behind his right and vice versa with short little stamps. Tonupasqua and Nompenekit swayed and shuffled for a minute longer and then they too joined in the dance, each of them taking up White Bird's long chant of vocables, interweaving the call with short grunts and shouts, and an occasional high whinny from Tonupasqua.
>
> My first reaction was to join in; involuntarily, almost, I felt my arm go up as soon as Nompenekit joined in the dance. But with Tonupasqua's whinnying filling the air, I began to worry slightly that someone across the lake would hear the chanting and call the police. For about ten minutes I was too distracted to appreciate the spectacle, then slowly, once again, I fell in with the ceremony and would have joined the dance had I not felt that I might violate the ritual. I moved farther into the woods, sat down again to watch, and then, for some reason, began to feel dizzy and almost frightened. The reality of what was going on,

the time scales that I felt I was witnessing, seemed too vast to comprehend, too much to handle at three in the morning. I felt that I was transported back into some indistinct period in the time before this time, when Menobozho, Hobomacho, the Bear, and the other mythological creatures walked over Scratch Flat. It was not an altogether pleasant revelation. What came to the forefront there was not the brilliantly lit Scratch Flat summer landscape, but the darker side of things, the horror and the mystery of the European Paleolithic death cults, rites of passage, and yet undiscovered rituals. Dark shuffling images flashed in front of me, unspeakable primal ceremonies, scarified, painted shamans, bear priests, wolf men and ritualistic sacrifices; and for a moment I thought I saw the actual form of a fourth figure dancing there. It was shorter, thicker than the others, and by the time I recognized the form as that of an upright bear, it had disappeared.

I realized then that I was not seeing Scratch Flat anymore. I had been carried it seemed to an earlier period, transported somehow to the Mal'ta peninsula on Lake Baikal in Siberia where the tribes of American Indians are believed to have originated. Whatever I saw there was the same thing that Cotton Mather and the other Puritan ministers so feared when they first encountered the aboriginal Americans. It was the fiery worm that flew by night, the dark ecstasies and Satanic figures that lurked in the howling wilderness and tempted wayward European travelers. I found there, it seemed to me later, the most essential Paleo artifact of all, the spirit that was born in the mind of the Paleolithic hunters two hundred thousand years ago, nurtured on the Mal'ta peninsula, carried across the Behring Sea land bridge, carried across the American continent, carried through fifteen thousand years of American history, and then deposited on a point of land on an obscure pond in the drainage of the Merrimack River on the northeastern coast of North America.

Although this incident took place in the late twentieth century, it captures the ancient essence of sacred dance. As a form of liturgy, dance precedes formal, written, and recited prayers by thousands, not hundreds, of years. More than mere time separates the Australian aboriginal men's dance or the African tribal ceremony from the recitation of "Our Father, who art in heaven," intoned by a dressed-up congregation with one eye on the clock. Indeed, it is probable that the primitive feelings dance can invoke is what so frightens hierarchical religious leaders.

One of the most effective descriptions of dance and the sacred prayer of life it depicts appears in Bill Moyers's introduction to Joseph Campbell's book *The Power of Myth:*

In Japan for an international conference on religion, Campbell overheard another American delegate, a social philosopher from New York, say to a Shinto priest, "We've been now to a good many ceremonies and have seen quite a few of your shrines. But I don't get your ideology.

I don't get your theology." The Japanese man paused as though in deep thought and then slowly shook his head. "I don't think we have ideology," he said. "We don't have theology. We dance."

Sources:

Campbell, Joseph. *The Power of Myth*. New York: Doubleday, 1988.

Mails, Thomas E. *Dancing in the Paths of the Ancestors*. New York: Marlowe & Company, 1983.

Mitchell, John Hanson. *Ceremonial Time*. New York: Warner Books, 1984.

Twofeathers, Manny. *The Road to Sundance: My Journey into Native Spirituality*. New York: Hyperion, 1994.

DAO

(See also Confucianism/Daoism; Lao Tzu)

Dao, sometimes spelled Tao, can be roughly translated to mean "the way." But no definition really captures the all-encompassing meaning of Dao. In the very first line of the Dao De Jing (or Tao Te Ching), Lao Tzu writes:

> The way (Dao) that can be spoken of
> Is not the constant way;
> The name that can be named
> Is not the constant name.
> The nameless was the beginning of heaven and earth;
> The named was the mother of the myriad creatures.
> Hence always rid yourself of desires in order to observe its secrets;
> But always allow yourself to have desires in order to observe its manifestations.

In China, if you ask what the Dao is, you will probably get the nebulous answer, "All ten thousand things." But in the West, if a practical definition of following the Dao could be attempted, it would probably say something like this: Daoism is the way to live the way.

The Dao is everything there is and the force that both brought it into existence and sustains it. In this sense, Dao is a noun. But it is also a verb. The Dao sustains everything and operates within the universe not only in its active, creating and sustaining force, but in the daily, moment-by-moment practice of all that live in it. It is at once everything and nothing, tangible and intangible.

The symbol of the Dao is the circle, divided into two halves. It is sometimes described as being two interlocking fish, one white, one black. But within the white fish is a black spot and within the black fish, a white spot. One symbolizes yin: the feminine, intuitive, instinctive force, the strength of which lies in yielding. Its sign is the tiger, and its celebration is at the time of the spring and fall equinoxes. The other symbolizes yang: the masculine, analytical, objective force the strength of which is in power and attack. Its sign is the dragon, seen in the parades of new year and midsummer festivals held in Chinese villages.

It should be emphasized here that the Western and Eastern dragon are two completely different symbols. In the West the dragon is a negative symbol. Western mythology sees the dragon as an evil force involved in two principal activities: dragons steal treasures and maidens. They don't do anything with either of them. They just guard them. In order to obtain the dragon's hoard and rescue the maiden, the gallant knight has to slay the dragon. Western psychological therapy consists of slaying the dragons of fear and resentment that guard the gold and innocence of our inner life. By skillful counseling, the therapist coaxes the dragon out into the light of day where it can be defeated, releasing the inner secrets of potentiality languishing in the caves of the psyche.

Eastern dragons, however, represent vitality. They are the masculine in both male and female that roars out into daylight, thumping its chest, ready for whatever challenges await.

In the West, snakes, a diminutive form of dragons, have always been something to destroy. In India, priestesses will actually lure a snake out of its lair and kiss it three times on the head to bring rain to the parched earth.

The principle of yin/yang is the basis of martial arts. Power is met with yielding, and yielding with power. Yin and yang operate as well within the human body, which must have feminine and masculine energy at balance in order to be healthy and strong.

Daoism as a religion is very ancient but has proved to be flexible, adapting with the times. A huge body of Daoist scripture exists. The Tao-tsang (Daoist canon) consists of more than one thousand volumes compiled over fifteen centuries. It is a mixture of Daoist, Buddhist, and Manichaean texts, with some Christian material thrown in for good measure.

Although myth and legend shroud Lao Tzu, ever since the fourth century BCE he has been studied, venerated, and sometimes worshiped, a fact that probably would have irritated the historical Lao Tzu no end. But his impact and his writings cannot be emphasized enough. The Dao permeates Confucianism, Buddhism, martial arts, New Age religion, and the *Star Wars* movies.

Sources:
Kung, Hans, and Julia Ching. *Christianity and Chinese Religions*. New York: Doubleday, 1989.
Lao Tzu. *Tao Te Ching*. Trans. D. C. Lau. New York: Penguin Books, 1963.

DAO DI JING *see* **Tao Te Ching**

DAVID, KING

He commits adultery and then has his lover's husband murdered. His legend is probably the most edited story in literature. Most Sunday-school teachers leave out the bad parts, and most pastors censor the verses not fit for Sunday morning consumption. Thus, by an unspoken conspiracy of the "keepers of the story," David is perhaps the most well known and revered but least understood character in the Bible. He has somehow managed a positive legacy. He wallowed in the sewer, but three thousand years after his death he still smells like a rose. As a leader he was right up there with George Washington and Abraham Lincoln. But he makes Bill Clinton, Richard Nixon, and John Kennedy all look like Boy Scouts.

How did he do it? Well, it helps to have good biographers. The consensus of modern biblical scholarship suggests that much of the Bible was put together from existing documents during his reign. Probably a lot of editing went on to cast him in a good light. The constant refrain during the book of Judges, for instance, that "there was no king and every man did what was right in his own eyes" goes a long way to setting him up as the hero who put Israel back together again. The last few chapters of Judges even put Saul, David's predecessor, in a bad light, possibly to bolster David's image by comparison.

But did the man at the center of the biblical stories really exist? Up to a few years ago the only witness was the Bible. Even the book of Leviticus demands two witnesses in a court of law. But archaeology has come to the rescue. "The House of David" has been discovered to have been a reality, for the words are found on no less than commercial bills of sale with no religious ax to grind. Evidence shows that people were trading with his merchants and doing business with his kingdom.

So we can turn to his biography with a fair amount of confidence that, except for a few exaggerations, the story emerging from the books of Samuel, Kings, and Chronicles is probably close to describing the historical figure. But there are problems. The author of 1 Samuel 17:50, for instance, tells us a youth named David killed Goliath with his slingshot. A few pages later, 2 Samuel 21:19 credits a man named Elhanan with the same deed. Were David and Elhanan one and the same, or are there two separate traditions at work here? Some Bible scholars have theorized that "David" is a title, and not a name. But that's a pretty far-ranging theory for such scant evidence. The truth is, we just don't know the answer. So the best guess now is that although editors, called "redactors," may have been at work, their honesty compels us to take what they wrote at face value. After all, if they had wanted to paint a strictly laudatory picture, they would have glossed over a lot more of David's foibles and his downright lewd, illegal behavior.

He was born in Bethlehem about a thousand years before his even more famous descendant, Jesus. His father, Jesse, was the grandson of Boaz and Ruth, whose story is told in the book bearing her name. The book of Luke lists forty-two generations separating David and Jesus (Luke 3), Matthew only twenty-eight (Matthew 1). But, to be fair, the two genealogies trace different sides of the family.

When we first meet David he is a shepherd, the "runt" of Jesse's litter. The prophet Samuel shows up one day on a secret mission from God. Saul, the appointed first king over Israel, is not working out. Samuel knows enough to find the new king's home but doesn't know which son is God's choice. Jesse, showing even less spiritual acumen than Samuel, leaves David out tending the sheep, figuring that he is not even in the running. Little did he know the kid with the unnatural red hair was going to grow up to be a giant-killer.

When Jesse musters the family sons, Samuel comes up empty. "Are these all the sons you have?" he asks (1 Samuel 16:11).

"There is still the youngest," says Jesse, "but he's out tending the sheep."

Recognizing David as the chosen one, Samuel anoints him king, but no one thinks to tell King Saul, who continues blithely on, fighting Philistines and running the kingdom into the ground. David, meanwhile, goes back to tending sheep. He will not assume his position as king until the death of Saul, years later.

When we next hear from him he is carrying food to his brothers, who are now fighting in Saul's army. The Israeli troops are bunkered down on a ridge facing the Philistine troops across the valley. In keeping with a rather sensible practice of the time, the Philistines had invoked the honorable custom of single combat, their champion against their opponents', winner take all. The only problem was that the Philistine champion was a nine-foot-tall giant named Goliath. Given his considerable size and reputation, no one wanted to take him on.

Until David, that is. "Who is this uncircumcised Philistine that he should defy the armies of the living God?" (1 Samuel 17:26)

Everyone knows what happened next—the young kid with the slingshot slew the nine-foot Philistine giant, and David became not only the most famous soldier in Israeli history but one of the most charismatic warriors in the history of the world. His fight became the universal symbol of every battle between entrenched power and the "little guy."

David appears next in quite a different guise. Saul is troubled by some kind of fit that is only soothed when David plays gentle music on the harp. The Bible makes it plain what's going on. "An evil spirit from God came forcefully upon Saul ... and he was afraid of David, because the Lord was with David but had left Saul" (1 Samuel 18:10–12). David was forced to flee when Saul tried to kill him. He rapidly became leader of his own band of troops, pursued by Saul throughout the hill country of Israel, always eluding him, but refusing to do him harm. After all, Saul was, according to David's reasoning, God's king.

Here, however, an interesting debate now rages. David and Saul's son Jonathan were best of friends. Jonathan served as David's spy, keeping David informed of Saul's plans and movements. But how close was their relationship? At Jonathan's memorial service, David preached the eulogy (2 Samuel 1:25–26):

> How the mighty have fallen in battle! ...
> I grieve for you, Jonathan my brother;
> you were very dear to me.
> Your love for me was wonderful,
> more wonderful than that of women.

Was Jonathan being "outed" at his own funeral? When the Bible says "the souls [of Jonathan and David] were knit together" (1 Samuel 18:1), is it implying a physical relationship as well, or at least a romantic one? According to Jonathan Kirsch in his book *The Harlot by the Side of the Road*, "these words from Holy Scripture were recently invoked in a debate in the Knesset, the national legislature of Israel, over the rights of gay men and women under Israeli law. Yael Dayan, daughter of another war hero of Israel [Moshe Dayan], succeeded in drawing the ire (and raising the blood pressure) of some of her fellow members of the Knesset by "outing" David; she argued, on the strength of David's eulogy of Jonathan, that the two were gay lovers."

David subsequently proved himself to be a rather lusty heterosexual fellow. But the debate persists, another example of how almost any opinion can be buttressed with biblical proof texts if you look hard enough. The truth is, we'll never know for sure if David was bisexual.

Sexual orientation aside, David eventually became king over Israel. He was the one who conquered Jerusalem and made it his capital city. Before this it was a Jebusite hill fortress. Ever since it has been called the City of David (2 Samuel 5:9). He soon brought the Ark of the Covenant to what would be its resting place in Solomon's Temple, defeated virtually all his enemies, and expanded the size of Israel to borders previously undreamed.

But one day he realized he had no new challenges and found himself bored. Enter Bathsheba.

"In the spring, at the time when kings go off to war," David decided to stay home (2 Samuel 11:1). Armies fought in the spring and summer, when they could be supplied by living off the land, but David was by this time too important to risk on the battlefield.

The Bible says that "one evening David got up from his bed and walked around on the roof of his palace. From the roof he saw a woman bathing" (2 Samuel 11:2). It was Bathsheba. It is a matter of debate who tempted whom, but the result was that Bathsheba became pregnant with David's child. Her husband was off fighting the wars David had stayed home from. So David quickly sent for him and tried to get him to sleep with Bathsheba so she could say the baby was his. But Uriah, Bathsheba's husband, turned out to be more honorable than David. He wouldn't go home to the comfort of his wife while his men were sleeping alone in tents, out in the field.

The next day, David tried to get him drunk. But a tipsy Uriah was more honorable than a sober David. There was only one thing left to do to prevent scandal. David sent Uriah back to the front carrying his own death sentence. Uriah's commander was ordered to put him in the thick of the fighting and then draw all the troops away. Death followed, of course, and every man in the army must have known something was up.

In the famous confrontation of 2 Samuel 12, Nathan, the king's chaplain, persuaded David finally to do the honorable thing. He confessed to his people, begged God's forgiveness, and married Bathsheba. The child born of the union died, the opinion of the editors of Samuel being that this was David's punishment for his sin. But the next child born to them is Solomon, leaving one to wonder. People had to have heard rumors about David's relationship with Bathsheba while she was married to another man. And the people of the kingdom might not have followed Solomon if he had been born the child of an illicit affair. Was the story of the first child's death included to clear Solomon of blame, setting the scene for his rule?

David had other family problems as well. His son, Absalom, murdered his half-brother Amnon for committing incest with their sister, and later he attempted to overthrow his father. David was actually forced to abdicate for a brief time, fleeing Jerusalem rather than fighting an attempted coup and being forced to kill his own son (2 Samuel 15).

The rest of David's story is one sordid event after another. Perhaps David was never quite the same after he realized the depth of depravity he had discovered in his soul. His final days are even worse. In his old age he found it difficult to stay warm at night, so a beauty contest was held. The winner got to sleep with the king to keep him warm, but the chroniclers are quick to point out that "he knew her not" (1 Kings 1:4).

Probably one of the most depressing scenes in the whole Bible is depicted in 1 Kings 2, where David meets with Solomon, who is about to be his successor. The two of them plot revenge against all the people David didn't want to kill while he was alive, but wanted to make sure followed him right after he died.

Finally, when we just don't want to hear any more about this side of David, he "rested with his fathers and was buried in the City of David," after having ruled Israel for forty years.

What are we left with? What is David's final legacy?

Was he an honorable youth? Yes. He was above reproach when he was young. There is no reason to doubt the facts since subsequent stories reveal plenty to criticize.

Was he a good general? Absolutely. His bravery is without question. His tactics have been studied by military leaders. His ferocity was tempered by compassion, though not nearly as much as we might like to hear about. But then again, those were brutal days.

A fine musician? Although many of the Psalms attributed to him were undoubtedly written by someone else, including almost certainly the beloved Twenty-third Psalm, there is enough substance left to say he certainly deserves his reputation as "the sweet singer of Israel" (2 Samuel 23:1).

Was he a shrewd politician? Most certainly. Between the lines of his fascinating story lie treaties and political alliances that laid the groundwork for his son Solomon's rule, the historical high point for Israeli influence.

Was he a devoutly religious man? If we can separate religion from morality he was one of the most profoundly religious persons not only of his day but of all time. He continually poured out his heart to God. He wore his feelings on his sleeve and wasn't afraid to show others his heartfelt devotion. Is it any wonder God called him "a man after my own heart" (1 Samuel 13:14)?

But speaking about morality—the temptation at this point is always to shrug the shoulders and say, "Well, those were different days." And they were. But that's why David manages to keep his reputation so spotless. The truth is, he was at times the most immoral character in the Bible, and that's saying something. He was capable of fits of rage during which he seemed to be bathed in blood. Sometimes he was capable of great mercy. Other times he demonstrated the heart of a ruthless terrorist, killing merely for shock value. He knew nothing about human rights when it served his purpose to be brutal.

He is a fascinating character and a fitting subject for the many books and movies he has inspired. From the standpoint of religion, psychology, warfare, music, poetry, politics, and human development he is a deep mine that will yield riches when approached carefully and plumbed with diligence. And whether or not he ever wrote the words, his memory comes alive whenever we hear, "Though I walk through the valley of the shadow of death I will fear no evil, for thou art with me.... Surely goodness and mercy will follow me all the days of life, and I will dwell in the house of the Lord forever" (Psalm 23).

Sources:

Bridger, David, ed. *The New Jewish Encyclopedia.* New York: Behrman House, 1962.

Bucke, Emory Stevens et al, eds. *The Interpreter's Dictionary of the Bible.* 4 vols. New York: Abingdon Press, 1962.

Kirsch, Jonathan. *The Harlot by the Side of the Road.* New York: Ballantine Books, 1997.

May, Herbert G., and Bruce M. Metzger, eds. *The New Oxford Annotated Bible with the Apocrypha.* Rev. ed. New York: Oxford University Press, 1973.

DEAD SEA SCROLLS

In 1947, a young Bedouin shepherd was searching the hills around the Dead Sea, looking for lost sheep. Finding a small crevice opening downward, he dropped a pebble to see how deep the cave might be. Instead of the expected "thunk," he heard the sound of broken pottery.

What he had found shook the world. Sealed up in the cave, stored in jars and clay pots, were scrolls hidden away ever since 70 CE, when Titus and his Roman Legions destroyed the Jerusalem Temple. The Qumran community was the home of the Essene brotherhood, a band of devoted right-wing Jews who lived during the time of Jesus. Archaeology has since discovered they had built a thriving school and a place of meditation and ritual. Perhaps even John the Baptist was one of their shining stars. They were patriots of the highest order, waiting for the coming of the Messiah who would drive out the Romans and restore the kingdom to Israel. When Titus arrived with his army, the Essenes hid their library, probably intending to return after the Roman threat was eliminated. But they never came back. For almost two thousand years the tablets and parchments that had instructed and informed their beliefs lay hidden in the ground until their discovery electrified scholars all over the world.

What was it that caused the excitement? Did the Dead Sea Scrolls offer new insights into Jewish belief? Were they proof that the Bible we now have is somehow wrong? Has Christianity been based on a lie? Did they contain shocking new revelations that would destroy the belief system of the Western world? Was there a cover-up conspiracy at work?

In a word, no. True, the scholars didn't help the situation much by immediately spiriting the scrolls away to secret locations and keeping the results of their academic studies quiet. But that situation had nothing to do with a cover-up.

First of all, some of the parchments were, understandably, very fragile. It takes a lot of time and painstaking work to open them without immediately crumbling them.

A section of the Psalms scroll, a liturgical collection of psalms and hymns and one of the Dead Sea Scrolls, believed to include the oldest surviving copies of the books of the Old Testament. *AP/Wide World Photos.*

Second, the constant problem of possession had to be addressed. The scrolls don't belong to the public. In a perfect world, the best experts could simply drop what they are doing and get to work. But, needless to say, this is not a perfect world.

Third, the academic community works under the "publish or perish" principle. Scholars, understandably, wanted an "exclusive." They wanted to keep their work quiet until they could write the definitive book and defend it before the academic court of inquiry.

All this took time, and the world, being what it is, was not patient. Conspiracy theories abounded. Novels were written and articles published claiming the scrolls contained some kind of "evidence" too delicate for the ears of the masses. Once that kind of thing starts it's hard to stop. Outlandish theories were advanced that the parchments told the story about aliens from outer space meeting secretly with the Essene brotherhood. Some said a book that they called "Q," from the German word for "source," was discovered. (This book probably existed. It is thought to have been the source the Gospel writers had before them when they wrote Matthew, Mark, and Luke. One author has even written a commentary on it, but it seems a bit far-fetched to write a commentary on a book no one has ever seen.)

Time has laid most of these theories to rest. But that in no way lessens the importance of the Dead Sea Scrolls. They are, without a doubt, the archaeological find of the twentieth century. To understand why, it is helpful to delve into the field of biblical translation.

Some fragments of the Hebrew Bible, that which Christians call the Old Testament, were probably written as early as a few thousand years BCE. But the majority of the canon wasn't written down until much later (see Bible). And until the twentieth century, the oldest complete copy of the Bible dated only to the ninth century CE. What existed before this time were copies of copies of copies. Granted, the process of hand copying was extremely regulated by scholars. Every word was counted and every page read by many people. Still, if a small mistake had been made once and then copied over and over, each time allowing for the possibility of further mistakes, a tenth- or even hundredth-generation copy could have been quite different from the original. So the question remained: How accurate, after all these years, was the Bible?

With the discovery of the Dead Sea Scrolls, scholars now had copies going back to before the time of Christ. The complete book of Isaiah was there, along with fragments from every single book except the book of Esther. Their importance lay in comparing them to modern translations. How close were they?

The answer is, very close indeed. The copyists down through the centuries had done their work amazingly well. So far, at least, there have been only very minor mistakes or differences discovered. The Dead Sea Scrolls have convinced scholars that modern Bibles are very faithful to the originals. Of course, the scrolls discovered at Qumran were not original either. They, too, are copies of copies. But their importance lies in the fact that they are so much closer in time to the originals. Not nearly as much time had passed to allow significant changes to have cropped up.

This is not nearly as exciting to most people as conspiracy theories and new religious philosophies. But to Bible scholars, it is the stuff of grand adventure.

Sources:
Kirsch, Jonathan. *The Harlot by the Side of the Road.* New York: Ballantine Books, 1997.
LaSor, William Sanford. *The Dead Sea Scrolls and the Christian Faith.* Chicago: Moody Press, 1956.

DEATH OF GOD THEOLOGY

In the 1960s, DOG, or "Death of God," theology became a buzzword. Completely missing the point of Harvard University's Harvey Cox in his popular book *The Secular City*, people jumped on the idea that DOG theology meant that what would come to be called "secular humanism" had triumphed. Conservative clergy heaped great scorn on those who even tried to understand what the so-called "DOG scholars" were trying to say.

Time magazine brought the issue to the front burner of public opinion when they placed Thomas Altizer of Emory University squarely in the hot seat. The bold cover story with the words "Is God Dead?" made Altizer a household name.

Charlotte Bruce Harvey, in *Emory Magazine*, recalls Altizer's interview on television's *Merv Griffin Show.*

As the theologian stood backstage in a New York theater waiting for the show's taping to begin, the producer approached him with the query, "So, what's your act?" Bemused, Altizer simply stared at the man.

"I mean, what do you do?" the producer tried again.

"I'm a theologian."

"You a pro?"

"Sure."

"Well, you know what to do, then. You have two minutes."

The orchestra struck up Griffin's theme song, the crowd clapped on command, and when Altizer's cue came he strode on stage and confidently launched into his two-minute homily on the death of God. He was, in many ways, the perfect talk-show guest: a handsome man in his late thirties with flashing green eyes, dark, wavy hair, and a movie star's sensuous lower lip (more than once compared to Glenn Ford), he exuded charm, quick wit and a flair for the dramatic. But as he stood on stage that day, the hot television lights bearing down on him, the audience responded not with applause but with the refrain, "Kill him! Kill him! Kill him!" Griffin pointedly disdained to shake his hand, and after taping was over, Altizer was shuffled out the theater's back door into a waiting taxicab, only to find the crowd reconvened, still chanting, "Kill him. Kill him."

That's life in America—God-fearing land of free speech and religious freedom.

Harvey continues:

"Tom just doesn't use moderate words," says Jack S. Boozer, who as chairman of the department of Bible and religion was Altizer's boss at the time. "We tried to get him to use another phrase than the death of God, because we thought it was a symbol that had such [far-reaching] implications for people, children included, that no one would understand what he was saying.... But he said no, so much is at stake that there is no other way to say it."

Most scholars who contributed to Death of God theology were trying to make an important point. Gabriel Vahanian, in *The Death of God* (1961) and *Wait without Idols* (1964), was trying to discover why belief in God had somehow become irrelevant in Western culture. Harvey Cox, in *The Secular City* (1965), made the point that modern culture was something to embrace and infuse with new meaning, not something to run away from in fear that it is somehow antithetical to traditional religion.

Both authors believed in a transcendent God who was "other," while still being present in human endeavor. They were joined by others who felt the crucifixion symbolized the end of the historical idea that God was just "out there" somewhere, uninvolved. If God is alive, they insisted, God must be found within human society and culture—imminent, not transcendent. The phrase "death of God" represented more a new understanding of God, or of the concept of God, than the destruction thereof. "God is dead," went the refrain. "Long live God."

All were attempting to redefine traditional understanding in terms of modern culture and experience. It is still not clear what their influence has been, but the suspicion is growing that, like many revolutionaries, they were not so much wrong as simply ahead of their time. People seeking to discover what it is to be religious in a secular/scientific age seem much more open to thinking about God in nontraditional terms.

Sources:

Douglas, J. D., ed. *The New International Dictionary of the Christian Church*. Grand Rapids, MI: Zondervan Publishing, 1974.

Harvey, Charlotte Bruce. "A Case of Academic Freedom," *Emory Magazine. Emory University.* http://www.emory.edu/history/altizer.html. September 14, 2003.

DEEP ECOLOGY

Is Deep Ecology a religion? Some people think so. As the new millennium dawned, a group of loggers from Minnesota brought a case before a federal district court judge in Minneapolis claiming a coalition of environmental groups were wrongly imposing the "religion" of deep ecology upon the U.S. Forest Service, thereby slowing down, and even bringing to a halt, logging in national forests. The loggers, it seems, were guilty of imposing on the ecologist's religious beliefs.

It was an interesting case. Is ecology a passion or a religion? And when does a passion become a religion?

The judge was not very impressed. Poking fun at the ecologists, he asked them what their religion consisted of. "Woody Allen said he first checked how many holidays they had before he picked a religion," he told them.

The ecologists were not amused. And they were not the first to believe the earth was alive and worthy of worship. Monotheists often pride themselves on "worshiping the Creator, not the creation." But for thousands of years of human history, the creation was the Creator, the womb of the goddess, the source of our being. Creation, viewed as the Earth Mother, gave birth to her children.

A story is told of Chief Seattle who, when told the Indians must learn to farm and plow like whites, replied, "What? Shall I drive a knife into my mother's womb?" Whether or not he actually said these words is relatively unimportant. What is important is understanding the sentiment behind them. Earth is alive. Earth is our creator and mother, the giver of life. If this is true, it follows that Earth is the goddess, the source of our being, and is to be considered both alive and divine. Ecology, then, when seen in this light, is a religion.

The term "Deep Ecology" was coined by Arne Naess, a Norwegian philosopher. In 1937 he built a small cabin on Hallingskarvet Mountain in central Norway. In this isolated region, he thought, meditated, and wrote. The results of his labor have influenced virtually everyone involved in ecological study and activism today.

The beginnings of the movement are usually credited to Rachel Carson and her 1962 book *Silent Spring*. But the ecological awakening of the 1960s was really a reawakening of religious movements that can be traced at least as far back as the Druids. Scientific types have even recognized the concept of "Mother Earth." In their attempt to describe Earth as a living, interrelated ecological system, they have recently invoked the name Gaia Principle, resurrecting an old name for the goddess (see Gaia Principle).

The problem, at least in America, is that the culture has for so long used the word "God" to represent a monotheistic, distant father figure that many cannot seem to understand that people from other traditions, including a few ecologists, use the term in quite a different fashion. Neo-pagans represented by Wiccans, Druids, and recently, more than a few Unitarians picture God in terms more like the "Power of Creation," not unlike the *Star Wars* concept of "the Force." Although no one knows how it got here or where it's going, they explain, the universe itself is the source of our being and worthy of our respect, if not our worship.

This principle is in direct opposition to the Judeo-Christian Bible, which tells us to "fill the earth and subdue it" (Genesis 1:28). Seen in these terms, the struggle between the philosophy of Deep Ecology and traditional monotheism is a holy war. Christians would never stand still if pagans moved heavy trucks into their cathedrals to demolish their altars. And neo-pagans are not about to watch from the sidelines when loggers cut down living trees considered to be sacred miracles of creation.

Pliny the Younger, way back in 111 CE, was faced with a similar problem, but the shoe was on the other foot. Christians were threatening his beloved paganism. The sacred groves were empty. No one was attending the festivals anymore. Recalling the "golden days" of his youth, he remarked, "The woods were formerly temples of the deities, and even now simple country folk dedicate a tall tree to a God with the ritual of olden times; and we adorn sacred groves and the very silence that reigns in them no less devoutly than images that gleam in gold and ivory."

Sources:

Harding, Stephan. "What Is Deep Ecology?" *Schumacher College*. http://www.schumacher college.org.uk/articles/college-articles/stephan/whatisdeepecology.html. September 14, 2003.

Myers, John. "Loggers Bring 'Ecology Religion' Case to Minnesota Federal Court." *Duluth News-Tribune*, January 15, 2000.

DELPHI, ORACLE OF

One day, so the story goes, Zeus decided to find the exact center of the world. He released two eagles, one from the east and one from the west, and let them fly toward one another. Wherever they met would mark the location of the world's exact midpoint. They met at Delphi, which everyone expected was going to happen anyway.

Even before Zeus' time, Delphi was a holy place. Nestled in the skirts of Mount Parnassus in Greece, the cave at Delphi had, since ancient times, been the home of a serpent goddess with the gift of prophetic divination. When Apollo, Zeus' faired-haired son, was still a young sun god, he killed the goddess, named Python, and took over her cave to build himself a temple, or oracle. (The term "oracle" can refer either to the shrine, the diviner who occupies it, or the prophesy itself.) Recognizing local tradition, he installed his own priestess, named Pythia.

But Greek gods have never been much for goddess worship, so he made sure a male priest attended her and translated all her prophecies. Sitting deep within the chamber at Delphi, the Pythia would enter a trancelike state that prepared her to be in touch with Apollo. She would then field questions put to her by the faithful, edited and interpreted by the priest. He would answer the questions in an enigmatic, metric, poetic form, perfecting the ancient art of political-speak—that is, being both obscure and ambiguous.

It was a great way to set Greek public policy, and the occasional individual received some answers, too. It worked for many, many years.

Sources:
Bolen, Jean Shinola, M.D. *Gods in Everyman*. San Francisco: Harper & Row Publishers, 1989.

DEVIL/DEMONS

> And though this world, with devils filled, should threaten to undo us,
> We will not fear, for God hath willed His truth to triumph through us.
> The prince of darkness grim, we tremble not for him;
> His rage we can endure, for lo, his doom is sure:
> One little word shall fell him.

Thus Martin Luther, in his famous hymn written in 1529, "A Mighty Fortress Is Our God," assured us we have nothing to fear from the devil as long as our hearts are in the right place.

Devils are not confined to Christianity. Almost all religions have some kind of devils, demons, evil tricksters, and things that go bump in the night as a vital part of their theology. In Western cultures, the term "devil" calls to mind Lucifer, the "Morning Star," or Satan (literally *the* Satan, meaning "the accuser").

In Christian, late Jewish, and Islamic theology, the devil ("Iblis" to Muslims) is a created being gone wrong. Always masculine, and thus referred to as "he," the devil is not the opposite of God. He is not all-powerful, all-knowing, or able to be in all places at the same time. Instead he is a personal, malignant being, not so much full of hate as empty of love. His power is limited and lies mostly in temptation and in the ability to cause fear. Although he is not, in Genesis at least, associated by name with the serpent in the Garden of Eden, later Christian writers read back into the early Jewish story their developing conception, calling him, in the Book of Revelation, "that old serpent, the devil."

In the book of Job he is the Satan, "the accuser of the brethren." Forced to report in with the rest of the angels after "roaming through the earth and going back and forth on it," he talks God into using the "upright and blameless" Job as a one-man testing ground wherein a cosmic battle of wills takes place between good and evil (Job 1:6–11).

The demon Eurynome, Prince of the Dead, from Collin De Plancy's *Dictionnaire Infernal*, 1863. *Fortean Picture Library.*

(It is interesting to note that the position of "accuser of the brethren" is still officially being filled on earth. When the Roman Catholic Congregation of Rites nominates someone for beatification or canonization, that person is represented before a papal court by a *promotor fidei*, or "promoter of the faith." To ensure proper procedure, however, they are opposed by an *advocatus diaboli*, a "devil's advocate" or "accuser of the brethren.")

It is in the New Testament that Satan comes into his own. There he tempts Jesus three times, trying to lure him away from his appointed task (Matthew 4). He tries to get the apostle Peter to talk Jesus out of going to Jerusalem. "Get behind me, Satan!" Jesus yells to a very surprised disciple (Matthew 16:23). After all, Peter had just a moment before heard Jesus say, "Blessings on you." Peter must have learned his lesson because in his first letter he warns Christians to watch out because their "adversary the devil prowls about like a hungry lion, seeking someone to devour" (1 Peter 5:8). It was Satan who "entered into Judas" (Luke 22:3), prompting him to betray Jesus. He is all over the apostle Paul in the book of Acts. James assures Christians that if they "resist the devil he will flee" (James 4:7).

And that's good news, because in Revelation things really heat up. The devil-inspired Antichrist takes over the world for a time. At the Second Coming, Satan is "chained" for a thousand years while Earth gets its breath back (Revelation 20:2). But he is released to try again (Revelation 20:7–10) before finally being thrown into "the lake of fire ... there to be tormented for ever and ever."

Who is this creature? Where did he come from and why does God allow all this carnage?

According to the Christian reading of the Hebrew scriptures, Satan once held the position of top angel. His name back then was Lucifer, "the Morning Star" or "Son of the Morning." In the famous lament of Ezekiel 28, God, while addressing the king of Tyre, speaks really to Lucifer when he says,

> You were the model of perfection,
> Full of wisdom and perfect in beauty.
> You were in Eden, the garden of God;
> Every precious stone adorned you ...
> On the day you were created they were prepared.

You were anointed as a guardian cherub, for so I ordained you.
You were on the holy mount of God …
You were blameless in your ways from the day you were created till wickedness
was found in you …
So I drove you in disgrace from the mount of God and I expelled you, O
guardian cherub …
Your heart became proud on account of your beauty …
So I threw you to earth.

Thus it is that Isaiah can cry:

How you have fallen from heaven,
O Lucifer, son of the morning.
You have been cast down to earth,
You who once laid low the nations!
You said in your heart,
"I will ascend to heaven,
I will raise my throne above the stars of God,
I will sit enthroned …
I will ascend,
I will make myself like the most high." (Isaiah 14:12–15)

But why does God allow Lucifer, now called Satan, to have such power? It's all
part of the plan, according to the apostle Paul.

The conservative explanation is this: God knew sin was bad because God
knows everything. But the rest of the angels had never seen sin before. They didn't
know why saying "I will" five times to God was such a bad thing. If Satan were simply
destroyed, the angels would spend eternity in fear, hoping they didn't get "zapped" like
Satan and his followers, the fallen angels now called demons. And God wants love in
heaven, not fear. So how does God show the angels how bad sin is without endanger-
ing heavenly harmony?

A planet is cleared off and prepared as a sin laboratory. Humans are created.
Satan is confined to work his wiles for a few thousand years—just long enough to
make a real impression. Yes, humans fall. But God shows he is big enough to take the
penalty himself. Jesus dies for humans and takes their punishment. After about six
thousand years, it's all over. Satan gets the punishment he richly deserves, and the
angels, called principalities and powers, come to understand. Satan and his demons
fell victim to temptation, but the lesson is eternally imprinted upon the minds of
those who keep the faith.

It's a little unclear exactly when Satan and his demonic host were cast out of
heaven. Some say it happened before the creation of humans, right in the middle of
the first verse of the Bible (see Creationism). But Jesus claims to have seen it happen
after the disciples were sent out on their first evangelistic mission in Luke 10:18.
Finally, in Revelation 12:9, we are told that "the great dragon was hurled down, that
ancient serpent called the devil or Satan, who leads the whole world astray. He was
hurled to the earth and his angels with him." This event doesn't happen until near the

end of human history. It is often argued that these are three views of the same event, seen from three different perspectives in time.

This is how Paul sums up the whole experiment in Ephesians 3:

> Although I am less than the least of all the apostles, this grace was given me: to preach to the Gentiles the unsearchable riches of Christ, and to make plain to everyone the administration of this mystery, which for ages past was kept hidden in God, who created all things. His intent was that now, through the church, the manifold wisdom of God should be made known to the principalities and powers in the heavenly realms, according to his eternal purpose which he accomplished in Christ Jesus our Lord.

Humans are rewarded, of course. After all, they were the innocent victims of the whole thing. In the end, angels are made to serve them. Angels, after all, are created beings. But humans, though also created beings, are adopted into God's own family as part of the plan that eventually destroys Satan.

Some questions remain, however.

1. Do all Christians accept this version of the story? Of course not. Christians don't all agree about anything.

2. Do any other religions have a similar story? Yes, Muslims have the same story. At least it starts out the same way. But they give it a different twist. In their version, Iblis, the Satan figure, loves God too much. When the angels are told to bow down to humans, Satan refuses. It's not because of pride, as in the Christian version. It's just that he loves God too much to bow down to anyone else. So Iblis is cast out of the presence of his Beloved. And how does he console himself for all eternity? By remembering the sound of his Beloved's voice and the last words his Beloved said to him. And what were those words? In effect, "Go to hell!"

3. If Satan is a personal being, a fallen angel, why doesn't he look like an angel? Throughout the years the image of Satan has changed with the times. Somewhere along the line, probably as a result of Christians associating him with pagan images, he developed horns, a forked tail, and a pitchfork. Lately he is seen in movies as a briefcase-toting lawyer type who has contracts for your soul available at a moment's notice. Often he takes great delight in torturing the damned in the fires of hell. But none of this is found in the Bible. Hell is his final punishment, not his domain. The deep-seated fears resulting from thousands of lurid stories have caused untold psychological damage to people raised on vivid tales of a loving God who sends people into eternal torment. And, the power of mythology being what it is, it is difficult to simply decide not to believe in, and thus not to fear, such a monster God.

Sources:
May, Herbert G., and Bruce M. Metzger, eds. *The New Oxford Annotated Bible with the Apocrypha.* Rev. ed. New York: Oxford University Press, 1973.

DHARMA

The Hindu understanding of the word "dharma" is difficult to translate. Roughly, it refers to the order of the world and the moral behavior of those in it. But that doesn't really capture its all-encompassing meaning. Hinduism is very comfortable with things that really can't be pinned down with a concise definition. After all, creation came before language, so it is only logical to think there are limitations in expression. Dharma includes all that there is, so it naturally follows that the basic concept of the word has fuzzy outer edges that can't quite be contained by scientific categories.

In Buddhism, however, the word is easier to grasp. The Buddha used the word to refer to the doctrine he taught, beginning with the Four Noble Truths, the Eightfold Path, and the Middle Way (see Buddhism).

Sources:
Fisher, Mary Pat. *Living Religions*. 3rd ed. Upper Saddle River, NJ: Prentice Hall, 1991.

DHIMMI

When Muhammad launched his aggressive push to spread Islam throughout the world, his armies were instructed to allow people in conquered cities the freedom to continue their religion, especially if they were "people of the book"—Jews and Christians.

Theoretically, non-Muslims still have the right to practice their religion in Muslim-controlled societies. These people are called dhimmi (pronounced de-hem-ee).

With the resurgence of radical, fundamentalist Islam in some Near Eastern countries, however, dhimmi have sometimes found it difficult to insist on their legal rights when faced by angry mobs, cultural pressures, or repressive regimes. With Muslim rulers focusing their rhetoric on the "devil" of American materialism and imperialism, it becomes difficult to control the actions of fervent, religious zealots who consider it their duty to defend their faith and way of life by focusing their anger on targets close at hand.

This problem is not limited to Islam. Jews, especially, have been victims of similar cultural forces, and witches and American Indians can attest to the same kind of persecution at the hands of Christians.

Sources:
Fisher, Mary Pat. *Living Religions*. 3rd ed. Upper Saddle River, NJ: Prentice Hall, 1991.

DISCIPLE/APOSTLE

Immediately after Jesus' baptism and period of temptation in the wilderness, he chose twelve followers—called disciples or apostles—to accompany him and witness his resurrection. One of his favorite teaching methods was to tell parables, short stories with a message. Often the crowds didn't understand what he was getting at, but in private he would explain to the disciples what he meant (Matthew 12:34–36).

The Last Supper of Jesus and his disciples on the eve of his betrayal by Judas Iscariot and condemnation by the Romans. *Fortean Picture Library.*

The word apostle comes from the Greek word *apostolos*, meaning "one who is sent." Frequently it is used interchangeably with the word "disciple." But technically any follower is a disciple. Buddha had disciples. So did the founders of all the great world religions. Apostle is the word used in the Bible specifically to refer to the twelve followers of Jesus who became the patriarchs of the Church.

As in all things biblical, there are problems trying to determine exactly who the twelve were. Different books of the Bible list different names. Still, a consensus developed very early in Church history as to who they were.

The Inner Circle

Peter, James, and John were present for some very special events in Jesus' ministry. By being invited to witness the raising from the dead of Jairus's daughter (Luke 8:51), the transfiguration on the mountain (Matthew 17), and Jesus praying in the garden before his death (Matthew 26:37), they seem to have been his most intimate associates. Although Peter was given the top leadership position in the early Church (Matthew 16:17), all three figured prominently in the new movement. John is credited with being the author of five books of the New Testament, James with one, and Peter with two. Peter preached the first Christian sermon (Acts 2). Although it is a matter of dispute, James might have been Jesus' brother or, more correctly, given the fact of the virgin birth, half-brother. At least his name appears in the list of his brothers and sisters given in Matthew 13:55.

The Undisputed Five

Andrew is the apostle who is always pictured bringing people to Jesus. He first followed John the Baptist, but he left with John's blessing to become an apostle of Jesus. Tradition says he later became an elder in the Jerusalem church.

Thomas, also called Didymus, was the doubter. His second name means "twin," but we have no idea who the other twin was. He became famous by refusing to believe Jesus had risen from the dead until he had seen the evidence with his own eyes, earning him the dubious title Doubting Thomas. But this seems to have been a part of his personality. In John 11 and 14, and twice in John 20, we are given evidence that he was a man who seemed to struggle with his faith.

James, sometimes called "the younger" or "the less" to distinguish him from James of the inner circle, seems to have been Matthew's brother. But because he is often identified with the Zealots, a radical group of Jewish patriots, he must have completely disagreed with his brother's politics, because Matthew was one of those "despised tax collectors" who were so hated by the common people.

Philip is the only apostle with a Greek name, probably indicating a rather liberal family upbringing.

Simon is known as "the Zealot." It follows that he was a Jewish idealist. Legend says he took the Gospel to England and preached there until the Romans crucified him.

The Apostles with Many Names

The name Bartholomew appears in Matthew, Mark, and Luke. In John, it suddenly changes to Nathaniel. If we accept the fact that there were only twelve apostles, a safe assumption given the number of times the group is referred to as "the Twelve," we have to conclude that Nathaniel and Bartholomew are one and the same. If this is the case, he was the oldest apostle and seems to have a delightful way of putting the "young whippersnapper" Jesus in his place. In John 1, Philip finds Nathaniel and announces they have found the promised Messiah. He is Jesus of Nazareth.

We can almost hear old Nathaniel say, "Humph!" "Can anything good come out of Nazareth?" he mutters. Jesus must have liked him, though. When he first sees Nathaniel, he says, "Behold—an Israelite in whom there is no guile!"

Jude's real name is even harder to pin down. "Jude" is the Latin form of "Judah." But Matthew calls him "Lebbaeus" and Mark calls him "Thaddaeus." Luke tells us he is called "Jude, son of James."

Maybe Saint Jerome had the right idea. He referred to him as "Trionius," the "man with three names." Of all the apostles, he is the man we know least about. He makes only one statement in the entire Bible (John 14:22), but it elicits the longest, most detailed response Jesus gives to any question ever asked him. Perhaps besides being a man of many names, he is a man of few words.

Matthew is also hard to pin down. In every list of apostles given in the Gospels he is called Matthew the tax collector. But in Luke 5, when Jesus calls a tax collector to be his apostle, he calls a man named Levi. Is "Levi the tax collector" the same as "Matthew the tax collector"? Again, by a process of elimination, we have to say, probably. At least that's how most commentators down through the ages have answered.

The Betrayer

The final apostle, of course, is Judas Iscariot, the one who betrayed Jesus for thirty pieces of silver. John calls him "the son of perdition" (John 17:12). Matthew says he would have been "better off not to have been born" (Matthew 26:24). The lists in all four Gospels add to his name the description, "the one who betrayed him."

Perhaps surprisingly, Jesus had made him the group's banker. What does this tell us? That money corrupts? That Jesus was trying to redeem him by giving him responsibility? The Bible is silent.

For two thousand years people have wondered. Did Judas have any choice? Did God foreordain him to be doomed? His betrayal had been prophesied. The prophet Zechariah had even foretold the amount of the betrayal, thirty pieces of silver.

As late as the 1960s, the staged opera *Jesus Christ, Superstar* pondered Judas's fate. Without him there would have been no betrayal, no cross, no resurrection—indeed, no Christianity. Was he the antihero? Or was he just a wicked sinner?

Even his death is a disputed one. In Matthew 27:3–10, we are told he "went out and hanged himself." In Acts 1:18–20, the story is that he took the silver, bought a field, "fell headlong, his body burst open, and his bowels spilled out." This discrepancy illustrates the lengths people will go to harmonize Bible stories. It is often said that Judas hung himself, but the rope broke and he fell forward, and so on—a conflation of the two versions of his death.

The Thirteenth Apostle

However Judas died, it left a vacancy. The remaining eleven members felt so strongly about filling the position that they immediately called a committee meeting in the first chapter of the book of Acts. They elected a man named Matthias and caused no end of controversy.

Matthias was never heard from again, prompting many to believe that in typical committee fashion they elected the wrong man. If they had waited patiently, the argument goes, they would have discovered God's real choice was a man who, at the time of the election, wasn't even a Christian. He was a fire-breathing Jewish patriot named Saul, and he even attended the trial of the first Christian martyr, "aiding and abetting" in his death.

When Saul converted and changed his name to Paul (see Paul, Saul of Tarsus), he apparently came to believe he was the man who was meant to be Judas's successor. Calling himself "the apostle abnormally born" (1 Corinthians 15:7) he went on to become the young Church's first missionary and greatest theologian.

Sources:

Douglas, J. D., ed. *The New International Dictionary of the Christian Church*. Grand Rapids, MI: Zondervan Publishing, 1974.

May, Herbert G., and Bruce M. Metzger, eds. *The New Oxford Annotated Bible with the Apocrypha*. Rev. ed. New York: Oxford University Press, 1973.

DISPENSATIONALISM

Dispensationalism is a theological system designed to give shape and organization to Bible history. Lewis Sperry Chafer (1871–1952) and Charles C. Ryrie (b. 1925) are perhaps the best-known defenders of the system. John Nelson Darby (1800–1882) is considered its founder, even though proponents claim it goes all the way back to Augustine in the fifth century CE.

Ryrie, in his book *Dispensationalism*, defines it this way:

Dispensationalism views the world as a household run by God. In His household-world God is dispensing or administering its affairs according to His own will and in various stages of revelation in the passage of time. These various stages mark off the distinguishably different economies in the outworking of His total purpose, and these different economies constitute the dispensation. The understanding of God's differing economies is essential to a proper interpretation of His revelation within those various economies.

In other words, when the ordinary person reads the Bible, he finds God behaving in different ways at different times. The angry God of the Old Testament who tells Joshua to kill all the Canaanites seems totally different from the Jesus of the New Testament who tells his followers to turn the other cheek. How to explain these differences?

Some have found the explanation by discovering "dispensations," periods of time when God acts in a certain way consistent with human development at the time, testing humans in respect to a specific revelation of the will of God. The *Scofield Reference Bible* and Dallas Theological Seminary have been at the forefront of dispensational theology, identifying seven different periods of time, seven different "dispensations," in which the Bible reveals the developing plan of God for the world and humankind.

According to the *Scofield Reference Bible*, these seven dispensations are as follows:

1. Innocence (before the fall described in Genesis 3)
2. Conscience (from the fall to Noah)
3. Human Government (from Noah to Abraham)
4. Promise (from Abraham to Moses)
5. Law (from Moses to Christ)
6. Grace (the Church age)
7. Kingdom (the millennium)

After the millennium, humankind enters the Eternal State.

Because Christians seem to have attacked each other as often as they have attacked the world, followers of dispensational theology and covenant theology (see Covenant) have often been at odds, with rhetoric appearing—at least to the uninitiated—to generate a lot more heat than light. Although it seems strange to the outsider, it demonstrates the devotion to a theological system that has been at the very core of the many different and competing Christian denominations in the world today.

Sources:
Lightner, Robert. "Covenantism and Dispensationalism." *The Journal of Ministry and Theology*, Dallas Theological Seminary, fall 1999.
Ryrie, Charles C. *Dispensationalism*. Chicago: Moody Press, 1965.
Scofield Reference Bible. Grand Rapids, MI: Zondervan Publishing, 1971.

DIVINATION

Divination is an attempt to read the future, determine the will of God, or give practitioners a feeling of being able to control fate. Probably every religion ever practiced has used some form of divination.

The Hebrew Bible absolutely condemns it, but priests nonetheless threw some sort of ritualistic dice called the Urim and Thummin. Romans sometimes went to war on the basis of what priests saw when they killed an animal and looked at its entrails. Different objects were thrown, rolled, dropped, tossed, or heated to get results.

Even today people read cards, tea leaves, or messages in newspaper astrology columns, convinced they can discover the future. Psychic telephone lines do a big business.

There are those who demonstrate with great effectiveness that they are able to locate water with a divining rod. Others claim they can locate lost people after holding a piece of clothing. Police forces occasionally employ such people, though usually very quietly.

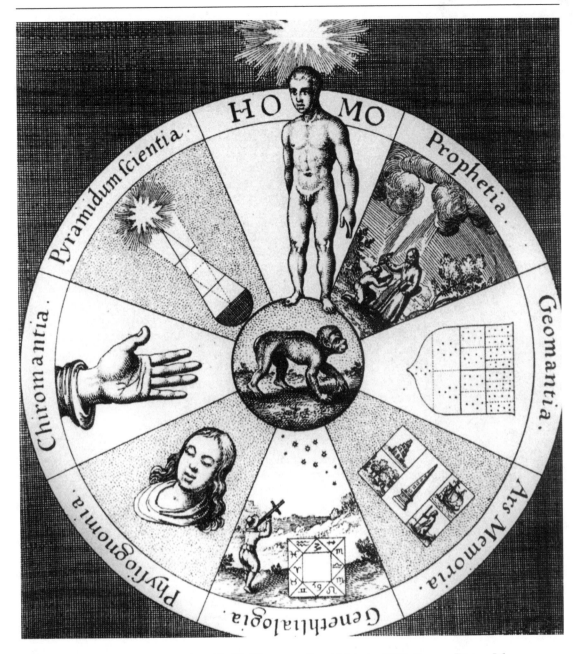

The eight divinatory arts, from Robert Fludd's *Utriusque Cosmi Maioris*, 1617. *Fortean Picture Library*.

Objections to divination range from simple scoffers to those who believe practitioners are in league with the devil. Christian religions especially have a history of punishing any who practice the art. If divination fails, the practitioners are ridiculed as fakes. If it is successful, they are accused of dealing with Satanic forces.

Whatever the techniques employed, divination is an ancient religious practice, probably dating to the very first person who prayed to a god and then asked for a sign as proof that the prayer was heard.

Sources:

Renard, John. *The Handy Religion Answer Book*. Detroit: Visible Ink Press, 2002.

DIVINE RIGHT OF KINGS

Although a much-maligned concept today, especially in democratic societies, the divine right of kings is actually a biblical idea. The apostle Paul explicitly states in Romans 13:1–5:

> Everyone must submit himself to the governing authorities, for there is no authority except that which God has established. The authorities that exist have been established by God. Consequently, he who rebels against authority is rebelling against what God has instituted, and those who do so will bring judgment against themselves. For rulers hold no terror for those who do right, but for those who do wrong. Do you want to be free from fear of the one in authority? Then do what is right and he will commend you. For he is God's servant to do you good. But if you do wrong, be afraid, for he does not bear the sword for nothing. He is God's servant, an agent of wrath to bring punishment on the wrongdoer. Therefore, it is necessary to submit to the authorities, not only because of possible punishment but also because of conscience.

A literal reading of the Bible seems to indicate that once a ruler is in place, people must believe that that ruler is God's choice. He has a divine right to rule.

True, the apostle goes on to warn the king that his is a great responsibility. But the fact remains, according to the Bible, that the king is God's implement of service on Earth.

There have been times in human history when this doctrine accomplished good things. It gave peasants comfort and provided kings the lever they needed to resist even papal commands in the days when church and state were not at all separate. But the dogma also caused great harm when rulers employed it to justify less than noble pursuits.

Taken to its logical conclusion, what does the doctrine mean to those who impose a literal interpretation of the Bible today? Does Paul forbid voting a president out of office? No one seems to take the verses that literally, but no one really explains why this passage can be neglected or labeled a cultural aberration while other verses must be followed exactly.

Sources:

Barzun, Jacques. *From Dawn to Decadence: 1500 Years to the Present*. New York: HarperCollins, 2000.

May, Herbert G., and Bruce M. Metzger, eds. *The New Oxford Annotated Bible with the Apocrypha*. Rev. ed. New York: Oxford University Press, 1973.

DOGMA

Although the word "dogma" was first used by the Greeks some four hundred years before Christ, it has come to be associated with the collective, intellectual theology of the Church. Dogma now refers to orthodoxy, that which must be believed because tradition has come to a consensus that it is true.

But dogma is always under fire. Whereas the Church of the third and fourth centuries met in council to determine its content, the Church of the nineteenth century subjected it to critical analysis.

In most civilized countries, those who disagree with Christian dogma are no longer subjected to inquisitors and papal courts of inquiry. Such is not the case, however, with other religions. When Salman Rushdie dared question Islamic dogma in his book *The Satanic Verses*, he discovered, much to the embarrassment and outright horror of many Muslims, that an Islamic bounty had been placed on his head, payable upon his death.

In Judaism, Christianity, and Islam, people have sometimes judged the dogmatic letter of the law so severely that they have overturned its spirit. Enforcing dogma is yet another example of how a good thing, meant to inform and support, can become a misguided tool of punishment.

Sources:
Douglas, J. D., ed. *The New International Dictionary of the Christian Church*. Grand Rapids, MI: Zondervan Publishing, 1974.

DOMINIC

Pope Innocent III (c. 1160–1216) was one of the most powerful and certainly one of the wisest pontiffs ever to rule in Rome. Two monastic orders began under his direction. Although he was at first reluctant to grant his approval, the world is richer because he finally did. Francis of Assisi (c. 1181–1226) and the Franciscans were the first (see Francis of Assisi). Dominic and the Order of Preachers—the Dominicans—were the second.

Dominic was twelve years older than Francis, but he began his work later. Those who followed him pursued his main objective of teaching, preaching, and study. Some great minds were trained under Dominican tutelage, including one of the greatest of all, Thomas Aquinas (1225–1274).

The order spread throughout Europe and influenced the main centers of theological study in Paris and Oxford. Dominican professors in universities around the world have sparked high levels of theological training and insight.

Their success did not come without blemish, however. From the very beginning, Dominicans had launched movements to convert Jews and Muslims. Unfortunately, their methods don't stand up to the hindsight of history. Force of arms and intrigue were sometimes employed, rather than the use of pen and pulpit. Crusaders were used against Muslims in Tripoli and Jews in Spain.

monasterium Sorianense

Saint Dominic, founder of the Order of Preachers, commonly known as the Dominican Order. *Fortean Picture Library.*

On the other hand, when Spanish forces terribly abused and exploited American Indians from Santo Domingo and Peru, Dominicans such as Antonio Montesinos preached boldly against the crown and its policies. As a result, the influential writer Bartolome de Las Casas converted and became a Dominican. His books caused a great stir, exposing the economic system of immorality that was being carried out under the guise of missionary work.

Unfortunately, things went from bad to worse. When Indian labor forces began to decline from the abuses heaped upon them, it was Las Casas who, in defense of the Indians he had grown to love, suggested slaves be imported from Africa. Although he later recanted and worked just as hard to free black slaves as he had indigenous Indians, the damage was done. Throughout the Caribbean, African slaves took the place of indigenous slaves, and to this day their descendants are more numerous than the people who once ruled the islands.

Although their labors are not given a lot of space in politically correct history books—the authors of which rightly seek to expose the barbarity of early fifteenth-century Caribbean slavery—the facts are that many Dominicans saw quickly and clearly what was happening in the Americas. They fought, unsuccessfully, to right the many sins European governments committed in their attempts to exploit the wealth of the New World.

It is significant that theologians of the time who wrote against slavery usually did so not on the basis of the inherent immorality of the system, but on the logic of how wealth would be distributed.

One would think religious orders would get along fairly well, but such is not always the case. One famous dispute took place after the Protestant Reformation. The Council of Trent, which lasted from 1545 to 1563, had condemned both Luther and Calvin on their views of grace and predestination, and many feared that the much respected Augustine, beloved of the reformers, would soon be condemned as well. Late in the sixteenth century the Jesuits produced a document stating that predestination (see Calvin, John, and Jacobus Arminius) was based on God's foreknowledge. One of the best Dominican theologians of the time countered the argument by stating that the Jesuits were anti-Augustine and ought to be condemned.

The trial went all the way to the top of the Inquisition. The Dominicans accused the Jesuits of being Pelagians (believers in free will). The Jesuits countered that the Dominicans were Calvinists (believers in predestination). The Inquisition turned the whole thing over to Rome, which, after a long time and many popes, told them both to go to their rooms and stop fighting.

Today, the various orders, though still competitive in a good-natured way, are usually a lot more polite to each other.

Sources:
Gonzalez, Justo L. *The Story of Christianity.* 2 vols. New York: Harper & Row, 1985.

DREAMS

It was the custom in ancient Britain, when a guest retired for the evening, to bestow a blessing upon him: "May the Gods send you a dream." It was understood in Celtic times that dreams were messages sent from the spirit world.

This belief seems to have been almost universal. Even in New Testament times, no one raised an eyebrow when the Magi, "being warned in a dream not to return to Herod, returned to their country by another way" (Matthew 2:12).

"An angel of the Lord, who appeared to him in a dream" (Matthew 1:20 and 2:19), regularly guided Joseph, husband to the mother of Jesus.

The urbane, educated apostle Paul had a dream one night wherein a man who seems to be Luke, the physician, appeared and called him to Macedonia (Acts 16:9).

Even in light of modern dream interpretation, there are still those who believe God communicates with us through our dreams, revealing the future or interpreting current events. The Australian Aborigines' whole concept of "Dreamtime" postulates a spiritual plain accessible through dreaming.

The latest theories tell us dreams come from our subconscious. When we have surrendered our conscious thought to rest and sleep, our subconscious is free to make known to us what we have experienced without our realization. Much more information comes to us each day than we can possibly process, so dreams originate in the intuitive, nonverbal portions of our minds. Viewing symbolic images thrown up on the screen of our relaxed consciousness, we can often discover in dreams what we already know but haven't yet visualized in a conscious manner. Inventions have come into being when a dream supplies the clue necessary to discovering the key ingredient of a new technology. Personal relationships come into focus when we suddenly discover something about an acquaintance that we saw but didn't quite process.

DREAMTIME

Australian Aborigines trace their religion into prehistoric times. In their belief system, everything that exists is part of a vast, interlocking network, a relationship beginning with the ancestors of the Dreamtime. The Dreamtime continues today and is accessible to people when they "dream the fire," or enter into spiritual communion with the reality of the invisible plane supporting the visible one. The power of Aboriginal spirituality has been called both telepathic and mystical, in direct contrast to

Illustration entitled "The Dream of Gilgamesh" by John Campbell, 1912. *Fortean Picture Library.*

typical Western pragmatism. When Australia was discovered and exploited by European society, the Aborigines were considered primitive, people in need of "elevation" to modern cultural standards. Typically, the rich Australian spiritual heritage, existing on a plane unappreciated, misunderstood, and underestimated by Europeans, was considered nothing more than superstition. Only in the last part of the twentieth century did it begin to dawn on Westerners that Aborigines understood the dangers inherent in the trajectory of modern Western society far better than their European counterparts. When anxieties and stresses built up, when life got to be too complex and perspective was needed, it was the habit in Australia to "go walkabout," to pare down and sort things out, to spend an open-ended amount of time simply "being" until perspective was regained. Aboriginal religion intuitively understood that life can sometimes layer up, making it difficult to remain in touch with the very essence of the Dreamtime connection, the feeling of what it means to be alive, in touch with all things in the web. Through mythology, through the ritual of the dance, accompanied by the unique sounds of the didgeridoo or clap sticks, through the very act of observing, living close upon the sparse land in ways no Westerner could, Aborigines lived their religion moment by moment. When they came together to share their histories, telling the old stories, they released the power of the Dreamtime into present-day reality, informing new generations and carrying on the wisdom of the ancestors who had lived for so long on the land.

It can be argued that Dreamtime was experienced when early pioneers told stories around fires in the Rocky Mountains and the Great Plains. Daniel Boone and Davy Crockett "went walkabout." American Indians danced and felt the presence of the divine in their environment. Indigenous Australians were no different.

Of course there existed those Aborigines who abused Dreamtime, walkabout, and the spiritual heritage that existed in Australia. There can be found, within the culture, abuse of women, laziness, drunkenness, and lack of direction. Probably no religious tradition has ever existed that personified a "golden age" when everyone was wise and spiritually fully developed. But spiritual traditions must be judged on their merits, not on their problem children. Dreamtime connected people with their heritage, supported and informed countless generations of people over the course of thousands of years, and is perfectly logical. Aboriginal customs have stood the test of time, coming to the aid of people who have seen their world turned upside down in a matter of a few short years. And, the greatest test of all, Dreamtime has been validated by people who feel the pressures of modern life and want to establish spiritual roots in a rapidly changing world. When the pressures of life build up and threaten to overcome us, when too much information floods our souls, perhaps we all need to "go walka-bout" or spend some quiet time "dreaming the fire."

Sources:
"The Dreamtime." *Aboriginal Art and Culture Centre.* http://aboriginalart.com.au/culture/dreamtime.html. September 14, 2003.

DRUIDS *see* Caesar, Julius; Celtic

DRUZE

In the early years of the eleventh century, a religious community came into existence that combined monotheism with beliefs about reincarnation. At first a secret sect with its own scriptures, the Druze allowed no religious conversion either in or out, insisting on marriage within the group. The sect was tied to their land and based on a close-knit family structure, with members obeying the word of the clan patriarchs.

The ancestry of the Druze is Arab. They split off from Islam when the sect migrated from Egypt to Lebanon. Very quickly they established themselves from Mount Hermon into the Galilee, and all the way to Syria. Today isolated communities may be found around the world. Many, especially in Israel, identify with Christianity, but wherever they are found they are famous for strict loyalty to their host nation. Known as the "Sons of Grace," they believe very strongly in the coexistence of all religions and ethnic groups. In religiously and culturally volatile places like Israel, this notion is becoming more and more difficult.

Sources:
Israel Druze Society. http://www.geocities.com/Baja/Outback/9277/d1.htm. September 14, 2003.

E

EASTERN ORTHODOX *see* Christianity, Development of

ECUMENICAL COUNCILS *see* Vatican Councils

ECUMENISM

"Ecumenical," according to Webster's dictionary, means "pertaining to the entire inhabited earth; universal in extent." The "ecumenical movement" began within Protestant Christianity, expanded through organizations like the World Council of Churches, and now, through grassroots clergy associations, is understood as a complete interfaith dialogue.

The movement began in the Christian mission field. Missionaries found themselves thrown together, forced to work in cultural situations that tended to downplay differences that might have seemed important and divisive back home. Baptists felt free to use Congregationalists' translations of the Bible in order to save the time involved in doing their own. Overseas, cooperation was almost mandatory. Whereas their American counterparts may have had the luxury of debating fine points of difference between predestination and free will, the overworked foreign missionaries just didn't have time for such luxuries.

Although ecumenism is, with a few exceptions (see below), accepted today as the norm, it was not always so. Before the Church grew so divided (see Christianity, Development of), the concept was both unheard-of and unneeded. Later, as individual denominations grew, it was a natural thing for people from different Christian traditions to band together when community projects outside the scope of any one denomination beckoned. Even there, however, it was the participation of moderate and liberal churches that formed the backbone of ministerial fellowships and Christian clergy associations. Fundamentalist pastors and Jewish rabbis were often left out, sometimes by their own choice but sometimes by a subtle (or not-so-subtle) attitude of exclusion on the part of traditional Methodists, Presbyterians, Baptists, and Congregationalists. By the 1960s, as mainstream America began to awaken to the realities of racial and ethnic segregation, and as the civil rights movement, largely sparked by Christian churches in both the south and the north, began to assert its influence, ecumenism flourished. Gradually, doors were opened and barriers broken down.

Even still, it took more than forty years for some groups to be included. As late as the 1990s, a clergy association in western Massachusetts brought down all kinds of criticism upon itself when it became one of the first in the nation to welcome a Druid priest and a neo-pagan witch into its membership. And shortly after the infamous September 11, 2001, terrorist attack on the World Trade Center in New York City, the Reverend David Benke, a high-ranking Lutheran pastor in the Missouri Synod, found himself suspended and ordered to apologize to all Christians after he participated in an interfaith prayer service held in New York's Yankee Stadium. Muslims, Jews, Sikhs, and Hindus all took part in the service, and this was unacceptable to twenty-one Lutheran synod pastors and congregations. In comments made to the *San Francisco Chronicle* by denominational spokesman David Mahsman, Benke was accused of "compromising the gospel of Jesus Christ" by appearing to place Jesus on an equal footing with Allah, Vishnu, "and whatever gods are involved."

Charges made against those who endorse ecumenism generally include "unionism" and "syncretism." Unionism involves mixing differing beliefs of Christian organizations. Syncretism pertains to joining together Christian and non-Christian religious views.

Perhaps the need for ecumenism in today's volatile world was best demonstrated at the very beginning of the movement. On August 2, 1914, a worldwide Christian conference was held to discuss ways churches of all denominations could work together for peace. It was felt this was a common cause that should unite people of all traditions. On that day, in the city of Constance, Germany, an ecumenical peace organization was founded, the World Alliance for Promoting International Friendship through the Churches, designed to be the first of its kind.

The organization never had a chance to meet, because that was the very day World War I began.

Sources:
Gonzalez, Justo L. *The Story of Christianity*. 2 vols. New York: Harper & Row, 1985.

EFFIGY *see* Healing Effigy/Amulet/Talisman/Fetish

EGYPTIAN GODS AND GODDESSES

For many generations, Heliopolis was the religious capital of Egypt. It was the city sacred to Ra, the Sun God. As the religion of Egypt grew, Ra developed a family—a sort of protective dynasty. The nine members of his family became the principal deities of the Egyptian pantheon called the Great Ennead of Heliopolis. Their names were Ra, Geb, Nut, Shu, Tefnut, Osiris, Isis, Set, and Nephythys.

Ra

The name "Ra" became an international household word after the "Ra Voyages" of the intrepid Norwegian adventurer and anthropologist Thor Heyerdahl in 1969 and 1970. Believing the history of Central America was influenced by ancient Egyptian sailors, Heyerdahl built a faithful replica of the kind of reed boats Egyptians had made. He then set out to prove pre-Columbian contact was at least possible. On his second try, sailing from Morocco to Barbados, he made it. The name painted on the sail of his boat was "Ra."

Ra was both creator and father to one of the most famous dysfunctional families in history. His family, as will soon be seen, were not only brothers and sisters, many of them were also husband and wife. They freely loved each other, murdered each other, and performed all kinds of mayhem. It is no wonder he decided to leave Earth and retire to become god of the sun and sky, leaving his grandson Osiris to rule the world.

Egyptian goddesses Isis and Nephys, attendants of Osiris, King of the Dead, from the *Egyptian Book of the Dead. Fortean Picture Library.*

Nut, Geb, and Shu

Nut and Geb were sister and brother as well as wife and husband. Their children were named Osiris, Isis, Set, and Nephthys. Nut was the goddess of the sky and the heavens. She is usually pictured with blue skin, covered with stars. Her husband, Geb, was god of the earth. His sacred animal was the goose.

But one day their brother, Shu, god of the atmosphere, caught them in a passionate embrace. He wasn't necessarily upset about the embrace. This was, after all, ancient Egypt, when gods did stuff like that. His problem was that they hadn't told him first. So he separated them. This perhaps explains how heaven and earth came to be separated by atmosphere.

Although the two brothers and one sister got into enough squabbles, it was their children who really carried the family quarrels to an extreme.

Osiris, Isis, Horus, and Set

One of the most important and well-known stories in Egyptian mythology explores the complicated relationship between these gods and goddesses.

Osiris ruled the world after Ra, his grandfather, left to take his new job ruling the sky. Osiris was married to his sister Isis, the most important goddess of the Egyptian pantheon. She was the goddess of motherhood, marital devotion, and healing. This last she was especially good at because she had coaxed her grandfather, Ra, into telling her his secret name, enabling her to perform all kinds of spells of enchantment.

Osiris and Isis had another brother named Set. He showed up at a party of gods once, carrying a coffin. As part of the entertainment, all the gods climbed into the coffin to see who it best fit. Unknown to Osiris, however, Set had the coffin made exactly to Osiris's measurements. It turns out he was jealous because Osiris had Ra's old job instead of him. Of course, when Osiris got into the coffin, it fit him like a glove. All Set had to do was close it up, seal it with lead, and kill Osiris by spiriting him off down the Nile River, into the Mediterranean Sea, and all the way to Phoenicia. Osiris, although dead by then, eventually found protection when a great, aromatic tree spread its roots about the coffin and enclosed him in its trunk. The problem came when the tree got cut down to form a pillar in the new palace of Astarte, daughter of Ra, in Phoenicia.

Isis was devastated. But eventually she found out about the great, sweet-smelling pillar in Astarte's new palace and immediately knew Osiris was inside. (Goddesses know these things.) Hieing herself off to Phoenicia, she got a job nursing Astarte's new baby.

She took such a shine to the young baby that she decided to burn off any mortality he might have so he could be immortal. While the fire slowly burned, she took on her favorite guise of a bird and, to pass the time while her magic was doing its work, flew around the room paying special attention to Osiris's coffin entombed in the pillar.

As you can well imagine, the child's mother wasn't too happy to discover what was going on when she burst into the room one afternoon, only to find her child in the fireplace while a bird flapped around the pillar.

But all's well that ends well. Isis persuaded Astarte that the pillar contained her husband, and she managed to get permission to put him on her barge and transport him back to Egypt. Of course she embalmed him first to prepare him for his death journey home. So imagine her surprise when she finally opened the casket, presumably to have sex with her dead husband, only to discover that somewhere back in the Nile River a crab had eaten his genitals! After a fascinating series of events, however, she finally managed to have sex with him and conceive a son, Horus.

At any rate, Osiris was brought back up the Nile in Isis's barge and, because he was the first living being ever to die, he soon landed a job as lord of the dead. Because he had been prepared for his final journey by being embalmed, he showed the ancients how to prepare for their own journeys after death.

Meanwhile Horus grew up and declared vengeance on his uncle Set—who once, somehow, a very long time ago, used to be his twin brother—for killing his father, Osiris.

At any rate, he eventually caught up with Set and castrated him before defeating him in battle. Some versions of the story have the battle still continuing—the battle between good and evil.

Horus went on to be reincarnated in every pharaoh. They were all seen as divine, sons of the gods. Horus was their prototype.

Nephthys

Nephthys was the youngest child of Nut and Geb. Although she was both sister and wife to Set, she left him when she discovered what he had done to her brother, and she was there to console her sister Isis upon the death of Osiris, who was both her brother and brother-in-law, being her sister's husband.

These gods and goddesses have served an important purpose in history. Almost certainly they represent the struggle between religious cults in prehistoric, ancient times. The cult of Set probably did go to war and eventually defeat their "brother" cult of Osiris. The cult of Isis probably did side with that of Osiris, and the sister cult of Nephthys probably did break allegiance with the Set cult to side with that of Isis. All these people were once "brothers and sisters," who once worshiped Ra, the Sun God, now remembered in ancient stories and myths. And if a "brother" from one cult married a "sister" from another cult, they could become the mother and father of a third cult. So it's really not as complicated as it at first seems to be.

By reading the myths in this way, we may be reading the real religious history of ancient Egypt. These myths may be the closest thing we have to a window on the past.

Sources:
Campbell, Joseph. *The Power of Myth*. New York: Doubleday, 1988.
"The Egyptian Pantheon." *Vibrani's One Source*. http://www.vibrani.com/gods.htm. June 3, 1997.

ELIOT, JOHN

The first Christian missionary outreach to the indigenous people of North America came about because John Eliot (1604–1690), "Apostle to the Indians," decided to take seriously the 1628 charter of the Massachusetts Bay Company. The charter said, in what hindsight simply has to qualify as sanctimonious terms, that part of the reason for coming to New England in the first place was "to win the natives of the country to the knowledge and obedience of the one true God and Savior of mankind." The official seal of the company pictured an Indian reciting the words of Acts 16:9, "Come over and help us." (This quotation comes from what is often called the apostle Paul's "Macedonian vision." Paul had a dream of these words one night that inspired the missionary journey he undertook, during which he met his faithful chronicler, Luke.) The first years the Pilgrims spent in Massachusetts Bay didn't see them spending much time saving Indians. Indeed, as is recounted every year at Thanksgiving time, the Indians spent the bulk of their days saving Pilgrims.

But in 1637 an English trader was killed, involving the Puritan community in an intertribal war between Narragansett and Pequot Indians, one of many that would later culminate in what has since been called King Philip's War. Being thrown together in a war opened the eyes of some Narragansett Indians to the God of the Puritans, who seemed ready and able to bless them with a lot of firepower and superior technology. John Eliot, pastor of the Roxbury church, had been in Massachusetts for six years, working hard to open a dialogue and establish a friendly relationship with local Indians. He had even managed to learn Algonquian, not an easy task by any means. But that was the language of trade spoken by all New England tribes. Although later missionary attempts involved teaching outward change, like wearing shoes and sitting on hard church benches during interminably long sermons, Eliot was more interested in inward change. He really loved his Christian God and he really loved his Indian friends. A true believer, Eliot taught the Indians what, in fact, he really believed—that God loved them and sent his son Jesus to die for their sins.

The Indians had some basic questions.

How, for instance, could God understand Indian prayers? As far as they knew, he spoke English and possibly a little French, not Algonquian. Eliot's answer? Just like the maker of an Indian basket knows straw and the properties of even unknown materials that make it up, God knows Indians and understands their hearts because he made all people.

The Indians also wondered whether even old Indians could convert, or if it was too late for them. Eliot responded that Jesus told a parable once about a man who hired workers even at the eleventh hour and paid them just as much as workers who had been in the field all day long.

But it was when Eliot undertook the translation of the whole Bible into Algonquian that he earned the respect of his Indian friends. To hear the "Holy Book" in their own language proved the key to persuading Indians that God really could communicate with them.

At this point, however, a few considerations have to be remembered. John Eliot was supported in his missionary work by the Society for Propagating the Gospel among the Natives of New England, funded from England. But correspondence left behind by early members of this society leaves no doubt they were not interested in converting Indians because they were Indians. They wanted to convert Indians because they thought the Indians were Jews.

Indians had a story similar to the flood story. They recognized Noah right away. They practiced circumcision. They danced. All of this was evidence, according to a popular theory of the time, that they were really descendants of the Ten Lost Tribes of Israel (see Abominable Snowman; Babylonian Captivity).

In 1660 Eliot wrote:

Truly the Bible says that the Ark landed on the eastward of the land of Eden, and if so, then surely into America, because that is part of the Western World. Hence why ought we not to believe a portion of the ten tribes landed in America?

This popular theory would be repeated in many forms over the next few centuries, culminating in the writing of the Book of Mormon (see Mormons/Church of Jesus Christ of Latter-day Saints).

This convinced some people that Indians were worth saving. As Edward Winslow, governor of Plymouth Colony, wrote in 1646, "Well, if they be Jewes [his spelling], they must not be neglected."

But whether John Eliot thought he was converting Indians or Jews, villages were established that became known as "praying Indian" towns. Eliot even reported, "the Indians have utterly forsaken their pow-wows." But this statement surely indicates more of what he wanted to believe than what was actually going on.

It was no easy task to produce "Um Biblum God," the first New World translation of the Bible. But it had a profound effect. Eliot had to invent words that were not a part of Algonquian dialect. When he needed a word to describe "great chiefs" such as Joshua or Samson, he used the word "mugwump." Much later, New Englanders began to fit the term to egotistic politicians. Still later, around 1884, Republicans called those who left "the party of Lincoln" mugwumps. Now it is sometimes applied to any person not officially affiliated with a political party.

By 1690, the year he died after enduring a long illness, John Eliot had written an Algonquian grammar, a primer, and a hymnbook. For generations, many of the descendants of the Indians so beloved by Eliot—though by now driven, in some cases, halfway across the country—would remember him when they sang and prayed in the manner in which they had been taught. "Singing Indians" and "praying Indians" were taken advantage of, persecuted, imprisoned, and killed along with other Indians in the years that followed his death, but there are still those who remember. In the last decade of the twentieth century, descendants of John Eliot's friends made the trip to New England from Minnesota to return, in his memory, an almost priceless first-edition hymnbook that had been given to them years before. Their thinking was that the man who cared so deeply should be remembered in the state that was his home. The book is now on display in a western Massachusetts museum.

Sources:

"John Eliot: Apostle to the Indians." *Christian History Institute.* http://www.gospelcom.net/chi/ GLIMPSEF/Glimpses/glmps024.shtml. September 15, 2003.

Kiefer, James E. "John Eliot, Missionary to the American Indians." *The Society of Archbishop Justus.* http://justus.anglican.org/resources/bio/164.html. September 15, 2003.

Mavor, James W., Jr., and Byron E. Dix. *Manitou.* Rochester, VT: Inner Traditions International, 1989.

EPIPHANY *see* **Christianity, Calendar of**

EPISCOPAL CHURCH

(See also Anglican Church)

Members of the Anglican Church faced a dilemma during and after the American Revolution.

On the one hand, they were members and faithful communicants of a church that acknowledged the King of England as its "supreme governor." They believed their church had practiced apostolic succession that continued in an unbroken line all the way back to the apostle Peter, and that if Henry VIII hadn't divorced his wife to marry Anne Boleyn they would all still be Catholic. Tied to England by strong ecclesiastical cords, they couldn't ordain clergy without an American bishop, and they didn't have any American bishops. Since most of their priests had returned to England, to the mother church, they were in desperate need to replenish the ranks.

On the other hand, they were loyal Americans. They believed in independence and wanted to stay in the country that many of their members had died to protect.

It seemed their cause was lost and Anglicanism would die out in the new United States.

Enter William White of Christ Church in Philadelphia, former chaplain to the Continental Congress. Almost singlehandedly, he laid the groundwork for a general convention, held in his hometown, in 1785. There, his fellow American Anglicans framed a constitution, revised the liturgy, and arranged for the consecration of bishops after the British Parliament made the necessary legal adjustments.

It all came together on February 4, 1787. White and Samuel Provost of New York were elevated to the Episcopal rank of bishop in England's Lambeth Chapel, thus forging a new American link in the long Protestant side of the apostolic chain. The Protestant Episcopal Church, though still facing trials inherent in any new endeavor, was born. Because of the historical position priests held and the tradition they represented, the Episcopal Church called its parish priests "Father," as was the case in both Catholic and Anglican tradition.

The Episcopal Church in America, although an independent entity, is still a part of the worldwide Anglican Communion. These historic ties, however, were recently threatened. In 1998 the Anglican Communion, including their Episcopalian representatives, approved a resolution "rejecting homosexual practice as incompatible with Scripture." But in July of 2003 the Episcopal Diocese of New Hampshire voted in their general convention to elect a gay bishop. The Reverend V. Gene Robinson is a divorced father of two grown children who has been living faithfully in openness with his male partner for thirteen years. This election represents the first time that a church claiming apostolic succession has elected an openly gay bishop. In response, conservatives in both the Anglican and Episcopalian denominations have threatened to break fellowship, but as of this writing, no such action has been taken.

Sources:
Hudson, Winthrop S. *Religion in America.* New York: Charles Scribner, 1965.

ESCHATOLOGY *see* **Antichrist; Apocalypse**

EUCHARIST

Then came the day of Unleavened Bread, called the Passover. Jesus sent Peter and John, saying, "Go and make preparations for us to eat the Passover." ... When the hour came, Jesus and his apostles reclined at the table. And he said to them, "I have eagerly desired to eat this Passover with you before I suffer." ... And he took bread, gave thanks and broke it, and gave it to them, saying, "This is my body, broken for you." ... In the same way ... he took the cup and said, "this is the cup of the new testament ... this is my blood, shed for you ... do this in remembrance of me" (Luke 22:7–21).

Whether it's called Eucharist, Communion, the Lord's Supper, or the Last Supper, this meal is the central ritual binding together all Christian churches. Every denomination considers it a sacrament, a "sacred mystery," and considers it central to the understanding of what it means to be a Christian. It is one of the two sacraments all Christians celebrate in common, the other being baptism.

Of course disagreements abound as to what Jesus meant, how to serve the meal, who can serve and partake, and what mystery occurs during its celebration. But this meal is the most universal and significant symbol in all of Christendom.

We begin with a question. What happened at the first Communion meal?

There is no question but that it came at the end of a Seder feast (see Passover). Luke makes it clear the disciples had met to celebrate a traditional Passover meal together. Not only were Jesus' instructions specific to that end, but the disciples were reclining around the table, typical even at contemporary Seder feasts, and it would have been perfectly normal for them to meet in this way at this time. They would typically have been remembering back over the last 1,500 years to the first Passover meal, eaten in haste by their ancestors in Egypt on the night before the Exodus. To them, this would have been a memorial feast, and Jews all over Jerusalem—indeed, all over the world—would have been meeting this night in similar fashion.

A Bishop raises the Eucharist, the embodiment of Christ in Catholicism, as part of the sacrament of Holy Communion. *AP/Wide World Photos.*

But this raises an interesting question. Passover instructions are quite explicit that the Seder is to be a family event. The whole purpose of the meal is to gather the family together to tell the old, old story. So where were the women? Mary, Jesus' mother, was in town the next day at the crucifixion. Where was she this night? It would have been unheard of, an absolutely disgraceful action, for a Jewish man to celebrate this meal without his mother present if she were anywhere nearby. The Passover ritual requires specific roles for women, men, and children who participate together. Granted, situations sometimes arise when exceptions have to be made. But who prepared the meal? The apostles Peter and John? Given the culture of that day, it is a decidedly improbable thesis.

But the Bible mentions no women present at all. Could the famous Leonardo Da Vinci, who pictured all thirteen men sitting on one side of a long table, the better to see everyone's face, have misled entire generations?

We are simply left to theorize. Perhaps Jesus wanted to be alone with the men who were closest to him. Maybe, even though it appears obvious, it wasn't a Passover Seder at all. Or maybe the women were there after all, but the Bible just doesn't mention them. Perhaps they were out in the kitchen by this time.

There are other mysteries surrounding this event. They seemed to drink a lot of wine that night. According to Luke, everyone seems to have had at least three portions, and there were probably many more served. Is it a coincidence that a few hours later they were all having trouble staying awake on the most important night of Jesus' life? In the immortal words of the rock opera *Jesus Christ, Superstar*, "What's that in the bread? It's gone to my head!" Were the disciples drunk?

And so the speculations continue. It is not even known what day of the week the Passover was celebrated that year. Tradition says it happened on a Thursday evening. But this raises serious chronological problems. If Jesus was arrested Thursday night and crucified Friday, how do we account for three days and nights in the tomb before Sunday morning, as Jesus prophesied (Matthew 12:40)? But if the meal took place earlier in the week we encounter more problems. The day after the crucifixion was a Sabbath. The story says specifically that Jesus had to be taken down from the cross before sundown just for this reason. So he must have been crucified on a Friday, unless the Sabbath referred to was the Passover itself. If the crucifixion took place on Wednesday and the Passover on Thursday, they would have had Friday to bury him before the regular Saturday Sabbath and an extra two days can be added to the scenario. But that can't be, first because the women who wanted to prepare his body for burial would have done so on Friday, with no reason to visit the tomb on Sunday morning (see Christ/Jesus of Nazareth), and second because Jesus' instructions specifically mentioned the Passover meal.

No single explanation has ever been offered that fits all the chronologies. We are left with the fact that we don't know when the meal took place, although Christians celebrate it on a Thursday. We don't know who attended, we do know they reclined at the table, but we picture them sitting up straight in modern chairs.

The events mark only the beginning of the problem. Significant debate arises when Christians try to decide what the whole thing means. There are four different interpretations held by the various Christian traditions.

Transubstantiation

This is the interpretation held by the Roman Catholic Church ever since the sixteenth-century Council of Trent. The council determined that Christ "is truly, really and substantially contained in the sacrament under the appearance of sensible things.... By the consequence of the bread and wine a change is brought about of the whole substance of the wine into the body of his blood. This change is called ... transubstantiation."

In this view, when the priest holds up the consecrated host and intones the words of the Mass, the wine and bread, although they appear unchanged, undergo a mystical process that actually transforms them into the very body and blood of the Christ.

During the Middle Ages, it became the custom for an altar boy to hold a plate or some such thing under the chin of the person receiving the host to prevent the body and blood of the Christ from accidentally falling on the floor where it might become lunch for a passing mouse.

It cannot be emphasized enough that the Roman Catholic Church revolves around the Eucharist. At the Second Vatican Ecumenical Council, the opinion was set down that "Truly partaking of the body of the Lord in the breaking of the Eucharistic bread, we are taken up into communion with Him and with one another.... No Christian community ... can be built up unless it has its basis and center in the celebration of the ... Eucharist."

Consubstantiation

Although the term doesn't appear in any of his writings, consubstantiation was the view of Martin Luther and remains the official position of the Lutheran Church today. Luther believed Christ is present "under or with (*con*) the species of bread and wine." In this view a union takes place between the heavenly and the earthly, even though the bread and wine are not changed in substance. Instead, they are infused with the reality of the divine.

Real Presence

In this view, held by many mainstream Protestant churches, the bread remains bread and the wine (many substitute grape juice) remains wine. But Christ, always present with the believer, is somehow represented in a way that is similar to, but at the same time different from, normal life activity. The "real presence" of Jesus is there when "two or more" believers gather together to break bread "in his name."

Memorial

In this view, held by many non-liturgical traditions, such as the many Baptist denominations, when Jesus said, "do this in remembrance of me," that's exactly what he meant. The communion meal is a memorial to what Jesus did on the cross. The bread and grape juice are symbols of his body and blood. They remind believers of Jesus, but nothing changes in terms of substance. Jesus is no more or no less with the believer than he always is.

Despite the differences in theological interpretation of the Eucharist, some consider the commonality of the ritual to be a miracle in itself. Christians cannot agree about the chronology or participation in the first ritual. They cannot agree as to what it means. In some cases they don't even allow Christians of different persuasions to come to their altars and receive the sacred elements. Like the caste system of ancient India, the higher you are on the theological ladder of Eucharistic social order, the less you tend to allow those of lesser purity to partake with you. But the miracle is that the communion service still is one that all Christians hold in common, and one ritual that allows believers to cling to their concept of "one, universal and apostolic church."

Sources:
Douglas, J. D., ed. *The New International Dictionary of the Christian Church*. Grand Rapids, MI: Zondervan Publishing, 1974.

EVANGELICAL

The strict meaning of "evangelical" refers to the Gospel. The Greek word from which it is derived, *euaggelion*, means "good news." So does the word "gospel." So in this sense, evangelical means "pertaining to the Gospel," or the story told by the four Gospels: Matthew, Mark, Luke, and John. They are the New Testament books that record the life of Jesus. Perhaps the apostle Paul best summarized the "evangel" in 1 Corinthians 15:1–8:

> Now brothers, I want to remind you of the gospel I preached to you, which you received and on which you have taken your stand. By this gospel you are saved, if you hold firmly to the word I preached to you. Otherwise you have believed in vain. For what I received I passed on to you as of first importance: that Christ died for our sins according to the Scriptures, that he was buried, that he was raised on the third day according to the Scriptures, and that he appeared to Peter, and then to the twelve. After that he appeared to more than five hundred of the brothers at the same time, most of whom are still living, although some have fallen asleep. Then he appeared to James, then to all the apostles, and last of all he appeared to me also, as to one abnormally born.

This is a synopsis of the story. The one who tells it, who brings the "good news," is called an evangelist.

All Christian churches use basically the same Bible and read the Gospels at their worship services. All accept what the apostle said in 1 Corinthians. So all claim to be evangelists and all claim to be evangelical. But some claim to be more evangelical than others.

Some Protestant churches began early on to differentiate between evangelical and evangelistic. "Evangelical" became a noun—something a Christian was if he or she believed the Gospel. But "evangelistic" described something the Christian did, something he or she lived for. Evangelistic churches purposely set out to convert souls to Christ. After a while, a liturgy developed, although most Evangelistic churches favor spontaneous rather than recited worship and would be mortified to admit they had a liturgy. Nonetheless, when the evangelist gave the altar call and the organist struck up the familiar strains of the hymn "Just As I Am," everyone knew what to do. They came forward to "get saved." It was the whole purpose of the service. It was what the liturgy called for.

This method of religious practice was completely different from what had become known as "High Church." In High Church, the emphasis was on liturgy and worship. No one ever asked if a worshiper was "born again." That would be prying. The person was a member of the church; he was there; he was a Christian. His name was on the rolls.

An evangelist, however, might say that being a Christian in name is not enough; one must be a Christian "in your heart." Testimonies began to be preached in Evangelical churches that went something like this: "I went to church all my life but I never accepted Jesus Christ as my personal savior. I was going to hell and I never knew it because I sang in the choir every week. But when Brother … came to town, I went forward and was born again."

Now there were, in effect, two different definitions of evangelical. All kinds of denominations arose that used the term "evangelical" in their title to advertise the fact that they were in the business of "doing" church instead of what they often called "playing" church. Evangelical had become a label differentiating what is now called conservative theology from liberal theology, even though both liberal and conservative churches still used the same word. It was a matter of interpretation. If a church believed in a literal reading of the Bible, rather than metaphorical; insisted on the individual's need for a personal experience of being "saved"; and sang the songs of John and Charles Wesley, it was "more evangelical" than those that didn't. The church might still have a formal worship service, but it would be considered Low Church rather than High Church. Many on both sides of the issue reveled in the difference.

The situation can be seen clearly in the formation of the Protestant Episcopalian Church in the late 1700s. Right from the beginning, High Church became Protestant Episcopalian. Low Church became Methodist Episcopal, eventually shortened to Methodist. Methodists considered themselves evangelical. So did Episcopalians, but not in the same sense. Style and theological substance were at odds with each other. When a person "converted" from one theology to the other, they tended to lump worship style into their bag of complaints about their former church home.

New Low Church adherents might have complained that their former congregation was just going through the motions, while established High Church folks might have lamented what they perceived as a lack of dignity and beauty in the worship.

It's important to remember that, at this point, no one was yet using the term "evangelical Christian" as a label. But everyone knew what the term meant. There were sermons being preached by Anglican and Episcopalian (typically High Church) ministers with titles such as, "We Are Evangelical." But Baptists and Methodists (typically Low Church) knew better.

By the 1920s the rift had grown into a chasm. Even those who were on the conservative side of what would soon be known as evangelicalism were suspicious of those more toward the center. With the publication of a series of pamphlets defining "the fundamentals" (see Fundamentalism) beginning in 1910, right-wing evangelicals began to call themselves fundamentalists. They wanted to distance themselves from what was being called "literary" or "higher criticism" (see Literary Criticism/Historical Critical Method) and from those who questioned the doctrine of the virgin birth, miracles, and the Second Coming of Jesus. Fundamentalism united the religious right against the form of liberal Christianity then called "modernism." The Scopes "Monkey Trial," held in Dayton, Tennessee, in 1925, pitted "modernist" Darwinism versus "fundamentalist" creationism. It generated such nationwide publicity that fundamentalism vs. modernism became a national debate (see Christianity).

Problems arise, however, whenever something as deeply felt as religious conviction comes to the surface. Fundamentalists took such pride in the purity of their beliefs, and modernists in their educated views and traditional worship, that the two sides simply stopped talking to each other.

THE RELIGION BOOK: PLACES, PROPHETS, SAINTS, AND SEERS

But by the 1950s fundamentalism had developed the appearance of an "attitude." Science had produced such a huge body of evidence supporting evolution that even though the fundamentalists had won the Scopes trial, it seemed they were losing the modernist war. Evolution, not Creation, was being taught in the public schools. Men returning from World War II were attending liberal colleges financed by the G.I. bill. Having been in contact with different cultures and religions, these men were not quite so quick to condemn others. Churches were booming, but many were moving to the suburbs, where Catholics, Episcopalians, Baptists, and Jews were all in the same bowling league.

The harder fundamentalists fought, the more their image became that of the preacher with the clenched fist, the unenlightened, the unbending.

Although it is difficult to document, a good argument can be put forth that it was fundamentalist objection to Billy Graham (b. 1918) that finally caused large groups of Christians to distance themselves from the fundamentalist title. The Reverend Billy Graham, arguably the most influential evangelical in America, was a fundamentalist, but he was open and inviting to everyone. He often welcomed civic leaders to sit on the front dais with him at rallies. This caused some fundamentalists to draw back in horror. How can believers associate with unbelievers?

Some fundamentalists began to picket Graham's famous rallies. They were called "separationists." Others were even more extreme. They not only disassociated from Billy Graham, they disassociated with those who associated with him. They were called "secondary separationists."

This incident was embarrassing to many who agreed with fundamentalist theology but didn't feel comfortable associating with fundamentalists. It became popular to declare one's theological position by announcing, "I am a fundamentalist in theology but not in attitude."

It was Harold Ockenga, pastor of Park Street Church in Boston, who coined the term "new evangelical." He preached a conservative form of theology but was greatly respected by the liberal intellectual community. When the popular periodical *Christianity Today* identified with the new label, and when the Billy Graham Evangelistic Association followed suit, the term "evangelical" stuck. It became the name for people of all denominations who followed a fairly conservative brand of Christian belief but felt free to associate with those who did not. At the same time, evangelicals sought to explore their faith unencumbered by the restraints of those who were suspicious of scientific inquiry and critical biblical scholarship.

Today's evangelicals can be found in every denomination and every local church. It is almost a separate denomination. Evangelical members of the United Church of Christ might attend conferences with evangelical Methodists and Baptists, feeling closer to them in the faith than they do with more liberal people in their own church. Probably every Protestant church in America has an evangelical wing in the congregation, even though they may not use the term.

Currently the labeling system is as follows (see Bible):

To the far right of the Christian spectrum lie those calling themselves fundamentalists. Moving toward the center, but still on the conservative right, lies the evangelical camp. In the center are those usually called "mainstream" or "middle of the road." To the left lie the liberals.

Notice that it makes little difference what the denomination is. Fundamentalists of the Missouri Synod Lutherans feel more comfortable with fundamentalist Orthodox Presbyterians than they do with liberal Lutherans. And Methodist evangelicals work together with American Baptist evangelicals when the Billy Graham organization comes to town. Evangelical student organizations are found in even the most liberal of seminaries and theological schools, for evangelicals consider themselves the heirs and modern expression of traditional fundamentalism—the essence of traditional Christianity.

Sources:

Douglas, J. D., ed. *The New International Dictionary of the Christian Church.* Grand Rapids, MI: Zondervan Publishing, 1974.

Gonzalez, Justo L. *The Story of Christianity.* 2 vols. New York: Harper & Row, 1985.

Hudson, Winthrop S. *Religion in America.* New York: Charles Scribner, 1965.

EVIL

(See also Devil/Demons)

"In the beginning, God created the heavens and the earth … and God saw all that he had made, and behold, it was very good" (Genesis 1:1).

So why are things so messed up today? Well, sin entered into the world. That's the point of the whole serpent-and-apple thing in Genesis 3 (see Adam and Eve).

But that doesn't really answer the question. If evil entered the world through Adam and Eve's sin, it doesn't account for the devil. And if we accept the explanation given in the Hebrew Bible, that "sin was found in [Lucifer]" when five times he declared he would "be like God," there is still the problem of God's part in all this. If God is all powerful, why does he allow sin to hurt so many innocent people? Why does the drunk driver walk away from the accident that kills the innocent child? Why do bad things happen to good people? If God is good, why doesn't he stop it? Maybe he can't. But if God is not all powerful, how can he be God?

Genesis even seems to paint a picture of a God who made a mistake: "The Lord was sorry that he had made humankind on the earth, and it grieved him to his heart" (Genesis 6:6).

If sin is in the world, it must be because God either *can't* stop it or *won't* stop it. And God loses both ways. Religion has to solve what is known as the "problem" of evil or it dies on the vine.

Considering the problem of evil, we discover three religious responses, with many variations.

Evil Is Part of Life's Duality

This approach is best explained by the Buddha. Evil is a part of life. No one put it here. It just is. How can there be good without its opposite? Good cannot exist without evil. How can there be a coin with just one side? It's impossible.

The way to handle evil is to accept it, just as we embrace good. Good is not necessarily "better" than evil, it is just more comfortable.

This view made it possible for some of the scientists who participated in the Manhattan Project to live with themselves after viewing the first atomic bomb explosion. The devastation released certainly was going to be a great evil for millions of people. But the end of the war, to say nothing of the perceived benefits of nuclear energy, was seen to be greater good for a greater number of people.

Evil Is Different from Misfortune

Many forms of American Indian religious belief differentiate between evil and misfortune. Misfortune occurs when a tree falls on your house. It isn't anybody's fault, unless you consider that you should have built your house somewhere else.

Evil, however, is caused by malignant spirits that have to be placated by a shaman or medicine person. No one knows how the spirits got that way. Perhaps they were just created evil to keep humans on their toes. The important thing is not so much to figure it all out as it is to take care of the problem. In American Indian and other traditions, there are spells to thwart evil spirits.

Evil Is Somehow a Part of God's Plan

This is where it gets sticky. To accept this view, one has to adopt the position of figuring out how God thinks. One Christian view is described in detail by the apostle Paul (see Devil/Demons). Simply put, the devil was allowed to sin because God gave him free choice, and he chose evil. In order to show the other angels the consequences of evil, God is allowing an experiment to continue for a short time on Earth that will prove once and for all what happens when free beings choose evil.

A variation on this theme transfers the blame squarely to humans: "Every inclination of [man's] heart is evil from childhood" (Genesis 8:21).

But both views lead to a philosophical quagmire. If created beings are free to choose evil, then the entity of evil must exist. God knew all about it, but neither the angels nor humans did. The mere fact that they were innocent, that they didn't know evil existed, however, does not deny its reality. If evil existed at all, even if God was the only one who knew about it, how did it get there? And why is it so important for God to go to such elaborate lengths to show its danger? Why didn't God just close the door and throw away the key? (Evil still would have existed, but at least only the philosophers and God would have had to worry about it.)

Many have wondered: Is evil so big that God cannot destroy it? If good cannot exist without its wicked twin, have we found a chink in God's all-powerful armor? Is there something God can't do?

Sources:
Deloria, Vine, Jr. *God Is Red*. Golden, CO: Fulcrum Publishing, 1994.
Hagen, Steve. *Buddhism Plain and Simple*. Boston: Charles E. Tuttle Co., 1997.
The Holy Bible, New International Version. Grand Rapids, MI: Zondervan Bible Publishers, 1978.

EXCOMMUNICATION/APOSTASY

Apostasy is the renunciation, either through words or actions, of a religious faith. One who commits apostasy is declared apostate, or excommunicated, by the church or religious institution. This means the person may no longer receive access to God by receiving communion or other sacraments. It is similar to the Amish practice of "shunning," although shunning means the apostate is completely ignored, even in civil intercourse. The object is the same. Wayward apostates are placed "outside the camp" to convince them of the error of their ways so they will eventually return. Biblical support for the practice is found in Paul's letters to the Corinthians, but it in fact preceded the Christian New Testament.

The term is first found in the Greek Septuagint version of scripture, used in various apocryphal books as well as in Joshua and Jeremiah. But it was commandeered early in the Christian era, first applied to no less a luminary than the apostle Paul himself in Acts 21:21. Paul turned the tables on his accusers when he wrote to the Thessalonians. In an apocalyptic passage later echoed by the author of 2 Peter, Paul assured Christians that the "apostasy" or rebellion must come first, before the return of the Lord. Since it certainly wasn't his own apostasy he was referring to, he was, in effect, calling his accusers apostate themselves.

Sources:
Bucke, Emory Stevens et al, eds. *The Interpreter's Dictionary of the Bible*. 4 vols. New York: Abingdon Press, 1962.
The Holy Bible, New International Version. Grand Rapids, MI: Zondervan Bible Publishers, 1978.
Webster's Third New International Dictionary and Seven Language Dictionary. 3 vols. Chicago: William Benton, 1966.

EXEGESIS

Exegesis is the science (some would call it an art or method of interpretation) of determining exactly the meaning of a particular passage of writing. This technique is used by all who study any writing, but especially by those who study religious scripture. Scriptures of all religions were written within the context of a particular culture and belief system. No one can write without having a certain frame of reference. Words mean different things to different people. Worldviews change. Even the meanings of words change over the years. Imagine the embarrassment a modern teenager feels when asked to stand up during a youth-group meeting of her peers and read the Kings James version of the Ten Commandments. What will she do when she gets to the part that says we are not to "covet our neighbor's ass"? She would have been on solid ground back in the seventeenth century. But the language is a bit awkward in the twenty-first.

Gabriel Fackre of Andover Newton Seminary has developed a formula that can be used by anyone who wants to do exegesis. This four-part system, outlined in Gabriel and Dorothy Fackre's book *Christian Basics*, works especially well when dealing with the Bible, but it can also be used by the student of mythology or any other ancient writing:

1. Common Sense: Start with its common-sense meaning—reading it just like a newspaper story.
2. Critical Sense: Next check out the ideas of some of the other students who have studied the passage's background, original language, and literary style.
3. Canonical Sense: Compare it to the rest of the author's writing. Is it consistent with the rest of the story?
4. Contextual Sense: What does the passage mean in terms of personal and contemporary culture?

The system will save the student from arriving at conclusions that might be "contemporary" or "politically correct" but totally at odds with what the original author really meant.

Sources:

Fackre, Dorothy, and Gabriel Fackre. *Christian Basics*. Grand Rapids, MI: William B. Eerdmans Publishing Co., 1991.

EXORCISM

Whenever a religion embraces a component involving evil, personal, spiritual entities, the possibility inevitably arises that those entities may inhabit human beings. Demons or devils, it seems, are never really happy until they have a material body in this dimension in which to carry out their diabolical plans.

The problem then becomes one of casting them out of their human host. Enter the exorcist, whose job it is to free the innocent victim of spiritual entities.

The motion picture industry has really had fun with exorcists. Beginning with the serious *Rosemary's Baby* and continuing through the light-hearted *Ghostbusters* and beyond, exorcism sells. There is even an exorcist on a Christian cable television network whose half-hour infomercial assures you that, for a fee, he will send you an instructional book and video and personally pray with you if you attend one of his religious services in which demons are driven out while the studio audience looks on. It costs a few thousand dollars, but there are payment plans available. If you can't afford that much, there is a cheaper plan that only costs about one thousand dollars. You get the book and video, and he will pray with you over the telephone. If that's still too much, you can get the book and video for sixty dollars or so.

When television evangelist Jimmy Swaggart was going through his trouble, facing allegations of soliciting prostitutes, his peer Oral Roberts swore he could see demons all over the poor evangelist. He prayed for him, and Swaggart came clean in his famous televised apology.

In an Associated Press report dated February 19, 2002, a Vatican spokesman neither confirmed nor denied a report that Pope John Paul II has carried out three

Seventeenth-century engraving of Jesus healing the possessed, by Matthaus Merian. *Fortean Picture Library.*

exorcisms during his papacy, the latest in September of that year. The Reverend Gabriele Amorth is an official exorcist for the Rome diocese. He did confirm that a young woman who appeared to be possessed was freed during one of the pope's general audiences. Cardinal Jacques Martin, a former papal aid, wrote in his memoirs about an exorcism performed by John Paul on an Italian woman in 1982. The AP report went on to say: "In 1999, the Vatican issued guidelines for driving out devils, stressing the power of evil. John Paul has repeatedly sought to convince the skeptical that the devil is very much in the world … and he wanted to give an example to his priests."

The Catholic Church has long practiced the ministry of exorcism, stressing the importance of remaining in accord with canon law. The whole process is outlined in the *Rituale Romanum*. The diagnosis of possession must be confirmed by the Ordinary of the Diocese, and the exorcist engaged is set apart for that ministry.

The charismatic movement, sweeping through all denominations, including Roman Catholicism, has caused discussion at the highest levels of the hierarchy. When listing spiritual gifts, Paul says the "gift of discernment" (see Charismatic Movement) enables those so gifted to spot demons. Jesus "cast out demons" (Luke

4:33) and promised that his followers would, too (Luke 9:1). So it follows, say those in the charismatic movement, that he meant for all those who were filled with the spirit to minister in this way.

But when people start indiscriminately to confront devils without benefit of clergy, all hell can break loose. So church officials recommend going through all the proper ecclesiastical channels.

Media outlets aside, Christians are not the only religious folks to cast out demons. Shinto, Native Americans, and most indigenous religions practice some sort of exorcism ritual. The key is found in the notion of a personal agent of evil, a personal devil or demon. Wherever you find this concept, you will find exorcisms performed by a shaman, priest, or medicine person. The rite may involve simple prayer or complex ritual, but the results sought are the same:

> A man called out, "Teacher, I beg you to look at my son, for he is my only child. A spirit seizes him and he suddenly screams; it throws him into convulsions so that he foams at the mouth. It scarcely ever leaves him and is destroying him...." Jesus replied ... "Bring your son here...." Jesus rebuked the evil spirit, healed the boy and gave him back to his father. And they were all amazed at the greatness of God. (Luke 9:37–43)

Sources:

The Holy Bible, New International Version. Grand Rapids, MI: Zondervan Bible Publishers, 1978.

Mahoney, J. "Exorcism and MPD from a Catholic Perspective." *Trauma and Chaplaincy.* http://jmahoney.com/exorcism.html. September 15, 2003.

"Report: Pope Performed Exorcism." *WWRN—WorldWide Religious News.* http://www.wwrn. org/sparse.php?idd=3921&c=98, February 19, 2002.

FAITH

"Faith," said the young Sunday school scholar, "is believing somethin' you know ain't true." And more than a few members of the choir quietly said, "Amen."

It's a safe bet that a lot of people, probably without ever stopping to think about it, have the same thought about faith. They don't cross their fingers behind their back while reciting the Apostles' Creed or slip quietly out the door after the Rabbi assures them Balaam's donkey talked his master out of cursing the children of Israel (Numbers 22:28). They don't really believe Allah is going to "get" them if they forget their morning prayer. But they still feel uncomfortable because they really can't convince themselves they believe what other members of the congregation seem to accept without question. If pressed, their best response might begin, "Well, I guess I believe it because it's in the scriptures, but...."

And many others in their community probably think the same way, but they are equally afraid to admit it because "a good Christian," "a good Jew," "a good Muslim" believes what they are expected to believe.

The English word translated as "faith" in the scriptures of modern monotheistic religions is one of three words used to translate the Greek word *pistis*. The word means "faith," but it also means "trust" and "belief." The problem is rooted in the long, historical process that gradually changed Western religious thoughts from the right side of our brains over to the left—from intuitive acceptance of the way things are to *thinking* about the way things are. Westerners have been taught that believing dogma and doctrine, accepted as the body of religious facts received, equals faith. In other words, Western religion has become more a process of believing "about" God rather than believing "in" God.

Religion probably originally consisted of living within a tribal framework that described and defined life in terms of day-to-day activity experienced by everyone in the community. This was certainly the case in early Judaism and in many indigenous traditions. The oral myths and stories were meant to teach moral lessons and history. Most of all, they were meant to be fun. Like stories of Santa Claus or George Washington chopping down his father's cherry tree, they ceased to be enjoyable when you stopped playing the game and started questioning the details. It wasn't the content that was important. It was the lesson.

But Western thought gradually shifted to the analytical. Because we're so used to it, it's hard to imagine that the way we think about religion is a relatively new product of the scientific era. Systematic thought has always been with us. We could never have moved past stone-age technology without it. But, as Robert M. Pirsig pointed out in his intriguing book *Zen and the Art of Motorcycle Maintenance*, a systematic approach didn't really consume philosophical thought until the time of the Greeks. And although the apostle Paul had a Greek education and employed its methodologies, systematic theology wasn't really practiced in the Western religious world until Thomas Aquinas rediscovered Aristotle's analytical method and introduced the world to Scholasticism (see Aquinas, Thomas). This resulted in a move from "thinking religiously" to "thinking about religion."

Monotheistic religions began to consist of "believing in" a series of systematic facts called doctrines. They were listed in statements of faith called creeds (see Creed). Those who accepted the creeds verbatim "had" faith. Those who did not accept them did not "have" faith. Peer pressure elevated those believers who embraced creeds most fervently, calling them people of "great faith." Sermons and homilies became talks aimed at convincing rather than converting. Indeed, conversion came to mean accepting at least enough truth to squeeze yourself into the kingdom of God. Faith became a matter of intellectual acceptance. Science, psychology, and philosophy, once a single package, separated from religion. People unable to accept their church's doctrines or creeds wholesale either faked it on Sunday morning or left their "community of faith" because they felt they were faithless. A "believer" became one who tried hard to accept something he or she knew wasn't true. An atheist was considered the honest one who wouldn't play the game.

Refreshingly, ever more religious scholars accept the scrutiny of doctrine and systematic theology, following truth wherever it may lead while still feeling very much at home in their lifelong community of faith. They are usually called "liberals" and must bear the slings and arrows of more conservative members of their congregations.

Such liberal believers assert that God is truth (not "knows" the truth or "speaks" the truth, but "is" the truth) and has big shoulders. So any honest search for truth, whether it takes place in the Bible or the test tube, is a search for God. And to the extent people discover truth, the liberals continue, they discover God. Indeed, it is the fact that they "have faith" that enables them to believe there is something to find.

FAITH HEALING *see* **Healing Effigy/Amulet/Talisman/Fetish**

FALUN GONG *see* **Cult**

FASTING

(See also Islam)

Fasting consists of voluntarily going without food for a period of time in order to sharpen the spiritual senses or prepare for religious ritual.

American Indian boys of some tribes would fast for four days as part of their vision quest, the ritual that earned them a new name and an adult's place in the tribe. Shamans of many indigenous traditions fasted before a particularly difficult healing or an important ritual involving the security of the tribe.

The Hebrew Day of Atonement is a prominent occasion for a public fast (Leviticus 16:9), and fasting (sawm) is one of the Five Pillars of Islam. During the month of Ramadan, Muslims are urged to refrain from food, drink, smoking, and sex during daylight hours.

Giving up something for Lent (see Christianity, Calendar of) is a time-honored Christian tradition designed to be a daily reminder to pray or meditate every time the urge arises for what was sacrificed.

Although Jesus spent a long time fasting in the wilderness in preparation for his public ministry, he spends very little time talking about the practice. In some cases he even seemed to discourage it (Matthew 6:16–18). This may account for the fact that the early Church doesn't seem to place nearly as much emphasis on fasting as the later Church does. (See Acts 13:2, 3 and 14:23 for the only examples of early Church fasting given in the Bible.) Undoubtedly the early Egyptian Monastic movement, with its emphasis on Christian asceticism (see Ascetic) gave fasting a jump-start in the developing Christian tradition.

Sources:

Douglas, J. D., ed. *The New International Dictionary of the Christian Church*. Grand Rapids, MI: Zondervan Publishing, 1974.

FATWA

An Islamic religious scholar is called an *'alim*, a word meaning "one who possesses knowledge." Specifically, it refers to a man who has extensively studied the Qur'an and related commentaries. Some *'ulama* (the plural of 'alim) specialize in learning the text from memory and reciting it in a ritualistic style known as *tajwid*. Others act as judges, basing their verdicts on Qur'anic texts. Such a judge is called a *faqih* ("one who understands deeply"). Other scholars are called *mufti*. These are the ones who define Muslim action in society. When a mufti pronounces a legally or morally binding Islamic law, the judgment is called a *fatwa*.

The Qur'an alone cannot possibly cover modern ethical dilemmas. What should a Muslim do, for instance, when given the responsibility to end life support for a loved one dying of cancer or heart failure—a choice Muhammad could never have conceived during his lifetime? Only one who has studied enough Muslim tradition to apply the "spirit" of older laws to the morality of new social issues can decide the question. The issuance of a *fatwa* helps establish a precedent for future cases, enabling Islam to change with the times while remaining true to its roots and tradition.

Sources:
Renard, John. *The Handy Religion Answer Book*. Detroit: Visible Ink Press, 2002.

FEMINIST THEOLOGY

It is safe to say that the five major world religions developed in the last four thousand years (Hinduism, Buddhism, Judaism, Christianity, and Islam) have been founded, shaped, organized, defined, and run by men.

The Hebrew Bible makes the claim, "So God created man in his own image, in the image of God he created them, male and female he created them" (Genesis 1:27). But while the first two clauses were taken very seriously, no one seems to have paid much attention to the third. The Christian New Testament states very clearly that "There is neither Jew nor Greek, slave nor free, male nor female, for you are all one in Christ Jesus" (Galatians 3:28). But the same author (Paul) who penned those words had a rather one-sided conception of equality, for after offering comments on how women should dress, he goes on to say, "A woman should learn in quietness and full submission. I do not permit a woman to teach or have authority over a man; she must be silent" (1 Timothy 2:9–15). This, he explains, is because "it was the woman who was deceived and became a sinner." After all, Eve was the first to eat the apple. Adam's only sin was in saying, "Yes, dear."

The Qur'an reminds us that "righteous women are devoutly obedient." And if they are not, there is a clearly defined and escalating process men should follow. "Admonish them (first), (next), refuse to share their beds, (and last) beat them (lightly)" (Surah 4, Aya 34). Both Hinduism and Buddhism have long traditions of warning men to watch out for the temptations women symbolize. Some traditions even urged men to cover their faces when women appeared on the street.

People attempting to defend their tradition from the accusation of male domination sometimes go to laughable extremes, dredging up a single prophetess or saint from hundreds or even thousands of years ago to "prove" women have been treated equally. But if Golda Meir is the only female political leader you can point to in the last two thousand years of your religion's history, you're in trouble. And Joan of Arc does not a tradition make. History has, indeed, been "his-story," not hers.

The past few decades have seen an attempt, at the very least, to alter the language of liturgy and hymnody. Inclusive-language hymnals have come up with various attempts to change the "Faith of Our Fathers" into the "Faith of Our Parents," but many claimed the effort was either too little, too late, or entirely misguided. When, for example, the new hymnal of the United Church of Christ messed with the iconic masculine imagery of everybody's favorite Christmas carol, there was weeping, wailing, and gnashing of teeth throughout the land. (The lyric was changed from "Hark! The herald angels sing glory to the newborn king" to "Hark! The herald angels sing. Glory to the Christ-child bring.")

If changing song words caused great consternation, however, it was a tempest in a teapot compared to what happened when tried and true words right out of the Bible were altered.

For two thousand years people have been baptized according to the ancient formula, "In the name of the Father, the Son, and the Holy Spirit." The distinct picture of a male God who is our "Father" became the focus of a developing storm of controversy when some priests began to baptize in the name of "the Creator, the Redeemer, and the Sustainer." Some male theologians complained that if the words are changed, the meaning is changed, and such an alteration would distort a two-thousand-year-old theological concept involving the nature of God and the Holy Trinity.

But the gender debate clouds an essential issue. At stake is an important truth that is far more complex than the relatively simple matter of correcting male-centered language. Language reflects and expresses how people think. It's fine to say God is above gender or that God embraces both masculine and feminine. But if people continue to talk about God in language that reduces God to a "Him"—something that's been done for thousands of years—it becomes plain that people have created God in a male image. And to the extent that has been done, many have missed the essential truth of who God is. Male theologians think like men. They use language unique to men. Male priests, male-centered theological language, and a male religious hierarchy means we have created a male God and male theology, to say nothing of male-centered traditions of worship. And that is simply too great an edifice of power to put aside simply by saying to women, "Oh, we mean you, too."

Feminist theologians of all religious traditions, upon finally attaining teaching positions of authority, set themselves to the task of redefining ancient traditions of entrenched power and understanding. It was, and continues to be, no easy task. The very definition of God, the essential center of religion, is being redefined. The idea of the goddess, long since buried by the religious "powers that be," is finally emerging from her long hibernation and is beginning to be recognized as a long-forgotten face of Truth.

One generation, even three or four, is probably not enough time to make much of a dent. Some progress, however, is being made in the church, the synagogue, the mosque, and society. Although it seems a painfully slow process, some comparative religion textbooks, such as Robert Ellwood and Barbara McGraw's *Many Peoples, Many Faiths*, are beginning to bear subtitles such as, "Women and Men in the World Religions." The pioneers, many of whom were persecuted and held back by academic and cultural prejudice, broke open the doors. Their daughters are pouring through in greater numbers each year. Most certainly, change will continue to come.

Sources:
Ellwood, Robert S., and Barbara A. McGraw. *Many Peoples, Many Faiths*. 6th ed. Upper Saddle River, NJ: Prentice Hall, 1999.

FENG SHUI

The Chinese tradition of feng shui and its Japanese equivalent kaso involve specialists who are called upon to design or redesign habitable structures in ways that will pro-

Custom-made home showing signs of the usage of feng shui, the ancient Chinese practice of aligning objects or living spaces with natural geographic features and energy fields to ensure harmony and good fortune. *AP/Wide World Photos.*

mote harmony and balance. Corporations in the West have recently discovered the tradition and increasingly employs feng shui consultants to create more psychologically friendly office spaces and reception areas.

When you walk into a space of any kind, your body receives thousands of unconscious signals, making you feel comfortable or uncomfortable. You might say something like, "This place has a nice feel" or a "conducive spirit."

The practitioner would say you are expressing exactly what feng shui is all about. The analogy of wind and water is often used. An obstruction causes both to change their movement and break their natural motion.

The sense of flow and natural movement was originally attributed to spirits. Furniture or architecture would obstruct spiritual entities, causing blockage and a feeling of tenseness or anxiety. But consultants now try to explain the feng shui concept in terms American business will understand. They seem to be succeeding. Office buildings and hospitals report increased efficiency and profitability when people sense the calmness of a strategically placed water garden or sculpture. Clients feel more at ease after a simple rearranging of furniture. Workers take fewer sick days. Peaceful surroundings promote *wa*, camaraderie between employees and company spirit.

Stripped of what American businesses might call the "smoke and mirrors" of Eastern spirituality, feng shui has been shown to improve the bottom line. It thus becomes yet another example of Eastern wisdom that, in terms of Western sensibilities, was way ahead of its time, a concept that was widely misunderstood in the West until it could be explained in a new context.

Sources:

Renard, John. *The Handy Religion Answer Book.* Detroit: Visible Ink Press, 2002.

FETISH *see* **Healing Effigy/Amulet/Talisman/Fetish**

FISH

If used as an acrostic, the Greek letters spelling out the word "fish" can form the phrase "Jesus Christ, Son of God, Savior." For this reason the fish became an early Christian symbol. It was a natural match. Some of the apostles were fishermen. Jesus told them he would make them "fishers of men" (Matthew 4:19). He fed the multitudes with five small loaves of bread and a couple of (probably pickled) fish, the caterer for the occasion being a generous little boy (John 6). The disciples' first meal together after the resurrection featured a fish course (John 21).

Used as a symbol representing Christ and belief in Christianity, the fish is seen in cross form in this late Roman mosaic. *Fortean Picture Library.*

A simple two-line drawing of a fish began to appear in out-of-the-way places, serving as a sort of Christian calling card and secret symbol. Its presence, to the initiated, meant, "Christian was here." Gradually the symbol worked its way into art and is still a popular motif on stained-glass windows, paintings, and bumper stickers.

Sources:

Douglas, J. D., ed. *The New International Dictionary of the Christian Church.* Grand Rapids, MI: Zondervan Publishing, 1974.

FIVE PILLARS *see* **Islam**

FLOOD *see* **Noah's Flood**

FRANCIS OF ASSISI

It makes for a wonderful story. Young man returns home from the Crusades a changed man; becomes disillusioned with his father's materialism and exploitation of workers;

throws away his privilege and walks naked into God's countryside; draws followers to him by virtue of his freshness and innocence; communes with animals; and eventually, by virtue of his simplicity and honesty, persuades Pope Innocent III to let him begin a new holy order called the Franciscans.

So runs the plot line of the movie *Brother Sun, Sister Moon*, the story of Saint Francis of Assisi. But like all things historical, the real story isn't quite that simply told.

The basic elements are true, however. Francis (c. 1181–1226) was the son of a wealthy textile merchant and probably did have a rather, at least for the time, carefree childhood. His name wasn't Francis, however. At his baptism he was christened Giovanni. His father, upon returning from a visit to France, gave him the nickname "Francesco"; had he not done so, the Franciscan Order might otherwise be called the "Giovannians."

Well educated, Francis enjoyed an uneventful upbringing until the day he participated, with youthful abandon, in a feud with the neighboring city of Perugia. As a result of his vociferous expression of childhood, an example of "our town against yours" chauvinism, he was arrested and spent the year 1205 in jail.

His downtime must have affected him. Upon his release he made a trip to Rome, after which he had a vision. He believed that God had told him to rebuild the church of Saint Damian, near Assisi. Selling his horse and some of his father's textiles, he gave the income to a priest to start a building fund. His father disowned him. Francis renounced worldly possessions and became a beggar, taking up collections to raise funds to rebuild more churches.

In 1209 Francis heard a sermon based on Matthew 10:7–10 that changed his life and set him on the course of immortality and sainthood. He felt a call to take up a life of apostolic poverty. He began preaching brotherly love, repentance, and spiritual innocence. The story is told that his followers found him alone and smiling one day, obviously very happy. They asked him what had happened to him. "I've married," he said. "To whom?" they rather anxiously inquired. "To Lady Poverty," was Francis's reply.

By 1212 his short rule of discipline had attracted enough followers for Innocent III to grant approval to the order that then called itself the Friars Minor. The Friars preached and cared for the sick, the elderly, and the poor. Also that year began a sister order for women, called the Poor Clares (named after Clare, their founder, who was an heiress and an early Francis disciple).

The new order grew quickly, perhaps too quickly. It soon became difficult to manage the Friars while staying true to the first, simple precepts. A new order, called Franciscans, was founded in 1223, but it had already begun to move away from Francis's original concepts of simplicity and a love of the whole of creation, a love that might be called naïve were it not such a profound expression of his vision.

Bowing in obedience to his successor, Francis abdicated leadership of the new order in 1223 and spent his remaining years in solitude and prayer. In his remaining years he composed *Canticle to the Sun*, *Admonitions*, and *Testament*. He is said to have received the sign of the stigmata before he died, and he was canonized by Pope Gregory IX only two years after his death.

His last words were reported to be, "I have done my duty. Now may Christ let you know yours. Welcome, sister death."

Saint Francis of Assisi has become a bridge between Catholics and Protestants. People of both traditions—indeed, even nonreligious people—seem equally to revere him. Statues of him are found in gardens and parks where people sit, feed small birds and animals, and feel at peace. And the famous "Prayer of Saint Francis," which may or may not have been written by him, is sung by church choirs everywhere:

> Lord, make me an instrument of thy peace.
> Where there is hatred, let me sow love.
> Where there is injury, thy pardon, Lord.
> Where there is doubt, let there be faith.
>
> Oh, Lord, make me an instrument of thy peace.
> Where there is despair, let me bring hope.
> Where there is darkness, let there be light,
> Where there is sadness, let there be joy.
>
> O divine Master, grant that I may not so much
> Seek to be consoled as to console.
> To be understood as to understand,
> To be loved as to love.
>
> Oh, Lord, make me an instrument of thy peace.
> Where there is hatred, let me sow love.
> For it is in giving that we receive,
> And it is in pardoning that we are pardoned.
> And it is in dying that we are born to eternal life.
> Lord, make me an instrument of thy peace.

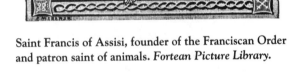

Saint Francis of Assisi, founder of the Franciscan Order and patron saint of animals. *Fortean Picture Library.*

Sources:
Douglas, J. D., ed. *The New International Dictionary of the Christian Church*. Grand Rapids, MI: Zondervan Publishing, 1974.
Gonzalez, Justo L. *The Story of Christianity*. 2 vols. New York: Harper & Row, 1985.

FREYJA *see* **Norse Gods and Goddesses**

FREYR *see* **Norse Gods and Goddesses**

FUNDAMENTALISM

The term *fundamentalist* can be applied to any who read the scriptures of their religion in a literal, non-metaphorical way, as defined by accepted, conservative, orthodox authorities. In the American mind, post–September 11, 2001, the word conjures up two images. The first is the old image of the Protestant Christian fundamentalist—the "Bible-believing, virgin-birth, born-again, second-coming" image. The second and more recent image is that of the Islamic fundamentalist who seeks to attack the United States, calling it a child of Satan.

In one important respect, both images illustrate the same word. If "faith" is understood in terms of accepting a body of facts called religious doctrine (see Faith), then a fundamentalist is one who has accepted his or her tradition's "fundamental" doctrines, as put forth by someone who is considered orthodox.

In the case of Christianity, the term was coined by a series of twelve small books published between 1910 and 1915 under the name *The Fundamentals*. The committee assembled to put the series together identified five key doctrines they believed to be the essential core beliefs that all Christians were required to accept. Sixty-four authors contributed to the project, B. B. Warfield of Princeton Seminary being the most prominent.

The five fundamentals were said to be:

The virgin birth of Christ
Jesus' deity and substitutionary atonement for sin
Christ's bodily resurrection
His literal second coming
The authority and inerrancy of the Bible

These booklets defined the kind of Christian orthodoxy that became known as fundamentalism.

Militant Islamics were given the name fundamentalists by the media shortly after their takeover of Iran in the 1970s. When the Qur'an became the law of the land, "Muslim fundamentalist" became a household term. Shi'ite Islam, the primary religion of Iran, has long housed within it a faction that reverenced martyrdom. In Sura 4:95 of the Qur'an, it says, "Not equal are those believers who sit (at home) and receive no hurt, and those who strive and fight in the cause of Allah with their goods and their persons. God hath granted a grade higher to those who strive and fight."

When "fight" is understood in terms of actual, flesh-and-blood warfare instead of spiritual warfare, when the Qur'an is read literally rather than metaphorically, the term fundamentalist is applied.

Sources:

Douglas, J. D., ed. *The New International Dictionary of the Christian Church*. Grand Rapids, MI: Zondervan Publishing, 1974.
Fisher, Mary Pat, and Lee W. Bailey. *An Anthology of Living Religions*. Upper Saddle River, NJ: Prentice Hall, 2000.

GAIA PRINCIPLE

The 1962 publication of Rachel Carson's *Silent Spring* was a dramatic wake-up call to environmentalists and the general public. Its detailed research regarding the consequences of pesticides, particularly DDT, had a profound effect on even the average American household. People began to question their attitude toward nature and wondered how it had come about. This book greatly influenced the modern environmental movement.

It wasn't long before theologians began to theorize that the problems Carson detailed so graphically stemmed from biblical monotheism. The early chapters of Genesis picture a unified creation in which humans dwell in harmony with their environment and all is declared by the Creator to be "very good." But the third chapter of Genesis clearly places humans and their environment at odds. Immediately following the first sin came God's declaration that "man" is to "rule over the earth and subdue it." Ever since that time, concurrent with the beginning of the historical Agricultural Revolution, the prevailing monotheistic worldview, especially as expressed in Western cultures, has been that the function of the created earth is to provide "natural resources" for humans, often at the expense of other species.

It has been argued, most influentially in Shepard Krech's *The Ecological Indian*, that indigenous Americans manipulated the landscape as well, long before they ever heard of Christianity, lacking only European technology to really complete the job. Indians used fire extensively, perhaps hunted mammoths to extinction, and were quite willing to stampede whole herds of bison over a cliff to obtain what they needed for consumption. But when Europeans arrived, bearing both the tools and a biblical mandate, the disaster so eloquently depicted in *Silent Spring* was only a few centuries away.

Clearly a new set of both physical and spiritual metaphors were needed to visualize the future. They were not long in coming. The environmental and ecological movements, the "second wave" of the feminist movement, animal rights groups, the "greening" of businesses and communities—all began the switch from mechanistic metaphors to organic ones. The rediscovery of native and indigenous spirituality helped as well.

But when Buckminster Fuller, the "scientist's scientist," coined the term "spaceship Earth," the stage was set for a metaphor that could be treated with respect by science while synthesizing both material and religious worldviews.

The spark was provided by James Lovelock and Lynn Margulis when they coined the term Gaia hypothesis, or principle. Invoking the ancient, pre–Indo-European, Neolithic name of the goddess "Mother Earth," they envisioned a living, breathing planet that was one interdependent organism, wherein all the separate systems, including humans, relied on one another. What happened to the oceans affected the climate. What happened to the climate affected crops. What happened to crops affected people. What people did to the oceans affected climate. And on and on the circle continues.

What was important was not the physical process the Gaia principle described. That was well known. But by employing the name of the goddess, both the religious and materialistic worldviews were united in common cause. It was a term all could embrace, the first universal religious metaphor at home in both church and science laboratory. Sidestepping the idea of "my God" or "my tribe" versus "your God" and "your tribe," it pointed to the entire human race as a single tribe, dependent on Mother Earth for survival. It was not a new religious outlook attempting to carve out a place from the competition. Instead, like a good mother, it embraced all of her warring children and said, in essence, "We're one family. We have to get along. Science and faith. East and West. Political left and right. Buddhist and Christian. Us and them. It makes no difference. We're in this together."

Sources:
Carson, Rachel. *Silent Spring*. Boston: Mariner Books, 2002.
Keck, L. Robert. *Sacred Quest: The Evolution and Future of the Human Soul*. West Chester, PA: Swedenbourg Foundation Publishers, Chrysalis Books, 2000.
Krech, Shepard, III. *The Ecological Indian: Myth and History*. New York: W.W. Norton & Company, 1999.

GALILEI, GALILEO

In 1616 the Roman Catholic Church was beset with problems. The new Protestant movement was growing by leaps and bounds. New worlds had been discovered, causing all manner of political, financial, and theological dilemmas. Intellectual Europe, awakening from its long slumber during the Middle Ages, was proposing all kinds of radical philosophies. Not least of these was the proposal that Earth was not, as previously thought, the fixed center of the universe. A free thinker named Nicolaus Copernicus (1473–1543) had dared to come up with a theory that planets orbited the sun, rather than the other way around. And a good Catholic churchman named Galileo Galilei (1564–1642) had gone and invented a telescope that he claimed proved Copernicus right. Ardent followers of Aristotelian logic had already been suspicious of Galileo. They had been pressing the Inquisition to ban Copernicus' book *De Revolutionibus*, and in 1616, the book was banned by decree. Galileo had made a trip to Rome to speak personally to them, trying to persuade folks in the church of what those outside the church were already excited about—namely, that when the plain words of the Bible conflicted with common sense, the Bible was probably being allegorical. In other words, it's perfectly okay to say "the sun rises in the east" without losing your theological footing if it turns out we suffer from an illusion every morning. But the church was afraid a scandal at this point would undermine its battle with Protestantism. So the Inquisition told Galileo to stop teaching Copernican nonsense and get back to being a faithful Catholic.

In 1623, however, Galileo thought he might have another chance. A longtime friend became pope. Galileo tried to get the 1616 decree revoked.

It didn't happen. But he did get permission to write a book discussing both the Aristotelian and Copernican worldviews. The understanding was that he could publish and teach as long as he promised to be impartial and not imply that God couldn't do whatever he wanted with his universe in ways humans couldn't possibly understand.

Galileo pioneered the experimental scientific method and was the first to use a refracting telescope to make important astronomical discoveries. *Fortean Picture Library.*

The resulting work was published in 1632 under the title *Dialogue Concerning the Two Chief World Systems,* and it was immediately hailed as a literary and philosophical masterpiece.

But Galileo's problems were only beginning. The new pope rightly deduced that people, especially liberal Protestants, were using the material to reinforce Copernican heresy. He declared that Galileo had broken his promise of 1616. The Inquisition sentenced him to house arrest for life and ordered him to publicly renounce Copernicus. The choice was to acquiesce or die by torture—not much of a choice. Galileo retired.

But his spirit was not broken. Four years before Galileo died, a copy of his manuscript was smuggled to liberal Holland and published under the name *Two New Sciences.* This book is considered the genesis of modern physics.

Galileo died in 1642. His life, perhaps more than any other, personified the modern perception of the separation of science and religion. Because of the human tendency to leap to black-and-white views, assuming every issue has only two sides, one is tempted to draw quick conclusions about the science/religion debate that oversimplify the argument.

Galileo was a loyal churchman all his life. At the same time, he believed his church was wrong about some issues. He obviously did not feel that religion was simply a way of explaining that which science does not yet understand. If that is all religion is, it is reduced to a form of mythology. To Galileo it was more than that. He saw no contradiction between religious belief and scientific inquiry. It is probable he viewed both as separate means to the same end. To picture him simply as a modern, radical "victim" of his "old-fashioned" church would be to rewrite history in accord with modern thought processes.

Of course the Inquisition was wrong. Modern popes have admitted it, long after such admissions could do Galileo any good. Galileo was bullied under threats of torture. But he also seems to have been a man of firm religious conviction. If so, he was certainly not the first to condemn his church while loving it still.

Sources:

Douglas, J. D., ed. *The New International Dictionary of the Christian Church*. Grand Rapids, MI: Zondervan Publishing, 1974.

Hawking, Stephen W. *A Brief History of Time: From the Big Bang to Black Holes*. New York: Bantam Books, 1988.

Sagan, Carl L. *Cosmos*. New York: Random House, 1980.

GANDHI, MAHATMA

Jainism and Buddhism both arose in the sixth century BCE in protest to Hinduism. Both offered alternatives to the caste system and denied that the Vedas (see Hinduism, Development of) were "inspired" scriptures.

The founder of Jainism (see Jainism), Mahavira, was a contemporary of the Buddha, Confucius, Lao Tzu, and the Hebrew prophets Jeremiah, Ezekiel, and Isaiah. Although most of these men did not know each other, of course, it points out the fact that this was a yeasty time of religious ferment. Of all the religions these people represent, Jainism, now considered to be a minority sect of Hinduism, is probably the least known in America, but it had a great effect upon late twentieth-century America.

Mohandas Karamchand Gandhi, later called Mahatma, the "Great Soul," was born in British-controlled Porbandar, India, on October 2, 1869. While studying law in London he became fascinated with the written works of religious and political leaders, among them Jesus Christ's Sermon on the Mount and Henry David Thoreau's book *Civil Disobedience*.

Although Gandhi was Hindu, he was very much influenced by the Jain practice of *ahimsa*, nonviolence to all living things. The Akaranga Sutra, a sacred Jain text, stated the principle very clearly:

> All breathing, existing, living, sentient creatures should not be slain, nor treated with violence, nor abused, nor tormented, nor driven away. This is the pure, unchangeable, eternal law.... Correctly understanding the law, one should arrive at indifference for the impressions of the senses, and not act on the motives of the world.

While fulfilling a one-year contract to do legal work in South Africa, Gandhi discovered that his British citizenship, like that of other Indians, was not honored by the British leadership. He stayed in South Africa for twenty-one years, developing strategies for Satyagraha, "truth and firmness," nonviolent protest. When he returned to India in 1915, these tactics led him to the forefront of the Indian nationalist movement. Although a member of the Vaishya, or merchant caste, he championed all people, especially the outcasts and the impoverished. Through public fasts and acts of civil disobedience, some of which landed him in prison, he simply refused to accept anything less than freedom for his people, who finally won independence from Britain in 1947.

His nonviolent civil disobedience tactics were studied by young Martin Luther King Jr., who employed them with great success during the American civil rights movement of the mid-twentieth century.

A line can thus be drawn from Hinduism through the Jainism of Mahavira, to Mahatma Gandhi, Martin Luther King Jr., and the Lyndon Johnson presidential administration's Civil Rights Act of 1964. Added to the ecumenical mix, of course, were Henry David Thoreau, the transcendentalist philosopher, and the Christian churches of many denominations that supported the civil rights movement and hosted prayer vigils before the "freedom riders" hit the streets.

Perhaps two quotations best mark this ecumenical journey.

Nonviolence is the greatest force at the disposal of mankind. It is mightier than the mightiest weapon of destruction devised by the ingenuity of man. (Mohandas Gandhi)

Gandhi was inevitable. If humanity is to progress, Gandhi is inescapable. He lived, thought and acted, inspired by the vision of humanity evolving toward a world of peace and harmony. We may ignore Gandhi at our own risk. (Martin Luther King Jr.)

As is so often the case in human history, there are other, more tragic parallels. Jesus Christ, studied by both Gandhi and King, and King himself, were assassinated. So was Mahatma Gandhi. On January 13, 1948, Gandhi began a fast to protest the riots that had broken out between Hindus and Muslims following the partitioning of India and Pakistan. Five days later, opposing leaders agreed to stop the fighting and begin peaceful negotiations. Twelve days after that, on January 30, Nathuram Godse, a Hindu fanatic who opposed Gandhi's tolerance for all creeds and religions, killed the Mahatma. Shot twice, Gandhi was heard to say, "Hey, Rama" ("Oh, God"). Then a third shot was fired, and Gandhi's voice was silenced forever.

Sources:

Fisher, Mary Pat, and Lee W. Bailey. *An Anthology of Living Religions*. Upper Saddle River, NJ: Prentice Hall, 2000.
"Mahatma Ghandi." *Engaged Buddhist-Dharma*. http://www.engagedpage.com/gandhi.html. September 15, 2003.

GANGES

The symbol of washing away impurities is prevalent throughout religious traditions, and a number of sacred rivers throughout the world have been used for this purpose.

River Ganges at Varanasi, India. The Indian religious belief system proffers much reverence to rivers as a gesture of acknowledgment of their life-sustaining abilities in their primarily agrarian society. *Fortean Picture Library.*

In Israel it was the Jordan. In Persia, the Tigres and Euphrates. In Egypt, the Nile. In India, it is the Ganges. Flowing from the head of Shiva, high in the Himalayas, down past Benares, the Ganges attracts legions who flock to its banks to bathe and purify themselves. It is considered a strong female presence, and its religious significance probably harks back to ancient times, predating the duality of pure and impure.

Sources:
Ellwood, Robert S., and Barbara A. McGraw. *Many Peoples, Many Faiths.* 6th ed. Upper Saddle River, NJ: Prentice Hall, 1999.

GEB *see* **Egyptian Gods and Goddesses**

GEMARA *see* **Tanakh**

GHETTO

Beginning with the Egyptian bondage and continuing through the Assyrian deportation, the Babylonian captivity, and the great Diaspora, Jewish people have found themselves living among Gentiles of many nationalities (see Judaism, Development of). Originating from the Latin word for "nations," "Gentile" simply means any non-Jewish person.

Frequently, especially in Europe beginning in the Middle Ages, Gentiles established Jewish-only quarters of the city called ghettos. This was not a new concept. Way back in the time of the Exodus, Jewish people were confined to the "land of Goshen" while building bricks for the Egyptians. Although the term is now used in a more generic sense, it often was the custom to wall in the Jewish ghetto at night and to completely lock it off during Christian Holy Days to prevent mixing between Christians and Jews.

Even under these harsh and demeaning circumstances, Jewish leaders attempted to run their communities according to Talmudic law, providing for the especially poor and fostering Jewish study and scholarship.

Among the most notorious ghettos were those established by the Nazis during World War II. One such ghetto was established in 1940, when the Nazis ordered all the Jews in Warsaw, Poland, to gather in a certain part of the city, then erected a ten-foot wall to seal off the area. An article published by the Public Broadcasting System describes the conditions: More than 400,000 Jews lived there, near starvation; 10 percent of the population died from disease by the end of the first year. Deportations of "non-productive" inhabitants began in 1942, and 300,000 Jews were deported that year, most of them to Treblinka death camp. In April of 1943, when the Nazis moved to liquidate the ghetto, the remaining inhabitants began their desperate, and hopeless, resistance. Shortly before his death in battle, resistance leader Mordecai Anielewicz wrote, "My life's dream has been realized. I have lived to see Jewish defense in the ghetto rally its greatness and glory."

Sources:

Fisher, Mary Pat, and Lee W. Bailey. *An Anthology of Living Religions*. Upper Saddle River, NJ: Prentice Hall, 2000.

"The Warsaw Ghetto Uprising (April 19–May 16, 1943)." http://www.pbs.org/wgbh/amex/holocaust/peopleevents/pandeAMEX103.html. October 5, 2003.

GHOST DANCE

Each year on Palm Sunday, Christians celebrate the day the people of Jerusalem welcomed and sang for the man they hoped would throw off the yoke of foreign oppression and restore the fortunes they had once known. Messianic movements have happened many times in many different religions, and a look at the Paiute Ghost Dance movement of the late nineteenth century reveals parallels with the Christian celebration of Palm Sunday, establishing a common reference point with one-third of the world's population. Such parallels remind us that we all are brothers and sisters with common dreams and aspirations; it is more difficult to dismiss one religion as superstition when one of the world's major religions has many of the same elements.

Consider the Sioux people in the year 1881. The great chief Sitting Bull had surrendered, ending a way of life and culture that had existed, in the minds of his people, forever. Forced to live on reservations, criticized because they either could not or would not learn to be farmers on worthless land white homesteaders didn't want, living off government subsidies that Congress reduced every year and that were often depleted by dishonest Indian agents, the proud people had, within a few short years, been defeated, slaughtered, ridiculed, and demeaned. The buffalo, central to their religion and economy, was destroyed not because the whites needed the food, but because of an intentional, governmental policy that knew the destruction of the great herds meant the destruction of the Indian people.

Seen in these terms, the Plains Indians were the victims of a religious war deliberately meant to destroy their heart and soul. It was sacrilege in the worst sense of the word—a war of aggression baptized under the rubric Manifest Destiny. The Sioux had been called idolaters and devils, deliberately chosen religious terms designed to brainwash the Christian population, many of whom considered it the work of God to kill Indians. It is a matter of public record that many sermons and newspapers of the time printed, in supposed justification of the slaughter, the Old Testament passages urging the destruction of women, children, and livestock that God is quoted as ordering from time to time against the enemies of Israel: "Now go, attack the Amalekites [Indians] and totally destroy everything that belongs to them. Do not spare them; put to death men and women, children and infants, cattle [buffalo] and sheep, camels [horses] and donkeys" (1 Samuel 15:3). When asked about the slaughter of Indian children, it became an editorial staple to repeat the quotation, "Nits make lice!"

In the midst of this despair an Indian religious movement began when a Paiute prophet named Wovoka had a vision in the Nevada desert. He saw a new age, marked by the return of the buffalo, the disappearance of the whites, and the resurrection of Indian ancestors. All this would be brought about if the people danced the Ghost Dance and dared to believe. It was a simple dance, marked by religious frenzy no different from that seen in Pentecostal holiness traditions, Sufi dervish cults, or Jewish Kabbalah mysticism. People would fall to the ground, perhaps speaking in tongues, and describe visions of a better tomorrow. The prophet didn't call the people to fight. There were certainly anti-white feelings expressed, but this was not a war dance. Indeed, the cult forbid the use of weapons, even against the white man. Instead, dancers wore sacred shirts they thought would protect them against bullets if they were attacked.

And this is what made newspaper reporters think the Indians were going to rise up against the settlements. Reservation officials felt their authority threatened as word of the new religious movement spread like wildfire. By 1890, Pine Ridge Reservation agent D. E. Royer called for troops. Right next door, James McLaughlin, agent at Standing Rock Reservation, ordered the arrest of his most famous ward, Sitting Bull, whom he mistakenly thought was the looked-for Messiah figure.

In the early morning of December 15th, forty-three Indian police surrounded the old medicine man's cabin and arrested him when he came outside. Although exactly what happened next is in dispute, fourteen people, including Sitting Bull, were killed. In fear of continued attacks that were immediately ordered, hundreds of people fled the reservation to seek the shelter of Big Foot, chief of the people camped at the Cheyenne River Reservation.

In the fear-shrouded days that followed, the people eventually surrendered and camped at a place called Wounded Knee. On December 28th, they were ordered to turn in their weapons. For a number of reasons, among them the need to hunt and the fear of what might happen next, some of the people refused. When a single shot was fired, probably by a frightened soldier, the army troops began to pour fire into the village. The cavalry, many of whom remembered what had by then become known as Custer's Last Stand, went berserk. Twenty-five soldiers were killed and thirty-nine wounded, most of them as a result of being caught in the cross fire of their own troops. They were buried with full military honors. But between 153 and 300 Indians, mostly women trying in vain to shield their babies, were killed and dumped in a common pit grave. Many of the bodies were mutilated by soldiers seeking grisly "souvenirs."

The Ghost Dance and hopes for renewal were massacred at Wounded Knee.

Not all whites were sympathetic to the "official" version reported to Washington and displayed across the country in newspaper headlines. A former Indian agent with the delightful name of Valentine McGillycuddy had issued an unheeded warning: "If the Seventh-day Adventists prepare for the coming of the Savior, the army is not put in motion. Why should not the Indians have the same privilege?" It was a question asked by many in private. But the public at large soon forgot.

Perhaps the best epitaph to the Ghost Dance's messianic dream was spoken at the sight of the common grave where the Indians were buried. A civilian worker, called in to help with the horrible task, later recalled his thoughts. "It was a thing to melt the heart of a man, if it was made of stone, to see those little children, with their bodies shot to pieces, thrown naked into the pit."

Sources:
America's Fascinating Indian Heritage. Pleasantville, NY: Reader's Digest Association, 1978.
Neihardt, John G. *Black Elk Speaks*. Lincoln: University of Nebraska Press, 1961.

GNOSTICISM

The word "Gnosticism" is derived from the Greek word *gnosis*, which means "knowledge." A lot of contemporary controversy surrounds this word, so it is important to lay some groundwork.

First of all, Gnosticism was not an early Christian "movement," later declared to be heretical. There were many non-Christian Gnostics. And there was no "movement" because Gnosticism was an amorphous philosophy, drifting through many systems of thought. It was not a particular theology taught by a particular person. It was not systematized at all, but rather a way of understanding the world that arose from Greek, pagan, and philosophical schools, interpreted in many different ways.

Gnosticism is an attempt to explain the nature of evil and the manner of salvation from it. There are so many different interpretations that what follows is only a rough guideline.

According to Gnostics, matter is at best unreal, and at worst, evil. Humans are really spiritual entities that have been trapped or imprisoned in a body. In the beginning, the Supreme Creator made a spiritual family consisting of (according to one system) 365 beings called "eons." One of these eons fell into sin. (One system of thought says that Wisdom, a spiritual eon, tried her hand at creation. Her "abortion" turned out to be the material world. According to this way of thinking, the world is an abortion of the spirit, not a divine creation.) But because the world was created as spirit, there are still bits and pieces of spirit in it. These have been imprisoned by what is called matter, and the only way to liberate them is to know the secret *gnosis*, or knowledge. A spiritual being must come from the other side and awaken humans from their spiritual slumber, their dream. Their spirits are asleep and need to be reminded of their true identity.

But the way is difficult. Humans are insulated from reality by many layers of heavenly realms, each ruled by an evil power who tries to bar the way to salvation. The messenger, thought by early Christian Gnostics to be Jesus Christ, holds the key that will unlock the bars. He had the spiritual "password," so to speak, and taught it to his disciples, who passed it on to others. In other words, Jesus came to Earth to remind people who they really were and to teach them how to return to that state.

This opened a tricky theological quagmire. Christ was a heavenly messenger. Since matter, including bodies, are evil, Christ could not have had a human body. Gnostics living at the time of Jesus pointed to the fact that before returning to heaven Jesus appeared in locked rooms and seemed to be in many far removed places without needing time to travel.

Orthodox critics were appalled at this thought. The whole point of the Gospel, according to them, was that God became a man just like the rest of humankind.

Maybe Jesus did have a body, countered the Gnostics, but it was certainly not like ours. That would have put him under the same power of evil that has entrapped humankind. Gospels were written claiming that one disciple or another noticed that sometimes Jesus seemed soft and airy and at other times rock hard. He only "seemed" to be human. These theories explaining Christ's body earned the Gnostics the title Docetists, which means "to seem."

Questions about the illusory or evil nature of matter naturally led to questions of ethics. How is a person to live? What are the rules of righteousness? Some Gnostics became extreme ascetics. They felt they needed to punish the body. Others became libertines. Since the body didn't matter, they let it follow its desires.

For a hundred years the battle persisted. Eventually, because the majority of Christian theologians thought Gnosticism denied such bedrock doctrines as Creation, incarnation, and resurrection, to say nothing of ethical behavior and lifestyle, a statement of faith was formulated to lay the controversy to rest.

In about 150 CE, probably in Rome, the series of questions then called a "symbol of faith" was composed and recited to baptism candidates to distinguish Gnostic Christians from what became known as orthodox Christianity.

Do you believe in God, the Father Almighty?

Do you believe in Christ Jesus, the Son of God, who was born of the Holy Ghost and of Mary the virgin, who was crucified under Pontius Pilate, and died, and rose again at the third day, living from among the dead, and ascended unto heaven and sat at the right hand of the Father, and will come again to judge the quick and the dead?

Do you believe in the Holy Ghost, the holy church, and the resurrection of the flesh?

Anyone who said "yes" to all three questions was baptized. This was the genesis of Christianity's oldest statement of faith, the Apostles' Creed.

It was supposed to mark the end of Gnosticism, but it didn't. One of the ideas that refused to die was that of Jesus teaching a secret wisdom to his disciples. If the apostles passed on this wisdom to others, it follows that those who received such wisdom would be the leaders of the church.

Even though bishops denied any secret wisdom and church leaders denied being entrusted with the *gnosis*, the idea persisted among the laity. Partly as a disclaimer, to show being appointed bishop was not about secret wisdom, churches began to keep lists, showing the unbroken line of orthodox apostles to present-day bishops. Thus, apostolic succession was born and continues to this very day in Roman Catholic and Anglican traditions. Second-century churches could thus show an unbroken line dating back to the time of Christ in a way Gnostics could not. This, by the way, was the beginning of the term "catholic." "Catholic" means "universal." By calling itself the Catholic, or universal, Church, early Christians were emphasizing the fact that they were the bearers of a message open to all, not just those who knew the secrets. Catholic also means "according to the whole." The message of Christ came through the complete message of all the disciples, not secret knowledge given only to one.

It is a supreme historical irony that this deliberate move to include all the apostles, this effort to become truly "catholic," would, centuries later, come to be centered on the person and authority of one disciple—the apostle Peter, considered to be the first pope.

Sources:
Gonzalez, Justo L. *The Story of Christianity.* 2 vols. New York: Harper & Row, 1985.

GOD

"God is love." "God is the eschatological hope." "God is the ground of our being." "God is my co-pilot." "God is a psychological crutch, a human invention." "My God! Did you see that?" "Oh God! What will we do now?"

All these expressions, and many more, have been employed to describe or invoke the name of the deity. Atheists have been known to ask the God in which they do not believe to "damn" someone, or send them to the hell they do not believe exists. The phrase "oh my God," expressed with the proper inflection, is always good for a laugh on the soundtrack of television sitcoms. "Oh God ..." can express horror, ecstasy, wonder, awe, and delight.

But who, or what, is God?

The answer depends, of course, on whom you ask. But most definitions may be lumped into one of five general categories.

God As Revealed Personality

This is the God of monotheistic religion, the God who exists outside of time and space but who stepped through the veil to reveal himself to humankind. (The masculine pronoun is used here because in this tradition, God has universally been pictured and referred to as male. Lately there is a movement, especially in traditionally liberal seminaries and denominations, toward gender-inclusive language. Such language would dictate the use of words such as "Godself" rather than "himself." But because of the overwhelming use of masculine language in historical monotheism, it has been retained here to better fit the tradition.)

In spite of the great separation, both of substance and sin, that exists between Creator and Creation, God "appeared."

In Judaism, God used various mediums to shade his appearance. Sometimes he spoke through angels, theophanies, or prophets. He spoke to Moses through a burning bush. Often he communicated to priests at the Tent of Meeting when they "cast the Urim and Thummim," which appear to be some sort of sacred dice. Once he spoke through Balaam's donkey.

All these intermediaries were not used because God was "playing hard to get" or being mysterious. There was a very practical reason God had to "filter" himself. In Exodus 33, Moses pleaded with God, "Show me your glory." God's reply was simple. "No one may see me and live."

Moses was hidden in the cleft of a rock and allowed to see God's "after glow." But from that time on, Moses would wear a veil over his face after he came from meetings with the Almighty because "his face was radiant."

In Christianity, God reveals himself further by "taking the form of a servant, being born in the likeness of men" (Philippians 2:7). "The Word was made flesh and lived for a while among us" (John 1:14). "The Son is the radiance of God's glory and the exact representation of his being" (Hebrews 1:3).

The primary revelation of Jesus Christ was followed by another revelation through the written word. "All Scripture is God-breathed, and is useful...." (2 Timothy 3:16).

Islam recognizes both of these revelations, even calling Jews and Christians "people of the book." The Qur'an reminds us, "We believe in ... what has been revealed to Abraham, Isma'il, Isaac, Jacob, and the tribes, and in the books given to Moses, Jesus, and the prophets, from their Lord" (Sura 3:84).

But Muhammad taught that both Jews and Christians rejected the revealed God. Islam teaches that a final revelation was given, that revelation being the holy Qur'an, dictated to Muhammad, who could neither read nor write, by an angel. The Qur'an obtained its final form over a period of only eighteen years after the Prophet's death. Allah, "the God," has made his final revelation, has called for the world to submit to his will ("Muslim" means "one who submits" to the will of Allah), and awaits the world's response.

Other world religions, to a lesser degree, contain an element of revelation. The "thirty-three million Gods" of Hinduism are all revelations of the face of the

Unknowable. Ahura Mazda spoke through the prophet Zarathustra. Indigenous religions often communicate with God through animal spirits.

But the common denominator of this expression of divinity is that such a great gulf exists between Creator and Creation that intermediaries, sent from the one who wishes to reveal himself, are necessary.

God As First Cause

This definition, often referred to as Deism, was popular in the eighteenth century and among the founding fathers of the United States. Although they are usually thought of as men of Christian convictions, Thomas Jefferson and the rest generally thought of God in terms described today as that of a watchmaker.

If you are walking down a lane and find a watch keeping perfect time, you have to assume someone made that watch, wound it up, got it going, and then, for whatever reason, walked away. It's simply too big a leap to think the watch was made by accident or somehow pulled itself together out of raw materials. Its function is obvious, and it works perfectly. The only conclusion any logical person can reach is that somewhere, hidden from view, is a watchmaker who made the watch and set it to working. Perhaps he is hiding somewhere behind a tree and watching to see what you do with his masterpiece. But since you can't see him anywhere, it could be that he simply left his creation behind and walked away to another task. You don't know anything about him except that he makes good watches. There is no evidence except for the watch he left behind. Even his existence is pure deduction. There seems to be no better way of explaining the watch you hold in your hand. The watchmaker is revealed only by his craftsmanship.

This theory illustrates the belief that God must be the first cause, the one before and behind the "Big Bang" of Creation. "The heavens reveal the glory of God," says the psalmist. "The skies proclaim the work of his hands" (Psalm 19:1). Those who hold this position believe it is too great a leap to conceive of Creation without a Creator. The universe is simply too complex not to have been planned by a mind. There may not be evidence that God is in communication with us. After all, we have only the word of prophets and preachers for that. But any logical person has to deduce that if a simple thing like a watch can't pull itself together out of nothing, certainly it's too much to expect of a universe.

This position has a way of creeping unnoticed into our minds. No less a scientist than Stephen Hawking, one of the preeminent astrophysicists of our day, ends his book, *A Brief History of Time*, with these words:

> However, if we do discover a complete theory [of Creation], it should in time be understood in broad principle by everyone, not just a few scientists. Then we shall all, philosophers, scientists, and just ordinary people, be able to take part in the discussion of the question of why it is that we and the universe exist. If we find the answer to that, it would be the ultimate triumph of human reason—for then we would know the mind of God.

God As Cultural Phenomenon

Man makes religion, religion does not make man.... Religion is the sigh of the oppressed creature, the heart of a heartless world, and the soul of soulless conditions. It is the opium of the people....

The religious world is but the reflex of the real world.

These words, written by Karl Marx, represent the view that God is a human invention, cast in different shapes by different cultures, usually to buttress systems of social power hierarchies. Sigmund Freud wrote that belief in God was a "universal obsessional neurosis." He considered God to be a cosmic projection of our love/hate relationship with our parents.

Others picture God as a cultural crutch, noting that when a president wants to persuade people that he means well, he ends his speech with the stirring words, "God bless America!" The president probably isn't being hypocritical. He really does want God to bless America. But the obligatory cheer doesn't hurt, either. After all, in the United States, where some polls say 88 percent of the people believe in God, who is going to argue against asking God to bless the "good guys"? It's subtle and sincere. And it works.

There are many reasons that some consider such cultural use of God harmful. In India, belief in God produced a caste system that kept people in their social place. The same thing happened in pre–Civil War America when many plantation owners believed God ordained slavery. Some believe the Roman Catholic Church culture and Islam's Allah invented a male God to subjugate women.

Because every culture has arguably produced a God created in its own image, it's easy to come to the conclusion that God is a cultural invention. Those who hold to this belief generally refer to themselves as atheists, declaring, just like Marx, that God is an invention of humankind, a cultural phenomenon.

God As Myth

Myths are guide paths into human experience, left by those who have gone before. They are stories illustrating truths, often richly layered. Adults often read highly entertaining children's stories on quite another layer than that of adventure story. Like poetry, sometimes they express the inexpressible.

Western society's math-and-science craze has produced a very literal-minded group of readers whose common conception is that myths are really nothing more than entertaining lies, and that the recording of history has always been a factual endeavor. Many insist, for example, that those who wrote scripture either were lying outright or must have been recording fact, even though the authors may have been writing within a mythological or metaphorical genre and didn't intend for their stories to be taken literally. Ample evidence supports the theory that even the author of Genesis did not think God really created the world in six days.

Jesus used to teach with great insight when he began his parable-myths with the phrase, "A certain man went out to...." He didn't warn his listeners he was making up the story. They knew that. What he was interested in was the truth the story conveyed.

So all this doesn't mean myths are not true. It means instead that they can be at least as true as literal fact. Poets and artists understand this. But many others do not. Myths can convey more insight through an "Aha!" experience than a straight telling of the facts because facts do not always convey the essence of the reality they are trying to express.

Such is the case, some believe, with the idea of God. It is not that calling God a myth means God does not exist. It just means that God exists in a form less expressible than mere facts can convey.

In Hindu thought, for instance, Brahman is completely indescribable (see Brahman/Atman). "No tongue can spoil it," is how the sages put it. Brahman is not even a God. Brahman is more a principle. Brahman came before language, so how can words pin him/her/it down? Even pronouns fail because Brahman is not just a noun. The thirty-three million gods of India are merely faces of the indescribable.

When Moses spoke to God at the burning bush, he asked, in essence, "Who are you?" The answer came back, "I Am."

Later, more literal scholars tried to insist God was really saying, "I cause to be." In other words, "I am the Creator." But that kind of scholarship misses the point and only confuses the insight of the original myth by adding a layer of cultural baggage.

Those who claim God is a myth are saying that God exists in a form we are unable to understand and describe, because God comes before language and patterns of thought. The only way to see God, according to this view, is to come at God obliquely through the lens of mythology. Not "God is …" but "God is like.…"

God As Expression of the Unknown

Historically, unanswered questions have been left to God. What caused a mountain to rise from a plain? Manitou. How did we get fire? Agni. What force was responsible for the disappearance of strange animals? Noah's flood. Who causes lightening? Thor.

Religions form along the borders of the unknown. The whole science vs. religion argument often has at its core the unstated assumption that as science pushes back the boundary of human knowledge, there is no longer any need for God. The expression "God of the gaps" arises from this notion: God resides in the gaps of human knowledge—gaps that are gradually decreasing in size as knowledge increases. People who hold this view generally believe God is the historical answer to questions better answered by scientific research. The place to find truth, they imply, is not in the church, synagogue, or mosque, but in the laboratory.

But another category of folks, who also see God as an expression of the unknown, see no threat from scientific knowledge to the notion of God. There exists in the cosmos, they say, that which cannot be analyzed under a microscope. What is love? Why does compassion still exist in this Darwinian survival-of-the-fittest universe? Why are some poems "better" than others? What is quality? Why, in spite of everything, do some people believe they actually talk to God? And, wonder of wonders, that God talks back? They aren't all crazy. How can it be explained?

These questions point to answers existing in the realm of the spiritual, not the material. And science is not equipped to examine things it cannot replicate in the laboratory under carefully prepared conditions.

This leads some people to the conclusion that there must be something out there greater than humans. To these people, "God" becomes a term to explain the unexplainable. Miracles, answered prayer, and coincidences compel us, according to this view, to believe we are not alone. God is not to be explained under this way of thinking. God's existence is simply to be accepted.

Many who belong to organized religions hold this belief, even when confronted by theologians and orthodox teachers. "In the unknown, God exists. And that settles it for me."

Sources:
Armstrong, Karen. *A History of God*. New York: Alfred A. Knopf, 1993.
Fisher, Mary Pat. *Living Religions*. 3rd ed. Upper Saddle River, NJ: Prentice Hall, 1991.
Hawking, Stephen W. *A Brief History of Time: From the Big Bang to Black Holes*. New York: Bantam Books, 1988.
Miles, Jack. *God, A Biography*. New York: Vintage Books, 1995.
Miller, Kenneth R. *Finding Darwin's God*. New York: HarperCollins, 2000.

GODDESS WORSHIP

Monotheistic religions have, from their inception, pictured God as masculine. Some may insist God is "above" or "embraces" gender. They may claim that in terms of leadership and importance gender doesn't matter to God and that women and men are equal in God's eyes. But anyone who reads the scriptures or peruses the religious history of monotheism soon comes to understand, beyond any shadow of a doubt, that God is masculine and men are in charge. It is so patently obvious that objections to the contrary are simply silly. Pronouns alone destroy any argument. God is a "He," a "Father," a "King," and a "Lord." End of story.

But it wasn't always that way. Many scholars believe that for the great majority of the time humans have existed on Earth, God was viewed as both male and female. And the most accessible, sometimes the highest ranking, and perhaps (and this is a big academic "perhaps") the most important god was the goddess.

The goddess is nature, the universal Mother. She is the source of fertility, the one who gives us birth and nurtures us. At times she gives us her caress in the gentle spring rain. But she is also capable of the monsoon and tornado. She is the unplowed field as well as the full harvest. She is as full of compassion and warmth as a day in June and as cold and heartless as a January snowstorm. Each month, the moon illustrates her progression from maiden to mother to crone. She is stability itself until she shows her dark side of fickleness and anger. She is wild, tempestuous, moody, and loving. She is nature, pleasant to view as long as you keep the screen door closed. At her best she is miraculous. At her worst she can kill. She is Gaia, the queen of heaven, the Divine Source, and the Great Mother.

We know virtually nothing about her worship, but legends do persist. Opinions are often stated as fact. We make assumptions based on archaeological finds and present-day theories of feminist psychology, but that is all they are. Some of these assumptions follow.

Hundreds, if not thousands, of prehistoric so-called Venus statues have been discovered from Spain to Siberia. They have wide hips and big breasts, so we assume they are fertility figures representing the goddess. It's probably a safe assumption, but the key word is "assumption." We don't know for sure. It's possible that they are merely erotic figurines.

Almost every religion in the world has built fences of "purity" around menstrual blood and has warned against contact between men and women during a woman's menstrual period. A woman's "power" has often been said to be strongest during this time. She has usually been confined by religious dogma to retire to a special place, perhaps a hut, "outside the camp" once a month. The Pentateuch of the Hebrew and Christian Bible is full of such passages that are rarely, if ever, read on Sunday mornings during Christian worship services. They are universally ignored in the Lectionary, the cycle of Bible readings designed to take both Catholic and Protestant worshipers through the whole Bible over the course of four years. It seems a safe bet that no one has ever read, for instance, Leviticus 15:19–30 from any pulpit, anywhere. We assume such passages refer to early patriarchal influence and male fear of the unknown and the, to men at least, mysterious processes of female biology.

In Judeo-Christian monotheism, the first sin is attributed to Eve. She ate the apple. She was deceived. Adam just went along because he loved his wife. Polynesian cultures often blame "first woman" for falling under the spell of a strange man. Inuit legends place a woman at the center of tales telling the story of how evil entered this world. Culture after culture blames the woman. We assume it's because men wanted to cement their power base by laying the cause for the world's problems at women's feet. Such an assumption seems to fit patterns of present-day psychology.

The truth of the matter is very complex. Worship of the goddess has been archaeologically proven, but the form of that worship has been so effectively wiped out by patriarchal religion that we simply don't know what it entailed. Many have tried to discover the goddess's power and duplicate what her worship might have entailed. But often, such attempts are simply pale imitations of typical patriarchal religious patterns. When that happens, they fail miserably. Then they are ridiculed.

The Salem witch trials, Nathaniel Hawthorne's classic book *The Scarlet Letter*, fear of pre-Christian Celtic rituals, Jewish attempts to resurrect female presence by offering the cup of Miriam along with the cup of Elijah, Islamic insistence on "proper" dress for women, Catholic and some Protestant refusal to ordain women based on the writing of Saint Paul—all offer the historic reminder that the goddess or women, possibly both, have been feared by men and kept under wraps.

Social customs echo the theme: Men ridicule and scorn prostitutes but keep them in business, year after year. America has yet to even consider electing a woman president.

THE RELIGION BOOK: PLACES, PROPHETS, SAINTS, AND SEERS

To all who will look with open eyes the message seems clear. Men are in control and afraid of the power of the goddess. They attempt through both religious and social means to keep her buried in the tomb to which they have confined her.

The balance of power is said to have shifted some six to ten thousand years ago (see Agricultural Revolution), before recorded history. Thus most of what we know about religious life for the majority of human existence is lost. So the question becomes whether men have always been in power or whether there was a metaphoric changing of the guard after a golden age of the goddess.

Attempts are underway to try to recover a semblance of balance. Wiccan scholars (see Wicca) have tried to read between the lines of what remains concerning the religion of those who worshiped the goddess. Feminist spirituality and neo-pagan movements, often referred to as "goddess movement" organizations, believe that prior to a patriarchal revolution, men and women lived in harmony with each other and with the environment, worshiping a Mother Goddess and Spirit Father who gave birth to human beings. They believe art proliferated and beauty was sublime until masculine, warlike energies destroyed the balance. They believe the worship of Mary in Catholic tradition represents goddess worship gone underground, awaiting future resurrection. Groups such as the California-based Temple of Isis flourish under the "New Age" rubric. Clarissa Pinkola Estes's *Women Who Run with the Wolves* (1992) was only one of many recent books daring to make the statement that women and men are different, and that that is a good thing.

But, irrespective of what both female and male feminists believe is right and just, was there an age of the goddess? Or was there even a time when male and female power were balanced and healthy?

The plain truth is, we just don't know. If, of course, by "goddess" and "god" people are referring to actual feminine and masculine personal deities, that is a religious view that must be accepted by faith or rejected through skepticism. But if the definition of "god" and "goddess" entails projected male and female images of the divine, although many might like to hope there was a time when their energies were in balance—when emotion, intuition, compassion, and other so-called female or right-brained energies balanced analysis, hierarchical, warlike, and so-called masculine or left-brained traits—then the archaeological jury is still out. The evidence is subject to broad interpretation.

But there seems to be a growing number of people in many different religious traditions making serious attempts to move toward balance. Only time will tell if the goddess has survived six thousand years of male domination to be resurrected in a new incarnation.

Sources:

Bolen, Jean Shinola, M.D. *Gods in Everyman*. San Francisco: Harper & Row Publishers, 1989.

Ellwood, Robert S., and Barbara A. McGraw. *Many Peoples, Many Faiths*. 6th ed. Upper Saddle River, NJ: Prentice Hall, 1999.

Estes, Clarissa Pinkola. *Women Who Run with the Wolves*. New York: Ballantine Books, 1992.

Lambert, Arnaud F. *Myths, Mothers and Matriarchies: The Archeology of the Goddess*. http://www.uiowa.edu/~anthro/webcourse/lost/godlong.htm. September 21, 2003.

GOLDEN AGE MOVEMENTS *see* **New Age Religions**

GOLDEN RULE

"Do unto others what you would have them do unto you," a staple of most religious traditions, is a philosophy known as the golden rule.

Sometimes it is cast in the negative:

Buddhism: Hurt not others in ways that you yourself would find hurtful (Udanavarga).

Confucianism: Do not unto others what you would not have them do unto you (Analects 15:2).

Hinduism: Do naught unto others [that] which would cause you pain if done to you (Mahabharata 5:1517).

Judaism: That which is hateful unto you, do not impose on others (Talmud, Shabbat 31a).

Other times it is put in positive terms:

Christianity: As you wish that men would do to you, do so to them (Luke 6:13).

Islam: No one of you is a believer until he desires for his brother that which he desires for himself (Sunan).

GOLGOTHA *see* **Calvary/Golgotha**

GOSPEL

The word "gospel" comes from the old English expression "good (or God's) spell." In other words, the good story or good news. The term has come to refer to the news of Jesus Christ's teachings about salvation and the kingdom of God. It refers as well to the four stories we have of Jesus in the Bible—Matthew, Mark, Luke (called Synoptic, or "similar" Gospels because of their similarity to one another), and John (see Bible). In this context, Christian churches that follow the universal lectionary readings each Sunday will always have a reading from the Old Testament, the New Testament (meaning the Epistles, or letters), and the Gospels. Often congregations will be invited to stand while the Gospel is being read. Each year a different Gospel is featured, over a three-year cycle. The Gospel reading is considered the controlling text; in other words, Old and New Testament readings are selected on the basis of the light they shed on the Gospel text.

In the 1950s, the Red Letter edition of the New Testament was published. This version printed all the words of Jesus in red. The idea behind this was that the Gospel would be differentiated from the words of the transcribers. It was an editorial method of highlighting the "Gospel truth."

Lately the word "gospel" has been used as a method of marketing churches preaching a conservative theology. A "Gospel-preaching church" is an evangelical or fundamentalist church, differentiating it from a liberal or mainline church. The distinction is one of semantics. All Christian churches believe they are preaching the Gospel. They just disagree as to what the Gospel is. Churches that believe the Gospel refers to a body of doctrines to be believed (the fundamentals, for instance; see Fundamentalism) refer to themselves as "Gospel-believing churches." Churches that emphasize the words of Jesus referring to outreach ("Give a cup of cold water in my name.... True worship is visiting the sick and feeding the hungry....") are often accused of preaching only the "social Gospel." Often it is said that the Gospel is summed up in one passage—John 3:16: "For God so loved the world that he gave his only begotten son; that whosoever believeth in him should not perish, but have everlasting life."

Sources:

May, Herbert G., and Bruce M. Metzger, eds. *The New Oxford Annotated Bible with the Apocrypha.* Rev. ed. New York: Oxford University Press, 1973.

Webster's Third New International Dictionary and Seven Language Dictionary. 3 vols. Chicago: William Benton, 1966.

GREAT AWAKENING

Its proponents claim it to be the most important revival in American history. They say it was a cross-denominational movement of God that changed the course of religion in America for the better, that it led to a new way of preaching, new forms of ministry, and a better understanding of God's purpose in the founding of America.

Its detractors call it a social phenomenon that split churches, ruined lives, demeaned the Reformation, and all but destroyed America's chance of ever being a real Christian nation.

It is called the Great Awakening and, for better or worse, America was changed after a Calvinist preacher named Jonathan Edwards preached a series of five sermons on the topic of "justification by faith alone." The scene was Northampton, Massachusetts, and the date was 1734. Edwards had been concerned by what he considered to be the complacent acceptance of Arminianism (see Calvin, John, and Jacobus Arminius) by the people in the Congregational church he served. He also noticed that the youth of Northampton were:

> very much addicted to night walking, and frequenting the tavern, and lewd practices.... It was their manner very frequently to get together in conventions of both sexes for mirth and jollity, which they called frolics, and they would often spend the greater part of the night in them.

The result of his sermons surprised everyone, especially Edwards. In his humble opinion they proved to be "a word spoken in season" and sparked "a very remarkable blessing of heaven to the souls of the people in town."

That was, to say the least, an understatement. A spiritual snowball started rolling down the cold hill of New England's religious life, enveloping folks who have been called by more than one writer "God's frozen people."

A young woman, said to have "questionable morals," became convinced of the evil of her ways. That inspired young people to follow her example of repentance. Conversions multiplied. According to Edwards, during the spring and summer of 1735, "the town seemed to be full of the presence of God. It was never so full of love, nor so full of joy, and yet so full of distress, as it was then."

By 1738 Edwards's book, bearing the descriptive title *Faithful Narrative of the Surprising Work of God in the Conversion of Many Hundreds of Souls in Northampton,* was the talk of London, England. It was reprinted in staid, conservative Boston. John Wesley read it during a walk from London to Oxford. George Whitefield read it during a trip to Georgia. By 1740, what was now being called a "Great Awakening," or religious revival, had spread from Georgia to Nova Scotia and out to what was then called the frontier. So great was the religious fervor and conviction of itinerant circuit preachers that it became common to declare, "The weather is so bad today that there's nothing moving except crows and Methodist ministers!"

Jonathan Edwards was not what we would today call a typical evangelist. He was a student who preached tightly knit expositions of scripture. For example, reading his famous sermon, "Sinners in the Hands of an Angry God," in which he keeps sinners suspended like spiders on webs over the fires of hell for all eternity, leads people to expect to hear the voice of a real fire-breathing, pulpit-pounding, brimstone-preaching evangelist. But Edwards read it word for word in a monotone, and he seemed almost embarrassed when people started to swoon in the aisles, swept up in their conviction of sin and despair. He was a theologian, not a natural speaker. (The preacher Edwards really admired was George Whitefield. It was said of Whitefield, after he was invited to fill the pulpit in Northampton, that by merely saying the word "Mesopotamia" he could move a congregation to tears.)

Whenever religious revivals begin, you can be sure detractors will follow. To some, the fervor of the Great Awakening was simply the "emotional babble" of lower-class, uneducated, simple folk who knew no better. Ministers who allowed such activity were not doing their duty. The detractors were called "Old Lights," and they were the essence of respectable, upper-class pillars of the community. Religion to them was to be expressed in contained, unemotional, intellectual, and academic terms. It was certainly nothing to get excited about.

The strange thing was that this was exactly the kind of man Jonathan Edwards was. He had graduated from Yale College. He believed in predestination. But people kept "choosing" to be saved when he preached. He was counted as one of the "New Lights," those who favored revival and reveled in the excesses the "Old Lights" so deplored.

The clergy and their churches were so split they completely rearranged the religious landscape. From the courthouse balcony in Philadelphia, Whitefield cried out:

Father Abraham, whom have you in heaven? Any Episcopalians? No! Any Presbyterians? No! Any Independents or Methodists? No, no, no! Whom have you there?

We don't know those names here. All who are here are Christians ...

Oh, is this the case? Then God help us to forget party names and to become Christians in deed and truth.

As time went on, it became a matter of more importance to side with the "Old Lights" or the "New Lights" than to belong to a particular church. Although the term "denomination" had been defined a century earlier, it now became widely used as a way to express the idea that people were Christians first, and members of a particular "brand" of the church second. Ever since then, denominationalisim has been a distinctly American tradition, even when transported to other countries.

We have to remember that the Great Awakening was called "Great" because it was general and universal. It changed the way many people thought about God in America and, to a lesser degree, in Europe. Its social ramifications alone changed the way America thought about itself. It unified American society and made people of differing religious traditions feel like one. Edwards and Whitefield were unifying names and rallying points a full thirty years before Washington and Jefferson were.

No one knows how many people started going to church, but the numbers were huge. Missions, especially to the American Indians, grew as never before. Education received a shot in the arm when the need for ministers schooled in the classics was seen. Universities—many of which, such as Princeton and Brown, still survive as respected secular institutions of learning—trace their beginnings to this time of religious fervent. The role of the laity in positions of leadership was enhanced. Ministerial authority was lessened, due to the fact that "New Light" ministers were pitted against their "Old Light" colleagues. Paradoxically, the profession was also enhanced due to the fame of "New Light" revivalists.

But all things come to an end. Gradually people returned to normal. Bickering and disillusionment increased. Jonathan Edwards was fired from his church when disagreements arose. A second Great Awakening arose during the first years of the nineteenth century, followed by religious high-water marks such as the 1950s church-building craze and the charismatic movement of the early 1970s, but a religious movement as significant as the Great Awakening has not been seen since.

Sources:
Hudson, Winthrop S. *Religion in America*. New York: Charles Scribner, 1965.

GREEK GODS AND GODDESSESS

Until fairly recently, serious study of mythology was limited to a narrow academic discipline known as "classical mythology." The key word is "classical," a code word for "Greek." Roman and Egyptian might be thrown in, with a little Celtic and Norse on the side, mostly because the stories seem interesting and entertain the students. But it all began with the Greeks.

Western philosophy and the thought processes leading to Western civilization began with the classical Greeks. The great philosopher George Whitehead once remarked that all of philosophy was merely footnotes to Plato (c. 428–c. 348 BCE). Ancient Greece's cultural dominance happened because of Alexander the Great (356–323 BCE), the young Greek ruler who conquered the Western world. He did something no other general before him had ever done. Rather than sack cities to bring home loot and slaves, Alexander left behind teachers and political leaders who superimposed Greek culture and language over every country they conquered. The result was called Hellenism. It worked so well that by the time of the Caesars, Roman rulers found it practical to leave the system in place. Greek became the language of com-

Gods and goddesses of Olympia as shown in this frontispiece from Jacopo Guarana's *Oracoli, Auguri, Aruspici, Sibillie, Indovinia dell Religiore Pagana, 1792. Fortean Picture Library.*

merce and economy. Anyone who was educated had to know how to speak and write Greek. It was called *koine* (common) Greek for that reason. The apostle Paul employed Greek systematic thinking during the formative years of Christianity. The New Testament was written in Greek. The Greek word *logos*, from which we get the

English word for systematic thinking, "logic," was chosen as an early title for Jesus. "In the beginning was the Word [*logos*]," are the first words of John's Gospel. "The Word [*logos*] became flesh," we are told. Seminarians today are taught systematic theology. Mathematicians are taught how to create logical proofs. Medicine works with Greek names for drugs. It's hard to imagine anything today, from the fields of math and science to religion and philosophy, that didn't originate with the Greeks and follow Greek patterns of thinking.

So in the field of Greek studies, it was long implied that nothing of any consequence began until the morning Plato was born. The rich history that had taken place before the classical age—the age of Plato—was largely ignored. Two authors, Robert Pirsig with his 1974 book, *Zen and the Art of Motorcycle Maintenance*, and Joseph Campbell with, among other books, *The Power of Myth*, helped to focus attention on pre-classical mythology. The old philosophical argument of *mythos* vs. *logos* was resurrected—the separation of mythology and logic, intuition and analysis.

Because logical, systematic thinking requires categories, most academic texts on the subject began with theories of mythological interpretation (systems explaining the meaning and evolution of Greek gods and goddesses), which consisted of three subdivisions: physical theories, historical allegories called euhemerism, and moral allegories.

In other words, Greek mythology and religion were understood to have been attempts to explain the physical world, understand human history, or teach ethics and morality. Much of civilization began to think differently after Plato and Aristotle. Their analytic, left-brained, philosophical system of thought, what we now call "scientific" or categorical thinking, has so dominated Western thought processes that most of us can't imagine there is any other way to think. Even in monotheistic religion, Aristotle was the darling of the reformers. Before him, our ancestors existed in the realm of the muses, classical mythology. So the study of Greek myths was seen as a specialized field of interesting historical academia, much as the teaching of classical Greek and Latin used to be considered important to a well-rounded education.

The late nineteenth century saw the beginning of the so-called "modern" period, with mythology divided into categories of romantic, anthropological (Edward Tylor's *Primitive Culture* and James Frazer's *Golden Bough* were both in vogue for a while), and linguistic.

When Sigmund Freud (1856–1939) advanced his psychological theory of myth interpretation, academia almost laughed him out of town. That is the point at which the two streams of modern mythological studies, classical and psychological, diverged. For the first time, somebody had dared suggest that myths might stem from the individual rather than the culture. This was a brand new way of thinking in the West, and it caused no end of academic consternation.

That consternation still lingers. Barry Powell is a respected scholar of mythology, as was the late Joseph Campbell (1904–1987). But Campbell rates only a footnote on page 650 of Powell's *Classical Myth* textbook used in many colleges. Here Powell acknowledges Campbell's "popularity" but assures students, "Although his works are interesting to read, they have limited value to scholars ... because of his eagerness to find a central hidden meaning [like so many before him] in all myths from all cultures."

When Carl Jung (1875–1961), Freud's protégé and associate, carried the psychological component further, delving into what he called the collective unconscious to find the primary source of the muse, even Freud backed off. But Jungian disciples from many disciplines began to discover the Greek pantheon.

In 1992 Clarissa Pinkola Estes wrote about the "wild woman" archetype in *Women Who Run with the Wolves*. Jean Shinoda Bolen popularized Jungian archetypes stemming from the Greek pantheon that were to be found in Everywoman and Everyman. It became an "in" thing at cocktail parties to know that the 2000 movie *O Brother, Where Art Thou?* was a retelling of Homer's *Odyssey*. And you could "one up" the person next to you if you knew that the mythical concept of water in the moving baptism scene was echoed by the archetypal "flood motif" at the end, signifying the return to the "real" world. Both Mikhail Baryshnikov, the ballet dancer, and Muhammad Ali, the boxer, have been described as representing the Greek mythical archetypes of "the Dancer," "the Lover," and "the Warrior." In short, Greek themes in popular culture as well as academia are pervasive.

So how does one enter the rich, instructive, convoluted world of the Greek pantheon known as classical mythology? Perhaps the easiest way to begin is with a Greek genealogy—a family tree, so to speak.

In the beginning, there was chaos, also called the void. Out of this void, Gaia (Mother Earth) materialized. She gave birth to the mountains and the sea, and also to Uranus, the sky, who became her husband.

Gaia and Uranus began bringing forth children. First came three monstrous creatures called Hecatoncheires. They each had fifty heads and a hundred arms. Next came three Cyclopes (the plural of Cyclops), each having only one big eye in the middle of its forehead. Finally came twelve Titans, who embodied all that was beautiful in the universe.

Uranus was proud of the Titans, but he feared the ferociousness of the first two sets of triplets. So he imprisoned the Cyclopes and Hecatoncheires in Tartarus, deep caves far beneath the surface of the earth.

Gaia, as any mother would be at the loss of her children, was heartbroken. She appealed to the Titans for aid. Only one, Cronos, was brave enough to help. Arming himself with a sickle, he lay in wait to attack his father. When Uranus came to lay with Gaia, Cronos attacked him and cut off his genitals, thus emasculating his father. (This image, by the way, is recalled each new year. Cronos, from where we get "time" words such as "chronometer" and "chronological," is pictured each January as "Father Time," marching off with his sickle.)

But Cronos decided not to free his entrapped brothers. They frightened even him. So Gaia was no better off. To make matters worse, Cronos was so afraid of competition that he took to swallowing each of the babies born to his new wife/sister, the Titan Rhea. (Again comes the image of time eventually "swallowing" all things.) When the sixth baby was born, a young child called Zeus, Rhea tricked Cronos into swallowing a stone wrapped in swaddling clothes. Zeus was smuggled in secret to the island of Crete, where he grew to adulthood.

Eventually, learning of the fate of his brothers, he prepared a powerful potion that he tricked Cronos into drinking. Cronos vomited up his swallowed children, who were now seen to have become magnificent adults. They began a war of retaliation with their father, Cronos. It lasted for centuries and almost destroyed the universe. In the end, it seemed as though Zeus was going to be defeated. But he finally gained victory by traveling alone into the underworld, releasing the fearsome Hecatoncheires and Cyclopes, who took his side in the war, eventually defeating the Titan army.

Jean Shinoda Bolen, in *Gods in Everyman*, tells how the spoils were divided:

After their victory, the three brother-gods—Zeus, Poseidon, and Hades—drew lots to divide the universe among them. Zeus won the sky, Poseidon the sea, and Hades the underworld. Although the earth and Mt. Olympus were supposedly shared territory, Zeus came to extend his rule over this terrain. (The three sisters had no property rights, consistent with the patriarchal Greek culture.)

Through his sexual liaisons, Zeus fathered the next generation of deities, as well as the demigods, who were the larger-than-life heroes of mythology. And while he actively begot children, he too, like his father before him, felt threatened by the possibility that a son would overthrow him. There was a prophecy that Metis, the first of his seven consorts, would give birth to two children, one of whom would be a son who would come to rule the gods and men. And so, when she became pregnant, he feared she was pregnant with this son, tricked her into becoming small, and swallowed her in order to abort this birth. As it turned out, the child was not a son, but a daughter—Athena—who eventually was born through Zeus's head.

Later generations, of course, saw the birth of legendary figures such as Oedipus, who killed his father, married his mother, and had a famous complex named after him. Homer's *Iliad* and *Odyssey*, written about 750 BCE, take us into the very heart of early Greek thinking and may even open a window through which to view actual historical events.

The question now becomes, what do we do with all this? What does it mean? There are at least three different traditional approaches to studying and interpreting Greek mythology.

Greek Myth As Western Cultural History

This view attempts to read history between the lines of the stories. The original inhabitants of Europe and Greece originally consisted of a stone-age culture of the type represented by goddess/Gaia-worshiping peoples found around the world. But with the Indo-European invasion (see Aryans; Hinduism), the patriarchal system began, represented by the Titans and their overthrow by the Olympians. Gaia, "Mother Earth," was replaced. Male gods, headed by Zeus, the warrior, prevailed. The "sky gods," patriarchal male figures who resided on mountaintops such as Olympus, often came down to Earth to take human wives. "Virgin births" were common—a union of the "Father god" with a human maiden. But the gods were primarily "up there" somewhere, and they needed to be appeased, most often by sacrifices. They certainly didn't have the intimacy common to the nurturing Mother Earth goddess. They were known to be treacherous and not to be trusted. Mostly, they were distant.

In short, the historical reading of Greek mythology is seen to represent the overthrow of matriarchal planters by patriarchal warriors, a process that is supported by considerable archaeological evidence. With the advent of the Indo-Europeans came the building of walled cities and implements of war. This perspective sets historical events upon the mythological stage and views history through a religious lens. "Our god against your god" is, even today, a common device used to justify wars of aggression.

Greek Myth As Human Psychology

The Greek gods and goddesses demonstrated unique traits evidenced in human psychological types, often called archetypes. Zeus, for instance, represents the CEO. Hermes is the marketing genius. Dionysus (the Roman Bacchus—see Alcohol) is the mystic and lover. Ares is the football linebacker. On and on the list goes, identifying every human personality with a member of the pantheon. By studying the gods and reading their stories, people often find religious/psychological clues to their personalities and discover ways to understand why they are the way they are and why they feel the way they feel.

Greek Myth As Morality Tale

England has good King Arthur. America, truthful George Washington and "Honest Abe" Lincoln. Greece had its heroes, too. "The face that launched a thousand ships," that of Helen of Troy, began the battle for Troy and involved gods who used to walk the earth alongside human warriors. They are great tales, and a child could do worse than to emulate the stalwart Ajax or the wise Penelope as they deal with forces greater than themselves. Seen in this light, the Greek gods offer ethical examples (sometimes good, sometimes bad) a whole lot more exciting than Washington chopping down a cherry tree and then admitting it. Many generations of children were raised on these tales.

In summary, the Greek gods and goddesses of classical mythology were the religious foundation of those who began Western civilization. Read at many levels, their stories cannot be discounted. They are not nearly as familiar as they once were, but their influence cannot be underestimated. It is safe to say that without them, civilization would look different. The people on whose shoulders Western civilization stands called forth the pantheon, either from the cosmos or their own psyches. The gods may be gone from Olympus, but their stories resonate today.

A wonderful *Star Trek* episode, "Who Weeps for Adonis," pictures the ancient Greek gods as visitors to planet Earth from outer space. No longer worshiped by humans, one by one they take flight to greener pastures. Adonis, the last god, interviews Captain Kirk, who presumes to speak for all people on the planet when he says, "We have no need of gods. The One is sufficient." And Adonis flies away.

WHO WERE THE OLYMPIANS?

Greek Name	Roman Name	Job Description	Family Entanglements
Aphrodite	Venus	Goddess of love	Married to Hepaestus, and beauty but had too many affairs to list.
Apollo	Apollo	Sun god (archer, lawgiver)	Son of Zeus and Leto
Ares	Mars	God of War	Son of Zeus and Hera; lover of Aphrodite, with whom he begat a daughter, Harmonia, and two sons, Fear and Panic (Deimos and Phobus)
Artemis	Minerva	Goddess of the hunt and moon	Daughter of Zeus and Leto, twin sister of Apollo
Athena	Minerva	Goddess of handicrafts	Daughter of Zeus and Metis
Demeter	Ceres	Goddess of grain	Mother of Persephone
Dionysus	Bacchus	God of wine and ecstasy	Son of Zeus and Semele
Hades	Pluto	God of the Underworld	Son of Rhea and Cronos, abductor and husband of Persephone, brother to Zeus and Poseidon
Hephaestus	Vulcan	Lame god of the forge	The only god who had a real job; married to Aphrodite, but she was never home
Hera	Juno	Goddess of marriage	Married to Zeus, portrayed as vindictive and jealous
Hermes	Mercury	Messenger of the gods	Supervised trade and travel, escorted people to Hades
Hestia	Vesta	Goddess of the hearth	Patron saint of "vestal virgins" and other good girls
Persephone	Proserpina	Queen of the Underworld	Abducted daughter of Demeter, mostly unwilling wife of Hades
Poseidon	Neptune	God of the Sea	Brother of Zeus and Hades
Zeus	Jupiter, Jove	Head god, god of thunder and lightning	Son of the Titans Rhea and Cronos; overthrew them and proceeded to have many affairs and numerous offspring while attending to his day job as CEO of Olympus

Important Titans

Greek Name	Roman Name	Job Description	Family Entanglements
Cronos	Saturn	Chief Titan	Son of Gaia and Uranus, husband of Rhea, father to six Olympians; the god who emasculated his father in order to attain his rule, and was in turn overpowered by Zeus, his youngest son
Gaia		Earth goddess	Mother and wife of Uranus, grandmother of the first-generation Olympians
Rhea			Daughter of Gaia and Uranus
Uranus		First sky god	Son and husband of Gaia

Sources:
Bolen, Jean Shinola, M.D. *Goddesses in Everywoman*. New York: Harper Perennial, 1971.
Bolen, Jean Shinola, M.D. *Gods in Everyman*. San Francisco: Harper & Row Publishers, 1989.
Campbell, Joseph. *The Power of Myth*. New York: Doubleday, 1988.
Campbell, Joseph. *Transformations of Myth through Time*. New York: Harper & Row, 1990.
Estes, Clarissa Pinkola. *Women Who Run with the Wolves*. New York: Ballantine Books, 1992.
Powell, Barry B. *Classical Myth*. 3rd ed. Upper Saddle River, NJ: Prentice Hall, 2001.
Rolleston, T. W. *Celtic Myths and Legends*. Mineola, NY: Dover Publications, 1990.
Rolleston, T. W. *Myths and Legends of the Celtic Race*. 2nd ed. London: Ballantyne Press.

GURU

In Hindu tradition, a guru is an enlightened, spiritual teacher. The word comes from a Sanskrit word that means "heavy" or "grave," and it is roughly translated as "the venerable." In other words, being a guru is serious business, involving leading people out of the darkness of ignorance.

You don't become a guru by studying or going to school. You become a guru by finding enlightenment. And once you become a guru you don't advertise for students. Students are drawn to you.

Ramakrishna, the great nineteenth-century guru, has written:

Anyone and everyone cannot become a guru. A huge timber floats on the water and can carry animals as well. But a piece of worthless wood sinks, if a man sits on it, and drowns him.

Stories abound about famous gurus. Ramana Maharshi died in 1951 but is remembered because he sat alone on a mountaintop, so absorbed by ultimate consciousness that he neither spoke nor ate. Finally he had to be force-fed by his followers. But his glance alone was said to illuminate those who came to see him, drawing out of them the answers to questions they didn't even know they had.

Generally speaking, a guru will not try to "teach" you anything directly. Unlike Western teachers who try to deliver a body of knowledge, a prospective student of a guru will be asked, "Do you have a question?" The guru is attempting to meet the student at the point of their need.

A popular metaphor is that of the glass and the pitcher of water. The glass represents the student. The pitcher, the guru. The water is spiritual wisdom. If a glass is full of stale water, nothing can be added. First the glass has to be emptied of its contents. Then, and only then, can fresh water be poured. (This lends insight to the contemporary observation, "He is certainly full of himself, isn't he?" Such a person cannot be taught.) If a glass is on the same level as the pitcher, water cannot be poured. So it is expected that the guru will be lifted up to a higher level, or venerated.

This kind of veneration can be abused by unscrupulous gurus. But the authentic wisdom teacher knows that the real guru is within; it is the self. Swami Satchidananda writes:

> What you wish to acquire is the way [the guru] lives, the serenity he has.... Ultimately all these forms and names should disappear into a formless and nameless One, who is the Absolute Guru.

Sources:
Fisher, Mary Pat. *Living Religions*. 3rd ed. Upper Saddle River, NJ: Prentice Hall, 1991.

H

HAIL MARY

Two great prayers of the Catholic tradition are known by their opening words. The first, often called the "Our Father," is addressed to God. The second, referred to as the "Hail Mary," is addressed to Mary, the mother of Jesus.

The words come from the salutation of the angel Gabriel when he appeared to Mary to announce the birth of Jesus: "Hail, favored one, the Lord is with thee. Blessed art thou among women" (Luke 1:28). These words became the opening line of the prayer: "Hail Mary, full of grace, the Lord is with thee."

The prayer seems to have begun to evolve in the Middle Ages when Mary, it is believed, began to appear to Christians, attesting to the life, death, and resurrection of Jesus. As years went by, the second portion of the prayer was added, a direct quote from Luke 1:42. Here, Elizabeth, "kinswoman" to Mary and the mother of John the Baptist, greets Mary with the words, "Blessed art thou among women and blessed is the fruit of thy womb."

Finally, some time in the fifteenth century, the final phrase was added: "Holy Mary, mother of God, pray for us sinners now and at the hour of our death."

At the crucifixion, Jesus entrusted his mother into the care of the disciple generally thought to be Saint John, the apostle. Jesus said to her, "Woman, behold thy son." But more important, he entrusted the disciple into the care of his mother when he said, "Behold thy mother." Catholics believe that act established a precedent. So the Hail Mary is now recited as a reminder and plea to Mary that she is to bring sinners into the presence of Christ upon their death.

During the sixteenth century it became the custom to recite the Hail Mary 150 times in a series of ten repetitions called a "decade," interspersed with prayers recalling the mysteries of Jesus' life, death, and resurrection. That was the practice

Figure of the Virgin Mary at a roadside shrine at Mamore Gap in County Donegal, Ireland. The prayer known as "Hail Mary" began to evolve during the Middle Ages. *Fortean Picture Library.*

that evolved into the great prayer cycle called the Rosary (see Rosary).

Sources:

Berry, George Ricker. *The Interlinear Literal Translation of the Greek New Testament.* Grand Rapids, MI: Zondervan Publishing, 1973.

Hoagland, Victor. "Lord, Teach Us How to Pray: The Hail Mary and the Rosary." *Bread on the Waters.* http://www.cptryon.org/prayer/rosary.html. September 15, 2003.

HAJJ *see* Islam

HALE-BOPP, COMET *see* Cult

HALF-WAY COVENANT

When the Puritans settled in New England, it soon became apparent that the whole European system of the parish church was going to be changed. According to the strict Calvinism they practiced (see Calvin, John, and Jacobus Arminius), people had to prove they had experienced new birth in order to be considered full, voting members of the congregation. This worked well in the first generation of New England Congregationalism (see Congregationalism). The people were already sifted by virtue of the fact that they had all immigrated for the same reasons. And since membership in the church was the requirement for voting in the parish, the pastor of the church being the town moderator, church and state were, for all practical purposes, one.

When their children were born it was understood that they were to be considered "half-way" members of the church, sealed by their baptism but not confirmed into full membership until they were old enough to demonstrate proof of Christian conversion. This was the established parish system. It was similar to the Jewish practice of circumcision. You were considered a "child of the covenant" because you were born to parents who were themselves members of the covenant.

But by the third generation, problems arose. Children were born to "half-way" church members, people who were baptized but had not yet demonstrated proof of conversion. What was the status of these children? Could they be allowed to vote in community matters?

Church members said no. Only full members should elect public officials. Such was the established pattern.

Non–church members called for disestablishment—the separation of church matters from civic concerns. They became known as "disestablishmentarianists."

Debate was heated because whatever decision was made would sacrifice a serious principle. If baptism and church membership were given to children of unregenerate parents, the church could no longer be considered a gathering of convinced believers. It would instead become a "mixed multitude," mocking the principles of Calvinism. But if baptism and church membership were denied, a growing number of people would be outside church discipline, and the whole dream of establishing a "Christian nation in the wilderness" would have come to naught.

This situation in 1657 prompted seventeen ministers from Massachusetts and Connecticut to meet in Boston and finally recommend that children of "half-way" covenanters be baptized. Charles Chauncey, president of Harvard College, virulently disagreed and headed up the opposition. The general court of Massachusetts eventually intervened in 1662, summoning a synod of churches to decide the issue once and for all. After a long debate, the Half-way Covenant was established. A person could be a voting member of the church and community simply by being baptized. One no longer had to exhibit proof of Christian conversion. And as long as a person's children were baptized and of legal age, they could vote, too.

Laxity resulting from the decision soon became apparent. When one domino fell, others followed. The Northampton Church began to allow children of unregenerate parents to take Communion. Two Harvard professors began to teach that all distinctions between regenerate and unregenerate believers be eliminated because such matters were a personal matter between the individual and God. The argument lasted for generations.

When the Salem witch trials began in 1692, some felt it was proof that God had deserted the people because they had opened the doors to sin and degradation. Others saw the whole disgusting episode as justification for the fact that the church has no business deciding civil matters in the first place.

Nowadays you can walk into a New England Congregational Church and just join up. In most cases they will welcome you with open arms and not even ask if your parents were ever baptized.

Sources:
Hudson, Winthrop S. *Religion in America*. New York: Charles Scribner, 1965.

HANUKKAH *see* **Judaism, Calendar of**

HARE KRISHNA MOVEMENT *see* **Cult**

HEALING EFFIGY/AMULET/TALISMAN/FETISH

An amulet is a charm, often a stone, gem, or relic, carried by an individual for religious reasons. Often called a talisman or fetish, sometimes amulets are thought to provide healing or protection from evil. In some indigenous traditions, they are called totems, given by animal spirit messengers for medicine power.

The terms are sometimes used interchangeably with the word effigy. But "effigy" is the technical term used for those objects carved or made from various materials to roughly resemble a specific person on whom the practitioner wants to work a spell. Sometimes called "Voodoo dolls," effigies are believed to contain the essence of their human counterpart. Usually a personal object or something like hair from the person is used in the effigy's construction. What is then done to the effigy is felt by the person. Fantastic stories are told of long-distance spells being carried out. Although modern, educated people may scoff, there may certainly be cases of a victim believing that he or she is the object of a spell and thereby persuading himself or herself that the spell has been effective.

To put it into perspective, in June 2002, National Public Radio broadcast a program describing what happened to a group of test subjects who were part of a study about knee operations. Half the subjects went through what was, in effect, a fake operation. Hospital staff went to great lengths to convince this test group that they had really undergone surgery.

An amazing thing happened. A good proportion of the test cases, those who had, in effect, received a "placebo operation," reported that their knee was much improved. Some were even "cured." No real explanation could be discovered except that these people, because they believed themselves cured, were cured.

This test case goes a long way toward explaining shamanic cures, Voodoo spells using effigies, "miraculous" Bible cures, and sudden cancer remissions. Even Christian "healers" such as Jim Jones have testified that they spiked their congregations with fake cripples who pretended to be cured so that the spectacle would "release the faith" of those who were really sick, helping them believe so that they could be miraculously cured.

Some posit that such faith healing can work for good, whether performed privately or by a religious leader such as a shaman or priest, and employing such cultural icons as effigies, amulets, or talismans, and such activities as chanting, hymn singing, or dancing.

Generally people of any given tradition do not call their own amulets by that name. A Roman Catholic might carry a saint's medal for luck while looking with scorn upon the superstition inherent in those who carry a Lakota medicine bag. Following the Crusades, many European towns had fragments of the True Cross brought home and displayed in honor, while they persecuted any woman caught with a mysterious gemstone hanging around her neck. And in the modern era, many nonreligious folk carry good-luck charms such as a rabbit's foot.

Sources:
Webster's Third New International Dictionary and Seven Language Dictionary. 3 vols. Chicago: William Benton, 1966.

HEAVEN *see* **Afterlife**

HEAVEN'S GATE *see* **Cult**

HEBREW PROPHETS

A priest, it is said, is one who represents people before God. A prophet is one who represents God before the people.

The Bible tells the story of the Hebrew nation (see Judaism, Development of). During much of that history the people rebelled against God by worshiping foreign gods and disobeying the law delivered at Sinai. The prophets were those who, seeing what was happening, delivered warnings and called the people to repentance. Some were successful in their endeavors. Others were not.

Those whose warnings were written down in canonical books (see Bible) bearing their names are known as the "classical" prophets. The four known as major prophets because of the length of their books are the prophets Isaiah, Jeremiah, Ezekiel, and Daniel. The twelve minor prophets are Hosea, Joel, Amos, Obadiah, Johah, Micah, Nahum, Habakkuk, Zephaniah, Haggai, Zechariah, and Malachi.

Their books have been studied, discussed, and written about in countless academic studies. Questions are legion: Did they ever really exist? Probably. Did they really write the books bearing their names? Some of them did. Are some of the prophetical books written by more than one author? Almost certainly. Were there other prophets whose work is lost to us? Emphatically yes. Who were they? Aside from those prophets represented in the Apocrypha (see Apocrypha), we'll never know.

Sources:
May, Herbert G., and Bruce M. Metzger, eds. *The New Oxford Annotated Bible with the Apocrypha.* Rev. ed. New York: Oxford University Press, 1973.

HEL (HOLLE OR HULDA) *see* **Norse Gods and Goddesses**

HELL *see* **Afterlife**

HERESY

When religions, especially in the case of historical Christianity, have established doctrines or dogmas that they insist must be accepted as true, people who don't accept them are declared heretical or heretics. They are guilty of heresy, or disagreeing with the accepted norm.

In the past, the Roman Catholic Church, for instance, established a whole department to "inquire" into questions of heresy. The Inquisition employed extreme measures to root out possible heretics (see Galilei, Galileo). The Puritans of New England used the same methods during the Salem witch trials.

The word has since come to be used outside of religion. Even Republicans and Democrats have been known to accuse those within their ranks as heretics.

Sources:
Webster's Third New International Dictionary and Seven Language Dictionary. 3 vols. Chicago: William Benton, 1966.

HERMENEUTICS

(See also Exegesis)

Hermeneutics is the art and science of biblical interpretation. It is art because it calls for nuance and craft; science because it demands technique and skill. There are accepted academic rules to follow that protect students from falling into the subjective trap of saying, "It seems to me...."

The Bible was written within a contextual and social tradition. It is easy to buttress one's present-day prejudices with verses that, taken from their textual and historical context, really do not pertain to situations their authors could never have conceived. A consistent position guards against that very common problem.

As an illustration of the use of hermeneutics, consider the famous commandment, "Thou shalt not kill." That seems very straightforward and easy to understand. But we soon run into textual difficulties when we discover that the same God who delivered this commandment instructs his people, just a few pages later, to enter the Promised Land and kill all the Canaanites. If we consider the word "kill" used in the commandments to be the same word used in the instructions to kill Canaanites, we deduce a God who is either fickle or schizophrenic. To retain a consistent view of God we have to look at the context of the two commands. And when we do so, we discover that one is given within the framework of a social contract dealing with neighbors, family, and community (the Ten Commandments). The other order is issued within the context of national war and political conquest (the command to take the land promised to Abraham).

So perhaps it would be best to translate the commandment, "Thou shalt not murder," which has a slightly different meaning. If a contemporary soldier, one who wishes to live his or her life according to the Ten Commandments, goes into battle with the idea that killing the enemy involves breaking one of those commandments, he or she might never pull a trigger. Soldiers are, after all, trained to kill. But they are not trained to murder. And that is the difference.

Sources:

Fackre, Dorothy, and Gabriel Fackre. *Christian Basics.* Grand Rapids, MI: William B. Eerdmans Publishing Co., 1991.

HINAYANA *see* **Buddhism, Development of**

HINDUISM

(See also Chakra; Guru)

It is probably correct to say that Hinduism is the oldest of the world's major religions, but it is just as correct to say it is the newest. Some might make the case that Hinduism is not a world religion at all. There are those who would go so far as to say there is really no such thing as "a religion" of Hinduism, at least not as religion is usually defined.

In the nineteenth century, British scholars began learning about Indian religions and forced them into a category they could understand, calling it "Hinduism" and arbitrarily determining that India was the home of a world religion that could be compared to Christianity. Largely as a result of their discussions with Brahmin priests, these scholars deduced a theologically coherent system of doctrine that was quite foreign to most Hindus, who usually felt little need for self-description at all, unless they needed to fill in the official bureaucratic forms imposed on them with the coming of British rule.

Hinduism is not so much a single religion as it is a family of religions. A Hindu might be pantheistic or polytheistic, monotheistic, agnostic, or atheist. He or she

Three Hindu gods, Brahma, Vishnu and Siva, 1873. *Fortean Picture Library.*

might live a very active life or be contemplative in the extreme. Hindus might visit a temple daily or never go at all. They may be very involved in family life or leave loved ones completely behind in a search for ultimate meaning. Until the end of the official caste system (see Caste System), their one social requirement was to abide by the rituals and rules of their particular caste in the hope that by doing so, their next birth might be a happier one and bring them one step closer to spiritual completion.

In the last years of the nineteenth century, Swami Vivekananda first helped Westerners begin to understand Hindu thought. His lectures in England and America convinced a huge following that Hinduism was steeped in ancient wisdom. But at the same time, he convinced Hindus to accept other points of view and open themselves up to Western-style scientific, intellectual methods of thought. The resulting blend of Eastern spirituality and Western materialism produced thinkers such as Deepak Chopra, a brilliant lecturer who also happens to be a fully accredited medical doctor and engaging author.

After saying all this, though, we are no closer to understanding Hinduism. So we must do what we have just accused the early British scholars of doing. We must attempt to bring the various strains of Hinduism together under one roof and then describe it as if it were a single structure.

According to Advaita Vedanta, one of Hinduism's influential schools, Hinduism, reduced to its simplest idea, is that everything is one reality—one profound unity (see Brahman/Atman). Brahman, the undefined principle ("Him the tongue cannot reach"), is one with the essence of humanity and all things. "Thou art that" is the declaration of the Upanishads, one of the Hindu scriptures. The soul, Atman, is one with Brahman, who is both the cause and the substance of the universe.

But while that statement expresses essential Hinduism, to leave it at that makes it sound much too simplistic. To delve deeper, we have to muddy the water in an attempt to clarify. When we do so, we discover that much of what modern quantum physicists are currently saying about the way the universe essentially works, expressing their findings in numbers and patterns of thought that seem quite contrary to logic, the Hindu rishis, or holy men, said through metaphor more than three thousand years ago.

We begin with the human experience of reality. The Hindu will say that everything humans see and experience is real. But because it is in a constant pattern of flux and change, it is ultimately an illusion (*maya*). The book you hold in your hand seems very solid and permanent. Drop it on your foot and you will experience that fact with painful consequences. But that experience is not the only reality, because the truth is that the book is made up of atoms, constantly in motion and never at rest, as is the foot you dropped the book on. All is motion. Nothing is solid at all. It just appears that way. If you leave the book out in the rain for a few years, you will see a different reality. Bury it in the earth and come back a thousand years from now and you will discover that what it appears to be now is only one stage on a journey that lasts forever. On a totally different level, does the reality of the book consist of material elements at all? Is it paper and ink, or the essence of the ideas that are written on the paper with the ink? In other words, does the book continue long after it is destroyed? Are the paper and ink simply one incarnation of eternal ideas that may someday take the form of governments or corporations that the words of the book define?

Scientists tell us energy cannot be manufactured or destroyed. It just changes form. The Hindu has no problem with that concept at all. The book was once an acorn and then a tree. It might someday become soil that nurtures a flower that produces energy for a honey bee that creates nourishment for a reader who will someday hold a book in her hand. The process continues forever. This is the wheel of samsara, the unending wheel of life.

Humans experience life in four stages of consciousness:

Ordinary Waking Consciousness. This is the consciousness you are experiencing right now. It is the condition in which we spend most of our time; it operates on the level of day-to-day activity that takes us through the process of living.

Imagination, Fantasy, and Dreams. You never know quite where someone really is. She might appear to be standing at a bench, putting widgets on gizmos all day. But in her mind she could be riding the Outback or climbing Mount Fuji. You can't tell because you can only see the body. Sometimes, when you read a good book or think deep thoughts, imagination and fantasy can be more real than the activity the body happens to be involved in.

Prajna ("Sleep without Dreams"). In this state, as in deep sleep without dreams, you are not limited to thinking about anything. When you think about something specific, you are limiting yourself, preventing yourself from thinking about an infinite variety of other things. So any thought is also a limitation, keeping you from being one with everything. Rather than being immersed in the One, you are entangled in the Many. This state escapes that limitation.

The Om State. "Om" was the initial sound by which the universe was breathed into existence. The Svetasvatara Upanishad puts it this way:

> The Self, whose symbol is Om, is the omniscient Lord. He is not born. He does not die. He is neither cause nor effect. This Ancient One is unborn, imperishable, eternal: though the body be destroyed, he is not killed.

> The Self is not known through study of scriptures, nor through subtlety of the intellect, nor through much learning; but by him who longs for him is he known. Verily unto him does the Self reveal his true being.

> By learning a man cannot know him, if he desist not from evil, if he control not his senses, if he quiet not his mind, and practice not meditation.

The self (Atman) is really Brahman, the only being, the universal being, the One. So the self, the ego, and the essence of the universe are really one. They just don't appear to be.

Put differently, we are the essence of the stars. We were both present at and formed by the Big Bang and will someday return to the singularity that began it all. The atoms in our body were once one with every single other atom ever formed and will again be one with all of them.

We don't experience it that way, but that's just because what we experience is an illusion. All we see is the present incarnation of atoms around us. The truth is that not one of them was present at our birth. Not one cell in our bodies is the same as those that formed us when we came into this life. And not a single cell now present in our bodies will accompany us to the grave.

So who is this illusion, the self, that feels so permanent? We can't point to anything that remains the same. It's all coming and going.

This is an example of very modern science and very old Hinduism saying exactly the same thing.

"I'm not the person I used to be," says the old-timer. Both the twenty-first-century scientist and the Hindu of three thousand years ago would agree.

We may know all of this, but we are usually not purposefully aware of it.

Why is it that a person will suddenly step in front of a speeding car to pull a baby to safety? He will risk his own life to save someone he has never seen before. Why? The Hindu would say that at the moment of extreme danger, the mind gets left behind and the senses take over. The person knows, in that moment of truth, that he and the baby are one, and that each is diminished if the other dies.

What is the purpose of a mountain with no one to appreciate it? What is the value of a person without a mountain to contemplate? The mountain and the person are one, engaged in a universal dance. Someday the person will be buried under the mountain and change form, adding to the bulk of the mountain while being reincarnated into a different form. The mountain will someday disappear. So will the person. But their essences will continue in different forms.

Sources:

Ellwood, Robert S., and Barbara A. McGraw. *Many Peoples, Many Faiths*. 6th ed. Upper Saddle River, NJ: Prentice Hall, 1999.

Mishra, Pankaj. "The God of New Things." *Boston Sunday Globe*, December 1, 2002.

HINDUISM, DEVELOPMENT OF

(See also Aryans)

Who were the first Hindus? When and where did they live? There are two different theories, and recent archeological discoveries have fueled a great deal of controversy.

The standard academic theory holds that 3,500 years ago, when Indo-European Aryans (see Aryans) either invaded or migrated to India by way of the famous Khyber Pass through the Himalayas, they found a stone-age people whose agricultural way of life was already ancient. Archaeologists have discovered many goddess figurines, usually an indication of religious agricultural/fertility practices, and even an ancient seal engraved with a figure sitting in a yoga position.

The Aryans brought with them the world's first scriptures, the Vedas (see Agni), which contained the stories and rituals of their people. These people were tribal and migratory. They had domesticated the horse and invented the chariot, so they must have been fierce competitors in battle.

The Vedas describe an enigmatic religious ritual called the fire sacrifice. We don't know much about it except that it consisted of drinking soma, a hallucinogenic drink, possibly derived from mushrooms. They also introduce us to Indra and Agni, two of the principal gods of Hinduism.

This historical period has been labeled the Vedic period, and it lasted until the beginning of the Brahmin period, about 300 BCE. During this time, social and religious systems began to develop. That period marked the beginning of numerous settled communities, the caste system, religious temples, and formal rituals of worship.

But there is another theory, and recent discoveries in the north of India seem to lend scientific support to it. Hinduism just might prove to be much older than scholars thought, and to have arisen completely independent of Aryan cultural influence—in fact, predating it by centuries.

In a country where history can be traced back more than five thousand years, it has long been the practice of rulers to link their regimes to the tales of glorious bygone eras. The notion of Aryan roots seems to smack of white, British influence.

The year 1947 had brought independence from British rule, and religion and politics have been intertwined ever since. Hindu pride caused nationalists to fight fiercely for positions of power in both spheres. In 1992, a sixteenth-century Muslim mosque was destroyed by an angry mob that was convinced the mosque had been built on the site of an ancient Hindu temple thought to be the birthplace of the supreme god, Rama. Two thousand people died in the ensuing riots. In 1998 a powerful coalition of Hindu nationalists began to combine religious fundamentalism with secular politics. One question at the heart of the conflicts is whether Hinduism could have a historical identity unique to the Indus Valley, predating any Aryan influence from outside.

Historians and scientists have used several methods in their attempts to discern the truth. One has been to examine ancient texts. Until recently most of them have been considered simply mythological in nature. The events they describe happened so long ago that they were thought to be made-up tales of an earlier time. One of them, for instance, describes a mythological causeway that connected India and Sri Lanka. According to the story, the causeway enabled Hanuman, the monkey god, free access to rescue a captured Hindu goddess. As soon as you have a story involving a "monkey god," it's easy to dismiss the whole story as a fanciful religious myth. But satellite images (whose veracity is questioned by some) have revealed what has been labeled Hanuman Bridge, ancient evidence that the supposedly mythological causeway did, indeed, exist. This possible discovery prompted the Indian government, in 2002, to launch an investigative expedition to plot the former course of the purportedly mythological Saraswati River, which was supposed to have disappeared thousands of years ago.

Perhaps the ancient texts were, indeed, describing an early Hindu culture that predated any Aryan invasion. If this proves to be so, the Aryans didn't "invent" early Hinduism. They merely conquered it. One aim of all this study is to "prove" the Hindu nationalists' belief that Hinduism developed independent of any outside help, right on the subcontinent of India, with no help from any Aryans. There have long been puzzling, nagging questions about the standard academic position. What about that stone age seal with the meditating yogi in the lotus position? If Hinduism formed after the Aryan invasion, where did this early, obviously religious figure fit into the scheme?

It has been said that there are thirty-three million gods in India. But it must be remembered that since Brahman is All (see Brahman/Atman), all gods are ultimately faces of Brahman. Brahman is not even a god. He is an undefined principle. So the gods are ways of expressing or visualizing the inexpressible.

Although we cannot possible identify all Hindu gods, there are a few who deserve special mention. Brahma (the masculine "a" ending distinguishes him from the neuter "n" of Brahman), Vishnu (see Avatar), and Shiva are the principal gods of the Trimurti ("Trio," or perhaps "Trinity"). These are the most important gods of the Hindu pantheon.

Brahma is the Creator. Although he is very respected, he has only about a half-dozen temples built in his honor. The reason is simply that he worked himself out of a job a long time ago. He is no longer present much on Earth because creation is finished, and he really doesn't have anything to do. He meditates on the lotus blossom growing from the navel of Vishnu, who sleeps on the cosmic ocean made up of the remains of the last universe before this one. When Brahma opens his eyes to look around, a world comes into existence. One day in the life of Brahma is four billion, three hundred and twenty years, or one world cycle. Then he closes his eyes, the world disappears, and when he opens them, another cycle begins. (Scientists believe the world is already about five billion years old. That's longer than one world cycle—Brahma may soon be stirring!)

Vishnu is the preserver. He is the god of goodness. An old story about him says that a sage was once sent to determine who was the strongest god. The sage came across Brahma, insulted him, and was severely trounced. So he moved on to Shiva, only to be soundly abused. By the time he finally found Vishnu, the sage was in no mood to put up with any more surly gods. Vishnu was asleep on the cosmic ocean, of course, so the sage marched right up and kicked him. When Vishnu woke up he immediately worried that the sage might have hurt his foot, kicking Vishnu awake. So Vishnu began to massage the sage's sore foot. The sage was impressed and declared Vishnu to be the most powerful God.

Vishnu comes to Earth when needed. His incarnations are called avatars (see Avatar). Hindus say there will be ten of them. Two of the most important are Rama and Krishna (see Bhagavad-Gita), heroes of old now worshiped as divine. The ninth avatar occurred when Vishnu was incarnated as the Buddha. The tenth is yet to come. In uncanny similarity with Revelation 19:11–19 of the Christian Bible, in his final incarnation Vishnu will appear as Kalkin, riding a white horse and wielding a flaming sword, to separate the righteous from the wicked.

Shiva is the destroyer, but not in an evil sense. It is more like the presence of death that comes to all things. The English poet Percy Bysshe Shelley wrote, "If Winter comes, can Spring be far behind?" Shiva is seen in the falling leaf and the dying breath. He is the God of yogis and ascetics.

He is also lord of the dance. Many statues picture him in this capacity, his four arms outstretched, dancing on the back of a turtle, which often has a human face. In this personification, he is called the Auspicious One who represents the Absolute Being. Shiva, as lord of the dance, pounds his drum louder and louder, accompanying all the changes of the world, until finally its vibrations shatter the cosmos into its primal elements; it then re-forms, as Brahma opens his eyes, into a new world.

When Shiva is visualized as a master yogi, he sits high in the Himalayas atop Mount Kallas. He is covered in white ash, the symbol of fire that has burned away passion. The holy Ganges River (see Ganges) flows from his matted hair. His concentration is such that the world would fade like a dream if he were to cease his meditation even for a moment. His wife, it is told, once came up quietly behind him and placed her hands over his eyes. Immediately the stars began to go out. She quickly left him to his meditation.

Shiva is also the life force represented by the phallic symbol of the lingam, the upright shaft around which the wheel of samsara turns. Here he is seen as life spirit, the will to live and continue.

Shiva is married to Shakti ("power"). Shakti, also called Kali or Parvati, Annapurna, and Durga, is the great goddess. Her symbol is the yoni, and she represents all that exists in the material world. She is the goddess in all her many and varied moods. She will give birth to a child, nurture it at her breast, and then wring its neck. Nature is fickle, indeed, and India revels in extremes. Light and dark are equally celebrated, for that is the nature of life.

Agni and Indra (see entries on each) are ancient gods who seem to have been Aryan imports. Agni, the god of fire, has been internalized to represent the power of the life force burning within. Indra, hero of what might be the prime Hindu myth, is a warrior god similar to Yahveh of the Hebrews or Zeus of the Greeks.

These are five of thirty-three million gods in India, but it cannot be emphasized enough that they are all faces of the one eternal, inexpressible principle called Brahman, the One.

So is Hinduism polytheistic, pantheistic, or monotheistic? The answer depends on how you choose to interpret the material.

In terms of how Hindus understand human beings and their place in the great scheme of things, perhaps it is most instructive to begin with three words: dharma, karma, and moksha.

Dharma refers to the order of the cosmos and the moral, ethical behavior of those in it. Karma describes the effects of our actions upon this life and all lives to come. Moksha is liberation of the soul from the illusion and suffering of samsara, the wheel of life. It is the final absorption of Atman into Brahman, the self into the One.

Dharma imposes karma until the release of moksha. Perhaps a simple illustration can best explain how the terms work together. Dharma describes what will happen if you fall off a cliff. Karma determines whether or not you fall. Moksha is the final step off the cliff.

Each lifetime determines karmic consequences for the next life and is the result of karmic consequences of the last. What you do effects what you will be. The idea is to build positive karmic consequences in this life so you don't have to relearn lessons for the next.

The scriptures of Hinduism reveal the slow development of its philosophy. The Vedas were written beginning about 1500 BCE. They tell of the gods and their myths. The Rig-Veda consists of religious poetry. More than one thousand hymns are addressed to the *devas*, or "shining ones." The Sama-Veda, Yagur-Veda, and Atharua-Veda, a compilation of incantations and spells, complete the set of four, combining to become the oldest scriptures in the world.

Sometime around 500 BCE, the Upanishads began to be written, probably as a response to Buddhism. They detail the Brahman-Atman philosophy, the practice of Om meditation, and the four levels of consciousness already discussed. These became the philosophical section of the Vedas, intended only for serious students. In effect, they moved Hinduism inward to the mind, thus embodying what is known as "intellectual" Hinduism.

The Upanishads describe two great principles: the Way of Society (the Laws of Manu) and the Way of the Yogi (Yogi Sutras).

The Way of Society (The Laws of Manu)

There are four "ends of man": kama (pleasure), artha (gain), dharma (righteousness), and moksha (liberation). These roughly correspond to the ashramas, the four stages of life: student, householder, hermit, and renunciant.

They work something like this over the course of a person's life:

When we are young our duty is to get an education and do the things young people must do. We sow our wild oats and try different philosophies. Above all, we gather like-minded friends about us and go about the business of embarking on the journey of life. We go to parties, debate our elders, meet potential mates, and generally have a good time.

But there comes a time when we realize it's time to settle down. We get married, have kids, move to the suburbs, buy a house, get a dog, put up a white picket fence, and join the PTA. We have entered the second stage of life. We are householders.

But after a few years this begins to pale. Mid-life crises begin. We turn inward. We start to ask what life is all about. We discover our spiritual side. We don't want to go out with the group as much. A night at home, reading a good book, starts to sound more exciting than the party down the street or the school committee meeting. We begin to realize our time is limited. There may be a lot of it left, but we come to understand that life is not eternal. People begin to ask, Where have you been keeping yourself these days? Well, we have entered the third stage of life. Our idea of a great vacation is to retire to a quiet room to read, unplug the phone, contemplate meaning, and practice our newfound spirituality. We begin to understand why some people go off to become hermits.

Finally, simply retiring from activity may not be enough. Although Western tradition has usually required people to stay at least somewhat active in community affairs, in India it was not uncommon for a man to renounce his possessions, leave his grown-up family, and hit the road, becoming a traveling *sannyasin*, a wandering monk who has cut himself off from society in order seek meaning and spiritual wisdom. It is said that the transformation of the renunciant is complete when he is given food and sustenance by one who was formerly his servant.

(Perhaps this understanding of the stages of life will help explain why there is such a vast difference between the social attitudes of America and those of such places as India. Traditional Hindus look upon a typical materialistic American lifestyle as stunted growth, evidence that such people have never grown up past the second stage of maturity and have not understood that it is impossible to accumulate enough goods to provide happiness. The average retired American lives off accumulated goods and investments. To traditional Hindus, this is backward. They do not respect a lifetime of accumulated wealth. Such a lifestyle represents spiritual poverty and is to be pitied. Meanwhile, many Westerners think of India as being full of impoverished people who can and should better themselves. As in all such sociopolitical issues, this is much too simplistic a generalization. But it points out a basic difference of religious opinion. Judeo-Christian tradition tends to view wealth as a proof of God's blessing. Hinduism sees it as the spiritual poverty of selfishness.)

The Way of the Yogi (Yogi Sutras)

This scripture details techniques of hatha yoga through a process consisting of eight steps, called limbs:

Nonviolence, truthfulness, non-stealing, celibacy, and non-greed

Purity, contentment, mortification, study, and devotion

Posture

Breath control

Withdrawal of attention from the senses

Concentration

Meditation

Contemplation

The limbs are envisioned as being "centered" and brought up through the seven chakras (see Chakra), or centers of energy located from the base of the spine to the top of the head, in a spiritual exercise of meditation called yoga.

The Way of Society and the Way of the Yogi come together in the scripture called Bhagavad-Gita, or Song of the Lord (see Bhagavad-Gita), itself a portion of a longer epic called Mahabharata, in which the lord Krishna specifies the method of spiritual progress.

To learn all that is contained in these scriptures involves the work of many lifetimes, and it helps to study under the guidance of a guru (see Guru), a spiritual teacher. In a tradition of devotional Hinduism that comes out of the Middle Ages, the guru will help determine the best *bhakti*, or spiritual path, that will aid you on your journey of spiritual discipline leading to moksha, when you finally lose your egocentricity and become one with Brahman.

Like most traditions, Hinduism has divided and changed, been added to and adapted. It has spawned great social evils, such as the caste system, and bettered countless lives. In some ways, it predated modern, scientific explanations for the origin of the cosmos and modern psychology by thousands of years. It has changed over the years, while at the same time retaining essential human truths, such as the stages of life, that go a long way toward explaining how to live in today's world. It has been described as an organic system, rather than a religion.

The lowly cobbler Ravidas, poet and mystic, in his *World of Illusion*, voices one view of what it is to be human in a world growing increasingly complex every day:

There is but One God. He is obtained by the True Guru's grace.
When there was egoism in me, Thou wert not with me.
Now that Thou art there, there is no egoism,
As huge waves are raised by the wind in the great ocean, but are only water in water.
O Lord of wealth, what should I say about this delusion?
What we deem a thing to be, in reality it is not like that.

And Lalla, a mystic of Kashmir, pens a very human response:

With the help of the gardeners Mind and Love, plucking the flower called Steady Contemplation, offering the water of the flood of the Self's own bliss, worship the Lord with the sacred formula of silence!

Sources:

Ellwood, Robert S., and Barbara A. McGraw. *Many Peoples, Many Faiths*. 6th ed. Upper Saddle River, NJ: Prentice Hall, 1999.

Fisher, Mary Pat, and Lee W. Bailey. *An Anthology of Living Religions*. Upper Saddle River, NJ: Prentice Hall, 2000.

HOLY WEEK *see* Christianity, Calendar of

HORUS *see* Egyptian Gods and Goddesses

I

I CHING *see* Confucian Texts

IMBOLC *see* Paganism, Calendar of

IMMACULATE CONCEPTION

For centuries Roman Catholic theologians pondered the question of how a normal human being, Mary, could give birth to a perfect human being, Jesus, who was born without sin, outside the restrictions of the "original sin" passed on from Adam and Eve to their progeny.

Finally, in 1854, the problem was solved. As with most religious pronouncements, there is a story behind the story.

Pope Pius IX served longer than any other pope in history, but it was during a time when the papacy was losing power. The political situation was such that he even had to leave Rome, unable to return until the French intervened. But Pius was determined to confirm the power of the office. Thus it was that in 1854 he issued the bull *Ineffabilis Deus*. It was the first time in history a pope said he was infallible and didn't need a council's approval if he spoke *ex cathedra* ("from the chair"). In the words of the first Vatican Council (see Vatican Councils), defining the conditions under which the pope is infallible:

> The Roman pontiff, when he speaks ex cathedra, that is, when in discharge of the office of pastor and doctor of all Christians, by virtue of his supreme Apostolic authority, he defines a doctrine regarding faith or morals to be held by the universal Church, by the divine assistance promised to him in blessed Peter, is possessed of that divine infallibility with which the divine Redeemer willed that his Church should be endowed for defining doctrine regarding faith or morals; and therefore such definitions are irreformable of themselves, and not from the consent of the Church.

Then he sat back to await developments. And nothing really happened. There was no great clamor from either pew or pulpit, so the doctrine of papal infallibility was determined.

The test case, so to speak, was the determination that Mary was born free from all taint of sin, including original sin. By virtue of the fact that she was chosen to be the mother of the Savior, the doctrine of the Immaculate Conception of Mary became official Church dogma. It was based on the idea that a person becomes truly conceived when a soul is created and fused with the body. In anticipation of what Mary was going to do when she conceived Jesus, she was, in effect, sanctified at the moment of her own conception. The original state of innocence did not free her from the consequences of sorrow, pain, and illness, but it did mean that she was sinless.

Sources:
Gonzalez, Justo L. *The Story of Christianity.* 2 vols. New York: Harper & Row, 1985.

INCARNATION

This doctrine, although it doesn't appear by name in the Bible, is the central tenet of Christianity. It states that Jesus Christ, the Second Person of the Trinity (see Arius), "took on" flesh (*in carne,* "in flesh"), or became a man. In other words, God became human, was born as a baby, and was later killed by humankind in order to become the substitute sacrifice for the propitiation of sin (see Christianity). This does not mean that God ceased to exist other than within the flesh of Jesus of Nazareth. It means that the eternal "Word" of God became the "Son" of God, present now in time. This concept is called the hypostatic union—perfect God and perfect man in one body. "The Word became flesh and dwelt among us" (John 1). Whenever the "other" steps across the line separating material from spiritual and becomes human, or "takes on" humanity, the divine is said to be "incarnate," or "in the flesh."

The term is used in a slightly different form outside of Christianity. Hindu belief, for instance, sees the human spirit (Atman) existing, over the course of many lifetimes, in many different bodies. When the spirit or soul incarnate in flesh takes on a new form, a new body, it is said to be reincarnate, or incarnated again. This is the doctrine of reincarnation.

Sources:
Douglas, J. D., ed. *The New International Dictionary of the Christian Church.* Grand Rapids, MI: Zondervan Publishing, 1974.

INDRA

The five principal deities of Hinduism are the three gods of the Trimurti (Brahma, Vishnu, and Shiva), Agni, and Indra.

Indra is the ancient god of war and storms, similar to the Greek Zeus or the Norse Odin. He often appears with a thunderbolt in his hand and is known as a slayer of demons.

We first read about him in the ancient hymns of the Vedas, so he probably came to India with the Aryan culture. But over the years this volatile god has, like so many Hindu gods, become internalized and tamed a bit. Originally born of heaven and Earth, he separated the two, bringing form out of chaos when he killed the great demon/serpent Vritra, who was threatening the whole planet.

But a prime myth of Hinduism reminds people that even such accomplishments amount to nothing in the great scheme of things unless they understand the fundamental meaning of what it is to be human.

The Upanishads, Hindu sacred texts, tell us that after slaying Vritra, Indra is understandably puffed up with pride. He ascends a great mountain and decides to build a palace worthy of such a great hero as himself. But the construction of the building just goes on and on. The head carpenter to the gods realizes he has signed on to an eternal contract. Clearly something must be done to whittle Indra down to size.

Upon consultation with Brahma, the god of creation, a curious plot is played out. A mysterious messenger appears at the palace door one day, and Indra proceeds to show him around the new construction. The messenger is properly impressed and remarks that this is certainly the finest palace any Indra has ever built. Indra is understandably confused. Any Indra? He thought he was the only one. The messenger from Brahma draws Indra's attention to a procession of ants walking in formation over the palace floor. "Those ants," he says, "are all former Indras!"

And that's the way it goes. A god in one world's lifetime is reincarnated as an ant in the next. It doesn't pay to get too cocky because you never know what kind of karma you're building.

Indra learns his lesson. He goes off to become a yogi. Of course he does everything to extremes, so he has to be taught another lesson. But he finally comes to understand that he is a manifestation of Brahman.

Sources:
Campbell, Joseph. *The Power of Myth*. New York: Doubleday, 1988.

INQUISITION

One of the darkest periods of Church history occurred over a period of about three hundred years, beginning with the appointment by Pope Gregory IX in 1231 of a special tribunal designed to root out and destroy heresy. A designated inquisitor, usually a Dominican or Franciscan, would typically come into town with great fanfare (accompanied by great dread) and announce that all heretics had a period of two to six weeks to confess their heresy. Those who repented were usually given light sentences. At the end of the grace period, the questioning began. It only took the testimony of two witnesses, whose identities were kept secret, to convict a supposed heretic. By the time of Pope Innocent IV in 1252, torture was allowed. The accused could be assisted by a counselor but could not be defended by a lawyer. These individuals were usually better off if they confessed to something, even if innocent, because the process of determining guilt was a painful one. Typically people were tortured until they pled guilty; then they were executed, often by burning at the stake, on the basis of their confession.

The Inquisition was not limited to the Catholic Church. Although it was not called by that name, New England Protestants did much the same thing during the Salem witch trials in Massachusetts.

As secular political power grew, the Inquisition gradually declined. Although it quite justifiably seems abhorrent to the modern mind, it must be remembered that similar human rights violations exist even today in some totalitarian states. Then as now, the Inquisition was more about entrenched power than religion.

Sources:

Douglas, J. D., ed. *The New International Dictionary of the Christian Church.* Grand Rapids, MI: Zondervan Publishing, 1974.

INTELLIGENT DESIGN THEORY *see* **Creationism**

INTERNATIONAL SOCIETY FOR KRISHNA CONSCIOUSNESS *see* **Cult**

ISIS *see* **Egyptian Gods and Goddesses**

ISLAM

(See also Caliphate)

The call is heard five times a day, coming from the graceful tower of the minaret. At sunrise, noon, afternoon, just after sunset, and at dark, the muezzin calls the faithful to pray:

> Allah is great! Allah is great!
> There is no God but Allah,
> And Muhammad is his prophet!
> Come to prayer! Come to prayer!
> Come to Abundance! Come to Abundance!

And to the dawn prayer is added:

> Prayer is better than sleep!
> Prayer is better than sleep!
> Allah is great! Allah is great!
> There is no God but Allah!

Some 1.2 billion people in the world, almost one out of every five, claim Islam as their religion and, five times a day, hear the cry, face toward Mecca, and recite their prayers. They are called Muslims ("submitters") because they have "submitted" to the will of Allah (see Allah).

Muslims belong to the religious tradition that is probably, in the words of author Robert Ellwood, "the most homogeneous and purposefully international of the other two giant cross-cultural faiths—Christianity and Buddhism." From the very beginning, Muhammad (see Muhammad), the founder of Islam, set out to spread the word around the world. And Islam, youngest of the world religions, is quickly fulfilling his vision.

His beliefs were quite simple and straightforward. But carrying them out can be difficult, and the intricacies of Islamic philosophy can be quite bewildering to Westerners.

Simply put, Muslims believe there is one God, Allah. He is the same God worshiped by other traditions but under different names. Allah has made himself (Muslims always use the masculine pronoun) known through many prophets, including Abraham, Moses, and Jesus. He has revealed himself through scriptures, such as the Bible. But the "people of the Book" (Christians and Jews) did not remain faithful. They didn't follow the directions. So Allah chose his last and greatest prophet, Muhammad, and dictated his final revelation, the Qur'an (see Qur'an), to give the world its final warning. People live only one life, and they will be judged on how well they submitted to the will of Allah.

That's all there is to it. There is good (submission) and there is evil (rejection). But to leave it there is to miss the subtlety and complexity of Islamic thought and practice.

There are five "pillars" of Islam—five requirements expected of all Muslims:

1. The Creed (Kalima)

La ilaha illa Allah; Muhammad rasul Allah—"There is no God but Allah and Muhammad is his messenger [or prophet]."

This is the *shahadah*, the "confession" that Muslims recite at least once every day and more frequently when necessary. They are often the very first words a baby hears whispered in his ear, and the last words to be uttered by a dying man. An action worthy of praise brings the response, *Alhamduli-llah*, "Praise be to Allah." Speculations about the future are always accompanied by the words, *Insha Allah*, "If Allah wills."

A Muslim visitor to the Dar al Islam mosque near Abiquiu, New Mexico, prays east toward Mecca during the midday prayer. *AP/Wide World Photos.*

Allah is definitely center stage, not Muhammad. The prophet insisted he was never to be worshiped. "Muhammad is not more than an Apostle; many were the Apostles that passed away before him" (Qur'an 3:144).

At Muhammad's funeral, when some believers found themselves hoping for a resurrection or Second Coming, Abu-Bakr, caliph ("successor") to the prophet, was quick to remind them: "O ye people, if anyone worships Muhammad, Muhammad is dead, but if anyone worships Allah, he is alive and dies not...."

Christianity considers its founder to be God, the Second Person of the Trinity. Muhammad wanted no such designation from Islam. There is only one God in this solidly monotheistic religion. That is Allah. Muhammad, the Holy Prophet, was just the messenger.

2. Daily Prayer (Salat)

The faithful are called to pray five times a day, though in America, at least, the two afternoon prayers can be combined. They ritually wash themselves (sand can be substituted for water in dry climates), face toward Mecca, and recite the Arabic prayers they learned in childhood. Hands will be raised to the side of the head as the words, *Allahu akbar,* "God is great," are spoken. Then the first *sura* of the Qur'an will be recited, followed by prayers and other verses. The worshiper will then bow, placing hands on knees, declare "glory to God," and, after again praising God in a standing position, descend to a posture of complete submission with knees, forehead, and hands on the ground, praying, "Glory to my Lord, the Most High!" After sitting and then repeating the posture of submission, the worshiper will resume a standing position, completing one full cycle of prayer. Two cycles are offered in the morning, four at noon, afternoon, and night, and three at sunset. After prayer the Muslim will turn his or her head to both sides and offer a blessing of peace to other Muslims and all who need God's guidance.

Men will often go to the mosque if it is convenient, pausing at the entrance to remove their shoes. Women usually pray at home, but in these more liberated times there is a separate area for them at the mosque. The women will, of course, first cover their head. Modest dress is a requirement for both men and women. Shorts and T-shirts are very definitely out of order. If it happens to be Friday, the holiest day of the week, the Imam, or prayer leader (sometimes called a sheik), will deliver a sermon. In America, the Imam is usually the administrator of the community as well, much like clergy of other traditions.

3. Almsgiving (Zakat)

Between 2 percent and 10 percent of income is to be shared with the poor of the community. This pillar emphasizes the need to remember less fortunate neighbors. It is to be given voluntarily. But, as in other traditions, it is usually collected (in some countries it is an actual tax) and a record is kept. Wealth is not frowned upon in Muslim communities. After all, Allah blesses the faithful. But it is to be shared in a way that is not demeaning to the recipient.

4. Fasting (Sawm)

During the month of Ramadan, no food (even medicine), drink, smoking, or sex is allowed during daylight hours. The hours are computed and published these days, but it used to be understood that day begins when there is enough light to distinguish between a black thread and a white thread.

After the sun goes down, however, it's time to joyfully feast with friends and family.

During Ramadan, Muslims greet one another by saying, "Ramadan Mubarak," which means "A Blessed Ramadan," or perhaps "Salaam," which means "peace."

5. Pilgrimage (Hajj)

At least once during their lifetime, during the month of Dhu-al-Hijjah (the "month of pilgrimage"), Muslims are expected to make a pilgrimage to Mecca in Saudi

Arabia, the birthplace of Muhammad and a holy city even before his time. Leaving home represents a kind of ritual death in which the pilgrim enters into a spiritual state known as *ihram*. Upon returning the pilgrim may add the title *hajji* to his name, marking a great spiritual achievement and entitling the bearer to great respect in the community. On pilgrimage the Muslim will join perhaps one million other pilgrims wearing special garments and sandals. They will circle the Kaaba, the shrine, seven times in a counterclockwise direction; they will view, and perhaps kiss, the sacred Black Stone (see Black Stone) at the Kaaba. They will visit the sacred well called Zamzam, the well of Hagar and Ishmael (see Abraham), and throw forty-nine stones at the pillar representing Iblis (see Devil/Demons). These were customs practiced even before Muhammad was born, but he sanctified them and gave them new meaning within the context of Islam.

For their whole lives, the pilgrims have faced Mecca during prayer. They have visualized this sacred spot of ground. Now they travel, for perhaps the only time in their lives, to the place of their dreams. For most of them, it is an intensely personal, holy moment, the climax of a lifetime.

Correct Living

If a Muslim is asked, "What is the meaning of life?" he or she will probably respond by affirming the central fact of the creed. Allah is Creator and the essential unity behind all that exists. Creation thus has dignity and value. The purpose of humankind is to seek understanding while submitting to Allah. It is difficult to stay on the straight path. People can be weak. Obedience demands structure. Humans are not partners with God. Allah is not our "buddy." To doubt or reject belief, to lie, steal, or deceive, to commit adultery or forbidden sex, to gossip or do damage to anyone or their feelings—that is sin. "For the insolent awaits an ill resort, Gehenna, wherein they are roasted—an evil cradling! All this; so let them taste it—boiling water and pus, and other torments of the like coupled together" (Qur'an 38:55–58).

How do the faithful walk the other path, the path of *iman* ("faith")? Faith is not a blind leap or a hoping against hope. Faith is based on rational intelligence, the highest form of knowledge. Humans are not "compelled" to believe the Qur'an. "No compulsion is there in religion" (Qur'an 2:256). But for those who study, reflect, and meditate on its message, Allah will lead them into all truth.

So to be a Muslim, a submitter, is a constant struggle and striving. It is a jihad, a holy war fought within the spirit. Humans aren't evil by nature. But neither are they perfect. So to live correctly means to constantly strive for goodness. The prophet Muhammad once returned from a battle and said, "We have returned from the small jihad to the great jihad," from the physical battle to the spiritual one.

But there are those within radical Islam who choose to interpret the jihad in terms of warfare against those who have blatantly rejected Islam, most particularly those in the materialistic West who oppose the idea of Islamic states, especially when those states control oil supplies. For those Muslims, the jihad is a fight to the death by whatever means can be appropriated. The idea of willingly dying for the faith, suicide bombing, is not unique to Islam. Japanese kamikaze ("divine wind") fighters used the same techniques in World War II. But it has wreaked havoc and tragedy in the West, especially in the case of the tragedies of September 11, 2001. Those who strap bombs to their chests and blow themselves up, along with innocent victims, are sometimes viewed as heroes in the Palestinian territories. Many point to the Prophet's declaration, "Not equal are those who sit at home and receive no hurt, and those who strive and fight in the cause of God with their goods and their persons. God hath granted a higher grade to those who strive and fight" (Qur'an 4:95).

But it cannot be emphasized enough that not all Muslims, or even anything approaching a majority, share this view.

Islam shares other rituals in common with Middle Eastern traditions, and it does not practice others despite popular misconception to the contrary.

Circumcision is practiced by Muslims as well as by Jews and many Christians. But in some localities around the world it is the tradition to perform what is often called female circumcision, or clitoridectomy. This practice is highly controversial, but those cultures that do it claim it is a ritual of purification. It is by no means common and, although it is often associated with Islam, it is not a Muslim or religious practice but a social one. It is widely practiced, for example, in primarily Christian countries such as Ethiopia and Kenya.

Certain events have created a negative impression on the general public. When Salman Rushdie published his 1988 book *The Satanic Verses*, in which he dared suggest the Qur'an was not necessarily what Islamic doctrine says it is, the Ayatollah Ruhollah Khomeini (1900–1989) of Iran accused him of blasphemy, sentenced him to death, and offered what was, in effect, a "contract" on his life. Osama bin Ladin (b. 1957), leader of Al Qaeda in Afghanistan, has called for a jihad, a holy war, against the United States.

While representative of the beliefs of a small minority, these kinds of very public actions have affected the perception of all Muslims among non-Muslims, straining relationships in pluralistic societies. What must be remembered is that these kinds of activities are not typical of a tradition that has contributed so much to human history. And Muslims around the world are just as angry as non-Muslims, perhaps more so, when their religion is abused or exploited by extremists.

Instead they would have the world remember the nature of Allah. "There is no God but he; that is the witness of Allah, His angels and those endued with knowledge, standing firm of justice. There is no God but he, the Exalted in Power, the Wise" (Qur'an 3:18).

Sources:

Ellwood, Robert S., and Barbara A. McGraw. *Many Peoples, Many Faiths.* 6th ed. Upper Saddle River, NJ: Prentice Hall, 1999.

Fisher, Mary Pat, and Lee W. Bailey. *An Anthology of Living Religions.* Upper Saddle River, NJ: Prentice Hall, 2000.

Ludwig, Theodore M. *The Sacred Paths: Understanding the Religions of the World.* 2nd ed. Upper Saddle River, NJ: Prentice Hall, 1996.

ISLAM, DEVELOPMENT OF

After the death of Muhammad (see Muhammad), Islam quickly spread out from its Arabian base. The first four caliphs ("successors"—see Caliphate) are often called the "rightly guided caliphs." Abu Bakr, 'Umar, 'Uthman, who was assassinated, and 'Ali, also a victim of assassination, were all early converts and followed the Prophet through the trials and tribulations of his seminal work.

If the movement's beginning seemed marred with violence, it continued with even more dissension and strife. From the very beginning there were those who thought 'Ali should have been the successor to the Prophet. They were known as Shia Ali, the party of Ali. This was later shortened to Shi'ite. By 1502 the Shi'ites became the official ruling body of Persia and today are the principal Islamic sect of Iran. They did not believe revelation ended with Muhammad but that it continued through a series (some say seven and others twelve) of Imams, or religious leaders.

Sunnis, on the other hand, are the traditionalists who believe Abu Bakr was the correct successor, and they attempt to follow the Qur'an and the rule of Islam as Muhammad established it.

A strict following of the Qur'an leads to difficulty in the modern world. Seventh-century Islamic practice, for instance, demands a literal "eye for an eye." It was the law to cut off the hand of a thief. If Islam is the rule of the land, this can be done. But a typical European or American court would not allow such a practice. So the law obviously had to be interpreted and modified. These interpretations are called *hadiths*, and they were based on the spirit of Qur'an law, rather than its letter. Gradually the Sunnis began to develop a tradition based on three great principles: the Qur'an, the Hadiths, and human reason brought to bear on specific circumstances. Facing the kind of cultural evolution later experienced by Christianity, Islam responded in the same way. It divided into factions. The Hanifites, Malikites, Shafi'ites, and Hanbalites each established geographical spheres of influence that continue to this day.

There are other similarities between the division of Islam and those of Christianity and Judaism. Each developed a mystical expression. Within Judaism it was the Kabbalah (see Kabbalah); within Christianity, the charismatic movement (see Charismatic Movement). Within Islam, it was the Sufi. This was the tradition so often depicted as that of the "Whirling Dervishes" and the Fakirs, those who could walk through live coals of fire.

The world has never experienced a growth in any world religion such as that demonstrated by early Islam. By 635 Damascus had fallen under Muslim control. A quick succession of countries followed: Persia by 636, Jerusalem in 638, and Egypt by 640. Spain, North Africa, the Middle East, India, Pakistan, and even parts of China quickly followed. Europe might have joined the procession had it not been for Charles Martel and the famous Battle of Tours in 732.

This was the "golden age" of Islam. The fabulous culture of Baghdad produced kings who ruled after the order of the *Arabian Nights*, tales such as that of 'Ali Baba and others. It bore little resemblance to the Islam of today but produced legends that would last for centuries. Lavish palaces, poets and slaves, harems: great wealth and luxury flowed into the hands of those at the top of the social ladder.

But even more important was the standard of scholarship practiced during this time. Libraries were built in which scholars translated Aristotle and Plato into Arabic.

The study of mathematics and philosophy grew by leaps and bounds. Much of what was later destroyed in the Alexandrian Library (see Alexandria) was saved only because Muslim scholars had translated the books there and had taken them to safety throughout the far-flung Islamic world.

The classic golden age of Islam came to an end in the eleventh and twelfth centuries. Turkish tribes from central Asia began to make incursions into Iran and Iraq. Baghdad fell, and the caliph there became a mere figurehead. When the fall of Palestine threatened Christian pilgrimages to the Holy Land, a series of Crusades (see Crusades) were launched that gradually drained the area of men and wealth. Jerusalem fell to the Crusaders in 1099. Although it was recaptured by Saladin in 1187, the Mongols were able to take advantage of the weakened state, advancing all the way to Baghdad by 1258. They proceeded to destroy the city and executed the last of the great caliphs. It was many years before new Islamic rulers could again carve out their spheres of influence in various parts of the world.

But by 1326, with the founding of the Ottoman Empire under the Turk Osman, Islam surged again. Mecca and Medina came under Muslim control and protection again. More important, Constantinople was captured in 1453 and renamed Istanbul. Music and art flourished, along with massive systems of law and architecture that still stand today. In the East, Persia came back under Shi'ite rule. Mongols converted to Islam in great numbers. India soon fell to the invaders, while leaders such as Babur, a descendant of Genghis Khan, and Akbar became known to the outside world. One of Akbar's successors built the famed Taj Mahal as a glowing example of Islamic art and architecture.

Such a history lesson points to the fact that religion influences politics to a very great degree. Sometimes it's hard to tell where one ends and the other begins. We have to wonder how much influence Islam would have on the modern world, for instance, if huge oil fields hadn't produced vast amounts of money. When Westerners poured into Iran to develop the oil fields, they brought Western culture, schools, towns, stores, and lifestyle. This led to a profound confrontation with Islamic customs and culture. Of course there was a reaction. Westerners thought they were liberating the common people, offering them opportunities they had never experienced before. But the Islamic leadership saw only decadence and loss of control.

When the Shi'ite leadership overthrew the Shah of Iran in 1979 and installed the Ayatollah Ruhollah Khomeini (1900–1989), a fundamentalist reaction affected the whole world. Even women in Cairo, used to wearing Western clothes and walking the streets unattended, now felt the need to wear traditional garb and stay away from compromising situations. Americans were at a loss to understand why the Muslim world of the Middle East looked upon the West with such seething resentment and outright hatred. They simply cannot understand why anyone would want to live under what they considered to be such a strict world of religious intolerance as they are told the Qur'an preaches.

Individual Muslims, as well, are at a loss. All they are told is that America is the great Satan. They do not see help offered. They see only restrictions imposed upon them as if they are a conquered people existing on handouts from America.

The debate following the infamous September 11, 2001, attacks on the World Trade Center in New York and the Pentagon in Washington, D.C., fostered a series of conferences and debates by leading scholars. A conference held in November 2002 at Harvard University was probably typical. Specialists in foreign policy and Islamic tradition debated for three days about the nature of conflict between militant Muslims and the West. Experts such as Bernard Lewis, author of the book *What Went Wrong? Western Impact and Middle Eastern Response*, and Samuel Huntington, a Harvard professor who argues that there is a "clash of civilizations" occurring between Islam and the West, were vocal about the need for America to understand the nature of the great gulf existing in the world today and the perception most Americans have about the problem.

While Americans would likely argue that they support the right of people worldwide to decide for themselves how to live, others might counter that this means the Americans want other countries to operate just like America. Of course, such an analysis is simplistic, only scratching the surface of a very real and difficult situation. One-third of Muslims living today reside in America and in countries in the former Soviet Union and Western Europe. It is impossible to fully practice the rituals and commandments of the Qur'an under these governments. And none of these nations is about to become an Islamic state. Can Muslim soldiers in such nations go to war against other Muslims in Islamic nations? What about personal persecution from neighbors who see Islam as a single entity, recognizing no difference between a terrorist organization such as Al Qaeda and the neighborhood mosque?

Sources:

Ellwood, Robert S., and Barbara A. McGraw. *Many Peoples, Many Faiths*. 6th ed. Upper Saddle River, NJ: Prentice Hall, 1999.

Fisher, Mary Pat, and Lee W. Bailey. *An Anthology of Living Religions*. Upper Saddle River, NJ: Prentice Hall, 2000.

Fudge, Bruce. "The Two Faces of Islamic Study." *Boston Globe*, December 15, 2002.

Ludwig, Theodore M. *The Sacred Paths: Understanding the Religions of the World*. 2nd ed. Upper Saddle River, NJ: Prentice Hall, 1996.

ISRAEL *see* **Babylonian Captivity; Judaism**

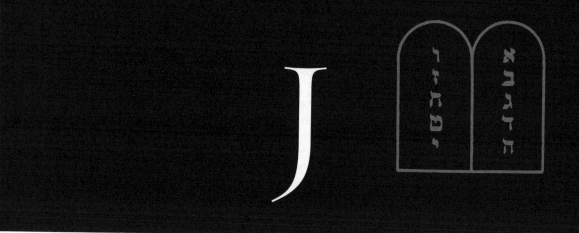

Jainism

Both Buddhism (see Buddhism, Development of) and Jainism developed in the sixth century BCE as a form of protest against Hinduism. They offered alternatives to the caste system (see Hinduism, Development of) and raised objections to the movement of the time that had begun to view the Vedas as holy scripture.

"Jain" means "conqueror." Its founder, Mahavira ("Great Hero"), was a contemporary of the Buddha, Confucius, Lao Tzu, and the Hebrew prophets Jeremiah, Ezekiel, and Isaiah. With the possible exception of Lao Tzu and Confucius, none of these men met or were influenced by each other, but the times certainly must have been ripe for spiritual movements.

Much like the Buddha, Mahavira's principal concept was that of dualism. The universe consists of the two opposing forces of good and evil. But where the Buddha discovered the Middle Way between the two, Mahavira proposed another philosophy. He understood the "good" in terms of soul, or life. Evil was lifeless, or matter. Soul or feelings exist in everything, even the dust of the ground or rocks of the landscape. But soul is entrapped in matter, "coated," so to speak, forming a material covering imposed by karma (see Hinduism). The human predicament is that the body (material, evil) is thus a form of prison for the soul (spiritual, good). So since karma placed you into this shell, the only way to break out is by extreme asceticism (see Ascetic).

This is to be carried out through five principal activities:

Non-injury to life
Truthfulness
Taking nothing unless it is offered
Celibacy
Renouncement of all attachments

Worshipers in a main hall gathered around a mandala in the Jain Temple in Bombay, India. *Fortean Picture Library.*

Pertaining to the first activity, Jains are vegetarians. Some even place screens over lamps to keep moths from hurting themselves in the flames. Others wear masks to keep from breathing in insects or sweep the path before them to avoid stepping on and crushing ants or bugs. This extreme form of attention is meant to avoid bad karmic repercussions in the next life.

Certainly the most well known of those influenced by Jainism was Mahatma Gandhi (see Gandhi, Mahatma). Mahavira's principles, especially those concerning non-injury, greatly shaped Gandhi's practice of nonviolent political opposition. Such practices proved to be a great influence on a young student named Martin Luther King Jr. So it can be argued that Jainism had a great deal to do with shaping the America we have known since the decade of the 1960s.

Today Jainism is considered a minority sect within Hinduism, but Mahavira has taken his place among the great religious founders of all time. There have only been nine of them in the history of the great world religions: Buddha (Buddhism), Confucius (Confucianism), Jesus (Christianity), Lao Tzu (Daoism), Mahavira (Jainism), Moses (Judaism), Muhammad (Islam), Nanak (Sikhism), and Zoroaster (Zoroastrianism).

Sources:
Ellwood, Robert S., and Barbara A. McGraw. *Many Peoples, Many Faiths.* 6th ed. Upper Saddle River, NJ: Prentice Hall, 1999.

JEHOVAH'S WITNESSES

The Fuller Brush man doesn't travel door to door anymore and vacuum cleaners are sold in stores these days. But door by door, one visit at a time, Jehovah's Witnesses quietly go about the business of what is probably the most audacious grassroots marketing campaign in history. In short, they are trying to reach, one at a time, six billion people with their message.

In June 2002 the Supreme Court of the United States ruled that, irrespective of local bylaws, the Jehovah's Witnesses have the right to ring every doorbell in the country. Their organizational structure is superb, their dedication inspiring, their numbers growing daily. Two by two, well-dressed, polite lay people who believe in their cause are out to talk personally to every soul in the world.

There are 945,689 Witnesses in the world right now. They spend an average of 189 hours per person per year getting the word out. There are 121,697 "pioneers" canvassing full time, adding daily to the membership of 11,582 congregations who meet in various Kingdom Halls around the world. Each member fills out a form documenting every house visited, with standard initials such as NH for "Not Home." During the year 2001, 179 million hours were catalogued at their headquarters in Brooklyn, New York.

The numbers alone tell the story. Through all kinds of weather, enduring vicious dogs, verbal abuse, and friendly, if evasive, chit-chat, they believe they have a story to tell and go about the business of telling it. They convert some people and irritate others. They are the brunt of jokes and slander, but they keep about their business.

Who are these people who care so much?

They are Jehovah's Witnesses. Their title comes from an Old Testament name for God. When you approach the Witnesses to find out what they are about, they will channel you into a home Bible study and introduce you to God. God has a name, just like anyone else. And if you want to get to know God you ought to first know his name. It's in the Bible, and is spelled YHVH. That's a little hard to enunciate. No one now living knows how it was pronounced. So we have to go with our best guess. Historically, the vowels that used to make the name pronounceable are "a," "o" and "e." That makes it Yahoveh. But the Hebrew letter that corresponds to the English "y" becomes "j," and somewhere along the line the original "a" became pronounced "e" in English and the final "e" began to be spelled as an "a." So meet Jehovah. Whenever the words "the Lord" appear in English-language Bibles, it's a translation of YHVH. Catholic and Protestant academics coined the name "Jehovah" long ago.

In the ninth chapter of the Gospel according to Luke, Jesus sent the disciples out into every town to preach the Gospel and be witnesses of the power of God. The order was never rescinded, so Jehovah's Witnesses believe they are simply doing what Jesus asked of his followers. They are witnesses of Jehovah. "Ye are my witnesses, saith Jehovah." Hence, the name.

But they have been called by many other names since their movement began in the days prior to 1872 when their founder, Charles Russell, began meeting with a small group of Christian believers to examine the scriptures "relative to the coming of Christ and kingdom." They have been known as Millennial Dawnists, International Bible Students, members of the Watchtower Bible and Tract Society, Russellites, and sometimes Rutherfordites.

It all began when Russell, a Congregationalist by religion and haberdasher by trade, "stumbled across," in his words, an Adventist preacher (see Seventh-day Adventism) who sparked his wavering faith. In 1879 Russell published his first book, *Food for Thinking Christians.* By 1884 his adherents had formed a movement called the Zion's Watchtower Society. (The name came from the third chapter of the book of Ezekiel. God warned the prophet that he was to be "as on a watchtower." If the enemy came and the watcher didn't warn the people, their blood would be on the hands of the watcher. But if the people were warned and didn't listen, at least the fault wouldn't lie with the watcher.)

Russell traveled incessantly and published a constant stream of pamphlets to help his followers. Like so many before him, he tried to figure out dates for the return of Christ. The year 1914 became the time when "the full establishment of the Kingdom of God would be established."

The year came and went without the coming of Christ. But upon reexamining scripture, Russell concluded that the date was right, it was only the interpretation of how the kingdom would come that was wrong. The year 1914 was when Christ returned "in Spirit," a prelude to the physical return. Armageddon would still take place, but not before those who responded to the call of the Spirit witnessed to that Spirit and became the "watchers" on the wall, warning the people of what was to come. (Some religious scholars and secular historians have noted that 1914, the year World War I began, was indeed a year that changed the world. Jesus warned of "wars and rumors of wars" in Matthew 18. They would come "before the time of the end.")

Pastor Russell died in 1917, and after a severe struggle among the 15,000 adherents, Joseph Franklin ("Judge") Rutherford assumed command. Under the popular slogan, "Millions now living will never die," the society rebounded from the scandals of Russell's divorce and his attempted sale of "miracle wheat." It was Rutherford who, in 1931, coined the term Jehovah's Witnesses and provided the witnesses with phonographs so they could play records of the judge's comments when they made their house calls. By 1942, when the judge died, a board of directors was appointed to lead the organization. The cult of personality disappeared, along with the phonographs. Now the Witnesses entered into their greatest period of growth.

The original message was very definitely aimed at those who were considered to be "culturally deprived." Satan's power, they said, is wielded through "the religious, commercial and political combine." These are the forces that oppress the righteous. One power structure does the bidding of the other. It is an evil conspiracy to defeat the righteous. Churches and religious organizations are "tools of Satan." Some ministers are probably well meaning, but duped. Others, backed by entrenched political forces, are out to steal the cash of their innocent congregations.

They have become famous for a few of the doctrines they espouse. Genesis 9:3 warns people not to "eat meat that has life blood in it," so many Witnesses are vegetarians. And Leviticus 17:14 says "the life of any creature is in the blood," so Witnesses refuse blood transfusions as well.

They are also forbidden to take part in ecumenical dialogues or events and are often criticized for believing their religion is the only correct one.

They believe Jesus Christ is God's son, the "first created" of all things, and so inferior to God. But he will return to Earth to rule.

So the Witnesses are issuing the warning. Some people are hearing the message, and the Witnesses believe it won't be long until Christ returns and the world will be restored. 144,000 Witnesses (the number comes from Revelation 14) will someday go to heaven. But the vast majority of the faithful, "a great multitude," will remain on Earth to live life the way it's supposed to be. "The wolf will live with the lamb ... they shall not hurt nor destroy" in all the earth (Isaiah 11).

Until then, Jehovah has his witnesses. They are passing out their magazine, the *Watchtower*. They offer books and lessons free of charge. They are dedicated, polite, and motivated.

Sources:
Bombardieri, Marcella. "Street Smart." *Boston Globe*, June 23, 2002.
Hudson, Winthrop S. *Religion in America*. New York: Charles Scribner, 1965.

JESUITS

The Society of Jesus, commonly known as the Jesuits, was founded by Ignatius of Loyola (1491–1556) and quickly became a response to the new conditions of the sixteenth century. The European discovery of America (see Columbus, Christopher), the Protestant Reformation (see Christianity, Development of), the invention of the printing press, and the end of the Middle Ages all demanded a different worldview. Ignatius, son of an illustrious, aristocratic Spanish family, thought to further the family name by becoming a warrior and military hero. Instead, a severe wound that caused a permanent limp forced him to reexamine his life. He turned to God and the Church. Referring to himself in the third person, he writes of the day he saw the light:

At that time he came to have much travail with scruples ... when he had such thoughts, very often the temptation came to him with great force, to jump from a big hole in his room, next to the place he prayed. But then, acknowledging that to kill himself would be a sin, he would cry out, "Lord, I shall do naught to offend thee."

Although he never described exactly what happened, when his eyes were fully opened to the mercy of God, he responded:

From that day on he was free of those scruples, being certain that our Lord had wished to free him by his mercy.

He tried to find his new vocation by making a pilgrimage to the Holy Land, hoping to find a place among the Franciscans as a missionary to the Turks. But his fiery temperament frightened the brothers, and his trip was a failure.

He next decided to become a hermit, but the lifestyle didn't fit him.

Deciding he needed education, the now-mature Loyola went back to school, mixing with young theology students and gaining a band of followers. His small flock swore obedience to the pope with such fervor that they were chosen by Pope Paul III to be the instrument by which the Catholic Church would challenge Protestantism at the Council of Trent. (It must be made clear that official Jesuit literature denies the Society of Jesus was formed to combat Protestantism. Such challenge nonetheless occurred, whether or not Pope Paul III or Loyola ever intended it.)

In the New World and in the Far East, Jesuits carried on a voluminous missionary activity, being known by their black robes and serious demeanor. Patterned after military organizations, the order was an efficient tool of a reformed papacy. Many of their brilliant young scholars contributed, in the words of historian Justo L. Gonzalez, "their knowledge to the polemic against Protestantism."

But this was by no means their only work. They established orphanages and houses for "reclaiming" prostitutes. They worked with the poor and outcast. By the time of Loyola's death, his order, about one thousand strong, was beginning to establish universities and other institutions of higher learning. The aristocracy began to take notice.

Their work was not without opposition, however. They were expelled from Portugal, France, and Spain, and Pope Clement XIV eventually suppressed the society, a ban that was not lifted until 1814.

The Society of Jesus today is a respected institution among leading academies and universities around the world.

Sources:

Douglas, J. D., ed. *The New International Dictionary of the Christian Church*. Grand Rapids, MI: Zondervan Publishing, 1974.

Gonzalez, Justo L. *The Story of Christianity*. 2 vols. New York: Harper & Row, 1985.

JESUS OF NAZARETH *see* **Christ/Jesus of Nazareth**

JIHAD

(See also Islam)

Jihad means "holy war." But how that word is interpreted is a matter of some debate, probably because Muhammad himself used the term in different ways. Sometimes he used *jihad* to describe the cultural and political spread of Islam. Sometimes he used it to refer to the spiritual war against evil both in society and in the human soul.

Following are a few passages from the Qur'an relating to jihad:

Not equal are those believers who sit (at home) and receive no hurt, and those who strive and fight in the cause of God with their goods and their persons. God hath granted a grade higher to those who strive and fight. (4:95)

Fight in the cause of God those who fight you, but do not transgress limits; for God loveth not transgressors. (2:190)

And fight them on until there is no more tumult or oppression, and there prevail justice and faith in God; but if they cease, let there be no hostility to those who practice oppression. (2:193)

And if any strive (with might and main), they do so for their own souls; for Allah is free of all needs from all creation. (29:6)

Let there be no compulsion in religion: Truth stands out clear from Error: whoever rejects evil and believes in Allah hath grasped the most trustworthy hand-hold, that never breaks. And Allah heareth and knoweth all things. (2:256)

Sources:

Fisher, Mary Pat and Lee W. Bailey. *An Anthology of Living Religions*. Upper Saddle River: Prentice Hall, 2000.

The Holy Qur'an, trans. with a commentary by Abdullah Yusuf Ali. Beirut, Lebenon: Dar Al Arabia, 1968.

JONES, JIM *see* **Cult**

JONESTOWN TRAGEDY *see* **Cult**

JOSEPH

Jacob, the grandson of Abraham, had twelve sons. Joseph, the eleventh, was his father's favorite. His story, made popular anew by the resounding success of Andrew Lloyd Webber and Tim Rice's stage show, *Joseph and the Amazing Technicolor Dreamcoat*, is told in a collection of stories found in Genesis, beginning in chapter 37. Joseph becomes the means by which the children of Abraham make the move from Canaan to Egypt.

Joseph was gifted with the ability to see the future in symbolic dreams. When Jacob gave his son a colorful coat as an expression of his love, the other sons became jealous. Joseph dreamed his brothers would someday bow down before him, and he made the mistake of telling them about it. In a fit of rage, they sought to kill him by throwing him into a dry well. At the last minute they changed their minds and sold him into slavery in Egypt, telling their father Joseph had died fighting a wild beast.

In Egypt Joseph became a respected attendant to a wealthy man named Potiphar. Potiphar's wife, however, had designs on more than Joseph's administrative talents, and she invited Joseph to her bed. Joseph refused, and in the ensuing struggle he escaped only by sliding out of his cloak and running from the room. To cover up her attempted seduction, she told her husband that Joseph had attacked her. Once again, Joseph found himself the victim of jealousy.

He was jailed and would have remained forgotten had he not interpreted the dreams of some of his cellmates. When one of them was restored to the company of Pharaoh's personal slaves, that man remembered Joseph when Pharaoh himself needed a dream interpreter. Joseph was summoned and prophesied a time of wealth followed by a period of famine. Pharaoh was so impressed he made Joseph second in command of all Egypt, in order to prepare for the hard times to come. When famine struck, Egypt was the only country ready for it.

Meanwhile, Joseph's family, back in Canaan, was in dire straits when their crops failed. They realized the only way they could get food was to travel to Egypt to beg for it. Not knowing their brother was the new Egyptian governor, they were tested by him and finally forgiven for their sins. After a few twists and turns of the story, the family is finally reunited in Egypt to live in luxury under the auspices of their powerful brother.

Four hundred years later, as the book of Exodus begins, their descendants are still there. But in the interim a "new king arose, who knew not Joseph." One of Jacob's greatest descendants, Moses, is also living in Egyptian luxury, unaware of his ancestry. This period of change happens between Genesis and Exodus. To close the pages of one book and open the next is to jump over four centuries of upheaval that sets the stage for the Passover (see Moses; Passover).

Sources:

May, Herbert G., and Bruce M. Metzger, eds. *The New Oxford Annotated Bible with the Apocrypha*. Rev. ed. New York: Oxford University Press, 1973.

JUDAISM

Hear, O Israel: The Lord our God, the Lord is One; and you shall love the Lord your God with all your heart, and with all your soul, and with all your might. (Deuteronomy 6:4–5)

Some say Judaism began when a man named Abraham (see Abraham) heard the voice of God calling him to a new land where his descendants would someday be as numerous as the stars of the sky and the grains of sand on the beach.

Those of a more worldly bent are apt to think it all began when a sheep-herding nomad arrived in Canaan with a new idea and a new God whose followers constituted a great nation and one of the world's major religions. For a brief time, about one thousand years before the most famous descendant of Abraham was born in a Bethle-

Jewish men, one wearing an Israeli flag, pray in front of the Western Wall, Judaism's holiest site. *AP/Wide World Photos.*

hem stable, this religion and people attained wealth and unified power rarely again seen in what later generations would call the Holy Land.

Others claim it all started when the descendants of Abraham, by now slaves in Egypt, huddled in their homes one night, dressed for a quick flight into the desert. They ate a meal of lamb, unleavened bread, and bitter herbs while they listened for the sounds of death coming from the homes of their Egyptian neighbors.

Or perhaps it really started when Moses, the great liberator, came down from Mount Sinai bearing tablets of stone containing directions on how to live a decent and moral life. Or when "Joshua commanded the children to shout, and the walls came tumbling down." Or when Solomon built a temple. Or when the people, slaves again but this time in Persia, experienced real monotheism for the first time.

Some students of history say it is simply the result of religion evolving from worship in the desert to worship in the city—the Canaanite Gods morphing into the universal Yahveh.

However it happened, and whatever or whomever was behind it, Judaism has shaped the world in a way no other religion has done. Together with its child, Christianity, and its brother, Islam, it forms the principle known as monotheism. This is the hallmark of Judaism. Underneath all the rituals and ceremonies, underneath the patriotism and vision, underneath the law, the religious and political squabbles, and all the history, lies the one, essential, and inescapable fact of Judaism: "Hear, O Israel: The Lord our God, the Lord is One."

Through eras of hardship and triumph, through the persecution of the Inquisition (see Inquisition) and the horror of the Nazi death camps, whether residing in Israel or declaring, "Next year in Jerusalem!" the descendants of Abraham have remembered the vow and the promise:

> I will make you into a great nation
>   And I will bless you.
> I will make your name great
>   And you will be a blessing.
> I will bless those who bless you
>   And whoever curses you I will curse.
> And all peoples on earth
>   Will be blessed through you. (Genesis 12:2–3)

The central point of Judaism is this: the Hebrew people felt called by God to be a unique people with a divine contract (see Covenant) and promise. This covenant earned them the nickname, sometimes used in a derogatory manner, "God's Chosen People." Their religion did not consist of striving for and attaining this position. Although education, teaching, and philosophy were important, they were not a means to an end.

The belief handed down from generation to generation was that they were Jews because they were born Jewish, children of the covenant. They were God's people because they were born to be God's people. All the rest came later.

Their story is told first and most importantly in the scriptures, the holy books called Tanakh, an acronym formed from the first letters of their three main sections or divisions—Torah (the five books of Moses), Nev'im (Prophets), and Kethurim (Writings). (Christians, breaking off from Judaism after the death of Christ, also used the Hebrew scriptures, eventually naming their version the Old Testament.)

But over the years the many interpretations, teachings, practices, and customs of Jewish life and religion became codified and written down in the great library of books known as Talmud. Talmudic scholars sought to adapt Judaism to their current times without sacrificing principle, an undertaking that kept the people united even while they were persecuted and driven from their homes time and again. Often criticized for interpreting the letter of the law while sacrificing its spirit, the scholars took the long view, realizing that over the centuries the sustaining power and discipline of the law was the force that protected their people. It was a hedge around them, a fence that served to keep the covenant people within the bounds of the promise while keeping their enemies at bay.

The sign of the covenant was chosen by Yahveh himself: "You are to undergo circumcision, and it will be a sign of the covenant between me and you ... any uncircumcised male who has not been circumcised in the flesh will be cut off from his people; he has broken my covenant" (Genesis 17:11, 14).

Even when it was inconvenient or dangerous to do so, most Jewish parents made sure their sons were circumcised on the eighth day of their life. During times of persecution, it might have meant their death if discovered, but death within the covenant of Yahveh was to be desired over life outside the promise.

If the Hebrew people came from Abraham, the Hebrew religion came through Moses. In the desert wilderness journey following their escape from Egypt (see Ark of the Covenant; Judaism, Development of), they received the law, both the Ten Commandments and the written law that filled page after page of the book of Leviticus. In the wilderness the religion was hammered out. Sacrifice began, the "burnt offering" of a lamb or other animal, recalling the day God provided a substitute for Abraham's son (Genesis 22). The plans for the Tabernacle (see Tabernacle in the Wilderness), later translated grandly into Solomon's Temple in Jerusalem, were spelled out in detail. The priesthood was instituted.

When the Jews settled in Canaan, they were prepared and ready to "sing a new song unto the Lord." It was a song never heard before. They are singing it still.

Sources:
The Holy Bible, New International Version. Grand Rapids, MI: Zondervan Bible Publishers, 1978.

Judaism, Calendar of

The calendar of Islam begins with a specific date, crucial to the beginning of the religion—the day the prophet Muhammad made his journey from Mecca to Medina (see Islam, Development of). The Christian calendar, appropriately, begins with the birth of Jesus of Nazareth, the founder. One would think, then, that the Jewish calendar would probably begin with the call of Abraham or the day Moses came down from Sinai bearing the tablets of the law. Judaism, however—first and oldest of the great monotheistic traditions, whose scriptures begin with the words "In the beginning"—traces its beginning to the beginning, the creation of the world.

Prior to the middle of the fourth century CE, only Jewish authorities knew the arrangement of the sacred calendar. They announced the arrival of special dates and advised the people about seasonal events. But the patriarch Hillel II changed all that. Using the dates and ages found in the biblical book of Genesis, he determined when the creation of the universe took place. Using that as his starting point, he began to compute dates anchored to that time. But the Jewish year is based on a lunar system rather than a solar one. The normal Jewish year consists of twelve months, each consisting of either thirty or twenty-nine days, adjusted to the phases of the moon. This falls short of the actual 365-day period it takes Earth to revolve around the sun. So adjustments have to be made. Jewish leap years occur in the 3rd, 6th, 8th, 11th, 14th, 17th, and 19th year of each 19-year cycle. Were it not for these adjustments, seasonal festivities would begin to creep too far forward of their appropriate time. It would be hard, for instance, to celebrate a feast of first fruits while the ground is still frozen hard. To illustrate further, Passover must be celebrated during the spring month of Abib (Nisan). But it cannot fall before the vernal equinox.

What all this means is that complicated adjustments are made continually, and Jewish lunar months rarely coincide with the present-day Gregorian calendar. This means that the Jewish New Year, Rosh Hashanah, for instance, always occurs in the Jewish month of Tishre. But some years it will fall in September and in others October.

No one knows for sure the exact date that Hillel II used to begin his reckoning. The one generally accepted is about 3,760 years before the common era. In other words, by adding 3,760 to the common secular calendar year, the result is pretty close to the Jewish date. The year 2000 CE, for instance, corresponds to the Jewish year 5760, or 5,760 years since the creation of the universe. (It is important to emphasize, however, that the acceptance of this date for the "beginning" is not a dogmatic requirement of modern Judaism. Most rabbis have no trouble holding to a religious date, with its appropriate symbolism, while simultaneously accepting a scientific date.)

THE JEWISH CALENDAR

Tishre (September–October)	Nisan (March–April)
Heshvan (October–November)	Iyar (April–May)
Kislev (November–December)	Sivan (May–June)
Tevet (December–January)	Tammuz (June–July)
Shevat (January–February)	Av (July–August)
Adar (February–March)	Elul (August–September)

Different systems have been used to determine how to list the months of the year, or when to begin the calendar. During the years of classical Judaism, apparently two versions were in use. One considered Nisan, then called the spring month or *Abib*, the beginning of the calendar year. The other version, Tishre. So we are apt to find disagreement when we read a typical scriptural reference that mentions, for example, "the first day of the second month." Which "second month" is the author referring to? We don't always know. It is recorded, however, that the two days of Rosh Hashanah (which translates literally to "the head of the year") were celebrated in the fall. This is the day traditionally considered to be the anniversary of the day of Creation. So it is common to begin with Tishre, the month when Rosh Hashanah occurs. The sounding of the shofar, the ram's horn, takes place in the synagogue each day during the month of Elul, to announce the coming of the new year. And before dawn of every day during the week before Rosh Hashanah, it is the custom to recite the Selihot, or penitential prayers.

Feasts of the Lord

Another calendar is described in the book of Leviticus, chapter 23. The Feasts of the Lord are commanded—seasonal celebrations based on an agrarian calendar that are also yearly reminders of God's dealings with Israel.

Feasts of the Lord	Historical Significance
Passover and unleavened bread	Redemption from slavery in Egypt
Firstfruits	Thanksgiving for the coming harvest
Feast of Weeks (Pentecost)	Thanksgiving for the first harvest
Summer	The time of work in the fields
Feast of Trumpets	Preparation for Day of Atonement
Day of Atonement (Yom Kippur)	Repentance
Feast of Tabernacles	Harvest celebration

As is the case with many Jewish traditions, Christians read prophesy where Jews read history. Since Christians believe themselves to be spiritual descendants of Abraham, they believe many of the events described in what they call the Old Testament really point to a later fulfillment described in the New Testament. In the case of the Feasts of the Lord, Christians believe them to be signposts pointing to the work of Jesus Christ.

In the Christian context, Passover symbolizes the crucifixion of "the Lamb of God." Unleavened bread refers to the sanctification Christ earned for them at the cross. The apostle Paul referred to Firstfruits as the resurrection, Christ being the "firstfruits" of the coming Gentile harvest. Pentecost corresponds to the birthday of the church, which occurred on that very day. Summer is the present two thousand–year period of laboring in the fields, preparing for the "harvest" of souls. The Feast of Trumpets is still to come, when "the trumpet shall sound," announcing the end of the harvest or the end of time. Yom Kippur, the Day of Atonement, will be fulfilled during the "Time of Tribulation" Jesus referred to in Matthew's Gospel, when the earth will be forced to repent of its sins. The Feast of Tabernacles will find its fulfillment during the millennium of peace and rejoicing.

Jewish people are understandably upset when Christians "take over" their traditions, in effect relegating them to a position of mere historical prelude to the "real" work of God, the Christian Church. And Christians have too often enforced this attitude with political power and anti-Semitism.

The problem is that the conflict cannot really be avoided because it is built into the Christian religion. Christian theology sees Judaism as a preparatory building block to God's "final revelation" of the Church. This was the position of the apostle Paul and virtually every Christian theologian since. Of course Jews are bothered by this. And this difference of opinion is one of the great stumbling blocks to the two religions ever really getting along. It is at the root of wars, millions of deaths, and the hardening of present-day political positions threatening to bring even more death into a "Holy Land" too familiar with war and destruction.

When the question arises about what can be done, the answer is: nothing—unless Christians are willing to completely dismantle two thousand years of history and theology.

In addition to those listed above, two other holidays have become important in the Jewish calendar. Both celebrate aspects of freedom.

Hanukkah

One of the reasons Hanukkah is such a big celebration is because it usually happens to fall in late December. Both internal and external forces have combined to raise the celebration of Hanukkah nearly to the level of hype associated with secular Christmas. It is common to hear greetings of "Merry Christmas and Happy Hanukkah," as if the two holidays were celebrations of one event by two different traditions. But they really have little in common.

Hanukkah commemorates a Jewish victory over the Syrian army in 165 BCE. Judas Maccabeus recaptured the Temple in Jerusalem, gaining a great victory over Antiochus, King of Syria. The story goes that when it came time to light the menorah (candelabrum) in the Holy Place (see Tabernacle in the Wilderness), there was only enough oil to last for one day. Runners were sent out to secure more, but there was no hope of keeping the sacred flame lit until they returned with a sufficient supply. But a miracle happened: the flame burned for eight days, until more oil was obtained.

Ever since that day, Hanukkah, the Festival of Lights, has been celebrated for eight days, beginning on the 25th day of Kislev. It lights up the short, dark days of December and serves as a reminder of the Jewish patriotic spirit that can never be put out. Children, especially, love the holiday because of the tradition of giving gifts each day of the celebration. Since the holiday of gift-giving and lights takes place so close to the worldwide celebration of Christmas, with its similar traditions and broad observance even among non-Christians, it was probably inevitable that Hanukkah and Christmas would come to be seen, at least through Gentile eyes, as similar traditions.

Purim

The other holiday celebrating Jewish freedom is Purim. The biblical book of Esther tells the story of how Esther, a young Jewish woman, saved her people from destruction during the Persian captivity. This victory over anti-Semitism, going all the way back to 500 BCE, is observed with parties and feasting. Even today, in places such as Tel Aviv, the celebration takes three days and can best be described as a carnival.

These two holidays, Hanukkah and Purim, celebrate Jewish freedom against anti-Semitic forces. They are patriotic holidays steeped in religious tradition. Held respectively in the fall and spring, they are a yearly reminder to those who struggle to keep the flame of freedom alive.

Sources:
Bridger, David, ed. *The New Jewish Encyclopedia.* New York: Behrman House, 1962.

JUDAISM, DEVELOPMENT OF

The story of early Judaism is found in Tanakh, the Hebrew scriptures (see Bible). It begins with the call of Abraham (see Abraham) and tells the story of the patriarchs, Abraham's descendants. These were his son Isaac and his grandson Jacob, whose name was later changed to Israel ("he wrestles with God") after he fought with the angel of

God all night long. Israel's children became forever known as *bene Yisrael*, "children of Israel." Israel was father to twelve sons, who became known as the twelve patriarchs of Israel. From each of these sons sprang a tribe of people, named after their "father" and collectively called the Twelve Tribes of Israel: Reuben, Simeon, Levi, Judah (from whom the Hebrew people would eventually come to be called Yehudi, "Judeans," eventually shortened to Jews), Dan, Naphtali, Gad, Asher, Issachar, Zebulon, Joseph, and Benjamin. Fifteen million people in the world now claim to be descendants of Abraham through one of these twelve patriarchs.

The stories of these men and their families make up the plot of the book of Genesis. In chapter eleven, Abraham is introduced. By chapter fifty the whole clan has moved to Egypt where, thanks to Joseph—now second in command to Pharaoh himself—they are welcomed and settle down to the good life. It makes for fascinating reading, and archaeologists still labor to uncover evidence of their existence and lifestyle (see Abraham; Joseph).

Exodus, the second book of the Bible, moves the action forward four hundred years. A new king has arisen "who knew not Joseph." The Hebrew people are forced to work as slaves, building bricks without straw for the latest Egyptian work project.

Under Moses, the people flee their captivity and begin their journey to the Promised Land (see Moses; Passover). During the forty years they spend in the wilderness between Egypt and Canaan, they receive the Ten Commandments (Exodus 20), build the Tabernacle (Exodus 26; see Tabernacle in the Wilderness), consecrate the priests of the new religion (Exodus 29), and receive the law (Leviticus). They experience tests and temptations (Numbers) and hear Moses' final words (Deuteronomy). By the time of Joshua they have been hardened by their trying experience and are ready for the wars ahead. They enter the land and begin the conquest of Canaan, city by city (Joshua).

After much fighting, they finally settle down and begin the process of self-government (Judges). Twelve different judges arise when their particular talents are needed. Some of their names have become legend: Othniel, Ehud, Shamgar, Deborah, Gideon, Abimelech (called a "false ruler" and not counted as a true judge), Tola, Jair, Jepthah, Ibzan, Elon, Abdon, and Samson.

By the end of the book of Judges, Israel is said to be "in confusion." Perhaps it was later editors who constructed the phrasing, but a litany runs throughout the narrative: this was a time "when each man did what seemed right in his own eyes." There were times when things ran smoothly, as indicated by the lovely idyll found in the book of Ruth. But it became apparent that a change was needed if the grand experiment was not to collapse into anarchy.

This change takes place in the book of 1 Samuel. The people call for a king and a unified monarchy. God warns them not to do it, but the people want to be like all the nations surrounding them. Saul is chosen as first king, but he fails miserably. His successor is David (see David, King). Under the rule of this poet, warrior, statesman, lover, musician, and visionary, the monarchy becomes a single nation. The stage is now set for Israel's glory years. The books of Samuel, Kings, and Chronicles tell the story of Solomon's empire (see Solomon), which is to last only until his death. His son, Rehoboam, has neither the head nor the heart to hold it all together. Civil war breaks out. Israel is divided into two nations. The northern nation, consisting of ten tribes still called Israel, lasts for only two hundred years, finally buckling under Assyrian pressure in 726 BCE. The people disappear into history, forever after being called the "Ten Lost Tribes of Israel." The southern kingdom, called Judea or Judah and comprising the two remaining tribes of Judah and Benjamin, lasts until the Babylonian captivity of 586 BCE (see Babylonian Captivity). When they finally return from this captivity, they will be known as Jews, children of the tribe and nation of Judah.

During their time of trouble, civil war, and social distress, God sent prophets (see Hebrew Prophets) to warn and instruct them—to call them back to the terms of the covenant. Some of the prophets have become legendary, men like Isaiah, Jeremiah, and Ezekiel. Others—like Jonah and the whale or Daniel in the lion's den—were less well known but still important.

The people returned to rebuild Jerusalem under the command of Ezra and Nehemiah, as told by the books that bear their names. But they were never again free from outside control. First they were under the thumb of the Persians. Then came the Greeks and the Romans.

They still had their scrolls. Poets and wise men had written songbooks (Psalms) and practical advice (Proverbs). They studied philosophy (Job, Ecclesiastes) and even wrote love poems (Song of Solomon).

Much later all these would be gathered together to form what the Jews call Tanakh. But while living in the land the Romans then called Palestine, Judaism was forced to begin a long process of change. Sadducees (politically conservative priests and wealthy businessmen) and Pharisees (political liberals who sought to apply the Torah to everyday life) vied with ultra-conservative groups such as the Essene Brotherhood, zealous patriots living in the Qumran settlement above the Dead Sea (see Dead Sea Scrolls). The situation was extremely flammable, awaiting only the right spark. Rome was losing its patience. Christianity, originally a reform sect of Judaism, had just begun, though hardly anyone knew about it yet. But hot, dusty, cantankerous Palestine was the place Caesar sent his generals who were out of favor. It was not considered a plum job.

Finally, in 70 CE, Titus and the Roman legions were ordered to put an end to rebellious Jewish influence once and for all. The people had refused to recognize Caesar as divine and place his statue in a public place in the capital.

"Is this too much to ask?" thundered Rome.

"Thou shalt have no other gods before me and build no graven images," was the retort from the rabbis.

So Titus burned the place to the ground. In the words of the Bible, "not one stone was left standing upon another." The Temple was gone, with the only remnant being an outer wall of the Temple Mount, now known as the Western Wall or Wailing Wall, perhaps the most sacred place today in all of Judaism. The people were led away into the great Diaspora, the dispersion, the captivity. The next two thousand years saw good times and bad, but the period was generally marked by heartache and persecution. With no Temple, the religion of Judaism delivered to Moses at Sinai could no longer be practiced. The sacrificial system of burnt offerings was limited to one spot of ground, the brazen altar in the Temple court (see Tabernacle in the Wilderness). That spot of ground was first in the hands of the Romans, then the Muslims, then, for a short time, the Christians.

This period of turmoil is precisely when Judaism proved its heart and backbone. The people reinvented themselves and the worship of Yahveh. They redefined what it was to be a child of Abraham under the covenant. The rabbis, inheritors of the Pharisee tradition, began teaching Torah under conditions that would have crushed lesser men. The Temple at Jerusalem was gone, so in its place grew the tradition of the synagogue, local congregations that sprang into place wherever there were ten men and a copy of the Torah.

The immense, living, evolving commentary called Talmud was compiled, line upon line and precept upon precept. Ever since the time of Ezra the Scribe, the oral law had been passed down, memories of ancient laws and traditions. By 200 CE, these were written down in a commentary called the Mishna.

During the Middle Ages, the mysteries of the Kabbalah (see Kabbalah) began to lead many Jews into a new spiritual path of mysticism.

The people simply refused to give up. In the history of the world, many people have been persecuted and tortured, ridiculed and destroyed. But perhaps no people have faced what the Jews faced and so staunchly retained their national and historic identity.

It has become quite popular, of late, to describe everything from ethnic cleansing to national war as a "holocaust." Usually the term is pronounced justified when numbers of the slain approach that of the six million Jews who were murdered by those who carried out Adolf Hitler's Final Solution. Thus we hear about the "Indian holocaust" or the "Serb holocaust." These were terrible, inhuman tragedies. But to use the term in this fashion is to miss the point. The Holocaust was not simply about numbers. If it were, the Roman Catholic–sponsored Inquisition and Crusades proportionately outdid Hitler. The point of the Holocaust of World War II was that it was one of many persecutions, hopefully the last and certainly the worst, that was targeted at a certain group and yet could not destroy the spirit and beliefs of a people who refused to let any earthly power destroy their religion and their faith. Such was the power of the unshaken covenant that Judaism actually grew stronger under the horrible persecution.

The world had never seen anything like it. The example set by people who refused to quit was so intrepid that in 1947, the United Nations, under the eye of a world just learning the full extent of what had happened in the Nazi death camps, was simply forced to recognize Zionism (see Zionism). By U.N. resolution, Palestine was partitioned into two states, one Arab, the other Jewish—a resolution that was accepted by the Jews in Palestine but rejected by the Arabs in Palestine and the Arab states. Israel thus became a Jewish state.

And that's what is at the root of the political turmoil that besets that tortured land today. Jews believe the land is theirs, given to Abraham and guaranteed by God to be their inheritance forever. Even nonreligious Jews believe the land has been consecrated by the blood of their ancestors.

But the Arabs have a point, too. They've lived there for many thousands of years. However nobly the battle has been fought, Judaism doesn't pertain to them. What about the rights of Arabs, whose ancestors lived in Canaan and worked the land ever since the first humans wandered up from Africa? Sentiment aside, they have a case. Even without the complexity of religious differences, historical and ethnic factors are at work. Many Palestinians are Jewish or Christian. Many Jews are nonbelievers. It isn't simply a religious war of "Orthodox Jew" against "Islamic terrorist," although that's often the way it is cast in the media.

In June 1967 the Jews recaptured the site of the old Temple. A Muslim mosque now stands there, the familiar Dome of the Rock that is seen in every skyline scene of Old Jerusalem. Treaties are made and broken. Palestinians are placed under house arrest and retaliate by sending suicide bombers against the enemy. Violence escalates. There is a war going on, and the world wrings its collective hands in helplessness. "What is the answer?" is the universal cry.

Perhaps there are no answers. Perhaps the scars are too severe, the historical issues too complex. Perhaps the feelings run too deep. Maybe history is going to prove stronger than politics.

Abraham never knew what he had begun when he journeyed to Canaan. Joshua didn't know what he was starting when he invaded the Promised Land. The battle between Jew and Palestinian continues still. And no end is in sight.

But Judaism doesn't exist just on one spot of ground. It has transformed itself. The lessons of the great Diaspora have broken down the boundaries of one land and one temple. All over the world, Judaism is flourishing.

Three main Jewish divisions carry on the tradition. But, as been the case repeatedly in other religions, often they don't get along at all.

The Orthodox are the traditionalists, holding to scripture and Talmud. They are often seen in their traditional garb of black suits and beards, black hats and prayer shawls, watching over the production of Kosher foods (see Kosher) and participating in ceremonies that go all the way back to early rabbinical times.

The Reform branch is the liberal branch, applying tradition to contemporary society and visualizing Judaism as a living, breathing tradition that must constantly reform to new social conditions.

The Conservative branch is a bit of a compromise, seeking to place rabbinical Judaism in a modern context.

Other, smaller branches of Judaism include Reconstructionist and Secular Humanistic Judaism.

Often the different groups disagree, sometimes violently. But at the core of each branch is the tradition, the love, and the history that binds them to the faith of their fathers.

Sources:

Bridger, David, ed. *The New Jewish Encyclopedia.* New York: Behrman House, 1962.

Josephus, Flavius. *The Works of Flavius Josephus.* Trans. William Whitson. New York: T. Nelson & Sons, 1873.

May, Herbert G., and Bruce M. Metzger, eds. *The New Oxford Annotated Bible with the Apocrypha.* Rev. ed. New York: Oxford University Press, 1973.

KAABA

(See also Abraham; Black Stone; Islam)

Kaaba means "square building" or "cube." It refers to the Islamic shrine in Mecca that Muslims face when they pray. The shrine is built around the famous Black Stone, and it is said to have been built by Abraham and his son, Ishmael. It is the focus and goal of all Muslim pilgrims when they make their way to Mecca during their pilgrimage.

Sources:
Fisher, Mary Pat. *Living Religions*. 3rd ed. Upper Saddle River, NJ: Prentice Hall, 1991.

KABBALAH

Kabbalah comes from the Hebrew letters qof-bet-lamed. When translated, it literally means "to accept" or "to receive." But it is usually translated as "tradition."

Kabbalah refers to a mystical branch of Judaism that traces its roots to the very beginnings of creation, but it was committed to writing in books such as the Zohar during the Middle Ages. This work was published in early-fourteenth-century Spain by Moses de Leon, but he attributed it to Rabbi Simeon ben Yohai, who lived in the second century CE. Many believe it to be a compilation of various streams of thought and teaching, and not the work of one man. The Zohar is a mystical commentary on the Pentateuch, the first five books of the Bible, and it is thought by Kabbalists to be equal in holiness to the Bible and the Talmud.

Kabbalah deals with five theological issues:

The Nature of God

Yahveh, God, is described as the Eternal—in Hebrew, Ein Sof (the Endless). (Kabbalists and other religious Jews believe the name of the deity to be so holy that it is not voiced. To refrain from speaking that name, vowels are not used. Hence the Hebrew name YHVH for Yahveh, and, in English, the rendering of God's name as G-d.) Because God is above all existence, he (in Kabbalah, the masculine pronoun is most often used) did not actually create the world. Instead, all forms of life, both above and below the plane we experience, are emanations from Ein Sof.

Ein Sof is not a name. It is rather a description of the absolute transcendence that is so far above us we can only depict it by describing what it is not (similar to the Hindu concept of Brahman; see Brahman/Atman). But even though Ein Sof is absolutely transcendent, he interacts with the universe through what Tracey Rich in her article "Kabbalah and Jewish Mysticism" refers to as "ten emanations from this essence." These are called Ten Sefirot, or the Ten Spheres. In English these spheres are translated as: crown, wisdom, intelligence (intuition, understanding), greatness, strength (power), beauty (glory), firmness (majesty), splendor, foundation, and kingdom (sovereignty).

1 Chronicles 10:11 quotes King David as he refers to the middle five of these emanations in order: "Yours, O Yahveh, is the greatness and the power and the glory and the majesty and the splendor, for everything in heaven and earth is yours." Perhaps this passage points to Kabbalah's ancient roots.

The names of these spheres, in Hebrew, allow for both masculine and feminine qualities, a characteristic that continues through much of Kabbalah theology. It is important to remember that the Ten Sefirot are not separate deities, but rather ways in which Ein Sof connects with the universe while at the same time remaining separate from it. Through these spheres God rules the world, and through them God's activities are explained.

The Creation of the Universe

If all that exists emanates from God and holds the universe together, then humans can interact with God by obeying the commandments and participating righteously within the framework of the intention of the Creator. The Hebrew people were given the law for that very reason. It was not just a law for them, it was the law for everyone. They were simply the ones chosen to demonstrate and preserve the universal law, which illustrates the very nature of the Creator.

The Destiny of Humanity

All souls were created at the same time and are the most important part of each person. Souls that remain pure after contact with human bodies become, at death, part of the divine, the ten spheres of God. Those souls that are impure, that do not obey the divine law, must continue to migrate from body to body until they have been completely purified (note the similarity to Hinduism—see Hinduism; Karma).

The Nature of Evil

Evil is not a separate entity. Instead, it is understood to be a cessation of the good. It can be overcome through prayer, repentance, self-affliction, and, most important, by strict observance of the law. In this sense, evil, even a great evil such as the Holocaust, is seen as a purging and reminder, a call to repentance, not just a punishment.

The Meaning of the Bible

The very text of the Bible is a code from God to humanity. It is filled with layers upon layers of messages only now beginning to be understood. Indeed, new computer studies seem to reveal hidden meanings never before discovered. Like a multi-dimension crossword puzzle, those who study Bible codes find predictions of historical events described by some as uncanny and by others as completely coincidental.

Michael Drosnin is not a Kabbalist, but his book *The Bible Code* documents many of the early messages computer analysis seems to reveal. On September 1, 1994, he flew to Israel and met with a close friend of Yitzhak Rabin, warning him that he had found the prime minister's name encoded in the Bible. Crossing that name were the words, "Assassin that will assassinate." The code even seemed to indicate the assassination would take place in the Hebrew year that began in September of 1995 of the common calendar. Its warning was ignored. Two months later, on November 4th, Rabin was murdered.

There are many other such warnings. The assassinations of John and Robert Kennedy and Martin Luther King Jr. are said to be there, as are the Holocaust, the World Wars, and the birth and rise to world power of America. As computers make the search easier, there seems to be mounting evidence of something the Kabbalists have been saying for centuries. Indeed, Drosnin now claims the World Trade Center tragedy of September 11, 2001, was prophesied. The latest edition of his book even goes so far as to predict the date of the end of the world (2004), assuming human beings don't wise up. Drosnin is not religious. He doesn't even claim a belief in God, let alone Kabbalah. He is interested only in what he deduces from his computer readouts, and he presents a compelling case for hidden meanings in scripture.

But not all Jews accept Kabbalah teachings, and some are extremely skeptical. Tracey Rich quotes an Orthodox Jewish scholar on the subject of Jewish mysticism: "It's nonsense, but it's Jewish nonsense, and the study of anything Jewish, even nonsense, is worthwhile."

Sources:

Bridger, David, ed. *The New Jewish Encyclopedia*. New York: Behrman House, 1962.

Drosnin, Michael. *The Bible Code*. New York: Simon and Schuster, 1997.

Rich, Tracey R. "Kabbalah and Jewish Mysticism." *Judaism 101*. http://www.jewfaq.org/kabbalah.htm. September 15, 2003.

KALIMA *see* **Islam**

KAMI

Kami is a Shinto word that is difficult to define without an understanding of the Eastern concept of the divine. It depicts, first of all, the invisible, sacred quality that causes human beings to respond with awe and wonder—the mysterious, the spiritual. It is what we feel but cannot express when, just for a moment, we see behind the curtain that separates spiritual from material. It is intuition—knowing without being able to say why we know.

But it is more than that. Kami also refers to the invisible essence called spirit, or more properly, spirits, that are born of this essence and inhabit another dimension of the world in which we live. In the West we are apt to call such a notion animism (see Animism), the belief that invisible spirits dwell within people or objects. Perhaps we might even go so far as to call it polytheism, belief in many gods. But neither really captures the idea.

In Western terms we are probably forced to define the word using theological constructs. Kami is the Shinto way of saying the divine is both immanent and transcendent, here and yet beyond. It is both singular and plural and can perhaps best be described as a quality rather than an essence. Japanese mythology describes it this way:

> In primeval ages, before the earth was formed, amorphous matter floated freely about like oil upon water. In time there arose in its midst a thing like a sprouting reedshoot, and from this a deity came forth of its own.

In time, this "deity" gave birth to the Kami, or spirits. Two of them, the Amatsu Kami, stood on the Floating Bridge of Heaven and stirred the oceans with a bejeweled spear. Over time the "cosmic soup" cooled into eight islands, forming mountains, rivers, plants, and trees. The Kami of the Sun, Amaterasu, came forth to rule this kingdom. Eventually the people of Japan came to be born in this land, never forgetting that they and all creation are from one source and share a common spirit.

Aside from the fact that, de-mythologized, this is a pretty good description of how modern science claims the world came to be, it means that in Shinto religious tradition it is hard to distinguish where nature ends and religion begins.

Kami is the force that keeps everything together. It is also the matter that is held together by the force. It is the mountain and the essence of the mountain that produces such awe in us. It is the tree and the feelings the tree invokes as we sit in its shade. It is the flower and that which we call the flower's beauty. It is the salmon swimming upstream and the mystery of why the salmon is there, swimming upstream. It is as abstract as creativity and as specific as a lightning bolt.

Kami are worshiped in shrines but experienced everywhere. They induce love and dread, peace and fear. They are the spiritual glue binding everything together in harmony—in a word, wholeness.

Sources:
Fisher, Mary Pat. *Living Religions*. 3rd ed. Upper Saddle River, NJ: Prentice Hall, 1991.
Picken, Stuart D. B. *Shinto: Japan's Spiritual Roots*. Tokyo: Kodansha International, 1980.

KARMA

In both Hinduism and Buddhism, every action has consequences. When a pebble falls into a pool, it produces rings that spread throughout the whole pool. A butterfly fluttering its wings can produce a typhoon, under the right conditions.

In the same way, our actions cause cosmic vibrations that affect not only this life but our lives to come. What we do not learn in this life must be learned in the next. Harm we cause in this life will come back to us in the next. The universe is relentless. It will not let us get away with anything.

At the same time, good things we do affect future lives as well. It is said that when the Buddha had his great moment of insight, he saw how all his past lives had prepared him for that moment. He understood how they were connected. All at once, he understood the great force of karma at work, propelling him to come to understand the Middle Way of the Four Noble Truths (see Buddhism). With this realization, karma had done its work. He was now complete.

And that, according to the teachings, is what karma does. It makes us complete, driving us forever, if need be, until we come to understand what we are. And with that understanding, we also come to know *who* we are. In this grand scheme of things, it is not that we wrestle with God. It is that God wrestles with us and says, in reverse of the words of Genesis 32, "I will not let you go until I bless you!"

Sources:
Hagen, Steve. *Buddhism Plain and Simple*. Boston: Charles E. Tuttle Co., 1997.

KIVA

Five thousand years after the last glacier melted enough to allow people to migrate by land to the Americas, a great civilization began to evolve complex cultural patterns in the Four Corners region of the American southwest.

By 1000 BCE the Anasazi people were beginning a settled, agricultural way of life that would develop for centuries. At the height of their golden age, 1100–1300 CE, settlements in what are now called Pueblo Bonito in Chaco Canyon, New Mexico, and Cliff Palace in Mesa Verde, Colorado, were cities housing up to seven thousand residents.

In the Navajo language, Anasazi means "enemy ancestors." Some translate it as "ancient ones" or "those who came before." The word describes a people who lived long ago and left a complex legacy, both mystical and material. A severe drought from 1276–1299 left their fields of corn high and dry, their irrigation ditches above water level. It is easy to speculate that a lack of firewood and heavy competition for resources drove the people to disband and drift away, either evolving different desert cultures or simply disappearing into legend. By 1300, all of their great settlements were deserted.

What they left behind, however, were monuments to their culture and rich religious mythology.

The Anasazi people believed they had entered this world through a hole in the ground from a world that had come before. This creation myth was reenacted every time they emerged from their kivas, underground chambers entered by ladder through a single entrance at the top. Although we don't know exactly what kind of religious rituals were enacted, the kiva was a central place of worship and initiation.

Kiva, a sacred underground gathering room, at Cliff Palace, Anasazi Indian settlement in Colorado's Mesa Verde National Park. *Fortean Picture Library.*

In 1934, when excavation began at the Kuaua Kiva, a fourteenth-century pueblo in New Mexico, murals were discovered on walls that had been replastered up to eighty times. Seventeen layers contained religious scenes immediately recognized by modern Navajos.

Clearly, the very architecture of the kiva represented a strong oral tradition that had been passed on for thousands of years.

Michael and Kathleen Gear, in their "First North Americans" series of novels, have attempted to harmonize modern archaeological thought with the ancient creation myth, speculating that the religion of the kiva did, indeed, represent historical reality.

When the Laurentide and Cordilleran ice sheets separated, opening a passageway south from the quickly disappearing Siberian land bridge, it is entirely possible that the first passageways to melt would have been underground, seasonal tunnels left by melting ice forming rivers under the glacier. If such a passage had been discovered and utilized by the first Americans, it could certainly have been remembered as an event of epic proportions. Stories would have been told for generations about a migration into a new world, where people encountered animals that had no fear of these new predators appearing suddenly through a hole in the ground.

This is, of course, speculation. But it is tempting to think that a religious tradition as strong as that of the kiva can be located and demonstrated in history.

Sources:
America's Fascinating Indian Heritage. Pleasantville, NY: The Reader's Digest Association, 1986.
Gear, W. Michael, and Kathleen O'Neal Gear. *People of the Wolf*. New York: Tor Books, 1990.

KOJIKI *see* Shinto Texts

KORAN *see* Qur'an

KORESH, DAVID *see* Cult

KOSHER

Jewish kosher foods are those that have been prepared under the supervision of Orthodox rabbis who have studied the dietary requirements of the Hebrew scriptures and will guarantee that the rules have been followed.

When matzah (bread made without leaven) is prepared, for example, the rule is ancient and simple: flour and water must be mixed together and put in the oven within seventeen minutes. Any longer than that and the bread has a chance to rise, at which point it is no longer unleavened bread. Every place in the kitchen that might possibly contain yeast residue is examined. Ovens and all utensils are thoroughly cleaned to remove any possible trace of leaven. Timers keep careful watch on the clock. Every Jew in the world knows that on Passover her bread is really unleavened if it is stamped with the kosher seal.

From wine to pickles, every food has its traditional rules. Animals have to be slaughtered in a certain ritualistic way. Some foods cannot be mixed.

Only flesh of animals that have a "cloven foot and chew the cud" are ritually pure. (Cattle and deer—yes. Pigs—no.) Water animals must have both fins and scales. (Fish—okay. Lobster—forbidden.) Birds of prey are out, as are reptiles. Blood from any animal is not kosher, and meat must be drained and salted before cooking. Meat and milk (and foods derived from each) must never be mixed. In other words, cheese on a hamburger is not kosher, nor is any kind of meat on a pizza. Foods such as fruits and vegetables occupy a neutral ground and are considered pareve.

Sources:
Bridger, David, ed. *The New Jewish Encyclopedia*. New York: Behrman House, 1962.

KWANZAA

Many people seem to think Kwanzaa is an ancient African holiday—another religious festival trying to get on the "holiday season" bandwagon. But Kwanzaa has only been around since 1966 and is not really African, although its symbols revolve around African motifs and the name is derived from the Swahili word that means "first fruits."

Kwanzaa is the brainchild of Dr. Maulana Karenga, the founder and present chair of the Black Nationalist Organization. He felt that significant advances among African Americans could not occur in the United States unless they happened within

Traditional music is played as the Chi Wara, right, an antelope that represents the new year, dances during the start of Kwanzaa. *AP/Wide World Photos.*

the context of a cultural base. If people are going to be moved, they need a sense of, in his words, "identity, purpose, and direction." It is not practical to think that will happen if your heritage and allegiance is to a nation that had enslaved your grandparents. The focus has to be on the future—what *can* happen instead of what *did* happen.

Kwanzaa is filled with symbols derived from Africa, but its purpose goes far beyond national remembrance. Through participation of Kwanzaa celebrations, African Americans come to understand their ancestral images, but the idea is to include people everywhere.

First Fruits originally was a holiday when African people would gather to celebrate the coming harvest. Most African Americans are urban dwellers and don't have many crops to harvest. But the joy of the season can be felt just the same. Seven principles are celebrated, and they are applied universally. Beginning on December 26th each year and continuing until January 1st, a candle is lit each day. Each candle symbolizes one of the Nguao Saba, the seven principles of Kwanzaa.

Umoja (Unity). The object of this principle is to strive for wholeness in the family, community, nation, and race.

Kujichagulia (Self Determination). The goal on this day is to seek definition, to create and speak for yourself rather than to allow others to speak for you.

Ujima (Responsibility). Here the emphasis is on maintaining community, to shoulder the responsibility for the problems of others and work together to solve them.

Ujamaa (Cooperative Economics). The object of this day is to work toward building and maintaining local stores, shops, and businesses so the community profits together.

Nia (Purpose). The ultimate purpose of Kwanzaa is now in sight. It is to collectively work toward the development of community in order to restore the community to its traditional greatness.

Kuumba (Creativity). Here the emphasis is on elevating the community, making it greater, more beautiful, and more beneficial each year.

Imani (Faith). The object here is to place trust in parents, teachers, leaders, and others, and also to strive for righteousness and its ultimate victory.

Sources:
"Kwanzaa: The First Fruit Celebration." *Afrocentricnews*. http://www.afrocentricnews.com/html/kwanza.htm. September 15, 2003.

LAO TZU

Lao Tzu (also transliterated as Lao-tzu or Laozi) is considered to be the architect of Daoism (also known as Taoism; see Confucianism/Daoism; Dao; Tao Te Ching). A contemporary of Confucius in the sixth century BCE, he was a native of the Ch'u Jen hamlet in the Li Village of Hu Hsian in the state of Ch'u.

It is said that Confucius once went to visit Lao Tzu, who was historian of the archives of Ch'u. Confucius was seeking instruction from the elder man. In this excerpt from Robert S. Ellwood and Barbara A. McGraw's *Many Peoples, Many Faiths*, we catch a glimpse of Lao Tzu's rather prickly personality:

> What you are talking about, *he told the young whippersnapper, Confucius,* concerns merely the words left by people who have rotted away along with their bones. Furthermore, when a gentleman is in sympathy with the times he goes out in a carriage, but drifts with the wind when the times are against him. I have heard it said that a good merchant hides his stores in a safe place and appears to be devoid of possessions, while a gentleman, though endowed with great virtue, wears a foolish countenance. Rid yourself of arrogance and your lustfulness, your ingratiating manners and your excessive ambition. These are all detrimental to your person. This is all I have to say to you!

Whereupon Confucius told his disciples:

> The dragon's ascent into heaven on the wind and the clouds is something which is beyond my knowledge. Today I have seen Lao-tzu, and he is a dragon!

Lao Tzu simply means "the old man." His surname was Li, his personal name was Erh, and he was styled Tan. He is known today largely because of a book that has had an influence way beyond its short length. It is called Tao Te Ching, and it was written, legends say, at the behest of the Keeper of the Pass before Lao Tzu left China for Tibet.

Although records are scanty at best, Lao Tzu seems to have been a historical person who supposedly had a good education and "kept a good table." But at the age of eighty or so he became thoroughly disgusted with the hypocrisy and striving of the world and became the world's first recorded "dropout." He mounted his water buffalo and headed for Tibet, stopping at the border only long enough to write what is perhaps the most famous book in Chinese history.

Put in a 1960s idiom, we might say he was a typical college graduate with a privileged education who enjoyed parties until, while contemplating the meaning of life, he decided to drop out, get on his Harley, and ride to California. Seen in this light, it's probably safe to say he was the original hippie.

Followers of Confucius like to belittle Lao Tzu, and Lao Tzu's followers disparage Confucius, but it seems fairly obvious that both philosophers were responding—in classic Chinese yin/yang fashion—to the same political situation (see Confucianism/Daoism). In modern terms, one was conservative, the other liberal.

Lao Tzu reveled in intuition and gentleness. When writing of the Dao, "the way," he said:

> The way that can be spoken of
> Is not the constant way;
> The name that can be named
> Is not the constant name.
> The nameless was the beginning of heaven and earth;
> The named was the mother of the myriad creatures.
> Hence always rid yourself of desires in order to observe its secrets;
> But always allow yourself to have desires in order to observe its manifestations.
> These two are the same
> But diverge as they issue forth.
> Being the same they are called mysteries,
> Mystery upon mystery—
> The gateway of the manifold secrets.

Words cannot explain the Dao. It must be grasped intuitively. And when grasped, it cannot be explained.

Daoism probably comes closest to expressing the attitudes of traditional Chinese religion, even though it is often downplayed. But maybe the best way to remember Lao Tzu is to listen to the final words of his classic book:

> The way of heaven benefits and does not harm; the way of the sage is bountiful and does not contend.

Sources:

Ellwood, Robert S., and Barbara A. McGraw. *Many Peoples, Many Faiths*. 6th ed. Upper Saddle River, NJ: Prentice Hall, 1999.

Lao Tzu. *Tao Te Ching*. Trans. D. C. Lau. New York: Penguin Books, 1963.

LAST SUPPER *see* Eucharist

LAWS OF MANU *see* Hinduism, Development of

LENT *see* Christianity, Calendar of

LEY LINES

Scattered all over the world are stone monuments left by people who lived during what we now call the megalithic age, the age of stone building. No one doubts the existence of Stonehenge or the megaliths of Easter Island, the pyramids of Peru or the dolmans of Ireland. They are there for all to see. Scientists have even speculated about and perhaps demonstrated how they were built. The unanswered question remains not how were they built, but why.

Why did a stone-age people, in the midst of their daily struggle to survive, feel the need to move megaton boulders miles over the landscape, sometimes even importing stones across vast bodies of water, just because rocks of a particular size and color were not available locally?

Current theories say the structures served as calendars or astrological observatories. But there are much simpler ways to construct such things. And why were they often placed at specific locations when it would have been much easier to build where the materials were found? Also, why do buildings of significance to one religion tend to be built upon the holy sites of earlier religions?

Aerial view of Sainbury ley, which runs three and a half miles in the Cotswalds in Gloucestershire, England. *Fortean Picture Library.*

It could very well be that the last person able to answer these questions was slaughtered by Julius Caesar (see Caesar, Julius) during his conquest of Gaul, when the indigenous religion of the Druids was wiped out. It could even be that the Druids arrived too late on the scene, the knowledge of the builders of the great monuments having already passed into obscurity.

But there are those living today who claim there is a geometry to holy places, a pattern to structures of England's Glastonbury Abbey and the rocks at Stonehenge. They believe this knowledge was known to the builders of the pyramids, to certain members of the first Freemason societies imported by King Solomon to build the Temple at Jerusalem, and to other ancient builders in tune with Earth rhythms. Those who believe this are called ley hunters, and they believe the earth either was or still is seamed through with lines of power, called ley lines. Where these lines intersect or rise close to the surface they can be detected, it is believed, by diviners (see Divination) and people attuned to the primitive forces that align our world. Whether they are naturally occurring fields of magnetic force, ancient rivers of glacial melt, or mystical veins of power is a matter of debate.

It is said that even people not in tune with ley lines can feel or intuit their power, a notion that explains why holy places remain holy. They "feel" sacred. Every year, thousands of modern Christians worship at the magnificent Cathedral of Chartres, unaware that they are standing upon the same ground where Druids once led sacrifices among the sacred oak groves of Gaul. And who has not entered a forest or climbed a mountain and felt, for a fleeting moment, an experience of reverence?

Sources:
Hitching, Francis. *Earth Magic*. New York: William Morrow and Company, 1977.

LIBERATION THEOLOGY

All the believers were one in heart and mind. No one claimed that any of his possessions was his own, but they shared everything they had.... There were no needy persons among them. From time to time those who owned lands or houses sold them, brought the money from the sales and put it at the apostle's feet, and it was distributed to anyone as he had need. (Acts 4:32–35)

You will know the truth, and the truth will set you free. (John 8:32)

These New Testament verses from the Bible, and many others like them, have inspired the study of what has formally been titled liberation theology. It is an understanding or Christian interpretation that insists that the purpose of the Gospel is to liberate the downtrodden and disenfranchised. In the past it was called the social Gospel, identified with liberalism and contrasted with a conservative theology stressing the need for individual salvation.

Martin Luther King Jr., for instance, was a Baptist, a tradition known for its emphasis on personal salvation. But in his published sermon, "An Experiment in Love," he argued that "It was Jesus of Nazareth that stirred the Negroes to protest with the creative weapon of love." He took his arguments to the streets where, armed with the weapon of liberation he had found in the words of the Bible, he guided the civil rights movement in mid-twentieth-century America.

What he said was not new. The whole genre of music once called the "Negro spiritual" was invented by African slaves who were forced to accept Christianity but were not allowed into white churches. Well-known songs such as "Jordan's Stormy Banks" and "Deep River" were testaments to the hope for freedom, even if that freedom came only at death. They were sung by black slaves out behind the barn while waiting for their white "masters" to finish the Sunday morning worship service inside the church.

But liberation theology, though long practiced by those who believed love had to have a social component, received its formal name in the 1960s after Vatican II (see Vatican Councils). Roman Catholic priests and nuns in Latin America began to very publicly side with the poor in their fight for social justice. Many of them paid the ultimate price for their struggles, murdered in places like Guatemala. Others were often criticized by Vatican conservatives such as Cardinal Ratzinger, who headed the Congregation for the Doctrine of the Faith. He claimed liberation theology emphasized liberation from poverty rather than sin. His arguments were countered by those who claimed that the very poverty prompting the need for liberation theology was brought about by sins the Christian Church had committed in the sixteenth century.

In the Americas and Africa, in Europe and the Far East, liberation theology still inspires Christians of all denominations to fight entrenched political forces that prevent freedom for all. It is still accused of being thinly disguised communism, as evidenced by the words of the book of Acts cited above. These words, especially during the anti-Communist McCarthy era of 1950s America, were an embarrassment to many conservative preachers, who wondered whether the early disciples were really communists.

But it seems obvious that liberation theology, along with the many evolving theologies, or methods of biblical interpretation, opening up today (feminist theology, narrative theology, historical theology, and so on), is here to stay. In the words of the song that has become the theme song of liberation theology, "Deep in my heart, I do believe we shall overcome someday."

Sources:
Fisher, Mary Pat. *Living Religions*. 3rd ed. Upper Saddle River, NJ: Prentice Hall, 1991.
The Holy Bible, New International Version. Grand Rapids, MI: Zondervan Bible Publishers, 1978.

LILITH

In the book of Genesis there appear to be two different versions of the story depicting the creation of man and woman.

In chapter 1, verse 27: "So God created man in his own image, in the image of God he created him; male and female he created them."

In chapter 2, verse 21: "So the Lord God caused the man to fall into a deep sleep; and while he was sleeping, he took one of the man's ribs … and made a woman … and brought her to the man."

Chapter 1 gives us the "dust of the earth" story while chapter 2 recounts the familiar "Adam's rib" account. It's difficult to harmonize them. Scholars who subscribe to literary criticism (see Literary Criticism/Historical Critical Method) simply see this as an example of two different traditions being woven into one story. But the Hebrew Talmudic scholars long ago formed an alternative tradition.

There are different versions of their story, but the general outline is that Eve was Adam's second wife. She is the woman of Genesis 2 and was created from Adam's rib. She accepted her role as being subservient. After all, her husband had come first and had given up a part of himself for her very life.

But the woman of Genesis 1, Adam's first wife, is quite another story. She was created from the same dust of the ground as Adam. (Some stories have her being created from dirty mud, rather than clean dust like Adam. This casts her in a sinister light.) As Adam's equal, the woman the Talmudic scholars named Lilith ("storm goddess" or "she of the night") was not about to play second fiddle to a man she considered her equal. When Adam "desired to lay on top of her," she refused. Why should she have to be on the bottom when she and the man were equal? So she flew off to the desert.

The key is that Adam had not yet been kicked out of the garden, so Lilith got away with eternal life. That's right. She's still out there. She consorted with demons and gave birth to demons—some stories say at the rate of more than a hundred a day. God sent three angels to bring her back, but she refused to come. The owl became her companion and symbol as she prowled the night, sometimes seducing sleeping men who thought they were dreaming.

She is pictured in Sumerian mythology as a goddess of desolation, part snake and part woman, with wings on her back similar to those of a dragon. She lives today in stereotypes of the "Dragon Lady," witch, and temptress.

Lilith, contrasted with Eve, no doubt gave the early Hebrew patriarchy of Middle Eastern tradition a valuable tool to keep women in their place.

Sources:
Cotterell, Arthur, and Rachel Storm. *The Ultimate Encyclopedia of Mythology*. China: Hermes House, 1999.

LINGAM/YONI

Sex is a basic human drive. Propagation is creation, an activity linked with the gods. But because it can so easily get out of control, most religions have a difficult time deciding how to deal with it. Some, such as traditional monotheistic religions, generally look upon sex as a necessary evil and tightly fence it in with rules and regulations.

Other religions, such as Hinduism, have tended to celebrate it, recognizing powerful divine forces at work. Shiva (see Hinduism) is the Hindu god most often pictured with the phallic symbols of lingam and yoni, stylizations of male and female sexual organs. The lingam is often pictured as the shaft upon which the wheel of samsara, the wheel of life, revolves. And archaeological sites going back to the very first humans display elaborate caves, opening into the "womb" of the earth, decorated with red ochre and described, in the polite jargon of academic texts, as being representations of "that opening through which we all enter the world."

Sources:
Fisher, Mary Pat. *Living Religions*. 3rd ed. Upper Saddle River, NJ: Prentice Hall, 1991.

LITERARY CRITICISM/
HISTORICAL CRITICAL METHOD

It's a shame the words "critical" and "criticism" carry such negative baggage. Or it's a shame better words couldn't have been chosen to describe a method of scriptural study that has been around for hundreds of years, but became recognized as a science only in the nineteenth century.

In this context, "criticism" doesn't mean "to criticize" in a negative sense, although that's exactly how many lay people interpret it when first confronted by the published results of biblical scholars. And to narrow the definition of literary criti-

Worshipers praying in front of lingam, snake stones, and a figure of Ganesa in southern India, from *Omens and Superstitions of Southern India* by Edgar Thurston, 1912. *Fortean Picture Library.*

cism, or the historical critical method, to biblical research is a mistake as well. Any document can be subject to this method of analysis.

But it is in the field of biblical research that literary criticism achieves perhaps its biggest popular audience. At face value, the idea behind the process is a simple one. It boils down to a single question: Is the Bible to be read like other books, or does it stand alone, above the field of human analysis?

Until the pioneers of biblical criticism, Karl Heinrich Graf and Julius Wellhausen (it didn't help any that they were from Germany and lived just before World War I), suggested that the Bible could be studied just like any other work of literature, most people accepted without question that the Bible was in a class by itself and was to be read at face value. If the first five books of the Bible were attributed to Moses, then that's who wrote them. The books of Daniel and Isaiah each must have been written by the person whose name appeared at the top of the first page. If the book of Colossians bore Paul's name, than Paul wrote it.

Throughout history, scholars have known better. Even the committees who put the Bible together (see Bible) used critical analysis to determine which books made the final cut. But the process was somehow, by universal consent, ignored by the vast majority of people who believed the Bible to be uniquely the work of God. If they acknowledged that too much human intervention occurred, it might detract from the power of God's word. Even today, many people are ignorant about how the Bible came to be, and they don't really want to know.

But once scholars began to subject the Bible to the same methods of analysis used to examine other ancient texts, the secret leaked out. The process could not be stopped. And the academic discipline of literary or historical criticism was born.

Its premise is, at root, that people wrote the Bible, not God. They may have been guided or inspired by God, but they were authors subject to the times and vocabulary in which they lived. Every scrap of evidence, including the words they used, other literature written at the same time, archaeological evidence, and literary techniques known to be prevalent in their day, must be studied to shed light on why the Bible is in the form it is.

People who study such things are trying to discover the truth. People who don't are afraid scholars might undercut the uniqueness of the Bible. Since critical evidence is almost always subject to interpretation, the debate will no doubt continue. Like all sciences, there are conservative and liberal approaches. There can be no doubt that some findings have found almost universal acceptance. But in today's "publish or perish" environment, extravagant claims have been made to justify a new book and ensure for its author a reputation in the field of literary criticism.

Let's examine an illustration to shed light on each of these two points of view: first, the traditional belief held by some that the author of one section of the Bible is the person who gives his name to that section; second, the biblical critical scholarship that points to evidence of multiple authors of that section, a view that finds wide, but certainly not universal, acceptance.

The Pentateuch, the first five books of the Hebrew Bible, or what Christians refer to as the Old Testament, is, in many Bibles, referred to as the Books of Moses. That is because Moses has historically been credited with their composition. Of course there is a small problem with the final chapter of Deuteronomy, which describes Moses' death. But this minor problem is usually explained away by saying either that Moses prophesied his own death or that his aide de camp, Joshua, completed the final words of Moses' farewell speech.

But by analyzing writing style and content, scholars began to detect layer upon layer of additions and "redactions," or editorial corrections. Literary fingerprints of many people began to appear. The Pentateuch seemed to be not so much a single blanket of one cloth, but a patchwork quilt sewn together by many hands.

The oldest strand woven into this quilt is attributed to an author named "J," or "the Yahwist." "J" is the English transliteration of the German "Y." This author calls God by the name YHVH (often spelled Yahveh) or, in English, the Lord, or Jehovah. Although corroborating evidence is very technical, suffice it to say a consensus of scholars has come to believe "J" lived in Judah, the southern kingdom (see Judaism, Development of) sometime after the reign of King David.

A second author refers to God by employing the name Elohim. This author is often referred to as "E," seems to be very appreciative of Moses, may have been a Levite priest, and probably lived a little later than "J," perhaps around 900–800 BCE. This is the author who wrote so much about Aaron (see Aaron), the first high priest, and the priesthood that followed him.

The many pages of laws and rituals found in Leviticus and parts of Exodus come from the author known as "P," for "priestly source." He may have been the one who edited the work of "J" and "E," molding it into the present form we know today, while adding his own commentary from time to time. "P," for instance, gives us Genesis 1 and the story of creation in which God seems a bit aloof, building the universe step by step, "decently and in order," as a good priest goes about his work. "J" gives us Genesis 2, a different account that has God getting right down into the dirt to create Adam and Eve. It's interesting that "P" never once uses the Hebrew word for "mercy." "P" seems to have been a kind of two-thousand-year-old Puritan.

The final author detected by literary criticism is the author named "D," the "Deuteronomist." This is the author of the book Deuteronomy, which seems to stand on its own, distinct in its own literary style. It purports to be the farewell address of Moses. Some see the hand of Jeremiah here. Others are not so sure. Some link Deuteronomy with the books of Joshua, Judges, 1 and 2 Samuel, and 1 and 2 Kings, forming a "Deuteronomistic history." Others don't buy it.

Besides these four authors, some scholars think various editors, or redactors, were at work, molding the final product, even putting editorial "spins" on some stories to make them fit in with whatever interpretation was in vogue at the time of the redactor. For instance, if the redactor lived at the time of King David, it might be considered patriotic and "politically correct" to prepare the way for David's reign by shading Saul's reputation just a bit. After all, Saul was David's predecessor.

Thus we have two conceptions of how the first five books of the Bible came to be. The first says Moses wrote it, working by himself. The second says the author was "JEPD," with perhaps "R," the redactor, contributing as well."

And this is just an illustration from the Pentateuch. The whole Bible has undergone this kind of analysis and is subject to the same kind of academic debate.

Biblical critical scholars take pains to point out that multiple authorship does not imply deceit. These authors were not trying to "put something over" on future generations, and there is no conspiracy going on. This was a perfectly normal practice of former times before the development of modern literary attitudes. Sometimes the authors wanted to humbly credit famous people. Sometimes they were simply doing what modern editors do today. Almost certainly none of them thought they were writing what would someday be considered scripture. They were just writing history as they saw it.

The point is that critical scholarship, using proven textual analysis that has been applied to everything from Shakespeare to Aristotle, has perhaps discovered how the Bible came to be written. Their results do not necessarily eliminate God's inspiration, though their deductions could allow for a strictly human approach, free of any divine inspiration. Many academics have accepted their findings, and even very conservative scholars have concluded that at least some of their conclusions are probably true.

But some scholars go further than even some liberal academics will accept. This happened when Harold Bloom and David Rosenberg published *The Book of J*, in which they concluded that the author "J" was a woman. The authors point out that "J" seems to have written a lot about women, unusual in a patriarchal society. She seems to cast women in a much lighter, almost playful, role than the other authors. Even more telling, "J" seems to have an easy and intimate knowledge of what the Bible calls "the manner of women," or menstruation. There is a wonderful story, for instance, in Genesis 31:30–35. Rachel, leaving home with her new husband, has stolen the household idols that she felt uncomfortable leaving behind. When her father begins searching for them, she eludes his search by placing them under the camel's saddle on which she is sitting and then tells her father she is having her period. He, of course, immediately backs off. Bloom and Rosenberg wonder: "Does this sound like the story a man would tell?"

Even some feminist critics, however, backed away from the possibility that a woman in those patriarchal times could ever have been allowed to write a book of the Bible. The questions and observations raised by Bloom and Rosenberg were good ones. But there is simply not enough evidence to convince the academic jury.

Another literary discipline that has captured a lot of ink in the public press is the concept of "demythologizing." To understand the principle, let's begin with a well-known myth. Every Christmas, Santa Claus flies down from the North Pole to deliver presents to all the good little boys and girls of the world. We all know the myth, embellished with reindeer and sleighs and elves and all. Only the very young among us accept the story as history. But no one who tells the story, not the television producer or the newspaper editor, begins with a disclaimer. When you go to a movie theater to see the latest incarnation of Tim Allen's *The Santa Clause*, there is no opening statement: "Warning! This is not a true story. In no way is it to be taken as historical fact!" We just know the myth and accept it as that. We don't have to belabor the point.

But suppose a culture existing two thousand years from now digs up a copy of *Rudolph, the Red-Nosed Reindeer*? At face value, they will have to assume the book is telling a historically true story because nowhere does the book claim to be anything different from that. Some future readers are going to choose to believe the story actually happened. They might even invent a "Santa Claus" religion.

Others will probably try to demythologize the story. In other words, they will try to get at the meaning of the myth after the fantasy is removed. They will decide that reindeer, for instance, can't really fly. They will produce statistical tables proving the improbability of one person getting to two billion homes in one evening. They will point out that not all homes even had chimneys.

The point is that after they remove the obvious embellishments, they will still be faced with a historical fact. Their archaeologists, after having discovered much evidence of Christmas trees and presents, will have to deduce that children did get Christmas presents on Christmas Eve in various locations around the world. So after demythologizing the story, they will be forced to decide that Santa Claus was a way to explain historical reality, buried under layers of myth. Christmas actually and historically happened in a way that the myth portrayed as metaphor. Will they still believe in Christmas? Absolutely. But will they believe it actually happened in the way the stories say it happened? Probably not. And unless some of us actually write down how we have fun with the story, and our future friends discover our writing, they will probably assume we were just primitive people who didn't know any better.

Here's the point. A lot happens in the Bible that is, shall we say, out of the ordinary. Jesus walks on the sea and changes water into wine. People are brought back from the dead. The Red Sea parts. Moses talks to a burning bush.

Did these things really happen? Or are they myths encapsulating historical truth? Is there a kernel of history at the heart of these myths? If so, what is more important—the story or the truth the story is trying convey?

Demythologizing is not an attempt to "disprove" the Bible. It is an attempt to recapture what the original author meant to convey within the context of his (or her) times.

These examples illustrate that critical scholarship is not, as detractors claim, some liberal conspiracy to destroy religion. It is a serious science that, like any other science, has to convince a majority of colleagues before it stands the test of time. Some conclusions pass the cut. Others do not. Wild assumptions may sell books, but it takes quite a persuasive piece of disciplined scholarship to become "gospel truth."

But the Bible is different from other works of literature in that most Shakespeare lovers don't really care if someone other than the Bard wrote his works. But Bible believers do care if the Bible is portrayed as simply another piece of literature written in ancient times. As long as those feelings are present, critical scholarship will continue to be a disputed academic discipline.

Sources:
Fackre, Dorothy, and Gabriel Fackre. *Christian Basics*. Grand Rapids, MI: William B. Eerdmans Publishing Co., 1991.
Kirsch, Jonathan. *The Harlot by the Side of the Road*. New York: Ballantine Books, 1997.
May, Herbert G., and Bruce M. Metzger, eds. *The New Oxford Annotated Bible with the Apocrypha*. Rev. ed. New York: Oxford University Press, 1973.

LITURGY

Derived from the Greek word *leitourgia* ("public duty"), liturgy has come to refer to the act of public worship, especially as it pertains to Christian church services. But its emphasis, though subtle, has quite literally changed the landscape and influenced daily life.

The kind of building we associate with the word "church" is a direct result of the liturgy it was designed for. The formal liturgical tradition of the Catholic Mass, for instance, called forth the Gothic cathedral. The simple tradition of the Quaker meeting produced a less formal design. The New England Meeting House places the preacher and his pulpit front and center, while many modern sanctuaries look more like "theaters in the round" with full-scale media rooms controlling sound and lighting equipment.

Beginning with the reforms of Vatican II (see Vatican Councils) in 1963, Roman Catholic liturgy forced a change in furniture placement. In an effort to include more lay participation, the priest now stood behind the altar, facing the people. Previously he had stood with his back to the people, facing the altar. Now the altar had to be moved away from the wall, enabling people to move behind it. While common now, back then it caused a furor.

When organs began to be used to accompany liturgy, churches were built around the demands of the instrument itself. Organ pipes began to be a recognizable part of liturgical furniture. Now, with many Protestant churches employing modern instruments, it is not uncommon for churches to be built around orchestra pits and stages, with giant screens behind the worship leader so as to project the words of songs or highlight the text of the lecturer's sermon.

Liturgy dictates architecture. Architecture displays theology. Theology demands liturgy. The three cannot be separated.

Sources:

Douglas, J. D., ed. *The New International Dictionary of the Christian Church*. Grand Rapids, MI: Zondervan Publishing, 1974.

LOKI *see* **Norse Gods and Goddesses**

LORD'S PRAYER

Although the term "Lord's Prayer" (Catholic tradition often refers to the prayer by its first words, calling it the "Our Father") is not used in the Bible, the prayer itself appears in two places. Both Matthew (chapter 6) and Luke (chapter 11) quote the well-known six petitions in much the same order, but neither, in its earliest text, contains the final doxology. These words were probably added as a liturgical element, a congregational response, as it were. They are often left out in Roman Catholic tradition.

Two theories address the fact that Matthew and Luke offer slightly different versions. One says Jesus taught the prayer twice, using slightly different words. The other is that Luke's version was the real one and that Matthew copied it, changing the words slightly. Amidst all the present-day controversy surrounding the question of what the historical Jesus really did or did not say, it is informative to note that most scholars believe this prayer comes to us directly from the lips of Jesus in pretty much the same form as his original utterance.

It is addressed to Abba, a Hebrew word translated as "father." But *abba* is a personal word meaning something closer to "daddy" or "papa."

The prayer is arranged as follows:

[Introduction:] Our father, which [who] art in heaven
[Petitions:] 1. Hallowed be thy name [May your name be made holy]—
2. Thy Kingdom come
3. Thy will de done on earth as it is in heaven

4. Give us this day our daily bread

5. Forgive us our trespasses ["debts" or "sins"] as we forgive those who trespass against us ["our debtors" or "those who sin against us"]

6. And lead us not into temptation but deliver us from evil

[Doxology:] For thine is the kingdom and the power and the glory forever [and ever].

Sources:

Bucke, Emory Stevens et al, eds. *The Interpreter's Dictionary of the Bible*. 4 vols. New York: Abingdon Press, 1962.

LORD'S SUPPER *see* **Eucharist**

LOST TRIBES OF ISRAEL *see* **Babylonian Captivity**

LUGHNASA *see* **Paganism, Calendar of**

LUTHER, MARTIN *see* **Christianity, Development of; Lutheranism**

LUTHERANISM

When Martin Luther (1483–1546) led the charge away from the Catholic Church during the Protestant Reformation (see Christianity, Development of), he was not interested in practical reform as much as doctrinal reform. He was appalled at the corruption in the Church, but that was not his main criticism. He was convinced that correct action could only follow correct belief. But within that correct belief, he recognized that there was room for disagreement.

Philipp Melanchthon (1497–1560), for instance, was a close friend of quite a different temperament who argued many of the same doctrinal points as Luther but was quiet enough not to be confrontational to the point of divisiveness. Luther considered his task in life to "remove the great boulders and cut down the trees," letting the more patient Melanchthon come behind to "plow and sow."

So after Luther's death, it was Melanchthon who carried out the interpretation of Lutheran theological thought. His systematic theology, commonly called Loci Theologici, became the standard "Lutheran" textbook of the times.

That caused problems, of course. This was, after all, a time of upheaval and religious argument. There were those who thought "Master Philipp," as Luther used to call him, had wandered from the path and was too close to the humanistic reform of Erasmus. Luther had rejected what he called "dirty reason." The Bible says, "There is a way that seems right to a man, but in the end it leads to death" (Proverbs 16:25). Luther believed scripture had to come first, even if it seemed unreasonable. The big proving ground, as far as he was concerned, was in the answer to the question "How are we saved?" Luther was convinced we are saved from sin and accepted into heaven solely on the grounds of God's grace. There was simply no room for good works or "earning" salvation by being a good person. The book of James seemed to disagree, or at least to soften this position, but Luther believed James held a nebulous place in scripture, calling it "a right straw-ey epistle," or "an epistle of straw."

Martin Luther, German priest, reformer, and founder of Lutheranism, painted c. 1529. *The Art Archive/Galleria degli Uffizi Florence/Dagli Orti.*

Some believed Melanchthon retreated too far from this position. Because there were other points of conflict as well, one of them concerning Christ's presence at the Communion (see Eucharist), in true Church tradition, a conference was held. This led to the Formula of Concord in 1577. The theological pattern following this declaration led to what is now known as Protestant scholasticism, a technical term that boils down to one point. Lutheran scholars believe Luther "got it right" and filter all doctrine through his lens. This position is summarized in the *Book of Concord*, a compilation of defining creeds, catechisms, and articles.

This triumph of doctrinal correctness has led to a lot of storyteller Garrison Keillor's "Lutheran jokes" on the *Prairie Home Companion* radio show, but it is an important component in understanding why Lutherans hold their denominational ties so dearly.

Lutheran church government, or "polity," tends to follow the original Roman Catholic organizational principle of the synod. This is a church deliberative body, originally a group of clergy, that decides policy and applies general canon law to particular situations. Presbyterian as well as Lutheran churches still follow this practice, as opposed to "congregational" church systems that emphasize local church autonomy (see Congregationalism). The synod has the authority to speak for the church. It is still common to hear Lutherans, before pronouncing judgment, exclaim, "What does synod say?"

On the other hand, church polity can lead to communication problems. In the 1990s, an extensive "pulpit and altar exchange" between Lutherans and members of the United Church of Christ, which practices congregational polity, almost broke down because some Lutherans couldn't quite figure out who spoke for the churches they were dealing with and wondered whether they had to each individual church.

To complicate matters, Lutherans do not comprise a single body. Within Lutheranism are various synods that operate independently of each other and differ on certain doctrinal points. Most Lutherans belong to one of two Lutheran denominations. The Evangelical Lutheran Church in America is the sixth largest Christian denomination in the United States, and the conservative Lutheran Church, Missouri Synod is the tenth largest.

Despite the divisions, there is a traditional position that unites worshipers and makes them distinctly Lutheran. It is best summed up by a phrase coming right out of the Reformation: *sola gratia* (only grace), *sola fide* (only faith), and *sola scriptura* (only scripture). This is what traditional Lutheranism is all about. Only God's grace, experienced through faith and understood through the scriptures, can save humans from sin. Good works are a proof of salvation, not the means by which it occurs. The two sacraments, baptism and the Lord's Supper, are defined and practiced not as simple memorial rituals but as unique means of grace through which God regenerates fallen humanity.

Lutherans, then, historically differentiate between law and Gospel. The law reveals God's wrath—"This is what you should be like. You have been tried in the balance and found wanting!" The Gospel reveals God's love—"But I love you anyway!" The Old Testament gave the law. The New Testament reveals God's love.

For Lutherans this is the central theological teaching and the essence of Christianity. All the rest comes later. Of course, there are other forces holding Lutherans together. Germany was the place Lutheranism began—its fatherland. When Germans and Scandinavians immigrated to America, it was only natural they would bring their faith with them. Worship services were conducted in their own language. It felt like home. This is the sense Garrison Keillor remembers in his Lake Wobegon material. He is not so much poking fun at Norwegian Lutherans in Minnesota as fondly remembering something meaningful. There is a shared tradition, an important tradition. It was the religion of both Johann Sebastian Bach and the everyman Midwestern farmer. It gave birth to the magnificent hymn "A Mighty Fortress Is Our God" as well as the rollicking "Good Christian Men Rejoice." It is carried out in great cathedrals and little prairie meeting houses.

Sources:

Douglas, J. D., ed. *The New International Dictionary of the Christian Church.* Grand Rapids, MI: Zondervan Publishing, 1974.
Gonzalez, Justo L. *The Story of Christianity.* 2 vols. New York: Harper & Row, 1985.

M

MAHABHARATA *see* Bhagavad-Gita

MAHAYANA *see* Buddhism, Development of

MANICHEISM *see* Augustine

MANITOU

Besides there is a generall Custome amongst them, at the apprehension of any Excellency in Men, Women, Beasts, Fish, etc., to cry out Manittoo, that is, it is a God, as if they see one man excell other in Wisdom, Valour, Strength, Activity etc., they cry out Manittoo, A God.

With these words, written from New England in 1643, Roger Williams introduced the Algonquian concept of Manitou to the world. It is one of those words that is very difficult to translate into English because our language doesn't contain proper categories to express American Indian thought. Manitou means "God," but that is not enough.

Perhaps the closest we can get to it is to trace the developing theology of Siberian shamanism, developed on the shores of Lake Bikal and transported thousands of miles across the wilderness where it was deposited in what would one day be called New England. There it awaited the coming confrontation with the Pilgrims' Christianity.

The people who would one day be called "Indians" believed in the Creator. They called him Kichtan or Kitchi-Manitou (the "Great Mystery"). Over a lot of time and across two continents they developed the belief that the Creator inhabited mountains and lakes, trees and animals, with a divine presence. Specific effigies or medicine bags were understood to be the home of spirits. The forest and sky, Turtle Island in North America—indeed, all of creation was the habitation of various Manitous, which were, in turn, an expression of the Great Mystery.

This three-fold realm of God—transcendent, immanent, and specific—is Manitou. People interact with Manitou because they are part of the creation. They are not separate from nature, as the Pilgrims believed. The Algonquians did not even believe humans were the crowning expression of the Creator's work. "Four-leggeds" and "two-leggeds" were equally a part of the whole. When a rock was removed from the seashore, something else was put in its place. When an animal was killed for food, an offering was returned. Balance and wholeness were the watchwords of Algonquian thought. When this wholeness was experienced or visualized, when an example of essential religion was seen in life, it was Manitou. With Manitou, the sacred fused with the secular.

Sources:

Johnston, Basil. *The Manitous: The Supernatural World of the Ojibway.* New York: Harper Perennial, 1995.

Mavor, James W., Jr., and Byron E. Dix. *Manitou.* Rochester, VT: Inner Traditions International, 1989.

MANU, LAWS OF *see* Hinduism, Development of

MASONS

What is Freemasonry? Who are the Masons? What goes on in the Masonic Lodge downtown? Is it a religion?

The answer to these questions depends entirely on whom you ask.

To some, Freemasonry is an ancient cult still going about the business of establishing a new world order. Log on to any Internet search engine and before you even get to an official Masonic Order website, you will discover page after page of essays that supposedly "expose" Freemasonry. According to the majority of Internet sites (sponsored mostly by conservative Christian groups), Masons continue the tradition and mission of the Kabbalah, Gnosticism, Rosicrucianism, and the Illuminati. They are the secret organization that is out to take control of your life. They always have been and always will be. They have duped their many members, who do not see the truth behind the Master Plan, and they have made many inroads. Does not the Great Seal of the United States of America, the one printed on the dollar bill in your wallet, consist of Masonic signs only Masons understand? Were not George Washington, Thomas Jefferson, Benjamin Franklin, and Paul Revere Masons? Even former U.S. president Gerald Ford, for heaven's sake. For many years it's been a not-too-well-kept secret that Mozart's opera *The Magic Flute* is based on Masonic symbolism. That must prove something! A cult that old must be involved in secrets the rest of us don't know anything about.

But talk to a Mason or attend a public night held at the Masonic Lodge and you will get quite a different story. Freemasonry, along with its orders of the Knight's Templar and DeMolay for men and boys, and the orders of Eastern Star and Rainbow Girls for women and girls, is the oldest fraternity in the world. It exists to make the world a better place. It fosters goodwill and good work. It builds hospitals and finances community projects. There are secrets, of course. All fraternities have rituals, handshakes, and emblems known only to members. Yes, a lot of very famous men have belonged, but that can be seen as proof that the organization is worth joining.

During a dark time in American Masonic history, in the early nineteenth century, the movement was discredited and ridiculed. In November of 1826, after a member threatened to reveal the order's secrets, he was kidnapped and murdered by fellow Masons. After a very public trial, thousands left the order. But that was then. This is now. And the movement certainly has recovered from a time that was not at all representative of the men who now meet at the lodge once a week.

No one knows when Masonry really began. Some trace it all the way back to ancient Persia and Egypt and the building of the ziggurats and pyramids. Others say it began with the building of Solomon's Temple about three thousand years ago. Whatever the case, it certainly has a long and illustrious history. The modern Masonic Lodge is often called a temple because it is built following the pattern of Solomon's Temple in Jerusalem and much of its ritual comes from those verses of the Bible that describe the construction.

The Masonic Knight's Templar trace their roots back to nine French knights who vowed to protect those who were on their way

Image of Masonic symbols by Oswald Wirth. *Fortean Picture Library.*

to the Crusades. They played an integral part in many battles during those times, earning a reputation for bravery. There are those who believe it was the Knights Templar who brought the Shroud of Turin, thought to be the burial shroud of Jesus, back to Europe and protected it down through the centuries. Some believe they had a part in the spiriting away of the Ark of the Covenant upon its disappearance (see Ark of the Covenant).

The first Masonic Grand Lodge was built in London in 1717. The order entered America through Boston in the eighteenth century. Many of America's founding fathers were Masons, and there is no question that many Masonic symbols found their way into the Great Seal and other national emblems.

The answer to the simple question, "Is Masonry a religion?" is not really straightforward. Masonry is not a religion. But Masons are religious. Although they will never try to convert anyone or change anyone's religion (by rule, it is forbidden), one has to believe in God in order to join the order. Meetings begin with prayer. Much of the ritual comes from the Old Testament of the Bible. Many Masons attend church on Sundays. Some of them nowadays may attend a synagogue.

Mayan pyramid, Kukulkan, at Chichen Itza, Mexico, photographed during the spring equinox when a shadow resembling a serpent moves down the side of the temple. *Fortean Picture Library.*

If you attend a Masonic Lodge in your town during one of their open meetings, you will certainly not find a group of secret conspirators out to take over the world. You will find an order that is dwindling, probably due more to cultural patterns of modern lifestyle than anything else, a group of people who genuinely enjoy the company of others while engaged in the task of doing good things for the community and participating in a tradition with a long history.

Sources:
Freemasonry Today. http://www.freemasonrytoday.co.uk/. September 15, 2003.

MAYA

Five hundred years before Abraham walked the deserts of the Middle East, or about 2500 BCE, the Mayan people were developing their own religious traditions in the rain forests of Guatemala. Their culture flourished all the way up to the Spanish invasion of the sixteenth century.

The Mayan lived in a world chock full of gods. Much of their average day was spent praying for health, rain, crops, luck, and fortune. But the central religious metaphor of Mayan religion was the *ceiba* tree, the tree of life. It existed in the three realms of earth, air, and atmosphere with its roots in the ground, trunk in the world, and branches in the heavens. Demonstrating its importance in the delicate climate of the rain forest, it literally exhaled the breath of Hunab K'U, the creative force. Gods and goddesses were associated with crops, especially corn, as well as rain, the sun, the moon, and stars, but the Maya knew that when the last tree was gone, people would perish from the earth.

There was a dark side to the religion. Powerful gods demanded powerful sacrifices to propitiate them (see Sacrifice). With great pomp and ceremony and before huge crowds, rituals were enacted during which humans were offered, with much shedding of blood, as tribute to gods who seemed to demand more and more each year. Pictures carved on stone altars often tell a gruesome story. Probably, though this is less certain, drugs were used to induce heightened states of spiritual awareness.

Such sacrificial ritual is a pattern common to many religious traditions. Perhaps because life was so mysterious they somehow felt the need to "pay the supreme sacrifice," or, more often, make someone else do it. It was central to Mayan religious life. But to judge the entire culture and religion on the grisly archaeology of one aspect of it is to miss the many positive attributes that informed an entire American civilization.

Sources:
Renard, John. *The Handy Religion Answer Book*. Detroit: Visible Ink Press, 2002.

MECCA *see* **Islam, Development of; Muhammad**

MEDICINE WHEELS

Scattered throughout the plains of western Canada and the United States are hundreds of prehistoric medicine wheels, circles of stones that seem to be aligned in patterns designed to represent astronomical sighting plains. When Europeans first discovered them, they naturally asked the Indians who built them. The answer was always the same: "The people who were here before." In other words, these were old—very old. They were considered sacred, protected by the spirits, and the destination of many a vision quest.

They remain so today. Many still travel to sit quietly, meditating on the circles which, by their very antiquity, provoke feelings of awe and wonder. Who built them? How were they used? And why are they here?

The pattern is not unique to America. Stone circles are found throughout the world, from Stonehenge, the "granddaddy" of them all, to the small, mountaintop circles of the American high desert that are known only to a few initiates.

The circle or sacred spiral pattern is also found consistently throughout the world's record of rock paintings. What does it mean? The standard theory is that astronomy figured heavily in its use. It is the common denominator in astrological alignments. Some speculate that the pattern is representative of the womb. But beyond that there seems to exist a spiritual component lost to modern humans. The best we can do is guess.

Medicine wheel in Sedona, Arizona. A Native American symbol, the wheel is a circle of stones with four spokes and a center. The outer circle is made up of sixteen stones, one for each of the twelve moons and one for each of the four spirit keepers, while the center represents the Great Spirit. *Fortean Picture Library.*

The question remains concerning the universality of the designs. Some consider it coincidence, believing the pattern represents a religious feeling we all must have in common. Whether we live in Siberia or Arizona, we all share the same human psychology. Others believe the design originated in one location and then spread throughout the world. This is the "diffusion" theory.

Sources:
Mavor, James W., Jr., and Byron E. Dix. *Manitou*. Rochester, VT: Inner Traditions International, 1989.

MEDITATION *see* Prayer/Meditation/Contemplation

MENCIUS *see* Confucian Texts

MENNONITES

Mennonites are the direct descendants of the Anabaptist movement (see Anabaptists) of the sixteenth century. Followers of the Swiss teacher Menno Simons (c. 1496–c. 1561),

A girl jumps onto first base as Mennonite children play baseball at recess outside their one-room schoolhouse in Lancaster County, Pennsylvania. *AP/Wide World Photos.*

from whom they got their name, they became an important religious force in the Netherlands and Germany, moved to the United States during colonial times, and eventually formed important communities in the prairie provinces of central and western Canada.

Like all denominations, they have suffered divisions over the years, the Amish being their most well known spiritual descendants.

Mennonites are considered to be conservative (see Evangelical) in theology. They practice the ritual of foot-washing, for instance, following the example and command of Jesus at the Last Supper (John 13). They require women to wear a head-covering during worship, following the advice of the apostle Paul (1 Corinthians 11:5). They forbid the taking of oaths, as in a court of law. Also forbidden is the holding of public office. They insist on plainness of dress and practice congregational polity. Each church is autonomous and calls its own minister.

One of the most important aspects of the Mennonite church is its peace witness. Along with Quakers and the Church of the Brethren, Mennonites are known for being pacifists. They forbid military service to their members, substituting civilian relief services overseen by the Mennonite Central Committee during times of war.

On any given Sunday, over one million Mennonites worldwide continue a 450-year-old worship tradition dating back to the time of the Protestant Reformation.

Sources:

Douglas, J. D., ed. *The New International Dictionary of the Christian Church.* Grand Rapids, MI: Zondervan Publishing, 1974.

MERLIN

(See also Arthur)

He that made with his hond
Wynd and water, wode and lond;
Geve heom alle good endyng
That wolon listne this talkyng,
And y schal telle, yow byfore,
How Merlyn was geten and bore
And of his wisdoms also
And othre happes mony mo
Sum whyle byfeol Engelonde. (*Of Arthour and Merlin*, c. 1260)

Did a historical Merlin really exist? Was there ever a mysterious Druid who stood as a hinge between the "old religion" and Christian Britain? Did he walk the sacred forests and counsel the young King Arthur? Did he rebuild Stonehenge as the final resting-place for his father, Ambrosias, bringing the capstone all the way from Ireland to serve as his memorial? Did he arrange both the conception and the coronation of the young king who would be a beacon to all kings? And does he sleep now in his crystal cave, awaiting the restoration of all things?

If not, we would probably have had to invent him. His is just too good a story to miss. Every year, it seems, someone comes out with a new twist, a new interpretation, a new way of understanding. He has been discovered by young boys who want to be knights of the round table, young girls who want to know more about the feminine presence in Avalon, new-age Druids who want to know more about magic, Wiccans who want to understand the natural world, and publishers who want to make more money by dipping again into the tried and true.

Some feel Merlin is completely a figure of British mythology, invented by Geoffrey of Monmouth in his *History of the Kings of Britain* to serve as a connection between the old Celtic religion of Druidism and King Arthur's acceptance of Christianity. Others feel the Merlin we know is a composite of any number of prophets and wizards who lived in the hills of ancient Britain. Still more believe that any story with such a long and illustrious history must be based in fact. And a few believe in Merlin just because they are unabashed, unrepentant romantics. (Ask any of the millions who flock to see the *Lord of the Rings* movies, in which Gandalf is a Merlin clone.)

Nikolai Tolstoy has written a book describing his quest to find the historical Merlin. He presents the thesis that Merlin did exist, though not as a contemporary to Arthur. After reading ancient manuscripts and walking the Scottish lowlands, he came to believe that Merlin was a Druid who lived in the north after Britain was left alone following the collapse of the Roman Empire. If this is the case, Merlin represents an old religion going back to prehistoric times when Bronze-Age Britain was dealing with the religious implications of the new Iron Age.

However Merlin is presented, the aspect of the hinge between two religious cultures, two spiritual worldviews, seems always to be present. When the new replaces the old, you need a guide. Merlin was that guide.

Think, for a moment, about the implications of this particular clash of religions. It required the people to completely change everything about the way they viewed the world. Celtic religion was all about connection with nature. Gods and spirits were everywhere. Nature itself was the church. The religious calendar was based on the position of the sun and the phases of the moon. Woodland sprites and fairies of the hill competed for the offerings left on roadside shrines. The environment *was* the religion. And humans were subject to it.

Then along came Christianity. Now humans were separate from nature. People were expected to subdue the earth, not to try to placate it. Fairies and woodland sprites became devils and demons.

It didn't help the confusion any when the church began to "baptize" Merlin's religion after discovering they couldn't root it out. Merlin's sacred groves were cut down, decorated with holly, and brought right into the house on Christmas Eve. His gods were made into saints. His sacred fire at the winter solstice became the Yule log fire. It took some getting used to. But Merlin, far-seeing prophet that he was, was there to guide the way. He knew the gods were just taking on a new incarnation. He knew the goddess would surface as Mary, the Mother of God. He knew Jesus was just another expression of the god taking on human form.

So he was there to soften the blow, accept the inevitable as the whim of God, and prepare the way for the new age.

Sources:
Tolstoy, Nikolai. *The Quest for Merlin*. Boston: Little, Brown, 1985.

MESSIAH

Waiting for a Messiah is a universal religious activity found throughout history. Jews and Zoroastrians say he hasn't come yet. Christians and Muslims say he came and no one paid any attention, so he'll be back. Some Native Americans believe a Messiah fashioned after Tecumseh will restore their lost fortunes. There are even those who believe a Messiah is Earth's only hope for survival and look for one to come from outer space.

A Messiah is so much a part of so many religions, especially monotheistic ones, that you have to use the word very carefully because people just assume you're talking about theirs. Whether he's called "Desire of Nations" or "the Son of God," people who believe in a Messiah believe that the divine will enter into history—that the eternal will step into time. Messianic aspirations offer hope: that somehow the world will have a happy ending and be either built anew or restored to a former glory.

In typically anthropocentric thought, the Messiah is always pictured as a human being, usually male, who will take charge and set things right. In essence, he is a benevolent monarch who represents God on Earth and is just like us, but without our shortcomings. To a certain degree, whenever a presidential candidate offers himself as the one who has answers to a set of national problems, he is appealing to people's messianic yearnings. The word itself comes from a Hebrew word that means "anointed." The Greek equivalent is Christos, from which is derived the name "Christ."

Sources:

Ludwig, Theodore M. *The Sacred Paths: Understanding the Religions of the World.* 2nd ed. Upper Saddle River, NJ: Prentice Hall, 1996.

MIDRASH *see* **Tanakh**

MIND-ONLY BUDDHISM *see* **Buddhism, Development of**

MISHNA *see* **Tanakh**

MITHRAISM

Mithras, God of the Morning, our trumpets waken the Wall!
Rome is above the nations, but Thou art over all! ("A Song to Mithras," by Rudyard Kipling)

Mithras, "the soldier's god," was worshiped in Rome for more than three hundred years. Because the rites were so secret, there is no written record and very little other evidence indicating what that worship consisted of. Tradition identifies him with a Persian god who belonged to the pantheon ruled over by the great god, Ahura Mazda (see Ahura Mazda/Ahriman), the god of goodness. Ahura Mazda fought the evil god Ahriman for the souls of humanity and the fate of the world. As the incarnation of Ahura-Mazda on earth, Mithras's job was to be the "judger of souls." He labored to protect the souls of the righteous from the demonic hoard of Ahriman. Persian tradition said Mithras was the one born of Anahita, the immaculate virgin called "the Mother of God." She conceived him from the seed of Zoroaster (later called Zarathustra by the Greeks) that had been preserved in the waters of Lake Hamun in the province of Sistan in Persia. Called "the Light of the World," Mithras was the mediator between heaven and Earth. Born in midwinter, he remained celibate all his life. Striding forth into the coldness of the world, he killed the sacred bull and offered the blood of the sacrifice to his followers. In ritual celebration, they drank wine that was said to have turned into blood and ate the bread of the sacrifice after an initiation ceremony consisting of a ritual baptism. They worshiped on Sunday and celebrated the birth of the Hero, Mithras, on December 25th. After Mithras finished the work he had been sent to do, he ate a last supper with his followers and ascended into heaven to watch over them until the Day of Judgment, when good and evil would be separated.

The resemblance to Christianity is remarkable. And Mithraism arose in the Roman world at the same time Christianity did. Origen and Jerome, early Church fathers, noted the amazing resemblance and commented on it.

Although no written records have survived, many inscriptions to Mithras have been discovered and a series of Mithraistic temples in Italy have been excavated, one existing right under the present Church of Saint Clemente, near the Coliseum in Rome.

No one has seriously suggested that Mithraism was the sole inspiration for Christianity. Early Christian sources are simply too well documented. But the resemblance and the timing is too perfect to be totally coincidental. Early Christianity borrowed from many religious traditions (see Christianity, Development of) and very probably was influenced in some way by Mithraism.

Sources:
Jones, Prudence, and Nigel Pennick. *A History of Pagan Europe*. New York: Routledge, 1995.

MOODY, DWIGHT L.

American "revivalism" is so much a part of the contemporary scene that people tend to think it's been around since Saint Paul. But the famous evangelist Billy Graham and his colleagues owe much of their success to a shoe clerk from Northfield, Massachusetts, named Dwight L. Moody (1837–1899), and to the American branch of the Young Men's Christian Association (see YMCA/YWCA). The movement, or process, they instigated has since been labeled "urban revivalism." Folks on the inside call it a movement of the Holy Spirit. Others tend to think of it as the "business" of evangelism. Whatever the case, Moody's experience with the Chicago YMCA and citywide evangelistic enterprises taught him that mass campaigns featuring big venues, good music, and inspiring preaching could produce revivals almost at will.

This is not to say Moody was a fake—far from it. He believed he was doing God's will by discovering new methods of reaching a lot of people in a very short time. But he was a businessman. He not only thought like a businessman, he dressed like one, talked like one, and acted like one. He was the first to "baptize" business techniques by using them on a mass scale in the preaching of the Gospel. He used his organizational, marketing, and promotional skills to raise vast sums of money, train a host of workers under executive direction, and in the process become the first of the breed of "professional evangelists."

If Moody had stayed in the shoe business, it's likely he would have carved out a fortune for himself, flowing in from a large business empire. But he forsook all that to follow what he believed to be his calling from God. As it was, he made a fortune in the field of religion. But he gave it all away. When he died, he left an estate containing a grand total of $500—which, by the way, he didn't know he had, or he would have donated that to the cause as well.

When he moved from Northfield to Boston, and then to Chicago, he never dreamed what his lot in life would be. He was active in starting the Sunday school movement and making it a part of the American church scene. He was active in the YMCA evangelistic campaigns. And in Chicago he realized what could happen if a few good people took seriously the "great commission" Jesus gave his church: "Go into all the world and preach the Gospel." Moody believed Jesus was talking to him personally, and he did exactly what his master told him. Known and respected, he became something of a Chicago civic institution. Operating on the basis that "it was better to get ten men to work than do the work of ten men," he had a host of projects, mostly connected to the YMCA, involving hundreds of workers. "We must ask for money for the Lord's work," he said. "Money, money, MONEY! at every meeting—not to support the Association as it now is, but to enlarge its operations."

When he took on a young song leader named Ira D. Sankey, the team was formed that would go down in history and set the pattern for Billy Graham and every other evangelist who ever lived. "Moody preaches the Gospel," it was said, "and Sankey sings the Gospel." Many of the most famous hymns to ever grace a hymnbook were made popular because of the success of the *Sankey and Moody Hymnbook*, used first in London and then in every citywide campaign the two put on together. It made them nationally recognized figures.

Through all the success and worldwide adulation, however, Moody remained a very humble man who never pretended to be more than a layman who loved God. A woman once confronted him, claiming to disagree with his theology. "My theology!" he exclaimed. "I didn't know I had any!" Everything he knew, he said, was related to the "Three R's: Ruin by sin—Redemption by Christ—Regeneration by the Holy Ghost." He believed solidly that people were free to choose their destiny, free to choose to believe in Jesus Christ as their savior. It was a simple religion, preached with homespun humor and humility. And people loved it.

But detractors grew. It became obvious that the people responding to his message at the revival meetings were not then joining local churches. Church membership remained fairly stagnant after he left town. Moody seemed to lift the morale of the regular churchgoers who came to see him, rather than attracting new believers. Eventually, as happens to all trends in America, people began to lose interest. But his conferences in Northfield were exciting for students because Moody would invite some of the greatest theological minds in the country to debate issues.

In 1879 he established the Northfield Seminary for Girls and, two years later, the Mount Hermon School for boys. Today the two institutions, now joined, host a Moody Bible Conference each summer at the Northfield campus. The Moody Bible Institute, formerly called the Chicago Evangelization Society, continues to turn out conservative Christian ministers and missionaries.

When he died in 1899, it was said that D. L. Moody had spoken to more than 100 million people, traveling more than a million miles to do it. Not bad for a simple shoe clerk who just wanted to teach Sunday school.

Sources:

Douglas, J. D., ed. *The New International Dictionary of the Christian Church*. Grand Rapids, MI: Zondervan Publishing, 1974.
Hudson, Winthrop S. *Religion in America*. New York: Charles Scribner, 1965.

MORMONS/CHURCH OF JESUS CHRIST OF LATTER-DAY SAINTS

In 1820 the little town of Palmyra, New York, was typical of the many mill towns dotting the famous Erie Canal. Religious revival had hit the area, the impact of which can still be seen in the small town famous for the fact that its main intersection features a church of a different denomination on each of the four corners. They surround

Statue of Brigham Young with the Mormon Temple in the background, Salt Lake City, Utah. *Fortean Picture Library.*

what was, until only a few years ago, Palmyra's only traffic light, making for some interesting ecumenical debates on Sunday morning at about 11 o'clock.

A young man named Joseph Smith, whose family had migrated down from Vermont, was caught up but confused by the religious questions of the day. Every preacher seemed to claim that his own church was the "right" church. Methodists vied with Presbyterians for new converts, and many other long-forgotten sects all added their voices to the spiritual mix. It was typical of the American melting-pot kind of frontier revival that often broke out during those times.

Smith decided he needed to go right to the source for guidance. He began to pray for help in knowing God's will concerning which church he should join:

> In the midst of this war of words and tumult of opinions, I often said to myself, what is to be done? Who of all these parties be right? Or are they wrong all together?

In a small grove of trees, now called the Sacred Grove and visited by many tourists every year, Smith received his answer. He later claimed that God the Father and Jesus Christ appeared to him, warning him not to join any church. Just as God had appeared to Moses and Paul in former times, he appeared to Smith with a message: The times were changing. Something new was about to happen.

Instructed to climb Hill Cumorah, a small glacial drumlin just north of Palmyra on the way to the little village of Manchester, Smith there met the angel Moroni, son of the great prophet, Mormon, who showed him where golden plates were buried that would answer Smith's questions. They were written in the language Smith described as "Reformed Egyptian Hieroglyphics," and he was able to translate because along with the plates he discovered a pair of "translating spectacles" that allowed him to read the lost language. When translated, they became *The Book of Mormon, Another Testament of Jesus Christ.*

The story they told changed Smith's life. When Jesus Christ walked the Galilee, he organized his church to be the vehicle whereby God, the heavenly father, would reveal himself to humanity and welcome them into heaven. The apostles continued this tradition and preached the Gospel during their lifetimes. They were the saints of the former days. But gradually the Church pulled away from the Gospel. It became apostate, and God withdrew the Church from Earth. Now, in these latter days, it was to be restored according to the prophecy given by the apostle Peter in Acts 3:19–21.

Mormon, the author of the record and one of the last of the prophets of ancient America, had buried the plates there in that hill centuries before. They described how Lehi, a prophet who had lived in Jerusalem some six hundred years before the birth of Christ, had sailed with a small group of people from the Mediterranean all the way to the American continent. They had built a great civilization in Central America while trading, and eventually warring, all the way north to the place of present-day Palmyra. After his resurrection in Jerusalem, Jesus Christ had appeared here in the Americas, preaching the Gospel to his "sheep of another fold." Alas, the people in America were no different from those in other places in the world where the Gospel had been preached and rejected. God raised up prophets, but they were ridiculed. War broke out. The last great battle between God's faithful and the apostate took place here at Hill Cumorah. The descendants of those who had fought were the very people Americans called Indians. Although remnants of history and snatches of language remained to hint of the history that taken place so many centuries before, the story was lost.

Lost, that is, until Smith translated the Golden Plates and revealed what had taken place here. He was able to do so, he said, because God was restoring the saints in these latter days, fulfilling the prophecy and preparing the way for the return of Jesus Christ.

Moroni concluded his book with a great promise. He said those who read his words and sincerely prayed about their meaning would be shown by the Holy Ghost that the words were true and that God's promise was being fulfilled. Smith believed. No one was allowed to see the plates except Smith, although he did reveal them to two different groups of witnesses so they could testify to their existence.

The Book of Mormon is used as a third Testament, as it were. It is not meant to replace the Bible but to be used as a companion to the Old and New Testaments. Mormons claim it predicts the history of the Americas for some twenty-five hundred years: the voyage of Christopher Columbus, the fate of American Indians, the coming of the Puritans, the Revolutionary War, and much more.

On April 6, 1830, ten years after Smith received the plates, translated them, and began to preach the newfound Gospel, the Church of Jesus Christ of Latter-day Saints was organized in Fayette, New York. It now boasts over eleven million members around the world.

But the church experienced persecution from the very beginning. Threatened and finally driven out of town, Smith led his followers west, joining the great western migration taking place at the time. In 1844 both Joseph Smith and his brother were killed by a mob while imprisoned in Carthage, Illinois, awaiting charges for the destruction of an anti-Mormon newspaper press. Brigham Young took control. Leading the people across more than one thousand miles of unsettled prairie, he finally arrived, in 1847, at the great Salt Lake Valley of present-day Utah. This, Young declared, would be the scene of the New Jerusalem. Salt Lake City was born. From this base, Mormon communities were established in Utah, Wyoming, Idaho, Colorado, New Mexico, Arizona, Nevada, California, north to Canada, and south into Mexico. They were united by the Bible, the Book of Mormon, and the Thirteen Articles of Faith that Smith had summarized concerning the beliefs of the new church.

Although the official name of the church is the Church of Jesus Christ of Latter-day Saints, they are often called "Mormons" after the name of the one of the authors of the text translated by Smith. They are a Christian church in that they follow Jesus Christ, but they do not consider themselves to be Protestant, because they feel that by the time of the Reformation the true Church had long since been withdrawn from Earth. Restored in the time of Joseph Smith, it now awaits the literal gathering of Israel and the restoration of the Ten Tribes, "lost" since the Assyrian invasion (see Babylonian Captivity; Judaism, Development of). Zion, the New Jerusalem, will be built on the American continent, where Jesus Christ will someday return to rule planet Earth.

It is probably very frustrating to church leaders that, in light of all this history and theology, people seem to have two questions they ask time and time again.

The first is probably more prurient than theological: "What is the Mormon position regarding polygamy?"

The church now forbids plural marriage. Its official position is that at various times in the past, God commanded a few men to take more than one wife. Abraham, Isaac, Jacob, Moses, David, and Solomon all did it. So when Joseph Smith and Brigham Young were told to take more than one wife, they questioned the practice but were faithful to God and followed his will. Since 1890, however, when Mormon president Wilford Woodruff received a revelation from God that the practice had to cease, it has been forbidden by official church policy.

Do some Mormons still practice plural marriage? Of course. There are fundamentalists in every religion who believe their church has become too liberal and who refuse to go along. But polygamists are excommunicated by the officially recognized church, the greatest punishment the church can deliver.

The second question comes as a result of recent lawsuits involving people researching their family trees. "Why does the Mormon Church keep such extensive genealogical records?"

Mormons believe in baptism by immersion. That's not much different from some other Protestant churches. But according to Mormon theology, you can baptize the dead by proxy, so to speak. You can stand in for them at the temple and be baptized in their stead. To identify deceased family members in order to baptize them, Mormons have established a huge genealogical data bank.

This project has caused some interesting news reports. Recently Mormons have put prison inmates in Utah to work transcribing, from German records released since the Holocaust, the names of Jewish people to be baptized. This practice has raised serious church/state separation problems, to say nothing of the fact that living Jewish relatives don't want their families being baptized, even if they did die long ago. They rightly feel it is disrespectful. A class-action lawsuit was supposed to have put an end to the practice, but it was recently discovered, according to Jewish complainants, that deceased Jews were still being baptized by proxy. The Mormons had apparently broken their word.

The church has stated that these people were baptized accidentally, claiming that the transcribers could not always tell whether the deceased were Jewish just from their names.

The principle at stake is this: Mormons believe families are united forever, even after death. It is very important to them to discover who their family is and make sure they are baptized, thus fulfilling God's requirements on Earth.

Meanwhile, a lot of Gentile genealogists, given free access to Mormon computer files, are at least happy with the result of the doctrine, regardless of their religious beliefs.

Mormons have endured quite a bit of persecution, yet most who come into contact with Mormons as a group come away with nothing but good things to say. The Mormon Tabernacle Choir is one of the most respected vocal ensembles in the world. Residents of Palmyra, New York, who each summer face an influx of thousands of Mormons arriving to attend the famous Mormon Pageant (a reenactment of the Mormon story that is held on Hill Cumorah), are unanimous in their praise of Mormon visitors. Townspeople claim Mormons are always well dressed, they are always well behaved, and they never drink or smoke. The church erects beautiful buildings and maintains an extremely polished website and visitor center, and its members strive always to be polite and helpful.

Conservative Christians, however, ridicule the religion, labeling it a dangerous cult. Its history is slandered in book and television exposés. Way back in 1832, Alexander Campbell published his *Delusions: An Analysis of the Book of Mormon*. In it he pointed out that the golden plates seem to have anticipated and given a definitive "answer to just about every error and truth discussed in New York for the last ten years." In other words, according to Campbell, the book was a hoax written by Smith, conveniently kept secret by not allowing witnesses to watch the "translation" process and designed to answer the current theological dilemmas of the day. The idea that American Indians were descended from the Ten Lost Tribes of Israel was a popular one and had been around for a long time. The late Vernal Holley, after a comprehensive study of the geography of the Book of Mormon, claims that a map of the "Holy Land according to Joseph Smith" can be placed right over a map of present-day New York. The two, he claims, including place names, rivers, lakes, and historic landmarks, are identical.

Some who have "come out" of Mormonism insist the public image and theology is a cover for a domineering sect that controls the lives of its members and teaches a totally different set of beliefs from those published for public consumption. Even Sherlock Holmes enters the picture. In Sir Arthur Conan Doyle's first adventure featuring the famous detective, *A Study in Scarlet*, Mormons are the evil enemy the fledgling detective has to defeat.

While the church has faced persecution since its inception, it continues to flourish and grow. Any visit to its newly completed visitor's center in Palmyra is a treat. Its television cable network is always informative. And its magnificent choir will no doubt continue to make definitive choral recordings for a long time.

Sources:

The Book of Mormon. Trans. Joseph Smith. Salt Lake City: The Church of Jesus Christ of Latter-day Saints, 1980.

The Church of Jesus Christ of Latter-day Saints. http://www.mormon.org. September 15, 2003.

Hudson, Winthrop S. *Religion in America*. New York: Charles Scribner, 1965.

Holley, Vernal. "In Search of Book of Mormon Geography." *Mazeministry.com*. http://www.mazeministry.com/mormonism/holley/holleymaps.htm.

MOSES

(See also Aaron; Passover)

According to biblical tradition, the extended Jewish family began with Abraham. But the religion of Judaism began with Mosheh Rabbenu, which translates as "Moses, our teacher." Moses was the lawgiver, the great liberator and reluctant servant of God. He is the most prominent figure, some say the author, of the Torah. Lists of the top ten most influential people of history are unanimous in recognizing his importance. Scholars may not be able to decide whether or not he really existed, but all are in agreement as to his importance.

Engraving, by Doré, of Moses breaking the Tables of the Law. *Fortean Picture Library.*

The problem with discovering the historical Moses is one common to religious heroes. All we really know about him comes from the Bible and nowhere else. He appears first in the book of Exodus, wrapped in a wonderful story about his birth and upbringing. A king, or pharaoh, had arisen in Egypt "who knew not Joseph," a Hebrew whose influence in Egypt had encouraged peace between the peoples (see Joseph). The Hebrews, so blessed at the end of Genesis, had, four hundred years later, fallen on hard times. Forced to serve as slaves living in the Egyptian ghetto town known as Goshen, they were punished severely if their daily quota of brick-making fell short.

Moses in Egypt

When Pharaoh ordered that the first-born sons of the Jewish slaves be killed, Moses' father and mother, Amram and Jochebed, gave him up to the hands of either fate or God. In the hope that someone would find the baby Moses and raise him, they wrapped him in swaddling clothes, placed him in a basket, and set him adrift on the Nile River.

Moses' sister kept careful watch on his progress downstream. It happened that Pharaoh's daughter was bathing at that moment and noticed the basket floating on the current. She did what many people do when picking up a helpless baby. She fell in love. She must have known that it was a Hebrew baby. And she must have suspected something was up when Moses' sister showed up just in time to tell her she knew of someone—Moses' mother—who was both willing and able to nurse the baby until he was old enough to move into Pharaoh's house.

Whatever happened—and the Bible characteristically leaves us free to decide for ourselves, thus guaranteeing endless centuries of people sitting around tables studying scripture—Moses was raised in the court of the king and grew to be one of the most important men in Egypt.

Therein lies one of the problems concerning Moses and the historical record. Egyptians have always been very good about recording history, especially the history of their kings. But there is no mention of Moses or the Hebrew people. None at all. Anywhere. Not even a defaced statue or a stray cuneiform tablet. Some explain Moses' absence by surmising that Egypt wasn't likely to record for posterity the humiliation of a Pharaoh who raised a very ungrateful Moses as his own. Others point out that one would at least expect to find that someone rewrote the story, slanting it in a way that would defend Pharaoh and cast aspersions on "Moses the ingrate," especially in light of what happens next in the story.

So far, all we have to go on is an account written possibly years, and more probably centuries, after the event. And any lawyer could persuade a jury that the testimony of the scriptures, written perhaps by Moses and certainly by Jewish authors, was biased toward the Hebrew point of view. But the tradition is so strong it refuses to go away. So it becomes, like so many other religious points of view, a matter of faith.

At any rate, Moses grew to adulthood thinking himself a very important person. But blood is thicker than Egyptian privilege. When Moses was about forty years old, he underwent a severe mid-life crisis. Seeing an Egyptian taskmaster beating a Hebrew slave, he was outraged and killed the Egyptian. Burying the body in the sands of the desert, he hoped the incident would pass unnoticed.

Of course, it didn't. A day later he became the talk of Goshen. Everyone knew what he had done. Moses was forced to flee for his life. In those days, you simply didn't defend Hebrew slaves. The thinking was that it tended to set a bad example.

Moses in Midian

So Moses went "home"—to the place where his ancestors had lived. He fled to Midian, where he spent another forty years tending the sheep of Jethro, the man whose daughter, Zipporah, became Moses' wife. Jethro is called "a priest of Midian," and here we find ourselves treading on some pretty believable historical ground. Given the subsequent warlike history between Israel and Midian, it's a fairly safe bet that later scribes wouldn't have invented a Midianite period for their beloved Moses unless such a story was widely believed to have been true. So if Moses really existed, chances are he stayed for a while in Midian.

Forty years, to be exact. We now have two periods consisting of one of the Bible's favorite symbolic numbers. Forty years in Egypt, forty years in Midian. But all quiet times come to an end in heroes' stories. And Moses was about to begin another forty-year period, the most important of his life.

Someone once said that Moses spent forty years thinking he was a somebody, forty years learning he was a nobody, and forty years discovering what God could do with a nobody. And it began in the most unlikely of places. If you were inventing this story, how could you ever think up a scenario in which Moses hears the voice of God coming out of a bush that "burned, but was not consumed" (see Burning Bush)? This is a real sticking point for Moses' detractors. The idea, which is so far-fetched it seems as though it must be a human invention, defies critical analysis just because it is so radical. Who would make up something like this if they wanted the story to appear believable?

But the Bible insists that it was by means of a burning bush that God gave Moses his marching orders, instructing Moses to tell Pharaoh to let God's people go. Moses was reluctant at first and full of excuses, pointing out that he was not a good speaker. God told him to bring his brother, Aaron, as his spokesperson. Moses finally agreed.

The Exodus

And so it began—the story retold every year by Jewish families celebrating Passover, perhaps the most famous liberation story ever told. It's called the Exodus (see Passover).

Moses traveled to Egypt to appear before the family that had raised him. Standing before Pharaoh, he declared God's intention to free the Israelites. Ten times Moses said, "Let my people go." Ten times Pharaoh refused. Ten times God sent plagues upon Egypt—the plagues that are recounted at every contemporary Passover celebration. The Nile was turned into blood. Frogs, gnats, and flies infested the land. Livestock died; boils broke out upon the people. Hail and locusts took their toll. Darkness covered the land. And still Pharaoh refused to release his slave laborers.

Finally the terrible tenth plague reaped its harvest. The firstborn of Egypt were killed by the angel of death. The Hebrew people had been warned, and those that heeded the word of God were prepared. They had carefully followed instructions that are, to this very day, remembered in symbol and story each Passover. A lamb had been slaughtered and roasted. Its blood had been sprinkled on the door posts and lintels of every Jewish house. The people were dressed for travel and had baked desert bread, unleavened bread, so they would be sustained on their journey into the wilderness.

Finally the moment of death was upon Egypt. Not even Pharaoh's firstborn son was spared. But as the Hebrew people listened to the eerie sounds of death spread from house to house throughout the land, they were spared when the angel of death, seeing the blood of the sacrificed lamb, "passed over" each Jewish home (hence the name of the Passover holiday) and went on to reap its deadly harvest.

Morning brought the glad news. They were free. They headed out toward the rising sun.

Upon reaching the Red Sea, however, they looked back to see that Pharaoh had changed his mind. The Egyptian soldiers in their chariots were in hot pursuit. The waters lay before the fleeing Jews. The armies were closing in from behind. Trapped between hammer and anvil, what could they do?

Moses showed them what to do, now and forever. "Trust in God!" was the message. "Have faith!" was the theme of the sermon. This moment was to be indelibly stamped upon their national memory and remembered when they later faced Assryian hoards, Babylonian armies, Roman butchers, and Nazi murderers.

"Remember this moment," said God.

And the impossible happened. With no hope in sight, they were forced to trust God. What they saw that day cemented them forever as the people of Abraham, Isaac, and Jacob—the chosen people of God. Moses stepped forward all alone and held up his staff. That's all. No incantations. No rituals. No elaborate preparations. Just acknowledge God and step back. Watch him go to work.

And the waters parted. Impossibly, the people found a path where a moment before there had been none. They crossed through on dry land. And with no human effort, with no human intervention at all, they were saved while Pharaoh and his armies drowned.

"Remember this moment," said God. And they did. Every year at Passover they still remember.

The story grew with the retelling. And therein lies the problem, at least for the literal minded. Did it ever happen? And if it did, did it happen like this?

Scholars are skeptical. The earliest account of the Exodus, they point out, doesn't mention Moses at all:

Sing to Yahveh, for he has triumphed gloriously;
The horse and his rider he has thrown into the sea. (Exodus 15:21)

And the ancient creed of Israel is similarly silent concerning the presence of Moses:

The Egyptians mistreated us and made us suffer, putting us to hard labor. Then we cried out to the Lord, the God of our fathers, and the Lord heard our voice and saw our misery, toil and oppression. So the Lord brought us out of Egypt with a mighty hand and an outstretched arm, with great terror and with miraculous signs and wonders. (Deuteronomy 26:5–8)

Conservatives point out that since Moses wrote both those passages, it stands to reason that he, a humble man, would decline to play up his own part in the drama. Liberals counter that Moses didn't write those passages, that they are examples of the earliest texts, woven into the fabric of the story much later by unknown scribes. In the end, some wonder, does it really matter? The story has inspired so many people and given hope to so many Jewish generations, let alone those of African slaves and Central American downtrodden masses, that its historical accuracy doesn't enter into the picture anymore. It has taken on a life of its own. In the end, the Exodus is a true story, whether or not it ever happened.

When literary criticism (see Literary Criticism/Historical Critical Method) began to filter down into Christian churches, it is said that a preacher tried to teach his congregation that the children of Israel really didn't cross through the Red Sea—it was the Sea of Reeds, only about a foot or so deep. The Hebrew people could go through because they were on foot. Pharaoh's armies bogged down because they were riding in heavy chariots.

"Hallelujah!" shouted one old saint from the back row. "That's an even bigger miracle. God drowned Pharaoh's whole army in only a foot of water!"

The story, like Moses, has a life of its own. And no one will ever disprove it.

The Wilderness and the Promised Land

Before Moses could lead the people into the Promised Land, they had to undergo basic training. For forty years they wandered in the wilderness. This is really where the religion of Judaism began. Moses received the law—both the Ten Commandments and the written law of Leviticus. Some ancient rabbis taught that Moses received a secret law as well, whispered in his ear by God himself. This law was passed on through Joshua to the scholars of later generations, who interpreted it and formed the rich oral traditions of Judaism. Plans for the great Temple were given in triplicate. The book of Exodus has God telling Moses how to build it, Moses telling the people what God said, and then a description of exactly how the instructions were carried out.

Ritual sacrifice began. Lessons were learned. Through it all, Moses built his reputation as prophet, priest, judge, lawgiver, intercessor, victor, exile, fugitive, shepherd, guide, healer, miracle worker, man of God, and rebel.

One psalmist wrote:

God made known his ways unto Moses,
His acts to the people of Israel. (Psalm 103:7)

One would think Moses would be given a hero's welcome into the Promised Land, carried there by ranks of heavenly hosts. But such was not the case. Moses, it seems, like all biblical heroes, had feet of clay. He never entered Canaan at all. And it wasn't a tragic accident that frustrated him. It was a punishment sent from God.

In Numbers 20, Moses had been told to give water to the people by speaking to a rock and calling forth the water. Instead, in his anger at the people for rebelling continually, he rather petulantly whacked the rock with his staff. Water came forth, all right, but Moses apparently angered God by not following directions.

"There on the mountain that you have climbed [Mount Nebo] you will die and be gathered to your people," God says to Moses. "This is because … you broke faith with me in the presence of the Israelites at the waters of Meribah Kadesh in the Desert of Zin and because you did not uphold my holiness among the Israelites" (Deuteronomy 32:50–52).

By this time in the story, after reading four books of the Bible, most readers are definitely on Moses' side and are appalled that God could be so strict in his judgment. After all Moses had done, couldn't God cut him some slack and let him set foot in the Holy Land at least once?"

Apparently not. God is a strict judge, and holiness is as holiness does. Moses got to look at Canaan, the Promised Land, from afar, but he wasn't allowed to set foot there.

God does give him a great obituary, though.

Since then no prophet has arisen in Israel like Moses, whom the Lord knew face to face, and who did all those miraculous signs and wonders the Lord sent him to do in Egypt.… No one has ever shown the mighty power or performed the awesome deeds that Moses did in the sight of all Israel. (Deuteronomy 34:10–12)

Moses' Influence

So what is the lesson? It's not always the arriving that's most important. Sometimes the prize is in the journey itself. Anwar Sadat once said, "He who cannot change the very fabric of his thought will never be able to change reality, and will never, therefore, make any progress." Moses changed the very fabric of Jewish thought. He not only freed the people from captivity, he set them on the road to becoming the first great monotheistic religion.

Some say Moses was influenced by a religious movement that arose during his time in Egypt. There was a brief period of Egyptian monotheism under Pharaoh Akhnaton from 1365 to 1355 BCE. If Moses lived during that time, goes the argument, he might have transferred the worship of the one Sun God to that of Yahveh.

Others believe Moses was not a monotheist at all. He just believed Yahveh, the god of the Jews, was the greatest god and would triumph over all other gods.

Perhaps there is something to this thought, because Moses' influence is not limited to Hebrew theology. Christians and Muslims have adopted him as a significant figure as well.

Christians point out that his very name points the way to Christianity. Moshea (the Hebrew name for Moses) means "Messiah," or "anointed one." It's the same as the Greek Christos or the English Christ. The English Jesus comes from the Latin Jesu, the Greek Iasous, and the Hebrew Joshua. So Jesus Christ is actually derived from Joshua/Moses. According to this typology, we have the team of Moses/Joshua, "Christ Jesus," freeing the people from slavery and leading them into the Promised Land.

Christians also put a different spin on why Moses couldn't enter the Promised Land himself. Moses represents the law—the Old Testament. It leads the way but cannot save anyone, according to Christian theology. Only grace can do that. So Moses, the law, leads people to a view of heaven but is not sufficient to let them enter.

According to Muslim theologians, Moses' ministry was to save his nation from slavery, equip them with a set of rules that would govern their society, establish a systematic corporate worship, and lead the people back to their homeland. But the people refused to submit. So God had to send yet another prophet, Muhammad.

Moses is revered by all three religions. Christians even look to a future appearance, bringing him back to finish what he started. In Matthew 17 he steps out of the pages of history to council Jesus atop the Mount of Transfiguration. In Revelation 11, though not mentioned by name, he appears to duplicate the miracle of turning water into blood, preparing the way for the Second Coming of Christ.

Perhaps these appearances are appropriate for one who died a suspicious death. All we learn from Deuteronomy is that Moses was buried by the hand of God somewhere in the mountains. In the New Testament book of Jude we read a strange passage about the archangel Michael "disputing with the devil about the body of Moses."

Ahad Ha'Am, a name used by Asher Ginzburg, an author, philosopher, and great leader of the Zionist movement, wrote these words about Moses, quoted in *An Anthology of Living Religions*:

> In my heart I dismiss all these questions [concerning the historical Moses] with one short and simple answer. This Moses, this hoary figure whose reality and essence you are trying to clarify, is not a matter for scholars such as you. We have a different Moses, our own Moses, the one whose form is writ large on the heart of our people from generation to generation and whose influence on our national life has not ceased from ancient times to now. Moses' historic reality does not depend upon your learned treatises. For even if you managed to prove beyond a shadow of a doubt that Moses the man never lived, or that he was not as he is depicted, this would not diminish by one iota the historical reality of the Moses ideal—the one who led us not only forty years through the Sinai desert, but thousands of years, through every desert we have crossed from the Exodus from Egypt to the present.

The following words, from Psalm 90, are attributed to Moses:

> Lord, you have been our dwelling place throughout all generations. Before the mountains were born or you brought forth the earth and the world, from everlasting to everlasting you are God. May the favor of the Lord rest upon us ... and establish the work of our hands.

Sources:

"Between Man and Fellow Man—Moses' Humility." *The Jewish Agency for Israel.* http://www.jafi.org.il/education/festivls/pesach/psruen04.html. September 15, 2003.

Bridger, David, ed. *The New Jewish Encyclopedia.* New York: Behrman House, 1962.

Bucke, Emory Stevens et al, eds. *The Interpreter's Dictionary of the Bible.* 4 vols. New York: Abingdon Press, 1962.

Fisher, Mary Pat and Lee W. Bailey. *An Anthology of Living Religions.* Upper Saddle River: Prentice Hall, 2000.

The Holy Bible, New International Version. Grand Rapids, MI: Zondervan Bible Publishers, 1978.

MOUNT OF TRANSFIGURATION *see* **Transfiguration, Mount of**

MUHAMMAD

(See also Islam)

Muhammad, founder of Islam, was born in 570 CE in Mecca, in what is now Saudi Arabia. At that time, Mecca was a commercial center, a cosmopolitan city filled with the hustle and bustle of caravans transporting fabulous wealth from Arabia all the way to Spain in the west and India in the east. It was also a city rich in sacred sites. The people had a vague idea that Abraham had traveled to Mecca with his son Ishmael. The Qur'an would later describe how the two of them had purified God's house, rebuilding the Kaaba (shrine) that had been destroyed by Noah's flood, but at this time it was a legend known only to a few. The black stone (probably a meteor; see Black Stone), which had fallen from heaven when Earth was cursed following the expulsion from Eden, was here. Even though the world had since experienced fifteen hundred years of ignorance, during which time God had tried in vain to get his unfaithful people to submit to his decrees, Mecca was full of religion. Situated right between two great world civilizations, the Byzantine and the Persian, almost every religion on Earth had been carried here by world travelers. Judea was not far away, and many Jews had fled here following the destruction of Jerusalem in 70 CE. Damascus, Caesarea, Antioch, and Alexandria were all flourishing Christian centers.

Christianity itself had recently been weakened by internal arguments about the nature of God. Christians couldn't seem to agree whether God was a trinity, three natures in one God, or a unity. Arguments, violent at times, were common when one camel driver would swear by the One, another would swear by the Three, and then both would begin swearing at each other. The fiercely monotheistic Zoroastrianism had its adherents, and many Bedouin people worshiped Allah, "the God," while recognizing many other local and cosmic Jinns (genies) as well. The moon, sun, trees, and sacred springs—like the mysterious well called Zamzam—all had their own spirits. At two special times during the year, all intertribal warfare ceased so that people could make a pilgrimage to Mecca, run back and forth between the two holy mountains, visit the standing stones, and participate in religious festivals.

All this is not to say there was any deeply held conviction about translating religion into ethical behavior. The people may have developed some highly sophisticated mathematics and poetry, but life was often violent, robbery was common, and even the most trivial incidents could spark tribal war that would last for generations.

The time was ripe for a new religion that would unify the Arabian tribes and bring order out of chaos while satisfying the spiritual hunger of the people.

In the midst of this volatile environment, a man named 'Abd al-Muttalib, who had a number of different wives from different clans, went searching for a bride for one

of his sixteen children. For his son 'Abdallah he obtained a woman named Amina. The newlyweds had only one child, and they named him Muhammad. 'Abdallah died, probably during Amina's pregnancy, so mother and child were left impoverished. Following the custom at such times, the child was given to a Bedouin clan so he could be introduced to desert culture. Muhammad was reunited with his mother when he was five years old, but she died soon after, so he grew up with his grandfather's people.

It must have been an exciting life for a young child. At least once he traveled with a caravan all the way to Syria. After that it was only natural for Muhammad to find employment in the caravan trade. He soon began to work for a wealthy widow who owned her own caravan "company," and it was not long before he so impressed his new boss that she married him. He was twenty-five years old and just starting out. She was fifteen years older than he, but she soon bore him six children, two of whom died in infancy.

Muhammad was now a respected member of Meccan society and might have remained a wealthy caravan merchant all his life were he not given to deep, spiritual contemplation. His wife's money allowed him the luxury of time to ponder religion and spirituality. He took to going out alone into the hills to spend hours, and then days, seeking God in the solitude of a cave on Mount Hira. On one of those trips his prayers were answered in a way even he could never have imagined. And the world has never been the same.

Eighteenth-century Turkish painting of Muhammad pledging daughter Fatimah to her cousin Ali in marriage. *The Art Archive/Turkish and Islamic Art Museum Istanbul/Harper Collins Publishers.*

Muslim tradition later would reveal that God had had his hand on this man from the very beginning. Mystical stories surround his conception and birth. 'Abdallah, it was recounted, had "a white blaze" between his eyes when he "went in to Amina," but it disappeared when Muhammad was conceived. The light of prophecy had been passed to the next generation. During Amina's pregnancy, a light shone from her that was so bright it could be seen as far away as Syria. At Muhammad's birth, two angels came to open his breast and clean his heart. They proceeded to put him on scales, balancing his life against one, then ten, then a hundred other men. Finally one angel cried out, "Leave him alone, for by God, if you weighed him against all his people he would outweigh them." A Christian monk named Bahira was said to have traveled to see him, discovering in the process that a "seal of prophecy" rested between Muhammad's shoulders.

These stories may sound fantastic, but they are no different from medieval stories surrounding the early years of Jesus, the Buddha, and Moses. They are typical of the legends that grow up around heroes.

Whether or not any of these things really happened, the story of Muhammad is spectacular enough to stand on its own. He was a deeply spiritual man who cared about God and understood that something needed to be done about the religious chaos of his times. Only a few men in history have been set apart to begin world religions or teach new ways of responding to the divine. Muhammad was one of them.

The Qur'an Revealed

When Muhammad was about forty years old he returned home late one night during the month of Ramadan. He had been visiting his cave of meditation and was deeply moved. He is reported to have said to his wife, "Cover me, Khadija, cover me!" He had had a vision. The angel Gabriel had appeared to him.

He came to me while I was asleep, with a coverlet of brocade whereon was some writing, and said, "Read!"

I said, "What shall I read?"

He pressed me with it so tightly that I thought it was death; then he let me go and said, "Read!"

I said, "What shall I read?"

He pressed me with it so tightly that I thought it was death; then he let me go and said, "Read!"

I said, "What shall I read?"

He pressed me with it the third time so that I thought it was death and said, "Read!"

I said, "What shall I read?"—and this I said only to deliver myself from him, lest he should do the same to me again.

He said,

"Read in the name of thy Lord who created,
Who created man of blood coagulated.
Read! Thy Lord is most beneficent,
Who taught by the pen,
Taught that which they knew not unto men." (Qur'an 96:1–5)

Throughout Muhammad's life he would continue to have these revelations. He would memorize them and later dictate them to a scribe who wrote them on parchment, stone, leaves, or anything else handy. Collected after Muhammad's death and bound in one volume, the world knows them today as the Qur'an, the holy scripture of Islam.

This kind of inspired writing is called oracular scripture. The words are understood by believers to come directly from the lips of God. Such is the holiness of such transcription that the words are never to be changed, even through translation. Many say they have read the Qur'an, but, according to Muslim tradition, unless they have read it in the original Arabic, they have not read it. All they have read is a translation. All quotations that claim to come from the Qur'an are not really holy scripture because they are translations, not the original as dictated from God through his angel.

The Early Years

As Muhammad grew in spiritual insight, it was only natural that he would try to teach his Meccan neighbors what he felt was Allah's message for them. But they refused to accept his teachings. His sermons were ridiculed. Although his wife, Khadija, believed him, along with his friend Abu Bakr, his cousin Ali, and Zayd, a freed slave, no one else would listen. After three years, the great world religion that was to become known as Islam had gained a total of about forty followers.

God had told Muhammad to preach ethical behavior. The people of Mecca were to give up the worship of false gods. They were to abstain from promiscuity and lust. They were to live virtuous lives, treating each other with fairness and kindness.

The reaction in the streets of Mecca was easy to predict. Such a manner of life would be bad for business. A lot of wealthy people had a lifestyle they enjoyed. They liked lust. Promiscuity was fun. Kindness was for wimps. Warfare was wholesome desert behavior. Muhammad? Who was he to try changing a way of life they had lived for centuries?

Muhammad preached at fairs and public meetings. He endured the taunts and jeers, eventually having to dodge rocks and stones thrown at him in anger. No one listened to him. The people wanted proof. They wanted to see a miracle.

"You have seen a miracle," was Muhammad's reply. "It is the Holy Qur'an."

"Not enough!" growled the crowds. And he was threatened with even more violence. They even tried to buy him off, but Muhammad insisted he wanted neither silver nor gold nor power. He just wanted them to repent and submit to the will of Allah.

In the midst of all this Muhammad continued to receive visions. One night Gabriel came to him, riding the magnificent steed al-Buraq, "white and long, larger than a donkey but smaller than a mule." Muhammad was taken to the "farthest mosque," and on to the seventh heaven wherein dwelt God himself. The first six levels were guarded by tested and famous personages such as Adam, Aaron, Moses, and Abraham. This mystical experience has become, for Muslims, a metaphor or model for the experience of the spiritual presence of God.

Islam Begins

Finally, in 622 CE, Muhammad realized he had to leave Mecca and establish a base somewhere else. The oasis town of Medina, about two hundred miles north of Mecca, had expressed an interest in the Prophet's message. On September 24, 622, Muhammad made his Hijrah, his pilgrimage, from Mecca to Medina. This is the date Islam is said to have begun, the first day of the Muslim calendar and the date from which all other time is measured. Muslims mark their calendar years AH, anno hegirae, "after the Hijrah."

Those who migrated with Muhammad were known as Muhajirun, the "emigrants." Those from Medina who received him were the Ansar, the "helpers." Together, they formed the community of Islam, the Ummah.

But there were those, even in Medina, who refused to accept Muhammad. The Jewish community understandably proved hostile to a new prophet. So most of the Jews were eventually expelled from the town. Some people accepted Muhammad's message only superficially and later came to be known as the party of the Hypocrites. Even within the faith there were disagreements. Some Ansar thought they were being treated less honorably than the Muhajirun.

Muhammad, however, continued to receive revelations, and Islam began to thrive. In only two years Muhammad felt the time was ripe to win Mecca to the true faith. The battle favored the Meccan army. Outnumbered three to one, the Islamic cause seemed to be lost. But the Prophet had received a message:

> Assuredly God will defend those who believe; surely God loves not any ungrateful traitor. Leave is given to those who fight because they were wronged—surely God is able to help them—who were expelled from their habitations without right, except that they say "Our Lord is God." (Qur'an 22:38–40)

In the battle of Badr, God gave the Medina Muslims victory. This was the turning point for the Muslim community, the proof that Allah would carry out his divine will through Muhammad and the new faith of Islam. The Arabian tribes were finally united. The jihad, the holy war against apostasy, had begun. Damascus fell in 635, Persia a year later, Jerusalem two years after that. Egypt, Spain, North Africa, the Middle East, India, even some of China soon followed. Europe remained free of Muslim control only because Charles Martel turned back the Islamic "desert riders" at the famous battle of Tours in 732.

Muhammad, meanwhile, continued to lead the new religion through moral example and extremely persuasive preaching. Emissaries were sent everywhere in the known world. "People of the Book," Jews and Christians, were asked to submit to the God they had ignored. The Holy Prophet's message was clear. There was to be no warfare, no killing, unless people simply refused to obey the commands of Allah. Only then was warfare justified.

Muhammad himself destroyed the idols of Mecca. His armies did the rest. Allah finally received the respect he deserved.

In March of 632 Muhammad made his final pilgrimage to Mecca. The city had by now been purged of all idolatry. Many of the ancient practices were now given new meaning. The people still circled the Kaaba seven times. They still kissed the Black Stone and ran back and forth between the two hills. They still threw pebbles at the stone pillars and drank from the sacred well of Zamzam. But these activities no longer were considered pagan rituals. They were now the sacred response of submission to Allah.

Shortly after returning to Medina, Muhammad became sick. Some say it was an aftereffect of an earlier assassination attempt by outraged members of the Jewish community. Others dismiss such a claim. Whatever it was, Muhammad recognized he was dying. In what proved to be his final sermon, he said:

> O men, the fire is kindled, and rebellions come like the darkness of night. By God, you can lay nothing to my charge. I allow only what the Qur'an allows and forbid only what the Qur'an forbids.

A few hours later, in June of 632 (AH 10), he died in the arms of his young wife, 'Aisha. A mosque was later built to mark the place of his burial.

The people naturally were confused. A messianic rumor began to circulate that somehow he would come back to life and return to lead the Muslim movement.

But Abu Bakr put such talk to rest. At Muhammad's funeral service, according to Robert S. Ellwood and Barbara A. McGraw in *Many Peoples, Many Faiths*, Abu Bakr cried out to the faithful:

> O ye people, if anyone worships Muhammad, Muhammad is dead, but if anyone worships Allah, he [Allah] is alive and dies not!

Muhammad was not divine or a son of God. He was simply a prophet. In this sense he is a model for every Muslim. He lived his life in submission to Allah, as all Muslims are called to do. He considered his religion to be the continuing evolution of Judaism into Christianity, and Christianity into Islam. During his final pilgrimage to Mecca he summed up his philosophy and outlined a path into the future:

> I have left you with something which if you hold fast to it you will never fall into error—a plain indication, the book of God and the practice of His prophet, so give good heed to what I say. Know that every Muslim is a Muslim's brother, and that the Muslims are brethren.

Sources:

Ellwood, Robert S., and Barbara A. McGraw. *Many Peoples, Many Faiths*. 6th ed. Upper Saddle River, NJ: Prentice Hall, 1999.

Fisher, Mary Pat, and Lee W. Bailey. *An Anthology of Living Religions*. Upper Saddle River, NJ: Prentice Hall, 2000.

The Holy Qur'an, trans. with a commentary by Abdullah Yusuf Ali. Beirut, Lebanon: Dar Al Arabia, 1968.

Ludwig, Theodore M. *The Sacred Paths: Understanding the Religions of the World*. 2nd ed. Upper Saddle River, NJ: Prentice Hall, 1996.

NATION OF ISLAM *see* Black Muslims

NATIVE AMERICAN CHURCH

In one sense, the Native American Church began in 1918, when James Mooney, an anthropologist from the Smithsonian Institution, testified before congressional hearings held concerning the issue of sacramental use of peyote by indigenous people in the American Southwest. As a result of those meetings, he advised members of various Oklahoma tribes to obtain a legal charter to protect their rights as an organized religion. The Native American Church was incorporated that very year.

But incorporation just expresses the official legal definition of when a religion begins. To better understand what the church is all about, we have to go back about ten thousand years to discover the first use of peyote.

Peyote is often called a mushroom, but it is actually a small, spineless cactus native to the American Southwest. Chances are it began to attract attention as soon as the first hunter-gatherers discovered that brewing it in a tea or chewing very small amounts produced an altered way of thinking that seemed to place the user in a heightened spiritual state. Peyote cactus buttons found in ancient human-occupied caves have been carbon-dated back as far as seven thousand years. The Huichol Indians of Mexico were making peyote-collecting pilgrimages into southern Texas by at least 200 BCE as part of a religious quest.

Some people view peyote simply as a hallucinogenic used by people who want to "get high" while using religion as their justification. Timothy Leary's reputation in the 1960s certainly gave that impression to folks in suburbia. But a careful study of the history of peyote use reveals a deeply sacramental ritual hedged in by religious rules and regulations going way back into ancient times. Some of these customs, adapted and filtered through Christian symbolism, have been rediscovered by the Native American Church, which now boasts some eighty chapters comprising members of at least seventy Native American nations.

Every state west of the Mississippi has at least one chapter, and the total membership of the church is estimated to be about 250,000 people. Much of the church's worship centers around singing, accompanied by small drums and gourd rattles. The singing is usually in a native language and dialect, but sometimes phrases like "Jesus is the Savior" will be heard in English. At these meetings, it is explained that peyote is a gift from God, a sacrament that not only places minds otherwise cluttered with cultural baggage and "busyness" into a spiritual state, but also counters cravings for alcohol and relieves day-to-day tensions. It is believed to cure various illnesses, many of them induced through the anxiety of poverty and hopelessness that has for so long been a fact of reservation life.

Peyote is not, however, usually taken just to induce visions. As a weak peyote tea is passed around, always clockwise according to Native American symbolism, participants are free to interpret Bible passages according to their own understanding, share their thoughts and beliefs, and express community through prayer vigils that usually last through the night. The idea is that the mind normally works in a manner conducive to everyday, waking reality. To contemplate spiritual things, it has to be moved out of its groove, so to speak, and elevated to a higher plane.

A typical response from non-Indian people is, "Sure. One big group trip!" It's difficult for people to respond to that which they have not experienced in the normal course of their daily lives. Perhaps it is impossible. So most Native Americans are justifiably careful when it comes to talking about their church meetings. It doesn't help, either, that certain well-publicized criminal court cases have been launched by Indian prisoners who may or may not simply be exploiting religious freedom to gain a temporary chemical release from prison drudgery. It would be a mistake, too, to think that peyote use among people of all races and religious traditions is limited to sacramental expression. Certainly it has a recreational following as well.

But ingesting peyote, to Native American Church members, is no different from Catholics drinking wine at Mass. Peyote is not just a plant. It is believed to be the very heart of the Creator, just as wine symbolizes the blood of the Creator in Christianity. The Creator had great compassion for his people. Christianity teaches that through his great love he entered the world as a man. Ancient Huichol belief was that the Creator died and was reborn as the peyote plant so that the people could obtain wisdom and understanding not possible in normal daily life. The Aztec people, culturally related to the Huichol, named the plant *peyoti*, which denoted the pericardium, or the lining of the heart. This reflects the Huichol belief that peyote embodies the Creator's heart.

When Spanish priests discovered what peyote was, they instituted the laws of the Inquisition to punish those who used it. It was strictly forbidden, but people kept secretly using it anyway. The religion migrated to the north, to the Apache, the Commanche, and the Kiowa people. By 1880 two religions were spreading throughout the Indian nations. One was the Ghost Dance (see Ghost Dance). The other was the peyote cult.

Perhaps it is easiest for people of non-Indian cultures to understand when they try to put themselves into the mind of a people who were defeated, slaughtered, and forced to live in what amounted to detention centers. Their religion was totally wiped out, and they were forced to daily bear the indignities of lost freedom and cultural identity. They searched for their roots, asking the question, "What do we do now?"

Their practical answer, like that of the African slaves in the American South, was to accept from Christian culture that which they felt was important, while at the same time adapting their own cultural symbols and producing a spiritual philosophy that satisfied them.

The Native American Church today stresses certain cultural truths and ethics. Abstaining from alcohol is one. Faithfulness to one's spouse and fulfilling family obligations is another. It is, for example, simply impossible for some Native Americans to understand how affluent white folks can leave grandma in a rest home somewhere. Self-sufficiency is an important doctrine, as are praying for the sick and, above all, praying for peace.

Sources:
Fikes, Jay. "A Brief History of the Native American Church." *Council on Spiritual Practices*.
   http://www.csp.org/communities/docs/fikes-nac_history.html. September 14, 2003.
Smith, Huston. *One Nation Under God*. Santa Fe, NM: Clear Light Publishers, 1998.

NAVAJO *see* **Kiva**

NEO-ORTHODOXY/NEO-PAGANISM

"Neo" means "new." So when someone chooses to use the word as a prefix to an established religious tradition, you can bet there are changes in store. The idea behind the use of the word is that traditions can easily get cemented in old-fashioned language and cultural habits. Things that made sense hundreds of years ago may sound, to twenty-first-century ears, quaint rather than intrinsically important.

Bishop James Ussher (1581–1656), for instance, thought the world was created over the course of one week in October in the year 4004 BCE (see Creationism). That was the orthodox view of his day, the early 1600s. Today there are people who disagree with his date, but not necessarily with his ideas about a higher power behind the creation of the universe. So they want to maintain certain Christian principles while updating their interpretation. In other words, they seek a "new" orthodoxy for today that unites eternal scriptural principles with modern scientific discoveries.

In the same way, orthodox pagans of ancient Europe probably personified deities of mountain and forest. Neo-pagans today are more apt to think in terms of nonpersonal forces at work in the cosmos. These powers are as real as gravity and electricity, but, unlike the ancient deities, they don't have faces and don't speak in an audible voice.

So whenever "neo" precedes a term describing a belief system, it reflects an attempt to maintain that belief system's underlying philosophical structure, perhaps even its practical application, while rethinking its language and cultural images.

Sources:
Ludwig, Theodore M. *The Sacred Paths: Understanding the Religions of the World.* 2nd ed. Upper Saddle River, NJ: Prentice Hall, 1996.

NEOPLATONISM *see* Augustine

NEPHTHYS *see* Egyptian Gods and Goddesses

NEW AGE RELIGIONS

A lot of ink is used up attempting to describe New Age religions. There are so many movements, groups, cults, and sects falling under the rubric that it is impossible to deal with them all. But certain categories do recur consistently.

Channeling

Many New Age movements believe spirit entities speak, or are "channeled," through receptive humans. In the popular series of "Seth" books, for instance, Jane Roberts claims to be channeling Seth. In *Seth Speaks*, Seth describes himself this way:

> If you believe firmly that your consciousness is locked up somewhere inside your skull and is powerless to escape it, if you feel that your consciousness ends at the boundaries of your body, then you sell yourself short, and you will think I am only a delusion. I am no more a delusion than you are.

> I can say this to each of my readers honestly: I am older than you are, at least in terms of age as you think of it.

> If a writer can qualify as any kind of authority on the basis of age, therefore, then I should get a medal. I am an energy personality essence, no longer focused in physical matter. As such, I am aware of some truths that many of you seem to have forgotten.

> I hope to remind you of these.

Whether the spiritual entities were once human, or whether they even once existed on Earth, they claim to have messages for the human race. Unable to physically put pen to paper, they must find receptive conduits through whom they are able to funnel their message. Because there are more and more entities being channeled into books nowadays, it is thought by many New Age believers that a cosmic shift of emphasis is upon us, and that the time of our particular mode of human understanding is getting short.

Eastern Movements

When the popular actress Shirley MacLaine published her best-selling memoir *Out on a Limb*, in which she claimed past life experiences, the Hindu concept of reincarnation (see Hinduism) was reintroduced to the mainstream American public. Since then, many Hindu and Buddhist practices, such as yoga and meditation techniques, have been given a Western twist and a new hearing. The Beatles came back from a trip to the East with sitar music and a guru, along with George Harrison's song

"My Sweet Lord," dedicated to Krishna. It didn't take long for the mainstream Christian population to adapt their religion, in the name of evangelism and attracting a younger audience. Soon Christian Bible study groups began to discover that David practiced transcendental meditation in the Psalms and John the Baptist was the reincarnated Elijah. "My Sweet Lord," cleaned up a little, began to appear regularly even in Roman Catholic liturgy. East had been brought West—Americanized, to the great dismay of an older generation—and a new trend began.

UFO Cults

On December 26, 2002, a group called the Raelian movement appeared on the cable television network CNN, claiming to have cloned the first human baby. Details were sketchy, at best, and the scientific community greeted the announcement with scorn. Five months later, Raja Mishra of the *Boston Globe* reported that "there are plenty of people who are gullible, who believe ... and may fall victim to their scheme." Indeed, dues-paying Raelian membership had increased by 10 percent, and dozens of people paid up to $200,000 apiece for the privilege of cloning themselves or loved ones when they learned that Raelian religious doctrine teaches that the human race began when a group of extraterrestrials began fiddling with our DNA a few million years ago.

Many have speculated that only a brush with beings from another planet could unite the populations of Earth. They may be on to something, because following the announcement by the Raelians, U.S. senators as far apart as the liberal Ted Kennedy from Massachusetts and the conservative Orrin Hatch from Utah partnered a bill aimed at banning human cloning. But not all religious groups followed the ecumenical lead of Kennedy and Hatch. The National Right to Life committee, in favor of the bill, found themselves opposing the Orthodox Jewish Congregations of America, who opposed it.

Other New Age UFO groups (see, for example, Heaven's Gate and Hale-Bopp in the Cult entry) look to the stars to define their religious beliefs. And their numbers seem to be multiplying with each passing year. Ever since Erich von Daniken's *Chariots of the Gods* became a popular success in the 1970s, introducing the theory that ancient Earth had been visited by aliens, many people have turned to the Bible to seek "proof" of alien visitations misunderstood by the biblical authors. Take, for example, the experience of Ezekiel, excerpted from Ezekiel 1:

> I saw a windstorm coming out of the north—an immense cloud with flashing lightning and surrounded by brilliant light. The center of the fire looked like glowing metal, and in the fire was what looked like four living creatures. In appearance their form was like that of a man.... I saw a wheel on the ground beside each creature ... they sparkled like chrysolite.... Their rims were high and awesome ... spread above their heads was what looked like an expanse, sparkling like ice and awesome. Above the expanse over their heads was what looked like a throne of sapphire, and high above on the throne was a figure like that of a man ... and I heard a voice speaking.

If this wasn't a passage from the revered Holy Bible but had just been discovered as a fragment of text from early times, an honest reading would certainly raise interesting questions.

This is not the only example. Elijah was taken up from Earth into the "heavens," or sky, by "a fiery chariot." He later appeared to three witnesses on a mountain (see Transfiguration, Mount of). Could this be a description of what we now call alien abduction? The story becomes more intriguing when we read of the solitary death of Moses. He walked up into the mountains following the command of a voice he heard speaking from the Ark of the Covenant. When he returned from the place where he communed with this voice, his face glowed as if from radiation or sunburn. Then he disappeared. No one saw him again until he appeared with Elijah to talk to Jesus on the mountain. There the two of them stepped out of and were surrounded by a great light, with glowing raiment covering their bodies. Separated from its sacred context, this might indeed sound like an extraterrestrial encounter.

Golden Age Movements

Did Atlantis really exist? And if so, did Atlantians know something about God we have forgotten? Was there an "age of the goddess" (see Goddess Worship)? Many New Age movements think so. For example, they are interested more in *why* Stonehenge was built than *how* it was built. Were ancient builders in tune with spiritual powers we need to understand today? Neo-paganism would like to see a return to a pre–Judeo-Christian/Roman age when people were supposedly more in tune with Mother Earth. An element of this kind of thinking appears in Judeo-Christian belief as well. Eden, was, after all, a "golden age" before sin entered the world.

Many other kinds of religious movements fall under the New Age category. Robert Ellwood and Barbara McGraw, in their book *Many Peoples, Many Faiths*, identify categories they label reactive movements, accommodationist movements, spirit movements, new revelation sects, import religions, and hybrid movements. They summarize these movements as follows:

> Basic features of new religious movements are likely to be: a different but recognizable doctrine; a practice centered on a single, simple, sure technique or a creative group process and practice; a charismatic founding and leadership and/or an intense, highly demanding group. On the other hand, they may involve a diffuse type of influence that is not directly competitive with mainstream religion. In every case, though, a new religious movement must offer inner rewards sufficiently effective and convincing to compensate for a break with conventional faith.

Sources:
Ellwood, Robert S., and Barbara A. McGraw. *Many Peoples, Many Faiths*. 6th ed. Upper Saddle River, NJ: Prentice Hall, 2002.
Neerguard, Lauren. "Cloning Ban to Face Debate." *Boston Sunday Globe*, December 29, 2002.
Roberts, Jane. *Seth Speaks*. San Rafael, CA: Amber-Allen Publishing and New World Library, 1994.

NICHIREN *see* **Buddhism, Development of**

NIHON SHOKI *see* Shinto Texts

NIHONGI *see* Shinto Texts

NOAH'S FLOOD

The Lord saw how great man's wickedness on the earth had become, and that every inclination of the thoughts of his heart was only evil all the time. The Lord was grieved that he had made man on the earth, and his heart was filled with pain. So the Lord said, "I will wipe mankind, whom I have created, from the face of the earth—men and animals, and creatures that move along the ground, and birds of the air—for I am grieved that I have made them." But Noah found favor in the eyes of the Lord.

Many religions have mythological flood epics recounting either local or worldwide deluges that destroyed Earth a long time ago. But the story of Noah's flood is possibly the most famous. It is found in the biblical book of Genesis, beginning in chapter five, and it can be summarized by categories.

The Reasons for the Flood

It is often said the flood was sent because of human wickedness. But the Bible throws in a mysterious verse that raises questions.

When men began to increase in numbers on the earth and daughters were born to them, the sons of God saw that the daughters of men were beautiful, and they married any of them they chose.... The Nephilim were on the earth in those days—and also afterward—when the sons of God went to the daughters of men and had children by them. They were the heroes of old, men of renown. The Lord saw how great man's wickedness on the earth had become....

Now what's this all about? Speculation runs rampant. Who are the "sons of God"? What are "Nephilim," a word often translated as "giants"?

It depends, of course, on your hermeneutics, your method of interpretation. Literalists say one thing, metaphorists another. Some insist the "sons of God" were demons, fallen angels. When they had sex with the "daughters of men," children of demonic fathers were born. These offspring were either monstrous "giants," or they were the inspiration for heroes of the various pantheons of gods later enshrined in myth by the Greeks and Romans. Others claim the "sons of God" were the offspring of the "godly" line of Seth, the son of Adam and Eve who was born after the death of Abel. The "daughters of men" were the offspring of the wicked Cain, who murdered his brother.

Still others, of course, insist the whole thing is simply another case of an author quoting from some long-lost source we don't know about, so we can never know the story that was probably familiar to the original audience.

For centuries the "giants of Genesis" were credited with all sorts of feats. They built Stonehenge. They set up the many standing stones that dot the eastern shores of Europe. Some stories even had them building the stone statues of Easter Island.

Whatever the reason, God didn't like what had happened. It wasn't just human sin that caused the great flood. Obviously the author of Genesis had something else in mind.

The Mechanics of the Flood

"Okay," say the skeptics. "Where did the water come from—and where did it go afterward?"

Well, there are many ideas floated about this, too.

If it was really just a local flood that was misunderstood to be worldwide in scope, perhaps we're reading about the formation of the Mediterranean Sea. Or maybe the Bible is telling us about flooding around the area of the Black Sea. Still others read into this story proof of the flood that destroyed Atlantis.

Others go a little further out on a limb. The Bible says this is a worldwide flood. That means we need to find a bigger source for all the water.

Perhaps Genesis 1 gives us a hint. The waters of creation were separated into the waters "above the firmament" and the waters "below the firmament." Maybe a water canopy, possible in the form of ice, surrounded the planet. Maybe Earth once had rings like Saturn. And for a trigger point, perhaps the whole planet was once perpendicular on its axis, creating a "greenhouse effect" with moderate, constant seasons from pole to pole. That would explain the climate of the Garden of Eden and perhaps even account for the longer life spans of the early heroes of Genesis. All God had to do to set the flood in motion was to tilt the Earth to its present twenty-three and a half degrees. Then the whole canopy would collapse in the form of rain for forty days. It's the tilt of the Earth that gives us seasons, after all, and that would explain why the author tells us that after the flood, Earth would forever after have "seed time and harvest, cold and heat, summer and winter … as long as the earth endures." It could also explain what happened to the dinosaurs, why there are marine fossils high in the Rocky Mountains, and where oil deposits came from.

But that's still a lot of water. Where did it all go? Perhaps it just settled back into its present location. Maybe Earth was originally mostly land. And it took a while for all that water to drain down to its proper depth. And, by the way, isn't coastal flooding what all the global warming people are warning us about? Maybe the waters of Noah's flood are locked up in the polar ice caps.

The Account of Noah

Genesis claims the entire population of the world was destroyed. All but eight people—Noah, Noah's wife, their three sons, and their sons' wives—perished. From Shem, Ham, and Japheth, the sons of Noah, descended all the modern races. Noah also took on board two of each of the "unclean" animals, those that weren't kosher, and seven of each of the "clean" animals. In other words, seven sheep but only two pigs; seven cows but only two lobsters (see Kosher). From this menagerie came every animal that now exists on Earth. Those that weren't included are now extinct.

They were crammed into an ark some 450 feet long, 75 feet wide, and 45 feet high. The boat was meant to float, not sail.

Is that big enough? Well, there are no end to models, both wood and computer generated, that have been built in order to "prove" it would be possible.

At any rate, the Bible insists it was Noah's home for the forty days and nights of rain, augmented by water from "all the springs of the great deep." The highest mountains were covered to "a depth of twenty feet." Then the waters took an additional "one hundred and fifty days" to recede. To find out when dry land was available to settle, Noah first sent out a raven, then a dove. The dove returned, unable to find a place to rest. A week later, another dove returned with an olive leaf in its beak. Finally, a third dove was sent out and failed to return. On the first month of Noah's 601st year, the earth was dry enough for him to come out of the ark, build an altar, offer a sacrifice, plant a vineyard, make some wine, and get drunk.

Does the Ark Still Exist?

Many books tell the stories of those who claim they have seen the remnants of the ark on Mount Ararat. Their descriptions have prompted a lot of high-powered excursions and well-funded expeditions. People take this seriously because Jesus said, in Matthew 24:37, "As it was in the days of Noah, so it will be at the coming of the Son of Man." In other words, the discovery of the ark would be a reminder, a good sign that the Second Coming is near. Besides this, it would support the conservative position that the Bible can be interpreted in a literal manner.

Although rumors of its final resting place are found way back in antiquity, the first modern sighting seems to have been reported by a Russian pilot in 1917. But his report was buried in government archives until the 1940s. In 1955 a French antiques dealer named Fernand Navarra claimed to have climbed to the site, removed some wood from a beam, and returned to have it analyzed. Initial reports said it was oak, at least 5,000 years old. Later, with the invention of radio carbon dating, estimates were upgraded to about 700 CE, far too late to have been from Noah's time.

Since then, "ark-aeologists" have built a whole cottage industry around finding what would be one of the greatest discoveries of all time. Various theories have been posed, the most popular being that the ark, now frozen in a glacier, has split into two halves, one of which has been carried farther down Mount Ararat. Satellite photos have been studied and some people claim a shadowy shape can be discerned during warm summers. But the ark remains an elusive goal.

So what can be said to summarize the search for the ark and the historical truth of Noah's flood?

As with all Bible stories, it comes down to interpretation. Those who read the Bible as they would a history text insist the flood was a real, worldwide catastrophe that happened just as Genesis says it did.

Others tend to think it may be a written rendition of oral history—memories of a long-forgotten local flood that was big enough to have seemed to be universal in scope to those who experienced it. A lot of flood stories exist, after all. Most religions around the world have similar myths. True, this may be proof of a universal flood. But it may also point to one big event that happened somewhere around the area of the

Middle East, the memory of which diffused with migrating people wherever they went. Still others believe the flood is a mythological rendering of the human psyche, perhaps arising out of our birth experience.

Sources:

The Holy Bible, New International Version. Grand Rapids, MI: Zondervan Bible Publishers, 1978.
James, Peter, and Nick Thorpe. *Ancient Mysteries.* New York: Ballantine Books, 1999.

NORNS *see* **Norse Gods and Goddesses**

NORSE GODS AND GODDESSES

A lot of early Norse religion is forever lost to us. Without a written record we can only speculate about what the Germanic and Slavic people of northern Europe thought of the hereafter, and about their interaction with gods and goddesses who appear briefly in the writings of early Christian monks.

But the time of the Vikings is recalled in the sagas written down by Snori Sturlson at the beginning of the thirteenth century. These sagas are full of heroic tales about Odin, Thor, and the Valkyries. They reveal a pre-Christian insight into the religion of the hardy Norsemen and -women.

The Norse pantheon was as rich and populated as that of Canaan, Babylon, and Egypt. But a few Norse gods and goddesses have been enshrined in popular imagination, thanks to the many paintings based on oral legends of the time and on the decorative beauty and grace of the famous dragon ships of Viking lore.

Norse theology was rich in ring lore—the famous Rings of Power that gave the bearer insights, strength, and magical abilities. They would bring good gifts if used wisely, but tragedy if they were used for greed or corruption. The plot of Richard Wagner's famous opera cycle, *The Ring of the Nibelung,* involves such a ring. The hero, Siegfried, won the cursed ring, Andvarinaut, after slaying the dragon, Fafnir. Although he himself was innocent, Siegfried got caught up in a tragedy involving Brynhild, the fallen Valkyrie. This tale inspired some of the greatest Wagnerian music ever written.

Odin (Woden or Wotan)

One-eyed Odin is the father of the gods and men. He is usually pictured wearing either a floppy hat, which makes him look something like author J. R. R. Tolkien's character Gandalf, or his famous horned Viking helmet. He keeps watch over the nine realms of the Nordic world with the help of his two ravens, Huginn and Munin ("Thought" and "Memory"), who fly daily through the heavens and return with the latest news. Odin is married to Frigga, the mother of all, who spins out daily life on her sacred distaff and knows the future. At least she says she does. No one knows for sure because she never tells anyone what it is.

They have a son named Baldur who is an interesting bridge to Christianity. He lived in Asgard, the home of the gods, with his wife, Nanna, goddess of joy. But he was sacrificed one midsummer when his half-brother Hodur, guided by Loki, the trickster, killed him with a dart made out of mistletoe. He will be reborn at Jul ("Yul") and cleanse Earth of evil at the end of time. Thus we see another religion wherein the good son of God is sacrificed by his evil counterpart, only to return in Messiah-like fashion to straighten things out in the end.

Odin is the god who gathers up the faithful who die in battle, transporting them to the great hall in Valhalla, where they will be available to fight in his army at the final battle of Ragnarok. Many of those fallen faithful were called *berserkers*, warriors who gave rise to the term "going berserk" because of their ritual battle lust and shield-biting frenzy.

We still remember Odin each week. Wednesday, which comes from the word Wodensdaeg, "Wodin's day," is his sacred day.

To gain knowledge and power, Odin once crucified himself, hanging for nine days on Yggdrasil, the World or Cosmic Tree, and cast his eye into Mimir's well in return for a drink that bestowed "immense wisdom." The parallels with Christianity—crucifixion and the "water of life"—have provoked a lot of interest.

Statue of Thor, Norse god of thunder, by B. E. Fogelberg. Thor is also the god of the common man who is called on for protection, health, agriculture, and justice. *Fortean Picture Library.*

Thor

Thor, the "Thunderer," was Odin's son. In some cultures he supplanted Odin as the favorite god. He was the one who produced thunder and lightning when he wielded his mighty hammer, Mjollnir. He is the personification of strength, and his chariot is pulled across the sky by two goats. Thor is the rugged individualist, prototype of the fierce Viking warrior. Thursday (Thorsdaeg, "Thor's day") is his sacred day.

Freyja and Freyr

Freyja is the goddess of love and beauty, which works out well because her twin brother Freyr is the horned god of fertility—a fortunate combination. Whereas both Odin and Thor were of the race of gods known as the Aesir, Freyja and Freyr are of the race known as the Vanir. The Vanir were thought to have been older than the Aesir, and the two races fought at first. But they made peace long enough to see the Vanir begin to fade. And that was a pity, because they were the ones associated with wealth, peace, and good weather. Apparently, as the Norse began to raid farther and farther afield, warlike tendencies replaced more peaceful pursuits.

Freyja is the queen of the Valkyries. The cat is her symbol, and her prized possession was the necklace Brisingamen, a gift she obtained when she slept with the four dwarves who made it. Friday (Frejyasdaeg, "Freyja's day") is her sacred day (though some say the day is named after Frigga, Odin's wife).

Freyja's brother Freyr is known as the King of the Elves. The boar is his sacred animal, and Gullenbursti, the "Golden Boar" or sun, is seen each morning at sunrise. Both the English and the Swedish are said to be his descendants.

Loki

Loki is the trickster as well as the god of fire. He is neither Aesir nor Vanir but comes from the race known as Ettins ("elementals"). As a result, he has both demonic and helpful qualities. On the one hand, he is capable of giving the gods fits. But sometimes he gets them out of trouble when they need a practical hand adjusting the weather or dealing with daily life in the world. He also creates some of the meanest monsters ever seen on the face of the earth.

The Norns

These are the fates. They determine the *orlogs* ("destinies") of both gods and humans, and they take care of Yggdrasil, the Sacred World or Cosmic Tree.

Hel (Holle or Hulda)

Hel is, as you might guess, the goddess of the afterlife. The Norse picture her as half dead and half alive, and view her, understandably, with great trepidation.

There are many other gods in the pantheon. Bragi is the bard and muse of poetry. Weiland is a smith and crafter of Odin's sword. Eostre (a good candidate for the root of the name Easter, the Christian spring holiday of Resurrection) is the goddess of spring and fertility. Her symbols are the Eostre bunny and Eostre egg. Also from this religious mythology come the stories of Beowulf, dwarves, elves, and the legend of Baba Yaga.

Did the Vikings ever carry any of these myths to America, leaving only stories, some runes, and blue-eyed children as evidence of their journey? Well, there are American Indian legends strikingly similar to some of these stories, and tales of blond, blue-eyed, metal-shirted gods are found from the Mississippi River valley and western Oklahoma all the way to Canada. There is even an interesting European DNA gene found in some New England Algonkian tribal ancestors. But until definitive archaeological proof is found, the legends remain mysteries lost in the mists of time.

Sources:
Cotterell, Arthur, and Rachel Storm. *The Ultimate Encyclopedia of Mythology*. China: The Annes Publishing Company, Hermes House, 1999.
"Meet the Gods and Goddesses of the Norse Pantheon." *Barbarian's Norse Religion Page*. http://www.wizardrealm.com/norse/gods.html. September 15, 2003.

Nun

Nun is a term used to describe a woman who has professed vows of poverty, chastity, and obedience within the Roman Catholic tradition. Technically it applies to women living in a cloistered community, but it is now often used to refer to religious women active in ministry to the world. The more traditional term for such women is "sister." Orders for women were established by Saints Basil, Benedict, Augustine, and Francis. Today nuns carry out much of the behind-the-scenes work of education and ministering to the sick and needy.

Sources:

Douglas, J. D., ed. *The New International Dictionary of the Christian Church.* Grand Rapids, MI: Zondervan Publishing, 1974.

NUT *see* **Egyptian Gods and Goddesses**

OCCULT

The word occult means "to hide from view" or "to conceal." Occult practices are those that claim to deal, in a secret or hidden manner, with supernatural forces or agencies. In the religious sense, "the occult" is usually applied to those secret rituals that attempt to worship, serve, or invoke the power of a devil or demonic figures.

This large and vague description, fitting a host of undefined but almost superstitiously feared practices, is revealing. Those who practice traditional, established religion tend to use the word "occult" whenever faced with describing something they don't understand, fear greatly, or wish to condemn.

Mary is dealing in the occult. Tom joined a Satan-worshiping group. Mike's son is hooked on the Dungeons and Dragons board game. Susan plays with Ouija boards. Voodoo and tarot cards deal in the occult. The implication is that the occult is evil, devil-worshiping, and demonically controlled. Unspeakable evils go on in dark places. Illicit sex with captured virgins is somehow implied, and black magic lurks at the center. The occult is always thought to be weaker than God but stronger than the power of one's own religious friends. Occultism, unproved but accepted as real, is viewed as an attempt to sell one's soul to the devil and bend supernatural powers to human control.

Perhaps the word's strongest power resides in the human tendency to keep mysteries in the dark by never examining them. At various times the secret rituals of the Masonic organization, the practice of being "slain in the spirit" in the Pentecostal Church down the street, and the mysterious rites of the Catholic Church have been all that are needed to accuse those organizations of practicing the occult.

The reality is that few people have ever experienced a real, dark occultic ritual, except in the movies. But the practice of using the word—covering the unknown in a veil of secrecy—leaves occultism in the dark. And, as with most fear-inducing

Occult method of communicating with the spirit world, this group consults the dead through a ouija board, which moves from letter to letter to spell out words. *Fortean Picture Library.*

things, the dark is where it is most powerful. In the light of day, the occult seems to disappear. Indeed, the most potent weapon of those who claim to practice occultism is secrecy itself.

ODIN (WODEN OR WOTAN) *see* **Norse Gods and Goddesses**

ORPHIC GODS

To understand Orphic religion we have to return to the time of the ancient Greeks. Bacchus (a.k.a. Dionysus; see Greek Gods and Goddesses) was the god of music, wine, and partying. His popular worship involved Bacchanalia: drinking a lot, running naked through the woods, and doing all the things associated with a good fraternity toga party.

But extreme religions usually come with a flip side. In this case it was Orphism. Orpheus may or may not have been a historical figure. He is most famous for accompanying Jason in the Argonaut expedition, searching for the golden fleece, when Orpheus's music-making got the group out of a serious jam. (Stories written much later picture Orpheus as a wandering philosopher engaged in a search for truth and knowledge.)

But Orpheus's main claim to fame, and the reason he spawned a religion, was that he married Eurydice. She died from a serpent bite, and Orpheus was so distraught he went down into Hades to get her back. Once again his music came into play. His performance so enraptured the gods that they let her go, with the condition that she never look back while on her journey back to the surface of the world. Of course she did.

Orpheus was so angry he decided to never have anything to do with women again. Hence, a religious myth directly opposed to the lusty Dionysus and the Bacchanal.

Over the course of time Orphic teaching began to establish a number of theological patterns. Music was important, of course, and many hymns were composed. The most committed Orphists were vegetarians, and wine was used only as a sacrament. But more important, life was viewed as an endless round of pain and suffering. The goal was to escape from earthly existence to eternal life. Afterlife became very important. In a Greek form of Karmic Hinduism and Buddhism (see Hinduism; Buddhism), Orphic religion sought escape from endless incarnations of suffering. They believed the universe was created by the great god Chronos, from which is derived the word chronology, a way of ordering time. Hence, time is the field in which we suffer. Only when we go "out of time" can we be free from pain.

The rather gloomy picture Orphism presents gave the world a great gift, for out of this background grew the Greek tragedy and the religious drama. Pythagorus, patron saint of mathematicians, was a devout follower of Orphism. Plato wrote concerning the concept of *soma*, or soul:

> The Orphic poets gave it this name with the idea that the soul is undergoing punishment for something; they think that it has the body as an enclosure to keep it safe, like a prison.

An early blues musician once wrote that there has never been a really good musician who had a happy childhood. Misery is the source of emotionally charged art. If that is the case, it helps explain Orpheus's musically ability. One song coming from the Orphic tradition is the beautiful hymn, "To Adonis":

> Many-named and best of Spirits hear my prayer, Golden-Haired lover of deserts,
> Infusing all with joy, by all desired, Many-Formed, male and female, charmed and beautiful Adonis,
> You rise and set with splendid fire, the glory of the skies,
> Two-Horned and lovely, much wept for are you,
> Sweet lover of Aphrodite, rejoicing in the chase, all-graceful,
> Son of Persephone,
> It is Your fate to descend to the realm of your Mother,
> Then rise and race through the illustrious heavens Your temporal glory restored.
> Come, Blessed Adonis, bring the fruits of Earth, and in these flames delight.

Sources:

Hodges, Miles. "The Greek Quest for Ideal Order: Dionysianism and Orphism." *New Geneva.* http://www.newgenevacenter.org/west/greek.htm. September 15, 2003.

"Orphism and Bacchism." *Orphika: The Greek Mysteries of Orpheus*. http://www.kristi.ca/orphika/bacchic.html. September 15, 2003.

"To Adonis." Virginia Stewart-Avalon, trans. *Sibylline Order*. http://www.sibyllinewicca.org/lib_writing/lib_oh_adonis.htm. September 15, 2003.

OSIRIS *see* **Egyptian Gods and Goddesses**

OUR FATHER *see* **Lord's Prayer**

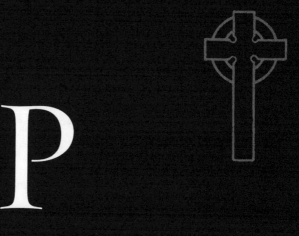

P

PAGANISM, CALENDAR OF

Because there is no single pagan religion, there is no single pagan calendar. The Baltic calendar is different from the Celtic, and both are different from, for instance, the Germanic. But there are four main festivals that were observed rather widely and are still celebrated by neo-pagans today.

Imbolc (February 1st)

This festival seems to be linked to the lactation of the ewes and the birth of the first lambs. It was the sacred day of Brigit (later adopted by the Christian Church as Saint Brigid), the goddess of healing and poetry, especially called upon during times of childbirth.

Beltain (May 1st)

This feast, associated with the new warmth of the sun, is often called the festival of Good Fire. This Irish festival, perhaps recognized in Welsh tales as well, is widely celebrated today. Fires were lit. Cattle were driven through the smoke to purify them. Brave people leaped through the flames with wild abandon, probably after the consumption of a lot of mead. This was the special time when the gods communicated with the world of humans. It may have received its name from the association with the sun god Belenos, who was worshiped in Gaul and Italy. The festival is kept alive today when we remember to dance around maypoles and deliver May baskets.

Lughnasa (August 1st)

Named after Lugh, the god of light, this harvest festival marked the baking of the first bread from new grain. It was a time for dancing outside in the moonlight and festive celebration of the harvest. The stage play and 1998 motion picture *Dancing at Lughnasa* eloquently capture the wild abandon still felt in rural Ireland during this festival.

Samhain (November 1st)

Perhaps the most important festival of the year, Samhain (pronounced sowen) marked the date the flocks were gathered together and harvested. It celebrated death and renewal. On this day the barrier was stretched thin between the otherworld and the world of humans. Kept alive today at Halloween, this festival was a night for spirits who needed to be placated lest they play their tricks. The tribes were gathered together. Winter was right around the corner. It was a solemn time, a holy but fearsome night.

Besides these festivals, most neo-pagans celebrate the equinoxes and solstices as well, further dividing the year into the traditional seasons of winter, spring, summer, and fall.

Most of the customs originating from these festivals have been both adopted and adapted by the Christian Church. The Celts and Gauls became Romans. The Romans became Christian. But the common people remembered the old ways. The Church, bowing to the inevitable, simply baptized the festivals and brought them into the sanctuary, where we now celebrate Christmas with Yule logs and evergreen trees, and Easter with bunnies and eggs.

Sources:
James, Simon. *The World of the Celts*. New York: Thames and Hudson, 1993.
Jones, Prudence, and Nigel Pennick. *A History of Pagan Europe*. New York: Routledge, 1995.

PANTHEISM *see* **Anthropocentrism**

PASSOVER

(See also Judaism, Calendar of; Judaism, Development of; Moses)

With good reason, Passover is perhaps the best-known Jewish holiday. Called Pesah in Hebrew, Passover marks the real birth of the Jewish religion that was established in the desert when Moses led the people out of bondage in Egypt.

Passover falls on the 15th day of Nisan (March or April of the common calendar) and lasts for eight days. The first two days and the last two are full holidays. The rest are called Hol ha-Moed, secular days of the holidays.

Passover begins with the family Seder, a word meaning "order." The family gathers around the table to partake of a ritual meal, each element of which carries a long history. From the time of the Exodus, layers of tradition have been added to the feast. Biblical times are represented. Rabbinical traditions are superimposed over those, with medieval and modern customs added to the mix. Jews figuratively eat their way through history, remembering their rich tradition. Family customs may vary, but the story is always the same. It follows the richly textured Haggadah, the order of the ritual.

The youngest member of the family asks the traditional Four Questions, preceded by the query, "Why is this night different?"

A young Jewish boy holds the Keira, a special plate of symbolic foods, for the Passover meal. *AP/Wide World Photos.*

The first question is, "Why do we eat matzah (unleavened bread) instead of leavened bread?" The answer is that matzah represents the desert bread, the "bread of affliction" the people took with them because they had to flee in such haste that the bread didn't have time to rise. Some families teach that haste was not the issue as much as the fact that the people knew they had to go into the desert. So, having faith that their escape was sure to happen, they prepared by taking the traditional desert bread with them.

The second question is, "Why do we eat bitter herbs?" The answer: They represent the bitterness of the forefathers who were forced to live under Egyptian bondage. It is a reminder that each generation must protect their precious freedom which, in the past, has often been suddenly taken away.

The third question in many traditions is, "Why do we dip herbs twice?" The dipping of parsley in salt water is a reminder that early generations dipped vegetables in water before partaking of a big meal. In addition, the parsley represents the growth of new life in springtime, and the salt water recollects the tears shed by enslaved Jews. Bitter herbs are also dipped into haroset, a mixture often consisting of apples, raisins, cinnamon, and nuts. This dipping of bitter herbs into the sweet haroset represents life's mixture of bitterness and sweetness. Furthermore, the haroset symbolizes the mortar used by the Israelites when they were forced to build for the Pharaoh.

The fourth question is, "Why do we sit in a reclining position during the meal?" The Bedouin people received the Israelites in the desert. Men of position reclined, following the ancient command, "Recline, and be at peace." Reclining is the desert custom, and the custom of reclining during the Passover meal is a reminder of the years of wandering. Many families, however, don't actually recline today; they sit in regular chairs at the table, sometimes placing a small pillow on the chair.

The main parts of the modern Seder consist of reciting the kiddush, the traditional prayer of blessing over the cup of wine; reading the Haggadah, the Exodus narrative that revolves around the four questions; partaking of the unleavened bread and bitter herbs, the festival meal; drinking the traditional four cups of wine at stated intervals during the celebration; and reciting the Hallel, the Song of Praise.

This celebration places a special emphasis on children. They are the recipients of the story as it is passed down from generation to generation. It is important to remember that this custom, the backbone of Judaism, goes back some 3,500 years. Jews have never forgotten. The individual family traditions that augment the feast and give it special character are repeated down through the generations. If Great-great-grandfather and Great-great-grandmother were suddenly to come alive and celebrate with the modern family, chances are they would feel right at home. And as the familiar, treasured customs are remembered each year, perhaps the ancestors do come alive, in the sense that their presence is certainly felt.

Sources:
Bridger, David, ed. *The New Jewish Encyclopedia.* New York: Behrman House, 1962.

PATRICK, SAINT

Did Saint Patrick really drive all the snakes out of Ireland? Did he convert the Irish by convincing them of the reality of the trinity by using the shamrock as an illustration? Did he convert Ireland all by himself?

Probably not.

The snake myth may refer to the fact that the Genesis serpent represented sin. And Patrick was a convincing preacher who was aided by a geographical situation that prevented snakes from reaching Ireland in the first place.

The shamrock was symbolic of the luck of the Irish. Patrick probably didn't even think of it—but as a teaching device, it works.

But none of this detracts from the legend. Patrick was an amazing missionary.

He was probably born in Scotland, perhaps of British ancestry and maybe in a village called Bannavem Taberniac. The other possibilities are Gaul or Kilpatrick, near Dunbarton. His father seems to have been a deacon or some kind of civic official. But his grandfather was a priest. The year was somewhere near 385 CE, and his name was Patricius Magonus Sucatus.

In 405 Patrick was captured by Irish raiders. He became a slave in Ireland, and it is unclear why he decided to go back there after he finally escaped and returned to his family, either seven or ten years later. Somehow, over the next fifteen years, he received some kind of training for the priesthood. He seems to have been ordained about 415 CE.

Stained-glass image of St. Patrick, the patron saint of Ireland, from the cloisters of Chester Cathedral. *Fortean Picture Library.*

If you count the "probably," "seems to have," "maybe," and "possibly" statements so far, you begin to get the idea we don't know a lot about what his early life was like. What we do know is that, whatever the cause and however it happened, he returned to Ireland and did great missionary work. His legend may have grown over the centuries, but it created for him an Irish reputation and legacy that cannot be discounted.

He was said to have been a bit of a mystic, seeing visions and hearing voices. But regardless of his methods, Ireland is Catholic because of him.

"I was like a stone lying in deep mire," he wrote. "And he that is mighty came, and in His mercy lifted me up, and verily raised me aloft and placed me on top of the wall."

He is said to have converted whole villages with his compassionate logic and ability to speak to Irish sensibilities. During Mass he once accidentally speared a potential convert in the foot when, lost in the beauty of the Mass, he pounded too hard with his bishop's mace. The convert thought it was part of the initiation rite and considered himself blessed to share in Christ's crucifixion.

Patrick was said to have baptized whole villages, a hundred or so at a time. He is probably the best-known and most beloved missionary the Roman Catholic Church ever sent forth. And the most successful.

His famous prayer reveals his spiritual center:

Christ be with me,
Christ within me,
Christ behind me,
Christ before me,
Christ beside me,
Christ to win me,
Christ to comfort and restore me.
Christ beneath me,
Christ above me,
Christ in quiet,
Christ in danger,
Christ in hearts of all that love me,
Christ in mouth of friend and stranger.

Sources:

Rabenstein, Katharine I. "Saint Patrick of Ireland." http://users.erols.com/saintpat/ss/0317 patr.htm. September 15, 2003.

PAUL, SAUL OF TARSUS

(See also Christianity, Development of)

Paul, a servant of Christ Jesus, called to be an apostle and set apart for the Gospel of God.... (Romans 1:1)

With these words, Paul introduces himself to the Roman Christians. He is credited with writing almost one-third of the New Testament. Many believe him to be the architect of the Christian Church, its first great missionary and theologian. Some call him saint and man of God. Others claim he perverted the vision of Jesus of Nazareth. He seems to have been hard to get along with. Even the apostle Peter, who called him "our dear brother Paul," is on record as saying that some of Paul's teachings are "hard to understand" (2 Peter 3). Some theologians refer to Paul as the "Moses" of the Christian Church, the one who set its doctrines in firm concrete. But did Jesus really mean to begin a whole new faith tradition, or was that Paul's idea?

The arguments swirl on and on. We won't solve them here. Probably no one ever will. But we can get an idea of what he thought about himself by reading closely his own autobiography, summarized in the first verse of the first chapter of the first book of the Bible that carries his signature.

Paul ...

Names used to mean something. Paul was born Saul of Tarsus, named after the first great king of Israel. His parents must have been fairly wealthy because, although born to a Jewish family of the tribe of Benjamin, he was an educated Roman citizen and a Pharisee, taught by none other than the great Rabbi Gamaliel.

That he was certain of his heritage and fervent in his patriotism is obvious. We first meet him in the seventh chapter of the book of Acts. Stephen, about to become the first Christian martyr, has just been found guilty of blasphemy because he accused his brother Jews of resisting, and then murdering, Jesus. They take him outside the city and proceed to stone him to death. Because it is easier to throw stones when your arms are unencumbered, they pile their cloaks "at the feet of a young man named Saul," who "gave approval to [Stephen's] death."

The execution must have had a great impact on Saul. When next we meet him he is on his way to Damascus, armed with letters from no less an authority than the high priest, giving him permission to arrest members of the new Christian cult and bring them back to Jerusalem for trial. Because of that fateful journey, his life, his name, and world history were forever changed. His name became Paul, which means little. (The only physical description we have of Paul is that of a small, very intense, bowlegged man whose eyebrows were so bushy that they met over his nose.)

Servant of Christ Jesus …

Paul traveled to Damascus with escorts. Their thoughts and impressions were not recorded, but it seems from what Paul later wrote that they didn't really understand what was happening when Saul was knocked from his horse and blinded by a great light. A voice spoke to him, "Saul, Saul, why do you persecute me?"

Paul responded with perhaps the dumbest question in the whole Bible. He even answered it himself. "Who is it, Lord?"

The men traveling with Saul were at a loss. They heard a sound, maybe even saw a light, but couldn't figure out what was happening. They managed to get Saul to Damascus. He was blind for the next three days and couldn't eat or drink anything. But a Christian named Ananias had been told by God to go to Saul, pray for him, and restore his sight.

Ananias was justifiably upset and tried to talk God out of it. "I have heard many reports about this man and all the harm he has done to your saints in Jerusalem. And he has come here with authority from the chief priests to arrest all who call on your name." Maybe it's a trick!

"But the Lord said to Ananias, 'Go! This man is my chosen instrument to carry my name before Gentiles and their kings.'" (Acts 9:15)

(There is great speculation concerning a physical ailment Paul referred to as his "thorn in the flesh." He believed God gave it to him to keep him humble. But he never says exactly what it is. He does hint, however. Although his usual method of writing was to dictate letters, he often wrote, in his own hand, a final closing paragraph. Sometimes he says, "See what large letters I am using," implying that he couldn't see well. Was the apostle almost blind? And did that blindness begin on the road to Damascus? It's another puzzle.)

Called to Be an Apostle ...

And so it began. Paul would later refer to himself as an apostle "born out of time." In other words, he considered himself equal in stature with the twelve apostles of Jesus, even though he was chosen after Jesus died.

This notion raises an interesting question. The first order of business on the apostles' agenda following the ascension was to hold an election to fill the place left open following the death of Judas. They elected a man named Matthias. We never hear from him again. Did Paul consider himself the proper candidate to fill the slot?

Paul began preaching right away. But he took his new job very seriously. He felt the need for training. So he studied a full fifteen years before he began the task that would occupy the rest of his life.

Set Apart for the Gospel of God ...

Paul accomplished more than anyone when it came to laying the foundation of the early Church. No one really knew how to go about it. So Paul just jumped in and began.

First he had to persuade the others that the Church was for Gentiles as well as Jews. Peter, who accompnied Jesus from the start and was the acknowledged leader of the Church in Jerusalem, was convinced people had to become Jewish before they could be Christian. That meant circumcision, a kosher table—the works.

Paul insisted this had to change. "There is neither Jew nor Greek, slave nor free, male nor female," he wrote to the Galatians (3:28), "for you are all one in Christ Jesus." (He later, however, promoted males over females and endorsed slavery.)

Having won his argument with Peter at the first Christian convention (Acts 15) he began what was to be his life's work. He undertook three great missionary journeys. In the back of almost every Bible there are a lot of maps hardly anyone ever looks at. One of them is called Paul's Missionary Journeys. It traces out the three trips with three different colors.

It was on the second of these journeys that Paul picked up his faithful chronicler, Luke, the physician. He was later assisted by young Timothy. Early on, his companion was a man named Barnabas, with whom Paul had some disagreements. But they seemed to have patched them up after Barnabas came around to Paul's way of thinking.

His method of operation was always the same. He would enter a town and proceed to preach about Christ at the local synagogue. Then he would get kicked out, often arrested, and have to stay at the home of a Christian sympathizer. But a group of believers would gather around him. A church would form. Later Paul would write letters of encouragement back to these churches. He wrote to the churches of Corinth, Galatia, Ephesus, Philippi, Colosse, and Thessalonica. Sometimes he wrote letters, called Epistles, to individual people such as Timothy or Titus. All these letters would circulate from church to church. One town would make a copy of the letter, substitute a neighbor's name in the address, and send it along. Eventually, when collected and perhaps edited, these letters became a substantial portion of the New Testament.

It was Paul's carefully constructed letters, as much as anything else, that set the foundation for Christian theology. He usually began with an extensive section of systematic theological presentation. Then he would say, "therefore ..." and begin to apply the teaching to everyday life. This set the pattern for most contemporary sermons. First theory, then application.

These letters didn't always bring good news and happy thoughts. When he wrote to the Galatians, for instance, he didn't even bother to begin with a polite greeting. "You foolish Galatians," he roars, "who has bewitched you?" And in what can best be described as Paul's gentlest letter, he mentions two Philippian women by name, Euodia and Syntyche, saying, right in front of the whole church, "Get along with each other, girls. Stop fighting!" (Philippians 4:2)

Paul's mission eventually began to cause too many problems to too many public officials. Even during his lifetime, Christians were being accused of "turning the whole world upside down" (Acts 17:6). When he returned home triumphant to Jerusalem, according to Acts 21, he was arrested. Here Paul's legal training came in handy. Taking advantage of his Roman citizenship, he summoned a higher court. He appealed to Caesar. This meant an all-expenses-paid trip to Rome, where he wanted to go anyway. After an exciting journey he finally arrived in the capital.

Roman law gave witnesses two years to show up and press charges. If they didn't come within that time, the accused went free. Maybe that's the reason Luke emphasizes, in the book of Acts, that Paul stayed for "two whole years in Rome." The implication is that he went free afterward.

But where did he go? That's the question. No one knows. Some legends have him going on to Spain; others back to Jerusalem. We don't know how he died. And perhaps that's the intent of the Bible. In many ways, Paul doesn't die. He lives on.

Love him or hate him, Paul has been a controversial figure since the beginning. Even while he was alive there were those who were jealous. They said he couldn't preach.

Paul was not above sarcasm. To those who wanted to hear a good sermon, he promised to bring along his friend Apollos, the "silver-tongued orator." But there was never any doubt whose ideas Apollos would be conveying.

Paul's was not an easy life. He was jailed, beaten, thrown out of town, stoned, and left for dead. He was ridiculed. At times he must have felt utterly forsaken. Sometimes he was a bit petulant—"Let no one cause me trouble, for I bear on my body the marks of Jesus" (Galatians 6:17). But at the end he could cry that he had "finished the race" and "kept the faith" (Timothy 4:7).

Sources:
The Holy Bible, New International Version. Grand Rapids, MI: Zondervan Bible Publishers, 1978.

PELAGIAN CONTROVERSY see Calvin, John, and Jacobus Arminius

PENTECOST see Christianity, Calendar of; Judaism, Calendar of

PENTECOSTALISM

(See also Charismatic Movement)

When the day of Pentecost came, they were all together in one place. Suddenly a sound like the blowing of a violent wind came from heaven and filled the whole house where they were sitting. They saw what seemed to be tongues of fire that separated and came to rest on each of them. All of them were filled with the Holy Spirit and began to speak in other tongues as the Spirit enabled them. (Acts 2:1–4)

It was the birthday of the Christian Church. The believers had gathered together to celebrate the Jewish feast day of Pentecost (see Judaism, Calendar of), and reports of what happened spread throughout the city of Jerusalem and, later, the whole world. Peter delivered the first Christian sermon. Three thousand people were reported to have been baptized on that day. And more flocked to join the new movement, for "the Lord added to their number daily those who were being saved."

Skip now to the year 1906. The Methodist Church is sponsoring a revival meeting at the Azusa Street Mission in Los Angeles, California. Those who attended later reported that it was as if Pentecost had happened again. The people were gripped by a force that felt "like a violent wind"; "They began to speak in other tongues as the Spirit enabled them." People were healed. People were converted. People felt they "were filled with the Holy Spirit."

Pentecostalism was born.

At first it was experienced in the rural south. Robert Duvall's brilliant 1997 movie, *The Apostle,* captures it perfectly. Pentecostalism was about revivals held in tents. There was singing, dancing in the aisles, and down-home preaching that was an art form in itself. Heavily influenced by the freedom of African American worship style, the preacher talked to the congregation, and the congregation answered right back. Not just the occasional "Amen!"—this was full-throated, throw-yourself-in-and-participate conversation. People moved. They were "slain in the Spirit," fainting dead away when the preacher put his hand on their forehead. No one looked at the clock. No one cared what time it was. The service was over when the Spirit stopped moving.

Pentecostalism is probably most famous for its practice of glossolalia, speaking in tongues. To outsiders, it sounds like gibberish—nonsense syllables. Sometimes it sounds like that to insiders, too. There is a difference of opinion as to what it means. To believers, it is often thought to be a heavenly language only God can understand. The Apostle Paul wrote about "tongues of men and of angels" (1 Corinthians 13). In other words, glossolalia is the language spoken by the angels in heaven.

But in the Bible it seems to be real languages that people could actually understand. On the day of Pentecost, for example, people had come together from many different countries to celebrate the holiday in Jerusalem. They all heard the Gospel proclaimed in their own language. Paul even put some boundaries around the use of glossolalia in the church. He said that when it occurs, only a few people should do it, one at a time, and not at all unless there is an interpretation given.

Some conservative theologians have theorized that "tongues speaking" was a foundational gift, needed at the beginning, to quickly reach a lot of people who would not otherwise have understood the apostle's language. So when the apostle Paul wrote, again in 1 Corinthians 13, "When the perfect comes, that which is imperfect shall pass away," he was saying that when the ability to provide translations had been perfected, as it has in our technological era, there would no longer be any use for the gift of glossolalia, and it would pass away.

But if that is the case, what is happening in Pentecostal churches when people speak in tongues today?

Well, say the doubters, it's just gibberish. Other religions do it, too. And there is even some clinical evidence that it can be learned and practiced until it becomes almost another language.

But believers disagree. There is no denying the fact that Pentecostal Christians believe glossolalia is a spiritual gift from God, proof of the "infilling" of the Holy Spirit. Some denominations do not even allow people to preach or become members until they demonstrate the ability to speak in tongues. It's proof that they have been both "saved" and "sanctified." Salvation is the first blessing. Sanctification, being cleansed by the Holy Spirit, is the second.

Pentecostalism has changed over the years. From the poor and rural South, it moved uptown in the charismatic movement (see Charismatic Movement) and into mainstream denominations such as the Assemblies of God (see Assemblies of God). But there are still parts of the country that look forward to the day the evangelist comes to town, sets up his tent or builds a "Holiness Temple," and invites them to "hit the sawdust trail," to walk down the aisle (usually consisting of sawdust spread on the ground under the revival tent) to get "saved" and "receive the blessing" of speaking in tongues.

Sources:
Hudson, Winthrop S. *Religion in America*. New York: Charles Scribner, 1965.

PILGRIMAGE (HAJJ) *see* **Islam**

Pow-wow

(See also Dance, Sacred)

Pow-wow is a North American Indian term with many meanings. It's difficult to translate directly into English because words represent thought patterns, and Indians traditionally thought quite differently from most Europeans.

Sometimes pow-wow means a holy person or shaman. Sometimes it refers to a tribal council. Often it refers to a ritual involving healing. Most often it refers to a celebration or ritual involving dance. The word conjures up community dancing, accompanied by the beat of drums and rattles and, usually, by singing rendered in the style modern musicologists have labeled "vocables," or ritualized chant.

Some of the customs practiced by Indian nations go back to antiquity and must be memorized exactly, so that an ancestor from a thousand years ago would know

A member of the Grand Traverse Band of Ottawa and Chippewa Indians performs a dance at their reservation in Peshawbestown, Michigan. Pow-wows draw upon ancient traditions of tribal gatherings that feature dance, music, storytelling, and ceremonies. *AP/Wide World Photos.*

precisely what was going on. Many of the songs are said to have been taught by "First Man" or "First Woman."

Some pow-wows are held today for the benefit of tourists. Others are sacred religious services.

Europeans tend to sit in straight rows when they go to church. Indians dance. Europeans are used to being "preached at." Indians participate. Europeans are used to organ music. Indians prefer the throbbing of the drums.

Prayer can take many shapes according to different religions, but it is the primary means of expressing faith and asking for gifts or graces from God. *Fortean Picture Library.*

I once asked an Ojibway elder how he was feeling. "Ninety-eight percent fine!" came the reply. "What would it take to fill in the last two percent?" I responded. "I'd have to hear the drums!" he said.

Sources:
Mails, Thomas E. *Dancing in the Paths of the Ancestors*. New York: Marlowe & Company, 1983.

PRAYER, DAILY (SALAT) *see* **Islam**

PRAYER/MEDITATION/CONTEMPLATION

These terms are used almost interchangeably, but there is a difference that must be understood when studying various religions with differing ways of approaching spirituality.

Prayer is directed toward a deity. A person prays to a particular god, goddess, or spiritual entity with the understanding that the entity is listening.

Meditation is "thinking about." Usually a particular idea or phrase, icon, or idol attracts the attention and involves the participant, who is seeking spiritual enlightenment or understanding.

Contemplation is a more open-ended meditation. The person contemplating doesn't try to understand as much as to experience.

A recent six-year study conducted at Duke University has come to the conclusion that prayer is good for one's health. Dr. Harold Koenig, directory of the University's Center for the Study of Religion/Spirituality and Health, reviewed the cases of some four thousand participants from various faith traditions and found that the relative risk of dying for those who frequently prayed was 46 percent lower than for those who didn't. Additionally, people over the age of sixty-four who prayed regularly had significantly lower blood pressure, survived heart surgery more often, and recovered more quickly from depression, alcoholism, hip surgery, drug addiction, stroke, rheumatoid arthritis, and bypass surgery.

No one knows why. Studies of this kind obviously cannot be used to "prove" divine intervention. The results could be psychosomatic. But they are undeniable.

Sources:
Hales, Dianne. "Why Prayer Could Be Good Medicine." *Boston Sunday Globe,* March 23, 2003.
Ludwig, Theodore M. *The Sacred Paths: Understanding the Religions of the World.* 2nd ed. Upper Saddle River, NJ: Prentice Hall, 1996.

PRESBYTERIAN

The Presbyterian Church, although divided into many denominations, traces its ancestry back to the Protestant Reformation (see Christianity, Development of). It began with Martin Luther, but some twenty years after he posted his famous Ninety-five Theses, John Calvin (see Calvin, John, and Jacobus Arminius) laid the basis for the theology that shapes the various Presbyterian churches existing today. John Knox studied with Calvin and took his theology first to Geneva and then, after a political exile, back to Scotland, where the first Presbyterian Church was formed.

Presbyterian doesn't refer to theology as much as it does to church polity. There isn't a lot of theological difference, for instance, between Presbyterians and Congregationalists (see Congregationalism). But there is a world of difference in the way the political hierarchy of the two churches work. Presbyterians are set up, politically, much the same way as the representative government of the United States. Individual churches elect representatives (presbyters) who represent them at a higher level (the presbytery). The presbytery owns the church buildings and has a say in who ministers to the local congregations. It, in turn, is responsible to the synod, elected from the various presbyteries. The presbytery does not go so far as to appoint bishops or individual ministers. The local church session has a lot of say in those matters. The highest elected body is the assembly, which serves the same kind of function as the U.S. Congress. So the Presbyterian political organization of representative government is somewhere in between an Episcopal system and a Congregationalist system.

The Presbyterian Church (USA) is the largest denomination in the United States. But theological differences, mostly involving biblical interpretation, have led to other denominations, such as the Presbyterian Church in America, the Cumberland Presbyterian Church, the Associate Reformed Presbyterian Church, and the Orthodox Presbyterian Church.

The Presbyterian Church is perhaps best known for its use of the Westminster Catechism, still widely used in confirmation classes.

Sources:
Gonzalez, Justo L. *The Story of Christianity.* 2 vols. New York: Harper & Row, 1985.

PROTESTANT REFORMATION *see* **Calvin, John, and Jacobus Arminius; Christianity, Development of**

PURE LAND BUDDHISM *see* **Buddhism, Development of**

PURGATORY

The Roman Catholic doctrine of purgatory (from the Latin word *purgare,* meaning "to make clean or purify") affirms that there is "a place or condition of temporal punishment for those who, departing this life in God's grace, are not entirely free from venial faults, or have not fully paid the satisfaction due to their transgressions."

"Venial faults" are those sins of human frailty that are not as serious as the more damning sins, such as murder, but still serve to render the person less than pure before God. Unrepented venial faults still need to be dealt with. That is the purpose of purgatory.

Purgatory, in accordance with Catholic teaching, is a temporary place or condition of punishment for those who, upon death, are not entirely free from venial sin. *Fortean Picture Library.*

Purgatory exists as a way-station on the path to heaven. Prayers of the faithful on Earth help lessen the time spent there, and indulgences, or forgiveness, can still be granted by the pope. But the doctrine points out the Catholic view of the seriousness of sin and the purity of God. Even though sin is atoned for by Christ, the results of that sin carry over into actions and attitudes, and these must be dealt with.

The official Church doctrine lists page after page of arguments from the Bible and tradition, but points out that the sixteenth-century Protestant reformers decided that purgatory did not exist. It was a figment of Catholic imagination. As such, it is a doctrine unique to Catholicism.

Sources:
"Purgatory." *Catholic Encyclopedia.* http://www.newadvent.org/cathen/12575a.htm. September 15, 2003.

PURIM *see* **Judaism, Calendar of**

QUAKERS/RELIGIOUS SOCIETY OF FRIENDS

In October of 1650, a young preacher who had a brand-new vision for the church was arrested in England and brought to trial on the charge of blasphemy. George Fox appeared before the magistrates and was asked questions concerning his orthodoxy. He believed in God. He believed in prayer. He believed most Christians tried to do the right thing. But he also believed something had gone terribly wrong with the way God's church was being conducted. He spoke the truth as he believed God revealed it to him. The reality of the presence of God was such that the magistrates should "tremble at the words of the Lord." When God spoke to him and to those who followed him, they "quaked" in the presence of divinity.

Whether the term "Quaker" was coined by one of the magistrates or adopted by Fox and his small band of believers is a matter of debate. But the term stuck. To this day, those who worship with the Religious Society of Friends are nicknamed Quakers.

Fox never intended to start a new religion or Christian sect. He just wanted people to be in touch with God and experience the divine presence directly. To this end, the Friends didn't appoint ministers or establish ritual patterns of worship. God spoke to each person individually. You could never predict when the word of the Lord would come. Meetings consisted of sitting quietly and waiting for the voice of the Holy Spirit to make itself heard. Friends would gather together in silence. Nothing might happen for minutes, even hours at a time. But then someone would stand and speak what he or she felt God had lain on their heart. Quiet minutes followed, during which the assembly would ponder the message. Then someone else would stand and speak.

And so the meeting would continue. No minister worked out a polished delivery. No clergy stood between the congregation and God. Each person was expected, as instructed in Philippians 2:12, individually to "work out your salvation with fear and trembling." There was no official creed or fixed set of doctrines.

The movement arrived in Boston in 1654. But the New England Puritans didn't want to be told they were stifling the spirit. They certainly didn't want to be told they were wrong in the way they conducted their church and its meetings. Quakers were persecuted, whipped, imprisoned, and run out of town. But they would not stop speaking what they considered the truth.

In 1672 the Friends received a real boost. William Penn, who counted himself one of their number, laid the foundation for Pennsylvania and the city of Philadelphia. Quakers gradually became part of the American mainstream. They preached pacifism as they always had, but it was mixed with a fierce sense of determination.

A wonderful story about peace-loving Quakers standing up for their rights concerns a Quaker who investigated the source of a noise in his house one night, only to discover a thief had broken in and was about to rob him. Holding his firearm firmly in his hand, he said to the intruder, "I would not harm thee for the world, my friend. But thee standeth where I am about to shoot!"

Quakers have been way out in front of just about every American cause concerning peace and justice. They were the first to permit women an equal part in worship. They were the first to protest the American government's treatment of Indians. They were the main force behind the Underground Railroad, helping runaway slaves find freedom in the North. They campaigned for voting rights, first for freed slaves and then for women. They protested the Nazi treatment of Jews before World War II and attempted to transport as many Jews as possible out of Germany.

Today the Friends have come a long way. They no longer dress in the familiar "plain" style made popular by the image on the box of Quaker Oats. They do not speak in the formal language of "thee" and "thou" as they used to. But they are still in the forefront of issues concerning peace and justice, still worship in the quiet style conducive to listening for the Divine Spirit, the "Inner Light," as they call it. And they continue to respect all religious perspectives.

Sources:

Hudson, Winthrop S. *Religion in America*. New York: Charles Scribner, 1965.
"The Quaker Religion." http://www.old.umassd.edu/specialprograms/dfinnerty/Quaker.html. September 24, 2003.

QUR'AN

(See also Islam)

Muhammad was illiterate. The text he received from Allah and dictated to scribes, compiled and referenced only eighteen years after his death in 632 CE, is called the Qur'an ("Recitation"; also transliterated as Koran). As one of the most recent of the world's scriptural texts, it has a strong historical basis. And because it cannot truthfully be translated from its original Arabic, we know exactly what Muhammad caused to be written, down to the very last word. For those who cannot read Arabic, it has, of course, been translated into various languages. But those translations are not considered to be valid copies of the Qur'an. They are simply aids.

The Qur'an is divided into 114 chapters (*suras*), which are further divided into a total of some 6,000 verses. In length, it is roughly the same as the Christian New Testament.

Sura 1 immediately places Allah at center stage:

In the name of God, Most gracious, Most Merciful,
Praise be to God, The Cherisher and Sustainer of the Worlds:
Most Gracious, Most merciful; Master of the Day of Judgment.
Thee do we worship, And Thine aid we seek.
Show us the straight way, The way of those on whom
Thou hast bestowed Thy Grace,
Those whose (portion) is not wrath, and who go not astray.

The Qur'an goes on to defines the quintessential monotheistic theological statement:

There is no God but [Allah]; That is the witness of Allah, His angels, and those endued with knowledge, standing firm on justice. There is no God but He, the Exalted in Power, the Wise (3:18)

Muhammad saw both Jews and Christians as people to whom God had spoken in the past. He called them People of the Book:

Mankind was one single nation, and Allah sent Messengers with glad tidings and warnings; and with them he sent the Book in truth, to judge between people in matters wherein they differed; but the People of the Book, after the clear Signs came to them, did not differ among themselves, except through selfish contumacy (2:213) ... Say, "O People of the Book! Come to common terms as between us and you: That we worship none but Allah" (3:64).

Many of the stories of the Jewish scriptures are told as well in the Qur'an:

He it is who created the heavens and the earth is Six Days. (57:4)

We said: O Adam! Dwell thou and they wife in the Garden; and eat of the bountiful things therein. (2:34)

And remember that Abraham was tried by his Lord with certain commands, which he fulfilled: He said, "I will make thee an Imam to the Nations." (2:124)

Behold! The angel said: "O Mary! Allah hath chosen thee and purified thee—chosen thee above the women of all nations." (3:42)

Then will Allah say: "O Jesus the son of Mary! Recount My favour to thee and to thy mother. Behold! I strengthened thee with the holy spirit, so that thou didst speak to the people in childhood and maturity." (5:110)

Many of the stories, of course, differ somewhat from their Jewish or Christian counterparts. Ishmael, Abraham's eldest son, is the one to whom a blessing is imparted, not Isaac, the youngest. Jesus is crucified and dies in the Christian scriptures. But in the Qur'an: "they killed him not, nor crucified him, but so it was made to appear to them, and those who differ therein are full of doubts, with no (certain) knowledge, but only conjecture to follow, for of a surety they killed him not: Nay, Allah raised him up unto himself: And Allah is exalted in power, Wise" (4:157–158).

These common stories probably mean that Muhammad's audience was already familiar with the stories of both the Hebrew and Christian scriptures. But the Qur'an is considered by Muslims to be the final revelation by God to humankind. It completes the divine revelation. It is God's final word until that day when "Allah reward[s] the righteous, (namely) those whose lives the angels take in a state of purity, saying (to them), 'Peace be on you; enter ye the garden, because of (the good) which ye did (in the world)'" (16:27–32).

Sources:

Fisher, Mary Pat and Lee W. Bailey. *An Anthology of Living Religions*. Upper Saddle River: Prentice Hall, 2000.

The Holy Qur'an, trans. with a commentary by Abdullah Yusuf Ali. Beirut, Lebenon: Dar Al Arabia, 1968.

R

RA *see* Egyptian Gods and Goddesses

RAMADAN *see* Islam

RASTAFARIANISM

Early James Bond movies made Sean Connery famous. The movies were set in the 1950s at the height of the Cold War. They painted a highly romanticized picture of Kingston, Jamaica. But what is obvious upon close inspection is that Kingston was romantic only if you were a white European with plenty of money. Thirty years earlier, it was even worse. In 1920 most people of African descent lived in abject poverty in what can best be described as slum conditions. Many justly blamed white imperialism for the destruction of their culture and the absence of hope.

Into this culture stepped Marcus Garvey, with a new philosophy he called "Back to Africa." It was a black self-empowerment movement that pictured a return to the idealized home of the ancestors: Africa. More to the point, Ethiopia. "Look to Africa," Garvey was fond of saying, "where a black man shall be crowned king, for the day of our deliverance is at hand!"

Ten years later his prophetic vision seemed to come to pass. A black African named Ras Tafari Makonnen was crowned emperor of Ethiopia. He took the title and name Emperor Haile Selassie the First. In Jamaica the news sparked rejoicing in the streets. They called Haile Selassie the "Lion of the Tribe of Judah." He claimed direct descent from King David himself, through David's son Solomon and the Queen of Sheba (thought to be an Ethiopian). When she visited Jerusalem and was swept away by Solomon's might and power (1 Kings 10), according to Haile Selassie, she came away with more than just gifts of gold and silver.

(Interestingly, Ethiopia is also thought by some to be the resting place of the lost Ark of the Covenant; see Ark of the Covenant.)

The people of Jamaica began to call themselves Rastafarians, after Ras Tafari Makonnen. They saw themselves as legitimate members of the tribe of Judah, one of the Twelve Tribes of Israel. They began to recognize Haile Selassie as a representative, perhaps even a manifestation of, Jah (God) on Earth.

According to their belief, there is no afterlife, so earthly life becomes very important. The "here and now" was what they were concerned about. They wanted an improvement in their social condition, and they didn't want to wait.

Rastafarians looked to the Hebrew scriptures to guide them in their beliefs, and in the book of Daniel they found the prophecy they needed to explain the events happening in Ethiopia. Daniel claimed to have had a vision. He saw a great statue. The statue, he said, had "hair like wool." Most theologians take this to mean the hair was white. Rastafarians thought it better described the hair of those with African ancestry. The statue had "feet like unto burning brass." This is generally thought to mean gold-colored, but Rastafarians saw it as meaning he had black skin.

A practitioner of Rastafarianism smokes a marijuana joint at the southern town of Vieux Fort, Saint Lucia, during the celebration of what Rastafarians call Ethiopian Christmas. *AP/Wide World Photos*.

It was a time of great patriotic, messianic excitement. The early Rastafarians despised white people. The culture of white imperialism was labeled "Babylon," after the "whore of Babylon" described in the book of Revelation. In this enigmatic passage, "the whore of Babylon" is said to be a city built on seven hills, the personification of all that is impure, evil, wealthy, and greedy.

(This was early Rastafarianism. A prophet calling himself Gad, leader of the Twelve Tribes of Israel movement, later opened the doors to whites. White people can never be Rastafarian leaders, however, because the scriptures point out that "the scepter will not depart from Judah, nor the ruler's staff from beneath his feet, until he comes to whom it belongs, and the obedience of the nations is his" [Genesis 49:10].)

From 1930 until 1974 Rastafarians waited, certain the Messiah would arise and life on Earth would change. But Haile Selassie died, and the Rasta world was shaken to the core. How could Jah die? Many of the elderly simply refused to believe the reports. They viewed the whole thing as a white media conspiracy. Others left the faith. Some taught that Jah went to sit on the highest point of Mount Zion with his empress, Menen.

Bob Marley became a prominent spokesman for the religion in the 1960s. He was a musician who came to be known as the "voice of Jamaica." His music, first called ska and later reggae, took the world by storm and exposed many of the injustices black Jamaicans have been forced to endure.

Today Rastafarianism has undergone a transition. Natural foods are very important. Most Rastas are vegetarians, though some do eat fish. Pork and alcohol are strictly forbidden. Coffee and salt are discouraged.

By far the most controversial aspect of Rastafarianism today, however, concerns an interpretation of a verse from the book of Psalms. Psalm 104:14 says, "He makes grass grow for the cattle, and plants for man to cultivate." Rastas translate it this way: "He causeth the grass to grow for the cattle, and herb for the service of man."

What is the "herb for the service of man"? Ganja, otherwise known as marijuana. Whenever the Bible says "plant," most Rastafarians read "herb." They use it not only for relaxation but also for religious ritual and medicinal purposes. The herb they smoke is a strain of Indian hemp, not the Mexican variety so familiar to many people in the United States. Ganja is much stronger, often producing religious visions. Those who smoke it say that under its influence they experience Jah, the same claim made by members of the Native American Church about peyote (see Native American Church). It has been declared an illegal substance in many countries. But that hasn't stopped its use.

Another distinction common to Rasta culture is the familiar hairstyle known as "dreadlocks." Dreadlocks symbolize the culture of African ancestry and, to Rastafarians, are deliberately meant to contrast with the straight, fine hair of most Caucasians. Rastas believe this hairstyle is commanded in the Bible. Leviticus 21:5 says, "Priests must not shave their heads or shave off the edges of their beards." This verse is also applied by many ultra-Orthodox Jews who wear a distinctive beard and hairstyle. For a head covering, the ultra-Orthodox wear tall black hats, while Rastas wear colorful crocheted caps.

Colors took on added importance after Marley became a superstar and public figure. He dressed in red to symbolize the "church triumphant"—Rastafarianism. Yellow stood for the wealth of the homeland. Green illustrated the beauty of Ethiopian vegetation. Black, of course, represented African ancestry.

Even the language changed for many Rastas. The beautiful, lilting language of the island is a joy to hear. But often a Rasta will say "I and I" instead of "you and me," because he truly believes all people are one.

Sources:
Fisher, Mary Pat. *Living Religions.* 3rd ed. Upper Saddle River, NJ: Prentice Hall, 1991.

RED PAINT PEOPLE

In the early decades of the twentieth century, archaeological discoveries along the Canadian Maritime Provinces and the Maine seacoast sparked a controversy that, one hundred years later, still rages. Burial sites lined with red ochre, some graves so old that the bones had disappeared, were found in coastal areas and islands separated by hundreds of miles. Who dug these graves and went to so much trouble to care for their departed loved ones?

The Red Paint People, as they came to be called, apparently had a religion with a high degree of ritual sophistication concerning afterlife. But if early dating estimates are reliable, they had developed this religion perhaps as early as two thousand years before the Egyptian pyramids were built.

In the years following the initial discoveries, further sites were found from the Canadian North Atlantic down to New York State, and all the way west to Lake Champlain, possibly even as far as the Great Lakes. The Red Paint people would have predated the elaborate Mound Builders of the Ohio Valley by some four thousand years.

Who were they? Where did they come from?

Conservative archaeologists immediately went to work. They insisted the estimated dates were wrong and that the sites couldn't be that old. (The partially tongue-in-cheek complaint of the traditional archaeologist is always, "But it can't be authentic because it isn't *supposed* to be here!") But with the invention of carbon dating, the original estimates were proved accurate.

Original theories had deduced Northern European ancestors for the Red Paint People. The same red ochre religious burial practices had been found ringing the North Atlantic all the way to Norway. Archaeological digs in Maine had turned up swordfish bones and other evidence suggesting the Red Paint People of the Americas had developed deepwater navigation and fishing techniques. The implication was that if people could fish way out in the cold waters of the North Atlantic, they could certainly cross it, perhaps following the glacier face and even camping along its base for long periods at a time.

But that flew in the face of an archaeological community that didn't even want to admit Viking presence in America until forced to do so by incontrovertible evidence discovered in the 1950s. If America was home to a pre-Columbian, pre-Norse civilization, it would mark a death blow to those who refused to accept the theory of "diffusion," of cultural transfer from place to place in ancient times.

Diffusion had become a discredited archaeological theory. The establishment refused to endorse it. Thor Heyerdahl had fought the good fight with his Kon-Tiki expedition in 1947, suggesting that ancient people did have the know-how and gumption to travel great distances over water, carrying their religion and technology with them. But even though his theories proved popular to the general public, the archaeological establishment refused to accept them.

So that was that. There was no European presence in the Americas before Columbus. End of story.

But the argument would not go away. So-called monks' caves, exact replicas of very early Christian monks' cells and prayer chapels, existing to this day along the west coasts of Ireland and the outer islands of Britain, were discovered all over New England. What were they?

Colonial storage cellars, said the experts; certainly nothing do with pre-Columbian Christianity, and absolutely nothing to do with ancient religion, either.

Others pointed out that they have doors that are much too small for storage cellars and that they have been called "monks' caves" from the beginning of colonial history. Furthermore, sometimes they seem to be placed with regard to solar alignments. But most of all, they look just like their European counterparts.

Detractors claim that any resemblance is purely coincidental because early Europeans could not have crossed the Atlantic, while proponents of the diffusion theory wonder why not and point to the monks' caves and grave sites of the Red Paint People as evidence of such crossing.

And on it goes. The big gun called "political correctness" has even been brought into play by the traditional archaeological community, who accuse diffusions theorists of implying that native peoples weren't smart enough to develop the religions and traditions of the Red Paint People. Further, they wonder why the theory persists that people traveled only from Europe to America, rather than the other way around.

Aside from the fact that oceanic currents don't flow that way, some reply that perhaps Native Americans did make the crossing, and that two-way traffic across the Atlantic be just one of the many things, including but not limited to Greek culture, that Europeans lost during the Dark Ages.

Transatlantic evidence seems to have a quirky persistence. A European DNA gene has been found floating around the New England Algonquian nation gene pool. Those monks' caves are still there (attracting, admittedly, mostly tourists with interests in the New Age). And the Red Paint People archaeological sites continue to offer up hints that sophisticated religious traditions involving life after death and associated burial practices entered this country from the East as well as the West, and maybe a very long time ago. Perhaps they even influenced the later "Indian" beliefs, not supplanting or even trying to usurp their religion, but just gently insinuating themselves into the culture, as can happen when people of different traditions meet and share ideas.

Picture a possible scenario:

Two brothers walk out of Africa and come to a parting of the ways on the large isthmus we now call the Holy Land.

One brother heads east and camps for a few thousand years on the shores of Lake Bikal. There he develops a rich shamanic spiritual tradition that he eventually carries across a land bridge, unfolding it upon the American continent in unique local expressions all the way from Alaska to Tierra del Fuego, and from California to New England.

The other brother travels west into Europe, eventually reaching the Atlantic Ocean. Not to be thwarted by a mere body of water, he soon learns how to build boats sufficient to carry him across, whereupon he meets his long-lost brother, who eyes him suspiciously from behind a tree. The two are reunited after their long journeys.

One is not "better" or "smarter" than the other. Each has evolved a unique way of viewing the world and a religion that teaches him how to live in it. One had to cross a big ocean. The other had to cross a whole continent. But they are still brothers! That's the point. They may have forgotten it, but they are still brothers—and always will be.

It would be wonderful, of course, to someday discover that the rich religious tradition of the Eastern Algonquians was an early example of what can happen when different traditions augment each other. If we could prove Siberian shamanism, North European paganism, Norse mythology, and early Christian mysticism all played a part in developing the culture that greeted the Pilgrims and helped them through their first Massachusetts winter, it would be a hopeful prototype for peace. Especially since, in our example, our two brothers parted company in the war-torn area of the Middle East.

Sad to say, we will probably never know, because the Puritans destroyed any chance of that ever happening. By the time of the clash of cultures now called King Philip's War (see Calvin, John, and Jacobus Arminius), any hope of mutual respect between Christians and Indians was lost for the next three hundred years. Besides that, the acceptable archaeological evidence needed to make such a claim simply has not been found.

Sources:
America's Fascinating Indian Heritage. Pleasantville, NY: Reader's Digest Association, 1978.
Braun, David P., and Esther K. Braun. *The First Peoples of the Northeast*. Lincoln: Moccasin Hill Press, 1994.

REFORMATION, PROTESTANT *see* Calvin, John,
and Jacobus Arminius; Christianity, Development of

REINCARNATION *see* Incarnation

RELIGION

What is religion? That's a hard question to answer. And the harder you try, the more difficult it becomes.

Is "religion" simply defined as the way we think about God? If so, Buddhism is not a religion, because many Buddhists don't believe in God. Nor do some Hindus and Unitarians and Jews. Add to those a lot of liberal Catholics who don't believe in God but won't admit it, plus a whole bunch of liberal Protestants whose definition of "God" is certainly not traditional.

Does "religion" mean simply living an ethical life? If so, then many good, nice, ethical atheists are religious.

Perhaps "religion" refers to an organized institution. But that can't be, because there are many religions (such as Quaker and Hindu sects) that resist any effort to organize. And many more religions that are not organized even though they think they are!

So in order to talk about "religion," it first becomes necessary to define the term.

One definition that seems to cut across many philosophical boundaries was developed by the sociologist Joachim Wach, who lived from 1898 to 1955. His "Three Forms of Religious Expression" comes close to capturing the elusive concept of religion.

Theoretical

This word refers to the fact that religions teach something. They have a "theoretical" component.

Religions teach by means of myths, doctrines, traditions, and customs. Sometimes it drives religious leaders crazy to hear from congregants, over and over again, "We've always done it this way!" But customs, stemming from myths and stories, cemented by doctrine, and interpreted by longstanding traditions, teach young people in ways they never quite outgrow. How many atheists, for instance, are still afraid of going to the hell in which they no longer believe? It's because the theoretical component of their childhood religion was so strong they cannot ever fully outgrow it.

Whenever we study a new religion, we ask about its teachings. That's what religions do. They teach something. They teach how the world was made, how humans came to be, what will happen in the future, how to live in the present. They pass on values and ethics by teaching children the social standards of their religious community. That's what Sunday school, catechism classes, and confirmation classes are for. That's why religious institutions of higher learning were formed.

Religions are all about teaching.

Practical

Religions also have developed ways of worshiping. "Practical" refers to what people in various religions actually do. Jews go to synagogues or observe family religious celebrations at home. Catholics go to Mass. Protestants attend church services. Muslims fulfill the Five Pillars.

Religious communities are known for their traditions. What makes us uncomfortable when we go to a worship service different from our own tradition is that we don't always know what is expected of us. We don't know the rituals. We don't know the customs. We are afraid of bumping into a "sacred cow."

Religions have a traditional practice, a "practical" component.

Sociological

Religions also attract a community. They have a sociological component. In New England, every town has a little white community church on the town common. In European cities, it's the cathedral that dominates the skyline. In Midwestern America, the "little brown church in the vale" is being replaced by the ultra-modern educational complex with an extensive bus ministry. California has its Crystal Cathedral. Jerusalem its Dome of the Rock. Mecca its Kaaba.

What kind of a community forms around a religion? The answer provides its sociological component.

So we might define "religion" in this way, using the words of Robert S. Ellwood, co-author of the textbook *Many Peoples, Many Faiths*:

> While the essence of religion may be beyond words, the religious experience … expresses itself in human life in three ways. These three forms of religious expression (are) theoretical, practical and sociological.

Sources:
Ellwood, Robert S., and Barbara A. McGraw. *Many Peoples, Many Faiths*. 6th ed. Upper Saddle River, NJ: Prentice Hall, 1999.

A rosary that belonged to an American soldier who was held captive during the Vietnam war. *The Art Archive/US Naval Museum Washington/The Art Archive.*

RELIGIOUS SOCIETY OF FRIENDS *see* Quakers/Religious Society of Friends

ROMAN CATHOLIC CHURCH *see* Catholicism

ROSARY

Roman Catholic tradition has developed prayers and meditations designed to immerse the believer in the mysteries of the faith. Sometimes various devices are used to aid in memorization. Perhaps the best-known prayer and memory device is the rosary and rosary beads.

John Renard, author of *The Handy Religion Answer Book*, summarizes the rosary meditation with these words:

> A "decade" of the rosary corresponds to each of the fifteen mysteries commemorated in the rosary. Ten Hail Marys are said for each decade; they are preceded by an Our Father and followed by a Glory Be to the Father. While reciting a decade of the rosary, one is to meditate on the particular mystery for that decade and on its meaning for life. The

entire rosary is divided into three chaplets: the joyful, the sorrowful, and the glorious mysteries. To "say a rosary" commonly means to pray one such chaplet of five mysteries. Commonly a chaplet is preceded by the recitation of the Apostles' Creed and of an Our Father and three Hail Marys. The Roman Catholic Church has long recommended this form of prayer as a convenient and effective way of meditating on the Christian mysteries of salvation.

The mysteries to be reflected on are the following.

The Joyful Mysteries
The Annunciation
The Visitation of Mary to her Cousin Elizabeth
The Birth of Jesus Christ
The Presentation of Jesus in the Temple in Jerusalem
The Finding of the Child Jesus in the Temple in Jerusalem

The Sorrowful Mysteries
The Agony of Jesus in the Garden of Gethsemane
The Scourging of Jesus at the Pillar
The Crowning with Thorns
The Carrying of the Cross
The Crucifixion

The Glorious Mysteries
The Resurrection of Jesus from the Dead
The Ascension of Jesus into Heaven
The Descent of the Holy Spirit upon the Apostles
The Assumption of Mary into Heaven
The Coronation of Mary as Queen of Heaven

Sources:
Renard, John. *The Handy Religion Answer Book*. Detroit: Visible Ink Press, 2002.

ROSH HASHANAH *see* **Judaism, Calendar of**

S

SABBATH

By the seventh day God had finished the work he had been doing; so on the seventh day he rested from all his work. And God blessed the seventh day and made it holy, because on it he rested from all the work of creating that he had done. (Genesis 2:2–3)

Remember the Sabbath day by keeping it holy. Six days you shall labor and do all your work, but the seventh day is a Sabbath to the Lord your God. On it you shall not do any work…. For in six days the Lord made the heavens and the earth … but he rested on the seventh day and made it holy. (Exodus 20:8–10)

These verses from the Hebrew scriptures constitute the driving command for Shabbat, or Jewish Sabbath, the weekly day of rest that begins with sunset on Friday and continues through sunset on Saturday evening.

The Talmud (see Judaism, Development of) outlines the laws and statutes tradition has regulated, defining what "work" is, what is and is not allowed, and how the day is to be celebrated. The Friday night kiddush, the benediction offered over wine and bread, ushers in the holy day that begins the weekly commemoration of creation. It is such a strong tradition that there have been times, such as during the Maccabean revolt, that Jews refused to defend themselves rather than break Shabbat.

The day is not viewed as a burden, something one must keep, but rather as a joy—something one gets to observe. The celebration of "Queen" Shabbat has, over the years, developed into a ritual.

On Friday night there is a blessing over candles, generally said or sung by the woman of the house, just before sunset. There is usually public worship at the synagogue. Evening and morning, after synagogue worship, a kiddush, or prayer of blessing, is spoken.

Three special meals are observed—the first on Friday evening, the second at noon on Saturday, and the third later in the afternoon. The Zemirot, one of many liturgical hymns, is often sung during these meals.

Shabbat is a time for study and reflection, usually of a section of Torah.

The day is concluded with the Havdalah ceremony, a separation ritual, on Saturday night.

Not all Jews hold to this strict observance, of course. Many families have developed their own traditions. But what has become known as the spirit of the Sabbath is very important. Even if traditional observances are not followed, a time of rest, refreshment, and remembrance is still observed even by many nonreligious Jews. Because the rest of the world does not recognize Saturday as a day of rest, many Jews—shopkeepers, for instance, or those who work at jobs requiring their presence on Saturdays—have had to make compromises.

In addition to the weekly Sabbaths, there are also anniversary Sabbaths held throughout the year, with yearly Sabbaths held every seventh year. Traditionally these were years set apart to let the land enjoy a Sabbath rest, to be replenished by lying fallow for a season.

There is a widely held belief that Sunday became a Christian Sabbath, a change in the day of rest. But Sunday is never referred to in the Bible by the name Sabbath. It was called the Lord's Day by early Christians, referring to the fact that Jesus was said to have risen on Sunday. It rapidly became a day of worship. But Shabbat continued to be a Jewish observance, and the early church never intended to supersede it.

Sources:
Bridger, David, ed. *The New Jewish Encyclopedia*. New York: Behrman House, 1962.

SACRAMENT

(See also Catholicism)

Augustine (354–430 CE) was the first to officially define the word sacrament, and his definition has stood the test of time. He said it was "an outward and temporal [visible] sign of an inward and enduring grace." In other words, a sacrament incorporates visible symbols that illustrate an invisible work of God. One example is baptism (see Baptism), which uses water to illustrate the theological premise that God "washes away" sin.

But some theological explanations go deeper than what is suggested by the word "illustrate." Some religions teach that the actual act, using the visible symbol, is what triggers the inward reality. In the case of baptism, for example, there are those who believe that without the outward act of cleansing, the inward reality never happens. In other words, if you are not baptized with water according to the rituals of the particular sect, you are not "saved."

A priest preparing the Eucharist, the embodiment of Christ, for the sacrament of Holy Communion. *Fortean Picture Library.*

Early on, the Roman Catholic Church recognized seven specific sacraments. Most Protestant denominations recognize only baptism and the Lord's Supper as sacraments. But even within these communities there is often disagreement as to the meaning, extent, and outward presentation of each sacrament.

THE RELIGION BOOK: PLACES, PROPHETS, SAINTS, AND SEERS

Sources:
Douglas, J. D., ed. *The New International Dictionary of the Christian Church*. Grand Rapids, MI: Zondervan Publishing, 1974.

SACRED DANCE *see* **Dance, Sacred**

SACRIFICE

The first "religious" act was probably ritual burial (see Burial Customs). The second might well have been sacrifice. No one knows why. All we can do is guess.

It could be that the human religious response to the unknown is to bargain. "If you do that, I will give you this." As in, "If you spare my crop, I will give you the first grain." But it could also be that human response to the unknown is to bribe. "How big an offering will it take to get you to spare my fields? My first fruits? My best lamb? My firstborn?"

All we know for sure is that sacrifice is found very early in the historical record. The disturbing fact is that human sacrifice is also found very early. And the practice seems to be universal. From Europe to China and all over the Americas, rising to the heights of gruesome ritual in Central America, animal as well as human sacrifice is well documented.

Even the biblical heroes, including David and Solomon, had the idea that the bigger the sacrifice, the deeper the sincerity. At the dedication of the Great Temple, Solomon offered a sacrifice consisting of "22,000 cattle and 120,000 sheep and goats" (1 Kings 8:63). With this kind of sentiment building, it is no wonder that the Hebrew psalmist laments, "You do not delight in sacrifice, or I would bring it; you do not take pleasure in burnt offerings. The sacrifices of God are a broken spirit; a broken and contrite heart" (Psalm 51:15–17).

We find the concept of sacrifice in every major religion. Practitioners of Buddhism and Hinduism tend to offer grain or vegetable sacrifices to specific deities. Those of Shinto and Confucianism tend to honor ancestors with sacrifices or offerings of fruit.

Judaism, Christianity, and Islam began with a human sacrifice—or at least an attempted one. The sacrifice of Isaac, or, according to Islamic tradition, Ishmael (see Abraham), marks the beginning of a long, involved theological journey to the present-day ritual of the Catholic Mass and the Protestant Communion service. Although Jewish sacrifices ceased with the destruction of the Jerusalem Temple in 70 CE (see Judaism, Development of), the practice is still symbolically remembered in Christianity. Jesus said, "This is my body ... This is my blood ... Take this in remembrance of me." The bread and wine used in these services point directly to what is understood as the sacrifice to end all sacrifices. God offered, in the closely reasoned logic of the author of the book of Hebrews, a final sacrifice that summed up all the animal sacrifices of the past (Hebrews 9 and 10). Modern Christians have "spruced up" the ritual so much that an observer might miss the meaning behind what is, in fact, the celebration of a very bloody, very painful sacrifice.

What tends to boggle the mind of most moderns, however, is that sacrifice was often seen as an honor. In Central American Indian traditions, those who were sacrificed were often willing victims. The winner of the ritual ball game (we don't really know what the rules were, but the stadiums have been excavated) joyfully accepted his death. Having proved his worthiness and received the adulation of his peers, the victim died at the very height of the greatest moment of his life. The modern equivalent would be to kill the quarterback who wins the Super Bowl. In other Central and South American villages, an innocent virgin, trained for her task, willingly gave up her life so that her grateful neighbors could have a bountiful harvest. She was honored, not pitied. At least, that's what the archaeological evidence and oral legends seem to indicate.

Even our language reveals the long history of sacrifice for the good of the tribe. In "America's game" of baseball, when a batter taps a ball down the first-base line, knowing he will be tagged out but at the same time advancing a teammate to a better scoring position, the strategy is called a "sacrifice bunt." And every Sunday afternoon during football season, a player praises a teammate who is "not afraid to sacrifice his body" for the good of the team.

Perhaps the altruistic idea of giving something up to gain something better for the community is behind the idea of ritual sacrifice. We simply don't know. What seems logical to us in this century might not even approach the reality of previous civilizations.

We will probably never know. Whatever the reasons, the practice of ritual sacrifice is one of the few universal religious rituals.

Sources:
Bridger, David, ed. *The New Jewish Encyclopedia*. New York: Behrman House, 1962.
Douglas, J. D., ed. *The New International Dictionary of the Christian Church*. Grand Rapids, MI: Zondervan Publishing, 1974.

SAINTS *see* **Catholicism**

SALAT *see* **Islam**

SALEM WITCH TRIALS

On the afternoon of January 20, 1692, Elizabeth Parris, age nine, and Abigail Williams, age eleven, began to scream obscenities, alternate between convulsive seizures and trancelike states, and exhibit other odd behaviors that quickly grabbed the attention of their neighbors in the town of Salem, Massachusetts. Over the next few days, other girls of about the same age began to act out in similar fashion. Within a month, when no other cause could be found to explain these actions, the townspeople decided the girls must have been bewitched by Satan.

The Reverend Samuel Parris, Elizabeth's father, led prayer services with the hope of exorcising the demons. Just to make sure all the religious bases were covered, a man named John Indian—probably not his real name—baked a cake featuring ingredients of rye meal and the girls' urine. This was "reverse magic" that was supposed to reveal the identities of the witches who had afflicted the girls.

Under such ecumenical influence, the girls confessed that a woman named Tituba, a Carib Indian slave "owned" by the Reverend Parris, was the witch. Later

Painting of the witch trial of George Jacobs, who was hanged based on the testimony of a child in Salem, Massachusetts, 1692. *Fortean Picture Library.*

confessions disclosed that Tituba was a member of a coven, along with Sarah Good and Susan Osborne.

On February 29th, warrants were issued for their arrest. Good and Osborne professed their innocence:

Judges Hathorne and Corwin: What evil spirit have you familiarity with?

Sarah Good: None.

Judges: Have you made no contract with the devil?

Good: No.

Judges: Why do you hurt these children?

Good: I do not hurt them. I scorn it.

Judges: Who do you employ then to do it?

Good: I employ no body.

Judges: What creature do you employ then?

Good: No creature. I am falsely accused.

But Tituba confessed that she often saw the devil, who looked "sometimes like a hog and sometimes like a great dog."

The trials continued throughout the spring and summer. By October 8th, more than twenty people, mostly women, had been found guilty and executed. Some were burned, others were hanged, and a few were squashed to death according to a quirky New England custom of building a sort of dance floor over the victim, and then holding a community party on it, involving people, horses, wagons, and anything else heavy. Many more faced the torture of being locked up in a jail cell and left to wonder what was going to happen to them.

Puritans of no less stature than the great Cotton Mather traveled from all over the area to witness the trials, taking back reports to their home churches. It was the talk of New England. Some people were probably just titillated. New England in 1692 could, after all, be a pretty dull place. And when women were publicly stripped to the waist and whipped to get them to confess, there must have been those who decided they would rather attend the public spectacle than hoe a long row of corn on a hot August afternoon. Even the courtroom debates were interesting.

But others, such as Thomas Brattle, were simply appalled. He wrote a highly articulate letter to the governor of the commonwealth, convincing him to make a declaration that no evidence of a supernatural nature could be allowed in a court of law.

That took the wind out of the sails of the prosecution, because all they had was supernatural evidence.

Then, on October 29th, Governor Phips dissolved the local court and ordered all further trials to be held before the State Superior Court. These took place in May of 1693. No one was convicted. The trials were over.

But the legend lingers on. Even today people flock to Salem to relive those scandalous ten months. Laurie Cabot (see Cabot, Laurie) has even made it her headquarters, the better to draw attention to the modern religion of Wicca (see Wicca).

Why did they do it? How could people have become so involved with supposed "witchcraft" and "devil worship" that they went so completely off the deep end of their religion? What happened to the words of Jesus about love and compassion?

Well, we might ask the same thing about the McCarthyism that swept the United States half a century ago. Mass hysteria is a terrible thing. But there were probably other reasons. Francis Hill, in her book *A Delusion of Satan*, suggests the witch trials my have been fueled by motives ranging from personal jealousy to post-traumatic stress syndrome experienced by those who fought in the American Indian wars. Fueled by sermons that questioned whether or not Indians had souls, ex-soldiers may have come to believe that the only reason the colonists suffered such bloody losses to "ignorant savages" was that Indians were in league with the devil. Now the devil was close at hand. In a classic case of misplaced aggression, they persecuted the innocent and helpless.

We'll probably never know. But of all the dark chapters in Christian history, the time of the Salem witch trials is undoubtedly one of the worst.

A volunteer rings the bell for the Salvation Army funds drive during the Christmas holiday season. The signature red collection bucket stands in the background. *AP/Wide World Photos.*

Sources:

Buckland, Raymond. *The Witch Book: The Encyclopedia of Witchcraft, Wicca, and Neo-paganism.* Detroit: Visible Ink Press, 2002.

Hill, Francis. *A Delusion of Satan: The Full Story of the Salem Witch Trials.* Cambridge, MA: Da Capo Press, 2002.

SALVATION ARMY

Within half an hour of the September 11, 2001, terrorist attack on the World Trade Center in New York, some 200 officers of the Salvation Army were on hand, offering coffee and hot meals, clothes, teddy bears to comfort children, and words of prayer and encouragement to anyone who needed them. The Salvation Army set up shop in more than twenty-four buildings, almost one million square feet of valuable Manhattan commercial space. Hundreds of trucks poured in and out of the city carrying sandwiches, hot dogs, food, water, and even eye drops. Every one of them bore the familiar logo of the Salvation Army, the same logo painted on the kettles that appear every Christmas in local shopping malls. No one will ever know for sure, but this effort may well go down as one of the greatest, most efficient, and most appreciated charity endeavors ever held on American soil.

The current leader of this $2.1 billion organization is a man by the name of Todd Bassett. He makes $13,000 a year. (To put this in perspective, Marsha Evans, CEO of the American Red Cross, made $450,000 in 2002.) According to the latest U.S. figures, that's poverty level. And his worldwide staff doesn't do any better. Obviously they're not in it for the money. They are committed Christians. The Salvation Army is a Christian church. Attend a worship service held in the auditorium of the Salvation Army building in your town and you will come away thinking you've just attended an evangelical Protestant church service. And you have. They are in the business of saving souls. That's where the "Salvation" part of the name comes from. The "Army" part comes from the fact that they are organized along the same lines as the military. The person who runs a local Salvation Army is probably called "Captain" or "Lieutenant," not Reverend.

But what makes the Salvation Army unique is that William Booth, its Methodist founder, believed way back in 1865 that you couldn't talk to someone about Christ if his or her stomach was growling. He decided to minister to the teeming denizens of London's slums, offering them "soup, soap, and salvation."

Thirty-five years later the movement jumped across the Atlantic, setting up shop in New York City's Battery Park. After that, it was only a matter of time and effort.

When a hurricane devastated Galveston, Texas, in 1900, the Salvation Army was there. Since then its members have offered assistance at every national tragedy and most neighborhood fires, answering the call for major disasters and for knocks on their door in the dead of night.

You may think they only appear during the holidays. You may even resent their very visible presence as volunteers ring bells, asking for donations during the busy shopping days before Christmas. But their records and statistics are public knowledge. There's no gimmick and no hidden agenda. They do it because they believe in their ministry.

Sources:
Hudson, Winthrop S. *Religion in America.* New York: Charles Scribner, 1965.
Sedgwick, John, and Loch Adamson. "The Bucket Brigade." *Reader's Digest,* December 2002.

SAMHAIN *see* **Paganism, Calendar of**

SAWM *see* **Islam**

SCAPEGOAT

The high priest is to take two goats and present them before the Lord at the entrance to the Tent of Meeting. He is to cast lots for the goats—one for the Lord and the other for "Azazel" (literally, "the goat of removal," the scapegoat).

These instructions are found in the biblical book of Leviticus, chapter 16. They describe actions that are to be taken by the high priest on the Day of Atonement (see Judaism, Calendar of). Two goats were to be brought before him. He would place his hands on their heads and confess the sins of the people. One would be slaughtered as a sacrifice to God. The other—well, that's where the problem lies.

The Bible says the second goat is to be offered "to Azazel," but no one knows for sure what that means. The most popular explanation is that Azazel means "scapegoat," and that's how most Bibles translate it. The idea behind the scapegoat is that he is to be sent out into the desert, separated from the people "as far as the east is from the west." He escapes death, but he carries the sins of the people with him to his dying day. They sinned, he suffers. They were guilty, he pays the price. That's what "scapegoat" has come to mean: an innocent person who is forced to take the blame.

We use the word all the time in politics. Officials mess something up so they need to find someone who is at fault. Vice President Spiro Agnew became President Richard Nixon's scapegoat. He resigned and was forced out into a political desert. President Jimmy Carter was blamed for not bringing home the prisoners of war from Vietnam, so he took the political rap and became the nation's scapegoat.

But is that what the Bible really says "Azazel" means?

Many scholars today disagree with the traditional interpretation. They believe "Azazel" doesn't refer to the goat at all. Instead it refers to either the place the goat was sent (the desert) or the demonic presence that inhabited the desert—in other words, Satan, the one who first caused humans to sin. That sin, these scholars say, is now returned to him, or put back upon him. This interpretation would mean the guilty party pays for the sin, not an innocent scapegoat.

If this second view proves to be correct, it would really cause a linguistic problem, because even those who have never read the Bible have learned what a scapegoat is. And sometimes a scapegoat is handy to have around. We use the concept whenever we want to shift blame away from ourselves. We place it on someone or something else, a scapegoat. So if proper interpretation someday forces us to throw our whole understanding of scapegoat out the window and we lose the biblical excuse to place fault on someone else when we mess up, remember to blame the theologians.

Sources:

Bucke, Emory Stevens et al, eds. *The Interpreter's Dictionary of the Bible*. 4 vols. New York: Abingdon Press, 1962.

SCIENTOLOGY

During the mid-1900s a man by the name of L. Ron Hubbard (1911–1986) began to study a field of metaphysics he called Dianetics, a word he coined to describe "what the soul is doing to the body." The book he wrote about his studies explained that humans have lost touch with their environment. People, he said, don't *have* spirits. They *are* spirits (literally *thetans*, from the Greek letter theta, which is often used as a symbol for spirit). What they have is a mind and a body. But they have forgotten this. They have forgotten who they really are. They live false lives, concentrating on all the wrong things. As a result, they suffer stress-related, psychosomatic illnesses and have lost the ability to be happy.

Drawing from what he estimated were some 50,000 years of religious wisdom, Hubbard believed he was the first to apply scientific methods and discoveries to the great questions of life: Who am I? Where did I come from? Where am I going?

In this sense, the Church of Scientology ("scientology" literally means "knowing how to know") is, according to its founder, the first religion that combines scientific principle with religious belief. It's a universal church for the new age, drawing from the fields of both science and religion.

His ideas were convincing enough to draw the attention of some very well known people. Actors John Travolta and Tom Cruise are among the most frequently mentioned high-profile members of the church.

Hubbard taught that humans were basically good, not evil. Experience and wrong thinking have taught them to commit evil deeds. Disagreeing with the Christian position first expressed by the apostle Paul (see Paul, Saul of Tarsus), Hubbard asserted that evil is not a part of basic human nature. It is something people do, rather than something they are.

What this means is that humans can improve by advancing spiritually. It takes work, training, and, according to critics, a lot of money, but it is something people can accomplish if they apply themselves.

As soon as Scientology began its phenomenal growth, attracting famous people and a big bank account, cries of "cult" began to be heard throughout the land.

Scientology has a lot in common with what people consider cults to be. It had a charismatic, high-profile leader. Stories about mind control and secret initiation rites began to circulate. People were said to be afraid to go against the wishes of the governing hierarchy. The high-profile adherents were called fronts or marketing tools.

Scientology has a lot of followers, and it is growing by leaps and bounds. It also has a lot of detractors, who say it will cost the average convert some $400,000 over the course of an average lifetime.

What Scientology calls therapy, its critics call brainwashing. What Scientology calls a church, its detractors label a cult. Scientology has been granted tax-exempt status as a church. L. Ron Hubbard is gone, but controversy still surrounds him.

Sources:
What Is Scientology? http://www.whatisscientology.org. September 14, 2003.

SET *see* Egyptian Gods and Goddesses

SEVENTH-DAY ADVENTISM

America has produced a host of people who have fanned the fires of messianic faith. The idea that a Messiah (see Messiah), most often identified as Jesus, will return to set things straight has spawned hope since the inception of the country.

One messianic group, known today as the Millerites, took the eastern states by storm ten years before the Civil War. William Miller (1782–1849), a farmer from Low Hampton, New York, had been converted in 1816. He was a Baptist who studied the Bible, trying to determine when Jesus would return. From evidence gathered from the generation tables listed in Genesis, the visions recorded by the prophet Daniel, and prophetic passages in the book of Revelation, he decided the return of Christ would happen "about the year 1843." His evidence seemed so overwhelming that some 50,000 people were convinced he was right. The target date he had determined was March 21st. Revival meetings were held as the time grew close. But when the day passed without incident, people began to despair. Miller, however, discovered he had made a crucial error. One of his followers pointed out that Habakkuk 2:3 and selected passages from Leviticus indicated that there would be a "tarrying time" before Christ would return. This gave the earth a second chance. October 22, 1844, was the actual date. It was "the tenth day of the seventh month" of the Jewish calendar. "Thank the Lord," said Miller, "I am almost home. Glory! Glory! I see the time is correct!"

Once again, it didn't happen. Miller's following, most of whom had sold homes and possessions, were despondent. Some of them became Shakers. Others just drifted away. Miller himself was excommunicated by the Baptist Church and died in 1849, a discredited and almost forgotten man. The whole episode was called the Great Disappointment.

But a few believers went back to their Bibles to figure out what had gone wrong. Some of them believed a minor miscalculation must have been made—a verse or two left out of the equation. They met in Albany, New York, in 1845 to form a new Protestant denomination, based on the premise that Christ would return according to a pattern prophesied in scripture. This new conference, following the pattern of many Protestant churches, later split into three factions. The largest remains today and is called the Advent Christian Church.

But some of Miller's followers began to think a woman named Ellen Gould White (1827–1915) had found the answer. Although only a young woman at the time of the Great Disappointment, after much study and prayer she began to preach a message that many were coming to believe. October 22, 1844, was the correct date. They hadn't miscalculated. They just had not interpreted correctly what was supposed to happen. Christ obviously didn't come back to Earth at that time. Instead, he entered the heavenly sanctuary to begin the second and last phase of his atoning ministry. Because the Church had neglected proper observance of the Sabbath, just as the Jews had done before the time of the Babylonian captivity (see Babylonian Captivity), Christ "was tarrying, not willing that any should perish." The world still had time. But there was a lot of work to do. Jesus would return shortly. But first people needed to know what was happening.

The name Seventh-day Adventist was chosen in 1860, but the denomination was officially formed on May 21, 1863. One hundred twenty-five churches and some 3,500 believers were now united as one Protestant, evangelical community who shared much in common with other fundamentalist Christian churches. What set the Adventists apart was their worship on what they called the true Sabbath, Saturday, the seventh day of the week.

White was a prominent author and gifted speaker. Her works are still studied today. The church believes she was given the spiritual gift of prophecy and was an integral part of God's plan concerning the return of Jesus Christ and the end of sin in the world.

Adventists, in common with many other fundamentalists, believe the Bible explains the plan of God. Satan was a created being, the greatest of the angels, who fell into sin. After the world was destroyed by the great flood as a result of that sin, God put into effect a plan to redeem it. The story is progressive. Little by little people began to understand more of the story as it unfolded. Throughout the Old Testament the plan was illustrated in type and symbol. The earthly sanctuary and its rules were a copy of the heavenly sanctuary. The rituals of the priests were a copy of what goes on in heaven. The laws showed God's plan for righteous living. When Christ, the Son of God, was born, humans rejected and crucified him. Christ's death on the cross was the ultimate, atoning sacrifice for sin. Jesus will return but is now serving in the heavenly sanctuary, fulfilling his role as high priest until, like the priest of old, he comes out of the sanctuary to minister to the people. That will be at the time of his Second Advent, or Second Coming. The dead will arise, Earth will be cleansed, and the heavenly sanctuary, the New Jerusalem, will literally come down from heaven to Earth. Some say it approaches even now down an immense "road," empty of stars, in the region of the constellation Orion.

Adventists have built a worldwide network of schools and hospitals, sending missionaries to every nation on Earth. They maintain their own publishing house and have been especially active in the fields of family life, health, and higher education, emphasizing excellent academic departments in the humanities.

Sources:
Hudson, Winthrop S. *Religion in America.* New York: Charles Scribner, 1965.
Seventh-Day Adventist Church. http://www.adventist.org. September 15, 2003.

SHAKERS/UNITED SOCIETY OF BELIEVERS

During the eighteenth century many Christian communities, sects, cults, and denominations were formed, each with its own expressive way of interpreting the Gospel.

In Manchester, England, a group led by James Wardley broke off from a Quaker community (see Quakers/Religious Society of Friends) because they wanted to practice a form of religious expression foreign to Quaker tradition. They believed in the ideals of simplicity and gender equality beloved by Quakers, but their services were often interrupted as members experienced ecstatic dance and trembling when filled with the Holy Spirit. Because of this habit, they became known as "Shaking Quakers." Understandably for the time, they were soon the objects of persecution and harassment.

One of the founders of the group was a young woman known as Ann Lee. During a long imprisonment she experienced a vision in which it was revealed to her that she was the Second Coming of Christ, the female component of "God the Father/Mother." Upon her release, "Mother Lee," as she came to be called, became the leader of the movement.

With a theology so radically different from mainstream Protestantism, the group, now called Shakers, were forced to immigrate to the United States, home of many diverse sects and cults. They arrived in New York City in May of 1774, gained some converts, and started a commune in Watervliet, New York.

Their timing couldn't have been worse. Persecution intensified, first because the Shakers were different, second because the bumptious Revolutionary War spirit so prevalent in America at this time was often directed at anyone who had recently come over from England, and third because the Shakers were pacifists.

They might have simply disappeared into history, forgotten like so many other small Christian cults, were it not for a religious revival called the New Light Stir that swept across New England beginning about the time of the signing of the Declaration of Independence. Other independent but like-minded sects united with the Shakers, impressed by the preaching of Mother Lee, who traveled and taught extensively in the western portions of Massachusetts and surrounding states. She died in 1784 having accomplished what she had set out to do. The Shaker religion was now firmly entrenched.

It wasn't just due to Mother Lee, however. "Father John" Meachim recognized early on the attraction many people had for Shaker furniture, music, dancing, and books, all of which demonstrated simple design and flawless craftsmanship. These industries began to finance the organization and served as marketing tools.

And it was good that they did, because the only way the Shaker religion was going to grow was by making converts. They couldn't "grow their own" like other religions because they practiced absolute celibacy. According to Mother Lee, sex was a gift given only for reproduction. It constituted the original sin in the Garden of Eden. The only way to grow spiritually was to return to the uncorrupted state of Adam and Eve before they started fooling around with something God had intended only as a reproductive duty.

Needless to say, no babies have ever been born into the Shaker religion. That tends to keep the numbers down.

By the 1880s Shakers had peaked in terms of numbers. They became sort of a tourist attraction that "worldly people" could observe. Their furniture and music were certainly in great demand. Ironically, there may have been more complicated musical arrangements of the Shaker tune "Simple Gifts" than of any other song. No less a luminary than Leonard Bernstein tried his hand. But probably Aaron Copland's ballet music, *Appalachian Spring,* takes the prize for the most musically complex and embellished setting of a tune written to celebrate simplicity. On the other hand, thanks to Martha Graham's choreography, at least people dance to it. Mother Lee would have appreciated that.

But all good things come to an end. Industrialization caught the fancy of the American public, and mass-produced chairs soon replaced the handcrafted Shaker furniture so sought after today by antique dealers. During the twentieth century the Shakers retreated into small communities, cutting way down on their contact with outsiders. In 1965 the group decided to accept no new members. Only two small communities, one in New Hampshire and the other in Maine, now remain. A few new members were received into the Maine community at Sabbath Lake during the 1990s, but some original members refused to recognize them. So, very soon, the Shakers will have no remaining presence save for their historical legacy and museum displays.

Sources:
Brown, Jane Roy. "In Hew Hampshire, an Orderly Shaker Kingdom." *Boston Globe,* June 30, 2002.
Hudson, Winthrop S. *Religion in America.* New York: Charles Scribner, 1965.
"The Shakers." *The Religious Movements Homepage at the University of Virginia.* http://religious-movements.lib.virginia.edu/nrms/Shakers.html. September 13, 2003.

SHINTO

Shinto means "the way of the gods" (*to* means "the way.") Its beginning in Japanese culture is lost in the mist of time, certainly going back into prehistory.

A visit to Japan, even in today's hustling and bustling, westernized, materialistic Japanese society, still reveals islands of peace and quiet in small shrines built to honor a local kami. (A Japanese concept, difficult to define, "kami" corresponds roughly to the Western notion of spirit; see Kami).

The four affirmations of Shinto revolve around tradition, joy, purity (as opposed to pollution), and festival. When the Olympic Games were held in Japan in 1998, television viewers were treated to this wonderful tradition as the opening ceremonies celebrated these affirmations in a uniquely Shinto fashion.

Even the famous Japanese sumo wrestling match is bound by Shinto tradition and follows specific rules. The rules, whether used for wrestling or any other ceremony, are easy to remember because in English they all begin with the letter "p."

Purification

In Shinto there is no concept of the "fall" of humanity. The world, the environment, and natural surroundings are all beautiful. But impurities and misfortunes, called *tsumi*, do arise. When this happens, rituals can invoke the kami to "carry the *tsumi* to the sea." Purification ceremonies are very important. They calm and cleanse, restoring a state of grace and beauty.

Presentation

Rituals became traditionalized long, long ago. A priest, after a purification ceremony, might take a very carefully arranged offering of fruit or vegetables into a shrine and present it before the altar of the kami of the shrine.

Prayer

Sometimes ritualistic dances are performed. Or the priest might intone a chant or traditional prayer.

The Heian Shinto shrine in Kyoto, Japan. *Fortean Picture Library.*

Participation

At the close of the service the participants are often presented with a small branch or some other natural gift, showing that they have participated in the ceremony. Sometimes a small sip of wine is offered.

If the ceremony is a civic celebration, of course, the order and style is blown up large. Parades and festivals accompanied by pageants draw people from miles away to participate.

Shinto has been influenced by other religions. Buddhism, particularly Zen Buddhism (see Buddhism, Development of), has made its mark, and westernization, especially since World War II, has made it difficult for Shinto to continue in its traditional forms. But the spirit of Shinto is so ingrained in Japanese culture that there will always be a place for tradition, peace, and unity with natural surroundings. There continue to be places in Japan where a visitor can be surrounded by such beautiful, natural harmony that, in the words of the late Joseph Campbell, "You can't even tell where art leaves off and nature begins."

Sources:
Ellwood, Robert S., and Barbara A. McGraw. *Many Peoples, Many Faiths*. 6th ed. Upper Saddle River, NJ: Prentice Hall, 1999.

SHINTO TEXTS

Shinto's oldest text was compiled in 712 CE by O No Yasamaro. It is called the Kojiki and tells the story of the creation of the world.

> Before the heavens came into existence, all was chaos, unimaginably limitless and without definite shape or form. Eon followed eon: and then, lo! Out of this boundless, shapeless mass something light and transparent rose up and formed the heaven. This was the Plain of High Heavens, in which materialized a deity called Ame-no-Minaka-Nushi-no-Mikoto (the Deity-of-the-August-Center-of-Heaven). Next the heavens gave birth to a deity named Takami-Musubi-no-Mikoto (the High-August-Producing-Wondrous-Deity), followed by a third called Kami-Musubi-no-Mikoto (the Divine-Producing-Wondrous-Deity). These three divine beings are called the Three Creating Deities.

In 720, the Kojiki was joined with the thirty-volume Nihongi or Nihon Shoki, the "Chronicle of Japan," which relates the history of Japan from its mythological inception to the coming of the Emperor in 697.

These texts are often coupled with the *yengishiki*, Shinto rituals related to the harvest, wind gods, fire, evil spirits, the road god, the sun goddess, and purification.

Writing didn't develop until quite late in Japanese history—sometime during the eighth century CE. Since "history" begins with writing, this means that virtually everything before that time has to be considered prehistoric. These early Shinto texts employed Chinese script and were probably influenced by Chinese history, but they are in character with the very early history of Japan, going back to 4500 BCE, when the first Japanese people lived in pit dwellings and survived by hunting and fishing. Many stone circles have been unearthed, indicating rituals involving sun worship. Because of this ancient history, Shinto texts show no history of "coming from" anywhere. The Kojiki and Nihonga assume the sacredness of the motherland, the womb from which the people sprang.

Sources:
Gengi Shibukawa. *Tales from the Kojiki*. http://www.wsu.edu:8080/~wldciv/world_civ_reader/world_civ_reader_1/kojiki.html. September 19, 2003.
Ludwig, Theodore M. *The Sacred Paths: Understanding the Religions of the World*. 2nd ed. Upper Saddle River: Prentice Hall, 1996.

SHU *see* Egyptian Gods and Goddesses

SIDDHARTHA *see* Buddha

SIKHISM

New religious movements are sometimes formed on the borders between two or more established religions. Voodoo (see Voodoo/Vodou/Vodun) is one example. Another is

Sikhism. Now numbering some eight million people, it began early in the sixteenth century when its founder, Nanak (1469–1539), had a vision. Steeped in both Muslim and Hindu tradition, Nanak was a mystic poet who believed that God—the all-encompassing God who is called by many names and who is above all understanding—had appeared to him in a vision. "There is no Hindu," he told his followers. "There is no Muslim." Sikhs call God Sat Nam, the True or Absolute Name. It is not important, claimed Nanak, to use only this particular term. God doesn't care what name you use. But it is important to understand that God is not limited by what name we choose to employ. The repetition of Sat Nam is true devotion, equal to any Muslim pilgrimage to Mecca or any Hindu journey to Benares. Freedom is found in submission to Sat Nam.

This is the essence of Sikhism. It combines the mystical tradition of Hinduism, the absolute devotion of ritualistic worship of Brahman, "He who cannot be named," with the fierce Muslim loyalty and submission to the one, all-encompassing Allah, "the God." The name of the religion means "learner."

Nanak thought of himself as a guru, a teacher of the new faith. Nine more gurus were to follow him, and after the death of the tenth and last, the scriptures of Sikhism were composed. They are called the Holy Granth and comprise poems and writings of the ten gurus.

> Those who believe in power,
> Sing of His power;
> Others chant of His gifts
> As His messages and emblems;
> Some sing of His greatness,
> And his gracious acts;
> Some sing of His wisdom
> Hard to understand;
> Some sing of Him as the fashioner of the body,
> Destroying what he has fashioned;
> Others praise Him for taking away life
> And restoring it anew.
> Some proclaim His Existence
> To be far, desperately far, from us;
> Others sing of Him
> As here and there a presence
> Meeting us face to face.
> To sing truly of the transcendent Lord
> Would exhaust all vocabularies, all human powers of expression,
> Myriads have sung of Him in innumerable strains.
> His gifts to us flow in such plenitude
> That man wearies of receiving what God bestows;
> Age on unending age, and lives on His bounty;
> Carefree, O Nanak, the Glorious Lord smiles.

Sikhism has no formal priesthood. Private worship at home in the morning and evening is encouraged. Worship services at the temple consist of hymns and prayers, readings from the Holy Granth, sermons, and the sharing of a sort of communion rite at the end of worship and in dinners following the service. For five hundred years, Sikhs sat on the floor while they dined after worship as a physical testimony to equality. During the twentieth century, however, some Sikh temples began to introduce tables and chairs, prompting accusations of elitism from more traditional worshipers.

Sikhism can best be understood as a mainstream, monotheistic religion with a strong emphasis on ethical behavior, seeing itself as a religion that transcends sectarian traditions.

Sources:

Ellwood, Robert S., and Barbara A. McGraw. *Many Peoples, Many Faiths.* 6th ed. Upper Saddle River, NJ: Prentice Hall, 1999.

Robinson, B. A. "Sikhism: History, Beliefs, Practices, Etc." *Ontario Consultants on Religious Tolerance.* http://www.religioustolerance.org/sikhism.htm. November 28, 2003.

Singh, Trilochan et al, *Adi-granth: Selections from the Sacred Writings of the Sikhs.* New York: Macmillan, 1960.

SOCIETY OF FRIENDS *see* Quakers/Religious Society of Friends

SOCIETY OF JESUS *see* Jesuits

SOLOMON

Israel reached its height of power and wealth about 1000 BCE during the reign of Solomon, its third king. Solomon was the son of the great King David and his famous queen, Bathsheba.

These were the years the first Great Temple and Solomon's palace were built (see also Masons). (Solomon's priorities, however, are a little suspect. He built the Great Temple in seven years. But 1 Kings 7:1 reads, "It took Solomon thirteen years, however, to complete the construction of his palace.") The so-called Wailing Wall, or Western Wall, now standing in Jerusalem is holy to the Jews. This center for prayer is the last remnant of the wall Solomon had built around the city three thousand years ago. Those who travel to this most holy Jewish place are awed by the fact that they can actually touch stones from Solomon's time.

But Solomon was more than a builder. He was a brilliant, and sometimes ruthless, political leader. Through a series of treaties and alliances, he expanded Israel's borders until the nation occupied more area than it had ever controlled before and more than it has possessed since. Commerce expanded greatly. Ships and caravans traveled throughout the whole known world, bringing wealth into a capital that was the talk of the whole Middle East. The "Queen of Sheba" (perhaps Ethiopia) is said to have traveled all the way north from her home just to get a glimpse of the great ruler of Israel. (Perhaps she got more than a glimpse; see Ark of the Covenant; Rastafarianism.)

His wisdom was reported to be far beyond that of normal kings. A famous story, retold in the Bible, is that two women were brought before him, each claiming to be the mother of a small child. He was asked to determine which was the true mother. He ordered the baby cut in two, so that each woman could take home half a child. One woman thought that sounded fair. The other was appalled and offered to give up her half so the baby could live. Solomon, being the smartest man in the world, immediately deduced that the second woman was the baby's mother.

Solomon is also credited with being a great philosopher. The biblical books of Proverbs ("Pride goes before destruction, and a haughty spirit before a fall"), Song of Solomon ("Let him kiss me with the kisses of his mouth"), and Ecclesiastes ("For everything there is a season, and a time for every purpose under Heaven") are all attributed to him, along with some of the Psalms.

All this empire building came at great cost, however. Taxes were so high and conscripted labor so extensive that only an iron-handed tyrant could hold the whole thing together. When Solomon died (probably of exhaustion—according to 1 Kings 11, he had seven hundred wives and three hundred concubines), his son Rehoboam saw the whole thing fall apart when the leaders of Solomon's old regime begged for some relief. Rehoboam made the mistake of thinking he could continue Solomon's policies forever. He decided even to outdo the master. It didn't happen, of course. Civil war broke out. The United Kingdom of Israel was torn in half (see Babylonian Captivity) and never recovered.

Perhaps Solomon saw it coming. Psalm 127 is attributed to him and seems very prophetic. It begins, "Unless the Lord builds the house, its builders labor in vain."

Sources:
The Holy Bible, New International Version. Grand Rapids, MI: Zondervan Bible Publishers, 1978.

SPIRITUALISM

Spiritualists do not "worship" spirits. Neither do they seek to commune with the devil. Some, as was the case with the clairvoyant Edgar Cayce (1877–1945), may be Methodist Sunday-school teachers. Others, as was true of Sir Arthur Conan Doyle (1859–1930), creator of the fictional detective Sherlock Holmes, may be best-selling authors.

But Spiritualists do seek contact with those who have crossed the border dividing the material world from the spiritual. Those who have died are still alive, according to Spiritualist belief, but in a different form.

God is real, but defined in different ways depending upon the individual's level of spiritual development. Often the phrase "the God of your understanding" is used to talk about divinity.

In order to contact "the other side" it is common to consult a person who has developed the gifts necessary to become a conduit to other planes of existence. Such a person is called a medium. Many Spiritualists believe that Jesus Christ was the greatest medium who ever lived on "the earthly plane." Mediums enter a passive, trancelike state and allow spirits to communicate through them. Such an experience is sometimes sought at a séance. (The great magician known to the world as Harry Houdini [1874–1926] tried all his life to discover if such things were really possible. He never attended an authentic séance. A gifted magician himself, he was always able to spot a charlatan. But he never gave up hope that the real thing existed. He promised his wife that when he died he would, if at all possible, communicate with her. He never did.

Photo of the largest spiritualist assembly in the world, at Forest Temple, Lily Dale, New York. *Fortean Picture Library.*

Séances were held every year on the anniversary of his death, but he never spoke to her. After many years, she finally gave up.)

Spiritualism has ancient routes. But its modern American incarnation seems to have begun, as with so many other religions, in upstate New York. In May 1848, Margaretta and Kate Fox were young sisters, eleven and eight years old. They claimed to hear a rapping emanating from an upstairs bedroom. They were able to work out a code and employ it to communicate with entities on "the other side." The news spread like wildfire. Soon the whole country was caught in the spell. "Rappings" were heard everywhere. Tables rose up from the ground and slowly revolved in circles. Voices were heard. Church attendance dwindled, and spiritualist séances exploded in every city and town across America. President Abraham Lincoln (1809–1865) even supported the movement.

But it wasn't long before frauds were uncovered. People who hoped to cash in on the movement through hoax and deception were exposed. The Civil War soon drew attention away from the fad.

But there were those who carried on, believing that just because fraudulent people tried to cash in on Spiritualism, it didn't mean the underlying principles were not real. Many Spiritualist churches had been formed and, just as in other religions, revivals have occurred from time to time. Spiritualist churches usually are formed around the psychic powers of one person, often a woman, who has cultivated her powers through practice and study. Services consist of listening for voices that speak from other planes of existence through mediums. Those who receive the messages then seek to act on them to improve understanding and contentment in this life.

Because the experience of communicating with spirits is an intensely personal one, it is difficult to define the word "spiritualism" with any degree of exactness with which all Spiritualists will agree. There are probably as many definitions as there are Spiritualists. The field is wide open. Of course that means there is still probably a high degree of fraud and deception. But there are those who have sincerely come to the conclusion that there is life after death. This is a belief common to many religions. Spiritualists just go one step further. They believe that those who have died want to be involved with and pass on their accumulated wisdom to loved ones.

Sources:
Ludwig, Theodore M. *The Sacred Paths: Understanding the Religions of the World.* 2nd ed. Upper Saddle River, NJ: Prentice Hall, 1996.

STONEHENGE *see* **Amesbury; Ley Lines**

T

TABERNACLE IN THE WILDERNESS

(See also Moses)

The first Passover had been observed. The children of Israel had left Egypt for good. They had passed through the Red Sea, having witnessed the defeat of Pharaoh's army. Now they were in the desert, headed for the fabled Promised Land. What would happen next?

In the wilderness, Moses, their leader, left camp and headed for the mountain called Sinai, accompanied only by his young aid, Joshua. They were gone for the obligatory forty days. During that time the people panicked, reverting to superstition and fear. They built a golden calf—a remembrance of Egypt and the old life. It was an idol, built in the shadow of Sinai where, at that very moment, Moses was receiving instructions forbidding such activity. Perhaps we can forgive them because they had cast off something old and not yet replaced it with anything new.

When Moses returned he overthrew the idol and presented the people with the foundations of what has become the religion we now call Judaism. In his hands he carried the law (see Ten Commandments). In his mind he carried instructions for the construction of the Tabernacle.

Because the children of Israel had a long way to go before they reached their final destination, the Tabernacle would be portable. It was a big tent, designed to be carried from place to place. Built of wood overlaid with gold leaf, it consisted of an outer court with only one entrance. The only entrance to Eden, they were reminded, was guarded by angels with flaming swords. There was only one way back into the presence of God. And before that way could be traversed, the flaming swords implied that something had to die first.

A worshiper stepping through the one entrance faced a large, bronze altar. Here he offered his sacrifice. The altar was a big barbecue pit, really, where the priests ministered. The worshiper would come, perhaps with a lamb, and stand before the priest. Placing his hands upon the head of his offering, the worshiper confessed his sins. The innocent victim, the lamb, became his substitute. Carrying the worshiper's sin, the lamb was ritually sacrificed and placed upon the altar.

From here, the priest took over. It was his job to represent the worshiper before God. He walked from the altar into the tabernacle itself. Here, too, there was just one entrance. It was the only way to enter into the presence of God. Before entering the front room of the tabernacle, the priest stopped at a bronze wash basin. Wearing the priestly breastplate upon which twelve precious stones were fastened, one for each tribe of Israel, he washed his hands and feet, symbolically cleansing himself.

After this duty was concluded he entered the first room of the Tabernacle. Overhead, sunlight filtered through a fourfold skin covering, the roof of the Tabernacle. The coverings were dyed red, representing blood; blue for the creation; purple for royalty; and white for purity. Three pieces of furniture stood before the priest. At his left hand was the menorah, the seven-fold candelabra that burned continually. At his right hand was a table containing twelve loaves of bread, baked fresh each day, representing the Twelve Tribes of Israel. Before him stood the altar of incense. When he paused here to pray, the smoke from the incense symbolically carried his prayers to heaven. Behind the altar hung the curtain through which he was not permitted entry unless it was the Day of Atonement and he was the priest selected to enter the Holy of Holies, the most holy place in the Tabernacle. Here, behind this curtain, rested the Ark of the Covenant (see Ark of the Covenant). This was where the very presence of God was to be found.

Five hundred years later, during the time of King Solomon, this Tabernacle would be reproduced in magnificent proportions in Jerusalem. But for now, it was the place the children of Israel called home. Wherever they went, they carried their Tabernacle, and their God, with them. They would never forget.

At the dedication ceremony, "a cloud covered the Tent of Meeting, and the glory of the Lord filled the Tabernacle. Moses could not enter the Tent of Meeting, because the cloud had settled upon it, and the glory of the Lord filled the Tabernacle" (Exodus 40:34–35).

Christian writers would later adapt their own theology to the symbolism inherent in this place. In this interpretation, as explained by the author of the New Testament book of Hebrews, Jesus was the High Priest. Only one entrance was possible because Jesus had said, "I am the door … I am the way." He was the "lamb of God," they would say, that was offered at the bronze altar ("This is my blood, shed for you"). And he was the High Priest who would pause before entering the Tabernacle, washing the feet of his disciples so they could enter the holy place with him. Only then, at the Last Supper—a Passover Seder—would they come to understand that he was the table of fresh baked bread ("I am that bread that came down from heaven … this is my body"). The Holy Spirit, working through them, was the menorah ("You are the light of the world"). Finally he uttered his High Priest prayer (John 17) as if he stood before the altar of incense. Then, after the crucifixion, "the veil of the Temple was torn in two." For the first time, everyone, Jew and Gentile alike, could gaze upon the Most

A morning t'ai chi session with San Francisco residents who gather to practice the Chinese exercise of moving meditation for physical and mental balance. *AP/Wide World Photos*.

Holy Place and see the face of God. Only then was his ministry, prefigured by the Tabernacle, complete.

So for both Jew and Christian, the Tabernacle in the Wilderness is remembered as a holy place indeed.

Sources:
The Holy Bible, New International Version. Grand Rapids, MI: Zondervan Bible Publishers, 1978.

T'AI CHI CH'UAN

One thousand years ago a "marriage" took place between an ancient philosophical religion and a new martial art. The religion was a unique form of Daoism (see Confucianism/Daoism) called Chi Kung ("excellence of energy"). It was devoted to physical health and peaceful, spiritual growth. But with warlords devastating the countryside and bandits coming down out of the mountains to prey upon the poor and helpless, even peaceful monks needed a way to defend themselves against aggression.

The result of this union, inspired by both peace and war, became known as T'ai Chi Ch'uan, or simply T'ai Chi. The movements of T'ai Chi, often described as "swimming in air," and the mental and spiritual focus required to perform them correctly, free the energies of the body to flow naturally. The physical movement is important, but of much more importance is the mental discipline. Human beings can do amazing things. But they usually don't. The reason, according to the practice of T'ai Chi, is that the energies needed to perform at peak capacity are blocked by negative thoughts and actions. The energy flow becomes dammed up, so to speak, and the resulting flood of health problems and mental fatigue can be overwhelming.

Western medicine usually tries to correct the illness at the point of the symptom. It treats, for instance, the symptom of depression with an active drug to counteract the depression. Chinese philosophy takes a different route. Depression is caused by a blockage of energy. It is not "natural" to be depressed. So the point of attack must come at the point of the blockage, not at the resultant symptom.

T'ai Chi sought to remove the blockage by letting nature fight the battle. Through martial art exercises it was discovered that the mind could be centered, fully involved in the present moment. When the mind is fully centered, fully at peace, the possibility to change, correct, and heal the body was realized. Change is natural. Everything changes constantly. But the human tendency is to resist change—to meet its force with more force. The resultant collision is typically Western. When someone hits us, we hit back, harder. The martial artist does the opposite. Force is resisted by yielding. The force of the opponent is thus used against him, to throw him off balance.

In the same manner, when illness strikes a blow, the Eastern approach is not to strike back with drugs, but to yield, to "go with the flow," throwing the illness off balance by yielding, allowing it to simply dissipate beneath the natural flow of energy, *chi*, which is the body's normal defense.

T'ai Chi is a ritual in which daily practice forms the habit of living fully in the moment and "going with the flow." The essence of T'ai Chi is not in learning a set of movements, although it may appear to observers that practitioners are doing just that. Neither is it in learning basic self-defense, although that can happen in the course of study. It is found instead in becoming aware of normal laws of flowing energy, of exploring natural health and wellness. That is why it is common to see, in the parks and public spaces of Chinese cities, people of all ages standing together at dawn and "swimming in air," practicing the movements they have learned, seemingly oblivious to one another. They are not "out there" somewhere. Just the opposite. They are "in here," totally in the moment, focused on the very essence of life, the energy that flows through us all.

Sources:

Perfetti, Ron. "Overview and Benefits of T'ai Chi Ch'uan." *T'ai Chi Ch'uan with Ron Perfetti.* http://www.ronperfetti.com/overview.html. September 13, 2003.

TALISMAN *see* **Healing Effigy/Amulet/Talisman/Fetish**

TALMUD *see* **Tanakh**

TANAKH

(See also Bible; Judaism, Development of)

The Hebrew scriptures are called Tanakh. This is an acronym based on the three sections comprising the whole. Each section contains books written by many different authors over many centuries. So the Tanakh can probably best be thought of as a library or collection, rather than a single volume. But it tells a unified story, a history of the Jewish people from the beginning of creation until about 400 BCE.

The first part is called Torah and consists of five books. These are called the Pentateuch (from *penta* for "five") or the Books of Moses (because they were purportedly given by God to Moses on Mount Sinai). Torah relates the history of the Hebrew people from Creation ("In the beginning, God created the heavens and the earth": Genesis 1:1) until the death of Moses ("Since then, no prophet has risen in Israel like Moses, whom the Lord knew face to face … For no one has ever shown the mighty power or performed the awesome deeds that Moses did in the sight of all Israel": Deuteronomy 34:10, 12).

The second part is called the Prophets (*Nev-im*). These books are said to be the work of men who were called by God over a period of centuries to speak the divine truth boldly and without equivocation. The prophets called for a return to the commandments through social change. They prophesied dire calamities, many of which later came to pass, if the people turned away from the guidelines set forth on Mount Sinai when Moses delivered the law. Many of them, Isaiah being the most prominent, foresaw the coming of a Messiah who would free the people from tyranny and usher in a day of peace and prosperity for the whole earth.

> A shoot will come up from the stump of Jesse; from his roots a branch will bear fruit. The Spirit of the Lord will rest upon him … The wolf will live with the lamb, the leopard will lie down with the goat, the calf and the lion and the yearling together, and a little child will lead them … They will neither harm nor destroy on all my holy mountain, for the earth will be full of the knowledge of the Lord as the waters cover the sea. (Isaiah 11:1–9)

The third part is called the Writings (*Kethuvim*). It consists of a very diverse selection of "wisdom literature" ranging from the poetry of the Psalms to the tragic drama of Job.

Much of the material comprising Tanakh consists of oral tradition, eventually written and edited by many hands during the centuries before 400 BCE. The documents were finally standardized in written form and translated into Greek in a volume called the Septuagint (the "work of the seventy scholars") in 250 BCE. Finally, in the years between 90 and 98 CE, rabbis meeting in the town of Jamania established the criteria that became the standard against which the various books were to be judged. The "final cut" depended on whether or not each individual book met three obligations:

1. Antiquity (written before 400 BCE)
2. Language (Hebrew, except for a few that were written in Aramaic)
3. Moral Integrity

The books that were rejected were Baruch, Tobit, Judith, Ecclesiasticus (Sirach), 1 and 2 Macabees, Wisdom of Solomon, and additions to Daniel and Esther (see Apocrypha). The books that were accepted now make up the Hebrew scriptures, called Tanakh by Jews and Old Testament by Christians.

As the centuries passed, rabbis and scholars produced an immense library of interpretations and commentaries. These came to be known as Midrash. The earliest Midrash text is probably a version of the Haggadah, a ritual used at every Passover meal (see Passover). One of the most quoted concerns an incident involving the famous Rabbi Hillel, as related in Nahum Glatzer's *Hammer on the Rock:*

> Once a heathen came before Shammai. He said to him: I will be converted, if you can teach me all the Torah while I stand on one leg. Shammai pushed him away with the builder's measure he had in his hand. The man came before Hillel. He converted him. He said to him: "What is hateful to you, do not do to your fellow. That is all the Torah. The rest is commentary—go and study."

The oral laws and rituals of Judaism, based on Tanakh, were eventually codified and became known as Mishna. These, too, developed their own commentaries, called Gemara. Together they comprise the great body of Jewish literature known as Talmud.

Some conclude that Tanakh, Midrash, and Talmud tie Judaism down to an ancient, out-of-date past; that they all seem to point to an old wisdom, out of touch with present-day reality. But Hebrew scripture takes the position that truth is an eternal reality. Michael Lerner, a philosopher and psychologist, is known as an advocate of Jewish liberation theology (see Liberation Theology). He writes eloquently of a reform movement within Judaism that is rooted in Torah. His language is modern and his ideas very contemporary. In his book *Jewish Renewal: A Path to Healing and Transformation,* he comes to this conclusion:

> If ever there was a category that seemed scary, it's this one: getting real. The more asleep people are, the more they feel threatened by the concept, dismiss it as New Age or flakey or contentless. The more awake you are, the more you've had experiences in which you've moved from being more unconscious to more conscious, and hence the more you understand what is being talked about.

Rabbi Hillel wouldn't have put it that way. But he would have understood.

Sources:

Bridger, David, ed. *The New Jewish Encyclopedia.* New York: Behrman House, 1962.

Fisher, Mary Pat and Lee W. Bailey. *An Anthology of Living Religions.* Upper Saddle River: Prentice Hall, 2000.

Glatzer, Nahum, ed. *Hammer on the Rock,* New York: Schoken, 1962.

Goldin, Judah, ed. and trans. *The Living Talmud,* New Haven: Yale University Press, 1957.

Lerner, Michael. *Jewish Renewal: A Path to Healing and Transformation.* New York: G. P. Putnam's Sons, 1994.

TAO TE CHING

(See also Confucianism/Daoism; Lao Tzu)

Lao Tzu's Tao Te Ching (or Dao Di Jing) just may win the prize for being the shortest book with the greatest influence in the history of the world. It is sometimes called "the book of five thousand characters," although in most versions it is slightly longer than that. Chinese readers have often considered it the classic expression of Daoist thought. But its many translations have brought it to the attention of Western readers as well, many of whom heard about it through the study of the spirituality underlying martial arts. Indeed, except for the Bible, it has been translated into more languages than any other text.

Although tradition has it that the work was written by Lao Tzu in the sixth century BCE, it must be noted that many contemporary scholars believe it was written by an unknown author or authors in the late fourth century or early third century BCE.

The text is usually divided into two sections, probably because Lao Tzu wrote that he had crafted a work "in two books" at the request of the "Keeper of the Pass." By the first century CE, the work was standardized into the thirty-seven chapters of Book 1 and forty-four chapters of Book 2. It was also at this time that the work became known by its present title. Before this is was commonly called *The Lao Tzu*.

The Tao Te Ching is now considered to be the defining text or scripture of Daoism. It begins with an introduction of a word—*Dao* ("the way")—that, by definition, cannot be defined:

> The way that can be spoken of
> Is not the constant way;
> The name that can be named
> Is not the constant name.
> The nameless was the beginning of heaven and earth;
> The named was the mother of myriad creatures.
> Hence rid yourself of desires in order to observe its secrets;
> But always allow yourself to have desires in order to observe its manifestations.
> These two are the same
> But diverge in name as they issue forth.
> Being the same they are called mysteries,
> Mystery upon mystery—
> The gateway of the manifold secrets. (Book 1:1–3a)

When author Robert Pirsig struggled to create his "metaphysics of quality" in his book *Zen and the Art of Motorcycle Maintenance*, he discovered that what the Greeks called *arete* and he called "quality" were very similar to what Lao Tzu had been writing about the Dao. Sometimes called simply "all ten thousand things," the Dao is undefinable, since it precedes even the language used to attempt a definition. But it makes for difficult reading to those accustomed only to Western thought patterns:

> Truthful words are not beautiful; beautiful words are not truthful. Good words are not persuasive; persuasive words are not good. He who knows has not wide learning; he who has wide learning does not know.

The sage does not hoard.
Having bestowed all he has on others, he has yet more;
Having given all he has to others, he is richer still.

The way of heaven benefits and does not harm; the way of the sage is bountiful and does not contend. (Book 2:194–196)

The countless people who have put the time and effort into studying the Tao Te Ching have been richly rewarded. But it does take time and effort, and even Confucius found Lao Tzu difficult to comprehend. After their famous meeting he was heard to exclaim, "Today I have seen Lao Tzu, and he is a dragon!"

Sources:

Fisher, Mary Pat and Lee W. Bailey. *An Anthology of Living Religions*. Upper Saddle River: Prentice Hall, 2000.

Lao Tzu. *Tao Te Ching*. Trans. D. C. Lau. New York: Penguin Books, 1963.

Ming-Dao, Deng. *365 Tao: Daily Meditations*. New York: Harper Collins, 1992.

Pirsig, Robert. *Zen and the Art of Motorcycle Maintenance*. New York: William Morrow and Company, 1974.

TAOISM *see* Confucianism/Daoism

TEN COMMANDMENTS

(See also Judaism, Development of; Passover)

I am the Lord your God:
You shall have no other Gods before me
You shall not worship idols
You shall not misuse the name of God
Remember the Sabbath, to keep it holy
Honor your father and mother
You shall not murder
You shall not commit adultery
You shall not steal
You shall not lie
You shall not covet

The above list is the Decalogue, the Ten Commandments Moses brought down from Mount Sinai after the children of Israel escaped from Egypt. Believed to have been written by the very finger of God on tablets of stone, they summarized the law that would define Israel and make her a unique nation of people. The commandments are not the whole law. That constitutes pages and pages of oral tradition and experience. But they summarize what God expects in human, ethical behavior—a kind of minimum daily requirement in righteousness.

The first four laws govern the way humans are to respond to God. They are summarized in Deuteronomy 6:5: "Love the Lord your God with all your heart and with all your soul and with all your strength." The next six describe how humans are to respond to each other. They are summarized in Leviticus 19:18: "Love your neighbor as yourself."

A memorial to the Ten Commandments, also known as the Tablets of the Law. *AP/Wide World Photos.*

Sources:

The Holy Bible, New International Version. Grand Rapids, MI: Zondervan Bible Publishers, 1978.

THEODICY

(See also Evil)

Why do bad things happen to good people? Why does the innocent child have to suffer when she gets hit by the car driven by a drunk driver, who proceeds to walk away without a scratch? On a much larger scale, why did six million innocent Jews die at the hands of Nazi criminals?

These tough questions are at the heart of the religious/philosophical discipline of study called theodicy. It is not a study involving pity, inherent in a question such as, "Why me?" Instead, it involves philosophical questions concerning the nature of God.

Who or what is God? If God is good, why does God allow bad things to happen? If God cannot prevent them, God is not all-powerful and we are left adrift in a sea of uncertainty. If God can prevent evil but chooses not to, then perhaps God is not good. Why else would God allow the innocent to suffer? How could a good, caring God do that? But if evil springs forth only from our free will, did that catch God by surprise? If so, God is not omniscient, "all-knowing."

What about evil? Is there an evil presence opposed to God, or is evil simply the absence of good? If either is so, God cannot be omnipresent, existing everywhere at once. Because if evil is the absence of good, and God "is" good, there must be a place of evil where God "is not."

The questions go on forever. Even a summary of the responses is really useless, because every argument has been successfully rebutted. There are those who simply throw up their hands and say the ultimate answer can be found only in the mind of God. Others see in the study of theodicy a crack in the armor of any kind of religious belief. Then there are those who like the chase so much they would be disappointed if we ever ran the quarry to the ground and answered the question, once and for all.

Sources:

Gerstner, John H. *The Problem of Pleasure: Why Good Things Happen to Bad People*. Morgan, PA: Soli Deo Gloria, 2003.

Kushner, Harold. *When Bad Things Happen to Good People*. New York: Schocken Books, 1989.

THEOSOPHY

There is a hidden side of reality that is controlled by masters of the occult: this is the premise of the Theosophical (divine wisdom) Society. Its founder and guiding light was a woman named Helena Petrovna Blavatsky (1831–1891). She spent more than twenty years traveling the world, meeting with experts in the occult. She was initiated into secret societies all over the globe. She studied in Egypt, Mexico, Tibet, Canada, and the United States, where she met Colonel Henry Olcott (1832–1907). He was a scientist and a lawyer who had been investigating the new phenomenon of Spiritualism (see Spiritualism) for years. The two of them formed the Theosophical Society in 1875, convinced science and the occult supernatural could expand both mind and spiritual power. In 1878 Blavatsky published *Isis*

Revealed, in which she looked to the wisdom of the ancient masters for guidance in the modern world.

It soon became obvious to them that real wisdom could only be found in the East. So the two traveled to India, where they established their headquarters in Madras, thereby linking their understanding of Theosophy with both Buddhism and Hinduism. They took such a proactive position for Indian independence from Britain that they were soon befriended by the local Hindu intellectual community, and Theosophy began to flourish.

Blavatsky published her most important work, *The Secret Doctrines*, in 1888, a work that she claimed was based on a lost text called *Stanzas of Dzyan*. It shows a lot of Hindu influence (see Brahman/Atman) with its imagery of the One universal principle, which flows through all things, pulsing through creation and then returning to the One. All reality is one universal consciousness. Humans, existing at different spiritual levels, are linked to the One.

Later Theosophical leaders developed a whole master hierarchy. Solar Logos rules the solar level. Sanat Kumara, "Lord of the World," resides in Shamballa, another dimension parallel to the one in which we live. The Buddha, the Bodhisattva, and Manu serve there as well. The Seven Rays govern all earthly life, each ruled by a different master. They have appeared from time to time throughout history. We know them by such names as Krishna, Jesus, and Roger Bacon.

Although Theosophy, as might be expected, splintered into many different movements, it is still active today, known by many names. It served a valuable function in that it introduced a lot of Westerners to Eastern thought. For this reason, a good argument can be made that Theosophy was the first of what is now called New Age Religion (see New Age Religions).

Sources:
Ludwig, Theodore M. *The Sacred Paths: Understanding the Religions of the World*. 2nd ed. Upper Saddle River, NJ: Prentice Hall, 1996.

THOR *see* **Norse Gods and Goddesses**

TOTEM *see* **Healing Effigy/Amulet/Talisman/Fetish**

TRANSFIGURATION, MOUNT OF

After six days Jesus took with him Peter, James and John the brother of James, and led them up a high mountain by themselves. There he was transfigured before them. His face shone like the sun, and his clothes became as white as the light. Just then there appeared before them Moses and Elijah, talking with Jesus.... Jesus instructed them, "Don't tell anyone what you have seen, until the Son of Man has been raised from the dead." (Matthew 17:1–9)

With these words the Bible tells the story of what happened on the Mount of Transfiguration. We have no idea where the mountain is or what really happened there. Some believe Mount Tabor was the site; others, the foothills of Mount Hermon. All we know is that from that time on, Jesus "set his face toward Jerusalem" and his death.

The story is full of mystery. Elijah and Moses both had died under suspicious conditions. We don't know what happened to Moses, only that he was buried secretly "by the hand of God" and "no one to this day" knows where. Later, the New Testament book of Jude reveals that the angel Michael, for some reason, "disputed with the devil about the body of Moses." Why did Satan want the body? We don't know.

Elijah's demise was even more spectacular. He never really died. He just went up to heaven in a fiery chariot.

Things get even more mysterious in the New Testament. First both Moses and Elijah appear on the Mount of Transfiguration. Then, in the final days of history, the book of Revelation presents two witnesses who come down to Earth to preach about Jesus. They have the power to "turn the waters into blood," just like Moses did in Egypt, and "shut up the sky so it will not rain," Elijah's most famous trick.

Peter was certainly impressed. Showing his typical pattern of speech before thought, Peter blurted out, "Lord, this is wonderful! Let us make three tents; one for you, one for Moses and one for Elijah."

No real explanation is ever given about why this particular meeting takes place. Given that Jesus, from that point on, began preparations for his crucifixion, it has been surmised that Moses and Elijah came to talk to him about death.

For those who approach passages like this with a bit more skepticism, the question is phrased a little differently. What is the author trying to tell us? What's the meaning behind the myth?

Again, we don't know. Early Christian writers liked to link both Testaments together, so maybe this was a device used to pull Moses and Elijah, both Hebrew heroes, into the new movement. There are prophecies in the Old Testament that say "Elijah must come" before Messiah appears. Matthew seems to say that John the Baptist was a sort of reincarnated Elijah, a type or symbol of the prophet himself. Perhaps that was what the author had in mind. Or perhaps Moses and Elijah were chosen because they represent "the law" (Moses) and "the prophets" (Elijah).

Then there is the matter of the enigmatic words just preceding this trip up the mountain. Jesus had said, "Some of you will not taste death before you see the Son of Man coming in his kingdom." The Gospels, written after most of those who knew Jesus had died, must have troubled believers who couldn't understand why Jesus, after predicting his return before the death of the disciples, had still not returned, even though the twelve were now gone. Had he been mistaken?

Matthew suggests that perhaps he was referring to the fact that at least three apostles were going to experience the eternal kingdom, meeting with three of its most distinguished residents high atop the Mount of Transfiguration. That would explain the reference.

Again, we just don't know. What we do know is that the Christian Church still celebrates the Transfiguration every August 6th. In the scripture reading for the day, Christians listen for the words God is said to have uttered on that mountain: "This is my Son, whom I love. With him I am well pleased. Listen to him."

Sources:
The Holy Bible, New International Version. Grand Rapids, MI: Zondervan Bible Publishers, 1978.

TRANSUBSTANTIATION *see* **Eucharist**

TRINITARIAN *see* **Congregationalism**

TRINITY *see* **Arius**

U

UFO CULTS *see* New Age Religions

UNITARIAN UNIVERSALIST ASSOCIATION

(See also Congregationalism)

In 1776 a spirit of independence that had been growing in the American colonies broke forth into the light of day. A century later, President Abraham Lincoln would claim it resulted in the birth of "a new nation, conceived in liberty." Every aspect of life in the colonies was affected, including religion. A lot of colonists saw their struggle as a God-inspired holy war.

But what kind of God? The new nation was proof of human progress. A rationalist ideology began to define "God" in terms of Providence—a force of nature that gave direction to human life and social evolution. The human race was "going" somewhere. It had a trajectory. Our destiny was in our hands. God was behind it, of course, and would help, perhaps, if our hearts were righteous and our motivations pure. It was the beginning of the politician's cliché that ended every speech, "With God's help, we shall prevail. God Bless America!"

This new way of thinking had a profound affect on the way people talked about God. A subtle line had been crossed. God was now seen to be "on our side," but as a helper behind the scenes. God and Truth were weapons in the fight for liberty and freedom, but humans were on the front lines, doing the real work. To read some of the speeches and published sermons of the day, one almost gets the idea that the writers of such works pictured God cringing in heaven, wringing his hands and fretting over whether or not George Washington would safely cross the Delaware on that fateful Christmas eve.

It wasn't long before religious attitudes began to change—some say for the better, others for the worse. Traditional Christianity, though not specifically identified with Britain, became part of the "yoke of tyranny" cast off after the writing of the Declaration of Independence. The feeling among many colonists was that they held their lives in their own hands. God was welcome to come along for the ride, but no bishop, no hierarchy, no priest, and certainly no pope was going to tell them what to do.

Not everyone felt this way. Bill after bill was submitted to Congress, trying to make the new nation a specifically Christian one. But the founding fathers resisted them all. Church and state were kept separate.

So, except for being a figurehead, God was kept out of politics. But the profound change that had occurred in the public mind cannot be ignored. People thought differently about religion after 1776, just as they thought differently about politics. Even in this, the twenth-first century, we still don't know where the revolution/evolution of religious thought is going to take us. Those tumultuous, heady days of freedom still cast a long shadow. We still don't know how to completely separate church and state. We forbid teacher-led prayer in public schools but open each congressional day with an appeal to the Almighty. We champion the atheist's cause with tax dollars bearing the motto, "In God we trust." We go to war only after assuring the nation that the "God of peace" is on our side.

It is necessary to paint this church/state picture in order to fully grasp the culture from which Unitarianism, and shortly after, Universalism, sprang. Both were movements originating directly from this period of history.

Unitarianism (see Congregationalism) is a theological system that pictures God as a unity rather than a trinity. Universalism is the belief that, in the end, all will be saved.

But that doesn't really explain these two movements. From the beginning, Unitarianism was considered a liberal Christian ideology subscribed to by Congregationalists and Anglicans who didn't intellectually accept "orthodox" views. Universalism was introduced shortly before the Revolution by people from the Methodist tradition. Independent churches following both ideologies formed after independence, but the two movements soon merged. They simply had too many points of common agreement between them to stay separated for long.

In the midst of this new association, the philosophical movement called transcendentalism began to flourish. Ralph Waldo Emerson and Henry David Thoreau wrote eloquent essays that powerfully combined rationalism with romanticism, "natural" religion with the science of nature. Self-knowledge was the new means by which people could begin to understand the universe.

To this day the Unitarian Universalist Association (UUA) affirms the principles championed during this turbulent, exciting time of American history. They "believe strongly in the inherent worth and dignity of every person" and seek "justice, equity and compassion in human relationships." They seek "acceptance of one another and the encouragement to spiritual growth in [their] congregations" along with "a free and responsible search for truth and meaning."

The above quotations, and what follows, are taken from the covenant, or promise, that binds UUA congregations within their association. They reveal the emphasis on pluralism and openness that has been a hallmark of both traditions from their inception:

> The living tradition which we share draws from many sources:

> Direct experience of that transcending mystery and wonder, affirmed in all cultures, which moves us to a renewal of the spirit and openness to the forces which create and uphold life;

> Words and deeds of prophetic women and men which challenge us to confront powers and structures of evil with justice, compassion, and the transforming power of love;

> Wisdom from the world's religions which inspires us in our ethical and spiritual life;

> Jewish and Christian teachings which call us to respond to God's love by loving our neighbors as ourselves;

> Humanist teachings which counsel us to heed the guidance of reason and the results of science, and warn us against idolatries of the mind and spirit;

> Spiritual teachings of earth-centered traditions which celebrate the sacred circle of life and instruct us to live in harmony with the rhythms of nature.

A contemporary UUA worship service typically includes many faith traditions. On any given Sunday morning a Buddhist might give a lecture about meditation, an environmentalist might talk about a pressing need for community involvement in the restoration of a local wetlands, or a priest might talk about meditation in the Franciscan tradition. Those sitting next to you might describe themselves as liberal Christian, agnostic, atheist, or any number of traditional religious labels. What you will most certainly not find is the recitation of a historic creed or "accepted" statement of faith. The individual is encouraged to question, to seek his or her own way, in the company of others on a similar journey.

Sources:
Gonzalez, Justo L. *The Story of Christianity.* 2 vols. New York: Harper & Row, 1985.
"Unitarian Universalist Association Principles and Purposes." *Unitarian Universalist Association.*
   http://www.uua.org. September 14, 2003.

UNITED CHURCH OF CHRIST

(See also Congregationalism)

In 1648 the Pilgrims of Plymouth Plantation and the Puritans of the Massachusetts Bay Colony decided they were in essential political and religious unity. They joined together under conditions outlined in a document called the Cambridge Platform.

More than one hundred years later, they joined together with a group called Christian Churches, which had formed a union in opposition to the perceived organizational rigidity practiced by their Methodist, Presbyterian, and Baptist neighbors.

The name chosen for the new denomination was Congregational Christian Churches (see Congregationalism).

Meanwhile, beginning about 1725, the Reformed Church in the United States began to draw together immigrants from Switzerland, Hungary, and other European countries. These people had grown up in the Reformed tradition (see Christianity, Development of). They joined with a denomination called the Evangelical Synod of North America, made up of mostly Lutheran and Reformed Christians from Germany. This new denomination became known as the Evangelical and Reformed Church.

In 1957 the four diverse traditions and two denominations united to form the United Church of Christ. It came as no surprise that their new logo bore the inscription, "That they all may be one." Their motto is simple: "In essentials, unity. In non-essentials, diversity. In all things, charity." Believing that "there is yet more light to break forth from God's holy Word," they set about doing their best to reverse the trend begun with the Protestant Reformation, in which churches divided and further divided into separate denominations. They began to teach that actions spoke louder than words. It was not enough to talk about faith. It had to be demonstrated. So the tempestuous 1960s saw marches and demonstrations as members of the new "liberal" denomination took to the streets with southern "freedom riders." They were shot at in Mississippi, where proactive UCC ministers went to help register black voters. They were ridiculed and lambasted from fundamentalist pulpits when they supported the infamous Angela Davis defense fund and refused to support Billy Graham in local crusades. Many conservative congregations departed the ranks, swelling the numbers of denominations such as the conservative Christian Congregational Churches. But the UCC persisted, convinced they were on the right side of history.

The story, in some ways, hasn't been a happy one since the 1960s. Membership has dwindled, churches have closed their doors, and struggling congregations have been unable to attract younger members.

New trends, however, have begun to offer hope for the denomination. The closing years of the twentieth century saw an increase of interested young families who found in the UCC a tradition in which they could raise their children. The very openness that drew criticism in the 1960s now attracted a new generation that appreciated a familiar church service, spruced up with inclusive language, new music, an interest in scientific thought, and even, in some cases, open and affirming acceptance of gay and lesbian people. That same openness, however, also provided the opportunity for traditional, conservative theologies to flourish. Groups such as the Biblical Witness Fellowship, devoted to an evangelical theology, began to form within the ranks, dedicated to restoring traditional values and ideologies.

It all makes for a yeasty mix. Conservative and liberal, gay and straight, evangelical and reformed—all can sometimes be found within the same local church. Sometimes it works. Sometimes it doesn't. There are now many more women seminarians than there are men. A lot of second-career senior citizens can be found studying for the ministry, sponsored by their local UCC Church. A typical state conference is apt to draw pickets protesting the guest speaker if he or she is considered to be either too liberal or too conservative. Big-time television personalities have been known to show up in small New England villages, broadcasting the final service of a particular reverend who is leaving to become pastor of a gay church, a fundamentalist church, an overseas mission group, or most anything else.

The point of all this is that the church deliberately refuses to dictate to its membership. Each congregation is free to pursue its own path. So is each conference. One person equals one vote. UCC theologians affirm the authority of God, but how that authority is defined and followed is up to the individual. Church leaders hold very definite beliefs and opinions, and they state them firmly. But a person is not going to be excommunicated for disagreeing. The denomination reserves the right to recognize, or not to recognize, the ordination of individual pastors. And if a local church wants to either ordain or hire a pastor not recognized by the UCC, it has the right to do so.

The United Church of Christ recognizes the challenge it faces. It summarizes that challenge in this way:

> We recognize our calling both as individuals and as a church to live in the world:
> To proclaim in word and action the Gospel of Jesus Christ
> To work for reconciliation and the unity of the broken Body of Christ
> To seek justice and liberation for all.
> This is the challenge of the United Church of Christ.

Sources:
"What Is the United Church of Christ?" *United Church of Christ*. http://www.ucc.org. September 14, 2003.

UNITED METHODIST CHURCH

People who study and label such things often refer to the theological spectrum in terms of opposite poles. On the "religious right" are the conservative, fundamental groups who often carry denominational brand names like Baptist, Pentecostal, or "Bible-believing."

On the "religious left" are the Unitarians, perhaps left-wing Episcopalians, or simply "liberals." In the middle are churches often called mainstream. These are the typical Protestant churches you will find in every city or town across America. Of this broad spectrum, perhaps no church is more representative than the United Methodist Church. How it got to be this way is an interesting, very involved, story. It began with a liberal Anglican priest and evolved into an American frontier church of whose clergy it used to be said, "The weather's so bad today there ain't nothin' out but crows and Methodist preachers!"

It all began because of a rainstorm.

In 1736 a group of Moravian missionaries set sail to begin work in the American colonies. The Moravians had just settled a longstanding argument with the German Lutherans and had begun to reach out to new boundaries. Traveling with them as ship's chaplain was an Anglican priest named John Wesley (1703–1791). They were headed for Georgia, where Wesley had been invited to serve as pastor of the Anglican

Church in Savannah. Wesley hoped to parlay this job into an opportunity to preach to Indians, who he was convinced were something like what Jean-Jacques Rousseau would ten years later call the "noble savage."

The voyage went well until they experienced a severe storm that split the main-mast and left the ship helpless. For a few minutes it appeared they were going to go down. The crew, including Wesley, would have completely panicked had it not been for the calm conviction of the Moravian contingent, who quietly sang hymns throughout the ordeal. John Wesley discovered, much to his chagrin, that he was more concerned with his own safety than anything else. He realized that he had witnessed, in the Moravians' reaction to imminent death, a religious conviction he did not have. Wesley began to doubt the sincerity of his own faith. He later wrote in great detail about the profound effect this demonstration had upon him. He had been converted and saved. He had been the leader of a group others derisively called the Holy Club, because members spent three hours every afternoon studying the Bible together. Now, at the very beginning of what was supposed to be a great career, he felt he had failed miserably.

What made things even worse was that he had expected great things of his new Savannah congregation. They, on the other hand, figured they were doing him a favor just by showing up on Sundays. The situation became too much for him. He sailed back to England, the whole experience festering in his soul.

In this frame of mind, as he later recalled, he attended a church service one night:

> In the evening I went very unwillingly to a society in Aldersgate Street, where one was reading Luther's preface to the Epistle to the Romans. About a quarter before nine, while he was describing the change which God works in the heart through faith in Christ, I felt my heart strangely warmed. I felt I *did* trust in Christ, Christ alone for salvation: And an assurance was given me, that he had taken away *my* sins, even *mine*, and saved *me* from the law of sin and death.

Wesley was changed forever. He had previously been "born again." Now he was "filled with the spirit."

During those days other momentous events were taking place. George Whitefield (1714–1770), another member of the Holy Club, had become a famous preacher, dividing his time between Georgia and England. He had begun to preach to his English audiences outdoors, just as he had done in Georgia. The crowds were growing. He needed help. He turned to Wesley.

Wesley didn't like outdoor revivals. He later said that at one time he was so concerned with doing everything "decently and in order," as the Bible dictates, that he questioned whether God could save anyone outside a church building. But he obliged, and eventually he learned to preach with such conviction and authority that people would weep, moan, and otherwise be convicted of sin. Turning their lives over to God, they would finally feel "cleansed of inequity."

Whitefield and Wesley disagreed about one important theological point. Whitefield was a Calvinist who believed in predestination (see Calvin, John, and

Jacobus Arminius). Wesley believed in free will. He was convinced people had to choose whether or not they would follow Christ. This disagreement eventually forced them to separate.

Wesley had no intention of starting a new denomination. He always thought of his outdoor preaching engagements as a means of introducing people to the Anglican Church. But "societies" formed. Religious groups met in members' houses, patterned after the Holy Club. Pretty soon they had their own buildings to meet in. Wesley's method of organization was so efficient that it wasn't long before outsiders began to mock them, calling them "Methodists." Later, his followers wore the name with pride.

To his dying day, Wesley reproved those who talked about splintering off, leaving the Anglican Church and forming a new denomination. But the group grew too large, too quickly. The break was inevitable.

While all this was taking place, however, two important things had happened. Methodism had "hopped the pond" to America where it was spreading by leaps and bounds along the borders of the new frontier. The common people had caught the revival bug. Not only did it speak to their souls, but they could be Methodists without being Anglican. The great western land rush carried the new faith far away from places where older, established churches were willing to go. Anglicanism was for downtown city streets, not the wilderness clearings served by Methodist "circuit riders."

This caused a problem. In 1777, Wesley had sent Francis Asbury (1745–1816) to the colonies to represent him. Asbury was the driving force of frontier evangelism. When the colonies declared their independence, Wesley strongly opposed the whole thing. But American Methodists, while still admiring Wesley, were not about to let religious organization keep them from fighting for their political freedom.

So American Methodists, now calling themselves the Methodist Episcopal Church, ironically became an official denomination even before their English counterparts. The word "Episcopal" comes from the Greek *episopus*, referring to church governments that place authority in the hands of a bishop. The "Episcopal" part of the new denomination's name, therefore, was derived from the fact that the American denomination appointed bishops without following strictly the Anglican rites. Wesley, still an Anglican, referred to himself as a "superintendent" rather than a "bishop" (see Anglican Church). Anglicans practiced the policy of apostolic succession. You didn't just bandy about the distinguished title "bishop" if you lived in England. But the Americans did. Wesley was furious when he discovered Asbury had called himself a bishop and appointed others without proper "laying on of hands" in the time-honored tradition. To this day, American Methodists have bishops. Their English counterparts do not.

Finally, after the inevitable struggles all denominations go through, the Methodist Church became a separate, Protestant denomination. Although originally distinguished from Calvinist traditions such as Congregationalism, Reformed, and Presbyterian by their belief in free will instead of predestination, at a typical Methodist service today, most people in the pews aren't even aware there is a theological distinction. The big difference between Methodists and Presbyterians, in the minds of many, is that the Methodists have a newer hymnbook. Also, their organization is different. They practice an Episcopalian form of church government. Their ministers are appointed and move more frequently than those of many other Protestant denomiations. But their choir members sing in the ecumenical chorus sponsored by the local council of churches. They have great potluck suppers, just like the Congregationalists. And their churches are apt to be federated—that is, two or three churches of different denominations have dwindled in size and found it easier to support a minister and carry on if they join together.

It was this similarity and common tradition that formed the United Methodist Church on April 23, 1968. Bishop Reuben H. Mueller, representing the Evangelical United Brethren Church (the EUB), and Bishop Lloyd C. Wicke, representing the Methodist Church, joined hands in Dallas, Texas. They prayed, "Lord of the Church, we are united in thee, in thy Church and now in the United Methodist Church." And the new United Methodist Church was born.

You might say it was a marriage made in heaven. Philip Otterbein (1726–1813), founder of the United Brethren in Christ, the spiritual parent of the EUB Church, had assisted in the ordination of Francis Asbury, way back in colonial times. Asbury had gone on to be the first "bishop" of the American Methodists.

John Wesley would turn over in his grave to hear it, but it seemed as if the two churches were "predestined" to become one.

Sources:
Gonzalez, Justo L. *The Story of Christianity*. 2 vols. New York: Harper & Row, 1985.
United Methodist Church. http://www.umc.org. September 14, 2003.

VATICAN COUNCILS

When most people refer to the Vatican Councils, they are usually thinking about the last two great Ecumenical Councils of the Roman Catholic Church. Depending on whom you talk to, there have been either seven or twenty-one of these councils held over the years.

Both Protestants and Catholics agree that there were seven great councils held between 325 CE and 787 CE: the councils of Nicea I (325), Constantinople I (381), Ephesus (431), Chalcedon (451), Constantinople II (553), Constantinople III (680–681), and Nicea II (787). These were the meetings that managed to hammer out so much of what is considered to be "orthodox" Christian belief.

The Roman Catholic Church adds fourteen more official councils to this list. The last two of these are called Vatican Councils.

Vatican I met in 1869 and 1870. Its primary function was to deal with concerns about what was then called "modernism." Probably the most famous result of this council was its ruling that when the pope spoke *ex cathedra*, that is, "when in discharge of the office of pastor and doctor of all Christians, by virtue of his supreme Apostolic authority, he defines a doctrine regarding faith or morals to be held by the universal Church," he spoke with the authority of papal infallibility. Up to then it had been assumed that all bishops, including the bishop of Rome, the pope, was under the rule of the whole church. But not after this. Now the power of infallibility rested in the papal office. When God spoke through the pope, the whole Catholic Church had to obey. (It comes as a surprise to many people that this famous doctrine is less than 150 years old.)

The council also passed resolutions regarding things like pantheism, materialism, and atheism. To no one's surprise, it condemned them all. It went on to talk about the new idea of evolution, reaffirming the role of God as Creator, and spoke out against "modernism" in general, calling it a "cancer in its ranks."

Nineteenth-century painting of the First Vatican Council in 1870. *The Art Archive/Museo Pio IX e Pinacoteca d'Arte Sacra Senigallia/Dagli Orti.*

Vatican II was held from 1962 to 1965. That was the council that "modernized" the church. Latin was almost totally replaced by the vernacular. The extent of lay participation in worship was increased. Greater friendliness with non-Catholic religions was encouraged and a greater concern for social involvement begun. The altar was moved out from the wall so the priest now faced the congregation. Guitars were heard more and more. "Folk masses" became popular. "Dialogue sermons" became all the rage. Right in the middle of the homily, an antagonist would stand up in the midst of the congregation and question something, speaking for the people. Of course, the whole episode was carefully scripted, so the priest eventually managed to "convince" his opponent and, by doing so, win over the congregation. Everyone knew what was going on, but congregants enjoyed it just the same.

There were, of course, strenuous objections to all this.

"The Father looks like he's doing a cooking demonstration. It's not Mass anymore!"

"If God had wanted the service to be in English, He wouldn't have written the Bible in Latin!"

"I just don't feel like it's church anymore!"

Others said the church had changed forever and folks just had to deal with it. Time seemed to be on their side.

But a strange current has moved through Vatican waters since the early seventies. There are those who think the tide may be turning back toward old-style Catholicism. The present pope has proved to be very conservative. Loud, strident voices can be heard on both sides of the debate.

What will happen still remains to be seen. Liberal American Catholicism is a very different religion from that practiced in other countries. What does the future hold, especially since the great clergy sexual-molestation scandals of 2002 and 2003? The future is very much in doubt.

Sources:
Radical Faith. http://homepages.which.net/~radical.faith/. September 14, 2003.

VEDAS *see* Aryans; Bhagavad-Gita; Hinduism, Development of

VISION QUEST

(See also Black Elk)

The vision quest is an important aspect of many indigenous religious traditions. Usually a young man undertook such a quest as part of his coming-of-age initiation, but often it became a ritual called upon when someone, usually a medicine person or shaman, needed spiritual guidance.

In many American Indian traditions, a young man would fast alone in the desert, mountains, or woods for four days. Four was considered to be a sacred number. He would pray for the Great Spirit to send him a vision. Perhaps a spirit from the animal powers would talk to him or send a sign. That animal would become the young man's totem, or spirit guide. A feather or claw, depending on the animal spirit, would be carried in the young man's medicine bag for the rest of his life. Perhaps he would even receive a new name as a result of his quest, with the name symbolizing a brand-new life.

When Christian missionaries began to read the Bible to Indian tribes, in many respects the native people had no trouble at all bridging the gap between their world and the world of the white Europeans. They felt right at home when they heard about Moses going up the mountain to talk to God or when they were told Abraham's name was changed after he received a vision from the Divine. Stories like these were very much a part of their tradition.

Often vision quests were undertaken by shamans who sought guidance. Sometimes a vision quest would be enhanced with the aid of hallucinogenic herbs. Other times, a ritualistic dance such as the Sundance would be an integral component. The idea was to place oneself in a receptive frame of mind and in a position conducive to hearing or seeing messages sent from the other side of life—the realm of the spirit.

Sources:
Twofeathers, Manny. *The Road to Sundance: My Journey into Native Spirituality.* New York: Hyperion, 1994.

Altar in the Voodoo Spiritual Temple of Mambo Miriam in New Orleans, Louisiana. *Fortean Picture Library.*

VOODOO/VODOU/VODUN

The term Voodoo is the most popular name for a religion developed in Haiti that is a combination of the religion of the West African Yoruba people and their Roman Catholic slave owners. Although it developed in the eighteenth and nineteenth centuries, the African elements may go back as far as five or six thousand years. Practitioners often use the Creole spellings "Vodou" or "Vodun" to distinguish the religion from the popular misconceptions of "voodoo" spells and black magic.

Because indigenous pagan beliefs were suppressed, the religion was forced underground and it developed in secret. Hollywood has managed to so infect the minds of most Westerners that it is almost impossible to join in honest discussion of Voodoo. "Everyone knows" it deals in black magic and incantations carried on in the dark of night by Obeah women who speak with musical Caribbean accents. "Everyone knows" it is involved with evil spells that produce zombies or "walking dead." And there is a very small kernel of truth in what "everyone knows." But mostly, what "everyone knows" comes out of fantasy movies, not reality.

The truth is that Voodoo is concerned primarily with veneration of the ancestors, as is the case with Japanese Shinto. It recognizes a pantheon of "nature" gods, similar to Hinduism. These vary from group to group; it is difficult to summarize Voodoo because there are so many different expressions. Anthropologists can't even agree who the principal deities are. Many have compiled lists of the different names for the gods, but no two lists are the same.

What is known is that Roman Catholicism has shaped Voodoo culture. Both believe in a Supreme Being. The Catholic saints are paralleled by the Voodoo *loa* or *lwa*, the spirits of people who had led exceptional lives. Both religions believe in an afterlife and have, as their centerpiece, a ritual sacrifice involving both flesh and blood. Both believe in the existence of evil, demonic, invisible spirits. Both believe in the existence of the human soul, which leaves the body at death to enter the place prepared for it. Both believe in exorcism. The many ceremonies, songs, and dances of Voodoo are performed primarily to honor worshipers' ancestors or the loa.

Sources:
Ellwood, Robert S., and Barbara A. McGraw. *Many Peoples, Many Faiths*. 6th ed. Upper Saddle River, NJ: Prentice Hall, 1999.
Gordon, Leah. *The Book of Vodou*. London, UK: Quarto Inc., 2000.

W

Wailing Wall

Israel reached its height of political power about 1000 BCE. Under the rule of King Solomon, Jerusalem was enlarged, a palace and the first great Temple were constructed, and a wall was built surrounding the city. Part of the wall still stands. The bottom two or three courses of stone along one side of the ancient city were preserved and are today a revered holy place where people flock to pray. Called the Wailing Wall because of the very vocal tradition of Hebrew prayer, and also known as the Western Wall for its directional position, Jews and tourists of many religious traditions can be found there at all times of the day. Wearing the traditional yarmulke, or skullcap, worn to cover the head while praying, most of them reach out to touch the ancient stones, writing their prayer requests on slips of paper to tuck into 3,000-year-old crevices. For those who can't get there in person, a fax machine has been set up to convey prayers to the Almighty.

WAY OF SOCIETY (THE LAWS OF MANU) *see* Hinduism, Development of

WAY OF THE YOGI (YOGI SUTRAS) *see* Hinduism, Development of

Wicca

Popular understanding has it that Wicca, also known as witchcraft or the "Old Religion," dates all the way back to Paleolithic times, echoing goddess worship, sacred festivals, and holy places.

Those overtones are certainly heard in the twenty-first-century version, but Wicca today is really part of the neo-pagan, or "new pagan," movement. Many people have reacted strongly against the monotheistic, patriarchal organizations and institutions comprising Western religion. They have tried to rediscover a spirituality that connects humans to their environment, rather than separating them from it. They have tried to find the feminine face of the divine, rather than just the masculine.

In 1921 Margaret Murray wrote *The Witch-Cult in Western Europe*. It proposed that witchcraft was a remnant of pre-Christian religion, barely surviving many purges but still continuing in many disguised traditions that the church "baptized" and adopted. Christmas and Easter are only two examples of Christian customs loaded with pre-Christian symbols (see Paganism, Calendar of).

By the time witchcraft laws were finally repealed in England in 1951, the Wiccan movement was well entrenched. Gerald Gardner (1884–1964), considered by some the father of modern Wicca, had already published his novel, *High Magic's Aid*, based on his experiences with Wicca, and in the 1950s he followed with the nonfiction *Witchcraft Today* and *The Meaning of Witchcraft*. Also influential was Robert Graves's (1885–1985) *The White Goddess*, published in 1959.

Wiccans believe that all nature is sacred and that human beings, rather than being nature's rulers, are very much a part of nature. Typically, Wiccan worship revolves around the goddess, but both male and female attributes comprise the sacred presence. The goddess is pictured in three forms—maiden, mother, crone—and these forms are seen monthly in the phases of the moon as it waxes and wanes. The male horned god, lord of the animals, is also an important metaphysical deity, born each year at the winter solstice. In the spring he is the lover and mate of the goddess, but he dies each fall, symbolized by the cold and dark of winter.

Wiccans form covens, small groups of typically twelve or thirteen people who meet to celebrate rituals and festivals. A typical meeting consists of "casting the circle," or defining a sacred space; purification rituals involving the four elements of fire, water, earth, and air; and the use of sacred implements such as the chalice, wand, and blade. Participants engage the ancient power of the dance and chant to form a "cone of power," channeling the collective power of the group to effect healing or transformation.

Wicca has provided a much-needed avenue in which to recover feminist spirituality and a healthy antidote to patriarchy. Goddess worship, emphasizing the sacredness inherent in Earth and nature, has even been recognized by scientists who coined the term Gaia Principle (see Gaia Principle), thus invoking the name of the goddess, "Mother Earth," to describe how things really work on this planet.

It is hard to know how many people practice Wicca today. The religion is, by design, not inclined to publish membership lists or hold annual meetings. But in 1993 the Parliament of the World Religions conference held in Chicago saw a very visible Wiccan presence. That presence sparked the formation of many more covens around the country. Many beginners are still feeling their way. It's not like there is a Wiccan manual to follow, though there has been talk in the Unitarian Universalist Association of training Wiccan clergy for military chaplaincy. But as experiences are shared and Wiccan wheat is separated from charlatan chaff, it is certain that the movement will continue to grow, develop, and gain acceptance.

Sources:

Buckland, Raymond. *The Witch Book: The Encyclopedia of Witchcraft, Wicca, and Neo-paganism.* Detroit: Visible Ink Press, 2002.

Ludwig, Theodore M. *The Sacred Paths: Understanding the Religions of the World.* 2nd ed. Upper Saddle River, NJ: Prentice Hall, 1996.

WORLD COUNCIL OF CHURCHES

The World Council of Churches (WCC) is "an international fellowship of Christian churches, built upon the foundation of encounter, dialogue, and collaboration." Formed as a result of the influence stemming from the ecumenical movement, it now consists of some 400 million Christians worldwide, most of whom probably don't even know they are members. About 340 denominations and individual churches belong. But when denominations send representatives, the individual churches of that denomination are included without necessarily being consulted. So aside from small items found occasionally in church newsletters, there has not been a whole lot of active participation from or even connection with individual Christians since the founding of the WCC in 1948.

Nevertheless, in numbers there is strength. The motto "One human family in justice and peace" resonates, even though only Christian churches are allowed to be a part of that family. This does not imply exclusion, however. The WCC simply sees itself as a Christian representative of some 120 countries on a mission to spark dialogue and involvement with all peoples. Its members accomplish a lot in terms of mission, charity, and disaster relief. Although they have been slandered by conservative churches and ignored by many liberal ones, they carry on a substantial ministry, and their presence is a constant reminder of those who struggle to overcome the history of splintering and division that is the legacy of much of Christendom.

Sources:

World Council of Churches. http://www.wcc-coe.org. September 15, 2003.

WOUNDED KNEE, BATTLE OF *see* **Ghost Dance**

WU JING *see* **Confucian Texts**

Y

YI JING *see* Confucian Texts

YIN/YANG *see* Dao

YMCA/YWCA

The Christian Church has a continuous history of urban outreach. From the time the apostle Paul took his message to the cities of the Roman Empire right up to present-day evangelists such as Billy Graham, there have been people dedicated to converting the teeming masses of the city.

One of these was Sir George Williams (1821–1905). In 1844, a meeting with twelve young men in his London apartment sparked the Young Men's Christian Association. From its first organizational meetings, Bible studies, and lectures at Exeter Hall, Williams, soon known as the driving force of the YMCA, was criticized because of his single-minded purposefulness and intolerance of smoking and games, along with his strict temperance code.

In 1855, with the adoption of a statement of faith they called the Paris Basis and strengthened by the Second Evangelical Awakening, the YMCA, now joined by the Young Women's Christian Association (YWCA), appeared ready to become another Protestant evangelical urban movement. By 1878 William Booth's Salvation Army seemed to fit the same mold with the same mission.

But something happened over the years. Gradually, recreational and relief work rose to replace evangelical concern. The familiar red triangle became well known to soldiers during war years. Hostels, gymnasiums, youth camps, and vocational training schools sprang up in American cities, the scene of its present strength. Today almost six million people avail themselves of YMCA/YWCA resources, most not even thinking about the organization's evangelical roots.

Sources:

Douglas, J. D., ed. *The New International Dictionary of the Christian Church*. Grand Rapids, MI: Zondervan Publishing, 1974.

Gonzalez, Justo L. *The Story of Christianity*. 2 vols. New York: Harper & Row, 1985.

YOGI SUTRAS *see* Hinduism, Development of

YOM KIPPUR *see* Judaism, Calendar of

ZAKAT *see* Islam

ZARATHUSTRA *see* Zoroastrianism

ZEN BUDDHISM *see* Buddhism, Development of

ZIONISM

The word "Zionism" was coined by Jewish nationalist Nathan Birnbaum (1864–1937) in 1893. Jews in Eastern Europe, having experienced centuries of persecution and suspecting more was coming, began to take literally the words spoken at every Seder meal, "Next year in Jerusalem!"

Zion is the traditional name for one of the hills in the city that was to become known as Jerusalem, the "City of Peace." It is the spiritual center of the Jewish universe, the Holy Land given to Abraham and his descendants forever. Ever since the destruction of their beloved Temple in 70 CE, Jews had longed to return, to establish Eretz Yisrael, the "Land of Israel."

But in the late nineteenth century the Holy Land was still known as Palestine. Jews had migrated there to live, work, and study. It was the destination of many a pilgrimage. But it wasn't home.

The first Zionist Congress was held in 1897, convened by the man who has come to be known as the "father" of political Zionism, Theodore Herzl (1860–1904). That first congress adopted the Basel Program, named after the town in which the representatives met. Their purpose was to establish in Palestine, then under Turkish rule, a permanent home for Jewish people. They formed the World Zionist Organization, the mission of which was to win approval for their cause by appealing to the leading world powers. It was an uphill battle all the way. The Balfour Declaration, passed by the British government in 1917, began the process. The next year, after

Britain received a League of Nations mandate to settle the area, saw an influx of Jewish migration. By the time World War II broke out, Jewish residents in Palestine numbered about 500,000.

No one knows what might have happened had the aftermath of the war not brought to the attention of the world the atrocities committed by the Nazis. But with the news of the Holocaust fresh in the public mind, in 1947 the newly formed United Nations overwhelmingly approved the establishment of a Jewish state in part of Palestine. The birth of the State of Israel was proclaimed on May 14, 1948 (the 5th day of the month of Iyar, in the year 5708 by the Jewish calendar).

Seven Arab nations promptly invaded the new state, and the first War of Liberation was soon underway. It continues to this day.

Not all Jews are pro-Zionist. A very vocal faction of Orthodox Jews, calling themselves "anti-Zionists," are happy Israel exists. It offers, after all, a safe haven for oppressed Jews to study Torah. But these ultra-Orthodox Jews believe very strongly that God pulls rank even over the United Nations. Israel must be divinely established and protected or it will not last.

The ultra-Orthodox point out that the Torah lists three oaths Israel took when it began its second exile back in the first century. Israel would not "go up like a wall." That is, massive force would not be used to restore the nation. God made Israel swear it would not rebel against the nations of the world. God made non-Jews promise not to oppress Israel "too much." Persecution is God's way of strengthening his people. The ultra-Orthodox feel that it's far more productive to study Torah and remain faithful. God will handle the details.

In deference to their religious beliefs, many ultra-Orthodox Jews living in Israel today are exempt from serving in the Israeli army; in addition, they receive other social benefits not extended to everyone. Their special status was established when the state of Israel first began and has been guaranteed over the years by their increasing political clout. This status infuriates less religious or secular Jews, many of whom fight for political rather than religious reasons. They wonder why they should fight and perhaps die to protect the ultra-Orthodox. While the religious political parties wield considerable power in Israel, in recent years those who support Zionism and oppose the military exemptions for the ultra-Orthodox have gained many followers. In Israel's 2003 January elections, the number of Knesset seats they won almost doubled their ranks in the government.

Numerous questions arise surrounding the issue of Zionism. Should Jews have their own homeland? Must faithful Jews live in Israel? Can you be a Jew without being religious? Are religious Jews hindering political progress and security? These are the kinds of questions Judaism has yet to answer. While the debate continues, war breaks out in the streets. Palestinians rightly claim they are being pushed out of their homes. Israelis justifiably feel grieved and outraged by the numerous suicide bombings carried out by Palestinian extremists. Americans debate which side they should support. And many people around the world wonder whether the Israelis have become the oppressors, rather than the oppressed.

Sources:

Bridger, David, ed. *The New Jewish Encyclopedia.* New York: Behrman House, 1962.

The Jewish Virtual Library. http://www.us-israel.org. September 14, 2003.

ZOROASTRIANISM

(See also Apocalypse)

About five centuries before the Common Era, the world's first true monotheistic religion began. Cyrus the Great (c. 585–c. 529 BCE) was king of Persia when Zoroaster (c. 628–c. 551 BCE)—Zarathustra, as he was later called by the Greeks—began to preach that a battle between good and evil, between the High God Ahura Mazda and the evil Ahriman (see Ahura Mazda/Ahriman), was being carried out on Earth. Ahriman had been lured into Earth's realm so he could be weakened and eventually destroyed at the end of time. History, viewed for perhaps the first time in a straightforward, linear fashion, was going to come to an end. After the destruction of Ahriman, the earth would be recycled and purified. Humans would be rewarded with paradise, an ideal heavenly realm with a divine court abiding over the blessed. Hell was awaiting the wicked. It was not eternal, but its fires would purify evildoers, just as they would purify the earth.

"The Resurrection of Zoroaster," drawing by Austin Osman Spare, 1905. *Fortean Picture Library.*

Just before that final day, Zoroaster would return (see Mithraism). A virgin, impregnated with Zoroaster's own seed—which had been preserved in a mountain lake identified as Lake Hamun—would conceive him. Until then, every thousand years a prophet would appear until the final restoration of the world. This final restoration, it was foretold, would occur three thousand years in the future, or about the year 2500 CE.

It is hard to overestimate the influence Zoroastrianism has had upon the world. The Jews first experienced it during the Babylonian captivity (see Babylonian Captivity). When they returned to their homeland, their religion had completely changed. That meant that Christianity and Islam were affected as well. The result was monotheism, the belief that transformed Western civilization.

Before the Babylonian captivity, Jewish religion was full of references to "other Gods." After they returned, there were none. Now there was only one God. The "gods" of other nations were merely idols, figments of the human imagination. The Dead Sea Scrolls (see Dead Sea Scrolls) are full of references to the "battle between light and dark," the Zoroastrian dualism so alive and well in our culture today. (So prevalent is dualism in our society that even the news media promise to tell us "both sides of the story," as if there were only two sides to present.)

Zoroastrian priests were called Magi. From them we get the word "magic." Magi were among the first to formally institutionalize the idea of astrology (see Astrology). They studied the skies for signs and portents. From their Ziggurat towers, they would nightly scan the stars and constellations. The biblical Gospel of Matthew has some of them journeying to Bethlehem at the time of the birth of Jesus, following a star that signified to them that "the King of the Jews" had been born.

At this point, a basic question must be posed. There is no doubt about Zoroastrian religion and its influence. But what about Zoroaster? Did he ever really live, or is he a character of mythology? Estimates of when he was born vary from the sixth century BCE all the way back to some six thousand years ago. But aside from his legacy we have no proof. One is certainly tempted, though, to think that such a legacy is proof in itself that he must have existed. Perhaps not with all the frills, bells, and whistles that accompany his legend. But where there is so much smoke, there must have been at least a small fire, and probably a big one, for Zoroastrianism became the official religion of Persia.

The religion still exists, even though Persia fell to Islamic invaders who reduced Zoroastrianism to a very small minority sect by 651 CE. As monotheists, they were "officially" respected by Muslims. But in practice they were ridiculed, labeled with the derogatory term *gabars,* or "unbelievers."

There have been Zoroastrian revivals over the years. The latest occurred between 1941 and 1979. But again Islam put it down. With the fall of the Shah of Iran in 1979, Muslims ended another Zoroastrian era.

Some believers migrated to India to escape persecution. Here they were known as Parsis, "Persians." Today the Parsis of India make up the bulk of the world's practicing Zoroastrians.

Although the Zoroastrians are few in number, their religion has had a tremendous impact, and the final vision of Zoroaster holds promise for the whole human race. Zoroaster believed good will triumph. These are words of his final prayer:

> And then may we be those who transfigure this world. O Mazda (and you other) Lords, be present to me with support and truth.
>
> Amen.

Sources:

Ellwood, Robert S., and Barbara A. McGraw. *Many Peoples, Many Faiths.* 6th ed. Upper Saddle River, NJ: Prentice Hall, 1999.

Ludwig, Theodore M. *The Sacred Paths: Understanding the Religions of the World.* 2nd ed. Upper Saddle River, NJ: Prentice Hall, 1996.

AFTERWORD

Once upon a time, villagers gathered to select a new shaman. A young woman, representing a new generation, had been selected to lead them into spiritual discoveries of benefit to all the people. It was an important day, and extensive preparations had been made. The young woman had undergone a thorough training. She had read and studied. She had learned myths from the old ones and could repeat them without a single mistake. She could weave together entertaining stories that made the whole village think more clearly about the important things of life—the things of the spirit. All that was needed now was the final ceremony that would bring together all she had learned. She was ready.

Or was she?

The elders summoned her to the village square, placed a blindfold over her eyes, and told her to stand before an ancient rock that bore an enigmatic message. Her blindfold was removed and the young woman was told she had only a short period of time to read the inscription. "Tell us its secret," the elders said, "and you will be worthy to lead us into new discoveries of the spirit."

Secure in all her training, she began. The villagers waited. The silence stretched on and on. And in the end, she couldn't do it. With anger and frustration she finally announced that the message carved in stone, inspired by an ancient wisdom, could not be translated. It was indecipherable.

The villagers were despondent. But it was even worse for the young woman. She retreated into herself, wondering why she had come up short. Where had she failed? Her training had been extensive. She had studied and learned about everything she could. Her active and fertile mind had probed and probed, seeking out answers to spiritual questions pondered by the elders. She thought she had learned all they had to offer. Now she was all alone.

The days of frustration stretched into weeks. A year passed.

Finally, at the low point of her despair, she wandered alone into the wilderness. There, at the boundary of the country she called home, she found a great tree. Beneath the tree rested a beautiful clay jar, painted and decorated with designs and symbols so mysterious and beckoning that she just knew it must contain something of great value. Perhaps this was the end of her journey. Perhaps here she would find the missing piece of her spiritual puzzle—the piece that would bring together into one all the mysteries of the elders, the ancient ones. After offering a wish and a prayer, she lifted the jar and gazed inside.

It was empty. There was absolutely nothing of value there at all. The jar that had looked so mysterious, that had promised so much of value on the outside, contained nothing of any value on the inside.

Shocked, she lost control of her emotions, her reactions, and her very grasp. The jar fell from her hands and shattered into a thousand pieces. It was broken beyond repair.

Into her mind flashed an image of the ancient rock standing in the village square. And in that instant she understood the meaning of the mystical inscription she had been told to translate.

Her value to the community lay not in her knowledge or her preparation. It didn't really matter whether she could tell entertaining stories or weave philosophical truths into a colorful, verbal tapestry. Her value lay not in her ability to explain signs and symbols that, perhaps, hinted of mystery and insight.

No. Her value lay in her brokenness. The beautiful clay jar, no matter how brightly decorated, no matter how large, was not sufficient to hold within itself the wealth of the elders. Their spiritual wisdom, gathered over millennia, could not be contained within the confines of a single vessel. Any vessel made for that purpose would have to have been fashioned with great pride. And pride is a dam across the mighty flow of the spirit river. The only way the clay jar, the only way the young woman, could release the power of the elders was to be broken. Only then could the river flow freely.

She had thought her talent sufficient, her training thorough. Now she realized it wasn't. Not for her. Not for anyone. And with that knowledge, she was content, and she could begin her work.

<hr />

I have devoted the last thirty years or so to studying and teaching in the field of religion. I've been a minister in the United Church of Christ since 1971. I've been a college professor of comparative religion since 1997. As I began compiling this book, I saw it as my chance to take everything I'd learned, put it between the covers of one book, and then die a happy man knowing I had left behind a summary of my life's work. It sounded easy.

Soon, however, I began to realize the extent of what I had undertaken. My problem very quickly became a matter of choice. Not about what to include. That was easy. I wanted to include everything. But rather, what had to be left out. Encapsulating at least twenty-five thousand years of human religious experience between the covers of one book, I found, becomes a daunting task.

For a whole year, I tried. There were times I felt directed by the powers of the cosmos. The muse spoke clearly and with conviction. But there were other times, I must admit, when I sat and stared at my computer screen, realizing I had utterly failed to capture in words a concept or tradition that had informed and illuminated whole civilizations.

That's when the words of the Biblical writer who called himself Quoheleth, "the preacher," came to mind: "All, all is vanity!"

And so I plodded on. At last it was time to draw things to a close. That's not to say the book was "finished." This kind of book is never finished. The best you can do is to say you've stopped writing. But anything that consumes this much of your time and attention is bound to leave a residual feeling of emptiness when the final paragraph is written, the last entry completed.

In that frame of mind I awoke one morning fresh from a vivid dream. I knew I had to write it down quickly, before the images faded. What I dreamed was the story of the shaman. The meaning was transparent. I found it fascinating first of all because I obviously identified with the "young woman" of the story but had never before cast my feminine side in the role of dream hero (or rather, heroine). I can only assume the Goddess is alive and kicking out there in the realm of the muse.

When the young woman is "blindfolded" before the villagers, it is symbolic of the fact that none of us can really "see" into the spirit world. The best we can manage is what the apostle Paul called glimpses "through a glass, darkly." The woman was trained, of course, which speaks of all the reading and studying one must do in this vast sea of religious wisdom. Although she had all the degrees and schooling, although she was a talented talker and teacher, in the end she discovered the only valid way to approach her task was in the spirit of "brokenness"—humility.

Zen Buddhists have a wonderful way of saying it. When a finger points to the moon, its object is to direct your attention to the moon, not to the finger pointing to the moon. The finger may glitter with rings and adornment. But if, in the end, you do not see the object to which it points, he who tried to direct your attention has failed.

That's what this book has tried to do. It merely points a finger in the hope that the reader will see the object to which it is pointing.

RESOURCES

American Folklore and Legend. Pleasantville, NY: Reader's Digest Association, 1978.

America's Fascinating Indian Heritage. Pleasantville, NY: Reader's Digest Association, 1978.

Armstrong, Karen. *Jerusalem: One City, Three Faiths.* New York: Ballantine Books, 1997.

Ashton, John and Tom Whyte. *The Quest for Paradise: Visions of Heaven and Eternity in the World's Myths and Religions.* San Francisco: HarperSanFrancisco, 2001.

Atlas of America. Pleasantville, NY: Reader's Digest Association, 1998

Barbour, Ian G. *When Science Meets Religion: Enemies, Strangers or Partners?* New York: HarperCollins, 2000.

Barzun, Jacques. *From Dawn to Decadence: 1500 Years to the Present.* New York: HarperCollins, 2000.

Bell, Catherine. *Ritual: Perspectives and Dimensions.* New York: Oxford University, 1997.

Berry, George Ricker. *The Interlinear Literal Translation of the Greek New Testament.* Grand Rapids, MI: Zondervan Publishing, 1973.

Bolen, Jean Shinoda, M.D. *Goddesses in Everywoman.* San Francisco: Harper & Row: 1985.

Bolen, Jean Shinoda, M.D. *Gods in Everyman: A New Psychology of Men's Lives and Loves.* San Francisco: Harper & Row, 1989.

The Book of Mormon. Trans. Joseph Smith. Salt Lake City: The Church of Jesus Christ of Latter-Day Saints, 1980.

Boslough, John. *Stephen Hawking's Universe.* New York: Avon Books, 1980.

Braun, David P. and Esther K. Braun. *The First Peoples of the Northeast.* Lincoln: Moccasin Hill Press, 1994.

Bridger, David, ed. *The New Jewish Encyclopedia.* New York: Behrman House, 1962.

Bucke, Emory Stevens, et al, eds. *The Interpreter's Dictionary of the Bible*. 4 vols. New York: Abingdon Press, 1962.

Buckland, Raymond. *The Witch Book: The Encyclopedia of Witchcraft, Wicca, and Neo-paganism*. Detroit: Visible Ink Press, 2002.

Campbell, Joseph. *The Inner Reaches of Outer Space: Metaphor As Myth and As Religion*. New York: Harper & Row, 1986.

Campbell, Joseph. *The Power of Myth*. New York: Doubleday, 1988.

Campbell, Joseph. *Transformations of Myth Through Time*. New York: Harper & Row, 1990.

Cotterell, Arthur and Rachel Storm. *The Ultimate Encyclopedia of Mythology*. Bath, Avon, UK: Anness Publishing, 1999.

Covell, Ralph R. *Confucius, the Buddha, and the Christ: A History of the Gospel in Chinese*. Maryknoll, NY: Orbis, 1986.

Deloria, Vine Jr. *God Is Red*. Golden, CO: Fulcrum Publishing, 1994.

Diamond, Jared. *Guns, Germs, and Steel: The Fates of Human Societies*. New York: W.W. Norton Company, 1997.

Douglas, J. D., ed. *The New International Dictionary of the Christian Church*. Grand Rapids, MI: Zondervan Publishing, 1974.

Dunne, John S. *The Way of All the Earth: Experiments in Truth and Religion*. New York: Macmillan, 1972.

Eller, Cynthia. *The Myth of Matriarchal Prehistory: Why an Invented Past Will Not Give Women a Future*. Boston, MA: Beacon Press, 2000.

Ellwood, Robert S. and Barbara A. McGraw. *Many Peoples, Many Faiths*. 6th ed. Upper Saddle River, NJ: Prentice Hall, 1999.

Estes, Clarissa Pinkola. *The Gift of Story*. New York: Ballantine Books, 1993.

Estes, Clarissa Pinkola. *Women Who Run With the Wolves*. New York: Ballantine Books, 1992.

Farb, Peter. *Man's Rise to Civilization: The Cultural Ascent of the Indians of North America*. New York: E.P. Dutton, 1968.

Fell, Barry. *America B.C.: Ancient Settlers in the New World*. New York: Pocket Books, 1976.

Fell, Barry. *Saga America*. New York: Times Books, 1980.

Fisher, Mary Pat. *Living Religions*. 3rd ed. Upper Saddle River, NJ: Prentice Hall, 1991.

Fisher, Mary Pat and Lee W. Bailey. *An Anthology of Living Religions*. Upper Saddle River, NJ: Prentice Hall, 2000.

Fitzgerald, Edward. *The Rubaiyat of Omar Khayyam*. London: Harrap Limited, 1984.

Gaskell, G. A. *Dictionary of All Scriptures and Myths*. New York: Gramercy Books, 1960.

General Association of Seventh-day Adventists. *Seventh-day Adventists Believe: A Biblical Exposition of 27 Fundamental Doctrines*. Hagerstown, MD: Review and Herald Publishing Association, 1988.

Gimbutas, Marija. *The Goddesses and Gods of Old Europe: 6500–3500 B.C.* Berkeley: University of California, 1982.

Gonzalez, Justo L. *The Story of Christianity.* 2 vols. New York: Harper & Row, 1985.

Good News Bible with Deuterocanonicals/Apocrypha. New York: American Bible Society, 1978.

Gould, Stephen Jay. *Rocks of Ages: Science and Religion in the Fullness of Life.* New York: Ballantine Publishing, 1999.

Graham, W. A. *Beyond the Written Word: Oral Aspects of Scripture in the History of Religion.* Cambridge: Cambridge University Press, 1993.

Guthrie, Stewart Elliott. *Faces in the Clouds: A New Theory of Religion.* New York, Oxford University Press, 1995.

Hagen, Steve. *Buddhism Plain and Simple.* Boston: Charles E. Tuttle Co., 1997.

Hauptman, Laurence M. and James D. Wherry, eds. *The Pequots in Southern New England.* Norman: University of Oklahoma Press, 1990.

Hawking, Stephen W. *A Brief History of Time: From the Big Bang to Black Holes.* New York: Bantam Books, 1988.

Helms, Randel McCraw. *Who Wrote the Gospels?* Altadena, CA: Millennium Press, 1997.

Hesse, Herman. *Siddhartha.* New York: Bantam Books, 1951.

Highwater, Jamake. *The Primal Mind: Vision and Reality in Indian America.* New York: Harper & Row, 1981.

Hill, Francis. *A Delusion of Satan: The Full Story of the Salem Witch Trials.* Cambridge, MA: DaCapo Press, 2002.

Hitching, Francis. *Earth Magic.* New York: William Morrow & Company, 1977.

The Holy Qur'an, trans. with a commentary by Abdullah Yusuf Ali. Beirut, Lebanon: Dar Al Arabia, 1968.

Houston, Jean. *The Hero and the Goddess: The Odyssey As Mystery and Initiation.* New York: Ballantine Books, 1992.

Hudson, Winthrop S. *Religion in America.* New York: Charles Scribner, 1965.

James, Peter and Nick Thorpe. *Ancient Mysteries.* New York: Ballantine Books, 1999.

James, Simon. *The World of the Celts.* New York: Thames and Hudson, 1993.

Johnson, Steven F. *Ninnuock (The People): The Algonkian People of New England.* Marlborough, MA: Bliss Publishing Company, 1995.

Johnston, Basil. *The Manitous: The Supernatural World of the Ojibway.* New York: Harper Perennial, 1995.

Jones, Prudence and Nigel Pennick. *A History of Pagan Europe.* New York: Routledge, 1995.

Josephus, Flavius. *The Works of Flavius Josephus.* Trans. William Whitson. New York: T. Nelson & Sons, 1873.

Josephy, Alvin M. and Richard M. Ketchum. *The American Heritage Book of the Pioneer Spirit.* New York: American Heritage Publishing Co., 1959.

Keck, L. Robert. *Sacred Quest: The Evolution and Future of the Human Soul.* West Chester, PA: Chrysalis Books, 2000.

Kirsch, Jonathan. *The Harlot by the Side of the Road.* New York, Ballantine Books, 1997.

THE RELIGION BOOK: PLACES, PROPHETS, SAINTS, AND SEERS

Krech, Shepard III. *The Ecological Indian: Myth and History*. New York: W.W. Norton & Company, 1999.

Kroeber, Theodora. *Ishi, the Last of His Tribe*. New York: Bantam Books, 1964.

Kung, Hans and Julia Ching. *Christianity and Chinese Religions*. New York: Doubleday, 1989.

Lao Tzu. *Tao Te Ching*. Trans. D. C. Lau. New York: Penguin, 1963.

LaSor, William Sanford. *The Dead Sea Scrolls and the Christian Faith*. Chicago: Moody Press, 1956.

The Last Two Million Years. Pleasantville, NY: Reader's Digest Association, 1973.

Lewis, James R. *The Astrology Book: The Encyclopedia of Heavenly Influences*. Detroit: Visible Ink Press, 2003.

Lewis, James R. *The Death and Afterlife Book*. Detroit: Visible Ink Press, 2001.

The Lost Books of the Bible and the Forgotten Books of Eden. Cleveland, OH: World Syndicate Publishing Company, 1926.

Ludwig, Theodore M. *The Sacred Paths: Understanding the Religions of the World*. 3rd ed. Upper Saddle River, NJ: Prentice Hall, 2001.

Mails, Thomas E. *Dancing in the Paths of the Ancestors*. New York: Marlowe & Company, 1983.

Mavor, James W. Jr. and Byron E. Dix. *Manitou*. Rochester: Inner Traditions International, 1989.

May, Herbert G. and Bruce M. Metzger, eds. *The New Oxford Annotated Bible with the Apocrypha*. Rev. ed. New York: Oxford University Press, 1973.

McDowell, Josh and Don Stewart. *Understanding Non-Christian Religions: Handbook of Today's Religions*. San Bernadino: Here's Life Publishers, 1982.

McDowell, Josh and Don Stewart. *Handbook of Today's Religions*. Nashville: Nelson Reference, 1992.

Miller, Kenneth R. *Finding Darwin's God*. New York: HarperCollins, 2000.

Ming-Dao, Deng. *Scholar Warrior: An Introduction to the Tao in Everyday Life*. San Francisco: HarperSanFrancisco, 1990.

Ming-Dao, Deng. *365 Tao: Daily Meditations*. New York: HarperCollins, 1992.

Morris, Desmond. *The Naked Ape: A Zoologist's Study of the Human Animal*. New York: Dell Publishing, 1967.

Mysteries of the Ancient Americas. Pleasantville, NY: Reader's Digest Association, 1986.

Mysteries of the Unknown: Mystic Places. Alexandria, VA: Time Life Books, 1987.

Neihardt, John G. *Black Elk Speaks*. Lincoln: University of Nebraska Press, 1961.

Peterson, Michael et al. *Reason and Religious Belief: An Introduction to the Philosophy of Religion*. 2nd ed. New York: Oxford University Press, 1998.

Powell, Barry B. *Classical Myth*. 3rd ed. Upper Saddle River, NJ: Prentice Hall, 2001.

Prabhupada, A. C. Bhaktivedanata Swami. *Bhagavad-Gita As It Is*. Los Angeles: Bhaktivedanta Book Trust, 1986.

Quinn, Daniel. *Ishmael*. New York: Bantam/Turner Books, 1995.

Renard, John. *The Handy Religion Answer Book*. Detroit: Visible Ink Press, 2002.

Renard, John. *Seven Doors to Islam: Spirituality and the Religious Life of Muslims*. Berkeley: University of California, 1996.

Rogerson, John. *Atlas of the Bible*. New York: Equinox, 1986.

Rolleston, T. W. *Myths and Legends of the Celtic Race*. 2nd ed. London: Constable & Co., 1987.

Russell, Howard S. *Indian New England Before the Mayflower*. Hanover: University Press of New England, 1980.

Sagan, Carl. *Cosmos*. New York: Random House, 1980.

Sagan, Carl. *The Dragons of Eden*. New York: Ballantine Books, 1977.

The Septuagint Version of the Old Testament, with an English Translation. Grand Rapids: Zondervan Publishing House, 1974.

Shah, Idries. *The Sufis*. London: Octagon Press, 1977.

Smart, Ninian. *Oxford Atlas of the World's Religions*. New York: Oxford University, 1999.

Smart, Ninian. *The Religious Experience*. 5th ed. Upper Saddle River: Prentice Hall, 1996.

Stewart, R. J. *The Living World of Faery*. Lake Toxaway: Mercury Publishing, 1999.

The Story of America. Pleasantville, NY: Reader's Digest Association, 1975.

Strong, James. *The Exhaustive Concordance of the Bible*. New York: Abingdon Press, 1890.

Teilhard de Chardin, Pierre. *The Appearance of Man*. New York: Harper & Row, 1956.

Teilhard de Chardin, Pierre. *The Phenomenon of Man*. New York: Harper & Row, 1959.

Tree, Christina. *How New England Happened*. Boston: Little, Brown & Company, 1976.

Twofeathers, Manny. *The Road to Sundance: My Journey into Native Spirituality*. New York: Hyperion, 1994.

Twofeathers, Manny. *Stone People Medicine*. Phoenix: Wo-Pila Publishing, 1996.

Weatherford, Jack. *Indian Givers: How the Indians of the Americas Transformed the World*. New York: Fawcett Columbine, 1988.

Wilson, A. *World Scripture: A Comparative Anthology of Sacred Texts*. New York: Paragon, 1991.

The World's Last Mysteries. Pleasantville, NY: Reader's Digest Association, 1978.

INDEX

Note: **Boldface** type indicates page numbers of main entries; (ill.) indicates photos and illustrations.

HWALY R
       200
       W734

WILLIS, JIM
   THE RELIGION BOOK

02/05